Human Resource Information Systems

Third Edition

*To my wife, Barbara, and my sons Sean, Colin, and Timothy,
and especially to my granddaughter, Isabella – M. J. K.*

To my wife, Kelley, and my daughters Rachel and Katherine – R. D. J.

Human Resource Information Systems

Basics, Applications, and Future Directions

Third Edition

Michael J. Kavanagh
University at Albany, State University of New York

Mohan Thite
Griffith University

Richard D. Johnson
University at Albany, State University of New York

Los Angeles | London | New Delhi
Singapore | Washington DC

Los Angeles | London | New Delhi
Singapore | Washington DC

FOR INFORMATION:

SAGE Publications, Inc.

2455 Teller Road

Thousand Oaks, California 91320

E-mail: order@sagepub.com

SAGE Publications Ltd.

1 Oliver's Yard

55 City Road

London EC1Y 1SP

United Kingdom

SAGE Publications India Pvt. Ltd.

B 1/I 1 Mohan Cooperative Industrial Area

Mathura Road, New Delhi 110 044

India

SAGE Publications Asia-Pacific Pte. Ltd.

3 Church Street

#10-04 Samsung Hub

Singapore 049483

Acquisitions Editor: Patricia Quinlin

Associate Editor: Maggie Stanley

Assistant Editor: Megan Koraly

Editorial Assistant: Dori Zweig

Production Editor: Stephanie Palermini

Copy Editor: Terri Lee Paulsen

Typesetter: C&M Digitals (P) Ltd.

Proofreader: Stefanie Storholt

Indexer: Will Ragsdale

Cover Designer: Glenn Vogel

Marketing Manager: Liz Thornton

Printed in the United States of America

Library of Congress Cataloging-in-Publication Data

Human resource information systems : basics, applications, and future directions / [edited by] Michael J. Kavanagh, State University of New York at Albany, Mohan Thite, Griffith University, Richard D. Johnson, State University of New York at Albany. — Third edition.

pages cm

Includes bibliographical references and index.

ISBN 978-1-4833-0693-3 (pbk. : alk. paper)

1. Personnel management—Information technology.
2. Personnel management—Data processing.
I. Kavanagh, Michael J. II. Thite, Mohan. III. Johnson, Richard D.

HF5549.5.D37H86 2015

658.300285—dc23   2013029735

This book is printed on acid-free paper.

Certified Chain of Custody
SUSTAINABLE FORESTRY INITIATIVE
Promoting Sustainable Forestry
www.sfiprogram.org
SFI-01268

SFI label applies to text stock

15 16 17 18 10 9 8 7 6 5 4 3 2

Contents

Part II: HRIS Effectiveness Measures and HRM Advice for HRIS Implementation   165

7. HR Metrics and Workforce Analytics   166

Kevin D. Carlson and Michael J. Kavanagh

14. Performance Management, Compensation, Benefits, Payroll, and the Human Resource Information System 452

Charles H. Fay and Renato E. Nardoni

15. Human Resource Information Systems and International Human Resource Management   488

Michael J. Kavanagh and John W. Michel

PART IV: SPECIAL TOPICS IN HUMAN RESOURCE INFORMATION SYSTEMS   529

16. HRIS Privacy and Security   530

Humayun Zafar and Dianna L. Stone

17. The Future of Human Resource Information Systems: Emerging Trends in HRM and IT 555

Richard D. Johnson and Michael J. Kavanagh

PREFACE

This third edition of *Human Resource Information Systems: Basics, Applications, and Future Directions* is written with two goals in mind. First, we wish to continue to improve the content and the usefulness of the content for faculty and students. Second, technology and human resource management (HRM) are continually evolving so the book must continue to evolve along with these changes. Although there have been several books on HRIS published, most authors have focused only on one aspect or dimension of the HRIS field, for example, on e-HR, Web-based HR, or HRIS in a global context.

The growing importance of HRIS is evidenced by the recognition of human resource management (HRM) practitioners, academics, and managers that information technology (IT) has become a critical aspect of developing and using HRM programs to better manage the human capital of an organization. Thus, a comprehensive education in the HRM field requires the knowledge and skills for developing, implementing, and maintaining a human resource information system. Despite this recognition, it has been personally frustrating for the editors and chapter authors to have to use several books and readings in teaching an HRIS course, because there was not a current or comprehensive textbook for the academic market. Many of the books in the area are now over 10 years old, and do not reflect the current state of either human resources or HRIS. As a result, faculty have had to rely on readings, parts of HRM and IT textbooks, and have had to develop much of their classroom materials on their own to cover the entire field of HRIS in their courses. After the first edition was published, we received very complimentary comments from faculty who used the book as well as informal communications with faculty in the HRIS field. As noted, this third edition of *Human Resource Information Systems: Basics, Applications, and Future Directions* is written with two goals in mind. First, we wish to continue to improve the content and the usefulness of the book for faculty and students. Thus, these are the reasons why we published the previous editions of this book, and remain the primary reasons for the publication of this third edition.

In the preface to the first edition of this book, we note that Kavanagh et al. (1990) stated that "among the most significant changes in the field of human resources management in the past decade has been the use of computers to develop what have become known as human resource information systems (HRIS)" (p. v). We also argued that the introduction of computers and IS/IT concepts to the field of HRM during the 1980s and early 1990s was a *revolutionary* change. That is, HRM paper systems in file cabinets were being replaced by the use of mainframes, PCs, and HRM software to computerize the HRM systems. To keep up with these technological changes in the HRM function, companies were forced to adapt, even though it was quite expensive, in order to remain competitive in their markets. However, it is our contention that advances in HR and IT as well as HRIS since the early 1990s have been evolutionary, that is, there have been constant improvements in the HRIS field in the last 20–25 years. From stand-alone applications on a PC, the field of HRIS now has seen the implementation of enterprise resource planning (ERP) configurations in HRM with extensive use of manager and employee self-portals. Today's systems are often web-based and connect extensively with social networking sites. Additionally, international firms have begun to use the power of an HRIS to expand their businesses because of the speed and accuracy of an HRIS.

Along with these changes in technology a revolution has come to the practice of human resources. The HR department in adopting this new technology has become a more important resource in the management of organizations. The changed role of HRM has evolved to the point that HRM managers and professionals are now seen as strategic partners, and sophistication in the use of computer technology to improve the delivery of HR programs and activities to management has grown immensely. Most critically, these changes have meant that there have been significant advances in the use of people resources in managerial decisions. These advances are due to the fact that people resources can be accessed more rapidly now than in 1990, and with a higher degree of accuracy. This marriage of HR with IT/IS in the development and improvement of an HRIS has increased the ability of management to use people knowledge to make better decisions on the human capital of their firms to gain a competitive advantage in the marketplace.

What these changes mean for the new learner with a background in HRM or IT, who is trying to understand the HRIS field, is that it is not sufficient to begin one's study with the improved products and processes that have occurred recently. For example, it would not be wise or fruitful to begin one's study of the HRIS field with a focus on new technologies such as service-oriented architecture (SOA), enterprise portals, N-tier architectures, cloud computing, or the use of Web 2.0 in HRM. This would be like starting with Chapter 17 of this book and then proceeding backward through the book. Unfortunately, many people do, in fact, focus on learning the technological advances in HRIS without understanding the basics first. Instead, to best understand how to effectively implement and use an HRIS, it is important to understand the *evolutional* changes to technology and how these changes have transformed HR practices (e.g. how HRM moved from using paper records in file cabinets to the computerization of the HR function). Only after understanding these changes will the learner be able to effectively understand how advances in technology can help their organization manage their HR function more effectively.

New Aspects of the Third Edition

First, two chapters (4 and 16) have been completely rewritten by new authors, both of whom have extensive knowledge obtained by teaching, researching, and practicing in the field of HRIS. In addition to adding new authors, Sage asked several faculty members who had adopted and used the previous edition to provide evaluations of the entire book as well as of each chapter. Their recommendations were very useful and led us to make a number of changes.

In terms of the content of this third edition, there are now four main parts of the book. Some chapters from the previous edition were moved and others replaced to meet the subject content of one of the four parts. For example, Chapter 8 was moved to become Chapter 6 because it fit better with the first five chapters than it did with Chapters 7, 8, and 9. The decision to create four new parts was based on feedback from the anonymous faculty reviewers as well as on our personal judgment that one of the major uses of an HRIS was to focus better on providing accurate and timely information for managerial decisions, both strategic and operational. Each part now focuses on one specific part of HRIS. As a result, the four parts of the book are now: Part I, Introduction to Human Resource Information Systems (HRIS): A Systems Perspective, which includes Chapters 1–6; Part II, HRIS Effectiveness Measures and HRM Advice for HRIS Implementation, which contains Chapter 7, 8, and 9; Part III: Human Resource Information Systems Applications, which consists of Chapters 10–15; and Part IV: Special Topics in Human Resource Information Systems, which consists of Chapters 16 and 17.

In addition to creating a four-part book, we made major revisions to Chapters 4, 7, 8, 11, 16, and 17. Again these revisions were based on feedback from the anonymous reviewers of the previous edition, which consisted of faculty teaching an HRIS course. These changes represent more general revisions throughout the third edition; that is, we updated the chapters so they present a survey of current knowledge and practice in IT, HRM, and HRIS. We retained our feature, "HRIS in Action," which faculty indicated their students enjoyed. Again based on positive feedback from faculty, new figures and tables were added to almost every chapter. We believe that a picture combined with text content improves the teaching and learning process. Many of the new figures are screenshots from a variety of HRIS software packages currently in use.

New cases were added to a number of the chapters, and we significantly expanded the chapter discussion questions. We did these things to improve the text as a learning and teaching tool—we wanted the text and each chapter within it to present a complete learning experience. Thus, we also continued the consistent structure across all chapters that was introduced in the previous edition. Chapters contain, in the following order: (1) an editors' note, (2) chapter objectives, (3) chapter content, (4) chapter summary, (5) a list of key terms, (6) chapter discussion questions, and (7) a case with student discussion questions. This internal *consistency* for each chapter was established by emphasizing the same chapter learning points for the chapter objectives, chapter summary, key terms, and chapter discussion questions. We felt that this within-chapter consistency would aid the learning process of the students and aid the faculty in identifying the important content of each chapter. For the student, the key terms are a guide, in the view of the editors, to the important aspects of the chapter, but they are not a glossary. Nor are all the key terms listed in the glossary in the appendix, which has been expanded and improved to include additional technical terms. Likewise the websites and additional readings in the appendix have been expanded because of recent changes in the field. In determining to make these changes in the book, the coeditors worked to make the third edition a textbook they would personally be comfortable using to teach their HRIS courses.

Third Edition Summary

In summary, in this third edition, we have described the major advances in the field of HRIS and the relation of HRIS to managerial decision making while, at the same time, exploring the basic concepts of developing, implementing, and maintaining an HRIS. The book represents the intersection of the best thinking and concepts from the two fields of HRM and IT. It was the early intersection of these two fields that changed the role of HR in organizations from record keeper to strategic partner. After introducing the basic concepts of an HRIS combined with new approaches to the operation of HRM in the organization, we then proceed to the more advanced, and evolutionary, technical changes. The basic philosophy of this book is that the integration or harmonization of technology with people management in an HRIS will create a distinct competitive advantage for organizations. We hope that you, the reader, gain this understanding and that you enjoy this book.

Companion Website

A password-protected instructor resources site includes PowerPoint presentations, test banks, detailed lecture outlines, discussion questions, suggested course projects, a variety of full-text SAGE journal articles selected to support and enhance the content of the book, and web resources. These materials are available at **www.sagepub.com/kavanagh3e**.

Students can also log on to the companion site and access the SAGE journal articles and web resources at **www.sagepub.com/kavanagh3e**.

Acknowledgments

Many individuals contributed in a variety of ways to provide assistance in the completion of this book, and we would like to thank them. First of all, we would like to thank all the authors who contributed chapters. We know how difficult it is to write a chapter for an edited book, particularly when the editors have defined the philosophy and approach to be used. In addition, special thanks go to those individuals who provided invaluable insights through their evaluations of the edition of this book and its chapters: Dr. Mesut Akdere, University of Wisconsin-Milwaukee; Dr. Yvonne Barry, John Tyler Community College; Gery Markova, W. Frank Barton School of Business, Wichita State University; Marc S. Miller, Adjunct at NYU-Poly—NYC and Long Island University; Frank J. Mueller, MSM, MS, Oakland City University; Jan Mason Rauk, MBA, University of Idaho; and M. Shane Tomblin, Marshall University, College of Business.

Again, we would like to thank Dianna Stone of the University of Texas at San Antonio for her support for the creation of this book, her assistance in helping find authors to write chapters, and her willingness to coauthor Chapter 16, "HRIS Privacy and Security." Our thanks go to the professionals in the International Association for Human Resource Information Management (IHRIM) and the Society for Human Resource Management (SHRM) who patiently listened and responded to our ideas regarding this book. We would also like to thank Katie Guarino for the understanding exhibited in her interactions with us as well as her suggestions for resolving technical issues we encountered in writing the book. Also, thanks to Patricia Quinlin for her guidance and patience during this long process. Finally, we would like to thank Terri Lee Paulsen and Stephanie Palermini for correcting our grammar as needed and finding those mistyped words and grammatical errors that were done by gremlins.

In particular, we would like to thank our families, who provided the warmth and support we needed when frustration and writer's block crept in!

Michael J. Kavanagh and Richard D. Johnson

Introduction to Human Resource Information Systems (HRIS)

A Systems Perspective

Evolution of Human Resource Management and Human Resource Information Systems

The Role of Information Technology

Michael J. Kavanagh and Richard D. Johnson

EDITORS' NOTE

*The purpose of this chapter is to provide an introduction to the fields of **human resource management (HRM)** and **information technology (IT)**, and the combination of these two fields into human resource information systems (HRIS). The history of the field of HRM and the impact of computer technology on HRM will be covered, as well as the advent of using a human resource information system and the subsequent effects on both HR and IT professionals. The different types of HR activities will be discussed as well as the different types of information systems used in HRIS. A central focus of this chapter is the use of data from the HRIS in support of managerial decision making. The development of the field of HRIS has had a significant impact on the emergence of strategic human resource management (**strategic HRM**), as is discussed in this chapter. This first chapter will lay the groundwork for the remainder of this book, and, consequently, it is important to understand thoroughly the concepts and ideas presented. This chapter contains definitions for a number of terms in common use in the HRM, IT, and HRIS fields. (Note that a glossary defining these terms is also provided at the back of this book.) The central themes of this book in terms of the development, implementation, and use of an HRIS will also be discussed. The chapter also presents a **model of organizational functioning** that provides an overview of an HRIS embedded within an organizational and global business environment, with a specific emphasis on its relationship to HR management and the strategic planning of an organization. A brief overview of the major sections of the book will be presented here as well; one discussing how each chapter is an integral part of the entire field of HRIS. Finally, you should note that the "Key Terms" used in this chapter are in bold and contained in a section after the chapter "Summary." The pattern of sections for this chapter will be consistent for all chapters of this book.*

CHAPTER Objectives

After completing this chapter, you should be able to

- Describe the historical evolution of HRM, including the changing role of the human resources (HR) professional

- Discuss the impact of the development of computer technology on the evolution of HRM and HRIS

- Describe the three types of HR activities

- Explain the purpose and nature of an HRIS as well as the differences between the types of information systems functionality in an HRIS

- Discuss how the information from an HRIS can assist in decision making in organizations

- Discuss how the developments in HRIS have led to HRM becoming a strategic partner in organizations and to the emergence of the field of strategic human resource management (strategic HRM)

- Be able to define Six Sigma, balanced scorecard, and the contingency perspective and fit model of HRM

- Describe the differences between e-HRM and HRIS

- Understand how HRM and HRIS fit within a comprehensive model of organizational functioning in global business environments

HRIS IN ACTION

Situation Description

To illustrate the importance and use of HRIS in contemporary HR departments, this vignette examines the typical memoranda that may appear in the in-box of HR professionals and managers. Assume you are the HR director of a medium-size organization that primarily maintains and uses manual HR records and systems. This morning, your in-box contains the following memos that *require action today.*

Memo 1: A note from the legal department indicates that some female staff members have filed an employment discrimination complaint with the local government agency responsible for the enforcement of equal opportunity employment. The female staff members allege that, for the past 10 years, they have been passed over for promotion because they are women. In order to respond to this allegation, the legal department requires historical data on the promotions of both males and females for the past 10 years for all jobs in the company broken down by department. It also needs the training records for all managers involved in personnel actions, such as promotions, to ascertain whether or not they have received training in equal employment provisions, especially in terms of unfair gender discrimination.

Memo 2: The second item is a complaint from employees working in a remote location of the company, about 150 miles away. The employees are complaining that their pay slips are not reaching them on time and that they are finding it difficult to get timely and accurate information on the most recent leave and benefits policies of the company.

Memo 3: A letter from the marketing manager states that he has not received any updated information on the status of his request, made three months ago, to recruit a new salesperson. The failure to recruit and hire a new salesperson has had a negative effect on the overall sales of the company's products over the past quarter.

Memo 4: A letter from the HR professional in charge of the southwest regional office says that she is swamped with HR administrative work, particularly personnel transactions on employees. As a result, she has not been able to meet employees in her region to describe and begin to implement the recent Employee Engagement Initiative as required by corporate headquarters.

Memo 5: A note from one of the production managers indicates that he has received a resignation letter from a highly regarded production engineer. She is resigning because she has not received the training on new technology that she was promised when hired. She notes that most of the other production engineers have attended this training program and have had very positive reactions to it.

Memo 6: A strongly worded note from the director of finance asks the HR department to justify the increasing costs associated with its operation. The note indicates that the HR director needs to develop a business plan for the overall operation of the HR department to include business plans for all of the HR programs, such as recruiting and training. Further, the finance director indicates that unless the business cases can demonstrate a positive **cost-benefit ratio**, the budget for the HR department will be reduced, which will lead to reductions in the HR department professional staff.

As the HR director, your first thought may be to resign since searching for the information required by these memos in the manual records on employees will require several days if not weeks to complete. However, you have just returned from a professional conference sponsored by the Society for Human Resources Management (SHRM) and remember how an HRIS may be what you need! As this chapter and the ones that follow will illustrate, an HRIS enables an HR department to streamline its activities and the demands placed on it by automating the HR data and processes necessary for the management of the human capital of the organization. This automation helps develop the capabilities to produce information and reports on the requests contained in the memos in the vignette, and these reports will facilitate efficient and effective managerial decision making. While an HRIS cannot make the judgment calls in terms of whom to recruit or promote, it can certainly facilitate better inputting, integration, and use of employee data, which will reduce the administrative burden of keeping detailed records and should aid and enhance decisions about strategic directions.

Need for an HRIS in Decision Situations

If you read the above memos again, you will recognize that each one has a request for HRM information that will be used in a decision situation. The information requested in Memo 1 will help the legal department determine the company's potential liability in a workplace gender discrimination situation. This information may help to determine whether the company should decide to rectify the situation in terms of an informal settlement with the female staff members or to defend the company's promotion procedures as valid—in court if necessary. The information required in Memo 2 may help the HR department decide to change its payroll procedures as well as its distribution of benefits information to remote company locations. The information needed to respond to Memo 3 will impact decisions by the HR department to change recruitment and selection programs. Obviously, the response to Memo 4 would greatly support the need for the acquisition of an HRIS. The information required to answer Memo 5 may help in decisions regarding the revision of recruiting and training procedures, especially for new engineers. The information that would be provided in response to Memo 6 will help decide the future of the HR department. As you go through this book, look at information on the capabilities of various human resource information systems, trying to find an HRIS that would allow you (as the HR director) to respond to each of the six memos in one day.

Introduction

Leading management thinkers suggest that "it is not technology, but the art of human- and humane-management" that is the continuing challenge for executives in the 21st century (Drucker, Dyson, Handy, Saffo, & Senge, 1997). Similarly, Smith and Kelly (1997) believe that "future economic and strategic advantage will rest with the organizations that can most effectively attract, develop and retain a diverse group of the best and the brightest human talent in the market place" (p. 200).

To maintain a competitive advantage in the marketplace, firms need to balance the resources available to the firm to achieve the desired results of profitability and survival. The resources that are available to the firm fall into three general categories: physical, organizational, and human. In discussing how to gain a competitive advantage in the global market, Porter (1990) notes that management of the human resources in the global economy is the most critical of the three. The idea of treating human resources as a means of gaining a competitive advantage in both the domestic and the global marketplace has been echoed by other authors as well. As Greer (1995) states,

> In a growing number of organizations human resources are now viewed as a source of competitive advantage. There is greater recognition that distinctive competencies are obtained through highly developed employee skills, distinctive organizational cultures, management processes, and systems. This is in contrast to the traditional emphasis on transferable resources such as equipment. . . . Increasingly, it is being recognized that competitive advantage can be obtained with a high quality work force that enables organizations to compete on the basis of market responsiveness, product and service quality, differentiated products, and technological innovation. (p. 105)

The effective management of human resources in a firm to gain a competitive advantage requires *timely and accurate information* on current employees and potential employees in the labor market. With the evolution of computer technology, meeting this information requirement has been greatly enhanced through the creation of HRIS. A basic assumption behind this book is that the effective management of employee information for decision makers will be the critical process that helps a firm maximize the use of its human resources and maintain competitiveness in its market.

The first purpose of this book is to provide information on the *development, implementation, and maintenance* of an HRIS. The second purpose is to demonstrate *how an HRIS can be used to support HRM functions,* such as in selecting and training employees, to make them more efficient and effective. The final purpose is to emphasize how an HRIS can provide **timely and accurate employee information** to assist decision makers at both the strategic and operational levels in an organization. As a consequence, the quality of employee information will have a strong effect on the overall effectiveness of the organization.

Historical Evolution of HRM and HRIS

One can analyze the historical trends of the HR function from different viewpoints: the evolution of HRM (human resource management) as a professional and scientific discipline, as an aid to management, as a political and economic conflict between management and employees, and as a growing movement of employee involvement influenced by developments in industrial, organizational, and social psychology. The historical analysis that follows will demonstrate the growing importance of employees from being just one of the replaceable parts in organizations in the 20th century industrial economy to being a key source of sustainable competitive advantage in the 21st century knowledge economy.

Since this is a book on HRIS, we will examine the development of the fields of both human resources and information technology in terms of their evolution since the early 20th century. This means examining the evolution of HRM intertwined with developments in IT and describing how IT has played an increasing role in the HRM function. This historical analysis will show how the role of HRM in the firm has changed over time from primarily being concerned with routine **transactional and traditional HR activities** to dealing with complex transformational ones. Transactional activities are the routine bookkeeping tasks— for example, changing an employee's home address or health care provider. Traditional HR activities are focused on HR programs like selection, compensation, and performance appraisal. However, **transformational HR activities** are those actions of an organization that "add value" to the consumption of the firm's product or service. An example of a transformational HR activity would be a training program for retail clerks to improve customer service behavior, which has been identified as a strategic goal for the organization. Thus, transformational activities increase the strategic importance and visibility of the HR function in the firm. This general change over time is illustrated in Figure 1.1 and will become evident as we trace the historical evolution of HRM in terms of five broad phases of the historical development of industry in the United States. For more information on this historical development, you should consult Kavanagh, Gueutal, and Tannenbaum (1990) or Walker (1982).

Pre–World War II

In the early 20th century and prior to World War II, the personnel function (the precursor of human resources management) was primarily involved in clerical record keeping of employee information; in other words, it fulfilled a **"caretaker" function**. During this period, the prevailing management philosophy was called **scientific management**. The central thrust of scientific management was to maximize employee productivity. It was thought that there was *one best way* to do any work, and this best way was determined

Figure 1.1 Historical Evolution of HRM and HRIS

Early Systems Mid-20th Century	Emerging Systems 21st Century
HR Role	*HR Role*
Employee Advocate	Strategic Management Partner
Maintain Accurate Employee Records	Evidence-Based HR
Legal Compliance	HR Data Supports Strategic Decision-Making
React to Organizational Change	External Focus: Serve "Customers"
Internal Focus: Serve Employees	Legal Compliance
⟶	
System Characteristics	*System Characteristics*
Inflexible	Flexible
"Islands of Technology"	Mobile
Batch Processing	Web-Deployed
Focused on Employee Record-Keeping	Integrated with Organizational System
	Real-time Processing
	Focused on Information Sharing

through time and motion studies that investigated the most efficient use of human capabilities in the production process. Then, the work could be divided into pieces, and the number of tasks to be completed by a worker during an average workday could be computed. These findings formed the basis of piece-rate pay systems, which were seen as the most efficient way to motivate employees at that time.

At this point in history, there were very few government influences in employment relations; consequently, employment terms, practices, and conditions were left to the owners of the firm. As a result, abuses such as child labor and unsafe working conditions were common. Some employers set up labor welfare and administration departments to look after the interests of workers by maintaining records on health and safety as well as recording hours worked and payroll. It is interesting to note that record keeping is one of the major functions built into the design of an HRIS today; however, there simply was no computer technology to automate the records at this time in history. Of course, paper records were kept, and we can still see paper record HR systems in many smaller firms today.

Post–World War II (1945–1960)

The mobilization and utilization of labor during the war had a great impact on the development of the personnel function. Managers realized that employee productivity and motivation had a significant impact on the profitability of the firm. The human relations movement after the war emphasized that employees were motivated not just by money but also by social and psychological factors, such as receiving recognition for work accomplished or for the achievement of work norms.

Due to the need for the classification of large numbers of individuals in military service during the war, systematic efforts began to classify workers around occupational categories in order to improve recruitment and selection procedures. The central aspect of these classification systems was the **job description**, which listed the tasks, duties, and responsibilities of any individual who held the job in question. These job description classification systems could also be used to design appropriate compensation programs, evaluate individual employee performance, and provide a basis for termination.

Because of the abusive worker practices prior to the war, employees started forming trade unions, which played an important role in bargaining for better employment terms and conditions. There were significant numbers of employment laws enacted in the United States that allowed the **establishment of labor unions** and defined their scope in relationship with management. Thus, personnel departments had to assume considerably more record keeping and reporting to governmental agencies. Because of these trends, the personnel department had to establish specialist divisions, such as recruitment, labor relations, training and benefits, and government relations.

With its changing and expanding role, the typical personnel department started keeping increasing numbers and types of employee records, and computer technology began to emerge as a possible way to store and retrieve employee information. In some cases in the defense industry, **job analysis** and classification data were inputted into computers to better understand, plan, and use employee skills against needs. For example, the U.S. Air Force conducted a thorough and systematic job analysis and classification through its Air Force Human Resources Laboratory (AFHRL), which resulted in a comprehensive occupational structure. The AFHRL collected data from thousands in jobs within the Air Force, and, through the use of a computer software program called the **Comprehensive Occupational Data Analysis Program (CODAP)**, it was able to establish more accurately a job description classification system for Air Force jobs.

Personnel departments outside the defense industry were not using computers at this time. Computers were being used for billing and inventory control, but there was very little use for them in the personnel function except for payroll. The payroll function was the first to be automated. Large firms began harvesting the benefits of new computer technology to keep track of employee compensation, but this function was usually outsourced to vendors since it was still extremely expensive for a firm to acquire or develop the necessary software for the payroll function. It was simpler to outsource this function. It is important to realize that computer technology was just beginning to be used at this time, and it was complex and costly. With increasing legislation on employment relations and employee unionization, industrial relations became one of the main foci of the personnel department. Union-management bargaining over employment contracts dominated the activity of the department, and these negotiations were not computer based. Record keeping was still done manually despite the growing use of computerized data processing in other departments, such as accounts and materials management. What resulted was an initial reluctance among personnel departments to acquire and use computer technology for their programs. This had a long-term effect in many firms when it came to adopting advancements in computer technology, even though this technology got cheaper and easier to use.

Social Issues Era (1963–1980)

This period witnessed an unprecedented increase in the amount of labor legislation in the United States, legislation that governed various parts of the employment relationship, such as the prohibition of discriminatory practices, the promotion of occupational health and safety, the provision of retirement benefits, and tax regulation. As a result, the personnel department was burdened with the additional responsibility of **legislative compliance** that required collection, analysis, and reporting of voluminous data to statutory authorities. For example, to demonstrate that there was no unfair discrimination in employment practices, a personnel department had to diligently collect, analyze, and store data pertaining to *all* employment functions, such as recruitment, training, compensation, and benefits. To avoid the threat of punitive damages for noncompliance, it had to ensure that the data were comprehensive, accurate, and up to date, which made it essential to automate the data collection, analysis, and report generation process. As you go through the chapters of this book, these varying laws and government guidelines will be covered within the specific HR topics.

It was about this time that personnel departments were beginning to be called human resources departments and the field of human resource management was born. The increasing need to be in compliance with numerous employee protection laws or suffer significant monetary penalties made senior managers aware of the importance of the HRM function. In other words, effective and correct practices in HRM were starting to affect the "bottom line" of the firms, so there was a significant growth of HR departments, and computer technology had advanced to the point where it was beginning to be used. As a result, there was an increasing demand for HR departments to adopt computer technology to process employee information more effectively and efficiently. This trend resulted in an explosion in the number of vendors who could assist HR departments in automating their programs in terms of both hardware and software.

Simultaneously, computer technology was evolving and delivering better productivity at lower costs. These technology developments and increased vendor activity led to the development of a comprehensive **management information system (MIS)** for HRM. The decreasing costs of computer technology versus the increasing costs of employee compensation and benefits made the acquisition of computer-based HR systems (HRIS) a necessary business decision. However, the personnel departments were still slow in adopting computer technology, even though it was inexpensive relative to the power it could deliver for the storage and retrieval of employee information in MIS reports. So, the major issue at this time in the historical development of HRIS was not the need for or capabilities of technology but how to best implement it.

Another factor was the booming economy in most industrialized countries. As a result, employee trade unions successfully bargained for better employment terms, such as health care and retirement benefits. Consequently, labor costs increased, which put pressure on personnel managers to justify cost increases against productivity improvements. With the increased emphasis on employee participation and empowerment, the role of personnel function transformed from a "protector" rather than a "caretaker" focus, shifting the focus away from maintenance to development of employees. Thus, the breadth and depth of HRM functions expanded, bringing about the need for strategic thinking and better delivery of HR services.

Cost-Effectiveness Era (1980 to the Early 1990s)

With increasing competition from emerging European and Asian economies, U.S. and other multinational firms increased their focus on cost reduction through automation and other productivity improvement measures. As regards HRM, the increased administrative burden intensified the need to fulfill a growing number of legislative requirements, while the overall functional focus shifted from employee administration to employee development and involvement. To improve effectiveness and efficiency in service delivery through cost reduction and value-added services, the HR departments came under pressure to harness technology that was becoming cheaper and more powerful.

In addition, there was a growing realization within management that people costs were a very significant part of a company's budget. Some companies estimated that personnel costs were as high as 80% of their operating costs. As a result, there was a growing demand on the HRM function to cost justify their employee programs and services. In one of the first books to address this growing need to cost justify the HRM function, Cascio (1984) indicates that the language of business is dollars and cents, and HR managers need to realize this fact. In a later edition of his book, Cascio (1991) quotes Jacques Fitz-enz (1980), who more accurately states the need for those responsible for human resource management to cost justify their function:

> Few human resource managers—even the most energetic—take the time to analyze the return on the corporation's personnel dollar. We feel we aren't valued in our own organizations, that we can't get the resources we need. We complain that management won't buy our proposals and wonder why our advice is so often ignored until the crisis stage. But the human resources manager seldom stands back to look at the total business and ask: Why am I at the bottom looking up? The answer is painfully apparent. We don't act like business managers—like entrepreneurs whose business happens to be people. (Fitz-enz, 1980, p. 41)

Even small and medium firms could afford computer-based HR systems that were run by increasingly user-friendly microcomputers and could be shown to be cost-effective. The prevailing management thinking regarding the use of computers in HR was not that their use would result in a reduction in the number of employees needed in HR departments but that employee activities and time could be shifted from transactional record keeping to more transformational activities that would add value to the organization. This change in the function of HRM could then be clearly measured in terms of cost-benefit ratios to the bottom line of the company.

Technological Advancement Era and the Emergence of Strategic HRM (1990 to Present)

The economic landscape underwent radical changes throughout the 1990s with increasing globalization, technological breakthroughs (particularly **Internet-enabled Web services**), and hyper competition. Business process reengineering exercises became more common and frequent, resulting in several initiatives, such as the rightsizing of employee numbers, reducing the layers of management, reducing the bureaucracy of organizational structures, creating autonomous work teams, and outsourcing. These changes to both human resources and the systems supporting HR are summarized in Figure 1.1.

Firms today realize that innovative and creative employees who hold the key to organizational knowledge provide a sustainable competitive advantage because, unlike other resources, intellectual capital is difficult for competitors to imitate. Accordingly, the people management function has become strategic in its importance and outlook and is geared to attract, retain, and engage talent. These developments have led to the creation of the **HR balanced scorecard** (Becker, Huselid, & Ulrich, 2001; Huselid, Becker, & Beatty, 2005), as well as to added emphasis on the **return on investment (ROI)** of the HR function and its programs (Cascio, 2000; Fitz-enz, 2000, 2002).

The increased use of technology and the changed focus of the HRM function, which shifted to adding value to the organization's product or service, led to the emergence of the HR department as a strategic partner. With the growing importance and recognition of people and people management in contemporary organizations, strategic human resource management (strategic HRM) has become critically important in management thinking and practice. Strategic HRM derives its theoretical significance from the resources-based view of the firm that treats **human capital** as a strategic asset and a competitive advantage in improving organizational performance (Becker & Huselid, 2006).

Reflecting the resource-based view, Becker and Huselid (2006) stress the importance of HR systems and structure—that is, the "systems, practices, competencies, and employee performance behaviors that reflect the development and management of the firm's strategic human capital"—for organizational performance (p. 899). Context is a crucial element in strategic HRM, and, therefore, researchers increasingly emphasize the **"best-fit" approach to strategic HRM** as opposed to the **"best-practice" approach to strategic HRM**. The success of strategic HRM is contingent on several factors, such as national and organizational culture, size, industry type, occupational category, and business strategy. Accordingly, Becker and Huselid (2006) argue that "it is the fit between the HR architecture and the strategic capabilities and business processes that implement strategy that is the basis of HR's contribution to competitive advantage" (p. 899).

A good example of the importance of HR and the information provided by an HRIS can be found in the **human resources planning (HRP)** function, which will be covered in greater detail in Chapter 11. HRP is primarily concerned with forecasting the need for additional employees in the future and the availability of those employees either inside or external to the company. Imagine, for example, that a company is considering a strategic decision to expand by establishing a production facility in a new location. Using the information recorded and analyzed in the HRIS, HRP can provide estimates of whether or not there are enough people available with the necessary skills in the external labor market of the new location to staff the new facility. Determining the availability of potential employees in the labor market may be critical to the strategic decision to build the new facility, and this, of course, could involve millions or billions of dollars.

In tracing the evolution of strategic HRM, M. L. Lengnick-Hall, C. A. Lengnick-Hall, Andrade, and Drake (2009) identify seven key themes:

- **HR contingency perspective** and fit: HR strategies are dependent on business strategies (cost reduction, quality improvement, and innovation) and business settings (manufacturing, services, public sector, and not for profit, as well as firm size)

- Shift in focus from managing people to creating strategic contributions, signifying the resource-based view of the firm and social capital

- HR system components and structure, focusing on HR system architecture and bundles of high-performance work practices

- Expanding the scope of HRM beyond the focal organization to include customers, suppliers, and competitors, both locally and internationally

- Achieving HR implementation and execution by translating the rhetoric into practice

- Measuring the outcomes of Strategic HRM by various means, such as the HR balanced scorecard approach

- Research methodological issues that stress the importance of evidence-based management

Another critical characteristic of Strategic HRM is the adoption and use of **HR metrics** (Cascio, 2000; Lawler & Mohrman, 2003). Most functional departments of an organization have utilized metrics for decades due to the nature of their business transactions. For example, the marketing department has set sales goals and the effectiveness metric that is used is the percentage of sales relative to the goal. But, for HR, the focus on the measurement of the cost effectiveness of programs is relatively recent. Despite the recent utilization of metrics, their use continues to grow and has deepened as organizations seek to compete globally.

Kaplan and Norton (1996) first popularized the concept of the *balanced scorecard* that goes beyond traditional financial measures to assess firm performance to include customer, internal process, and learning perspectives. Incorporating the principles of the balanced scorecard approach, Beatty, Huselid, and Schneier (2003) developed the HR balanced scorecard that seeks to achieve the key HR deliverables (workforce mindset, technical knowledge, and workforce behavior) by aligning, integrating, and differentiating the HR systems. In addition, Lawler, Levenson, and Boudreau (2004) emphasize that three types of metrics are important to evaluate the HR function. The first type is *efficiency metrics* for administrative tasks such as "time to fill" jobs. The second type is *effectiveness metrics* for HR practices such as the cost to fill a job vacancy. The third type is *impact metrics* for HR programs and practices that focus on the overall objective of developing and optimizing workforce capabilities and competencies. For example, an organization could assess the cost per hire comparing current-year cost relative to the costs in previous years or after a major change to recruitment practices. HR metrics combined with IT knowledge and applications has given organizations a significant tool to utilize the human capital in their organizations.

The most recent development related to the role of HRM in Strategic HRM has been the application of HRIS-enabled **Six Sigma** processes to HRM. Most professionals associate Six Sigma with General Electric, as the company was the first major user of the Six Sigma approach. In general, Six Sigma refers to streamlining operations through business process reengineering and has been structured around five key processes—define, measure, analyze, improve, and control (DMAIC). The DMAIC approach uses an assortment of statistical tools to reengineer business processes, improve decision making, and improve customer service. Six Sigma will be discussed in terms of project management in Chapter 6.

As we will see in the ensuing chapters, information technology is a key enabler of Strategic HRM (Haines & Lafleur, 2008). However, in determining the strategic fit between technology and HR, it is *not the strategy per se that leads to competitive advantage but rather how well it is "implemented,"* taking into account the environmental realities that can be unique to each organization and, indeed, between units and functions of the organization. A critical aspect of an HRIS in supporting the implementation of strategic plans is using it to make decisions about employees, human capital programs, and initiatives. All of these HRM decisions are aided by the ability of the HRIS to generate reports, for example, the number of new employees needed for a specific job. Thus, in the section entitled "A Primer on HRIS" later in this chapter, you will note the generation of reports to be a key benefit of an HRIS. HRM reports are central to decisions involving the human capital of an organization, and they enable the translation of strategic plans to operational decisions. As you go through the chapters in this book, you will see how reports are used in a variety of HRM programs and activities.

HR Activities

Typical HR programs involve things such as record keeping, recruiting, selection, training, employee relations, and compensation. However, all these programs involve multiple activities, and these HR activities can be classified into three broad categories: transactional, traditional, and transformational (Wright, McMahan, Snell, & Gerhart, 1998). Transactional activities involve day-to-day transactions that have to deal mostly with record keeping— for example, entering payroll information, tracking employee status changes, and the administration of employee benefits. Traditional activities involve HR programs such as planning, recruiting, selection, training, compensation, and performance management. These activities can have strategic value for the organization if their results or outcomes are consistent with the strategic goals of the organization. Transformational activities are those activities that add value to the organization—for example, cultural or organizational change, structural realignment, strategic redirection, and increasing innovation.

Wright et al. (1998) estimated that most HR departments spend approximately 65% to 75% of their time on transactional activities, 15% to 30% on traditional activities, and 5% to 15% on transformational activities. One of the major purposes of the design, development, and implementation of an HRIS is to reduce the amount of time HR employees have to spend on transactional activities, allowing the staff to spend more time on traditional and transformational activities. This notion of using technology to improve transactional activities and accomplish them more efficiently is the central theme of this book and provides one of the primary justifications for a computer-based system. In later chapters that discuss various HR programs such as selection and training, we will see how a computer-based system can aid in both traditional and transformational activities to make them consistent with the strategic goals of the organization.

In terms of the broad roles of HR, Ulrich (1998) identifies four main roles, namely, strategic business partner, administrative expert, employee champion, and change agent. Ulrich, Younger, and Brockbank (2008) stress that, in the 21st century, the HR organization should function as a business within a business, shifting its focus from activities to outcomes and capabilities and its structure so that it mirrors that of the business.

Interface Between HR and Technology

Technology-driven automation (IT) and the redesign of work processes certainly help reduce costs and cycle times as well as improve quality. Information systems (IS) can further help decision makers to make and implement strategic decisions. However, IT is only a tool and can only complement, not substitute for, the people who use it. Often, organizations mistake IT as a message and not the messenger, so they divert time, effort, and money away from a long-term investment in people to developing and deploying information technologies (Thite, 2004). In fact, the critical success factors in information systems project implementation are often nontechnical and due more to political, social, and managerial issues rather than technical issues (Martinsons & Chong, 1999). This topic is covered in detail in Chapters 8 and 9.

With the increasing use of information technologies in HR planning and delivery, the way people in organizations look at the nature and role of HR itself may change (Roehling et al., 2005). With HR data and reports now readily available on their desktops, will managers interact less with the HR department and see it as being less important? If that is so, how will it affect the attitude of HR professionals toward their jobs and profession? Will they resist the adoption of technology if they perceive that this technology lessens their status?

In traditional organizations with silo mentalities, turf wars between operational departments and functions acting as independent entities are common. Therefore, top management needs to be mindful of organizational politics in managing change. This awareness can be particularly important when developing and implementing an HRIS. Through most of its evolution, HRM has had an administrative and caretaker focus in its delivery, and, even today, this administrative and caretaker focus is important. But, with technology significantly decreasing the time required for administrative tasks, HR departments will begin to allocate resources to more complex, strategic, and transformative activities. Through these changes, the role of HRM is redefined and transformed through value-added, strategic initiatives and interventions. This also means that HR professionals will need to learn new skills and rethink the way the HR department is organized and delivers its services. With the improved job skills of HR professionals, technology will be seen as HR's "partner in progress." While having an advanced, full-fledged system will not automatically make HR a strategic business partner, this system acts as a building block and an effective aid in the process (Lawler & Mohrman, 2003).

A Primer on HRIS

What Is an HRIS?

After reviewing the many definitions of an HRIS, we define it as a system used to acquire, store, manipulate, analyze, retrieve, and distribute information regarding an organization's human resources to support HRM and managerial decisions. An HRIS is not simply computer hardware and associated HR-related software. It requires cooperation among departments for its best use. That is, it includes hardware and software; it also includes people, forms, policies and procedures, and data.

It is important to note that a company that does not have a computerized system still has a human resource information system, but the system exists on paper (e.g., stored in files or folders). The paper systems that most companies used before the development of computer technology were still comparable with an HRIS, but the management of employee information was not done as quickly as in a computerized system, nor did it provide the wealth of data that today's HRIS provides. If these companies had not had paper systems, the development and implementation of computerized systems would have been extremely difficult. For the purpose of this book, however, we will use the term *HRIS* to refer to a computerized system designed to manage the company's HR.

The primary purpose of the HRIS is to provide service, in the form of *accurate and timely information,* to the "clients" of the system. There are a variety of potential clients, as HR information may be used for strategic, tactical, and operational decision making (e.g., planning for needed employees in a merger); to avoid litigation (e.g., identifying discrimination problems in hiring); to evaluate programs, policies, or practices (e.g., evaluating the effectiveness of a training program); and to support daily operations (e.g., helping managers monitor the work time and attendance of their employees). All these uses mean that there is a mandatory requirement that data and reports be accurate and timely and that the client can understand how to use the information.

Because of the complexity and data intensiveness of the HRM function, it is one of the last management functions to be targeted for automation (Bussler & Davis, 2001/2002). This fact does not mean that an HRIS is not important; it just indicates the difficulty of developing and implementing it compared with other business functions—for example, the billing and accounting systems. Powered by information systems and the Internet, almost every process in every function of HRM has been computerized today. A sample employee home screen for an HRIS is shown in Figure 1.2

The systems and process focus helps organizations keep the customer perspective in mind, since quality is primarily defined and operationalized in terms of total customer satisfaction (Evans, 2005). Today's competitive environment requires organizations to integrate the

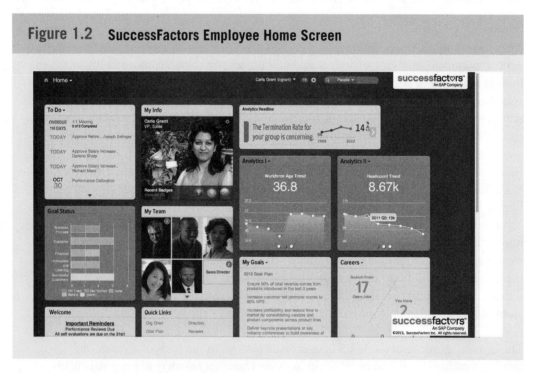

Figure 1.2 SuccessFactors Employee Home Screen

activities of each functional department while keeping the customer in mind. An effective HRIS helps by providing the technology to generate accurate and timely employee information to fulfill this objective.

e-HRM and HRIS

Confusion can arise concerning the distinction between e-HRM and HRIS. Electronic human resource management, or e-HRM, reflects a philosophy for the delivery of HR; it uses information technology, particularly the Web, as the central component of delivering efficient and effective HR services. This philosophy can be best seen through the words of Gueutal and Stone (2005): "Things will look a bit different here. No longer will you deal with an HR professional. . . . The HR portal will take care of you" (p. xv). Essentially, technology becomes the nerve center for disseminating, connecting, and conducting human resources (Strohmeier, 2007). Organizations embracing an e-HRM approach don't simply utilize technology in the support of human resources but instead see technology as enabling the HR function to be done differently by modifying "information flows, social interaction patterns, and communication processes" (Stone & Lukaszewski, 2009, p. 136).

Conversely, as conceptualized in this book, an HRIS comprises the technology and processes underlying this new way of conducting human resource management. An HRIS can include technologies such as databases, small functional systems focused on a single HR application (e.g., performance management), or a large-scale, integrated **enterprise resource planning (ERP) architecture** and Web-based applications. In today's environment, it can even be devices such as smartphones and social networking tools that enable employees to access HR data remotely or to connect with others in the organization. Another way of looking at the differences between e-HRM and HRIS is that e-HRM tends to be more focused on how HR functionality is delivered (e.g., e-recruitment and e-training), and an HRIS is more focused on the systems and technology underlying the design and acquisition of systems supporting the move to e-HRM.

Why Do We Need HRIS?

Using HRIS gives firms several advantages (Beckers & Bsat, 2002). They include

- providing a comprehensive information picture as a single, integrated database; this enables organizations to provide structural connectivity across units and activities and to increase the speed of information transactions (C. A. Lengnick-Hall & Lengnick-Hall, 2006);

- increasing competitiveness by improving HR operations and management processes;

- collecting appropriate data and converting them to information and knowledge for improved timeliness and quality of decision making;

- producing a greater number and variety of accurate and real-time HR-related reports;

- streamlining and enhancing the efficiency and effectiveness of HR administrative functions;

- shifting the focus of HR from the processing of transactions to strategic HRM;

- reengineering HR processes and functions; and

- improving employee satisfaction by delivering HR services more quickly and accurately.

The ability of firms to harness the potential of HRIS depends on a variety of factors, such as

- the size of the organization, with large firms generally reaping greater benefits;

- the amount of top management support and commitment;

- the availability of resources (time, money, and personnel);

- the HR philosophy of the company as well as its vision, organizational culture, structure, and systems;

- managerial competence in cross-functional decision making, employee involvement, and coaching; and

- the ability and motivation of employees in adopting change, such as increased automation across and between functions (Ngai & Wat, 2004).

In assessing the benefits and impact of an HRIS to an organization, typical accounting methods do not work with the HRM function (Becker et al., 2001; Cascio, 2000; Fitz-enz, 2000, 2002; Huselid et al., 2005; Thite, 2004; Ulrich & Smallwood, 2005). While there are several tangible benefits in implementing an HRIS, such as payroll efficiencies and a reduction in labor costs due to automation, there are several intangible or hidden benefits as well (Roberts, 1999). They include employee satisfaction with streamlined and efficient HR processes and freeing up HR from routine, administrative matters to focus on strategic goals.

Furthermore, HR practices can help organizations untangle the rigidity and inertia associated with the mechanistic, routine nature of enterprise resource planning (ERP). ERP software applications are a set of integrated database applications or modules that carry out the most common business functions, including HR, general ledger, accounts payable, accounts receivable, order management, inventory control, and customer relationship management. Obviously, HRM's emphasis on knowledge management, human capital stewardship, and relationship building can provide considerable assistance in the implementation and use of ERPs (C. A. Lengnick-Hall & Lengnick-Hall, 2006). Therefore, active engagement of HR professionals in the introduction and ongoing functioning of an ERP is important so that organizations can realize the strategic benefits associated with these systems (Dery & Wailes, 2005).

Different Types of HRIS

Although there are multiple typologies for the classification of computer-based systems, we are going to define the most basic types of systems that are most readily applied to the HR context and for use within an HRIS. Although there are many ways of categorizing information systems, one of the most common ways of doing this is to focus on what level of organizational processing the system supports: daily operations, managerial functioning, executive-level processes and strategies, and those that span organizational levels. Table 1.1 catalogs the major types of information systems, lists their major focus and goals, and provides examples of how they can be used to support human resources.

As seen in Table 1.1, specific computer-based systems have been created to support HRM at different organizational levels with applications for HRM. Although large, global organizations have likely implemented most, if not all, of these types of systems, it would be unusual for small to midsized organizations to have the resources to do so. Despite this, most organizations would have some of these systems in place and would depend on them to support operations and decision making. As you go through this book, these systems and their HR examples will be discussed, and you should refer back to this table as needed.

System Development Process for an HRIS

According to engineering and information processing literature, the formal design of any information processing system is supposed to follow a set of steps labeled the **systems development life cycle (SDLC)**. However, as Sprague and Carlson (1982) and other writers (Aktas, 1987; Davis, 1983) have noted, the traditional SDLC is somewhat difficult to use as originally specified. But there is agreement that the SDLC has five general phases: (1) planning, (2) analysis, (3) design, (4) implementation, and (5) maintenance. As will be seen, particularly in Parts I and II of this book, there are multiple references to the SDLC and its phases.

Kavanagh et al. (1990), applying the main concepts and phases of the traditional SDLC to the HRM function, recommend the following system development process for an HRIS: "The HRIS development process refers to the steps taken from the time a company considers computerizing its human resources functions through the analysis, design, development,

Table 1.1   Information Systems Providing Support for HRM

Organizational Level	Type of System	Major Goals and Focus	HRM Examples
Operational	Transaction Processing System	Improved transaction speed and accuracy Improved efficiency in the processing of daily business transactions Automation of routine transactions Reduced transaction costs	Payroll processing Time and attendance entry Online creation and dissemination of application forms
Managerial	Management Information System	Provides key data to managers Supports regular and ongoing decisions Provides defined and ad-hoc reporting	Producing EEO3 reports Calculating yield ratios for recruiting Calculating per-capita merit increases
Executive	Executive Information System	Provides aggregate, high-level data Helps managers with long-range planning Supports strategic direction and decisions	Succession planning Aggregate data on balanced scorecard
Boundary Spanning	Decision Support System	Interactive and iterative managerial decision making Supports forecasting and "what-if" analysis Supports business simulations	Staffing needs assessment Labor market analysis Employee skills assessment

	Expert System	Embed human knowledge into information systems Automate decisions with technology	Resume keyword searches
	Office Automation Systems	Designing documents Scheduling shared resources Communication	E-mail training-room scheduling
	Collaboration Technologies	Supports electronic communication and collaboration between employees Supports virtual teams	Communication support for e-learning Online meetings and shared documents HR departmental wikis
	Enterprise Resources Planning System	Integration and centralization of corporate data Share data across functional boundaries Single data source and common technology architecture	OrangeHRM Oracle/PeopleSoft Lawson HRM SAP

implementation, maintenance, evaluation, and improvement of the system" (pp. 92–93). This system development process is quite similar to the one proposed by Walker (1982). He indicates that development of an effective HRIS should follow seven stages: "Proposal to Management, Needs Analysis, System Specifications, System Design, System Development, Installation and Conversion, and Evaluation" (p. 38).

Although this book will cover all the phases in the development and implementation of an HRIS, there are two *critical* points to be emphasized from these descriptions of the phases or stages of system development. One, the system development process *begins* when the company first begins to consider computerizing its HR functions. It is important to *document* this beginning of the process so that it can be considered when the system is being evaluated and maintained. The second critical point is the *importance of the evaluation* and, as needed, the improvement of the system. This evaluation must be continuous and occur not only after the system has been implemented but also at every stage of the development. The quality of these evaluations of the system will depend heavily on the documentation of the stages of the entire system development process. The documentation of the planning and development of a system is one of the most important determinants of successful system implementation, as well as of continued system improvement.

A Model of Organizational Functioning

As stated in the previous paragraph, the documentation and evaluation of HRIS development and implementation are critical since we envision the effective functioning of any organization as dependent on the effective management of its employees. The use of computer technology to improve the management of employees is centered on the creation and maintenance of an HRIS. Figure 1.3 depicts an overview of an HRIS within the organizational and a global business environment.

This figure shows at its center the Human Resources environment and the major components of that environment (e.g., HR Programs). The next layer in the figure represents the organizational environment and its components. Outside the organizational environment is the global business environment, which directly influences the organizational environment and indirectly affects the HR environment. Each of these layers mutually influences each other and together can impact the development and implementation of the HRIS. For example, differing labor laws across countries mean that different HR policies may be implemented and may affect the type of data collected by the HRIS and reported to regulatory agencies in different companies. The figure also indicates the interrelatedness between the strategic management system; the strategic HRM system; and the performance, business, and HR goals that are generated during the strategic planning process. As will be emphasized throughout this book, the *alignment* between the global business environment, the strategic management system, the strategic HR management system, the business goals, the HR goals, and the HR programs is critical to the organization's maintenance of its competitiveness in the market (Evans & Davis, 2005; Huselid, Jackson, & Schuler, 1997).

There are several aspects of this model that are critical. First, this model is a framework to use in reading, organizing, and understanding the information given in this book. Second, this is a systems model; that is, it is organic and can change over time, as the

Figure 1.3 Overview of an HRIS Embedded in Organizational and Global Business Environments

Global Business Environment

Organizational Environment

Government Regulations

Strategic Management System

Organizational Information System

Human Resources Environment

Societal Concerns

HR Knowledge

IT Knowledge

Technology

HR Evaluation HR Scorecard, HR Metrics, ROI, etc.

Human Resource Information System

HR Programs Recruitment, Selection, Training, Employee Safety, etc.

Competitors

Strategic human resource management

HR Goals Retention, Climate/ Morale, Productivity, etc.

Labor Markets

Research-Based Best HR Practices

environment changes (e.g., the increasing focus on unfair discrimination in society and in the workforce will affect the HR environment and will, in turn, affect the organizational and global business environments). Third, the model is centered on the use of an HRIS as critical to the efficient operation of the organization. Note that if the HRIS were removed it would still represent a model of organizational functioning. However, it is our contention that an organization operating without an HRIS at its core would not be able to compete as effectively. The costs of managing HR data would just be too expensive in relation to its competitors. Fourth, the HRIS and the HR program evaluation results, in terms of HR metrics and cost-benefit results (value added and return on investment—ROI), are in continual interaction. This emphasis is consistent with current thinking in the HRM field (Cascio, 2000; Fitz-enz, 2000, 2002) and has generated the **HR workforce scorecard** (Becker et al., 2001; Huselid et al., 2005). Finally, it is important to note that the *successful* design, development, and implementation of an HRIS *depend equally on IT and on HR knowledge,* which is the basic philosophy of this entire book.

Themes of the Book

The *overall theme* of this book is that the HR and IT functions operate separately and together in an HRIS and are focused on providing accurate and timely information for managerial decisions, both strategic and operational. There are other themes that are emphasized in this book, which can also be seen in Figure 1.3. These themes are the major factors that influence the effective operation of the organization through their impact on managerial decisions. In addition, they directly affect the success of both the HRM programs and the use of the HRIS. These factors are as follows:

1. The effective alignment between the strategy of the firm, the HR strategy, and HR programs,

2. The importance of tying HRM programs to IT applications and databases,

3. The importance of legal considerations in all HR programs and functions,

4. The need for a cooperative relationship between HR and IT professionals, and

5. The critical need for the creation and use of HR metrics to guide decision making and evaluate the cost-effectiveness of the HR strategy and programs.

All the chapters of this book will contain some reference to some or all of these factors, and their effects will be discussed in detail in each chapter.

SUMMARY

The primary purpose of this chapter was to introduce the academic and practitioner field of human resource information systems (HRIS), emphasizing that an HRIS is at the intersection of IT and HRM. The evolution of the field of HRIS, from its initial role of a record keeper concerned with only transactional HR activities, such as changing addresses on employee records, to one of becoming a strategic partner was covered in detail. This evolution demonstrated that, as IT improved over time, so did HRM, and these improvements made their marriage into HRIS that much easier. The advances in the field of HRIS also led to a reduction in the percentage of time that HR professionals spent on routine transactional and traditional activities and an increase in the percentage of time spent on transformational ones. The increase in time spent on transformational activities improves the "value added" by HRM programs to the strategic plan of an organization.

A basic primer on HRIS was presented, and the different types of human resource information systems were discussed, showing how the different types are needed for decision making at different levels in the organization. The distinction between HRIS and e-HRM was explained to help the reader avoid confusing these terms when they appear in the remainder of the book. In addition, the chapter discussed the development of HRIS and how it has helped enable HRM to become a strategic partner in organizations, which then led to the emergence of strategic HRM as a field of study. Various strategic approaches were discussed, such as HR in a contingency model, the HR balanced scorecard, and the use of Six Sigma in HR.

A model of organizational functioning in organizational and global business environments was covered. This model is centered on an HRIS and focuses on how the feedback from results generated by an HRIS can influence the operation of the entire organization. The central themes of this book were emphasized, and the reader was alerted to the fact that these themes will occur throughout the chapters of the book. Finally, an overview of the structure of the book was provided to demonstrate the connections between the chapters of the book.

KEY TERMS

DISCUSSION QUESTIONS _____

1. What are the factors that changed the primary role of HRM from a caretaker of records to a strategic partner?

2. Describe the historical evolution of HRM and HRIS in terms of the changing role of HRM and the influence of computer technology on HRM.

3. What is required for the effective management of human resources in a firm to gain a competitive advantage in the marketplace?

4. Describe the emergence of strategic HRM and the influence of computer technology. What are some of the approaches used in HRM to facilitate the use of Strategic HRM in a firm's business strategy?

5. How does technology help deliver transactional, traditional, and transformational HR activities more efficiently and effectively?

6. Justify the need for an HRIS.

7. Describe and differentiate the major types of information systems.

8. Using the organizational model presented in this chapter, explain why and how the global business environment and organizational environment influence the nature and importance of the HRIS function.

CASE STUDY: POSITION DESCRIPTION AND SPECIFICATION FOR AN HRIS ADMINISTRATOR _____

One way to assess the nature and importance of a particular function or position in an organization is to examine the job description and job specifications for this position, as they tell us what activities, duties, and tasks are involved in the job as well as what knowledge, skills, and abilities (KSA) are required to perform the job. The following is an actual advertisement for an HRIS administrator. A large corporation placed this ad in the "Job Central" section of the Internet site for the International Association for Human Resources Information Management[1] (http://www.ihrim.org).

HRIS Administrator

Job Level: Senior (5+ Years), Full time

Reports to: Senior Director of Human Resources Operations

Position Summary

MOMIRI, LLC is an Alabama Native Owned Corporation, providing shared services to the MOMIRI family of companies and planning and incubating the next generation of companies serving federal and commercial customers. MOMIRI companies offer core expertise in telecommunications, information technology, product development, major program management, open source software, construction management, facility operations, and operations support. MOMIRI companies realize that quality personnel are the key to our success. An excellent benefits package, professional working environment, and outstanding leaders are all keys to retaining top professionals.

Primary Function

The incumbent will serve as a key member of the HR Support Services department and provide professional human resources support in specific functions or disciplines to management and staff for the MOMIRI family of companies. This position is viewed as going to a midlevel professional who assists management and staff with HR programs at the tactical level and performs all essential duties and responsibilities at the direction of the Manager of HR Operations.

Essential Duties and Responsibilities

- Provides technical assistance to senior-level HR staff and management on several HR programs to include employee relations, compensation, EEO compliance, company policies and procedures, disability programs (STD, LTD, FMLA, ADA), federal and state employment laws, and personnel actions as needed.

- Supports and maintains the Human Resources Information System (HRIS) in addition to other systems supported by the management of enterprise applications.

- Serves as technical point-of-contact for assigned functional areas and assists subject matter experts with ensuring data integrity, testing of system changes, report writing and analyzing data flows for process improvement opportunities.

- Supports HRIS and other enterprise systems' upgrades, patches, testing and other technical projects as assigned.

- Recommends process/customer service improvements, innovative solutions, policy changes and/or major variations from established policy.

- Serves as key systems liaison with other departments and process stakeholders (e.g., Payroll).

- Writes, maintains, and supports a variety of reports or queries utilizing appropriate reporting tools. Assists in development of standard reports for ongoing customer needs.

- Maintains data integrity in ATS, HRIS, and other enterprise systems by running queries and analyzing and fully auditing data across all HR departments.

- Conducts new hire in-processing to include systems training for new employees and entering new employee information in Costpoint.

- Conducts termination out-processing to include entering employee separation information in Costpoint and reporting attrition data.

- Develops user procedures, guidelines, and documentation for HR-related systems. Trains system users on new processes/functionality.

- Provides HR tools and resources for management and staff to accomplish their goals and objectives.

- Processes personnel actions (hires, terminations, pay & title changes, promotions, employment status, etc.) to include entering data into HRIS.

- Assists with special HR-related projects and provides training to other staff members as required.

- Performs other duties as assigned.

Requirements

Specialized Knowledge and Skills

- Experience working with a multiple-site workforce.

- Working knowledge of federal and state employment laws and related acts.

- Advanced to expert level computer skills.

- Excellent verbal and written communication and presentation skills.

- Great interpersonal skills.

- Strong time-management and prioritization skills.

Qualifications

- Bachelor's degree in HR and/or equivalent professional experience.

- 3–5 years of technical HRIS experience in professional HR environment.

- Self-directed, highly responsive, and detail oriented.

- Ability to maintain absolute confidentiality in all business matters.

- Government contracting experience is a plus.

Case Study Questions

1. How does this position help the HR function become a strategic partner of the organization?

2. From the position description, identify the traditional, transactional, and transformational HR activities that this position is involved with.

3. Using the key responsibilities identified for this position, explain why and how the HRIS function plays a pivotal role in the organizational model as described in this chapter.

STUDENT STUDY SITE _____

Visit the Student Study Site at **http://www.sagepub.com/kavanagh3e** for additional learning tools such as access to SAGE journal articles and related web resources.

NOTE _____

1. The name of the company in the advertisement has been changed.

REFERENCES _____

Aktas, A. Z. (1987). *Structured analysis and design of information systems.* Englewood Cliffs, NJ: Prentice Hall.

Beatty, R. W., Huselid, M. A., & Schneier, C. E. (2003). New HR metrics: Scoring on the business scorecard. *Organizational Dynamics, 32*(2), 107–121.

Becker, B. E., & Huselid, M. A. (2006). Strategic human resource management: Where do we go from here? *Journal of Management, 32*(6), 898–925.

Becker, B. E., Huselid, M. A., & Ulrich, D. (2001). *The HR scorecard: Linking people, strategy, and performance.* Boston: Harvard Business School Press.

Beckers, A. M., & Bsat, M. Z. (2002). A DSS classification model for research in human resource information systems. *Information Systems Management, 19*(3), 41–50.

Bussler, L., & Davis, E. (2001/2002). Information systems: The quiet revolution in human resource management. *Journal of Computer Information Systems, 42*(2), 17–20.

Cascio, W. F. (1984). *Costing human resources: The financial impact of behavior in organizations.* Boston: PWS-Kent.

Cascio, W. F. (1991). *Costing human resources: The financial impact of behavior in organizations* (3rd ed.). Boston: PWS-Kent.

Cascio, W. F. (2000). *Costing human resources: The financial impact of behavior in organizations* (4th ed.). Cincinnati, OH: South-Western College.

Davis, W. S. (1983). *Systems analysis and design: A structured approach.* Reading, MA: Addison-Wesley.

Dery, K., & Wailes, N. (2005). Necessary but not sufficient: ERPs and strategic HRM. *Strategic Change, 14,* 265–272.

Drucker, P. F., Dyson, E., Handy, C., Saffo, P., & Senge, P. M. (1997). Looking ahead: Implications of the present. *Harvard Business Review, 75*(5), 18–24.

Evans, J. R. (2005). *Total quality.* Toronto, ON: Thomson.

Evans, W. R., & Davis, W. D. (2005). High-performance work systems and organizational performance: The mediating role of internal social structure. *Journal of Management, 31,* 758–775.

Fitz-enz, J. (1980). Quantifying the human resources function. *Personnel, 57*(3), 41–52.

Fitz-enz, J. (2000). *The ROI of human capital: Measuring the economic value of employee performance.* New York: AMACOM/ American Management Association.

Fitz-enz, J. (2002). *How to measure human resource management* (3rd ed.). New York: McGraw-Hill.

Greer, C. (1995). *Strategy and human resources: A general managerial perspective.* Englewood Cliffs, NJ: Prentice Hall.

Gueutal, H. G., & Stone, D. L. (2005). *The brave new world of eHR: Human resources management in the digital age.* San Francisco: Jossey-Bass.

Haines, V. Y., & Lafleur, G. (2008). Information technology usage & human resource roles & effectiveness. *Human Resource Management, 47*(3), 525–540.

Huselid, M. A., Becker, B. E., & Beatty, R. W. (2005). *The workforce scorecard: Managing human capital to execute strategy.* Boston: Harvard Business School Press.

Huselid, M. A., Jackson, S. E., & Schuler, R. S. (1997). Technical and strategic human resource management effectiveness as determinants of firm performance. *Academy of Management Journal, 40,* 171–188.

Kaplan, R. S., & Norton, D. P. (1996). Linking the balanced scorecard to strategy. *California Management Review, 39*(1), 53–79.

Kavanagh, M. J., Gueutal, H. G., & Tannenbaum, S. I. (1990). *Human resource information systems.* Boston: PWS-Kent.

Lawler, E. E., Levenson, A., & Boudreau, J. W. (2004). HR metrics and analytics: Use and impact. *Human Resource Planning, 27*(4), 27–35.

Lawler, E. E., & Mohrman, S. A. (2003). HR as a strategic business partner: What does it take to make it happen? *Human Resource Planning, 26*(3), 15–29.

Lengnick-Hall, C. A., & Lengnick-Hall, M. L. (2006). HR, ERP, and knowledge for competitive advantage. *Human Resource Management, 45*(2), 179–194.

Lengnick-Hall, M. L., Lengnick-Hall, C. A., Andrade, L. S., & Drake, B. (2009). Strategic Human Resource Management: The evolution of the field. *Human Resource Management Review, 19,* 64–85.

Martinsons, M. G., & Chong, P. K. C. (1999). The influence of human factors and specialist involvement on information systems success. *Human Relations, 52*(1), 123–152.

Ngai, E. W. T., & Wat, F. K. T. (2004). Human resource information systems: A review and empirical analysis. *Personnel Review, 35*(3), 297–314.

Porter, M. E. (1990). *The competitive advantage of nations.* Boston: Free Press.

Roberts, B. (1999). Calculating return on investment for HRIS. *HR Magazine, 44*(13), 122–127.

Roehling, M. V., Boswell, W. R., Caligiuri, P., Feldman, D., Graham, M. E., Guthrie, J. P., et al. (2005). The future of HR management: Research needs and directions. *Human Resource Management, 44*(2), 207–216.

Smith, A. F., & Kelly, T. (1997). Human capital in the digital economy. In F. Hesselbein, M. Goldsmith, & R. Beckhard (Eds.), *The organization of the future* (pp. 199–212). San Francisco: Jossey-Bass.

Sprague, R. H., & Carlson, E. D. (1982). *Building effective decision support systems.* Englewood Cliffs, NJ: Prentice Hall.

Stone, D. L., & Lukaszewski, K. M. (2009). An expanded model of the factors affecting the acceptance and effectiveness of electronic human resource management systems. *Human Resource Management Review, 19,* 134–143.

Strohmeier, S. (2007). Research in e-HRM: Review and implications. *Human Resource Management Review, 17*(1), 19–37.

Thite, M. (2004). *Managing people in the new economy.* New Delhi, India: Sage.

Ulrich, D. (1998). A new mandate for human resources. *Harvard Business Review, 76*(1), 124–135.

Ulrich, D., & Smallwood, N. (2005). HR's new ROI: Return on intangibles. *Human Resources Management, 44*(2), 137–142.

Ulrich, D., Younger, J., & Brockbank, W. (2008). The twenty-first-century HR organization. *Human Resource Management, 47*(4), 829–850.

Walker, A. J. (1982). *HRIS development: A project team guide to building an effective personnel information system.* New York: Van Nostrand Reinhold.

Wright, P., McMahan, G., Snell, S., & Gerhart, B. (1998). *Strategic human resource management: Building human capital and organizational capacity* (Technical report). Ithaca, NY: Cornell University.

CHAPTER 2

Database Concepts and Applications in Human Resource Information Systems

Janet H. Marler and Barry D. Floyd

EDITORS' NOTE

As mentioned in the book overview in Chapter 1, this chapter is focused on understanding databases and the applications of IT to the development and use of an HRIS. Although this chapter may be a review for some students, the material in it is critical to understanding the remaining chapters of the book. As such, students may want to refer to this chapter as they are studying subsequent chapters. This introductory chapter is also an excellent example of the contribution of IT to the field of HRM in building an HRIS.

CHAPTER Objectives

After completing this chapter, you should be able to

- Discuss the difference between data, information, and knowledge
- Identify problems with early database structures
- Understand what a relational database is and why it is better than older database structures
- Discuss three types of data sharing and why they are important
- Know where data in a database are stored
- Know the different ways in which data can be delivered to the end user
- Know what a query is and discuss three different types of queries
- Discuss how queries are used to support decision making
- Discuss the key steps involved in designing a simple database in Microsoft (MS) Access
- Know what the top HR databases are
- Identify key data fields in an HR database
- Understand the difference between operational databases and a data warehouse
- Discuss how business intelligence software can support HR decision making

Introduction

Whether an organization purchases, leases, or develops its HRIS, the data and the information it produces are stored and retrieved through a database. Today's HRIS have as their foundation electronic databases that work in conjunction with **business applications** to transform data into information that is essential for business operations and for decision making. Many believe that managing electronic databases and turning data into accessible and actionable information is a competency necessary to succeed in today's marketplace. Indeed, data are produced, stored, updated, and shared by HR employees and managers on a daily basis. This process is so pervasive that it often goes unnoticed. Yet, the effective collection, storage, integration, and use of data are essential for any business, and the most successful organizations are masters of this process!

In this chapter, we provide an insight into how commercially delivered HRIS databases work. We define key **relational database** terminology, describe how a database is structured, and show how to develop a basic database using **MS Access**, a basic **database management system (DBMS)**, as an example. We discuss how DBMSs provide the capability to integrate HR data and to link this data with other data essential to the operations of a business. We close by providing examples of HRIS built on MS Access to provide a basic understanding of larger, more complex commercially developed HRIS databases.

Data, Information, and Knowledge

Data are the lifeblood of an organization. The production and maintenance of data are critical to the smooth operation of every part of the organization. Data represent the "facts" of transactions that occur on a daily basis. A transaction can be thought of as an event of consequence, such as hiring a new employee for a particular position for a specified salary. The organization attempts to capture the data (facts) associated with each of these transactions, such as the date hired, the name of the person hired, the title of the position, the location where the new hire will work, and so on, and then store these data for future use.

Information, on the other hand, is the interpretation of these data. An interpretation of data always has some goal and context such as making a hiring decision for a particular department or understanding the performance of an employee to make a promotion decision. Note that sometimes the data themselves can be informative without any additional transformation (e.g., the salary range of the job). But other times, we must do additional work (e.g., calculating totals or presenting the data in some order) to turn the data into information to answer important questions such as "What is our full-time employee headcount in Corporate Sales?" or "Which employee should be promoted?"

Knowledge is information that has been given meaning (Whitehill, 1997). Knowledge is different from data and information. More than what and why, knowledge is about *how*. Knowledge, therefore, consists of the procedures one follows to use data and information to make decisions and conduct business. In many instances, such procedural knowledge is mostly hidden, residing in the minds of individuals and groups in the organization. For example, in HRIS, facts about age, gender, and education are the data. Information created from these data includes average age, gender ratio, and number and types of graduates at the business unit level. Such data and information help HR managers plan recruitment, schedule training programs to bridge skill gaps, and identify whether there may be employee discrimination. Knowledge represents how HR managers can execute the recruitment plan, decide which training programs are best to bridge skill gaps, or determine what to do if employee discrimination exists. In the HR function, *data* about employees and jobs are the foundation of most of the *information* that is critical to analyzing and making HR decisions. *Knowledge,* on the other hand, constitutes knowing what information is needed from a database and how to use it to achieve HR objectives.

Database Management Systems

A DBMS is a set of software applications (i.e., computer programs) combined with a database. A DBMS electronically allows organizations to effectively manage data. Managing data means

- identifying the data needed to create information that is necessary to make HR decisions,

- defining the characteristics of that data (e.g., number data vs. character data),

- organizing those data in a manner that promotes integration, data quality and accessibility, and finally

- restricting access to the data to the right personnel.

By performing these functions effectively, a DBMS turns data into an organizational resource.

A database is a set of organized data. Importantly, it is a permanent, self-descriptive store of interrelated data items that can be processed by one or more business applications. *Self-descriptive* means that the database knows about the characteristics of the data (e.g., the length of an employee's last name can be no greater than 30 characters) or that a paycheck can only be associated with one employee. *Interrelated* means that there are "links" between different sets of data in the database. For example, there can be a link between the data about employees and the jobs that they have. There can also be links between HR data and other data in the organization, such as linking a managerial position to specific company facility resources such as office space or a production facility. As a central repository of data, many different business applications and users can access the data, making an organization's database a very valuable organizational asset that, therefore, needs to be managed appropriately.

The main functions of a DBMS are to create the database; insert, read, update, and delete database data; maintain data integrity (i.e., making sure that the data are correct) and security (i.e., making sure that only the right people have access to the data); and prevent data from being lost by providing backup and recovery capabilities. Database management systems are also designed to have high performance, allowing data to be retrieved quickly by the many users in the organization.

DBMSs and databases work in conjunction with business applications, such as **transaction processing systems (TPS)**, to make organizations run smoothly. As shown in Figure 2.1, these business applications consist of a set of one or more computer programs that serve as an intermediary between the user and the DBMS while providing the "functions" or "tasks" that the user wants performed (e.g., store data about a new hire) (Kroenke, 2003). The business application must talk both to the user sitting at a computer terminal in an easy-to-use manner and to the database in a way that is very efficient. For example, a payroll business application involves collecting data from an employee's time card, storing these data in a database, and then retrieving and manipulating these data to produce a paycheck. Data from this transaction processing system can also be used to generate reports on monthly personnel expenses. These reports are the basis of **management reporting systems (MRS)**. We'll talk more about these later in the chapter.

Figure 2.1 Database, Database Management System, and Business Applications

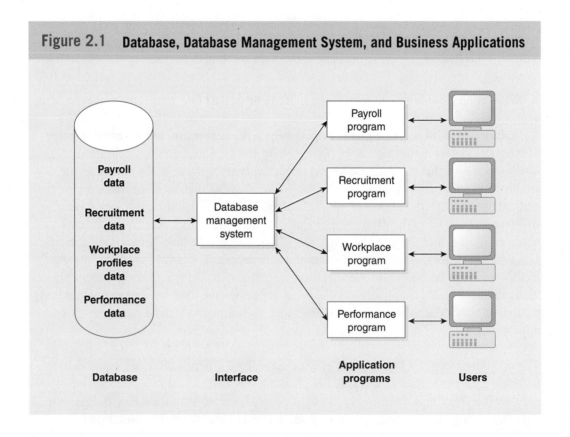

There are thousands of commercially available business applications that work in conjunction with a DBMS to process business transactions. In a 2000 census of comprehensive HR software for the HR function, Richard Frantzreb catalogued more than 150 HR applications (Meade, 2003). In another census of specialized HR products under headings such as employment management, Equal Employment Opportunity (EEO), training management, career development, HR planning, performance management, personnel policy, survey processing, employee scheduling, attendance/timekeeping, payroll, and so on, Frantzreb counted 2,500 HR software products from about 1,700 vendors (Meade, 2003).

Early DBMSs[1]

Early DBMSs were simply data-processing systems that performed record-keeping functions that mimicked existing manual procedures. Thus, electronic data were stored in computers in much the same way that they were stored in paper filing systems. Paper filing systems typically consisted of a filing cabinet and a drawer for each type of business document (e.g., an employee personnel form). These documents were also called "records." Inside would be paper documents with each document being a "record" of a transaction (e.g., promoting Susan to senior manager). Computer systems mimicked this, creating individual computer files, typically one for each type of document. For example, there would be an Employee File with employee records, a Time Card File with time card records, multiple Employee Benefit Files with their associated documents, and so on. The main objective of these file-processing systems was to process transactions such as update payroll records and produce payroll checks as efficiently as possible. The goal was not on data sharing among different business applications and users.

These traditional **file-oriented data structures** had a number of shortcomings. These shortcomings included: (a) data redundancy—an employee's name and address could be stored in many different files; (b) poor data control—if you had access to the file you had access to *all* the data in the file, which may not be desirable because you may want to restrict the data viewed by a particular user; (c) inadequate data manipulation capabilities—it was very difficult to combine the data across files and to easily update and to add new data; and (d) excessive programming effort—any change in the structure of the data (e.g., adding a new field such as a mobile phone number or a screen name to an employee record) required extensive changes in the software program that accessed the data.

In general, early file systems were good at specialized transaction processing. They were not designed to easily and quickly provide information to answer questions such as "What was the average hourly wage for female programmers last year compared with this year?" because the data to answer the more complicated questions came from different files; for example, employee gender and salary would be in the **master file on employees**, and hours worked would be in the time-card transaction file. Difficulties also arose when managers in the organization wanted to share data across applications: Fundamentally, there was no easy way to "link" information. For example, managers could not connect information about employee salaries and sales projections.

To overcome the shortcomings of file-oriented structures, *hierarchical and network database systems* evolved in the mid-1960s and early 1970s. The key to these systems was that relationships between different records were explicitly maintained. Although relationships among the data were created between sets of data, as illustrated in Figure 2.2, the relationships were created based on where the data were stored (e.g., the job records for Employee X are located in Sector 3 of Disk 4). Thus, only the very knowledgeable technical staff was able to effectively interact with the database. These database systems also required an excessive programming effort and suffered from inadequate data manipulation capabilities if the program was poorly designed.

The advent of *relational database management systems* addressed the many problems associated with these older DBMSs and database structures.

Relational DBMSs

In 1970, E. F. Codd introduced the notion that rather than programming relationships between data based on physical location, the information needed to integrate data should

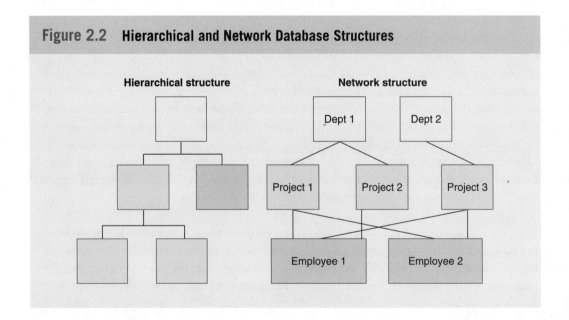

Figure 2.2   Hierarchical and Network Database Structures

Hierarchical structure   Network structure

Dept 1   Dept 2

Project 1   Project 2   Project 3

Employee 1   Employee 2

reside within the data (Hansen & Hansen, 1996). Included in Codd's proposal was that data be stored in tables where each table represented one "entity" in the real world and the information associated with that "entity'" be stored only in that table. For example, a company could have an employee table (i.e., employee is an "entity"), and so information about the employee, such as name, address, and date of hire, would only be stored in that table and nowhere else. Such an idea removed problems with redundancies such as storing the employee's address in many locations and then not knowing which one is the correct one, if the employee's address is changed in one location and not in the other location. These tables were called relations, and from this model came the name *relational database*.

In relational database systems, retrieval of data from different tables was based on logical relationships built into the table structures, which made feasible the creation of a query capability that was much more accessible to end users who generally had limited programming experience. This technique also allowed for relationships to be easily built among all the entities in the organization. We'll talk more about this a bit later in the chapter.

Perhaps, the most significant difference between a file-based system and a relational database system is that data are easily shared. There are three types of *data sharing*: (1) data sharing between functional units, (2) data sharing between management levels, and (3) data sharing across geographically dispersed locations. Data sharing requires a major change in end-user thinking, particularly in those employees who are accustomed to owning their own data on their PCs. Fundamentally, sharing data means sharing power because both data and information are power. Sharing data also means being a good citizen and making certain that the data you enter is correct.

Data Sharing Between Different Functions

Relational DBMSs facilitate data integration across different functions such that each function might have access not only to its own data but also to other data as well. Thus, the HR department is able to maintain its employee database but also access cost information from the accounting department's database. As a result, relational database technology increased the feasibility and popularity of integrated business applications. These integrated applications used in large organizations are referred to as **enterprise resource planning (ERP)** business applications.

ERP software applications are a set of integrated database applications, or modules, that carry out the most common business functions, including HR, general ledger, accounts payable, accounts receivable, order management, inventory control, and customer relationship management. ERP modules are integrated, primarily through a common set of definitions and a common database (Martin, Brown, DeHayes, Hoffer, & Perkins, 1999).

Data Sharing Between Different Levels

Operational employees, managers, and executives also share data but have different objectives and, thus, different information needs. Operational employees focus on data-processing transactions to ensure smooth operation of critical business transactions. A common business transaction is processing the information from an employee's timecard. At this level, transaction-processing information systems help conduct business on a day-to-day basis to provide timely and accurate information to managers and executives. For example, transaction-processing systems update employee work history, attendance, and work hours. Operational employees are concerned with the accuracy and efficiency with which these data are processed.

Managers, on the other hand, are more interested in summary data, such as reports generated from daily operational data that can be summarized into daily, weekly, or monthly reports on hours worked by employee or absences by employee.

Executives rely on information produced at an even more aggregated level to evaluate trends and develop business strategies. For example, executives might ask for reports that compare turnover statistics across business groups and over time.

These three different levels of use correspond to three different types of software systems that have evolved over the past three decades: transaction processing systems (TPS), management reporting systems (MRS), and **decision support systems (DSS)** (Hansen & Hansen, 1996). TPS were first applied to lower operational levels of the organization to automate manual processes such as payroll. Their basic characteristics include (a) a focus on data storage, processing, and flows at the daily operational level; (b) efficient transaction processing; and (c) summary reports for management (Sprague & Watson, 1989). Early ERP applications were used primarily for their transaction processing functionality.

Note the similarity between the categorization of information systems into electronic data processing (EDP), management information systems (MIS), and decision support systems (DSS) discussed in Chapter 1 (Sprague & Carlson, 1982). These terms correspond to TPS, MRS, and DSS in this chapter. As you may recall from Chapter 1, an additional information system was identified—the human resources management decision system (HRMDS). The HRMDS was described as consisting of the reports managers and HR professionals receive on a regular basis but that are actually used in their daily work, *particularly in their decision-making capacity*. The HRMDS could be classified as a special instance of an MRS or MIS system but focused specifically on information used in decision making—a central theme of this book.

In addition to TPS capabilities, relational databases can also provide MRS capability. Characteristics of an MRS include (1) information aimed at middle managers; (2) integration of TPS data by business functions such as manufacturing, marketing, and HR; and

(3) inquiry and report generation from the database (Sprague & Watson, 1989). Management reporting systems can be designed to provide daily, monthly, quarterly, or annual summary reports of key transactions such as employee headcounts by department or distribution of employee performance reports to meet budgets and manage performance.

Decision support systems assist senior managers and business professionals in making business decisions. Data mining, data analytics, and **business intelligence (BI)** are examples of information derived from a DSS, which relies on data warehouses. Data warehouses represent aggregated data (e.g., the total salary information by department by month) collected from various databases available to a business.

Data Sharing Across Locations

In today's global environment, access to data from any physical location in the world is increasingly important. Teams of employees may be stationed in Thailand, India, and the United States. Two issues arise when data are shared across wide geographic locations. These are (1) managing the day/time of a transaction and (2) determining where to store the various components of the business application, DBMS, and database.

To deal with day/time, developers of DBMSs such as Oracle, MS SQL Server, and IBM DB2 are building the capability to deal with recording dates and times according to the time zone in which the data originated. So, for example, if a database is stored in London and an employee records a transaction while sitting at a terminal in Los Angeles, in addition to the time (say 1 P.M. in Los Angeles), the time zone (-08:00 from Greenwich Mean Time) is also stored with the transaction.

As part of a global information system design, organizations have chosen to break their business application and DBMS into components, often called "tiers." More detail on tiers will also be covered in Chapter 3. Traditional client-server architectures broke an application into two tiers, typically with the user interface and some business logic on the user's computer, such as a PC (the client) and the database and mainstream parts of the application stored on a server. In today's global environment with high-speed data networks, **N-tier architectures** exist with databases and applications being distributed among many different computers around the world. So if, for example, you are in an Internet café in Bangkok trying to get information about your benefit election, the hosting computer may be in London and the data may be located on a computer in Chicago. In sum, computer networks are created that provide instant access to these operational data, allowing real-time managerial decision capability regardless of physical location.

A centralized database allows a company to confine its data to a single location and, therefore, more easily control data integrity, updating, backup, query, and control access to the database. A company with many locations and telecommuters, however, must develop a communications infrastructure to facilitate data sharing over a wide geographical area. The advent of the Internet and a standardized communication protocol made the centralized database structures and geographically dispersed data sharing feasible.

Key Relational Database Terminology

As discussed earlier, relational DBMSs are used to store data important to the organization. Key terms in relational database management include entities, attributes, tables, primary keys, foreign keys and relationships, queries, forms, and reports. Below we define each term and describe its function in a database.

Entities and Attributes

Entities are things such as employees, jobs, promotion transactions, positions in company, and so on. They include both physical things such as desks and conceptual things such as bank accounts. A company must analyze its business operations and identify all the entities that it believes are important.

Each of these entities is made up of "attributes." An attribute is a characteristic of the entity. For example, an employee has a name, address, phone number, education, and so on. Attributes also have characteristics such as the type of data (e.g., date, number, or character) and size (e.g., number of characters or the largest number that can be stored).

In addition to identifying the entities and attributes, the relationships among the entities must be defined. For example, a company may have an employee entity and a department entity. Then the company must define the relationship between the employee entity and the department entity (e.g., Does an employee have to be assigned to a department? Can an employee be assigned to more than one department?).

Tables

How does this information fit into a relational DBMS? Tables are used to store information about entities. As illustrated in Figure 2.3, one table is created for each entity—in this example, driver table, car table, moving violation table, and parking violation table. Attributes are stored as the columns (also called fields) in the table. As noted earlier, attributes represent a single data element or characteristic of the data table. For example, a table of driver data would have the following columns or characteristics: first name, last

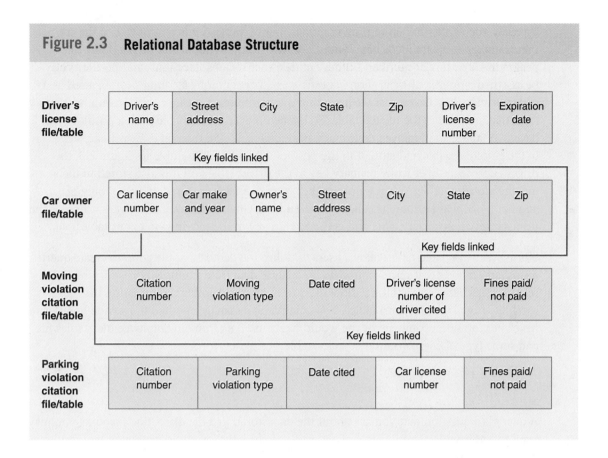

Figure 2.3   Relational Database Structure

Driver's license file/table	Driver's name	Street address	City	State	Zip	Driver's license number	Expiration date

Key fields linked

Car owner file/table	Car license number	Car make and year	Owner's name	Street address	City	State	Zip

Key fields linked

Moving violation citation file/table	Citation number	Moving violation type	Date cited	Driver's license number of driver cited	Fines paid/ not paid

Key fields linked

Parking violation citation file/table	Citation number	Parking violation type	Date cited	Car license number	Fines paid/ not paid

name, street address, city, state, driver license number, expiration, and so on. Each of these characteristics represents an attribute or field of the table.

Each table in a database contains rows. Rows are also referred to as records and represent an "instance" of the entity. For example, in the driver table, each row contains data about a particular driver, and each column contains data that represent an attribute of that driver, such as name, phone number, and license number.

Relationships, Primary Keys, and Foreign Keys

To represent the relationships among the tables, we have to do a bit more work. In a relational DBMS, relationships are created by having the same attribute in each table with the value of the attribute being the same in each table. Most often this is done by taking the "primary key" of one table and including it in the related table. What is a primary key?

Typically, each entity has an attribute that has unique values for each instance of the entity. For example, each employee has a Social Security number that is unique (i.e., only one person has a particular number). Other entities, such as jobs, locations, and positions can be assigned a unique number if one doesn't exist. These unique attributes can be used as a table's primary key. Given that we have a unique attribute, to create a relationship, we simply store that attribute in the related table. So if an employee is associated with a position, we have two tables, an employee table and a positions table. We then take the primary key of the employee table and store it in the position table. In the example in Figure 2.3, the driver's license number is the primary key in the driver table and it is also stored in the moving violation table. When a primary key from one table is stored as an attribute of another table, that attribute is called a **foreign key**. Thus, in Figure 2.3, driver's license is the primary key in the driver table and is the foreign key in the moving violations table.

Storing data in related tables allows users to utilize the database application to create queries, forms, and reports that retrieve, update, or analyze data from multiple tables together. The relationships between the tables allow users to accurately combine information that "go together" from two (or more) tables. For example, if a manager wished to provide bonuses to his or her top salespeople, he or she would likely use data from an employee file, a sales file, and some type of compensation criterion table.

Queries[2]

A query is a question that you ask about the data stored in a database. For example, you may want to know which employees live within a specific city. You could generate these results by scrolling through the relevant table or by sorting the table by city and then looking at the result, but this is both time-consuming and you would have to do this task each time you wished to find the answer to your question. A better approach is to create a query. A query is a structured way of posing your question to the DBMS in a language the DBMSs understand. This definition (e.g., show all employees with city Albany) can be saved in the database and used again and again. Importantly, each time the query is executed it searches through the *current* table records and lists the results. The results of a query on a table(s) are always displayed in something that looks just like another table. However, this result table is only temporary and is not stored in the database. It is important to note that queries do not store data! All data are stored in tables. Queries only report on data currently in the table.

There are three different kinds of queries: select queries, action queries, and cross-tab queries. A **select query** allows you to ask a question based on one or more tables in a database. This is the most commonly used query. These queries can be quite general or quite specific. For example, a general query might extract all employees from the database who have reached retirement age. A more specific query might retrieve employees who have reached retirement age and who live in New York and are engineers.

An **action query** performs an action on the table on which it is based. Actions include updating data in the table (e.g., increasing the base salary of all employees who were rated above average in the latest performance rating), deleting records from the table (e.g., removing employees from the employees table if they no longer work at the company), or inserting records (e.g., the query may add a new set of benefits to the benefits table). You can also use this type of query to create new tables.

A **cross-tab query** performs calculations on the values in a field and displays the results in a datasheet. The reason it is called "cross-tab" is that it tabulates the data for a set of descriptor attributes, contrasting them or crossing them in a table format. For example, we might want to see the total personnel count by gender by region. So we would see the gender on the left-hand side and the different regions listed across the top of a table. A cross-tab query could display different aspects of the data, including sums or averages or minimum or maximum values. As another example, a cross-tab query could determine headcount by department or determine pay range maximums and minimums in pay grades by department.

Select queries and cross-tab queries provide the information that managers and executives expect from IT. These queries can serve as the foundation for MRS and DSS information and decision making. Action queries, on the other hand, improve the operational efficiency of managing and maintaining a database and are most closely associated with TPS. These tasks are important to the operational staff but of less interest to HR managers and executives.

Queries are also used as the basis for forms and reports. In addition to retrieving data, they can add, update, and delete records in tables. You can define fields in a query that perform calculations, such as sums and averages. The following list summarizes the typical capabilities of queries (Bast, Cygman, Flynn, & Tidwell, 2006):

- Display selected fields and records from a table
- Sort records on one or multiple fields
- Perform calculations
- Generate data for forms, reports, and other queries
- Update data in the tables of a database
- Find and display data from two or more tables
- Create new tables
- Delete records in a table based on one or more criteria

Forms[3]

A form is an object in a database that you can use to maintain, view, and print records in a database in a more "structured" manner. Although you can perform these same functions with tables and queries, forms can present data in many customized and useful ways. For example, you can design a form to look like the time sheet submitted by an employee. Well-designed forms can improve data input efficiency and accuracy. Consequently, forms represent the main mechanism for creating end-user interfaces.

A form can be based on a table, multiple tables, or queries. A form can display one record at a time or many records. Often, we select only one record and then create a nice-looking, easy-to-use layout to work with the data in that one record. To view and maintain or add data using a form, you must know how to move from field to field and from record to record. Forms provide navigation buttons that facilitate moving from field to field and from record to record. Data that are entered or changed in a form automatically change the values in the underlying table once you save the changes.

Reports

A report is a formatted presentation of data from a table, multiple tables, or queries that is created as a printout or to be viewed on screen. Data displayed in a report are dynamic, reflecting the latest data from the tables on which the report is based. Unlike forms, however, you cannot change the data or add a new record in a report. You can only view the data in a report.

Although you can print data appearing in tables, queries, and forms, reports provide you with the greatest flexibility for formatting printed output. As with forms, you can design your own reports or use a report wizard to create reports automatically.[4]

Introduction to MS Access

MS Access is a relational DBMS in which data are organized as a collection of tables. Like any relational database, the data in tables can be queried. MS Access also makes it easy to create forms and reports through the use of form or report wizards. A form or report wizard is a computer program or tool that guides you through the creation of a form by asking you a series of questions. For example, which table is the form to be created from, and which attributes do you want to be displayed on the form? The form or report is created based on your answers.

MS Access is designed for relatively small databases and assumes limited knowledge of database programming. MS Access provides the following functions (Adamski & Finnegan, 2005):

- It allows you to create databases containing tables and table relationships.
- It lets you easily add new records, change table values in existing records, and delete records.

- It contains a built-in query language, which lets you obtain immediate answers to questions you ask about your data.

- It contains a built-in report generator and report wizard, which lets you produce professional-looking, formatted reports from your data.

- It provides protection of databases through security, control, and recovery facilities.

Data in an MS Access table or query can be exported to other database applications or to spreadsheet programs such as Excel or Lotus 123. Once these records are in a spreadsheet program, then further analyses may be conducted and graphs and charts constructed to enhance analytical HR metric reports. Data can be exported by simply opening the database that has the object—for example, table or query—that you want to export. Then select File, Export from the database menu. Select the type of file—for example, .xls—you want the object to be saved to and specify a name. Click Save. Now you can open the file in Excel. You may also "link" the data in the database to the spreadsheet. When the spreadsheet is opened, the most recent data from the database are retrieved and presented in the spreadsheet.

Unlike spreadsheet software programs, MS Access handles substantially more data and contains the ability to model relationships. Each MS Access database, for example, can be up to 2 GB in size and can contain up to 32,768 objects, including tables, queries, forms, reports, and so on.

Designing an MS Access Database

The design process begins with an analysis of the data and information that the users of the database will need to have stored and retrieved in order to accomplish their work. Typically, we think of work as consisting of tasks within a business process, and so we can think of the data that will be required to be stored in a database and of the information that will need to be extracted. We find out the data to be stored by interviewing the intended end users of the database. We ask about entities that they need to keep information on, the attributes of those entities, and also how the entities are related. In addition, we may watch users at work and look at the forms, reports, and other business documents that they use to be successful. Gathering copies of all existing forms and reports currently used may also act as guidelines for creating forms and reports, though sometimes our intention is to change how they are doing business, and so some of these documents may be significantly changed or even discarded.

In general, the database design process can be broken down into several steps that are somewhat sequential but oftentimes have to be repeated until the database meets the users' needs:

- Determine what the users want from the database: What questions need to be answered? What information needs to be tracked? What reports are produced? What data are needed to provide the basis for those results?

- Identify the data fields needed to produce the required information; in doing so, we also identify rules that define the integrity of the data, including data type (number, character) and data limits (e.g., if we are storing days, we might only allow the numbers 1 to 31).

- Group related fields into tables (entities).

- Determine each table's primary key.

- Normalize the data: Make sure the data for an entity are really associated with only that entity.

- Determine how the tables are related to one another and include common keys.

- Create the relationships among the different entities and insure referential integrity.

- Create queries to define data needs that are not handled by only looking at individual tables.

- Create reports to provide a structured view of the data.

- Create forms, and in doing so, identify a common design for the forms: Typically, we create a form for each table along with a "main menu" form that allows the user to navigate to each form associated with a table and to view queries and reports.

- Enter test data to verify the quality/accuracy of the system design.

- Test the system: Do all the queries work correctly? Are the forms easy to use? Are the end users happy?

- Enter or populate the database.

HR Database Application Using MS Access

For small companies, generally with fewer than 1,000 employees, there are commercially available HR database applications based on MS Access. One such system, popular in the United States, is HRSource from Auxillium West (www.auxillium.com). Both software products offer wide breadth of functionality and flexibility to import and export data from and to Excel and to integrate with other database applications, particularly payroll. Both provide a centralized relational database with basic transaction processing and management reporting systems.

Both HRSource and HRVantage have familiar MS Access forms as user interfaces. They both allow users to create custom queries and reports. However, the database applications also come with preconfigured reports and queries. For example, HRVantage provides more than 150 standard reports, which include Absence reports, EEO reports and graphs, termination analyses, employee skill searches, employee profiles, OSHA reports, employee performance reports, and many others. HRSource offers users 70 built-in reports. Customers also claim that with a little expertise in MS Access, they are able to mine their HR information in a way that they never could before they centralized on one HRIS database (Meade, 2003).

Other HR Databases

A few decades ago, database application programs were often written by companies for their particular use; in today's business environment, customized application programs termed *legacy systems* are being replaced by commercially developed HR systems supported by enterprise database application programs (e.g., PeopleSoft Enterprise HCM, MySAP ERP HCM, Lawson HCM, Epicor HCM, SuccessFactors Employee Central, UltiPro HR, Workday). The most well-known HR database applications have the capability to operate on various DBMS platforms (e.g., Oracle, SQL Server, DBS2). These commercial database application programs can either be licensed and installed onto computer hardware a company buys themselves, or they can be accessed remotely through an approach called software as a service or "SaaS" The SaaS approach to HRIS is discussed further in Chapters 3 and 17.

Regardless of how complex your HRIS DBMS is, you must ensure that you know what information can be derived from any database. To know this, one must have an idea of what tables and attributes (fields) are in the database. Software vendors should be able to provide this information to end users; however, for the large, complex HR applications, this may run into thousands of tables and fields! Auxillium West, makers of a low-priced HRIS, offer a document to prospective customers that lists the data items commonly tracked. Their most commonly tracked HR fields are listed in Table 2.1 (Meade, 2003).

Although the list in Table 2.1 appears to be comprehensive, in fact, it is quite sparse when compared with more complex database applications. More complex database applications will also have fields that relate to business processes other than HR, such as accounting and finance. Integrated databases allow sophisticated queries and analytical reports, such as hours spent on recruiting, recruiters' hourly pay, job board posting costs, number of positions filled, number of declined offers, number of open positions, number of voluntary terminations, and number of involuntary terminations.

Data Integration: Database Warehouses, Business Intelligence, and Data Mining

An organization's ability to generate meaningful information to make good decisions is only as good as its underlying database. As Dr. John Sullivan notes, "I have found that the

Table 2.1 Examples of Common Fields in an HR Database

Employee ID	Job Code/Title
First Name	Pay Rate Type
Last Name	Rate Effective Date
Address	Salary
City	Bonuses
State	Status
ZIP Code	Category (full-time/part-time)
Home Phone Number	Contract Employee Status
Gender	Department
Ethnic Code	Office Information
Birth Date	Manager
Veteran Status	Division/Location
Visa Expiration Date	Company Property
Education	Emergency Contact
Past Employment	Time-Off Accruals
Skill Code	Benefits
Training/Certification	Work-Related Injuries
Performance Rating	Disability
Next Review Date	
Hire Date	
Termination Date	
Termination Reason	
Rehire Date as Applicable	

largest single difference between a great HR department and an average one is the use of metrics" (Gur, 2006). Metrics are measures of organizational performance outcomes that are derived from measures of important individual and organizational outcomes (e.g., individual job performance and absentee rate). As was discussed in Chapter 1, the current emphasis in HRM is functioning as a strategic business partner. A prerequisite for meeting this goal is the use of metrics to assess and monitor quantitative data from HRM programs like recruiting and training effectiveness. The primary objective of measuring HR metrics is to improve individual and organizational effectiveness. The use of metrics in HRM programs will be discussed in greater detail in Chapter 6. Chapter 7 will describe how to use these metrics to compute cost-benefit analyses (CBAs) and return on investment (ROI) calculations.

Much of the measurement data to create HR metrics will come from an organization's data warehouse. A data warehouse is a special type of database that is optimized for reporting and analysis and is the raw material for management's decision support system. Business intelligence, BI, is a broad category of business applications and technologies for creating data warehouses to analyze and provide easy access to these data in order to help organizational users make better business decisions. BI applications include the activities of decision support systems, query and reporting, statistical analysis, forecasting, and data mining.

BI systems allow organizations to improve business performance by leveraging information about customers, suppliers, and internal business operations from databases across functions and organizational boundaries. Essentially, BI systems retrieve specified data from multiple databases, including old legacy file database systems, and store these data into a new database, which becomes that data warehouse. The data in the data warehouse can then be accessed via queries and used to uncover patterns and diagnose problems.

Patterns in large data sets are identified through data mining, which involves statistically analyzing large data sets to identify recurring relationships. For example, data mining an employee database might reveal that most employees reside within a group of particular ZIP codes. This may help if the organization wants to supply transportation or encourage car pooling. Data mining is relatively new to business analytics and has not yet been widely used for HRM decisions.

BI systems also provide reporting tools and interfaces (e.g., forms) that distribute the information to Excel spreadsheets, Internet-based portals, PDF files, or hard copies. These results can also be distributed to key executives in specialized formats known as executive dashboards, which are becoming a popular executive decision support tool.

A major reason for a DBMS is to provide information from various parts of the organization in an "ad hoc" manner. Ad hoc means that a user can ask a question of the data that no one has thought about yet. The user can sign into the data and pose his or her question in the form of a query. This is a very powerful concept that enables all levels of the organization. Data warehouses and BI software enable managers to create information from an even greater store of data.

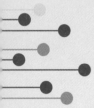

SUMMARY

In this chapter, we have described the key aspects of current DBMS technologies and how they work to create, store, and manage critical data about an organization. Data are transformed into information by relational DBMSs and business applications that work together. The underlying data in a database are collected from business transactions and stored in tables that are related to each other through shared fields called primary and foreign keys. Queries represent questions asked of the data and are used to access specific data stored in tables. The results of queries can be viewed in forms or reports that are customized so that the end user can better interpret the data that are retrieved from the database. More sophisticated data analyses and reports such as executive dashboards are produced from specialized databases called data warehouses and business application software called BI software.

Most HRIS rely on an underlying database. Understanding how database systems work, therefore, is relevant to HR decision makers because knowledge about how to create, store, and access data can be a key differentiator in a competitive environment. Small HR databases can be created using MS Access, or more sophisticated ones can be purchased from software vendors. There are literally hundreds of HR database business applications that create, process, and analyze HR data. The challenge is to find one that can most cost-effectively collect and share data from which meaningful information can be extracted to support making good decisions.

KEY TERMS

action query 47

business applications 35

business intelligence (BI) 43

cross-tab query 47

database management system (DBMS) 36

decision support systems (DSS) 42

enterprise resource planning (ERP) 41

file-oriented data structures 39

foreign key 46

management reporting systems (MRS) 38

master file on employees 39

MS Access 36

N-tier architectures 43

relational database 36

select query 46

transaction processing systems (TPS) 38

DISCUSSION QUESTIONS

1. Explain the differences between data, information, and knowledge.

2. What are the main functions of a database management system,

and how is it different from a
database?

3. What were the shortcomings of early
file-oriented database structures?

4. What are the three types of data
sharing?

5. Define the key terms in a relational
database.

6. What is the difference between a
primary key and a foreign key?

7. What are the three types of queries?

8. How are forms and reports similar, and
how are they different?

9. Take the list of HR database common
fields and group them into tables.

10. What are the differences between
data warehouses, BI, and data
mining?

11. Can knowledge be turned into a
database?

CASE STUDY

You have been asked to create an applicant database for a small recruiting firm that
specializes in recruiting HR professionals for small to medium-sized firms. Describe the
process that you would use to design this database. Use MS Access to develop a prototype of
the database that you could show your manager.

STUDENT STUDY SITE

Visit the Student Study Site at **http://www.sagepub.com/kavanagh3e** for additional learning
tools such as access to SAGE journal articles and related web resources.

NOTES

1. For a more detailed discussion, see Hansen and Hansen (1996, pp. 52–56).

2. For a more detailed discussion, see Bast et al. (2006, chap. 3).

3. For a more detailed treatment, see Tutorials 4 and 5 in Adamski and Finnegan
(2005).

4. For a more detailed treatment, see Tutorials 4 and 6 in Adamski and Finnegan (2005).

REFERENCES

Adamski, J., & Finnegan, K. (2005). *New perspectives on Microsoft Access 2003.* Boston: Course Technology Thomson Learning.

Bast, K., Cygman, L., Flynn, G., & Tidwell, R. (2006). *Succeeding in business with Microsoft Office Access 2003.* Boston: Course Technology Thomson Learning.

Gur, Z. (2006, June/July). Up.link. IHRIM. *link,* 5.

Hansen, G. W., & Hansen, J. V. (1996). *Database management and design.* Upper Saddle River, NJ: Prentice Hall.

Kroenke, D. M. (2003). *Database concepts.* Upper Saddle River, NJ: Prentice Hall.

Martin, E., Brown, C., DeHayes, D., Hoffer, J., & Perkins, W. (1999). *Managing information technology.* Upper Saddle River, NJ: Prentice Hall.

Meade, J. (2003). *The human resources software handbook.* San Francisco: Jossey-Bass.

Sprague, R. H., & Carlson, E. D. (1982). *Building effective decision support systems.* Englewood Cliffs, NJ: Prentice Hall.

Sprague, R., & Watson, H. (1989). *Decision support systems* (2nd ed.). Englewood Cliffs, NJ: Prentice Hall.

Whitehill, M. (1997). Knowledge-based strategy to deliver sustained competitive advantage. *Long Range Planning, 30*(4), 621–627.

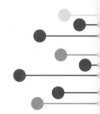

CHAPTER

3

Systems Considerations in the Design of a Human Resource Information System

Planning for Implementation

Michael D. Bedell and Michael L. Canniff

EDITORS' NOTE

This chapter covers the information necessary to understand the system development process for HRIS in more depth in order to improve the design of the HRIS. As mentioned in Chapter 1, the system development process involves multiple stages from initial design to implementation and evaluation. Failure to follow these steps or rushing through them will result in a poorly designed system that will ultimately fail when it is implemented. Thus, this chapter begins to identify some of the information that is critical for the eventual implementation and evaluation of an HRIS. The authors start with a focus on the users of the system to help the system development and design process in its beginning steps. The types of information about the users or customers of the HRIS, the sorting of HRIS data into categories of human capital, and the main concepts of hardware and database **security** *are covered.*

CHAPTER Objectives

After completing this chapter, you should be able to

- Understand the different types of users or customers of the implemented HRIS and their different data needs
- Discuss the differences between the five general hardware architectures that are presented, from "dinosaur" to "cloud computing" to "bring your own device"
- Discuss, very generally, the main concepts of hardware and database security
- Discuss the "best of breed" approach to HRIS acquisition and the various options available for each functional area of HR
- Develop an understanding of the general steps and factors that affect system implementation
- Understand the pros and cons of implementing a changeover from one software system to another

HRIS IN ACTION

A billion-dollar retailer with 4,000+ stores finds that it cannot move fast enough to beat out the competition. The organization's senior management arrives at the conclusion that it would be easier to achieve the strategic goals enumerated by the board of directors if the various organizational functions would share information. Shared information would enable them to develop and deploy new actions and tactics more quickly. The CEO and president have therefore ordered the major functions to update their information systems immediately so that data sharing is possible. The **senior vice presidents (SVPs)** of accounting and human resources immediately conclude that the only solution is to decide jointly on an **enterprise resource planning (ERP)** product. An ERP software application is a set of integrated database applications or modules that carry out the most common business functions, including human resources, general ledger, accounts payable, accounts receivable, order management, inventory control, and customer relationship management (see www.erpsupersite .com). To speed the installation along, the SVPs decide on a rapid-implementation methodology that a company down the street used. The goal is to have the new systems operational in nine months.

Shortly after this decision has been made, the SVP of HR calls you into his office and tells you that you will be management sponsor for this project. You have to decide on everything. You sit back in your nice office and think:

What's the problem with this scenario? It shouldn't be difficult to select a vendor and then borrow the methodology from down the street. It worked for them; it should work for us! We'll call a few vendors in the morning and find out about cost, time frame, and implementation methods. In the meantime, I should find out a little more about how to do this and who will be using the ERP. I remember from my information systems class in college that this is a reasonable first step when it comes to buying software.

What do you think your response would be to this inquiry? As you go through this chapter's material, keep this vignette in mind, and see if your answer changes.

Introduction

Successful implementation is the central goal of every HRIS project, and it begins with a comprehensive design for the system. As the steps in the system development process are covered in this chapter, the foundation knowledge that is critical to the implementation process will be emphasized. Only by understanding the users/customers of the HRIS, the technical possibilities, the software solution parameters, and the systems implementation process can we increase the probability that the completed software installation will adequately meet the needs of the **human resource management (HRM)** function and the organization. The chapter will begin by identifying the potential users and the kind of information that the HRIS will be managing and storing to facilitate decision making. The chapter will next discuss the technical infrastructure, how the technical infrastructure has evolved, and the many choices that the organization must make. After the technology is discussed, the systems implementation process will be presented.

Those who have participated in a system implementation will tell you that success is the result of careful planning, a dedicated team, top-management support, and an awareness of potential pitfalls. These same people will also tell you that the implementation process provides a host of opportunities to reengineer and systematically improve nonsoftware processes to reflect best practices in HRM. These opportunities should not be ignored, as they can benefit the organization as much as implementing the software will. Finally, the **implementation team** members will tell you that getting the system up and running was the most intense six months, year, or two years of their work life but that they learned a lot and every moment of the experience was worth the time.

There are four things that should be remembered throughout the chapter:

1. It is important to keep in mind the customer of the data, the process, and the decisions that will be made.

2. Everything about HRM is a system of processes designed to support the achievement of strategic organizational goals. The HRIS, in turn, supports and helps manage these HR processes.

3. An HRIS implementation done poorly will result in an HRIS that fails to meet the needs of the HR function.

4. Successful implementation requires careful attention to every step in the system design process. However, done well, the implementation process is full of opportunities to improve the organization and processes. More consistent processes will contribute to enhanced organizational performance.

HRIS Customers/Users: Data Importance

Individuals who will be using the HRIS can be split into two general groups: employees and nonemployees. The employee category includes

- managers who rely on the HRIS and the data analyzed by the analyst or power user to make decisions;

- analysts or power users who use the HRIS to evaluate potential decision choices and opportunities;

- technical staff who are responsible for providing a system that is usable and up to date for each user, or clerical employees who largely engage in data entry; and

- employees who use the HRIS on a self-service basis to obtain personal information, for example, to look up paycheck information, to make choices about benefits during open enrollment, or to see how much vacation time they have available.

The nonemployee group includes potential employees, suppliers, and partners. Potential employees are those who might log in via a Web portal to search for and apply for a position. Suppliers and partners are organizations that interface with the HR function for a variety of purposes, from recruiting to benefits administration and payroll.

Employees

Managers

The **managers** referred to within this section may have a variety of titles: manager, director, vice president, and even CEO. What they all have in common is that their primary HRIS need is to have real-time access to accurate data that facilitate decision making with regard to their people (Miller, 1998). The HRIS provides the manager with data for performance management, recruiting and retention, team management, project management, and employee development (Fein, 2001). The HRIS must also provide the information necessary to help the functional manager make decisions that will contribute to the achievement of the unit's strategic goals and objectives (Hendrickson, 2003). Easy access to accurate employee data enables the manager for each employee to view and engage in employee life cycle changes such as salary decisions, job requisitions, hiring, disciplinary action, promotions, and training program enrollment (Walker, 2001; Zampetti & Adamson, 2001).

Many HRIS products provide real-time reporting and screen-based historical information that can provide managers with information about their employees or their functional units. There are also several third-party software products available that provide managers with almost continuous data about the status of their unit and the organization—much as a dashboard on a car provides immediate information. The analysis of more complex situations is beyond the capabilities of many of these reporting and query tools. To facilitate decision making on complex issues, the manager, before making a decision, usually relies on the analyst or power user to complete some type of analysis.

Analysts (Power Users)

The **analysts or power users** is perhaps the most demanding user of the HRIS. The primary role of the analyst is to acquire as much relevant data as possible, examine it, and provide reasonable alternatives with appropriate supporting information to facilitate the decision process of the manager. The analyst is referred to as a power user because this person accesses more areas of the HRIS than almost any other user. Analysts must be proficient with reporting and query tools. Analysts must also understand the process used to collect the data, how new data are verified, and how the HRIS and the employee life cycle interact. They also need to understand the data definitions in terms of what data exist, the structure of the data, and what data fields are up to date and complete. Some HRISs also provide tools that the analyst can use to model scenarios or perform "what-if" analyses on questions of interest.

As an example, a recruiting analyst might be asked to provide a short list of potential internal candidates for a position that opened in the marketing function of a large retailer.

The potential candidates' characteristics of interest are queried and may include (1) when they were last promoted, (2) whether they have engaged in continuous personal-skills development, (3) what their undergraduate degrees were, and (4) whether they have ever expressed any interest in marketing. The analyst would query appropriate tables and develop a list of internal candidates.

Another example might have the HR analyst completing an analysis of corporate headquarters turnover to determine if a particular function or salary issue is the cause of the problem. This information would be drawn from existing reports, ad hoc queries, and available salary information. Data could be compiled into categories by salary, function, gender, or organizational level and examined to determine if the cause of the turnover can be pinpointed and then countered.

Technicians (HRIS Experts)

Technicians (HRIS experts) straddle the boundary of two functions. Their role is to ensure that appropriate HR staff members have all the access, information, and tools necessary to do their jobs. HRIS experts do this by understanding what is needed from an HR-process standpoint and then translating that into technical language, so the technical employees—programmers, database administrators, and application administrators—know exactly what to do. When the technical staff is planning to install the latest update and one of the results will be a change in functionality, the HRIS expert must take what the technical staff provides and translate that into language HR users understand, so as to indicate how processes and activities might change. For example, if an HR professional required that a new report be generated every other Tuesday, the HRIS expert would learn what data the report requires—perhaps mock the report up with the user—and then explain to the technical people how to make sure that this report is automatically generated on the time schedule.

Clerical Employees

Much like power users, **clerical employees** also spend a significant portion of their day interacting with the HRIS. The difference is one of depth. The clerical employee must understand the process required to enter information into the HRIS and may also need to start the process or generate periodic reports. While clerical staff members in the HR employment department do not generally provide input about whether to hire an individual to a particular position, they bear considerable responsibility for seeing that the new employee gets paid properly. Hiring a new employee requires that someone, for example, a clerical employee, enter the appropriate information into the HRIS—such as the reporting relationship of the new employee as well as his or her benefits, salary, and direct deposit information.

Organizational Employees

Organizational employees are essentially all the other employees throughout the organization who interact with the HRIS. These employees serve in roles such as bank teller, nurse, machinist, salesperson, and accountant. These employees are not involved in human resources and are not likely to make decisions with HR data, but they may utilize the HRIS to help manage their personal information. Typically, all the employees in the organization may interface with the HRIS through a self-service Web portal or secure employee kiosk, removing the necessity of an HR clerk or staff member assisting with many routine HR record modifications (Walker, 2001). Self-service capabilities encourage employees to manage their personal HR profiles with respect to a variety of functions, such as benefit and retirement plan monitoring or computerized training, in addition to using HRIS-based systems to complete numerous personnel forms (Adamson & Zampetti, 2001; Zampetti & Adamson, 2001). Typical self-service applications are accessible most of the day throughout the week. Employees log on to the system, where their identity is authenticated and verified. Then appropriate change options are offered to the employee based on certain parameters that control the areas where the employee is allowed to make valid alterations to the HRIS—such as personnel data updates, job postings, or desired training enrollments (Adamson & Zampetti, 2001; Zampetti & Adamson, 2001). One fairly large financial-services organization noted that self-service options significantly enabled them to reduce the annual benefits open-enrollment process by reducing the paper documents generated, reducing necessary mailings, and reducing the data that had to be read and entered into the HRIS. Data entry time alone was reduced from six to two weeks (Bedell, 2003b).

Nonemployees

Job Seekers

It is estimated that 70% to 90% of large organizations use online recruitment, and that number continues to increase (Stone, Lukaszewski, & Isenhour, 2005). Online recruiting tends to attract individuals who are well educated, Internet savvy, and searching for higher-level positions (McManus & Ferguson, 2003). Online recruitment also attracts people born since 1980, who have grown up with computers and are therefore comfortable with obtaining information on the Internet (Zusman & Landis, 2002). A successful recruitment website needs to be user-friendly and easy to navigate, while attracting candidates to apply to an organization by clearly communicating the benefits of joining it.

Typical **job seekers** have little or no prior information about how to interface with the HRIS and have had nearly zero training opportunities with it. Therefore, the recruiting portal needs to provide ease of use and ease of access to up-to-date job information. The Web form that is used to collect applicant data must also be reliably entered into the appropriate fields within the company's HRIS database. This online recruiting activity will facilitate searches for new employees to fill existing and future positions.

Sourcing Partner Organizations

The partner organizations to HR functions require certain information to complete their tasks. **Sourcing partner organizations** such as Monster.com, Adecco, and most executive recruiting firms require information about vacant positions, including a position description, job specifications, desired candidate competencies, potential salary range, and contact information. The information provided is limited to specific searches for open jobs and is updated as needed.

Business partners that are the recipients of decisions to outsource portions of the HR function (e.g., benefit management firms) or that facilitate process completion on behalf of the employee (e.g., banks) require information that is related to current employees. This requirement increases the need for accurate data, training, and specialized security assurances, as employee information is leaving the organization.

Important Data

As is evident in the previous sections, each customer or user of the HRIS has slightly different needs with regard to what information he or she will be using. Some users simply input data and information, a few simply look at data and information provided in the form of reports, while a few others analyze the data and information to make decisions. What these users all have in common is that all the information is about potential and current employees with a focus on managing the organization's human capital to improve decision making and help to achieve strategic organizational goals. Specific data from the HRIS database fit into three categories:

1. Information about people, such as biographical information and competencies (knowledge, skills, abilities, and other factors)

2. Information about the organization, such as jobs, positions, job specifications, organizational structure, compensation, employee/labor relations, and legally required data

3. Data that are created as a result of the interaction of the first two categories: for example, individual job history, performance appraisals, and compensation information

HRIS Architecture

The HRIS "Dinosaur"

In the early days of human resource applications (just 30 years ago), large "dinosaurs" roamed the IT landscape. These were called mainframe computers and were primarily built by International Business Machines (IBM). These large systems hosted the payroll applications for most enterprises. Users of the mainframe system, which mainly consisted of IT personnel and HRMS administrators, executed large batch processes while directly logged onto the mainframe. Although access to the mainframe could be done via a desktop monitor, no processing was done locally. This architecture is commonly called a single-tier computing system. Everything (user interface, application processing, and data storage) resided on the mainframe and had to be accessed by the client company locally.

Client-Server (Two-Tier) Architecture

During the 1980s, it was discovered that many typical HR functions (such as employee benefits, recruiting, training) did not require such high-powered and expensive processing available on the mainframe computers. With the advent of the **personal computer (PC)**, many of these functions could be re-allocated to the local processing power of the PC. By the end of the decade, HRIS software vendors such as PeopleSoft began using the power of PCs and created the **client-server (two-tier) architecture** (see Figure 3.1).

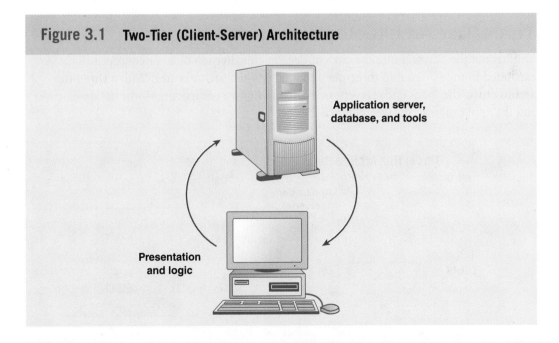

Figure 3.1   Two-Tier (Client-Server) Architecture

Application server, database, and tools

Presentation and logic

The purpose of the two-tier (client-server) architecture was to spread out low-powered processing capability to the dozens of PCs now being used across the enterprise. High-performance applications such as payroll would still be run in a batch process on the mainframe (or large Unix server). But the day-to-day processing could be implemented on the PC. In this case, an application's logic or set of business rules would run on the local machine. Issues such as validating dates, addresses, and name formats would be checked instantly at the PC (without looking up the business rule at the server). Even more complex checks such as term of employment, salary deduction calculations, and employees' health plans could be done on the local PC. In addition, software applications could use the graphical user interface (GUI) of the Windows environment. Ease of computer usage was a driving factor to include individuals with lower levels of technology experience.

Finally, the HR software application technology could be divorced from the database technology. This separation simplified the HR application and allowed an enterprise to select the most appropriate database management system (DBMS) for their needs. Refer to Chapter 2 for comprehension discussion of DBMSs. The most common database design is the relational model. This model standardizes how data is physically stored on the computer and provides standard data access via the Structured Query Language (SQL). In fact, most software products are able to communicate to a variety of DBMS Servers. Utilizing a standard called Open Database Connectivity (ODBC), applications became database servers. This two-tier architecture was a huge leap forward in exposing HR to serve many more employees—data was still located in a centralized database, but logic could be distributed to the PC that needed to run the specific application and usability increased!

Three-Tier Architecture

Throughout the '90s and into the current decade, this division of labor concept has expanded from two-tier into three-tier and finally N-tier architectures. With a **three-tier architecture**, the "back end" servers are divided into two components—the database server and the application server (see Figure 3.2).

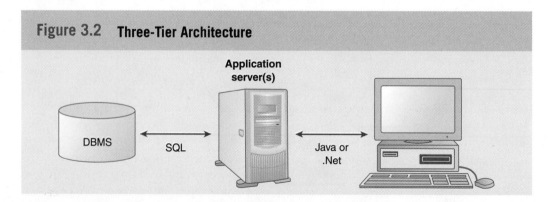

Figure 3.2   Three-Tier Architecture

Application server(s)

DBMS — SQL — Java or .Net

The client still managed the user interface, but more demanding processing occurred in the middle—the application server tier. **Middleware** products such as BEA's Tuxedo transaction processor implemented transaction logic to maintain data reliability. For example, if two recruiters updated the same job position at the same time, a transaction processor would ensure that both updates are committed to the database (if possible). This allowed many simultaneous users to access the central database. There are a couple of drawbacks with both two-tier and three-tier systems. First, there exists a large amount of network traffic or "**bandwidth**" required to execute database transactions between the client and the server. Secondly, the user interface client needs to be installed (along with database drivers) on every PC that needs to access the HRIS (with a corollary issue being that employees need to be trained on this application). Therefore, HRIS access tended to be limited to employees within the "four walls" of the enterprise (residing within the local area network). Low-bandwidth access, such as Internet dial-up, was impractical.

To truly provide for employee self-service (ESS) portals (discussed in detail in Chapter 10), the Web browser was adopted to solve the above issues. First, the browser created a "thin client" environment as opposed to the "thick client" environment described in the two-tier model. An Internet Web browser comes installed on all major **operating systems** (OS; e.g., Windows, Mac OS, Linux, even Palm OS). The browser's user interface has become universal. Therefore, very little employee training is required to use a browser-based application. Finally, a browser works well in a low-bandwidth network environment. So now the typical HRIS application architecture looks like Figure 3.3.

A standard Web server, such as Microsoft's Internet Information Server (IIS) or Apache's Web Server, manages **HTML (Hyper Text Markup Language)** communication between the browser and the application server. The application server manages multiple user sessions logged onto the system at the same time as well as more complex business rule execution. And the application server also issues transactions to the centralized database server. Instead of just limiting ourselves to a four-tier label, this has been labeled **N-tier architecture** for the following reasons:

- It is expandable to multiple Web servers and application servers to handle **load balancing**.

- Web servers can be geographically dispersed to provide world wide access.

- Additional file servers can be added to save documents, reports, error logs, and employee data, which are generated on a daily basis.

- Multiple print servers or specialized printers can be added as needed. For example, payroll check printing requires a security enabled toner called MICR to print encoded checks for bank cashing. These check printers can be physically located in a secure environment, but connected to the HRIS N-tier architecture like any other printer.

- Additional "process schedulers" can be added to handle large batch jobs such as payroll cycles. These servers offload "heavy" processing from the main application server so that user interaction is not impacted.

N-Tier Architecture With Enterprise Resource Planning

The architecture diagram becomes even more complicated when other ERP components are added. HRISs do not exist in a vacuum. They interact with other business operations within the company. For example, when payroll is run, these financial-related transactions need to be registered in the company's general ledger (GL) application. Typically, GL exists within the financial/accounting component of large ERP systems from SAP, Oracle, and Microsoft.

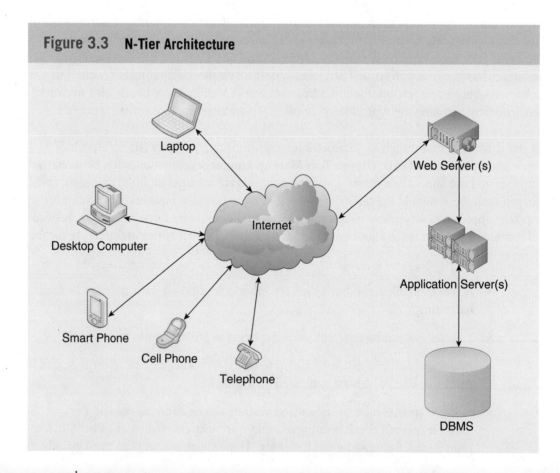

Figure 3.3   N-Tier Architecture

Therefore, GL transactions must be interfaced between payroll and these systems. So additional application servers and databases enter the picture, depicted in Figure 3.3. There exist many variations on this diagram—in some cases databases can be shared (in this situation the HRIS is subsumed within the enterprise resource planning [ERP] system), in other cases Internet technologies such as **XML (eXtensible Markup Language)** and Web services are used to integrated HRISs and ERP. The ultimate goal is to provide a *single data truth* so that all enterprise data can be accessed by users (employees, partners, suppliers, managers) wherever and whenever needed. Data should not be duplicated, re-entered, or copied to multiple systems. ERP applications provide the infrastructure to avoid this problem. So even though the architecture may be more complicated, the logical view of the system remains relatively simple and this complexity is hidden from the end user. For example, a consultant for a large IT services company can travel throughout the world, work with multiple clients, but still be able to record his or her time and expense reports with a single browser application from any hotel room.

Cloud Computing—Back to the Future!?

In the latter half of the 2000 decade, a new architectural model has become prevalent, called **cloud computing**. Cloud computing can be defined as a computing architecture that uses the Internet and central remote servers to maintain data and applications. Hosted services are then delivered over the Internet. Cloud computing technology allows businesses to use applications without having to go through the complex installation process. It is notable that the "cloud" in "cloud computing" was inspired by the cloud symbol that one uses to represent the Internet in flow charts and diagrams. There exist three general service categories commonly recognized in cloud computing. These include:

- **Infrastructure as a Service (IaaS)**—This type of service basically provides access to an operating system (such as Microsoft Windows or Linux) or cluster of connected systems. Amazon Elastic Cloud Compute (EC2) provides access to on-demand operating systems.

- **Platform as a Service (PaaS)**—The next level of services include application and Web server technology prebuilt into the leased computer. Enterprises still build out custom applications on top of these servers. Microsoft Azure is an example of PaaS.

- **Software as a Service (SaaS)**—In this case, a complete application is delivered over the Internet. This can be as simple as an e-mail service (think Google Mail) or as complex as the entire HRIS application (see Workday, Inc. website at www .workday.com).

The underlying goal with cloud computing is to reduce the resources needed by companies in maintaining and running databases and applications. To achieve this, a server "cloud," or group of computers are operated off site and accessed through the Internet. In this way, a company can utilize the processing and storage powers of these "clouds" of computers without actually having to own and invest in them. This can reduce software and equipment capital outlays as the company does not need to keep purchasing new software or hardware to keep pace with technology changes. That investment becomes the responsibility of the vendor offering the cloud computing services. Cloud computing can be sold on demand, by the minute or the hour, and is elastic—meaning that an enterprise can consume as much or as little of a service as they want at any given time. From an accounting perspective, an enterprise leases a preset amount of computing power over an annual period. This can be budgeted in a similar manner as telephony or electrical expenses. Computing charges then become part of operational budget expense as opposed to large capital investments.

In a sense, cloud computing is a return to the single-tier model of the 1980s. Instead of a single, large mainframe running all of the applications, the Internet is acting as the "super computer," providing the application runtime environment. And instead of a "dumb" terminal accessing the mainframe payroll system, the browser now provides the interface to the entire set of human resources applications. In the ancient history of mainframe applications, human resources departments had to rely upon corporate data centers (or IBM) to provide high-performing and up-to-date applications. With cloud computing, the burden lies with software vendors such as Workday or Oracle's Taleo (www.taleo .com—a hosted recruiting and talent management solution) to provide the updating. And of course, leveraging the cloud requires solid, high-performance Internet access all of the time. Finally, the cloud service providers now maintain sensitive corporate data. So when choosing a cloud solution, the evaluation process must include a thorough security analysis.

Security Challenges

Security ranks as a top priority for any human resource information system. Security needs to be addressed to handle the following situations:

- Exposure of sensitive payroll and benefits data between employees

- Loss of sensitive personnel data outside the enterprise (such as Social Security numbers)

- Unauthorized updates of key data such as salary amounts, stock options (both quantity and dates), etc.

- Sharing of personnel or applicant review comments with unauthorized employees

- Sharing data with external organizations and service providers

Security for the HRIS is so important that there is an entire chapter that covers this topic in detail. If interested at this point, read and examine Chapter 16 for a comprehensive discussion on HRIS security.

Best of Breed

An HRIS, as discussed in the previous section, often exists as one of the main parts of an overall ERP software solution for the company. Yet the HRIS is not a monolithic solution even within HR business processes. There exist alternative software applications that solve specific HR business problems. This section addresses these types of solutions, the pros and cons of using multiple applications, and technical infrastructure. In general, an architecture that combines products from multiple vendors is called **best of breed (BOB)**.

The most well-known example of these BOB architectures comes from the audio industry— surround-sound receivers combined with CD players, DVD players, high-end speakers, and even the occasional retro turntable. All these components "plug and play" with each other to provide the best-possible sound experience. This architecture works because of the standards that have been established for decades and that enable different devices to work together. We will see below that BOB software components for an HRIS still need to mature somewhat to reach the capability of the analog audio components. Yet the goal remains the same: deliver the best-possible point solution to meet the business need.

For this synergy to work properly, three conditions need to be present for each software solution:

- First, there should be a perceived need for a specialized solution. For example, if a company expects to receive electronic job applications over the Internet 90% or more of the time, an **optical character recognition (OCR)** program, which scans handwritten or typewritten forms into an electronic format, would not be needed for resume scanning.

- Second, a universally agreed-on set of guidelines for interoperability must exist between applications. This exists at both the syntactical and the semantic levels. The **syntactical level** refers to the base "alphabet" used to describe an interface. For any two applications to communicate, they will need to share data. This data exchange can be done through databases, simple text files (such as Excel), or, increasingly, XML. Basically, XML is similar to HTML, which is used in all Internet browsers. XML files can be shared or transmitted between most software applications today. XML presents a structured syntax— an alphabet—to describe any data elements within an HRIS.

An HR example would consist of selecting the most robust HR software applications—regardless of vendor—for each need and then using the XML language to move data efficiently among those applications. The HR department might select Resumix software for resume tracking, Oracle's PeopleSoft for most HR applications and data management, Chronos software for time and labor tracking, ADP software for payroll purposes, and a proprietary vendor product for outsourced HR benefits administration.

- Third, applications need to "speak the same language." Just as the Roman alphabet allows the spelling of words in multiple languages and formats, XML enables data to be described with many different tags. At the **semantic level**, the language needs to map between software applications. An employee's data description may consist of various tagged fields, such as Name, Address, Birth Date, Phone, Title, Location, and so on. If one of the applications does not have most of the same set of XML tags, it will not be able to exchange employee data. As important as the shared data semantics between applications is having analogous business process semantics. For example, a time-keeping system may define a pay period differently from the payroll application that actually prints employee checks.

If the above conditions are met, HRIS applications should be able to interoperate with many point solutions. What are the typical solutions found in an HRIS implementation? The following sections will detail examples of solutions for some of the HR programs in an organization.

Recruitment

The business process to recruit new employees for a company has many BOB opportunities. Large HRIS applications tend to focus on the internal hiring processes of the company—creating and approving job requisitions, saving applicant data, scheduling interviews, capturing interview results, and, finally, hiring the new employee. Yet there exist other software applications to "fine-tune" the hiring process. OCR scanning applications can eliminate the rekeying of applicant data from paper-based resumes, and other applications can perform applicant database searches, post job requisitions directly to Internet job sites, and run applicant background checks. These examples of specific functionality are typically not provided in an HRIS.

Time Collection

Most companies require employees to submit time-keeping data each pay period. For hourly employees, this typically means using a punch card and time clock to track hours. Some solutions use employee badges with magnetic stripes, thereby enabling employees to clock in and out. Again, most HRIS vendors do not provide the hardware needed to track time. Time-keeping systems will capture the hourly data from various readers throughout a site. Employee scheduling for various shift coverages can be implemented with time collection or planning software. For example, transit districts schedule bus operators to cover a very complex route system throughout the week. Unionized rules force certain break periods and preferences for senior operators. Driver schedules are posted for future pay periods; and actual hours worked, reported sick, taken as vacation time, and so on, are collected for prior pay periods. Such data will be reviewed each pay period prior to being transmitted to the HRIS payroll application.

Payroll

In some cases, the entire payroll process may be outsourced to another vendor, such as ADP. ADP specializes in providing payroll services for companies of all sizes. For some enterprises, the cost of maintaining a payroll application and staff in-house may outweigh the benefits of controlling the process. In this case, employee time data, pay rate, and benefit information would be transmitted to ADP for processing. This choice of using an outside provider is conceptually the reverse of the typical BOB motivation. The enterprise is not looking for the *best* technical or functional solution but for a provider offering a commodity service at the *lowest* cost. In the case of a large multinational corporation with lots of employee levels, it would probably be prudent to purchase the HRIS payroll application.

Benefits

Each year, most employers present their employees with what is called the benefits open enrollment period during which signing up for benefits is similar to course enrollment for students each semester. Instead of enrolling in courses, though, employees enroll for major medical, dental, and insurance benefits. For example, employees choose between health care providers such as Kaiser or Blue Cross for their medical insurance. These providers support interfaces with the major HRIS applications so that, as employees log into the enrollment software, they can review offerings tailored to their company's plan. Thus, when employees select a particular insurance program, they can then transmit enrollment data to the provider through their organization's HRIS.

As one can see in Figure 3.4, BOB solutions introduce additional complexity into the software architecture. This complexity can add IT expense in the form of new software licensing and programming charges. The justification for the added functionality needs to compensate for these additional costs. So a cost-benefit analysis should be performed by the HR function to determine whether the BOB alternative is to be used. Detailed procedures to compute a cost-benefit analysis are covered in Chapter 7.

In summary, BOB options can create a much more powerful solution than a stand-alone HRIS. The BOB alternative also creates system flexibility, as each application can be managed and upgraded independently. Yet this power and flexibility may end up costing the IT department by giving rise to more complex systems administration issues.

Planning for System Implementation

A variety of authors, consultants, and others have discussed implementation methods for information systems. Rampton, Turnbull, and Doran (1999) discuss 13 steps in the implementation process. Jessup and Valacich (1999) divide the implementation of a system into five steps, with a focus on the systems side of the process. Regan and O'Conner (2002) provide eight steps for implementing information systems. Some organizations have proprietary processes that they use for all implementations. Points to remember in regard to system implementation as this section is examined are as follows: (1) this is a process that will take a team of individuals anywhere from six weeks to three years to complete; (2) a variety of ways to manage this process may be attempted, so long as the key issues are examined and organizational goals for the implementation are achieved; and (3) there is no single definitive approach to be used in all situations.

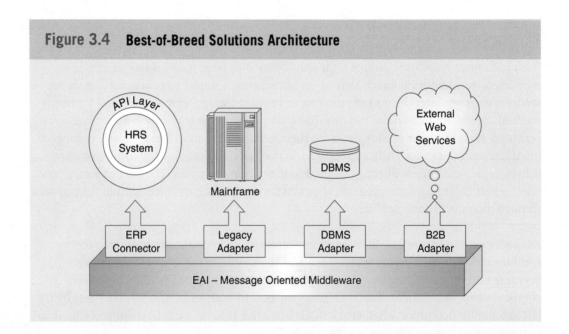

Figure 3.4   Best-of-Breed Solutions Architecture

The first key step is planning. This is an absolutely critical step in any business process and especially in the design of any large-scale software implementation involving multiple-process interfaces. Note that the planning process doesn't guarantee success—rather, it increases the probability that the implementation will be successful. The systematic examination of the following topics provides the organization with the opportunity to see how the implementation will work—to peer into the crystal ball—and identify some contingencies for implementation steps that might not go perfectly. In other words, a robust planning process provides a framework within which the implementation team can proceed, and it provides some decision-making parameters for any unforeseen difficulties that might appear (Bedell, 2003a).

The topics that need to be discussed during the various steps of the planning process include, but are not limited to, the following:

- Project manager
- Steering committee/project charter
- Implementation team
- Project scope
- Management sponsorship
- Process mapping
- Software implementation
- Customization (vanilla vs. custom)
- Change management
- "Go live"
- Project evaluation
- Potential pitfalls

Rather than go into a lengthy discussion of all of the topics above regarding system implementation by using project management techniques, the reader should check Chapter 6 "Project Management and Human Resource Management Advice for Human Resource Information Systems Implementation." Chapter 6 provides a comprehensive discussion of project management techniques of system implementation in terms of advice from both IT and HRM viewpoints, and discusses critical IT and HRM factors for successful project management and system implementation.

SUMMARY

The implementation of an HRIS goes beyond simply placing a new technology into the organization. This chapter focuses on several of the many different organizational, people, and technical issues that must be addressed. The first section considers the important internal and external users or customers of the HRIS and organizational goals. In the second section, four different types of HRIS architectures are enumerated. The evolution of technology, from legacy "dinosaur" systems to contemporary N-tier architectures and cloud computing, has dramatically affected the scope and influence of HRISs in organizations. Therefore the strengths and weaknesses of each architecture are discussed. Next, a brief overview of hardware and database security is provided to make the reader aware of their importance in any HRIS adoption process. The third section of the chapter discusses the best-of-breed approach to HRIS adoption and the pros and cons of this approach in different functional areas. Finally, the chapter concludes with a general discussion of the steps that organizations might take to plan and implement an HRIS and of the factors that can affect these processes. A brief discussion of the conversion approaches to "going live" with the new HRIS illustrates the choices available to organizations when switching over to the new system. In summary, organizations that are able to manage the people, processes, and technology involved in an HRIS implementation should be more likely to find that the new HRIS is able to meet their goals more effectively in terms of budget, functionality, and usability.

KEY TERMS

analysts or power users 61

bandwidth 67

best of breed (BOB) 71

clerical employees 62

cloud computing 69

enterprise resource planning (ERP) 58

eXtensible Markup Language (XML) 69

human resource management (HRM) 59

Hyper Text Markup Language (HTML) 67

implementation team 59

infrastructure as a service (IaaS) 69

job seekers 63

load balancing 67

managers 61

middleware 67

N-tier architecture 67

operating systems (OS) 67

optical character recognition (OCR) 71

organizational employees 63

personal computer (PC) 65

platform as a service (PaaS) 69

security 57

semantic level 72

senior vice presidents (SVPs) 58

DISCUSSION QUESTIONS _____

1. Identify the various types of users or customers of an HRIS.

2. What are the three broad categories of data that an HRIS manages?

3. How does network bandwidth affect a two-tier (client-server) architecture?

4. How does an N-tier architecture simplify the IT department's task of maintaining client software?

5. Research various middleware products from IBM, BEA, or Oracle, and discuss how these products can be leveraged in an HRIS.

6. Research www.hr-xml.org. How many transactions or interfaces do the standards support? How many software vendors are involved with the organization?

7. Take a specific industry, say the K–12 education industry. How might HireRight's integration with Oracle's PeopleSoft assist the process of hiring employees such as bus drivers, janitors, or campus security?

8. When might BOB not be "best"?

9. The systems development process has been discussed by many. Name five discussion topics that need to be completed during the planning process.

10. Complete a flowchart of the process you follow to enroll in classes and pay your tuition. Then apply the process template in the section "Planning for System Implementation."

11. Why do employees fear change? Give some examples of how you might eliminate the fear of change.

12. How does network bandwidth impact a Two Tier Client Server architecture?

13. How does an N-Tier simplify IT departments' task of maintaining client software?

14. Discuss Row Level Security—How does this work? Why may this be more important to an HRIS system versus a manufacturing software solution?

15. Research various middleware products from IBM, BEA, or Oracle and discuss how these products can be leveraged in an HRIS system.

CASE STUDY: VIGNETTE REVISITED _____

This case is revisited with some additional information that involves the understanding of the material in this chapter. The additional information will be added to the situation described in the vignette at the beginning of this chapter.

A billion-dollar retailer with more than 4,000 stores finds that it cannot move fast enough to beat the competition. The organization's senior management arrives at the conclusion that it would be easier to achieve the strategic goals enumerated by the board of directors if the various organizational functions would share information. Shared information would enable them to develop and deploy new actions and tactics more quickly. The CEO and the president have therefore ordered the major functions to immediately update their information systems so that data sharing is possible. The senior vice presidents (SVPs) of accounting and human resources immediately decide that the only solution is to decide jointly on an ERP product. ERP software applications are a set of integrated database applications, or modules, that carry out the most common business functions, including human resources, general ledger, accounts payable, accounts receivable, order management, inventory control, and customer relationship management. To speed the installation along, they will install it using a rapid implementation methodology that a company down the street used. The goal is to have the new systems operational in nine months.

Shortly after this decision is made, the SVP of HR calls you into his office and tells you that you will be management sponsor for this project. You have to decide on everything. You sit back in your nice office and think:

> What's the problem with this scenario? It shouldn't be difficult to select a vendor and then borrow the methodology from down the street. It worked for them; it should work for us! We'll call a few vendors in the morning and find out about cost, time frame, and implementation methods. In the meantime, I should find out a little more about how to do this and who will be using it. I remember from my information systems class in college that this is a reasonable first step when it comes to buying software.

What do you think your response would be to this inquiry? Has your response changed now that you have read this chapter? If so, how?

New Information for the Case: Part 1

After some discussions with department heads from all the departments in the organization, you realize that there are a large number of people (stakeholders) who will be affected by the new systems. Furthermore, you come to realize how important HR data really are to these stakeholders. Based on this information, you think, "Wow, there are far more people who could be potentially using this information system than I expected!" The old textbook and the vendor information should provide a lot to think about.

Using the information from the section of this chapter titled "HRIS Customers/Users: Data Importance," please answer the following questions:

1. Identify some of the customers who would be logical members of the implementation team and explain why.

2. Think through an HR process and sketch out what data are necessary to complete your sample process well. How much history does the organization need to convert to continue functioning?

3. Pick one area of the HR function (e.g., recruiting), and make a list of processes that will need to be mapped and possibly reengineered during this implementation.

New Information for the Case: Part 2

Over the next month, as you continue to obtain information about the design and implementation of the new system, you are still somewhat confused about what to do. Once again, we find you in your office thinking:

> There are so many potential decisions to make with regard to hardware! I wonder what we need to schedule, if we need to buy hardware, and how we should configure the servers to ensure maximum security. And this "bring your own device" stuff is going to drive us nuts! It's time to make another list of questions!

Based on the information in the section of the chapter titled "HRIS Architecture," please respond to the following:

1. Make a list of questions for each of the following individuals: lead hardware technical expert, network manager, and chief software manager.

2. What configuration should the company use? Make a suggestion and support it!

3. Make some recommendations about security and bring your own device.

New Information for the Case: Part 3

As part of your investigation, you have uncovered a system concept called "best of breed." You are in your office again trying to decide what to do, and you think, "Perhaps best of breed might be the easiest and best way to go."

1. Make a recommendation as to whether a BOB option should be chosen or a more standardized option with simpler interfaces between hardware and software should be selected.

2. Think about what the best answer should be when you have to connect your system with accounting and finance. Make a recommendation and support it!

New Information for the Case: Part 4

You have just sat down in your office feeling as if there is way too much to do! Your IS software professional has given you the information from one of the potential vendors about the various steps that need to be taken in implementation of the HRIS. Your immediate reaction is, "Man, am I going to be at work late for the next many months!"

Case Study Questions

Based on the information in this chapter, answer the following questions:

1. Develop the first few steps of the project plan.

2. Discuss the potential political necessities outlined in this section as they relate to this type of implementation.

3. Think about and create a list of steps that make sense for your organization.

4. Is the nine-month rapid-implementation time frame feasible? Or will it just lead to failure?

STUDENT STUDY SITE _____

Visit the Student Study Site at **http://www.sagepub.com/kavanagh3e** for additional learning tools such as access to SAGE journal articles and related web resources.

REFERENCES

Adamson, L., & Zampetti, R. (2001). Web-based manager self-service. In A. J. Walker (Ed.), *Web-based human resources* (pp. 24–35). New York: McGraw-Hill.

Bedell, M. (2003a). Human resources information systems. In H. Bidgoli (Ed.), *The encyclopedia of information systems* (Vol. 2, pp. 537–549). Burlington, MA: Academic Press.

Bedell, M. (2003b). *An identification of the cost savings resulting from an HR information system implementation.* Paper presented at the meeting of the American Society of Business and Behavioral Sciences, Las Vegas, NV.

Fein, S. (2001). Preface. In A. J. Walker (Ed.), *Web-based human resources* (pp. vii–x). New York: McGraw-Hill.

Hendrickson, A. R. (2003). Human resource information systems: Backbone technology of contemporary human resources. *Journal of Labor Research, 24*(3), 381–394.

Jessup, L., & Valacich, J. (1999). Information systems foundations. In L. Jessup & J. Valacich (Eds.), *Que education & training* (pp. 4–10). Indianapolis, IN: Macmillan.

McManus, M. A., & Ferguson, M. W. (2003). Biodata, personality, and demographic differences of recruits from three sources. *International Journal of Selection and Assessment, 11,* 175–183.

Miller, M. S. (1998). Great expectations: Is your HRIS meeting them? *HR Focus, 75,* 1–2.

Rampton, G. M., Turnbull, J., & Doran, J. A. (1999). *Human resources management systems: A practical approach* (p. 142). Toronto, ON: Carswell.

Regan, E., & O'Conner, B. (2002). *End-user information systems: Implementing individual and work group technologies* (pp. 26–28, 368–369). Upper Saddle River, NJ: Prentice Hall.

Stone, D. L., Lukaszewski, K. M., & Isenhour, L. C. (2005). e-Recruiting: Online strategies for attracting talent. In H. B. Gueutal & D. L. Stone (Eds.), *The brave new world of eHR.* San Francisco: Jossey-Bass.

Walker, A. J. (2001). Best practices in HR technology. In A. J. Walker (Ed.). *Web-based human resources* (pp. 3–12). New York: McGraw-Hill.

Zampetti, R., & Adamson, L. (2001). Web-based employee self-service (pp. 15–23). In A. J. Walker (Ed.), *Web-based human resources.* New York: McGraw-Hill.

Zusman, R. R., & Landis, R. S. (2002). Applicant preferences for Web-based versus traditional job postings. *Computers in Human Behavior, 18,* 285–296.

CHAPTER 4

The Systems Development Life Cycle and HRIS Needs Analysis

Lisa M. Plantamura and Richard D. Johnson

EDITORS' NOTE

This chapter begins the section of the book focused on how to determine the needs for an HRIS and how that determination affects the design of the HRIS. The idea that there will be different users of the HRIS with various data and information needs was introduced briefly in Chapter 3. In this chapter, you will see the importance of the initial needs analysis and how it is done. In keeping with the holistic nature of HRIS, the systems development life cycle (SDLC) is introduced; however, this chapter focuses heavily on the **analysis phase** *of the SDLC, as the remaining parts, namely, planning, design, implementation, and maintenance, are discussed in subsequent chapters. The authors emphasize that the needs analysis begins the process of HRIS design, but that this analysis is also done continuously throughout the system design process. This notion of continuously updating the needs analysis recognizes the possibility of both organizational and technology changes during the development and implementation of the HRIS. In addition, it is important to complete an accurate and comprehensive needs analysis because this will provide the blueprint for the evaluation of the HRIS after it is implemented.*

CHAPTER Objectives

The learning goals for this chapter are listed below. At the end of this chapter, you should be able to address the following questions:

- What is a systems development life cycle (SDLC)?
- How does the analysis phase of an SDLC inform the needs analysis process?
- What is a needs analysis, and why is it important?
- What are the main stages of the needs analysis?
- What is involved in an HRIS needs analysis? What types of activities are performed?
- Who is typically involved in an HRIS needs analysis?
- What are the key deliverables of an HRIS needs analysis?

HRIS IN ACTION

Failing to Plan Is Planning to Fail

A multimedia company planned to offer a special benefits package to a select group of employees. The purpose of the package was to encourage some employees to retire early, which would provide cost savings to the company, as well as meet some of its other needs, such as providing promotional opportunities to help attract and retain younger employees. The special package included granting additional years of service for the purposes of calculating retirement and retiree medical benefits, granting additional age to employees to be used in the calculation of eligibility for early retirement incentives from the pension plan, and eliminating some portion of the normal reductions in pension plan benefits for those taking early retirement. The cost of implementing these changes in the existing system for the estimated eligible group of just over 500 employees was prohibitive due to the complex nature of the calculations involved.

The project was in danger of being canceled until a careful needs analysis was done. For 500 employees, did the solution need to be fully automated? Did employees need to be able to model their retirement benefits on the Internet? How much manual work could be relied on to handle the workload? Did the project need to be repeatable?

The answer for the multimedia company was to build a simple solution outside its HRIS using spreadsheet and word merge applications and to couple that simple solution with a high-touch customer service group that was able to respond to the needs of program participants, manage the increased manual paperwork requirements, and perform the interventions into the system to make the components that had to be automated, such as the payment of benefits, function properly. The program that had nearly been canceled was a success, so much so that it was repeated just the next year in another company division.

Implementing the changes in the existing HRIS would have been the obvious solution, but creating a one-time solution when it appeared there would be little future need for a complicated implementation was the right choice in this case. Careful, honest, and practical needs analysis made possible what had been impractical due to cost concerns. It should be noted, however, that the HRIS provider recognized the need the multimedia company had expressed and later made a decision to augment its software to include features that would provide greater flexibility for future offerings, meeting a need the provider hadn't recognized during its own original planning and needs analysis.

Introduction

This chapter briefly introduces the systems development life cycle (SDLC) and provides readers with an in-depth look at one of its most important activities, needs analysis. Although similar in nature to the implementation process described in Chapter 3, the SDLC focuses on the activities across all aspects of the development project. The overlap between these chapters is deliberate because the specific details on both needs analysis and implementation are complementary and represent two important parts of the development and design of an HRIS. The second part of the chapter focuses on a specific activity within the analysis phase of the SDLC, needs analysis. **Needs analysis** refers to the process of thoroughly gathering, prioritizing, and documenting an organization's HR information requirements, and it serves as a necessary input for the subsequent design and implementation of an HRIS.

An HRIS needs analysis usually takes on a particularly prominent role in the analysis phase of an HRIS development project, prior to significant design and implementation activities. It is important to note, however, that the needs analysis for the HRIS continues through the entire systems development process because each stage in the process could lead to the identification of new needs for the HRIS.

Consider some of the potential costs of not planning and conducting a thorough needs analysis:

- Users reject an HRIS that fails to provide the functionality they need.

- Vendor software packages are selected based on incomplete, inaccurate, or irrelevant criteria.

- Costly custom systems are developed and built based on arbitrary data.

- Custom additions to the HRIS are required to fill needs after implementation, as these needs were not properly identified during the needs analysis.

- Scope creep occurs because of growth in the goals, functionality, and requirements of the HRIS without adjustments to the time, cost, or resources allocated to the project.

Consequently, needs analysis is not something that HRIS project personnel *choose* to do; it is something they *must* do. The following sections in this chapter provide a road map for conducting a needs analysis. First, we discuss the systems development life cycle.

The Systems Development Life Cycle

The **systems development life cycle (SDLC)** is a formal, multistage process through which information systems are implemented. Specific phases include planning, analysis, design, implementation, and maintenance (Figure 4.1). Just as each organization has a unique culture, so, too, the SDLC is often tailored to the need of each organization. Some organizations may choose to codify over 20 phases in their life cycle, while others may use only the five phases listed above. Despite the variation in the number of phases, most scholars and practitioners would agree that the activities outlined in the five-phase SDLC introduced here contain the major system development activities.

This phased approach to system design has multiple advantages. First, it allows the organization to focus on a limited set of issues. Second, it contains many activities within one phase and allows organizations to make "go, no-go" decisions at the end of each phase. At any time the project is seen as not meeting objectives, it can be terminated, with the work to-date providing a baseline if conditions merit moving forward.

We encourage readers to take particular note of the dashed lines. The dashed lines represent the idea that you may find it necessary to revisit previous phases of the life cycle if conditions change or if details were missed. The problem is that just like

Figure 4.1   A Typical Systems Development Life Cycle (SDLC)

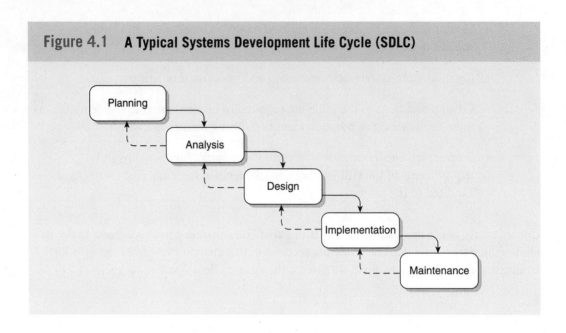

climbing a real waterfall, moving back up the life cycle can be costly, challenging, and full of effort. Just ask salmon how hard it is to swim upstream! Each of the five phases in the SDLC is important, and skipping any specific phase can have negative impact on the success of your project. Let us consider more closely the SDLC phases depicted in Figure 4.1:

1. *Planning:* The **planning phase** of the SDLC includes both long-range or strategic planning and short-range operational planning. During the planning phase, HR will determine the existing technological and system capabilities and develop a general plan for adapting, upgrading, or changing these plans. In a sense, HR is conducting an analysis of their future human capital strategies and assessing what may need to be done technologically to ensure that these strategies may occur. As this phase is at a strategic level, the planning is very high level and not as detailed. At the end of this phase, an organization should have a general idea of the issues they need to address and may have developed a plan to move forward.

2. *Analysis:* It is in the **analysis phase** that an organization's current capabilities are documented, new needs are identified, and the scope of an HRIS is determined. In many systems projects, this phase can be the most time-consuming and important phase of the SDLC. The analysis phase of the SDLC encompasses steps such as reviewing the current system processes, looking for opportunities

for improvement, exploring and justifying change, developing requirements for the new system (needs analysis), and prioritizing those needs. At the end of this phase, a formal requirements definition report should be completed and available for use in systems design or vendor evaluation. Because needs analysis is such an integral part of the analysis phase, we devote an entire section of the chapter to it below.

3. *Design:* In the **design phase**, the "blueprint" for the system is finalized. Whereas the analysis phase finalizes the needs or requirements for the HRIS, here, the detailed specifications for the final system are laid out. It is often during the design phase that the final vendor evaluation and selection occurs. (This topic is covered in detail in the next chapter.) Using the results of the needs analysis, the current human resources processes may be changed and updated to reflect current organizational needs and potentially industry best practices. Organizations have many options in design, and these options are covered more extensively in the next chapter.

4. *Implementation:* During the **implementation phase**, the HRIS is built, tested, and readied for actual rollout, or the "go live" stage—the point in the SDLC at which the old system is turned off and the new system is put into operation. Two common approaches to switching from the old system to the new system used by many organizations is to either pilot the new HRIS in one location before fully going live, or to turn on limited functions and then continue to add functionality. There is not one single optimal approach, but instead, the approach used by your organization should reflect your needs and context. Key steps in implementation include coding or configuring modules, system testing, finalizing procedures, converting old data for use in the new system, documentation, and training end users.

5. *Maintenance:* The SDLC does not end once the go-live date arrives. The **maintenance phase**, sometimes referred to as the "forgotten phase" (Smith, 2001), is that phase in the life of an HRIS during which the primary objective is to prolong the useful life of the HRIS, and it begins once the new system is put into operation. Consequently, a crucial part of maintenance is the evaluation of the HRIS. Does it meet the needs of all users as determined during the earlier phase of the SDLC? Has it been accepted by the users? Is the HRIS being used properly? Maintenance serves four main purposes:

   a) **Corrective Maintenance**—There will be times that despite the best efforts of designers and implementers, something in the system doesn't work properly and must be fixed (e.g., computer bugs, misinterpreted designs, incorrectly specified designs, or identified needs ignored).

b) **Adaptive Maintenance**—The human resources environment is always changing and evolving. For example, new government regulations affecting HR practices, such as legislation addressing racial and gender discrimination, can prompt new requirements or alter the old requirements of the system.

c) **Perfective Maintenance**—The goal of perfective maintenance is to tweak or improve on the existing system. For example, a more efficient routine that speeds up processing times could be developed in the maintenance phase.

d) **Preventative Maintenance**—Preventative maintenance focuses on the ongoing requirements of maintaining the hardware and software than runs the HRIS. Such a maintenance action will prevent future system crashes due to inadequate hardware.

Having briefly reviewed the SDLC, we will focus the remaining discussion on needs analysis. Although needs analysis is important throughout the life of a project, it is particularly important early in the project—in the planning and analysis phases.

Analysis

As noted above, the analysis phase of the SDLC encompasses multiple steps, including conducting a needs analysis and the writing of a formal requirements definition report. Organizations sometimes skip over analysis, progressing directly to solutions, as people may be influenced by the marketing materials and promises made by software vendors. It is not unheard of for HR representatives, after attending trade shows and viewing potential HRIS solutions, to make a purchasing decision based on what they have seen, rather than what their organization really needs.

This phase is particularly important because, unless the requirements are specified in detail, the organization cannot select the best vendor package or design their own system effectively. HRIS software is expensive, regardless of whether it is built or bought, so the investment made should be in the definitive system. When an organization does not conduct a proper needs analysis, it may expend considerable effort reworking the solution because it does not meet their needs. In fact, it has been argued that the costs to fix errors increase exponentially through the life cycle. What this means is that a $100 fix during analysis could be a $10,000 fix during the implementation. Additionally, time is wasted, as it takes longer to get to a solution that works for the organization. A proper needs analysis provides the organization with information focused on the essential areas, which is then used to document the functional system requirements. Do not underestimate the importance of the analysis. Remember, it is easier (and less expensive!) to fix a problem now before the new system is designed, rather than when it has been implemented.

Needs Analysis

As noted above, needs analysis focuses on the process of thoroughly gathering, prioritizing, and documenting an organization's HR information requirements. The first question that you may want to ask is why would you undertake a needs analysis? Essentially, the purpose of needs analysis is to collect and document information related to making changes connected to

- Current system performance issues;
- The introduction of a new system, application, task, or technology; or
- Any opportunities perceived to benefit the organization.

The process of conducting a needs analysis is systematic, and it should progress in a logical, methodical fashion, as each stage affects those that follow. An effective needs analysis consists of five main stages, each of which has activities that will be discussed in detail:

1. Needs Analysis Planning
2. Observation
3. Exploration
4. Evaluation
5. Reporting

Regardless of the type of system desired, all stages should be completed, although more detail may be required when, for example, a system is being built in-house rather than purchased from a vendor.[1] The resulting HRIS will be better formulated, executed, accepted by employees, and used if time and effort is invested in this early phase. At the end of needs analysis, there will a detailed and prioritized list and description of HR's current and future functional automation support needs.

1. Needs Analysis Planning

During this first stage of the needs analysis process, **needs analysis planning**, the team is assembled and prepares to investigate the current and desired system applications and functions. Once the team is in place, they can begin arranging to conduct a thorough investigation. There are four major activities that need to be completed during this stage. Each is discussed in turn.

Organize the Needs Analysis Team

The needs analysis is generally conducted by a team led by HRIS analysts and involving human resources and information technology staff. The team must work with current systems users and associated constituents and **stakeholders** to identify problems clearly, research possible ways of addressing the problems, and report their findings in order to support a decision on the most appropriate solutions. There are several key personnel who need to be part of this team. For example, a senior-level manager, preferably with HRIS analysis experience, should have overall accountability for needs analysis. In addition, an information technology professional should be included, along with at least one employee who has knowledge of the present HRIS (if there is one) or current HR processes. Finally, for large-scale projects, teams may wish to involve an external consultant. If an outside consultant will be involved in the needs analysis, it is important that he or she be integrated early in the assignment.

In addition to this core project team, a task force of constituents from the functional areas is needed to speak for the stakeholders. This group should include representatives from each area of HR, payroll, and any other areas that may use the HRIS directly. Table 4.1 provides a list of several common stakeholders in many large organizations. These people will participate in review and verification of findings, as well as serving as liaisons for their departments or functions. They should support the core team and care about the project.

Determine Management's Role

The involvement of upper management is also important to ensure successful needs analysis outcomes. If top management support has not already been obtained, getting their active involvement and buy-in of other stakeholders can be difficult. Senior management sponsorship and a visible presence are critical to the success of the project, and mutual respect and honesty will allow the team to acquire the information needed to perform the analysis and make suitable recommendations. This group acts as a steering committee that will guide the team, resolve issues, and set priorities.

Define the Goals

Once the needs analysis team is in place, the next step in planning is to define, clarify, and gain management acceptance on the goals for needs analysis. Goals give focus; they provide a standard against which performance and achievement may be measured. It is essential at this point that the team knows what it hopes to achieve, how it plans to work, and the anticipated schedule, as well as how the completed needs analysis document will look. In addition to overall systems scope and processes, these goals may also include timing, budget, staffing, and any other factors that could affect system selection, development, implementation, and

Table 4.1 Common Organizational Stakeholders

Human Resources Stakeholders	Other Stakeholders
Benefits Administration	Payroll
Compensation	Corporate Security
Diversity Management	Auditing
EEO/Affirmative Action	Organizational Subsidiaries
Employment	Service Bureaus and Third-Party Processors
Employee Relations	Retirees
Ethics and Sustainability	General Ledger
Global HR	Telephone Directories
Health and Safety	Medical
HR Consulting	Legal
Incentive Programs	Company Store
Labor Relations	Community Relations
Pension Administration	Relocation Services
Profit Sharing	Emergency Services
Relocation	Corporate Strategy
Staffing Management	Mail Room
Succession Planning	
HR Technology	
Training and Employee Development	
Workers' Compensation	

operations. Like other goals, they should be specific, measurable, attainable, relevant, and timely (SMART). At this phase, the requirements should be phrased in terms of what the system should accomplish rather than how it will work; details will be determined later.

Determine Tools and Techniques to Be Used

Specific information-gathering tools and techniques should be used when conducting a needs analysis. Each organization and project will require its own combination of observation, exploration, analysis, and reporting approaches. The tools may run the gamut from simple paper and pen note taking for smaller projects through complex documentation systems for corporate-wide systems. Whatever the size of the project, it is important to choose tools that are easy to manage and allow the organization to gather the data needed to ensure that the organization can move into the design mode with accurate and timely data.

It is important to note, that although these tools and techniques assist analysts in examining every indicator, it is also important that the analyst verify all data and consider each alternative objectively before making any conclusions. In addition to identifying the tools and techniques to be used, it is also important to establish performance standards and criteria to measure the results of the process. This way, stakeholders can be satisfied that the recommendations are based on thorough, rigorous research. We will discuss some of these tools and approaches later in the chapter.

2. Observation

During the **observation** stage, analysts impartially observe the current systems and processes, forming the basis for later recommendations. At this point, the investigation is at a high level; more detailed data will be gathered later, during the exploration stage. It is important for the analysts to interact with employees at all levels in the areas that may be affected by the changes during observation. In fact, involving employees now provides a great opportunity for them to voice their concerns and for the analysts to determine what they consider strengths and weaknesses of their current systems and operations. Research has shown that the more involved the users are in the analysis, design, and implementation of new systems, the more successful these systems will be. Involving the users can create a sense of ownership, can lead to better communication and idea sharing, and has been shown to relate to more successful systems (cf. Harris & Weistroffer, 2009). Trends may become apparent, which could be helpful later. The observation stage also consists of multiple steps, each of which is discussed below.

Analyze the Current Situation

This activity begins by assessing the current state of HR systems and processes. Before embarking on the detailed exploration of any new system, analysts must first develop a picture of present HR operations, including any problems and issues involved in each area or function. As part of this activity, analysts must consider the existing processes and current organizational results and compare these to the organization's expectations for what they anticipate in the future. Once a clear, objective understanding of the current processes are obtained, this phase continues with a definition of needs. As an example, a tool such as the one shown in Figure 4.2 might be helpful during this stage to help organize the analysis.

Figure 4.2 Example Preliminary Systems Review Document

Functional Area	Task	Current Process	Desired Process	Performance Issues
Compensation	Performance Reviews			
	Annual Salary Increases			
	Job Analysis			
	Salary Evaluation			
Benefits	Annual Benefits Enrollment			
	Claims Administration			
	Paid Time Off			
Employment	Employment Planning			
	Recruitment			
	Staffing			
Training and Development	Workforce Training			
	Career Development			
	Succession Planning			
	Performance Management			

Define the Needs

The next step in the observation stage is to define the needs that the new system must meet. The objective of this activity is to determine how those within HR believe their operations should occur, to evaluate industry best practices, and to begin investigating what changes or updates to the system may be valuable to adopt. As part of this step, organizational policies, procedures, and standards must be considered, along with any regulatory requirements. Essentially, the goal of this activity is to determine what the new system should accomplish based on the above information.

Identify Performance Gaps

Once you understand your current operating environment and have gained a strong understanding of the "ideal" operating environment, the team can conduct a gap analysis. Comparing the current situation to the desired situation allows the organization to identify and outline any **performance gaps**. These gaps, or areas of mismatch between the existing and required processes, form the basis for developing the systems requirements that are developed during the analysis and reporting stages.

Classify the Data

Once the data has been gathered, they need to be organized. It is important to separate the data into categories (e.g., by function, process, and other groupings that makes sense for your environment), and to separate technical and process systems issues from other organizational issues. For example, if there are problems with a specific function due to lack of knowledge on how the current process works, this may reflect a training issue rather than a system issue. In addition, the analysis team should seek to separate the real problems from symptoms when reviewing the effects of one process on another. For example, late filings of mandated reports may be considered a problem, but it may actually be a symptom of the real issue, which might be lack of data needed to generate the report. Finally, consider the scope of the issue; does it affect a few employees or the entire management staff?

Determine the Priorities

Using the information above, the team can now set the priorities for the needs that have been identified. The needs may be ranked based on scope, cost-benefit analysis, time to implement, and/or potential impact if ignored, as management will be interested in these assessments when reviewing the results of the preliminary analysis. Before presenting the results to management, it is a good idea to have the task force review priorities to ensure that the assessment is accurate.

Note that both *needs* and *requirements* are strong words in the sense that they imply something that the organization, and therefore the HRIS, *must have.* It is important to recognize that as needs are being identified a process should be put into place to prioritize them. This ranking will result in a list of needs that fall along a continuum from high-priority or critical needs, those that definitely will be built into the system, to medium-priority needs, which are likely to be included, to low-priority needs, which may be incorporated if time and resources allow. More on this is discussed in the following sections.

Review With Management

When presenting the preliminary findings to management, the team should be prepared to adjust priorities as requested, clarify any remaining questions, and discuss the next phase of the project in order to gain management's continued commitment. When reviewing the analysis with management, it is important to work with them to define the task, agree on the process, state the desired outcome, and establish shared responsibility for the continuation of the project. The analysis team should also ensure that management understands that the full needs analysis takes time to design, develop, and accomplish. How long this will take depends on the complexity of the organization. It is critical *not* to promise more than can be delivered. One of the challenges is that the analysis phase is time consuming and complex, yet HR and management will likely push the team to finish the phase as quickly as possible. Therefore, the analysis team should be prepared to defend the phase and educate stakeholders on what the phase entails and why it should be completed before moving forward. Ultimately, though, management's commitment is essential to fund, staff, and support the next stage. Thus, it is important to receive formal management support and agreement (e.g., memo, contract, etc.) before moving forward.

3. Exploration

The **exploration** stage of the needs analysis process builds on the analysis completed in the observation stage and involves gathering additional and more detailed data regarding HR processes. Remember that the problems must be defined clearly before any suitable solutions may be determined.

Collect the Data

The data collected during exploration provide the foundation for the development of goals that the organization wishes to achieve with the new system. This data also help the organization align their new system with key HR objectives. It is important to keep in mind that the data collected during the needs analysis may be used for other purposes after the system is developed and implemented, so it pays to do a good job now. In other words, good documentation now means fewer problems later!

Multiple techniques should be used to collect data for the needs analysis, including questionnaires, observations, interviews, focus groups, and reviews of job descriptions, policies, procedures, and other documentation. Regardless of the methods chosen, it is critical to develop a concise problem statement that documents the causes of the issues to be resolved and separate facts from opinions.

Interviews

The goal of conducting **interviews** is to find representative employees that can effectively communicate the key HR practices and processes to the analysis team so that they can develop a thorough understanding of current HR operations. A variety of different interview types may be used when conducting a needs analysis. These types can run the gamut from completely unstructured interviews, where a general topic is introduced for discussion and the interviewer lets the interview progress naturally, to thoroughly structured interviews, where the interviewer asks specific questions in a predetermined order and respondents select from a set of alternative answers. An example of a structured interview script/guide is shown in Figure 4.3.

The results of interviews can be compiled by functional area experts and reviewed by that area's management to make certain that all tasks are covered and represented correctly. Although interviews are time and labor intensive, when conducted well, they can contain the required data needed to assess the system requirements as well as being a rich source of opinions, ideas, and suggestions. It is also important that the interviewer reviews his or

Figure 4.3   Interview Guide

Interviewee:	
Date:	
Position:	
Function:	
Phone:	
E-mail:	
System/Activity:	
Staffing (FT, PT, Temps, etc.):	
Brief Description:	
Technology/Software in Use:	
Status:	
Which data are collected, stored, and/or used by this function?	
Which of these data are automated, and in which systems?	
Which additional data could be automated, and in which systems?	
What problems do you experience with your current systems?	
How often have you observed this problem, or how often does it occur?	
Interviewer:	

her notes soon after completing the interview to ensure that the information recorded is complete and accurate. The longer you go without writing down and reviewing your notes, the harder it will be to ensure that your notes are accurate.

Questionnaires

Questionnaires are structured data-collection tools that must be designed and implemented carefully in order to obtain usable results. Before the questionnaire is implemented, the purpose and importance of each question should be determined. Employee time is valuable, and no question should be included unless it serves a clear purpose that helps the analysts better understand HR data or processes. In addition, from a statistical standpoint, it is important that the questions are reliable and valid so that any analysis of the captured data can be trusted. As you would expect, it is important to design a professional-looking document (or Web survey, if administering the questionnaire online), to use clear instructions, and to focus on developing a document that is easy to use. Before launching the questionnaire to employees, the questionnaire should be tested to ensure that the questions are clear and understandable, and that they are collecting the needed data. Finally, throughout the process, it is important to not only ensure that respondent's answers remain confidential, but also that they understand that their responses will remain confidential.

As with interviews, questionnaires also have several advantages and disadvantages. For example, one advantage of questionnaires is they can be distributed to large groups quickly and easily. In addition, questionnaires are much less time-consuming than observing or interviewing employees. Questionnaires also lend themselves to easier analysis and can be more convenient for employees (i.e., they can be completed at a time of their choosing). Finally, because questionnaires can be viewed as more anonymous, it increases the likelihood that you may obtain more accurate and honest responses.

Questionnaires do have shortcomings, though. Compared to interviews, questionnaires have much lower response rates. Many employees may not perceive that they have the time to complete them, or they may feel that their responses do not matter. Unlike an interview, questionnaires contain less rich data because there are no opportunities for an interviewer to focus on any nonverbal cues or to engage in follow-up questions as needed. In addition, questionnaires can be used less effectively to increase employee or management buy-in. People like to have their opinions valued, and interviews can reinforce their feelings of worth. When employees believe that their feelings and perceptions are valued and they are involved in the decision processes, they feel greater ownership in the new system (Wu & Marakas, 2006).

Observation

Another excellent way to gather data regarding HR processes is to observe personnel as they do their jobs. Because observation takes place in the actual work environment, information is obtained within the context in which HR activities occur. Observation is most useful when trying to determine what employees do and in what order. Further, it can be used to identify potential causes of performance issues. Although observation has the advantage of minimizing interruption of routine functions, observers must be skilled in observation and knowledgeable of the process itself.

Prior to observing employees in the work setting, it is important to determine the activity to be studied and to collect and review any documentation available (e.g., mission statements, organization charts, position descriptions, current systems processes, policies, etc.). In addition, try to remain as unobtrusive as possible, take notes for later clarification, and refrain from disturbing the employees' work.

Observation has its limitations, though. First, it is important to account for the fact that even with a well-trained and effective observer who attempts to remain unobtrusive, his or her presence alone may subtly affect how the employees go about their work. Second, observation is not as effective for high-level jobs where the process and outcome of work is not as easily seen. For example, complex tasks that require an employee or manager to make decisions are not easily observed and may require interviewing the employee to better understand the actual decision-making process. Therefore, observation may be best for simpler tasks, tasks in which data is not as accurately articulated by employees, or tasks where it may be easy to inadvertently miss key processes using other data collection techniques.

Focus Groups

Focus groups consist of a sample of people representing a larger population who gather together to discuss a topic; in this case, the topic would relate to the HRIS. Focus groups are important because they can provide as deep of information as interviews, but it has the added advantage of bringing people together, which can lead to greater and more effective information sharing than if only interviews were utilized. Participants in focus groups are asked for their opinions and attitudes, and the results can help to shape system requirements. Although it can seem challenging to pull together the perfect combination of people at the same time, small discussion groups such as these may uncover needs not previously found and help the analysts identify new requirements. Recommendations for effective focus groups include the following:

- Limit the size of the group to no more than 8 to 12 people.

- Allow sufficient time to cover the material, generally one to two hours, and keep the meeting focused to make good use of everyone's time. Consider having a moderator to keep the meeting focused.

- Before starting the focus group, explain the objectives clearly.

- Encourage group members to speak freely, and ensure that everyone participates. An icebreaker exercise can be a great way of opening up group communication.

- Use a variety of group facilitation methods, such as brainstorming, prioritizing, and consensus building to encourage and promote discussion on differences of opinion and to clarify issues.

- Take notes and/or video or audio tape the session, so that nothing is lost.

- Thank participants for their time and ideas.

4. Evaluation

Several activities occur during the **evaluation** stage of needs analysis. Once the data have been collected, they must be reviewed and assessed to create a clear picture of the current and desired processes, data sources, and issues. Next, the data should be arranged in a format useful for the next phase of the SDLC: design. Third, the data should be reviewed by the project team to gain additional perspective and encourage suggestions, noting any duplications or omissions. For example, consider whether data must be collected and stored in the new system or if it could be calculated from data already in the system. For example, if employer-paid life insurance is twice an employee's annual salary, there is no need to store that value in the system, as it can simply be calculated from the existing salary data. In addition, it is important to consider how other areas of business interface with human resources and how HR data may come from, and be sent to, other systems. As an example, production or sales data may be used by HR as part of a performance appraisal or compensation process, but they would likely be provided from a non-HR module or system.

There are several ways of assessing and analyzing the system data, functions, and processes, and these may be organized in any way that assists in this process. For example, visual representation of priorities may be displayed in check sheets, graphs, Pareto charts, flowcharts, or data flow diagrams to support and summarize the analysis. When this information is organized, it can then be prioritized according to, for example, the time when it must be present or the level of importance, as shown below. The prioritization method is up to each organization.

Priority	Description
1	Must be present at implementation
2	Must be present within six months of implementation
3	Nice to have, but not essential
4	Not needed in the near future, but may be needed due to environmental changes

Importance	Description
1	Mandatory
2	Strongly desired
3	Nice to have

The result should be an operational depiction of the HR system needs, including a visual representation and descriptive text that lists the particular processing required to support each function. These documents will serve as the primary reference for the remainder of the project, and they also serve as a key communication tool for HR staff, consultants, vendor representatives, and technical staff. For example, given that no organization has unlimited budget to implement all functionality desired by the organization, prioritizing ensures that the most important functionality will be given first focus. In fact, for many projects, desired functionality will often have to be eliminated because of budget or time constraints.

5. Reporting

The final stage of the needs analysis process, **reporting**, involves preparing a report that summarizes the findings and presents recommendations for the design phase. The final report should include an overview of the current systems and processes, along with a description of how a new system could address the issues and weaknesses with which the function deals. This report should contain the formalized **requirements definition**, the document that lists each of the prioritized requirements for the new system. The requirement definition can include specifications geared toward solving problems identified in the analysis as well as any that focus on new functionality that HR requires in the new system. These requirements should be written in such a way that when the new system is tested, each requirement can be verified as being met.

Although the report can be, and often is, viewed as a sales presentation to management and other constituents that presents a business justification for continuing the project, it is also a roadmap for moving forward. The report becomes the basis upon which the new system will be designed. There is no standard format for the requirements report. Instead, the format will depend on the intended audience and corporate and/or information technology reporting standards. A potential outline for the report is shown in Figure 4.4. The written report is generally accompanied by an oral presentation where stakeholders can ask questions and receive additional information about the project.

Figure 4.4   Sample Report Outline

1. Executive Summary

2. Project Background

    2.1. Project Initiation

    2.2. Project Charter

    2.3. Project Scope

    2.4. Project Team

    2.5. Steering Committee

    2.6. Project Schedule

3. Current Systems

    3.1. Description

    3.2. Components and Functions

    3.3. Interfaces

    3.4. Strengths and Weaknesses

4. General Operational Requirements

5. Functional Requirements

    5.1. Function 1

        5.1.1.   Function 1 Description

        5.1.2.   Function 1 Requirements

    5.2. Function 2

        5.2.1.   Function 2 Description

        5.2.2.   Function 2 Requirements

    5.3. Etc.

6. Information Technology Requirements

7. Support Requirements

8. Next Steps

9. Appendices

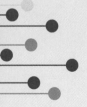

SUMMARY

Organizations faced with the need to update, upgrade, or implement changes to HR processes and to consider new software should follow a formalized, structured process to give them the best chance to succeed. In this chapter, we briefly introduced this structured process: the systems development life cycle that helps organizations better manage the design and implementation of new or upgraded systems.

The chapter further focuses on the analysis phase of the SDLC, particularly on the needs analysis portion of this phase. Needs analysis is designed to help the organization discover the disparity between the organization's present HR system(s) and desired HR systems. The chapter outlines an effective, formal, multistaged approach that starts with naming the project team, reviewing current processes and systems, and determining future needs and priorities. The resulting requirements definition can provide the ongoing project team responsible for vendor evaluation and/or system design with a clear picture of what the organization requires and when it must be delivered. It establishes the structure for future phases of this project, as well as a framework for ongoing operations. Needs analysis can, therefore, rightfully be viewed as one of the most critical to the success of the entire project.

KEY TERMS

adaptive maintenance 88

analysis phase 82

corrective maintenance 87

design phase 87

evaluation 99

exploration 95

focus groups 98

implementation phase 87

interviews 95

maintenance phase 87

needs analysis 84

needs analysis planning 89

observation 92

perfective maintenance 88

performance gaps 94

planning phase 86

preventative maintenance 88

questionnaires 97

reporting 100

requirements definition 100

SDLC (systems development life cycle) 000

stakeholders 90

DISCUSSION QUESTIONS

1. What are some critical success factors for effectively conducting an analysis of HRIS needs?

2. Explain how planning and analysis integrate and inform further steps in the systems development life cycle (SDLC).

3. Compare and contrast the different methods of data collection, explaining the conditions under which each is most effective.

4. Which prioritization method is most useful in establishing the appropriate values for system requirements, and why?

CASE STUDY: "PLANNING THE NEEDS OF OTHER ORGANIZATIONS" _____

If you think a thorough, high-quality needs analysis is daunting on an internal project, imagine if you were an HRIS vendor and your job was to provide a "best of breed" system (see Chapter 3) that meets most of your many different clients' needs. Such an approach makes planning and needs analysis more challenging because difficult choices must be made as to the functionality that is sufficiently broad to go into a general market package. It is costly to vendors, and indeed may be infeasible, to include functionality that is so specific that only a small portion of a system's client base benefits from the function.

Consider the following hypothetical company, Benefast Partners, which provides a specific market niche HRIS product: benefits administration software. Its challenge: Provide comprehensive benefits administration software that meets the needs of a growing and complex benefits marketplace. According to Davis Hunter, a former employee of Benefast,

"Benefast Partners (name changed to protect confidentiality) was only doing defined benefit pension plans for large employers (20,000+ employees). When you focus your business opportunities on *Fortune* 100 companies, it limits your potential for growth to small and midsized markets. Given that there is competition in the market for small, medium, and large clients, there was no real way to expand. We were, however, doing 401(k) retirement plan administration both on our proprietary system, designed and marketed for large employers, and on a purchased platform for smaller companies. We had interest from existing 401(k) clients to take on administration of their defined benefit plans, and we felt we had lost 401(k) business in the past because we didn't offer total retirement outsourcing, just 401(k).

It wasn't possible to charge small employers the kinds of fees necessary to implement their plans on our proprietary system, so our efforts centered on what could be done with the purchased system used for small to midsized 401(k) plans. We quickly determined that the purchased system's defined benefits platform wasn't sophisticated enough from a calculation standpoint to handle most of the complexity of defined benefit plans, so we decided to use a combination of the purchased system with the calculation engine component for the proprietary system.

We had a lot of needs analysis conversations with our colleagues in another office who were running the project. Given the multiple platforms involved, processing time was a huge concern. We decided to segment the market and serve only those customers who met a fairly stringent set of requirements. Basically, we built a system to serve clients whose plans were easy to administer. In other words,

1. No multiplan clients

2. No retirement modeling

3. No coordination of benefits, for example, no combination of 401(k) and defined benefit plans

4. Limited Web interface

So, based on this segmentation, we launched our new product with one of our parent companies (a bank). By the time we had signed our third client, we had already begun to move toward a fairly complex multiplan environment. Our fourth and fifth clients were even more complex. We were over budget and off schedule on everything, and then we started trying to figure out how to do coordination of benefits. We built a system for plans that were easy to administer—but plans that are easy to administer are few and far between in the marketplace, and those that exist aren't typically managed by organizations shopping for benefits vendors."

Case Study Questions

1. How would you evaluate Benefast Partners' strategy?

2. What changes (if any) would you make going forward?

3. What methods would you employ to ensure that an HRIS package meets the majority of your clients' needs?

STUDENT STUDY SITE _____

Visit the Student Study Site at **http://www.sagepub.com/kavanagh3e** for additional learning tools such as access to SAGE journal articles and related web resources.

NOTE _____

1. Although most organizations no longer build full systems from scratch, many organizations find it necessary to customize their systems by building their own

modules or apps. Thus, the same need and logic would apply to these small-scale changes.

REFERENCES

Harris, M. A., & Weistroffer, H. R. (2009). A new look at the relationship between user involvement in systems development and system success. *Communications of the Association for Information Systems, 24*(42), 739–756.

Smith, J. (2001, February/March). Knowledge transfer: The forgotten phase. IHRIM.*link*, 6, 53.

Wu, J., & Marakas, G. (2006). The impact of operational user participation on perceived system implementation success: An empirical investigation. *Journal of Computer Information Systems, 46*(5), 127–140.

RECOMMENDED READINGS

How to select HRIS software—& defend your planned purchase. (2009, September). *HR Focus, 86*(9), 3–4.

Swedberg, J. (2009). The technological touch. *Credit Union Management, 32*(2), 30–33.

System Design and Acquisition

Richard D. Johnson and James H. Dulebohn

EDITORS' NOTE

Building on Chapters 3 and 4, this chapter focuses on the design and acquisition of an HRIS. Thus, the focus of this chapter is on the "design" phase of the systems development life cycle (SDLC), as illustrated in Figure 4.1. The authors differentiate between the logical and the physical design of an HRIS, as well as emphasizing the differences between the data and process views of a computer system. As will be discussed in this chapter, these differences are critical for the effective design of an HRIS that will meet the needs of the various stakeholders of the system, that is, HR and information technology (IT) professionals, managers, and employees. Data flow diagramming is discussed as a tool used to analyze the process design characteristics prior to the actual physical design of the HRIS. In addition, the three choices or options that organizations face when moving into physical design are examined. All the effort involved in completing an accurate and comprehensive logical and physical design of the HRIS helps ensure that the acquisition of the system will be done properly. The chapter concludes with a discussion of how to develop a request for proposal (RFP) and how to evaluate proposals received from outside vendors. This last section is a good lead-in to Chapters 6 and 7, which are focused on using HR metrics and analytics to calculate cost-benefit analysis for the acquisition of an HRIS.

CHAPTER Objectives

After completing this chapter, the reader should be able to

- Understand the difference between the data and process views of a system
- Understand the purpose and components of the data flow diagram (DFD)
- Understand the hierarchy of DFDs and the concept of DFD balancing
- Understand the three choices or options that organizations have when moving into physical design
- Understand the purpose of an RFP and what information should be included in it
- Understand the various criteria used to evaluate vendor proposals
- Describe the various types of feasibility and their purpose in evaluating potential solutions

HRIS IN ACTION

Larson Property Management Company is one of the largest property-management companies in California, with more than 1,000 employees. The company provides a full array of commercial management and development services. These activities include complete management services for commercial office and retail buildings and apartment complexes; the construction, repair, and maintenance of commercial properties; and financial management and billing services for commercial real estate clients. The company has experienced significant expansion over the past five years in response to the growth in apartment and commercial construction in southern California, and this expansion has resulted in the need to hire a large number of employees on an ongoing basis to staff its operations.

Larson Property Management has depended on a legacy HRIS to manage its applicant and employee databases. The system runs on a client-server computer system. The system was implemented approximately 10 years ago, prior to the rapid growth of the company and when the organization had fewer than 100 employees. The system's functionality is limited to the storage and retrieval of employee and applicant data. For recruiting purposes, the system requires a clerk to manually enter basic applicant data, the results of the application test, and whether or not an offer of employment has been made. Prior to this, applicants' files were passed around to those who reviewed the materials and were sometimes misplaced, so trying to locate a particular applicant's file was often a problem. The current HRIS has limited file storage capability for applicant and employee records and currently has reached its storage capacity.

Larson Property Management has decided to replace its legacy HRIS. One application module in the new HRIS that the company wants is a sophisticated applicant-tracking system (ATS). The primary objective of the ATS will be to provide a paperless hiring process. The basic functions of the new system will be managing the requisition and approval of job openings, storing resumes and job applications and retrieving through query functions the names of applicants who match job requirements, tracking a candidate's progress through the recruiting and selection process, and providing automated reporting functions. The company's managers also want an e-HR functionality that includes the Internet posting of job openings through the company's website and external job-posting services, application and resume submission through the Web and through kiosks at various office locations, staff ability to access and use the system remotely through a Web browser, and online resume- and application-scanning capabilities.

Part of the design phase is modeling the processes that will be used in the system for applicant tracking. For Larson Property Management, this modeling will allow the system analysts to design an efficient paperless hiring process.

Case note: As you read this chapter, keep the situation at Larson Property Management in mind. It will be the basis of the case analysis at the end of the chapter.

Introduction

> Never tell people how to do things.
>
> Tell them what to do and they will surprise you with their ingenuity.
>
> —General George S. Patton (1947/1995)

The goal of this chapter is to provide a deeper understanding of the process through which an HRIS is designed and acquired. This design and acquisition of an HRIS comprises but one phase in a larger systems development process. As noted in previous chapters, the larger development process is called the **systems development life cycle (SDLC)**. As seen in Chapter 4 (Figure 4.1), the five generic phases of the SDLC are planning, analysis, design, implementation, and maintenance. This chapter focuses on the design phase by discussing briefly the role and features of the structuring of a system's requirements through process system modeling, during which analysts create data flow diagrams (DFDs) to model both the business processes that the system will use to capture, store, manipulate, and distribute data and the options facing the HR department as it moves into design. Next, the vendor-management relationship is covered, including the creation and use of a request for a proposal (RFP), the evaluation of vendor responses, and the choice of a vendor or vendors. Finally, the chapter ends with a discussion of the HRIS feasibility criteria.

Design Considerations During the Systems Development Life Cycle

As discussed in previous chapters, the SDLC is a structured set of phases focused on the analysis and design of information systems. The goal of the SDLC is to provide those organizations updating existing systems or designing new ones with a stronger, more structured process to follow. A report by the Standish Group (2004) provides evidence that, as the use of structured development techniques is increasingly practiced, system quality improves. At the same time, this report also found that fewer than 30% of systems projects are successful and more than 50% go live later than planned and are over budget. Given the wide variety of program needs in the HR department, such as recruiting, selection, training, performance management, and compensation, and the complexity of these needs, the importance of following a structured approach to the development of an HRIS cannot be overstated.

Although each phase in the life cycle is important, the goal of this chapter is to focus specifically on the activities associated with designing the HRIS. The design of the HRIS can occur in two phases: logical and physical design. The design phase is separated into two components because each has a different aim and perspective. The **logical design** of a system focuses on the translation of business requirements into improved business processes, irrespective of any technological implementation. For example, a business requirement for organizations such as Larson Property Management is the acquisition of new employees. HR business processes typically include (1) identifying jobs requiring new employees and approving those jobs; (2) analyzing the requirements of those jobs; (3) posting those positions and recruiting applicants from the labor market; (4) tracking applicants through the recruiting process, (5) selecting from the recruiting pool, through the use of selection tools such as interviews, applicants that best fit the job requirements; and (6) bringing new hires on board and placing them in their jobs. The HR programs associated with these processes are (1) HR planning, (2) job analysis, (3) recruiting, (4) applicant tracking, (5) selection, (6) placement, and (7) record keeping.

Conversely, the focus and goal of **physical design** is determining the most effective means of translating these business processes into a physical system that includes hardware and software. To merge the phases together can invite the temptation to focus heavily on the physical aspects of the new system (hardware and software) at the expense of improved business processes. In addition, focusing on the physical aspects of a system can lead to premature decisions and the selection of physical solutions that may not be the most effective ones for the business processes identified.

For example, a new and improved version of software may appear on the market. Imagine that this software is designed to automate and help manage compensation systems based on a combination of base pay administrative features along with merit modeling, reporting and analysis, and bonus pay plan tools. However, a company purchasing this software because of its elegance may have made a serious error if the company's top management is planning to drop the bonus program in two years as part of the company's new strategic plan. Another example would be the failure to acquire needed software features due to lack of attention on processes. Of course, adequate logical design enables effective physical design. Revisiting the example of Larson Property Management, we can imagine a design scenario related to staffing and the acquisition of new employees in which a thorough and careful analysis of the staffing process (logical design) would permit the company to determine that it needs a particular level of work-flow processing and Web enablement to track applicants and allow the posting of jobs online and online application to posted jobs (physical design).

Logical Design

As discussed in Chapter 4, once an organization has completed the analysis phase of the SDLC, which results in a comprehensive process analysis for the new HRIS, one of the key tasks facing the HR staff and development teams is to model the needs for the new system. There are two ways in which the system can be modeled: the physical model and the logical model. The physical model focuses on the computer technology for the HRIS, that is, on the hardware, software, networking plans, and technical manuals. The strength of this type of model is that it focuses on how the system will actually operate. In turn, this strength also becomes its weakness because, by focusing on the actual way the system will be implemented in terms of technology, analysts and HR staff may be constrained by the current, operational physical model. That is, HR staff members are familiar with the functioning of the current (i.e., legacy) HRIS they are using but, typically, not with the technological aspects of new systems or with the current technology available.

Therefore, system developers like to focus on the essence of the business processes independent of any technological implementation. To do this, logical models of the system are created. Logical models are HRIS models that could be operationalized in multiple ways in terms of the technology. For example, in the logical model, an organization might focus on receiving and processing applicant files. There are several physical ways in which an organization could implement this process. It could use a Web portal in an HRIS, a kiosk at a retail outlet, direct e-mail, or physical mail. The strength of using logical models is that the HR staff and developers can focus specifically on the business processes, policies, and procedures instead of on technology. Marakas (2006) refers to this as "separating the 'what' from the 'how'" (p. 116). By focusing on what the system does or needs to be able to do, the analyst and HR staff will be less likely to be distracted by or to focus on a single technology platform. In turn, they will be more likely to design a stronger solution.

Essentially, a **logical model** is similar to the blueprints for a home or an airplane. It provides the organization with an outline of the key business processes and goals for the system. Then, as the physical system is designed, these are translated into the hardware and software platforms that best fit the business's needs. For an HRIS, there are two types of models created for the system: those focused on the system processes and those focused on the data the system captures.

Two Ways to View an HRIS: Data Versus Process

For any HRIS, the organization must look at the total HR system from two different perspectives: the data perspective and the process perspective.

The **data perspective** focuses on an analysis of what data the organization captures and uses, and on the definitions and relationships of the data, while ignoring how or where the data are used by the organization. For example, a system whose aim is employee recruiting would need data about the applicants and their knowledge, skills, and abilities (e.g., name, address, degrees received, work experience). The data perspective would focus on the important data to be captured but would not be concerned with how the data are to be used within the organization. In addition, the data perspective focuses on the most efficient and effective way to capture the data to ensure accuracy.

The **process perspective**, conversely, focuses on the business processes and activities in which the organization engages and on how data flow through the HRIS. For example, a recruiting module from this perspective would consider business activities, such as receiving applications, sorting and scanning resumes to determine the interview pool, scheduling interviews, reporting candidate information for legal purposes, and so on, but not the data definitions and relationships. The designer would focus on the specific business processes, including the input of the data into the system, the flow of data through the system, and the storage of the data, but not on precisely what data are captured and how they are best organized or stored. Essentially, process modeling uses tools to describe the processes that are carried out by a system.

A key question that the reader might be asking is "Why should I care about these distinctions?" The reason the distinction between the process and data perspectives is important is that each represents a portion of the total HRIS but neither provides the complete picture. By modeling each separately, the organization is better able to understand and communicate its needs to the technical staff (e.g., the project management team responsible for designing and implementing the HRIS and any external consultants, vendors, or software developers). In addition, while processes may change in the future, data generally represent the most permanent and stable part of a system. For example, employee data from prior systems are often converted into the new HRIS data format and transferred into the new system. This data conversion and migration process is a critical step in the implementation phase, and it provides a bridge and continuity between the legacy system and the new HRIS. This permanency of data and the more dynamic aspect of processes suggest the importance of dealing with each separately.

Over the past three decades, a well-established procedure for modeling information systems has been developed. The procedure is based on a process perspective that uses data flow diagramming. A common aspect of all design methodologies is the use of diagrammatic modeling techniques. While the style of the charting symbols varies, the fundamentals are well established. Our focus in this chapter is on the creation and use of process models.

Logical Process Modeling With Data Flow Diagrams

A **process model** describes and represents the key business processes or activities conducted by the organization, such as applicant tracking. The specific type of process model typically used by organizations is a **data flow diagram (DFD)**. A DFD is a graphical representation of the key business activities and processes in the HR system, the boundaries of this system, the data that flow through the system, and any external individuals or departments that interact with the system.

The focus of a DFD is on the movement of data between external entities (such as a job applicant) and processes (the applicant-tracking process) and between processes and data stores. Kendall and Kendall (2008) argue that DFDs have four distinct advantages over narrative (e.g., written) descriptions:

1. There is freedom from committing to the technical implementation of the system too early.

2. They provide a deeper understanding of the interrelatedness of systems and subsystems.

3. They allow for stronger communication of system knowledge to the employees, since the diagrams are in pictorial form.

4. They ensure a deeper analysis of the proposed system to determine if all business processes have been identified.

A DFD consists of four symbols (see Figure 5.1). These include the entity, the data flow, the process, and the data store. The **entity** represents any external agent (e.g., an individual, department, business, system) that either receives or supplies data to the HR system. For example, in an **applicant-tracking system (ATS)**, a manager could request that a job opening be posted, or an applicant could submit her resume online. In this scenario both the manager and applicant are entities. Other examples of an entity are a manager inputting merit pay raise information on an employee into the payroll system or the production/ manufacturing system inputting piece-rate production data about the number of products produced by an employee into the payroll system. Similarly, the time-and-labor module, which provides time-card information on employees and their start and end times on workdays, represents an entity for payroll systems. Because entities represent a specific person, place, system, or department, they are labeled with a noun in the DFD.

The **data flow** represents the movement of a single piece of data from point to point through the system (e.g., from process to process, entity to process, or process to data store). As a data flow represents data about a person, place, or thing, it should also be labeled with a noun. The label of a data flow should describe exactly what data are contained in the flow. For example, a data flow labeled "Time Sheet" would represent an

Figure 5.1   Symbols of the DFD

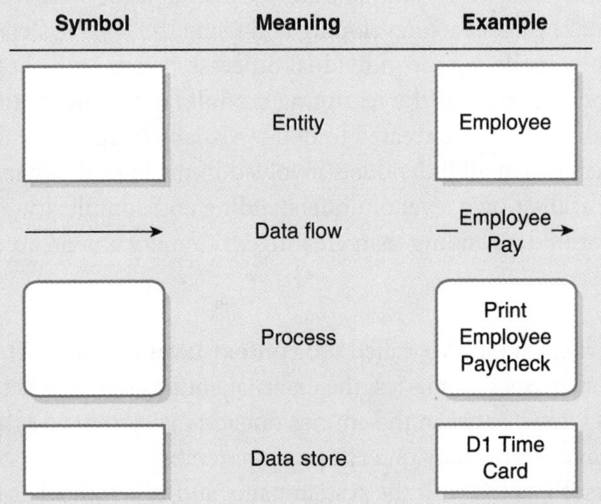

Symbol	Meaning	Example
☐	Entity	Employee
→	Data flow	Employee Pay →
☐	Process	Print Employee Paycheck
☐	Data store	D1 Time Card

employee's time sheet, and the exact data contained in the flow would be precisely defined as part of the diagramming process. Because DFDs describe the key business processes and the flow of data between them, *an important rule to remember is that all data flows must begin or end at a process.*

The third component of a DFD is the **process**. A process represents a business activity. The goal of each process is to change or transform inputted data into a useful output (e.g., creating an applicant record, updating an employee record, creating a recruiting yield ratio report, reporting Equal Employment Opportunity Commission data on applicants). Since data are transformed as part of these processes, they should be labeled with action verbs, for example, *calculate, send, print,* or *verify.*

The final symbol represents the **data store**, in other words, the data at rest in the system or a repository of data. This repository could be a filing cabinet, a file on a desk, a computer file, or a database table. A data store contains data about a person, place, or department and should be labeled with a noun. Examples of data stores include employee files, applicant files, employee records, and customer or current benefits records. Data stores are typically identified with a "D*n*," where D identifies that what is labeled is a data store and *n* is a number reflecting the data store's unique identifier (D1, D2, etc.). The symbols and their use are illustrated in Figure 5.1.

Creating and Using the DFD

Most DFDs for integrated business systems are very complex, consisting of hundreds to thousands of processes, data flows, and data stores. If all of these were included on a single diagram, it would make the task of developing and using the DFD too complex. Therefore, DFDs are organized by modeling the individual processes (such as the applicant-tracking process) and components (such as the recruiting module) of an information system. Furthermore, a series of DFDs are created to depict visually increasingly detailed views. The value of this approach is that all individuals involved in the logical design of the system can view the model at their own level of understanding and complexity. Viewing the model provides much better understanding than creating written documents to describe the model and all the processes.

The highest-level DFD developed is called the **context-level diagram**. This diagram describes the full system, its boundaries, the external entities that interact with the system, and the primary data flows between the entities outside the system and the system itself. The context level diagram contains only one HR process, representing the system, data flows, and entities. This process is labeled with the system name and is identified as the context-level diagram. A sample context-level diagram for an ATS is shown in Figure 5.2.

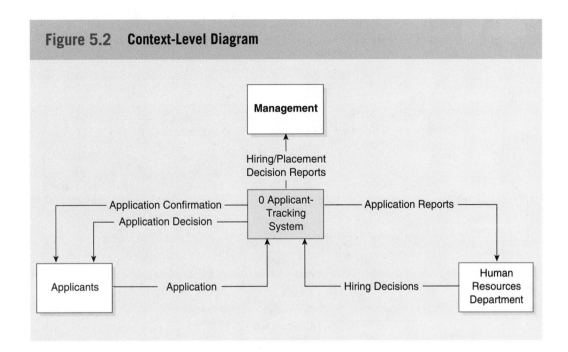

Figure 5.2   Context-Level Diagram

The single HR process in the context-level diagram is then broken into greater detail on the **level 0 diagram** to provide a clearer picture of the HR business process. The level 0 diagram contains the major system processes and the data that flow between them. Each process should be labeled with a verb that reflects the action that the process conducts. In addition, each process is numbered consecutively starting with 1.0 (1.0, 2.0, 3.0, 4.0, etc.). It is important to note at this point that the context-level diagram and the level 0 diagrams should reflect and communicate the same information (see Figure 5.3).

This concept is called the **balancing** of DFDs. Notice that, although the level 0 diagram shown in Figure 5.3 has more detail than the context-level diagram, it contains the same inflows and outflows from management, applicants, and human resources. For example, on both levels, the three flows, "Application," "Application Confirmation," and "Application Decision," flow between the Applicant entity and the system in the same way. Balancing DFDs is important because we want to ensure that all individuals are viewing and using the same model of the system. Otherwise, there is the risk that the system will not be designed appropriately.

In the same manner that the context level can be decomposed into a level 0 diagram, the level 0 diagram can be decomposed into *additional-level diagrams*. As with the context-level diagram, the level 0 diagram in Figure 5.3 also hides specific details about all the processing tasks within the HR system. Thus, the next-level diagram (the level 1 diagram) would break

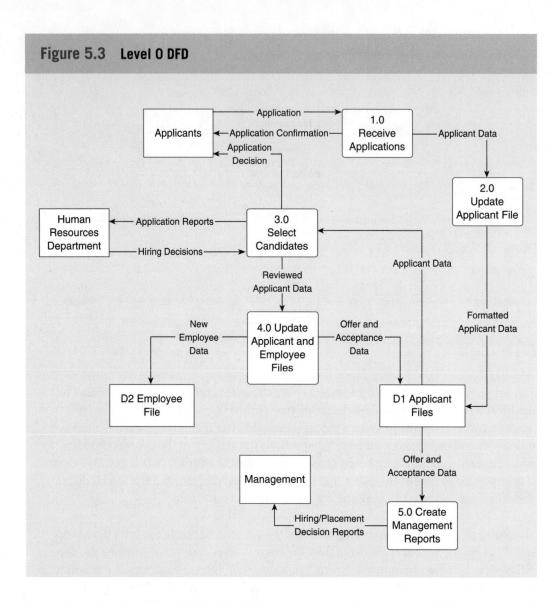

Figure 5.3   Level 0 DFD

down the processes within the level 0 diagram to better portray and help staff to understand the HR processes in the system. This level of detail will, in turn, improve the accuracy of the logical design of the system. The same process of decomposition could occur at successive levels (level 2, level 3, etc.); however, this diagramming becomes a very complex task and is beyond the scope of this book.[1] The DFD is considered complete when it includes all the components necessary for the system being modeled.

The DFD can also be used as a tool for analyzing the current system versus the desired system. In addition, DFDs are often used for business process reengineering, in an effort to improve the system. For example, through the DFD, the analysts designing the ATS for Larson Property Management might discover that data (e.g., rating scores) from a lower-level manager's interview of job candidates currently flow back to the HR department for approval prior to allowing the applicant file to proceed to the next-level manager. Through this analysis, they could find that this step is unnecessary in the new HRIS because the system would use a decision rule, based on the minimum score needed to proceed, to forward the applicant data to the next manager automatically upon an applicant receiving a passing score.

Physical Design

As was discussed in earlier chapters of this book, the acquisition of a system is the culmination of a series of important steps. By this point, the organization should have a strong understanding of its current operations, a set of requirements for the new system, and a new logical model for how it wishes the system to operate. Once the new system has been designed and logical models of the new system have been tested against the business requirements, the organization will move to the **physical design** phase. The major goal of this phase of the SDLC is to translate the logical model and requirements into a physical system, including all hardware, software, and networking.

Major activities in this phase include (1) determining whether or not there is value in continuing the system design and actual implementation processes, (2) determining hardware and software options and requirements, (3) determining where to obtain the hardware and software (e.g., by in-house development or commercial software purchase), (4) developing an implementation schedule, and (5) working with potential vendors to assess and select software if system software is to be obtained externally. For most organizations, these activities will typically mean that the HR staff specialists (e.g., the recruiting manager) will work closely with HRIS specialists and the internal **information technology (IT)** staff, as well as with software vendors and any external consultants brought in to help with the physical design of the system. The extent of involvement of these various stakeholders depends on the size, scope, and type of HRIS developed.

During the physical design phase, the HRIS and IT staff will focus heavily on how any new software and hardware will fit within the current **IT architecture**. In addition, IT and HRIS staff will provide technical recommendations on the relative value and cost of building the system internally or purchasing an off-the-shelf package from a commercial vendor. The HR staff will also work with the external vendors to ensure that the focus of the system is on the business requirements and not the technology itself. It is also important at this point to remind the HR staff to be very careful of scope creep (which was discussed in detail in Chapter 4).

Three Choices in Physical Design

The first step in this design phase is to determine how to proceed with physical design. First, the organization has the option of doing nothing. Although this may seem to be counterintuitive because much time and money typically have been spent on the analysis and design process to date, there may be important organizational or environmental reasons for not proceeding. For example, on completion of a thorough analysis and logical redesign of the HR processes, a small organization in the southern United States was faced with a public lawsuit, and it was forced to delay the final design and implementation of the project until this was settled. In other instances, companies have postponed proceeding after learning that a target software vendor was in the process of a major revision of the software product.

The second option is to *make changes to only the HR business processes without implementing new or upgraded technology.* Before any time or money is spent on new technology, it is important that the organization address all proposed business process changes and determine if these processes can be handled using the current HRIS technology. In the book *Good to Great,* Collins (2001) suggests that one important difference between good companies and great companies is that good companies view technology as a solution, whereas great companies see technology as a tool to be used to support great business processes. Furthermore, Brynjolfsson and Hitt (1998) found that organizations were much more likely to increase productivity and performance when they coupled any technology changes with business process changes.

At this point in the process, it can be easy to forget that the goal for the development of the new system should be to use technology to support HR practices, making them more efficient and adding value to the organization; an organization should not get so caught up in the promise of a new technology with industry "best practices" that it ignores actual needs. In HR or IT, although using best practices is desirable, if these practices are not compatible with the specific needs of your organization as identified in the needs analysis, any business process and technical changes are likely to be less effective.

The final option that an organization can choose is to *implement the business process changes along with new or upgraded technology.* There are three basic ways that this can be done: build it, buy it, or outsource the development. Organizations that choose the first approach—to build the technology internally—will take responsibility for the development of the software and hardware. The advantage of this approach is that the organization will control all aspects of the development, including the look and feel and functionality. Using this approach, the organization will be able to write software to meet 100% of the business's requirements. Finally, internally building the software can also provide increased flexibility and creative solutions for the issues within the HR business processes.

There are several shortcomings in building the HR system internally from scratch. First, it can be much more expensive to implement than an off-the-shelf solution. In addition, since it is a unique application, the amount of software testing and the developmental risk are much higher with this approach than for an off-the-shelf system. Further, for this approach to work, the organization must already have or readily be able to obtain the technical, functional, and project management skills necessary to build the system effectively. For most organizations, obtaining what is needed to build the system is a daunting task because software development is generally not part of their **core competency**, and they likely do not have the staff and resources available to complete such an undertaking. Finally, since an HRIS is typically one of at least several core modules that are part of the overall **enterprise resource planning (ERP)** system, building the module in-house often leads to issues and challenges associated with integrating the HRIS with the other core modules, including the data warehouse component used to integrate data as a basis for business intelligence features.

For most organizations, the second approach of buying prepackaged, **commercial off-the-shelf (COTS) software** fits many needs. These systems can range from small, single-function applications costing a few thousand dollars to large-scale, ERP software packages costing millions of dollars. The advantage of using this approach to acquiring software is that the systems are well tested and proven and can be purchased and implemented in a short period. For this reason, most of the HR software adopted and used today is COTS. The good news for organizations considering the adoption of a COTS solution is that most business operations are fairly generic, so there are applications available that should meet the majority of the needs of most organizations. The bad news is that even the best system will rarely meet all the specific needs of the organization, with most meeting about 70% of the organization's needs. Thus, organizations choosing to purchase a COTS solution should be prepared either to work with the vendor to customize the system to meet their unique needs or to change their processes to fit with the software (and thereby opt for what is referred to as the "vanilla" approach). As mentioned briefly before, the risk of adapting your business processes to the software is that the business processes supported by the software may be incompatible with the way your organization operates, which can result in increased costs or reduced competitive advantage. In addition, when an organization implements a vendor's upgrade in the future, it will likely be necessary to redo whatever customization was done during the initial implementation.

ALLIANCE PROGRAMS

To assist organizations that wish to implement a customized solution, most of the major HRIS software vendors (e.g., Oracle, SAP, Infor) supplement their mainline enterprise solutions by investing in alliances with other independent software vendors (ISVs).

(Continued)

The primary goal of these **alliance programs** is to provide a total solution to make both vendors' products more attractive and effective for their customer base. A secondary goal for the HRIS vendors is to create an "ecosystem" of solutions that can compete more effectively with other HRIS applications. The larger the ecosystem or number of partners in a program, the bigger the footprint the HRIS application will have. A side effect is that the HRIS provider appears to be more "open" from a technical perspective. In fact, Oracle and SAP are actively selling their technical integration capabilities (middleware) alongside their HR applications.

The final approach to developing the software is to outsource the development to an external company or to obtain access to existing software through an **application service provider (ASP)**. The greatest advantage of outsourcing is that an external software development can bring vast resources, experiences, and technical skills to design a much more effective solution than would otherwise be possible. However, outsourcing the development can be risky. For example, by outsourcing, the firm may expose confidential internal information and business processes to an external organization. Second, outsourcing may not lead to reduced time and expense for the organization because many of the tasks that would need to be completed if the software were developed in-house would still need to be completed *with* the external software developer.

As can be seen from the previous discussion, there are advantages and disadvantages to each approach for software development. Thus, the decision as to which approach to use will be based on multiple factors and may differ from organization to organization and project to project. In addition, an organization need not rely on a single approach. For most organizations, the solution chosen is often a combination of in-house and external development. The decision regarding which approach to choose is based on a series of factors, including the nature of the business process; the size, technical skills, and project management skills of the software staff; and the development time frame. Table 5.1 contains a matrix of how these different factors may influence the approach chosen.

If the decision is made to purchase and customize COTS or to outsource development, the organization will need to work closely with external software vendors. Thus, vendor selection becomes a very important decision.

Working With Vendors

Although building a new HRIS from scratch with internal resources may be a viable option for some organizations, by far the most common decision that the HR department will make

Table 5.1   Software Acquisition Strategies

| | Development Strategy | | |
	In-House	COTS	Outsource
Business need	Unique	Standard	Noncore function
In-house skills	Functional and technical expertise exists	Functional expertise exists	Functional and technical expertise not in-house
Project management skills	Project has skilled and experienced project manager	Project has a manager with experience to coordinate and manage vendor relationship	Project has manager with experience to manage an outsourcing relationship
Time frame	Flexible	Short	Flexible or short

Source: Adapted from Dennis, Wixom, and Roth (2006).

is to work with an external vendor to develop or acquire the system. To do this, the HR staff will need to work closely with both the internal IT department and external vendors to ensure that the business process requirements and all technical requirements are presented to the vendor. The first step in this process is to develop a **request for proposal (RFP)**.

An RFP is a document that solicits proposals and bids for proposed work from potential consultants or vendors. An RFP defines the organization's goals and requirements for the new information system. It provides the details that define hardware, software, and services requirements. For the organization, it provides a structured approach that minimizes the chance of omitting important criteria. On return from vendors or consultants, it simplifies the vendor comparison process by providing a format to elicit consistent and complete responses.

The RFP provides an opportunity for the HR department to record systematically what its staff will need the system to do. As part of this process, any remaining implicit assumptions should be made explicit. Basically, the RFP will define what is needed and what is not needed in the system. In addition, the RFP begins the communication process and relationship building with vendors.

Although there are many different factors that will determine precisely what should be included in the RFP, experts in the field have argued for the inclusion of a key set of components. Table 5.2 presents an example of these key factors, adapted from recommendations made by the Society for Human Resource Management and the work of Hinojos and Miller (1998).

Table 5.2 is an excellent starting point for developing an RFP, but it should not be taken to include all items that may be required. Those developing an RFP for an organization should keep in mind their unique situation and add or subtract what is included as appropriate for their needs. The information in this table is also very general in nature, and how it is developed will be different for each organization.

When developing the RFP, organizations should keep several things in mind. The first recommendation is to *focus on the business requirements*. Given that the system is being considered in association with business process changes, an excellent place to begin the development for the vendor is to review the requirements and logical redesign of the business processes. These should then be communicated to each vendor.

Associated with this requirement, the second recommendation is to *be specific*. After all the effort given to the needs analysis and the redesign of business processes, very specific requirements will be available and should be included in the RFP. It is important to be specific as to your organization's needs because, if you are not specific, you risk allowing the vendors to determine what is included in the final system. Although it is desirable to work with a vendor to develop the final system, it is important that the system be developed to meet your specific business needs, not just designed to match the system a vendor has available. Furthermore, an RFP that is too general may not be screened in sufficient detail by the vendor, leading to a product that has too much detail and is too complex and too expensive for the business's needs. The overall objective of the RFP is to have the vendors propose system hardware and software to meet the specific requirements you have identified for your new system.

The third recommendation is to *keep it simple*. One of the temptations in developing an RFP is to include all possible business and technical requirements in it. The problem with including many technical details in the plan is that vendors may review the RFP and screen themselves out because they think they cannot fill the needs outlined in the RFP. For example, it would be important to ask whether a benefits system allows for benefits reports, benefits administration, and so on. Conversely, the RFP would want to stay away from

Table 5.2 Recommended Components of a Request for Proposal

- Data about you
  - Who you are as a business
    - Company name, size, scope, industry, annual sales, locations, etc.
  - Business requirements
    - Required business processes, functionality, and project scope
  - Technical requirements
    - Does it need to work with a particular operating system, existing organization systems, etc.?
  - Delivery time frame needed
    - Is there a desired target implementation date?
- Requested data from vendor
  - Vendor details
    - Company name, size, scope, annual sales, experience, etc.
    - Number of implemented applications
  - System pricing
    - May include license fees, maintenance charges, training costs, implementation costs, and support costs
  - System details
    - Functionality included in the system
  - If customization is necessary, how will this be addressed (timing, delivery, cost, support, etc.)?
    - Supported technology now and in the near future
    - Customer support options
    - Training options
  - Customer references
    - Find out user and organizational experiences with the system.
    - Ask these references for other companies they know using the system to broaden your knowledge (after all, the vendor is likely to provide you with clients who have had positive experiences).
  - Sample contract terms

including requirements as to length of fields, types of passwords used, and so on, which do not focus on business needs but instead are focused on technical and physical design issues. Essentially, if something is not important to the HR department and reflective of the business processes modeled in the DFDs, it is best not to include it.

This point leads to the fourth recommendation, which is to *work closely with the HRIS and IT staff* as the RFP is developed. The professional staff will be responsible for working with the vendor to ensure the smooth installation and maintenance of the HRIS. Therefore, it is important for the HR staff to work closely with the information systems professional staff to make sure that any essential technical considerations are included. For example, if there are existing systems that need to provide information to or receive information from the system, then this should be included. In addition, if there is a certain platform (e.g., UNIX, Windows) that the organization has experience with and with which it would like the system to integrate, this too should be included.

Vendor Selection

After the RFPs are sent, the vendors will then evaluate them to determine if they have a product that would fit the company's needs. If the HR and IT staff have put together a strong RFP, then they should get a set of vendors who have a better understanding of the company's specific needs and who can provide a better-tailored response and proposal for the HRIS. After receiving the vendor responses, you will have the opportunity to evaluate the relative strengths and weaknesses of each vendor. To do this, you should consider several things and assess software options according to a number of criteria. These are described below.

Functionality

As you assess the different vendor responses, it is important to evaluate how fully the functionality of the HRIS meets the HR needs. For example, a software product that meets 70% of the organization's needs will be less desirable than one that meets 98% of its requirements. On the other hand, software that meets 98% of the organization's needs but has no additional functionality may not provide the organization with the opportunity to grow and expand its options in the future, so it may be less attractive than a product that meets 90% of your HR needs but allows for growth over time. It is important that the HRIS implemented today is able to change as the organization grows. Otherwise, within a few years, the organization will have to go through the entire systems development process and purchase or develop an entirely new solution. Finally, an HRIS that will meet your organization's needs with minimal customization for actual use would be more attractive than one requiring significant customization.

IT Architecture and IT Integration

The next issue focuses on the IT architecture for the HRIS. The organization will need to know whether the HRIS will be a stand-alone system or a networked system or a Web-based one, and so on. In addition, the organization will want to know with what technology or platform the HRIS has been developed (e.g., UNIX, Linux, Windows). Finally, as important as knowing the answers to these questions is understanding the extent to which the HRIS will integrate within the broader corporate IT architecture. An HRIS that can more readily interact and communicate with operations, manufacturing, and sales can provide a much stronger return for the company than one that stands as an isolated entity. The easier the integration with the broader IT architecture, the easier it will be to implement and use the system. In today's environment of employee self-service and Web portals, the ability to provide remote access to employees can also be a plus as different systems are considered. Finally, if functional HR systems are being considered from multiple vendors, the extent to which they can be integrated and communicate with each other also becomes important.

Price

Although price will ultimately play a very large role in the selection of an HRIS, price should be secondary to the goal of finding a system that meets your process needs. At the same time, price will ultimately determine which system is selected. The ultimate cost of the system will include the visible costs, such as the cost of hardware and software, as well as the less visible costs, such as customization costs, employee training costs, licensing fees (e.g., site licenses, per seat licenses), upgrade costs, and the cost of system operation and maintenance over time. HRIS costs and cost-benefit analyses are covered in more detail in Chapter 7.

Vendor Longevity and Viability

As with any purchase decision, it is important to evaluate the quality of the vendor itself. The good news is that many vendors have been in business for 10 to 20 years, so vendor longevity is usually not an issue. In today's environment, the viability of vendors can often be assessed through their responsiveness to existing clients and their history of providing timely upgrades and increasingly flexible systems. Furthermore, the HRIS vendor marketplace has been undergoing some consolidation as companies seek to better position themselves to provide value-added services across the HR functional spectrum, so the vendor you sign with today may end up merging with another company. A listing of several sample vendors can be found in Table 5.3. In addition, IHRIM provides an online buyers guide for those interested in adopting HR software. (http://www.ihrimpublications.com/Buyers_Guide/BG.php)

Table 5.3 Sample Vendors

Vendor Name	Website	Twitter	Focus
Infor	www.infor.com	@Infor	ERP
Oracle	www.oracle.com	@OracleHCM	ERP
SAP	www.sap.com	@SAPHCM	ERP
Ceridian	www.ceridian.com	@ceridian_US	Core HRIS
SuccessFactors	www.SuccessFactors.com	@successfactors	Core HRIS
Workday	www.workday.com	@Workday	Core HRIS
Peoplefluent	www.peoplefluent.com	@Peoplefluent	Core HRIS
OrangeHRM	www.orangeHRM.com	@orangeHRM	Open Source CORE HRIS
Myco Portal	www.mycoportal.com	@MycoPortal	Small Business

Assessing System Feasibility

At this point in the design process, it is very important that you stop and consider whether or not the system will work for you. Although the system may meet all the requirements as defined in the requirements document, it still may not be feasible to implement for several reasons. Therefore, it is important to conduct a thorough feasibility assessment of the project. A feasibility assessment should go beyond the traditional economic metrics and should include multiple dimensions, such as technical, operational, human factors, legal, political, and economic.

Technical Feasibility

Technical feasibility focuses on the current technological capabilities of the organization and the technological capabilities required for the implementation of the proposed system. As part of any assessment of technical feasibility, the HR staff must work closely with systems analysts and technical staff to determine whether or not the current technology can be upgraded to meet the needs of the organization or whether an entirely new technological architecture will be needed to implement the proposed system changes.

Typical questions an organization might ask as part of a technical feasibility assessment are as follows:

1. Do the hardware and software exist to implement this system? Are they practical to obtain?

2. Do we add on or patch the current software or start from scratch?

3. Does our organization have the ability to construct this system?

4. Can we integrate the new system with our current systems?

Operational Feasibility

Operational feasibility focuses on how well the proposed system fits in with the current and future organizational environment. For example, a system, despite meeting technical feasibility criteria, may make such a drastic change in how the organization operates that it may not have a strong chance of being successfully implemented. For example, a series of research studies in information systems has found that the more compatible a system is with an employee's current ways of working, the more likely the employee will be to use the system (Agarwal, 2000). Therefore, when a new system is highly incompatible with current practices, HR staff or designers might seek to change or decrease the scope of the project to reduce these incompatibilities.

In addition, operational feasibility assesses the extent to which the project fits within the overall strategic plans of the HR and IT departments as well as within the organization's overall strategy. Other areas addressed as part of the assessment of operational feasibility include the likelihood of meeting the proposed implementation schedule and delivery date. The HR staff and developers must work together to ensure that the schedule will meet any critical operational deadlines, that resources are sufficient to meet the schedule, and that the schedule takes into account key organization dates (e.g., annual budgeting). The techniques used in project management are very important and will be discussed in detail in Chapter 8.

A second area of operational feasibility focuses on human factors. An assessment of the human factors feasibility focuses on how the employee uses and works with the system, on the system's usability, and on the training the employee receives. The usability of the system reflects the effectiveness and efficiency of the system to the employee and is often characterized by the usefulness of the system to the employee and the ease with which he or she can use the system. It can reflect how intuitive the interface is to navigate, the effort an employee must put into learning to use the system, and how effective the system is in supporting the employee's work.

Do not underestimate the importance of human factors in determining the operational feasibility and ultimate success of a system. Over the past 20 years, hundreds of studies have found that the usefulness and ease of use of a system play a large role in system use and adoption.[2] In addition, recent research has found that usefulness estimations can be accurately assessed by employees early in the development process but that perceptions of ease of use may evolve as employees gain direct experience with the software (Davis & Venkatesh, 2004). These human factor considerations will be covered in Chapter 9 in more detail, along with suggestions as to how to solve the acceptability issue.

Typical questions asked as part of the assessment of operational feasibility would include the following:

1. How well does the system fit within our organizational context? Will this make us better?

2. How much will our organization change because of the new business and technical changes?

3. How long will this take to do, and does the schedule fit our business's needs?

4. If we have to squeeze, what might we be able to eliminate?

5. Do we have or can we get the personnel to do this?

6. Can people use the system?

7. What kind of training do we need?

Legal and Political Feasibility

Legal and political issues also play a very important role in assessing the feasibility of an HRIS. The best-designed and -implemented system can end up causing major headaches for the organization if it violates existing laws and regulations. This point is even truer for an HRIS than for many other types of information systems because existing laws and regulations play a larger role in HR than in other core business functions (as will be discussed in Chapter 10). For example, if the HRIS fails to maintain specific employee performance records correctly, legal challenges of wrongful discharges will be more difficult for the company to defend against.

Political feasibility focuses on the political environment of the organization in which the HRIS is being implemented. Issues such as power redistribution involving loss of individual or department control can have major political implications that can affect the effectiveness of the implementation. What is interesting is that political issues can undermine the implementation of a new HRIS more quickly and completely than any technical shortcomings. The challenge here is that, while political feasibility may be fairly easy to identify, it can be challenging to effectively address. Individuals who are negatively affected by the implementation of the system (or who perceive themselves to be negatively affected) are likely to undermine, resist, or disrupt its implementation, either overtly or covertly. Thus, it is important to understand and anticipate the political consequences of a system implementation at this point, before implementation is started. Again, these issues are discussed more fully in Chapter 9.

Typical questions asked as part of a **legal and political feasibility** analysis include the following:

1. Does the implementation of this system infringe on existing copyrights?

2. Are we violating any antitrust issues by implementing the system?

3. Do we have contracts with other companies that don't allow use of the new software?

4. Does the system violate any governmental policies?

5. Does the system violate any foreign laws? (This question would be significant for global companies who have operations in multiple countries where different laws require different practices supporting the capture and use of HR data, for example.)

6. Who is likely to resist the implementation of the system?

7. Who may "win" or "lose" as a result of this implementation?

8. What is the risk of system sabotage?

Economic Feasibility

The final aspect of a feasibility assessment is evaluating **economic feasibility**. The goal of an economic feasibility analysis is to determine whether the costs of developing, implementing, and running the system are worth the benefits derived from its use. To do this, an analyst would identify the appropriate costs and benefits of the HRIS and assign precise values to each. Then, these costs and benefits should be subjected to a thorough cost-benefit analysis. As mentioned earlier, Chapter 7 provides comprehensive coverage of how to assess the costs and benefits of an HRIS.

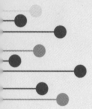

SUMMARY

The goal of this chapter was to discuss the factors that contribute to a more effective system design strategy. First, we discussed how the HR staff and consultants translate the requirements from previous phases of the SDLC into improved logical business processes. We then discussed how these new processes are modeled through logical modeling tools such as the DFD. DFDs are important because they allow the HR staff, consultants, and programmers to have a common model of the system from which to work and because they can be used to identify potential shortcomings not yet identified in the new system. In addition, because DFDs are hierarchical in approach, they allow for the system to be viewed at multiple levels of specificity. This makes them a useful tool for communicating with all relevant actors in the systems development process while also being technical enough to allow developers to best determine how to translate business requirements into the new HRIS. Given that the cost of making changes becomes significantly more expensive once the physical design of the system has been undertaken, it is important that these models be as effective and accurate as possible to avoid system rework.

Third, we discussed the options available for the firm when developing the final physical design for the new system. One option available to firms is not to change their existing practices. Other options include building the software internally or sourcing the software through external vendors. The chapter also briefly outlined the steps of working with a vendor, from the RFP through the selection of the vendor, and it provided several suggestions for getting the most out of the RFP and the vendor selection process. Finally, whatever approach is chosen for the final design, any selected physical system must be assessed as to its feasibility. Although budgeting committees will pay especially close attention to the profitability of the system, we also explained the importance of considering different types of system feasibility. Although this phase of the SDLC can be complex and challenging to manage, we believe that following a structured and disciplined approach such as the one outlined will result in the development or acquisition of a system that is a stronger fit for the organization.

KEY TERMS

DISCUSSION QUESTIONS

1. What is the difference between the data view of a system and the process view of a system? Why is this distinction important when designing a new system?

2. Discuss four reasons that a DFD is a stronger tool than a written narrative of the business processes.

3. How do companies use an RFP when sourcing software? What are the key items that should be included in the RFP?

4. If you were advising a firm on developing an RFP, what would be some key suggestions you would make for improving the effectiveness of the RFP?

5. When evaluating vendor offerings, what are the key factors that will help your firm determine the best software product to acquire?

6. Even if a system pays for itself financially, an organization must conduct a thorough feasibility study. What types of feasibility should be assessed, and what information does each type of feasibility assessment provide the organization?

CASE STUDY[3]

Larson Property Management Company is one of the largest property management companies in California, with more than 1,000 employees. The company provides a full array of commercial management and development services. These activities include complete management services for commercial office and retail buildings and apartment complexes; construction, repair, and maintenance of commercial properties; and financial management and billing services for commercial real estate clients. The company has experienced significant expansion over the past five years in response to the growth in apartment and commercial construction in southern California, and this expansion has resulted in the need to hire a large number of employees on an ongoing basis to staff its operations.

Larson Property Management has depended on a legacy HRIS to manage its applicant and employee databases. The system runs on a client-server computer system. The system was implemented approximately 10 years ago, prior to the company's rapid growth and when it employed fewer than 100 employees. The system's functionality is limited to the storage and retrieval of employee and applicant data. For recruiting purposes, the system requires a clerk to manually enter basic applicant data, the results of the application test, and whether or not an offer of employment has been made. Prior to this, applicants' files were passed around to those who reviewed the materials and were sometimes misplaced, so trying to locate a particular applicant's file was often a problem. The current HRIS has limited file storage capability for applicant and employee records and currently has reached its storage capacity.

Larson Property Management has decided to replace its legacy HRIS. One application module in the new HRIS that the company wants is a sophisticated applicant-tracking system (ATS). The primary objective of the ATS will be to provide a paperless hiring process. The basic functions of the new system will be managing the requisition and approval of job openings, storing resumes and job applications and retrieving through query functions the names of applicants who match job requirements, tracking a candidate's progress through the recruiting and selection process, and providing automated reporting functions. The company's managers also want an e-HR functionality that includes the Internet posting of job openings through the company's website and external job-posting services, application and resume submission through the Web and through kiosks at various office locations, staff ability to access and use the system remotely through a Web browser, and online resume- and application-scanning capabilities.

Part of the design phase is modeling the processes that will be used in the system for applicant tracking. For Larson Property Management, this modeling will allow the system analysts to design an efficient paperless hiring process.

Larson Property management is well aware that the design stage of the SDLC is critical for the successful implementation of the new ATS. However, there is considerable confusion about how to proceed with this phase. The HR and IT professionals assigned to the ATS committee have been meeting to plan the new system. From their planning and needs analysis, it is clear that a new HRIS application is needed, can save considerable time, and can result in more accurate storage and retrieval of applicant data for cost-benefit and other management reports.

The company has had several vendors provide presentations, with each vendor outlining its particular approach to the design of an ATS. But these presentations were primarily focused on the physical design of the new ATS. The HR and IT committees must now begin the design process, which must be completed in three months.

Case Study Questions

1. Based on the material in this chapter, design a three-month operational plan for the ATS.

   a. In your plan, make certain you differentiate between the logical and physical design of the ATS. Which one should be done first? Which one is more important?

   b. Describe the importance of the data view versus the process view for the design of the new ATS.

   c. Who are the important stakeholders to be considered in the design of the ATS?

   d. How will you determine whether these stakeholders need the information that the new ATS will deliver?

   e. Based on your personal knowledge of recruiting by companies, develop a DFD with at least two levels.

2. Based on the work you have completed for Question 1, provide a brief outline of the RFP that is to be sent to the HRIS vendors.

STUDENT STUDY SITE

Visit the Student Study Site at **http://www.sagepub.com/kavanagh3e** for additional learning tools such as access to SAGE journal articles and related web resources.

NOTES

1. The interested reader seeking more information on developing DFDs, including the rules for their completion as well as the decomposition process, can check out the following resources: *The Structured Analysis Wiki,* written by Ed Yourdon (http://yourdon.com/strucanalysis/wiki/index.php?title=Introduction), or any of the systems analysis and design textbooks listed in the reference sections of this book.

2. Interested readers are encouraged to read Ma and Liu (2004) for a thorough review of this research.

3. Note that this is the case from the vignette, plus added material.

REFERENCES

Agarwal, R. (2000). Individual acceptance of information technologies. In R. W. Zmud (Ed.), *Framing the domains of IT management* (pp. 85–104). Cincinnati, OH: Pinnaflex Educational Resources.

Brynjolfsson, E., & Hitt, L. M. (1998). Beyond the productivity paradox. *Communications of the ACM, 41*(8), 49–55.

Collins, J. (2001). *Good to great: Why some companies make the leap . . . and others don't.* New York: HarperCollins.

Davis, F. D., & Venkatesh, V. (2004). Toward preprototype user acceptance testing of new information systems: Implications for software project management. *IEEE Transactions on Engineering Management, 51*(1), 31–46.

Dennis, A. R., Wixom, B. H., & Roth, R. M. (2006). *Systems analysis and design* (3rd ed.). Hoboken, NJ: John Wiley & Sons.

Hinojos, J. A., & Miller, M. (1998, July/August). Methodologies for selecting the right vendor. *Benefits & Compensation Solutions,* 38–42.

Kendall, K. E., & Kendall, J. E. (2008). *Systems analysis and design* (7th ed.). Upper Saddle River, NJ: Pearson.

Ma, Q., & Liu, L. (2004). The technology acceptance model: A meta-analysis of empirical findings. *Journal of End User Computing, 16*(1), 59–72.

Marakas, G. M. (2006). *Systems analysis and design: An active approach* (2nd ed.). New York: McGraw-Hill.

Patton, G. S. (1995). *War as I knew it.* Boston: Houghton Mifflin. (Original work published 1947)

Standish Group. (2004). *The chaos report.* Boston: Author.

Project Management and Human Resource Management Advice for Human Resource Information Systems Implementation

Michael J. Kavanagh

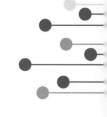

EDITORS' NOTE

This chapter focuses on the implementation and maintenance of the HRIS, the final two stages of the systems development life cycle (SDLC). Although these topics have been discussed in Chapters 3, 4, and 5, the use of the **project management (PM)** *tools and processes covered in this chapter will ensure that the implementation of the HRIS will be more orderly and completed on time. Chapter 9 will extend the information technology (IT) approaches outlined in this chapter's discussion of PM and examine critical issues involved in the implementation, acceptance, and maintenance of an HRIS from a behavioral view. Project management involves a planned set of procedures to accomplish a specific (and usually) one-time effort—for example, changing a maternity leave policy or implementing a new HRIS. PM includes the following components: (1) develop a project plan, (2) determine project goals and objectives, (3) define tasks to achieve goals, (4) identify the resources (people and money) needed, and (5) estimate a budget and timeline for completion. The use of PM in the development of an HRIS project involves combining knowledge from both HRM and IT to ensure successful implementation. The foremost organization for professionals in PM is the Project Management Institute (PMI). PMI provides training for certification as a Certified Associate in PM (CAPM) and a Project Management Professional (PMP). On the one hand, IT provides us with PM technical approaches, techniques, and tools, while HRM provides behavioral knowledge, team management, leadership advice, and change management techniques. Following formal PM procedures and recommendations is important for the successful development and implementation of the HRIS. More important, the use of PM techniques and tools should begin in the early stages of the development of the HRIS, that is, prior to senior man-agement's approval of the initial proposal. The interrelatedness of the content of this chapter with that* *of Chapters 3, 4, and 5 is important to acknowledge because it illustrates how effective management of an HRIS project requires the cooperation and skills of both IT and HR professionals. In addition, HR metrics and workforce analytics (Chapter 6) and the cost-benefit analysis (CBA, Chapter 7) are critical elements of a PM development and implementation plan for an HRIS.* **Critical success factors** *in the management, implementation, and acceptance of the HRIS project are also covered at the end of this chapter.*

CHAPTER Objectives

After completing this chapter, you should be able to

- Understand how the use of PM approaches, techniques, and tools helps throughout the entire SDLC

- Be able to describe and define the factors that are used to develop the performance evaluation and review technique (PERT), the critical path method (CPM), and Gantt charts

- Understand how monitoring the project activities carefully on a Gantt chart will ensure project completion on time

- Be able to construct a Gantt chart

- Be aware the existence of the Project Management Institute (PMI) and the training programs for professional certification

- Understand how Six Sigma can be used in HR and project management

- Understand how the combination of knowledge from the IT and HRM fields makes the development and implementation of the HRIS successful

- Be able to describe how IT factors can affect HRIS project success

- Understand how knowledge from the HRM literature provides guidance for handling the behavioral problems and issues that arise in HRIS development

- Understand the different roles of the steering committee, the CBA team, and the PM team in the HRIS project

- Be able to describe how training and documentation are crucial to both the development and the implementation of an HRIS

- Be able to describe how critical success factors affect the success or failure of an HRIS project

HRIS IN ACTION

In a national organization with 24 plant locations within the United States, a new software package for use in recruiting and selecting new employees, that is, for applicant tracking, was being developed and implemented as an add-on to the firm's current HRIS. The software was created by an external vendor; however, the implementation was being done by the internal HR and IT staff. As part of the contract, the vendor agreed to make modifications to the software as needed, until the management of the organization felt the software was operating properly. (This feature of an external vendor contract is typically required in the request for proposal [RFP].)

The project team had used one project management technique, PERT, and a specific visual device—the Gantt chart. These PM tools will be described later in this chapter. Their plan included (1) a project plan, (2) project goals and objectives, (3) tasks or activities to achieve goals, (4) an outline of people and dollar resources needed, and (5) a budget and a timeline for completion. As a critical part of the PM plan for this firm, a steering committee and a project team were established at the corporate level; and each company location was to form parallel steering committees and project teams at their location, teams that included IT and HR professionals.

The initial phase of the implementation involved a small-scale pilot test of the first version of the new software in two plant locations in order to make changes to the software if there were any problems. This initial phase took three months to complete, and the necessary modifications to the software were made. The next phase, to be accomplished over the next three months, was to field-test the revised version of the software in all company locations. It was decided to have the corporate-level leader of the HRIS project teams visit each location to meet with the HR and IT staff on the local project team to answer questions and generally assist with any problems during the field test. The feedback from this field test was to be sent to the vendor, so any necessary additional modifications of the software could be made.

In most of the firm's locations, the meetings with the HR and IT staff went fairly well, and the managers at these locations were pleased with their progress in implementing the new software. In 11 of the company locations, however, no formal meetings on the field test had been held. In these locations, the HR and the IT departments have had many difficulties cooperating, and each blamed the other for the lack of action on the current project. In addition, there were very few meetings in these 11 plant locations, and the project manager did not really understand the PERT analysis and the Gantt chart. Local project teams had been appointed that had both HR and IT professionals as members, but, unfortunately, the teams had only a few meetings. The corporate project team leader conducted interviews at the local plants to determine the source of these problems.

The results of these interviews revealed several problems. Even though the local staff meetings in the 11 plant locations had been scheduled by the local project leader, there were always key personnel, IT or HR, missing at each meeting, and this situation led to a cancellation of the meetings. Unfortunately, which key personnel were missing changed from meeting to meeting, making the accomplishment of the field test near impossible. Thus, it appeared obvious that the project charter and the steering committee (see Chapter 3 and later in this chapter) were poorly done, which, in this case, resulted in poor coordination between the corporate team leader and local team managers. There was also very little preparation or training in the use of PM tools or techniques for the PM team. In addition, there was no project or team training done for this project.

After intervention by senior management and 10 months of struggling with this problem in the 11 company locations, the field test was finally completed. This set the timetable for the total software implementation to 10 months longer than antici-pated. The project was completed 10 months late, which led to a major cost overrun of 153%. As a further negative result, it appeared that there were going to be layoffs to counter the additional costs for this project.

What was the central problem in this situation? Even though the corporate project team had used well-tested IT approaches and techniques from the PM field, the lack of a clear project charter and the poor selection of local steering committees in the 11 "problem" locations led to project failure. The information in this chapter will focus on the *necessity* of having well-tested PM techniques, good HRM programs, and team leadership training to enhance the effective management of the project team, as well as on recognizing the needs of all stakeholders in the organization, in order to ensure that the project is implemented properly and within the defined timeline.

Introduction

Statistics measuring the success of systems development efforts are not very encouraging. The failures of systems implementation have been well documented in the past. Browne and Rogich (2001) assert that "despite good faith efforts by organizations, analysts, and users, a majority of systems are either abandoned before completion or fail to meet user requirements." Inordinate delays and excessive budget overruns as well as user dissatisfaction, late deliveries, and customer dissatisfaction are some of the most cited reasons for the failure of HRIS projects. It has been estimated that this problem costs organizations in the United States alone at least $100 billion a year (Ewusi-Mensah, 1997). Of those systems that are completed, more than 55% will exceed cost and time estimates by a factor of 2. Even more troubling is the fact that only 13% of the IS projects that are completed are considered successful by the executives who sponsor them (Lemon, Bowitz, Burn, & Hackney, 2002).

Recent reports of the failures of HRIS implementation in major corporations indicate that these projects need to be more closely monitored due to the significant failure rates (Bondarouk & Meijerink, 2010; Dery, Hall, & Wiblen, 2010; Dulebohn, 2010; Grant, Newell, & Kavanagh, 2010; Tansley, 2010). The failure to deliver successful systems poses risks not only to those whose operations depend on these systems but also to those responsible for delivery. The inability to employ "quality" systems can prevent the firm from performing critical operations satisfactorily. In most cases of these failures to implement systems, the use of project management (PM) tools, techniques, and management procedures, as well as advice from the HRM "organizational change" literature, was largely ignored.

A classic example is the well-documented failure of Hershey Foods' $112 million computer system (Nelson & Ramstad, 1999). Due to the poor design and implementation of this new system, Hershey was unable to fill an order for 20,000 pounds of candy placed by a regional distributor in mid-September in anticipation of Halloween demand. The distributor, in turn, could not satisfy 100 of his 700 retail customers. The journal article describing the debacle further quoted a candy buyer for Lowes Foods, a chain of supermarkets, who advised stores to stop reordering Hershey candies and switch to a competitor. Although Hershey claimed that it lost only a small percentage of its market share, others contended that the shelf space the company lost would be difficult to win back. Many of these problems could have been avoided if an effective PM methodology had been utilized.

Project management is a systematic and structured approach to planning and properly executing a specific, and usually one-time, objective. The objective of any project can range from planning a social event like a college-wide picnic to the implementation of a complex, multimillion-dollar computer-based system like an HRIS. In both of these examples, the IT and HRM tools are absolutely necessary to ensure the project objective is achieved.

This need for effective management of an HRIS development project was extensively discussed by Walker (1982) when he identified the 10 most common mistakes in developing an HRIS. One of the major issues that he identified was **loose project control**, which was a central problem in the situation described in the vignette at the beginning of this chapter. Likewise, Kavanagh, Gueutal, and Tannenbaum (1990) provided a list of 14 recommendations based on an extensive review of the HRIS literature. Prominent among these recommendations was the "need to make a detailed plan" and to "develop a checklist to monitor implementation"; as well, they noted that "documentation . . . is critical for successful implementing and maintaining of the HRIS" and that HR and IT managers should "audit the new system periodically for maintenance" (p. 191). This chapter focuses on describing the approaches and techniques you can use to meet these recommendations and successfully develop and implement an HRIS.

Project Management Cooperation

Effective PM for the HRIS depends completely on a positive relationship between the IT and HR departments. As seen in the vignette, a poor relationship between these departments caused the project to fail in 11 company locations. Without this necessary cooperation, the HRIS development and implementation will fail. In the next several sections of this chapter, the contributions from the fields of IT and HR will be described along with a prescribed approach to combine them to make the HRIS fulfill the needs of all end users.

The IT Perspective

Project Management Processes

An examination of the project management literature reveals a number of methodologies for managing an HRIS project. Information on PM in general and PM techniques and tools can be found at the websites of the State of Kansas (www.da.ks.gov/kito/ITPMM.htm) and the Project Management Institute (www.pmi.org). Although there are a number of PM approaches and methods described in these websites, detailed coverage of each is beyond the scope of this book. However, Josler and Burger (2005) provide an excellent description of the use of PM methodology in the successful implementation of an HRIS in a university setting.

Regardless of the methodology employed, each approach has four general **project management process phases** in common. These phases are quite similar to the stages of the systems development life cycle (SDLC) for an HRIS project and, basically, parallel the various steps and requirements in the development and implementation of an HRIS as covered in Chapters 3 to 5. However, it is important to examine project phases from the perspective of the IT discipline since this examination can uncover additional issues regarding the success of an HRIS project.

The PM methodologies all begin with the **project initiation phase**. In this phase, a **project concept** and a **project proposal** are developed. The project concept describes the key stakeholders and seeks to ensure that the right questions are asked so that the right problem is solved. In the initial stages of an HRIS, this information is critical. The project proposal, also called a **project charter**, contains objectives and performance targets (e.g., cost, time, scope). The project concept and charter must be approved by top management to fulfill the requirements of this initial phase and begin the development of an HRIS. Without a firm and continuing commitment from top management on the project timeline and budget, the HRIS project will likely fail.

The second phase of project planning identifies the tasks that must be performed. A **work breakdown structure (WBS)** is created along with **work packages** (i.e., what must be done, by whom, using what resources, in what time, and at what cost). During this phase, the time order in which activities, tasks, and jobs are to be performed is planned, and specific checks or monitoring points are established. These monitoring points could have important effects on the direction, scope, or requirements of the HRIS project, and, thus, designating monitoring points on the timeline is critical.

As discussed in the IT field, the third phase is called **project execution**. In this phase, the HRIS project is tracked, and periodic progress reports are prepared for management and the project team. During this phase, five key factors are assessed: schedule, budget, open issues, risks, and communication. PM approaches such as the PERT (performance evaluation and review) and the CPM (critical path method) are used in conjunction with visual tools such as Gantt and bar charts during project execution. A description of the use of these approaches and tools is available on the Internet (http://en.wikipedia.org/wiki/Project_management_software).

The final phase is **project closeout**, which involves the implementation, evaluation, documentation, and maintenance of the HRIS. This phase includes the following goals and activities:

1. Accepting the project's products (indicated by user sign-off)

2. Completing the **post-implementation evaluation report (PIER)**

3. Disbursing resources (staff, facilities, and automated systems)

4. Conducting a "lessons learned" session

5. Completing and archiving project records

6. Recognizing outstanding achievement

7. Celebrating project completion

The celebration of the project's completion is as important as the initial proposal since it will help employees feel more committed to making the new HRIS operate properly.

As can be seen, the IT field offers a number of techniques and approaches to PM developed by professionals. Using these techniques, one can develop an **overall work plan** based on the work breakdown structure and work packages described previously. This overall work plan is a written time schedule of tasks and responsibilities with deadlines so that the HRIS project will be done in the total time allotted. Note, however, that the orientation of this plan is toward the management of the project itself, not the people who are responsible for the development and implementation of the HRIS.

The management of the people involved—the project team, end users, and organizational managers—is contained in advice from the HRM and HRIS fields. This distinction between the IT and HR fields is sometimes referred to as the *gap* between the IT capabilities of the organization and the use of these capabilities by HR professionals. Frequently, there is a mismatch—positive or negative—between what the HR department wants and the capabilities available through the IT department. This fact, as seen in the opening vignette, underscores the need for cooperation between these departments in staffing the project team. The next section discusses some of these issues regarding the formation and operation of the project team.

Project Management Approaches and Tools

The IT field has provided some powerful approaches and tools to be used in managing any project. **Performance evaluation and review technique (PERT)** is a method for analyzing the tasks involved in completing a given project, the time needed to complete each task, and the minimum time needed to complete the total project. It was invented in 1958 by the U.S. Department of Defense's U.S. Navy Special Projects Office and was intended for complex, one-of-a-kind projects such as its first application—developing the Polaris mobile submarine-launched ballistic missile.

The **critical path method (CPM)**, meanwhile, uses a mathematically based algorithm for scheduling a set of project activities and was developed by DuPont and the Remington Rand Corporation for managing plant maintenance projects. CPM is used to construct a project model that includes the following:

1. A list of all activities required to complete the project

2. The time (duration) that each activity will take to complete

3. The dependencies among the activities

Using these values, CPM calculates the starting and ending times for each activity and determines which activities are critical to the completion of a project (called the critical path) and which activities have "float time" (are less critical). In PM, a **critical path** is the sequence or project network that determines the shortest time possible to complete the project. Any delay in activity on the critical path directly affects the planned project completion date (i.e., there is no float on the critical path). A project can have several, parallel critical paths. An additional parallel path through the network with a total duration shorter than the critical path is called a subcritical or noncritical path.

Finally, one can develop a **Gantt chart**, which is a graphical representation of the duration of tasks against the progression of time in a project. *Wikipedia* defines a Gantt chart as follows:

> A Gantt chart is a type of bar chart that illustrates a project schedule. Gantt charts illustrate the start and finish dates of the terminal elements and summary elements of a project. Terminal elements and summary elements comprise the work breakdown structure of the project. ("Gantt chart," 2011)

An example of a Gantt chart can be viewed in Figure 6.1.[1] As can be seen, there is a requirement for all the tasks to be represented in the Gantt chart as well as estimates of time to complete tasks. From the three time estimates, the expected time to complete the tasks can be computed. These expected times listed in Figure 6.1would be very useful in monitoring whether or not each task is completed in the time expected. For example, if a number of the tasks were taking 25% longer than expected, the project plan may have to be altered.

Figure 6.1   Gantt Chart Example

In the following example there are seven tasks, labeled *A* through *G*. Some tasks can be done concurrently (*A* and *B*) while others cannot be done until their predecessor task is complete (*C* cannot begin until *A* is complete). Additionally, each task has three time estimates: the optimistic time estimate (*O*), the most likely or normal time estimate (*M*), and the pessimistic time estimate (*P*). The expected time (T_E) is computed using the beta probability distribution for the time estimates, using the formula ($O + 4M + P$) ÷ 6.

Activity	Predecessor	Time estimates			Expected time
		Opt. (*O*)	Normal (*M*)	Pess. (*P*)	
A	—	2	4	6	4.00
B	—	3	5	9	5.33
C	A	4	5	7	5.17
D	A	4	6	10	6.33
E	B, C	4	5	7	5.17
F	D	3	4	8	4.50
G	E	3	5	8	5.17

Figure 6.2   Construct Gantt Chart

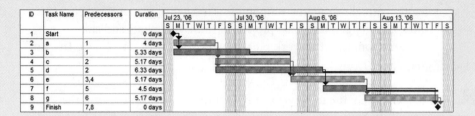

A Gantt chart created using Microsoft Project (MSP). Note (1) the critical path is in red, (2) the slack is the black lines connected to noncritical activities, (3) since Saturday and Sunday are not work days and are thus excluded from the schedule, some bars on the Gantt chart are longer if they cut through a weekend (Gantt chart, 2011).

As noted in Note 1, the instructions for how to develop a Gantt chart and then covert it to a bar graph with a time dimension (as in Figure 6. 2) would make an excellent planning tool for any project. This example is from Wikipedia, but there are numerous websites on the Internet if you search for "Gantt chart." A good exercise would be to create a Gantt chart for planning a party. There are *several tasks* that need to be done: shopping for groceries, ordering special items such as a birthday cake, shopping for invitations or sending e-mail invitations, and of course, making sure there are adequate beverages purchased. In fact, your instructor may assign this project to groups of students in the class.

There are multiple advantages in using these PM approaches and tools; the major one is a tighter control over the process to ensure successful implementation of the HRIS. This tighter control is attained by the following means:

1. Definition of all activities to be accomplished to complete the project

2. Establishment of a specific schedule for activities that includes an estimate of when each activity will start and end

3. Project milestones that are used to monitor specific activities set by this schedule

4. Assignment of resources in terms of equipment, people, and, thus, costs for all activities

5. Computation of the total budget and allocation of the budget needed to accomplish each activity

6. A graphical picture of the entire project showing all activities, their costs, and their milestones

Extending these IT ideas and providing more detail for the management of an HRIS project, Rampton, Turnbull, and Doran (1999) indicate that every project has resource limits and specifications in the following categories:

- Time—start and end dates
- People—identification, specific skills they bring to project, availability, costs
- Tools—equipment, software
- Money—budget (p. 76)

In addition, they note that PM also brings a critical capability to the HRIS project—namely, evaluation of the project's performance by monitoring progress against the planned timetable. This monitoring allows for periodic adjustments as well as ensuring that project creep is not occurring.

Software has been developed for all the PM approaches and tools—CPM, PERT, and Gantt charts. The interested reader can consult *Wikipedia: The Free Encyclopedia* (http://en.wikipedia.org/wiki/Project_management_software) for a fairly comprehensive listing of different types of software. Software applications *will not be recommended* in this book since each organization's situation will vary, and choosing software and hardware for HRIS decisions is a complicated matter. The International Association for Human Resource Information Management (IHRIM) has a buyers' guide for HRIS software that is available to members, and, if any outside consultants are used, they usually have information on the most current and effective PM software for the HRIS project.

For a more detailed and technical explanation of PERT, CPM, and Gantt charts, consult one of the several good texts available (O'Brien, Crnkovic, & Belardo, 2006; Wiest & Levy, 1969). In addition, Jon Peltier (2008) has developed a method using Microsoft Excel to build Gantt charts.

General IT Factors Affecting PM Success

Rather than presenting a detailed discussion of the various stages and templates found on the Project Management Institute and State of Kansas websites, this chapter will consider three general issues that must be addressed and that are critical to the success of any of these PM methodologies. The *first issue* is the importance of *solving the right problem*. All too often, IT developers create systems that they *think* end users want. The end users are frequently dissatisfied with the results, which accounts for the dismal statistics cited previously. The *second issue* involves having people with *the right knowledge to solve the right problem.* Frequently, IT system developers do not understand the HRM domain and its problems and constraints adequately. It is necessary to have systems developers who are sensitive to HR issues and willing to learn about the constraints in HR functionality. With such systems developers, the information requirements phase can be completed within the time frame and budget constraints specified by the project plan. In most organizations, this problem can be solved by having both IT and HR professionals on the project team. Obviously, if the organization has an HRIS professional, this problem will be greatly reduced. The *third issue* involves having project managers, from either an IT or an HR department, who *understand the dynamic nature of any HRIS project* and how the interrelations among various factors might render decisions ineffective or even counterproductive. For example, studies have shown that assigning more people to an overdue project might actually delay project completion.

In addition to these three issues, the three general factors that affect successful PM are time, cost, and scope. The cost of project development depends on a number of variables, including labor rates, material, plant resources (e.g., buildings, machines), equipment, and profit. In addition to the total fixed and variable costs are contingency costs and time to completion, which can be broken down into the units of time required to complete each task. Scope refers to what the project is supposed to accomplish and what the end result should be (i.e., what the end user wants). Time and cost are process measures of performance and, therefore, measures of efficiency. Scope, on the other hand, is about effectiveness and is measured by whether the right questions have been asked and whether the right problem is being addressed. Staying within the project costs, time, and scope depends highly on the ability of the project team to gather the correct information requirements for the HRIS project during the needs analysis, which was described in Chapter 4.

As can be seen, the IT field offers a number of techniques and approaches to PM developed by professionals. The PM4HR framework assists in successfully completing projects. Using these techniques, one can develop an overall work plan based on the work breakdown structure and work packages described previously. This overall work plan is a written time schedule of tasks and responsibilities with deadlines so that the HRIS project will be done in the total time allotted. Note, however, that the orientation of this plan is toward the management of the project itself, not the people who are responsible for the development and implementation of the HRIS. HR metrics, covered in Chapter 7, can also be used to measure success at different stages in effective project management. Spirgi (2009) identifies the following five levels of the measurement and use of HR metrics to guide the project management processes:

> Level 1: Program Management: Metrics that monitor the success of your project practices, for example: accomplishing a stated number of meetings and timeliness of project reporting.

Level 2: Deployment: Metrics that monitor your ability to effectively launch your initiative to all stakeholders with the right tools and techniques—and on time/on budget, for example: Training delivery on time/on budget and training effectiveness.

Level 3: Adoption: Metrics that monitor your ability to successfully launch your initiative and drive user adoption and acceptance, for example: Usage of system and employee engagement.

Level 4: HR Operational Strategies and Efficiencies: Metrics that monitor your HR function's ability to perform more effectively due to process improvements and automation, for example: Improved speed to hire and improved payroll accuracy.

Level 5: ROI Value-Based: Metrics that monitor your program's ability to impact performance levers based on your defined business case, for example: Business performance/productivity and reduced turnover (p. 8).

The Human Resource Management Perspective

The techniques of PM from the IT literature will ensure the development of an overall written work plan for the HRIS project. However, there are still a number of organizational requirements involved in the successful completion of the HRIS project. Grossman (2009) has a number of recommendations regarding how to manage the people who manage the projects. In addition, the HRM literature provides guidance on how to handle the behavioral and management issues that arise in fulfilling these requirements during the HRIS project. The organizational and management requirements include the following:

1. Identification of steering committee and project charter
2. Configuring the PM team
3. Identification of available resources and constraints
4. Controlling project creep
5. Selection of the implementation team
6. Training and documentation

Each of these requirements and their use in PM will be described in the following sections.

Identification of the Steering Committee and Project Charter

During the initial considerations for the development of an HRIS, typically, there are strategic goals set for the project. Often this process is referred to as "making the business case" for the HRIS project, which would include estimating both the costs and the benefits of the new system—that is, estimating its cost-effectiveness (see Chapter 7). Consequently, a subset of members from the project team must be selected to develop an investment analysis, as described in Chapter 7, that is, a cost-benefit analysis (CBA). However, the central focus before project initiation would be on both strategic and operational goals. For example, some possible goals could be (1) reducing the transaction costs in HR processing; (2) improving the quality of HR information for managerial decisions; or (3) improving the HR processes of talent management, which includes the recruiting and selecting of new employees as well as the retention of valued ones. Regardless of the specific strategic and operational goals for the new system, the project will still have constraints in terms of resources available.

Because of these goals and constraints, the **steering committee** must include representatives of senior management from HR, finance, IT systems, marketing, research and development, and operations. The steering committee members must be selected on the basis of their competence in project management as well as their availability (Grossman, 2009). A crucial player is the senior management member who is selected as the **project sponsor**, since this person typically has overall fiscal responsibility for the project. The primary responsibility of the steering committee is the *oversight of the project* in terms of progress toward meeting strategic goals and staying within the project budget. Thus, the steering committee does not get involved in the day-to-day activities and operations associated with the development of the HRIS. This is the role of the project team, which will be covered later.

One important task for the steering committee is the development of the project charter. The project charter was discussed in Chapter 3, and it does the following:

- It makes the case for the implementation.
- It shows connection to organizational goals and strategies.
- It has a plan for end users' involvement and participation.
- It provides identification of **project scope**.
- It identifies implementation team members.
- It identifies additional expertise that might be available.
- It provides a training plan.

- It explains the agreed-on decision-making process.

- It discusses the process by which customization requests will be reviewed and acted on.

- It covers the PM methods used.

- It defines reporting requirements.

- It identifies deliverables.

- It defines political relationships of importance to project success.

The development of the project charter and the coordination of the members of the steering committee involve a great deal of communication and interpersonal skills on the part of the project sponsor, who serves as the chair. As Rampton et al. (1999) note, the communication of project planning and project status in the steering committee and throughout the organization involves an inordinate amount of time. Thus, when it comes to the project sponsor and the steering committee, being patient while keeping an eye on meeting project deadlines is an art. Having well-done PM tools such as CPM, PERT, or Gantt charts is an absolute necessity for the HR project. However, it is people, not the existence of the charts, that make the project successful (Dulebohn, 2010; Grant et al., 2010). Merely sending a memorandum indicating progress on a Gantt chart will not ensure cooperation from either the steering committee or the project team members. It is necessary to both train project managers and, more specifically, provide team training in communications and interpersonal relationships for the steering committee members. As noted earlier, Spirgi (2009) has identified five levels of the measurement and use of HR metrics to guide and monitor the project management processes. Steering committees often will also hire outside "process consultants" to help develop and maintain good working relationships within the steering committee, with the **project team**, and with the end users in the organization.

Configuring the PM Team

A central idea that has been discussed through the first seven chapters of this book is that **end-user involvement** and participation is crucial if the HRIS project is to be successful. In systems development, getting the end users to tell a system developer what they know about their domain (e.g., HR programs and processes) and their information and decision requirements largely depends on the developer's ability to ask the right questions. If the systems developer knows how to ask the right questions, knowledge of the users' domain and their unique problems and needs will be easier to obtain. Thus, Belardo, Ballou, and Pazer (2004) contend that it is necessary to educate developers regarding how to ask the right questions and to teach them how to develop the interpersonal skills necessary to gain the cooperation of the users.

Whereas the steering committee oversees the entire HRIS project, the PM team is involved in the day-to-day activities necessary to develop and implement the new HRIS. Its members have the job of completing the activities specified by the CPM, PERT, or Gantt chart according to the defined timetable. The team must be capable of estimating the actual resources, both personnel and monetary, needed to complete the project. A major responsibility of the team is to communicate—by way of written reports on a regular (weekly or monthly) basis—with both the steering committee and the important stakeholders, for example, the vice president of HR, regarding progress on the HRIS project. If the organization has a newsletter or a company bulletin board, these should be used to keep all members of the organization apprised of the progress of the HRIS project.

The PM team should be comprised of representatives from the functional units affected, most notably the HR and IT departments. There may be other units affected, for example, operations, marketing, or finance, and a judgment must be made whether to include representatives from these functional units or simply supply regular update reports on the project to them. The HR professionals chosen for the team should have significant functional knowledge of how to measure the metrics of the project, some technical proficiency, and a positive status within their department and the organization. An example might be the manager of employment or compensation. Likewise, IT professionals could include systems analysts, hardware and software specialists, and HRIS professionals, all of whom should be respected members of the organization.

One of the critical issues faced by the PM team is the selection of the team **project manager**. This person should have strong communication skills, including the ability to speak, listen, and write effectively. The project manager must ensure that the team members understand the importance of regular communication with their supervisors. Team training is an absolute necessity for the project team. Many of the failed HRIS projects were the result of poor team cooperation and interpersonal difficulties (Grant et al., 2010). Furthermore, to be successful in implementing the new HRIS, all potential users must be made aware of the project's progress and how it will affect them. Feedback loops should be developed so that users can provide valuable information to the project team during development and implementation. Kavanagh (2001) used surveys to assess users' attitudes regarding the implementation of a new system. The results of these surveys were then used to guide the development and implementation of the new system as well as to provide feedback to members of the organization.

Quality Processes in Project Management

Quality considerations are also important in the design of any new business process or information system, and an HRIS is no exception. In addition to effective communications in pursuit of quality processes, many organizations are adopting a Six Sigma approach to assessing the effectiveness of HR processes. Although originally developed by Motorola,

USA in 1981, and famously applied by General Electric to improve the quality of its manufacturing processes, Six Sigma is now being applied to a wide variety of production and service processes. It has become one of the most widely recognized quality improvement methods used in businesses today. A recent issue of the *Workforce Solutions Review* (Martinez, 2010) defined Six Sigma as "a data-driven philosophy and methodology initially developed as a means for eliminating manufacturing defects by driving towards six standard deviations between the mean and the nearest specification limit in any process. The statistical representation of Six Sigma describes quantitatively how a process is performing" (p. 6).

Six Sigma thus focuses on business process reengineering with the goal of improving the quality of process outputs, for example, the annual turnover rate of employees, by identifying and removing the causes of defects (errors) and minimizing variability in business processes. Six Sigma is a structured approach for improving business (HR) processes through a step-by-step method labeled DMAIC, which stands for define, measure, analyze, improve, and control. The **DMAIC approach** uses an assortment of statistical tools to reengineer business processes, and HRM processes such as recruiting, training, and compensating employees, can be examined using this approach. "The DMAIC project methodology has the following five phases":

- *Define* the problem, the voice of the customer, and the project goals, specifically.

- *Measure* key aspects of the current process and collect relevant data.

- *Analyze* the data to investigate and verify cause-and-effect relationships. Determine what the relationships are, and attempt to ensure that all factors have been considered. Seek out the root cause of the defect under investigation.

- *Improve* or optimize the current process based upon data analysis using techniques, such as design of experiments . . . or mistake proofing, and standardize work to create a new, future state process. Set up pilot runs to establish process capability.

- *Control* the future state process to ensure that any deviations from target are corrected before they result in defects. Implement control systems . . . and continuously monitor the process. ("Six Sigma," 2010)

The management of the people involved—the project team, end users, and organizational managers—is contained in advice from the HRM (PM4HR) and HRIS fields. This distinction between the IT and HR fields is sometimes referred to as the *gap* between the IT capabilities of the organization and the use of these capabilities by HR professionals. Frequently, there is a mismatch—positive or negative—between what the HR department wants and the capabilities available through the IT department. This fact, as seen in the opening vignette, underscores the need for cooperation between these departments in staffing the project team. The next section discusses some of these issues regarding the formation and operation of the project team.

Identification of Available Resources and Constraints

The steering committee, by way of the project charter, will have established preliminary estimates of available resources for the project and constraints on its scope. Except in unusual situations, the constraints established by the steering committee cannot be altered. However, sometimes it may be necessary to change the initial identification of needed resources, that is, personnel time and other costs. One of the major tasks of the PM team is to identify the need for more resources in the early phases of the project, particularly if legitimate project creep occurs because the initial plans for the HRIS project missed some important aspects of the project. As a result, the project manager must be in constant communication with team members regarding any unforeseen difficulties—for example, if a project team member leaves the organization. In situations where project resources change, the project manager has the responsibility to inform the steering committee chair immediately.

Controlling Project Creep

Project creep is defined as the enlargement of the original boundaries of the project as defined in the project charter. As noted previously, project creep (also known as "scope creep") may be legitimate if a major aspect of the project was omitted at the early planning stage. However, other forms of project creep can easily occur as end users see the potential usefulness of computerization. If effective communications have been established within the project team as well as with the entire organization, project creep can be contained by frequent updates on the project's progress, updates that include a definition of the project charter. In addition, using PM tools such as a Gantt chart ensures that the project is meeting its goals and not being extended into activities not contained on the Gantt chart. Surveys of users, as noted, are also useful to ascertain if system users' perceptions of the project have started to creep. In other words, continuous and regular communication is the key to avoiding project creep.

Selection of the Implementation Team

In some cases, the entire PM team, plus the steering committee, will serve as the implementation team. A more common configuration is that a subset of individuals from the PM team is tasked with focusing on implementation issues, such as employee cooperation and training, as well as on change management techniques. It is not unusual to have an external consultant provide technical assistance on implementation using change management techniques such as survey-guided feedback and focus groups. The implementation team also has primary responsibility for communication with the entire organization and, as noted in Chapter 3, begins this communication with the initial planning for new system development. The implementation team should include professionals from HR and IT, as well as representatives of all functional departments in the organization. It is also important to have a senior manager serve as the leader of the implementation team. Note that these additional people can be added as the project enters its actual implementation phase; however, these individuals must be in the communication loop throughout the entire project.

Software Implementation

Although there are many activities to be completed when implementing the new or upgraded HRIS, we focus on three specific tasks of particular importance: data migration, software testing, and system conversion. **Data migration** (or conversion) involves identifying which data should be migrated and how much historical data should be included, as well as the actual process of moving the data. Developers will need to determine when and how to convert the data, the time needed to allocate for data conversion, and any implications for data conversion on system downtime. Decisions must be made in regard to how far back to convert data and how to convert the data from the older system data structures to the new system's data structures.

Another important task to be completed during implementation is software testing. The goal of *software testing* is to verify that the new or upgraded HRIS meets the requirements outlined during analysis and design, and to ensure that it does so with as few errors or bugs in the program as possible. Consider an example from payroll. The testing team may work with the HR staff to ensure that the payroll module functions function properly, that it avoids double payments or missing payments, and makes sure that checks print.

The third task we will briefly discuss is system conversion. *System conversion* focuses on how the new or upgraded HRIS will be introduced into the organization, that is, how it will be implemented. There are four types of conversion approaches to implementation that an organization can utilize when implementing a new or upgraded HRIS. In a *direct conversion* the old HRIS or nontechnical processes are turned off and the new one is turned on. This is the quickest and often the least expensive implementation approach. At the same time, this is the most risky approach. Regardless of training and the change management process, there is an organization-wide learning curve while the users adjust to the new software. In addition there is no other option if the system has errors or delays. As illustrated by Hershey's choice to use this conversion option in 1999 when implementing a new distribution system, if there are significant problems, significant profits may be destroyed as well. In Hershey's case, the company could not deliver $100 million of inventory to stores during the Halloween sales season (Koch, 2002).

In a *parallel conversion*, the new software is on for a period of time before the old software is turned off. The time period in question is usually a meaningful business cycle to the organization (e.g., a month or a quarter). During this time, both software systems are functioning, receiving input, running reports, and being queried. The positive of a parallel conversion is that there is enormous testing that goes on before the old software disappears. The negatives are that there is a risk that employees will try to use the old system processes rather than fully committing to the new system, and there will have to be dual data entry performed for every task.

The final two implementation approaches focus on a phased or piloted approach to implementation. In a *pilot conversion*, the new system is implemented in a single, pilot location. In large organizations with business units positioned across geographic locations, it may be necessary to use multiple locations as pilot locations during the conversion. The advantages of a piloted approach are that a representative location (or locations) can be selected to test out the new system while minimizing risk. Any needed adjustments can be made to the system before going live across the entire organization. In a *phased conversion*, the system is brought on line through a series of functional components. For example, the organization may wish to turn on the core HRIS first and then bring on recruitment and learning management later.

Nestlé USA, the California-based food company, opted for a gradual, phased-in implementation rather than going live all at once. The company started by implementing a new payroll system—first to a small group of 600 employees, then to other business units over time. "'By focusing on a small group first, we were able to address many of our interface and reporting needs upfront with a small population of employees. . . . Demonstrating successes and celebrating them along the way reinforced senior management's decision to fund the project, and motivated our team to keep going,' says [Mike] Benson [director of HRIS]" (Henson, 1996, p. 5).

Training and Documentation

There are a variety of activities involved in training for the new system and its documentation. However, without the necessary training, usually provided by the external vendor who supplies the software, the system will either fail to be developed properly or fail during its implementation. Likewise complete, accurate, and **up-to-date documentation** of the system is critical for the implementation of a successful HRIS. Documentation in terms of notes, diaries, memorandums, and reports created during the development and implementation of the HRIS will be invaluable when updates to the system are needed.

There are several different training programs that are necessary for the development and use of the new HRIS. As discussed earlier, one of the first considerations when beginning the HRIS project is to develop a project plan using CPM, PERT, or Gantt charts. It is desirable to use an employee (from IT or HR) who is certified by the Project Management Institute (www.pmi.org/) or who has taken seminars on PM from the American Management Association (www.amanet.org/). Obviously, without a carefully developed project plan using PM techniques, no amount of communication or employee involvement will suffice to make the HRIS a success. When they have no internal employees with PM skills, companies frequently use outside consultants to develop the project plan.

It is also recommended that the PM team receive training in group processes such as decision making and in communication skills. Furthermore, it is necessary that the project team leader and the implementation team members be trained in the use of planned change or "change management" methods. **Change management** is a structured approach to changing individuals, groups, and organizations to accept new ideas and processes, that is, a new HRIS. Lewin (1951) described change management as involving three phases—unfreezing current attitudes and behaviors, changing to new attitudes and behaviors, and refreezing these new attitudes and behaviors. There are other change management approaches in the literature (Kotter, 1996; Luecke, 2003). The important point is that these approaches work and are absolutely critical for the successful implementation and use of the HRIS. These approaches will be covered in detail in Chapter 9.

The final training that needs to be done is training on the new system. Most vendors of new software will provide training on the new system and more extensive training at an additional cost. The additional cost depends on the level of training needed for the users. To determine the amount and type of training needed for users, the organization should complete an analysis of the training needs and follow the recommended phases for effective training (Wexley & Latham, 2002). In most organizations, the HR department will have training professionals who should be used to complete the training phases. It is important that this training effort be included in the project plan in terms of time needed for the training and the costs. Premature introduction of a new HRIS or introducing it without appropriate training will lead to failure (Kavanagh et al., 1990).

Critical Success Factors for IT and HRM Issues

Several authors have discussed critical success factors in HRIS development and implementation (Ceriello & Freeman, 1991; Kavanagh et al., 1990; Rampton et al., 1999; Walker, 1982).

These lists of success factors and mistakes serve as both cautions and recommendations for a successful HRIS project. Some of these mistakes and success factors have been mentioned in previous chapters as well as earlier in this chapter. However, for your convenience, we present here a compilation of critical success factors:

1. *Top management support:* Simply stated, the project must have **top management support** at the beginning and throughout implementation and evaluation. The top management, that is, the CEO and department or unit heads, must be willing to provide the necessary resources and authority for project success.

2. *Provision of adequate and timely resources:* These resources include technology, money, time, and personnel. Without a carefully constructed PM plan, organizations will typically have inadequate resources to develop and implement the HRIS. The development of a "business plan" for the HRIS project is an absolute necessity for success. Chapter 7 provides excellent approaches to the development of a business plan for the HRIS, one that includes a cost-benefit analysis (CBA).

3. *Ongoing communication:* Everybody involved in and affected by the HRIS project needs to be informed regularly about the goals, progress or lack of it, issues, and challenges throughout the life of the project, so there is less room for organizational politics, rumor mongering, and misapprehensions. Constant monitoring and frequent feedback are integral parts of the communication process.

4. *Conducive organizational culture:* The culture of the organization will be strongly affected by the history of changes in the organization and how they were accomplished. Contrast an organization in which change was dictated by management versus one in which there was extensive participation by employees in the change effort. You will discover that the organization with the more participatory culture accepted change more readily. When it comes to change, then, this organization has a more **conducive organizational culture**. In addition, the training on the new system will not transfer to the users of the new HRIS unless there is a supportive organizational culture for learning (Lance, Kavanagh, & Brink, 2002; Tracey, Tannenbaum, & Kavanagh, 1995; Velada, Caetano, Michel, Lyons, & Kavanagh, 2007).

5. *User involvement:* As indicated in Chapters 3 and 4, user involvement is critical to the effective development and implementation of the HRIS. This ensures that the project is designed and implemented in accordance with user requirements and, therefore, will have a better chance of being accepted. User involvement will be discussed in more detail in Chapter 9.

6. *Project champions:* The best-possible situation would be to have two **project champions** for the HRIS project—the steering committee chair and the project team manager. Obviously, this means that the selection of these individuals must be done carefully, and the persons selected should enjoy a good reputation and status in the organization.

7. *Organizational structure:* Typically, the implementation of a new HRIS will require changes in reporting lines of authority as well as changing responsibilities for HR and IT. If the departments are not used to cooperation and collaboration, they will develop a "silo mentality" and will compete against each other to the detriment of the organization.

8. *Change management methodology:* The assumption that employees will "love" the new system because of its sophisticated features is naive. Communication and user involvement throughout the development and implementation phases of the project, as well as good training on the new HRIS, are critical to success.

9. *Project control and monitoring:* Trying to execute an HRIS project without a written project plan—for example, the Gantt chart—will lead to failure. Likewise, the project team's failure to communicate project milestones and progress will severely damage the project effort. This loose project control could also be the result of a weak project team or steering committee. The necessary communication from both of these groups will ensure strong project control. As noted earlier, Spirgi (2009) has identified five levels of the measurement and use of HR metrics to guide and monitor the project management processes. These metrics should provide excellent feedback to the project team in monitoring the progress of the project.

10. *Cross integration between business systems:* Poor integration between systems is usually the result of poor communication across functional departments during the development of the HRIS. Without effective communication, the HRIS will be unable to interface with other business systems, such as the financial, operations, or marketing systems.

SUMMARY

This chapter has been concerned with understanding the value and use of project management (PM) and HR change practices throughout the entire SDLC as a new or upgraded HRIS is developed and implemented. The use of PM tools and techniques such as CPM, PERT, and Gantt charts was covered in detail. The factors involved in developing these PM tools were discussed. Software for the development of a Gantt chart based on the human resources, tasks, and timelines was

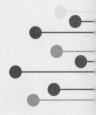

identified as well. Finally, the IT factors that can affect project success negatively or positively were identified, and their effects on an HRIS project were discussed.

A dynamic perspective of HRIS project management has been presented that uses the joint contribution of IT and HRM approaches, and the chapter argues strongly those organizations cannot rely only on IT approaches such as CPM, PERT, and Gantt charts, thereby excluding the useful behavioral approaches found in the HRM literature. Likewise, using only the behavioral, group, and organizational approaches from the HRM literature without a written plan provided by a bar or Gantt chart will result in either a poorly designed HRIS, expensive cost overruns, or the abandonment of the project. The importance of a project charter and scope management were discussed. Further, the importance of carefully selecting the project team and steering committee was covered in light of how these planners affect project completion.

In general, this chapter has not only focused on PM tools from IT but also identified how HRM knowledge and practices can help handle the behavioral problems and issues that can arise during the development and implementation of an HRIS. Team training of the project team and steering committee was described as crucial to HRIS project success. In addition, the use of continuous documentation through the four PM stages was covered, and behavioral techniques were discussed that address the challenges faced by all project managers—namely, how to improve project effectiveness and efficiency.

Finally, 10 critical success factors for overall HRIS project management have been identified from both the IT and the HRM literature. In discussing these 10 factors, we explained how each should be used in the development and implementation of an HRIS. Throughout, the chapter has emphasized the importance of documentation by and communications from and to the steering committee and the PM team. Also, documentation and communication were linked to the implementation processes for the HRIS; however, a complete discussion of implementation processes will be provided in Chapter 9.

KEY TERMS

DISCUSSION QUESTIONS

1. What are the advantages of using a PM approach from the IT literature for the management of an HRIS project?

2. How does the behavioral advice from the HRM literature complement the formal IT tools, such as a Gantt chart?

3. What is the information needed to construct a CPM, PERT, or Gantt chart?

4. Construct a Gantt chart for planning a surprise birthday party for your mother or father.

5. In which phases of the SDLC is documentation important? Why?

6. Do the critical success factors from the IT and HRM literature complement each other? Or is there disagreement between the recommendations from these two fields? Explain your answer.

7. Discuss the organizational factors that might affect the quality of the HRIS being developed. For example, how does a change in organizational structure or in project leadership influence the outcome of an HRIS development project?

CASE STUDY: IMPLEMENTING AN HRIS

ABC Finance provides financial services to customers and employs around 2,500 staff. The organization is currently facing major changes in its environment, both internally and externally. Externally, factors such as increasing globalization, new and innovative technologies, changing demographics and demands of customers, increasing deregulation, and competition in the industry have forced the firm to be more competitive by reducing costs and offering innovative services—by doing more with less. Internally, there has been a shift over the past few years to a client focus from a product focus, continued growth in the organization resulting in geographical dispersion across the country, and a move toward the delivery of online services. Historically, different functional departments within the firm have rarely collaborated with each other to solve organizational issues. The organization is cautious and consultative in its decision making and could best be described as bureaucratic.

The organization has made a decision to implement a new HRIS along with a new finance system and a new customer relationship management (CRM) system. The existing systems are all more than 10 years old and do not support the current or future environments in which the organization sees itself operating. The existing HRIS will be unsupported by the current vendor in the next six months, and there is an urgent need to implement the new system as soon as possible. The implementation has the support of key senior people in the organization. The HR, finance, and customer relations business units see this implementation as a business project with the software and IT resources as the enabler of better and more effective services.

The organization has two support units—corporate services (HR, finance, operations, CRM) and information services—and three business lines: retail services, commercial services, and investment products. A major organizational restructuring took place only two years ago. The introduction of this structure was largely successful, particularly in the corporate services units. However, there was little emphasis on managing the change issues during restructuring, and, as a result, some of the areas in the business lines are still coming to terms with the change and have become highly suspicious of new programs and initiatives that emanate from corporate services and information services. There is a perception that the "head office" is too concerned with it and does not take into account the needs of other areas and locations. In the past, employees and managers from various geographic locations have complained that the central administration has done a poor job of including or consulting them when decisions are being considered.

The organization includes an HR function and a separate payroll function that reports through to the finance function. HR and payroll currently use the same HRIS. The HR function was, until two years ago, a decentralized function, with many HR services staff reporting through to different business lines. Following the company-wide restructuring, the HR function was predominantly centralized so that the majority of staff now report through to the HR director. Some areas were not centralized and continue reporting to the relevant head of a business unit. After implementation, a new business model may be required to assist with a more complex and integrated system, particularly as the HRIS and the CRM system will share some aspects of the same database.

A major factor affecting the CRM system implementation is that the firm currently does not have staff sufficiently skilled in project management or in implementing a system of this size and complexity. It has looked to external organizations to assist it in implementing the new systems. ABC Finance expects to gain a transfer of skills, knowledge, and methodologies to its own staff for the ongoing maintenance of the production system, so it may manage future upgrades and implementations.

The existing HRIS was poorly documented when it was implemented, and the vendor provided limited documentation. Because of the decentralized history of HR, data were input with various codes and into various fields; that is, there was no consistency in the way data were recorded. It is a well-known fact that the data in the current IS are neither up to date nor correct. The HR data in the current system carry little credibility in the company.

Furthermore, the software vendor has advised of an upgrade to its product that is nearing completion. This upgrade will provide for additional functionality that will support the objectives of process efficiency, cost reduction, and the use of the Web and work flow management tools at no extra cost. It is known that the software provider has a history of not delivering new versions on time and that these can sometimes be shipped with "bugs."

The project has a fixed budget. Although there are some contingency funds, it is expected that these will be for emergency issues only, such as unforeseen costs within the existing scope. Although the HRIS/CRM implementation is still some time off, the PM team needs to make a decision soon on the postproduction support model. Previously, each system had its own support team. The team is considering an integrated support model in which staff members are multiskilled in each of the major areas—HR/payroll, finance, and CRM. This model would necessitate another round of company-wide restructuring.

Obviously, ABC Finance has undergone significant change in the past few years, and all staff are feeling some change fatigue. However, there is a significant commitment to managing the change process as part of this project. A change management team has been appointed comprising training and communication staff.

Case Study Questions

1. What PM approaches, techniques, and tools that have been discussed in this chapter can be applied to aid this organization in successfully managing the HRIS project?

2. It is often said that people factors are more important in technical project success than technology. From this perspective, explain the contribution that the HRM department can make to the management of this project.

3. Prepare a list of critical success factors that you think are most important for this project and compare them with the list presented in this chapter.

STUDENT STUDY SITE

Visit the Student Study Site at **http://www.sagepub.com/kavanagh3e** for additional learning tools such as access to SAGE journal articles and related web resources.

NOTE

1. This example of a Gantt chart, Figures 6.1 and Figure 6.2, was obtained from Wikipedia (http://en.wikipedia.org/wiki/Gantt_chart, accessed February 5, 2013).

REFERENCES

Belardo, S., Ballou, D. P., & Pazer, H. L. (2004). Analysis and design of information systems: A knowledge quality perspective. In K. V. Anderson & M. T. Vendelo (Eds.), *The past and future of information systems* (pp. 43–60). New York: Elsevier.

Bondarouk, T., & Meijerink, J. (2010, August). *Implementation of an HR portal: Results of a qualitative study from a public sector organization.* Paper presented at the annual meeting of the Academy of Management, Montreal.

Browne, G. J., & Rogich, M. B. (2001). An empirical investigation of user requirements elicitation: Comparing the effectiveness of prompting techniques. *Journal of Management Information Systems, 17*(4), 223–249.

Ceriello, V. R., & Freeman, C. (1991). *Human resource management systems: Strategies, tactics, and techniques.* New York: Lexington Books.

Dery, K., Hall, R., & Wiblen, S. (2010, August). *Human resource information systems: Constraining human agency and implications for HR skills.* Paper presented at the annual meeting of the Academy of Management, Montreal.

Dulebohn, J. (2010, August). *Assessing cross-functional teams in ERP/eHR implementation projects.* Paper presented at the annual meeting of the Academy of Management, Montreal.

Ewusi-Mensah, K. (1997). Critical issues in abandoned information systems projects. *Communications of the ACM, 40*(9), 74–80.

Gantt chart. (2011). *Wikipedia: The free encyclopedia.* Retrieved from http://en.wikipedia.org/wiki/Gantt_chart

Grant, D., Newell, S., & Kavanagh, M. J. (2010, August). *Realizing the potential of an HRIS: Unintended consequences, human agency, and the HR function.* Symposium presented at the annual meeting of the Academy of Management, Montreal.

Grossman, R. J. (2009). Managing the people who manage the projects. *HR Magazine, 54*(8), 12–16.

Henson, R. (1996, November). HRIMS for dummies: A practical guide to technology implementation in human resource information management system. *HR Focus, 73*(11), 3–5.

Josler, C., & Burger, J. (2005). Project management methodology in human resources management. *College and*

University Professionals HR Journal, 56(2), 25–30.

Kavanagh, M. J. (Chair & Presenter). (2001, August). *Planned change of information technology in the NYS probation department.* Professional Development Workshop presented at the annual meeting of the Academy of Management, Washington, DC.

Kavanagh, M. J., Gueutal, H. G., & Tannenbaum, S. I. (1990). *Human resource information systems.* Boston: PWS-Kent.

Koch, C. (2002). Hershey's bittersweet lesson [Electronic version]. *CIO Magazine.* Retrieved from http://www.cio.com/article/31518

Kotter, J. P. (1996). *Leading change.* Boston: Harvard Business School Press.

Lance, C. E., Kavanagh, M. J., & Brink, K. E. (2002). Retraining climate as a predictor of retraining success and as a moderator of the relationship between cross-job retraining time estimates and time to proficiency in the new job. *Group & Organization Management, 27,* 294–316.

Lemon, W. F., Bowitz, J., Burn, J., & Hackney, R. (2002). Information systems project failures: A comparative study of two countries. *Journal of Global Management, 10*(2), 28.

Lewin, K. (1951). *Field theory in social science.* New York: Harper & Row.

Luecke, R. (2003). *Managing change and transition.* Boston: Harvard Business School Press.

Martinez, C. (2010). Strengthen your company's pulse with six sigma tools and methodologies. *Workforce Solutions Review,* 1, 6–12.

Nelson, E., & Ramstad, E. (1999, October 29). Trick or treat: Hershey's biggest dud has turned out to be its new technology—at the worst possible time, it can't fill its orders, even as inventory grows—kisses in the air for Kmart. *The Wall Street Journal,* A1.

O'Brien, J. A., Crnkovic, J., & Belardo, S. (2006). *Management information systems.* New York: McGraw-Hill.

Peltier, J. (2008). Gantt charts in Microsoft EXCEL. *TechTrax, 3*(4), Article 3. Retrieved from http://pubs.logicalexpressions.com/Pub0009/LPMArticle.asp?ID=343

Rampton, G. M., Turnbull, I. J., & Doran, J. A. (1999). *Human resources management systems: A practical approach.* Scarborough, ON: Carswell.

Six Sigma. (2010). *Wikipedia: The free encyclopedia.* Retrieved from http://en.wikipedia.org/wiki/Six_sigma

Spirgi, H. (2009). Charting a new course for your human capital management journey. *IHRIM.link, 14 (June/July),* 5–8.

Tansley, C. (2010, August). *Project team branding on global human resources information systems projects.* Paper presented at the annual meeting of the Academy of Management, Montreal.

Tracey, B., Tannenbaum, S. I., & Kavanagh, M. J. (1995). Applying trained skills on the job: The importance of the work environment. *Journal of Applied Psychology, 80,* 239–252.

Velada, R., Caetano, A., Michel, J. W., Lyons, B. D., & Kavanagh, M. J. (2007). The effects of training design, individual characteristics, and work environment on transfer of training. *International Journal of Training and Development, 11*(4), 282–295.

Walker, A. J. (1982). *HRIS development: A project team guide to building an effective personnel information system.* New York: Van Nostrand Reinhold.

Wexley, K. N., & Latham, G. P. (2002). *Developing and training human resources in organizations* (3rd ed.). Upper Saddle River, NJ: Prentice Hall.

Wiest, D., & Levy, J. (1969). *A management guide to PERT/CPM.* Englewood Cliffs, NJ: Prentice Hall.

HRIS Effectiveness Measures and HRM Advice for HRIS Implementation

CHAPTER 7

HR Metrics and Workforce Analytics

Kevin D. Carlson and Michael J. Kavanagh

EDITORS' NOTE

The capacity to manage is limited by the type and quality of data available to managers. Better information about the expectations of customers, the actions of competitors, and the state of the economy provides strong foundations for setting the strategic direction of organizations. Information about levels of output, for example, numbers of defects and efficiency of processes, positions line managers to produce high-quality products in the right amounts at the right time to meet customer needs. The same is true for the effective management of human capital in organizations. In "Future Insights" the Society for Human Resources argues "The development of deeper levels of analysis to monitor metric outcomes, identify trends, leverage positive outcomes and intervene in or mitigate negative outcomes will lead to better overall human capital management" (Society for Human Resource Management [SHRM], 2012, p. 6). As discussed in this chapter, effective approaches to the measurement of human capital and its impact on organization processes enables both HRM professionals and line managers to make better decisions about HRM programs, like recruitment, for example, to increasing organizational effectiveness. This is accomplished by focusing on the development of systems of workforce analytics and supporting HR metrics that meet the needs of organization decision makers. This chapter offers a brief history of the efforts involved in the development of HR metrics and workforce analytics and of how these efforts have been enhanced by the advent of integrated human resource information systems.[1] From benchmarking to operational experiments, the HRIS field is rapidly evolving on many fronts. These advances are changing how HR metrics and analytics are used in organizations, and, subsequently, their impact on organization effectiveness. The use of HR metrics and workforce analytics will help managers and organizations balance the costs and benefits consequences of decisions. These cost-benefit analyses are covered in Chapter 8.

CHAPTER Objectives

After completing this chapter, you should be able to

- Discuss the factors that have led to increased organizational interest in HR metrics and workforce analytics

- Discuss why the information from numeric systems like HR metrics and workforce analytics may fail to generate a return on investment (ROI) unless they lead to improved better decision making

- Discuss the difference between metrics and analytics

- Describe the limitations of the traditional HR metrics

- Discuss the historical role of benchmarking and its strengths and weakness today

- Discuss the roles that activities such as data mining, predictive analytics, and operational experiments play in increasing organizational effectiveness

- Discuss the differences between metrics and analytics used to assess efficiency, operational effectiveness, and organizational realignment, and offer examples of each

- Describe which characteristics of HR metrics and workforce analytics are most likely to have an organizational impact

HRIS IN ACTION

When Dan Hilbert arrived as manager of Employment Services at Valero Energy, he wasn't quite sure what he wanted or needed to do. Coming from a background in operations, he was used to having information about the effectiveness of all current operations; yet, as he quickly learned, these data were not available for HR operations and programs, nor were there systems in place to generate them. He recognized the potential value of having even simple descriptive statistics about the organization's people, and its operations—to highlight potential opportunities and how changes in these values could signal potential problems. However, since these data were not currently available or easily developed, he created a small team, consisting of one HR staff member who could help get access to data from the organization's current systems and a graduate student with a statistical background, who was hired as a part-time employee. The team's assignment was to collect data about the human capital in the organization in an effort to learn more about the organization and its people, which Dan was now charged with supporting.

The team's analysis highlighted a unique characteristic of the Valero workforce—all of its refinery managers were at least 55 years old. This meant that these managers, each with long tenure in one of the most critical positions for assuring operating success, would be eligible to retire in fewer than 10 years. Further, given that these managers had all joined the company at roughly the same time and had held these refinery manager positions for many years, the promotion pipeline for succession to this position was limited. In other words, promising managers who had joined the organization at lower managerial positions decided to leave the company when it was clear that upward opportunities were limited.

When Hilbert presented the results of this analysis and his conclusions to senior managers, they were shocked. No one had considered this issue of the aging of refinery managers, and, likely, management would not have become aware of the situation until the refinery managers began to retire. By then, it would have been too late to act to get immediate replacements. Interestingly, as Valero's success increased and the stock price increased, the retirement age lowered, compounding the problem. The pipeline of trained managers capable of filling these positions internally would not have been sufficient to meet the demand created by the mass retirements, and the time to train them as refinery managers was lengthy. As a result, the computation of relatively simple metrics and analytics provided new insights on the current retirement status of employees. This data allowed management to engage in the training and development needed to build internal bench strength for this critical position prior to these managers retiring, likely saving the refinery millions in salary expense and reduced refinery performance.

Introduction[2]

> I have found that the largest single difference between a great HR department and an average one is the use of metrics . . . bar none, there is nothing you can do to improve yours and your department's performance that exceeds the impact of using metrics.
>
> John Sullivan (2003)

Human resources (HR) metrics and **workforce analytics** have become a hot topic in organizations of all sizes. Interest is rising, and organizations are reaching out to learn more about, useful metrics and analytics and how they can use them to improve organizational effectiveness. Although the use of HR metrics and workforce analytics is not new, various factors are driving increased interest. An important driver is the widespread implementation of integrated HRISs. The adoption of these systems shifted what had been primarily paper-and-pencil processes to electronic processes and, as a result, greatly increased the capacity of organizations to access and examine transaction-level data. Today's HRIS builds on the capabilities of faster and more capable computers, improved connectivity through organizational networks and the Internet, and the availability of user-friendly analytics software. These changes have fundamentally altered the dynamics of human capital assessment in organizations, driving the marginal cost of assessment lower while providing the potential for near real-time analysis and distribution of information. These factors, combined with recent and growing interest in evidence-based management, account for the rapidly growing interest in HR metrics and workforce analytics.

A Brief History of HR Metrics and Analytics

Systematic work on the development of measures to capture the effectiveness of an organization's employees can be traced as far back as the days of scientific management (Taylor, 1911) and industrial and organizational psychology (Munsterberg, 1913). Methods of quantitative analysis and its use in decision making were developed during the build-up of both men and matériel occasioned by World War II. Further study and development occurred during the great post-war industrial expansion in the United States that continued into the 1970s. Many of the HR metrics used today were first considered and developed during this period (e.g., Hawk, 1967).

Widespread assessment of HR metrics did not occur until the pioneering work of Dr. Jac Fitz-enz and the early benchmarking work he conducted through the Saratoga Institute. In 1984, Fitz-enz published *How to Measure Human Resources Management,* currently in its third edition (Fitz-enz & Davidson, 2002), which is still a highly valued overview of many HR metrics and the formulas used to calculate them. A set of 30 metrics were developed through the joint efforts of the Saratoga Institute and the American Society for Personnel Administration (ASPA), the forerunner of the current Society for Human Resource Management (SHRM). These metrics are listed in Table 7.1. Initially, HR metrics were primarily used to measure or audit aspects of HR programs and activities as described by Cascio (1987) and Fitz-enz and Davidson (2002). Next, metrics began to be used to measure HR effectiveness. SHRM has identified a number of metrics that organizations can use in this way. These metrics comprise the HR Metrics Toolbox seen in Table 7.2 (SHRM, 2010). For example, absence rate, a measure of the extent to which employees are present each day to complete their work (Hollmann, 2002), can be calculated as follows:

[(# days absent in month) divided by (Avg. # of employees during mo.) times (# of workdays)] times 100 (Hollmann, 2002; Kuzmits, 1979). Another useful metric is cost per hire, which can be calculated as Cost per Hire (CPH) = the sum of external costs (recruiting) and internal costs (training new employees) divided by the total number of starts in a time period (SHRM, 2010). There are also more detailed approaches for the measuring and benchmarking of employees' behaviors such as turnover (Cascio, 2000),

Table 7.1 HR Metrics Toolkit (2010)

HR Metrics

Absence rate	[(No. of days absent in mo.)/ (Ave. no. of employees during mo.) × (No. of workdays)] × 100	Measures absenteeism. Determines if your company has an absenteeism problem. Analyzes why and how to address the issue. Analyzes further for effectiveness of attendance policy and effectiveness of management in applying policy. (See Hollmann, (2002)
Cost per hire	(Advertising + Agency fees + Employee referrals + Travel cost of applicants and staff + Relocation costs + Recruiter pay and benefits)/No. of hires	Costs involved with a new hire. Use *EMA/Cost per Hire Staffing Metrics Survey* as a benchmark for your organization. Can be used as a measurement to show any substantial improvements to savings in recruitment/retention costs. Determines what your recruiting function can do to increase savings/reduce costs, etc.
Health care costs per employee	Total cost of health care/Total employees	Per capita cost of employee benefits. Indicates cost of health care per employee. For benefit data from the Bureau of Labor Statistics (BLS). See BLS's publications titled *Employer Costs for Employee Compensation and Measuring Trends In The Structure And Levels Of Employer Costs For Employee Compensation* for additional information on this topic.

HR Metrics

HR expense factor	HR expense/Total operating expense	HR expenses in relation to the total operating expenses of the organization. In addition, determines if expenditures exceeded, met, or fell below budget.
		Analyzes HR practices that contributed to savings, if any.
Human capital ROI	(Revenue— (Operating expense –[Compensation cost + Benefit cost]))/ (Compensation cost + Benefit cost)	ROI ratio for employees. Did organization get a return on their investment? Analyzes causes of positive/negative ROI metric.
		Uses analysis as an opportunity to optimize investment with HR practices such as recruitment, motivation, training, and development.
		Evaluates if HR practices have a causal relationship in positive changes to improving metric.
Human capital value added	(Revenue— (Operating Expense –[Compensation cost + Benefit Cost]))/Total no. of FTE	Value of workforce's knowledge, skill, and performance. This measurement illustrates how employees add value to an organization.
Prorating merit increases	(No. of mos. actually worked/No. of mos. under the current increase policy) × Increase in percentage the person would otherwise be entitled to	The basic steps to calculate an employee's pay increase appropriate to the period of time worked.

(Continued)

Table 7.1 (Continued)

HR Metrics

Revenue factor	Revenue/Total no. of FTE	Benchmark to indicate effectiveness of company and to show employees as capital rather than as an expense. Human capital can be viewed as an investment.
Time to fill	Total days elapsed to fill requisitions/ No. hired	Number of days from which job requisition was approved to new hire start date. How efficient/ productive is recruiting function? This is also a process measurement. See *EMA/Cost per Hire Staffing Metrics Survey* for more information.
Training investment factor	Total training cost/ Headcount	Training cost per employee. Analyzes training function further for effectiveness of training (e.g., Has productivity increased as a result of acquiring new skills and knowledge? Have accidents decreased?). If not, evaluate the causes.
Training (ROI)	(Total benefit − Total costs) × 100	The total financial gain/benefit an organization realizes from a particular training program less the total direct and indirect costs incurred to develop, produce, and deliver the training program (see white paper Four Steps to Computing *Training ROI* [Lilly, 2001] for more information on this topic).
Turnover costs	Total of the costs of separation + vacancy + replacement + training	The separation, vacancy, replacement, and training costs resulting from employee turnover. This formula can be used to calculate the turnover cost for one position, a class code, a division, or the entire organization. *Exit interviews* (Drake & Robb, 2002) are a useful tool in determining why employees are leaving your organization (see white paper *Employee Turnover Hurts Small and Large Company Profitability* [Galbreath, 2000] for more information on this topic).

		Implements retention efforts. Evaluates if HR practices are having a causal relationship in positive changes to improving cost of turnover.
Turnover rate (monthly)	(No. of separations during mo./Avg. no. of employees during mo.) × 100	Calculates and compares metric with national average, using business and legal reports at www.bls.gov/jlt/home.htm. This measures the rate at which employees leave a company. Is there a trend? Has metric increased/decreased? Analyzes what has caused increase/decrease to metric.
		Determines what an organization can do to improve retention efforts. Evaluates if HR practices have a causal relationship in positive changes to improving metric. (See white paper titled *Employee Turnover: Analyzing Employee Movement Out of the Organization.*)
Turnover rate (annual)	([No. of employees exiting the job/Avg. actual no. of employees during the period] × 12)/No. of mos. in period	Calculates and compares metric with national average, using business and legal reports at www.bls.gov/jlt/home.htm. This measures the rate at which employees leave a company. Is there a trend? Has metric increased/decreased? Analyze what has caused increase/decrease to metric. Determines what organization can do to improve retention efforts. Evaluates if HR practices have a causal relationship in positive changes to improving metric. (See white paper titled Employee Turnover: Analyzing Employee Movement Out of the Organization.)
Vacancy costs	Total of the costs of temporary workers + independent contractors + other	The cost of having work completed that would have been performed by the former employee or employees less the wages and benefits that would have been paid to the vacant position(s).

(Continued)

Table 7.1 **(Continued)**

HR Metrics

	outsourcing + overtime—Wages and benefits not paid for vacant position(s)	This formula may be used to calculate the vacancy cost for one position, a group, a division, or the entire organization.
Vacancy rate	(Total no. of vacant positions as of today/Total no. of positions as of today) × 100	Measures the organization's vacancy rates resulting from employee turnover. This formula can be used to calculate the vacancy rate for one position, a class code, a division, or the entire organization.
Workers' compensation cost per employee	Total WC cost for year/Average no. of employees	Analyzes and compares (e.g., Year 1 to Year 2, etc.) on a regular basis. You can also analyze workers' compensation further to determine trends in types of injuries, injuries by department, jobs, and so forth. HR practices such as safety training, *disability management*, and incentives can reduce costs. Use metric as benchmark to show causal relationship between HR practices and reduced workers' compensation costs.
Workers' compensation incident rate	(No. of injuries and/or illnesses per 100 FTE/Total hours worked by all employees during the calendar year) × 200,000	The "incident rate" is the *number of injuries and/or illnesses* per 100 full-time workers. 200,000 is the base for 100 FTE workers (working 40 hours/week, 50 weeks/year.) The calculated rate can be modified depending on the *nature* of the injuries and/or illnesses. For example, if you wished to determine the lost workday case rate, you would include only the cases that involved *days away from work*.
Workers' compensation severity rate	(No. of days away from work per 100 FTE/Total hours worked by all	The "severity rate" is the number of days away from work per 100 FTE. To calculate the severity rate, replace the number of injuries and/or illnesses per 100 FTE from

HR Metrics

	employees during the calendar year) × 200,000	the incident rate calculation with the number of days away from work per 100 FTE. More information is available regarding the types of injuries, incident rates, and comparison with other SIC codes at www.bls.gov/iif/oshdef .htm#incidence.
Yield ratio	Percentage of applicants from a recruitment source that make it to the next stage of the selection process (e.g., 100 resumes received, 50 found acceptable = 50% yield)	A comparison of the number of applicants at one stage of the recruiting process with the number at the next stage. (*Note: Success ratio* is the proportion of selected applicants who are later judged as being successful on the job.)

Source: Adapted from Fitz-Enz, J. (1995) How to Measure Human Resources Management, 2nd Edition. New York, NY: McGraw-Hill, Inc.

as well as for creating HR metrics for programs such as employee assistance and work-life programs (Cascio, 2000).

Kaplan and Norton's (1996) introduction of the **balanced scorecard** (see Chapter 10) further refined managers' thinking about metrics. The balanced scorecard recognizes the limitations of organizations' heavy reliance on financial indicators of performance. Such measures focus on what has already happened rather than providing managers information about what *will* happen. Balanced scorecards focus on developing leading indicators of performance from several important perspectives, including customer satisfaction, process effectiveness, and employee development, as well as financial performance. In addition, the thinking required to develop balanced scorecards help managers identify sequences believed to lead to critical organizational outcomes.

About the same time, Huselid's 1995 work on high-performance work systems demonstrated that the systematic management of human resources was associated with significant differences in organizational effectiveness. This work provided evidence that human resource management did indeed have strategic potential. Becker, Huselid, and Ulrich (2001) helped

Table 7.2 **Measures in the Saratoga Institute/SHRM Human Resources Effectiveness Report**

Revenue per Employee

Expense per Employee

Compensation as a Percentage of Revenue

Compensation as a Percentage of Expense

Benefit Cost as a Percentage of Revenue

Benefit Cost as a Percentage of Expense

Benefit Cost as a Percentage of Compensation

Retiree Benefit Cost per Retiree

Retiree Benefit Cost as a Percentage of Expense

Hires as a Percentage of Total Employees

Cost of Hire

Time to Fill Jobs

Time to Start Jobs

HR Department Expense as a Percentage of Company Expense

HR Headcount Ratio—HR Employees: Company Employees

HR Department Expense per Company Employee

Supervisory Compensation Percentage

Workers' Compensation Cost as a Percentage of Expense

Workers' Compensation Cost per Employee

Workers' Compensation Cost per Claim

Absence Rate

Involuntary Separation

Voluntary Separation

Voluntary Separation by Length of Service

Ratio of Offers Made to Acceptances

Source: Adapted from Fitz-enz, J. (1995). *How to measure human resources management* (2nd ed.). New York: McGraw-Hill.

bring these ideas together in the HR scorecard, which highlights how the alignment of HR activities with both corporate strategy and activity improve organizational outcomes.

Limitations of Traditional HR Metrics

Unfortunately, while the computing, communications, and software infrastructure supporting HR metrics and analytics has undergone dramatic change since the late 1990s, the metrics themselves have not. Current computing operations are capable of capturing data on a wide range of electronically supported HR processes, extracting, analyzing, and then distributing that information in real time to managers throughout the organization. However, currently popular HR metrics were developed before current computing infrastructures existed. As a consequence, recognizing what data most organizations could easily and inexpensively gather played an important role in identifying which metrics could reasonably be included in benchmark studies. A quick perusal of the metrics listed in Table 7.1 highlights the early emphasis on readily available data, most of which came from accounting systems.

Consequently, these metrics emphasize costs or easily calculated counts (e.g., headcount, turnover) that often serve as proxies for costs. Every managerial decision has **cost and benefit consequences**, whether we recognize them or not. As a result, when metrics and analytics systems only provide information about costs, they are of limited value to managers. If managers are only provided information about costs, with little or no information about benefits, costs are likely to become the primary driver of managerial decisions. This perpetuates the still-common perception of HR as a "cost center." Thus, information on benefits from a managerial decision must also be known in order to conduct an estimated return on investment (ROI) for the decision.

A second limitation of early metrics efforts is that they tended to aggregate data to the level of the organization. As such, they offer limited information that could be used to identify and diagnose within-organization differences. Organizational turnover rates, for example, are heavily influenced by the turnover rate in the organization's dominant job category, masking any differences in turnover rates for jobs with fewer incumbents.

Finally, early efforts only provided data after events had occurred. This results in slow responses to problems or opportunities. Because they provide data "after the fact," these are described as "feedback" metrics. Feedback metrics can be effectively used to signal problems, but they are suboptimal as a primary source of data because they do not support real-time remedial action to minimize any negative effects.

Contemporary HR Metrics
and Workforce Analytics

Using HR Metrics and Workforce Analytics

While benchmarking is still done, the field of HR metrics and workforce analytics is expanding and evolving. Workforce analytics has become an umbrella term that encompasses a wide range of activities and processes.

HR Metrics

There is a fundamental distinction between HR metrics and workforce analytics. HR metrics are data (numbers) that reflect some descriptive detail about given processes or outcomes, for example, success in recruiting new employees. In the domain of human resources, these reflect characteristics of the organization's HR programs and activities.

Workforce Analytics

Workforce analytics refer to strategies for combining data elements into metrics and for examining relationships or changes in metrics. Understanding these combinations is done to inform managers about the current or changing state of human capital in an organization in a way that can impact managerial decision making. The importance of this view is that the analytics an organization needs depend on the problems and opportunities that currently face its managers. Understanding what opportunities and problems managers face suggest relevant analyses that can support better decisions. These analyses then determine what metrics the organization needs in order to compute these analyses and how those metrics should be calculated.

Benchmarking

The Saratoga Institute's **benchmarking** efforts were the first to develop information on standard HR metrics regarding the use and management of human capital. Benchmarking data is useful in that it provides insights into what is possible. However, a challenge in using HR metrics as benchmark data is that an organization's human resource practices and the use of its HR staff reflect current challenges facing that organization. As a result, most organizations have an HR department, but the specific functions performed by these departments vary widely across organizations. Consequently, direct comparisons of HR benchmarking data from one's own organization to data from other organizations may not provide realistic guidelines for either goal setting or forecasting the potential effectiveness of remedial actions an organization might undertake.

Data Mining and "Big" data

Interest in data mining human capital information has been on the rise since the implementation of integrated HRISs and digitized HRM processes. **Data mining** refers to efforts to identify patterns that exist within data and that may identify unrecognized causal mechanisms that can be used to enhance decision making. To identify these causal mechanisms, data mining uses correlation and multiple regression methods to identify patterns of relationships in extremely large datasets. An example would be the identification of a correlation between employee job satisfaction and employee turnover. Data mining has a number of important applications, but the caveat with its use is that it can also uncover spurious and nonsensical relationships (e.g., taller employees make better leaders; older employees have longer tenures).

Current interest in **big data** reflects efforts to analyze the extremely large datasets created by many transaction systems. Often these datasets can be many terabytes (2^{10} gigabytes) or more. Many Web-based applications and transaction sites, like those generated by Amazon.com, Google, and many social media sites, generate large numbers of transactions. Efforts in big data reflect attempts to mine these very large datasets for patterns that can provide addition insight for managers about customer preferences or process characteristics that managers can use to drive greater sales, increase customer satisfaction, and reduce costs. In many cases, this process involves analyses of quantitative data as well as qualitative analysis of unformatted text.

Predictive Analyses

Predictive analysis is the goal of many metrics and analytics efforts. Predictive analysis involves attempts to develop models of organizational systems that can be used to predict future outcomes and understand the consequences of hypothetical changes in organizations, for example, a change in existing organizational systems. To continue the simple example above, if the organization discovered a correlation between employee job satisfaction and turnover, HR could use this data to suggest modifications to the employees' work situation or their benefits. Efforts to develop balanced scorecards are examples of elementary predictive systems. They involve identifying leading indicators of important organizational outcomes and the nature of the relationships expected to lead to them. Engaging in efforts to test the assumptions in these models over time can lead to enhancements in the quality of the models' underlying predictive analyses, either by identifying additional leading indicators or better specifying the nature of the relationships between predictors and outcomes.

Operational Experiments

The evidence-based management movement argues that managers should base their decisions on data drawn from the organization and evidence about the actual functioning of its systems rather than using personal philosophies or untested personal models or assumptions about "how things work." One of the most effective methods for developing the evidence on which to base decisions is through **operational experiments** conducted within the organization. Ayres (2007) describes how Google uses operational experiments to test the effectiveness of the ad words used on its website. Rather than simply relying on intuition or "expert judgment" about which ad wording is more effective, it creates an experiment. It configures its site to alternate the presentation of competing ad text to visitors to its site and then tracks the number of "click-throughs" on the ad for a period of time. Given the large number of daily hits, Google can get objective data on the effectiveness of the various ads in a relatively short time and then adopt the ad wording demonstrated to be most effective.

Workforce Modeling

Workforce modeling attempts to understand how an organization's human capital needs would change as a function of some expected change in the organization's environment. This change may be a shift in the demand for the organization's product, entry into a new market, divestiture of one of the organization's businesses, or a pending acquisition of or merger with another organization. This process involves establishing a human resources planning (HRP) program, which is covered in more detail in Chapter 11.

HR Metrics, Workforce Analytics, and Organizational Effectiveness

Changes in both the analyses conducted and the metrics utilized allow organizations to take advantage of today's more capable assessment infrastructures. Despite reporting more metrics with greater frequency to a wider group of managers, many HR professionals tasked with this reporting question whether these efforts have had a significant impact on organization effectiveness. Often, these individuals report frustration with their inability to get managers to (a) tell them what information they need, (b) use the HR metrics information included in existing reports, or (c) even acknowledge receipt of the reports. These perceptions represent a fundamental opportunity to improve the approach organizations take toward the utilization of metrics and analytics.

A Common and Troublesome View

Many managers perceive the increased interest in metrics and analytics as simply a mandate to compute and report more metrics. The assumption behind this perception is that assessing and reporting HR metrics results in better organizational performance. But it is not clear that generating and reporting more HR metrics will necessarily result in better individual, unit, or organizational performance. In fact, this link between HR metrics, for example, between voluntary turnover and an organizational performance metrics like **revenue per employee (RPE)**, has not been very well established.

In addition, a common perspective adopted in many organizations is that data elements lead to metrics. These metrics can then be combined in various analyses that can then be reported to managers who use the information in these analyses to drive decision making. This view was dominant in the development of many metrics and analytics over the last decade. However, the problem with this approach is that it is not clear which data elements are relevant, and there is no basis for guiding how they should be combined into metrics, or how those metrics should contribute to analytics. These types of approaches to metrics have two common and predictable outcomes. First, individuals tasked with developing and reporting HR metrics in organizations struggle to determine which metrics to report and how those metrics should be calculated. Second, as a result of the first outcome, these organizations subsequently report large numbers of metrics, which ultimately have little or no impact on decision making and, therefore, offer no return to the organization.

A more effective approach is to start with the problems or opportunities faced by the organization and develop an understanding of what information is likely to be useful to managerial decisions. An understanding of these problems permits organizations to determine effectively the analytics that are most likely to be useful in improving organizational effectiveness. These analytics then determine which metrics are relevant to the analysis and which data elements need to be incorporated into the analysis. The difference in these two approaches is dramatic. The latter one is targeted at specific managerial decision situations while the first one does not have this focus.

This approach is reflected in Figure 7.1. All organizations have ultimate outcomes of interest. For profit businesses, these ultimate outcomes center on some combination of revenues and costs. But how those outcomes are achieved is often the result of complex sequences of processes that form causal chains producing the outcome of interest. For example, generating a high-performing sales force requires that high-potential salespeople first recognize sales as a potential career, then they must apply for sales positions when they become available, and they must be recognized as potential high performers during selection processes. Next, they must accept job offers when they are extended, be effectively on-boarded to the organization, trained effectively, and appropriately supervised so that they choose to remain with the organization. Each of these data points reflects an intermediate outcome that may be influenced by earlier outcomes and may influence subsequent outcomes. Further, each outcome itself may be capable of being influenced by the actions of an organization's employees. Linking these outcomes creates a framework of useful organizational metrics and analytics. These intermediate outcomes are potential avenues for influencing ultimate outcomes, and tracking relevant metrics can give managers the capability to determine where managerial intervention may be most effective.

Figure 7.1 is a graphic display of this sequencing from data points to HR metrics and finally to organizational metrics—the Ultimate Outcome in Figure 7.1. For example, it has been argued that RPE is not a good organizational metric because it does not reflect the investment effort or input required to achieve the output (Lermusiaux, 2006). Lermusiaux argues for a new metric, **return on workforce (ROW)**, which monitors and best reflects the value that the total talent returns to the organization. ROW is calculated as: Return on workforce = Operating income divided by/total labor cost. This organizational metric could start with data points, for example, successful recruiting ratio defined as total recruiting/successful hires, which would begin the action-outcome sequence seen in Figure 7.1. Then the identification of the action-outcome sequence leading to ROW could be determined by working backward from ROW, which would constitute the Ultimate Outcome. Of course, there are statistical analyses, like regression, that could be used to define the outcomes at each step, but they require historical data on all the HR programs.

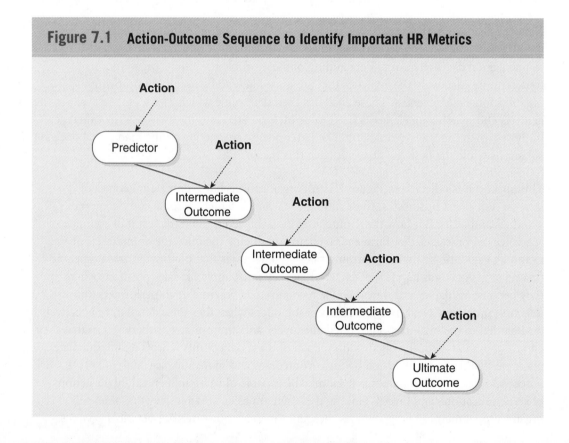

Figure 7.1   Action-Outcome Sequence to Identify Important HR Metrics

Better Problem Solving and Decision Making

HR metrics and analytics comprise an information system, and information systems can only have an impact on organizations if, as a result of the information they receive, managers make different and better decisions than they would have without that information. No information system, including HR metrics and analytics, generates any return on the investment unless managers change their decision behavior for the better. If managers do not make different and better decisions as a result of the information reported to them, the time and effort expended in conducting and reporting HR metrics and analytics is wasted.

The emphasis on improving managerial decisions changes the dynamics driving metrics and analytics assessment efforts; that is, it raises the bar. It is not simply good enough to "do" metrics and analytics. These activities need to be approached in a way that increases the possibility that access to the information from these efforts will change managerial decisions, making them more effective. A fundamental problem is that many of the currently popular HR metrics do not provide a clear impact on important managerial decisions. The challenge, therefore, is to identify metrics and analytics that provide managers with the information they need to make better decisions regarding the acquisition and deployment of an organization's human capital.

In organizations, decisions result in tactical choices. These choices may be among alternative tactics to achieve specific outcomes or in response to specific problems. The choices could also involve the decision to adopt a standard response, as compared to trying something new, or to take no action at all. Making these decisions requires three things: (1) understanding the outcomes that one is attempting to achieve, (2) understanding the factors that influence those outcomes and their current states, and (3) knowing available tactical options and their costs. For any information system, including an HRIS that can produce metrics and analytics, improving decision making requires that these sources of information influence decision makers to choose to make different and better decisions.

Opportunity Domains of HR Expertise

Excellence in human resources functioning requires three sets of expertise. These are depicted in Figure 7.2. *First,* an organization must have access to the knowledge in **HR centers of excellence** to potentially change the activities of HRM. This access to knowledge does not refer to information systems, but rather to the "know-how" required to deploy available human resource programs and tactics in recruitment, selection, job design, development, motivation, compensation, performance management, retention, safety, benefits, and regulatory compliance to accomplish the objectives of the organization and to improve organizational effectiveness. This knowledge exists in HR experts who understand new advancements in these programs and activities, as well as how and when they might be employed to improve effectiveness. This HR expertise might exist within an organization's full-time staff, or it might be found in consultants hired on a contract basis to assist the organization or in third-party vendors who take on responsibility for improving outsourced organization processes.

A *second* set of expertise exists in **HR business partners**. Whereas the centers of excellence represent the technical expertise of internal HRM professionals, these external business partners can work with managers from other functional departments (e.g., production, marketing) to examine the organization's business and processes to understand how HR programs can support these processes. This understanding allows them to identify opportunities to change HR programs and processes in ways that overcome problems affecting the operational functioning of their departments or that capture new opportunities. HR business partners can translate the activities of HRM to their situations in order to meet the specific needs of the organization. They work to identify when and how changes to HRM programs and processes can enhance organizational effectiveness. These business partners, along with the HR staff, can also use Six Sigma. **Six Sigma** focuses on business process reengineering, with the goal of improving the quality of process outputs (e.g., the annual turnover rate of employees) by identifying and removing the causes of defects (errors) and minimizing variability in business processes. Six Sigma is a structured approach for improving business (HR) processes through a step-by-step method labeled DMAIC, which stands for define, measure, analyze, improve, and control.

The *third* set of expertise is **administrative process efficiency**. This sort of **HR efficiency** refers to the capacity to conduct existing HRM processes accurately and on time while minimizing costs. Centralizing certain HRM processes, for example, recruiting new employees, offers process efficiency benefits. Only a limited number of individuals need to be trained on how to complete complex or detailed processes. This centralization is particularly valuable when a process is subject to dynamic legislative or administrative guidelines determined outside the organization. Centralizing processes can result in greater emphasis on continuous quality process improvement. The increased repetition of specific processes also fosters learning that can result in faster and more error-free execution.

HR Process Efficiency

Each of these three areas of expertise represents a separate domain in which organizations can conduct both metrics and analytics work. Currently, most metrics focus on the third set of expertise—administrative process efficiency. These metrics focus on how well the HR department accomplishes its critical processes to support organizational effectiveness.

Figure 7.2 Components of HR Functionality

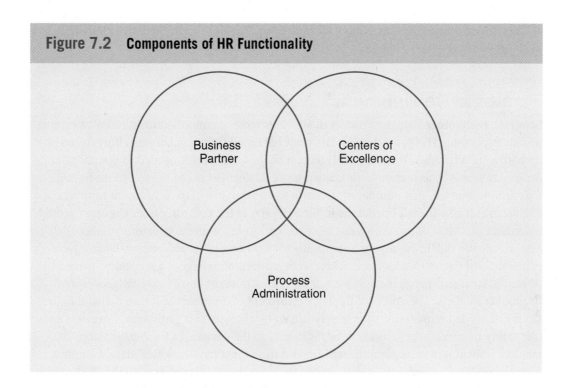

Metrics in this area might include cost per hire, days to fill positions, percentage of performance reviews completed on time, and HR department costs as a percentage of total costs or sales. However, process administration is only desired when the organizational processes are those that best support the company's operating departments in pursuit of their goals.

Organizational Effectiveness

HR metrics and workforce analytics focused on organizational process improvement are primarily focused outside the HR department. Here, the objective is to utilize the technical competence of the HR professionals in HRM regarding their understanding of how best to recruit, select, deploy, train, design jobs for, motivate, develop, evaluate, and retain employees in order to help organizational units more effectively accomplish their objectives. The outcomes are the business units' operational metrics, that is, percentage of on-time deliveries, operational downtime, lost time accidents, units sold, or cost per unit. Analyses will attempt to identify what changes in HRM practices can help organizations or specific business units improve their **operational effectiveness**. HR managers need to first identify what processes most effectively accomplish organizational objectives at multiple unit levels and then find ways to maximize the efficiency and effectiveness of the implementation of those processes in the organization. This task requires close coordination with the HR business partners in the company.

Strategic Realignment

Strategic realignment involves the set of activities most commonly known today as human resources planning (HRP; for more detail, see Chapter 11). These planning efforts focus on both long-term plans to assure replacement of the labor power needed to operate as an organization as well as planning for needed strategic changes in the organization. Boeing, for example, engages in a number of efforts to assure that it will have sufficient numbers of engineers available to staff operations in future years, as the company faces the approaching retirement of a large portion of its engineering workforce. Strategic realignment also extends the use of HRM analytics to planning for new situations and circumstances. New situations and circumstances occur when an organization undergoes a strategic change in direction, such as through merger, acquisition, divestiture, or entry into new geographic or product markets. The ability of the HR department to estimate the future demand and supply of needed human capital is largely driven by changes in organizational strategy, and this ability to forecast these future needs is crucial to the survival of the organization. To conduct human resources planning, the organization must have historical data, 10 years or more, on labor availability as well as section and turnover data of employees. In sum, all three areas of expertise are important. HR managers must be able to demonstrate their capacity to use metrics and analytics to manage their own operations well, and then others will be more likely to listen to their recommendations. HR managers and professionals must also work closely with their business partners in operational departments to help improve their capability to achieve their desired outcomes. Finally, using HR metrics and workforce analytics to improve decision making related to organizational effectiveness and strategic realignment can affect the organization's bottom line.

Measurement, Metrics, and Analytics Basics

Getting Started

When undertaking a metrics and analytics effort, the first question the organization needs to answer is, what problems in the organization are worth solving or what opportunities for enhancing organizational effectiveness exist? Organizations are awash in opportunities for increased effectiveness. Due to current improvements in computing and communications infrastructures, the effort and costs required to develop metrics for different opportunities may not differ dramatically. Thus, choosing to spend your time on projects with a greater potential return for the company makes good business sense. Given that most organizations' capabilities in HR metrics and analytics may not be well developed at this point, focusing on a limited number of potentially high-payback opportunities may be the best strategy associated with developing any new capability.

Once a problem and an opportunity are identified, the first step is to determine the organizational outcome that is associated with the problem. For instance, if the organization is struggling with getting orders shipped to its customers on time, an appropriate outcome metric will measure the extent to which the organization ships its orders on time. If an organization is concerned with the amount of time positions remain vacant before a new employee is hired, a measure of the amount of time positions remain vacant or the total time required to fill positions may be the appropriate outcome measure.

Outcome measures capture the extent to which a problem exists and should provide an indication of the extent to which actions taken by the organization are successful. Organizations are also interested in factors that cause these outcomes, and we will turn our attention to these shortly. Our first focus, though, is identifying the outcomes that matter.

The Role of "Why?"

Management scholars have theories of how organizations work. Most organizational members have their own personal theories regarding how their companies work. These theories provide a framework for identifying potentially important information, focusing attention on environmental stimuli, and strengthening the capacity to identify the tactics that can be used to solve problems. However, choices for outcome measures to assess are often based on personal theories about how things work in the organization, theories that may not reflect reality. For example, company employees often identify intermediate outcomes, such as implementation of flexible work hours (flextime) or changes in supervisors, as outcomes of interest. Intermediate outcomes are those that are more immediate indicators of things that employees believe lead to more important outcomes, for example, changes in the two previous intermediate outcomes leading to a "much happier" workplace. However, in some cases, the intermediate outcomes may not be the best ones on which to focus. This situation occurs when changes in decisions impact intermediate outcomes but do not have the expected impact on the ultimate or distal outcomes.

An important test of the appropriateness of outcome metrics is the "why" test. When one considers a potential outcome variable, it is useful to ask why the organization is interested in that particular outcome. If the answer is because it impacts some other variable that influences an important outcome, for example, profitability, then care must be taken to assure that changing the intermediate (or proximal) outcome also impacts the distal outcome. Organizational factors such as pay and working conditions that have influence through their effects on intermediate variables are reasonable targets for assessment, particularly if we understand the subsequent impact these factors have on ultimate, distal, and more important outcomes. Often, changing factors such as pay and working conditions will impact intermediate outcomes but may not produce any effect on the ultimate outcome of company profitability.

Employee turnover of valued employees, for example, is often identified as an important organizational outcome due to the costs associated with it (Cascio, 2000). It is among the most frequently assessed and reported HR metrics in organizations. Most managers agree that excessive turnover is a significant problem. High levels of turnover are disruptive to operations and can cause organizations to lose the critical expertise and capabilities of employees that leave. The answer to "why" turnover is important is that it disrupts operations and leads to potential loss of knowledge and important skill sets. But, in many cases, it is not clear whether the departure of specific employees actually results in decreasing profits. In some cases, a departing employee is replaced by a stronger performer, which will enhance profits. At a minimum, asking "why" helps highlight the potential causal sequence through which these intermediate variable effects are expected to have their influence. These analyses can highlight which metrics are likely to be more critical and provide a framework for understanding how change in these metrics should be interpreted.

Putting HR Metrics and Analytics Data in Context

Reporting HR metrics data alone is ineffective in leading to improvement in managerial decision making. Data points representing important organizational outcomes become useful when the decision maker can attach some meaning to them. Often data will need to be placed in context. For example, knowing that an organization's turnover level for newly hired management trainees is 13% is more meaningful when it can be placed in the context of the organization's previous turnover history for this position. Is turnover rising or falling for this position, and, if so, how quickly? Reporting trend information for metrics is one way to provide the context that gives meaning to the data, thus creating useful information.

Benchmarking is a second method for adding context to an organization's metrics. Data on metrics from other organizations in the same industry can provide information that offers insight into an organization's performance relative to its peers. However, not all companies are organized in the same way. As a result, and particularly for HR metrics, how the HRM function is structured in an organization can have a significant impact on the value of HR efficiency metrics. A department with a more centralized structure of HR functions typically has lower efficiency metrics than HR departments structured such that more of the responsibility for HR processes and activities exists in operating units. As a result, HR benchmarking data need to be considered in the context of how the organization has structured the HR function. Senior management needs to ensure that the HRM function is supporting organizational effectiveness. Then, the HR organization can be structured in order to maximize HRM effectiveness in supporting organizational objectives. HR effectiveness measures can then be maximized within the context of that structure.

For these reasons, internal rather than external benchmarking will often provide more appropriate data for establishing operational objectives for the HR efficiency benchmarks. Although external data is useful, care needs to be taken to understand how HR functions and activities are structured in the organizations providing this data.

Reporting What We Find

In discussions with individuals who construct metrics and analytics reports, we hear a common concern: These individuals wonder *whether anyone pays any attention* to the reports they produce. Often, they send reports to managers and professionals and receive no feedback. Among those who do get positive feedback from the benchmark information are HR professionals who embed this data in an interpretation of what they mean for the organization. Reporting data in context is a key component of their success stories.

A substantial amount of metrics and analytics effort has focused on reporting. **Reporting** incorporates decisions about (a) what metrics will be reported; (b) how these metrics will be packaged; and (c) how, (d) when, and (e) to whom they should be reported. Effort has focused on attempting to identify what metrics an organization should use. However, trying to identifying what metrics should be reported without considering an organization's problems and opportunities misses the reasons for the metrics. How metrics should be reported focuses on depicting metrics for decision makers so that the "message" relevant to them has a greater probability of being understood.

How questions deal with choosing between distributing metrics to decision makers using e-mail or creating opportunities for decision makers to extract metrics as needed. This latter approach can be done by posting the metrics on company websites.

When questions deal with the timing and frequency of metrics reports. In some cases, reporting is currently done annually, quarterly, or monthly. Some organizations are also considering the possibility of real-time updating for some metrics.

To whom questions address who receives metrics data. To date, it is most common for metrics and analytics to be reported first to senior executives. However, there is a growing recognition that managers at lower levels of the organization may be able to make more immediate use of the information contained in these data in order to assist in tactical, operational decisions.

For individuals conducting metrics and analytics work, paying attention to the capabilities and needs of the targeted audience is critically important. The information reported must be relevant to the issues facing the managers who receive it. Further, simply providing numbers to managers is unlikely to be of much use to them until they can understand the meaning of the information for their decision situations. Consequently, the HR analyst must report the numbers but also provide an interpretation of what the data means for the manager's decision situation. Some HR analysts argue that the interpretation of metrics results is the central message that speaks to managers, which, in turn, is then supported by the numbers. When packaging a metrics analysis, then, we must understand the needs of the recipients and fit the data to the information needs of the decision maker.

HR metrics and analytics information can be reported in a number of ways. Generally, a combination of "push" and "pull" means of communication will work for most organizations. Push communications channels, such as e-mail, actively push information and analyses to the attention of managers. These channels are used for information that is time critical or that the manager is unaware of. **Push systems** are excellent for getting information to decision makers. However, sending irrelevant or poorly timed information through push systems can contribute to information overload and reduce managers' sensitivity to messages. As a result, they may only skim the information sent through push systems or, even worse, not attend to it at all.

Pull systems are ways of making information available to managers so that they can access any of it at a point in time when it will be most useful for their decision making. Examples include (1) posting HR metrics and analytics analyses and reports on internal company websites, (2) offering access to searchable information repositories, or (3) providing access to analytics tools as examples. These "pull" methods avoid the e-mail clutter associated with push systems, but pull systems can be ineffective because managers may not know what information is available or when or where to look for the information.

How frequently data are analyzed and reported is also an important consideration. The existence of an integrated HRIS, faster computing capabilities, more effective software, and advanced internal communication systems creates the capability to analyze and report information in real time for managers. How frequently data are reported and how narrowly data are packaged are also critical to supporting effective decision making. Creating reporting cycles that are too long risks losing opportunities to make changes in operations on the basis of the reported information. Aggregating too much data from subunits to higher-level units can result in the problem of causing differences between operating units, departments, or functions to be buried in the aggregated averages for the higher unit. This information for managers' work units must be available to support decision making.

HR Dashboards

A common form of reporting HR analytics data is in the form of a dashboard. Dashboards are an enriched component of reporting. **Dashboards** reflect efforts to align real-time analysis of organizational and HR processes as well as an increased capacity to aggregate organizational data. Dashboards also contain business unit analyses to permit managers to drill down to examine metrics on several levels within the organization. The dashboard allows users to maintain a current snapshot of key HR metrics. An example dashboard is found in Figure 7.3. Notice how the dashboard provides summarized graphical and tabular information for the executive, which they can use to make HR and employee decisions.

Infographs

In many instances, pictures can provide a more compelling way to present the story resulting from an analysis, particularly when that story is based on complex analyses that build upon insights from a number of different data sources. In those situations, many organizations find that **infographics** offer an effective alternative. Infographs combine a number of data

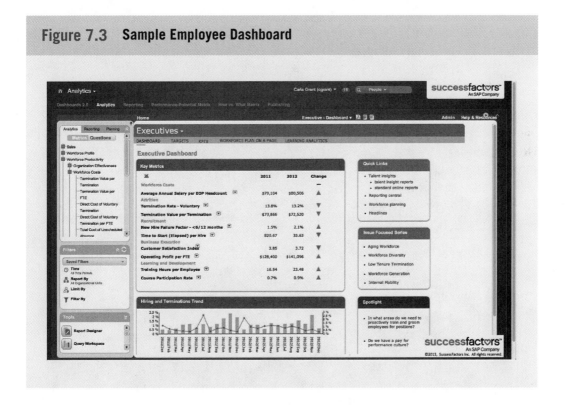

Figure 7.3 Sample Employee Dashboard

elements often incorporating pictures, figures, tables, and text to help tell a story more effectively than can be done by any of these elements. Some organizations, like the Pamplim Career Services at Virginia Tech, have used infographics like the one shown in Figure 7.4 to present data effectively in order to gain buy-in or to provide complex combinations of evidence needed to raise the awareness of managers about specific organizational opportunities or needed organizational changes.

Useful Things to Remember About HR Metrics and Analytics

Don't "Do Metrics"

The *primary objective* of developing capabilities in HR metrics and workforce analytics is *to increase organizational effectiveness.* It is not simply to generate a static menu of HR metrics reports. Simply conducting the analysis and developing reports are activities, and activities raise costs. Developing HR metrics and workforce analytics to be used by managers and

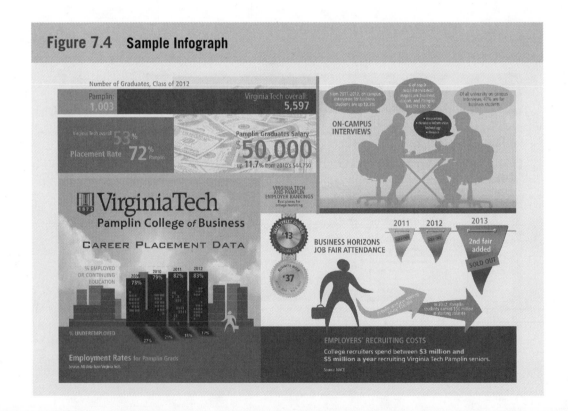

Figure 7.4 Sample Infograph

professionals must involve a return on the organization's investment. The real test of the value of HR metrics and workforce analytics is whether managers who have access to the information provided by these analyses make different and better decisions.

Bigger Is Not Always Better

The success of any metrics and analytics project is not measured by how many people are involved, how many metrics the project tracks, or how many people receive reports. It is gauged by the impact that the project's results have on managerial decisions. Many successful efforts have been focused on small, narrowly targeted metrics and analyses that have addressed organizationally important questions.

Small metrics and analytics projects have several advantages over the multimillion-dollar implementation projects that include integrated prepackaged analytics systems. First, they cost less and require fewer resources in terms of time and materials. Second, they are less visible during the initial start-up while the project team is learning through trial and error. These two aspects provide the project team with opportunities to focus on critical HR metrics while giving them the flexibility to work through the necessary trials and errors.

HR Metrics and Analytics Is a Journey—Not a Destination

Because the focus is on identifying and responding to opportunities and problems, useful and effective HR metrics and workforce analytics projects change over time. Markets for both products and labor will change, as will organizational processes. These changes will require adjustments in the ideal size, skill requirements, and deployment of an organization's human capital. If organizations are successful in solving operational problems or capturing opportunities, the focus for managers naturally shifts to other problems or new opportunities. These problems are unlikely to require the same analytics and therefore may depend on identifying new metrics.

Be Willing to Learn

Organizations that have an HR metrics and analytics function will develop a bias for experimentation to try out new HR activities, programs, or processes. One consequence of organizational life is the ongoing opportunity to recognize that there may be a better way to do things than your current approach. This point is true not only for the organization's operational processes but also for its metrics and analytics efforts. The organization should develop a metrics and analytics "laboratory" where the HRM professionals can experiment with new analyses and test existing assumptions about the requirements of the organization's current systems. This examination can foster new approaches and allow new metrics and analytics to be created.

Avoid the Temptation to Measure Everything Aggressively

Not every HR function, process, or metric that can be analyzed should be. Successful efforts will focus on those things, at a given point in time, that are most likely to have the greatest impact on managerial decision making. The intensity of an assessment project should be matched to how much opportunity it offers for improvements, and the project itself should be focused on factors, processes, and functions related to those things that are likely to have the greatest impact on organization effectiveness.

HR Metrics and the Future

The development of useful and effective HR metrics and workforce analytics is likely to be viewed in the future as a very significant source of competitive advantage. We now have the tools and the computing infrastructure to handle these projects that can help us understand organizations and support effective organizational functioning. By using HR metrics and workforce analytics, decision makers will acquire the ability to more effectively manage and improve HR programs and processes as well as to improve the effectiveness of HRIS use. Using this acquired ability, managerial decision makers may be able to modify entire employment systems to manage the company's human capital more effectively. Bintliff-Ritchie (2006) notes the following managerial benefits of metrics for organizations:

- Operational reporting is more efficient and cost-effective because the data from individual applications is integrated and accessed through a single solution.

- Graphically rich information is available to the people who need to make decisions and show metrics-based results.

- Real-time analytics demonstrate the true relationship between workforce investments and the organization's bottom-line financial, customer, and operational results.

- Human resources practices and investments can be optimized to meet enterprise performance goals.

As a result, organizations that make investments in internal human capital assessment resulting in useful HR metrics and workforce analytics will become less willing to share their knowledge with other organizations in their industry. Benchmarking, which has been a staple of HR metrics and workforce analytics for almost three decades, will become more difficult to access and develop as organizations recognize the competitive value of these capabilities.

SUMMARY

The central focus of this chapter was to define the domain of HR metrics and workforce analytics and discuss how they can contribute to improving organizational effectiveness. HR metrics are data elements that contribute to analyses that provide information to help decision makers in organizations make better decisions. HR metrics and analytics activities provide no return on the organization's investment unless managers make different and more effective decisions as a result of the information provided by metrics and analytics reports. Therefore, focusing the development of HR metrics and workforce analytics around organizationally important problems and opportunities is likely to increase the possibility of significant returns for the organization.

This chapter also highlights the wide range of activities that fall within the domain of HR metrics and workforce analytics. Although classic metrics still have value, new **computing infrastructures** offer tremendous opportunities to change both the metrics and types of analyses organizations undertake. We can expect the types of metrics organizations used in the future to change as the needs of decision makers change, and as these analyses continue to work toward effectively balancing the cost and benefit consequences of decisions (see Chapter 8). Components of this continued evolution of metrics and analytics capabilities are driven by increased use of both push and pull reporting systems, more extensive use of predictive analytics and operational experiments, and the development of organizational expertise in metrics and analytics capabilities. As these skills mature, organizations will be able to move beyond simple analyses of HR efficiency metrics to a greater emphasis on operational effectiveness and organizational realignment analyses, which will further enhance the value of HR metrics and workforce analysis systems.

KEY TERMS

DISCUSSION QUESTIONS

1. What factors have led to increased organizational interest in HR metrics and workforce analytics?

2. When might the information from numeric information systems such as HR metrics and workforce analytics *not* generate any return on investment (ROI)?

3. What relationships should exist between the metrics an organization chooses to calculate and report and the types of analyses it conducts?

4. What are some of the limitations of the traditional HR metrics?

5. Discuss the historical role of HR benchmarking and its strengths and weaknesses as part of a metrics and analytics program in organizations today.

6. What roles might more recent analysis activities, such as data mining, predictive statistical analyses, and operational experiments, play in increasing organizational effectiveness?

7. What differences exist between metrics and analytics that focus on HR efficiency, operational effectiveness, and organizational realignment? Offer examples of each.

8. Describe which characteristics of HR metrics and workforce analytics are likely to result in greater organizational impact.

CASE STUDY

Regional Hospital is a 500-bed hospital and several associated clinics in a major East Coast metropolitan area. It has been an aggressive adopter of computing technologies in efforts to decrease costs and improve operational efficiencies. A critical challenge facing the hospital is meeting its ongoing challenges to staff the hospital and allied clinics effectively, given the ongoing shortage of nurses; uncertainty in health care legislation; emphasis on shortening hospital stays to reduce costs, which causes the daily census (numbers of patients in various departments) to vary dramatically from day to day and shift to shift; the continued aging of the population in its primary care area; and the unending competition for employees with key skill sets. Employee expenses represent more than 80% of the overall costs of operation for the hospital, so identifying ways to match optimal skills and numbers of employees to the appropriate shifts is critical to achieving consistent success. However, individual shift managers struggle to make effective staffing decisions, resulting in consistent overstaffing or understaffing of shifts and departments. These staffing problems potentially increase the high costs of varied levels of patient care and satisfaction and potentially increase the risk that staff turnover may escalate because of dissatisfaction with the continuing inability of managers to match staffing needs to demand.

Company managers recognize the potential that HR metrics and analytics might have for their organization, and they have come to you for help. They are hearing from their peers in other hospitals that metrics can help in this area but are not quite sure where to start. They are looking for you to offer guidance on how to do HR metrics and workforce analytics.

Case Study Questions

1. Do you believe that a program of HR metrics and workforce analytics might be useful in Regional Hospital? If so, why?

2. What opportunities do you see regarding "where" and "how" metrics and analytics might be applied in this organization?

3. Identify three analyses and associated metrics you think might be useful for Regional Hospital to consider.

4. How might Regional Hospital utilize benchmarking as a part of its metrics and analytics effort, if at all?

5. What advice would you offer to the managers at Regional Hospital about developing a program of HR metrics and workforce analytics?

6. What potential problems might occur in the establishment of an HR metrics and workforce analytics program for Regional Hospital managers about which you would want to alert them prior to beginning this project?

STUDENT STUDY SITE _____

Visit the Student Study Site at **http://www.sagepub.com/kavanagh3e** for additional learning tools such as access to SAGE journal articles and related web resources.

NOTES _____

1. Throughout this chapter we will often refer to HR metrics and workforce analytics in a shorter form, as metrics and analytics. The meaning is the same.

2. The content of this chapter was based in part on two articles published in the *IHRIM Journal* (Carlson, 2004a, 2004b).

REFERENCES

Ayres, I. (2007). *Super crunchers: Why thinking-by-numbers is the new way to be smart.* New York: Bantam.

Becker, B. E., Huselid, M. A., & Ulrich, D. (2001). *The HR scorecard: Linking people, strategy and performance.* Boston: Harvard Business School Press.

Bintliff-Ritchie, J. (2006). Finding hidden gold using business intelligence to mine workforce data. IHRIM.*link,* June/July, 12–15.

Carlson, K. D. (2004a). Estimating the value of the indirect benefits of new HR technology. *IHRIM Journal, 8*(4), 22–28.

Carlson, K. D. (2004b). Justifying HRIS investments post Y2K: Identifying sources of value. *IHRIM Journal, 8*(1), 21–27.

Cascio, W. F. (1987). *Costing human resources: The financial impact of behavior in organizations* (2nd ed.). Boston: Kent.

Cascio, W. F. (2000). *Costing human resources: The financial impact of behavior in organizations* (4th ed.). Boston: Kent.

Drake, N., & Robb, I. (2002). *Exit interviews* (SHRM White Paper). Alexandria, VA: Society for Human Resource Management.

Fitz-enz, J. (1995). *How to measure human resources management* (2nd ed.). New York: McGraw-Hill.

Fitz-enz, J., & Davidson, B. (2002). *How to measure human resources management* (3rd ed.). New York: McGraw-Hill.

Galbreath, R. (2000). *Employee turnover hurts small and large company profitability* (SHRM White Paper). Alexandria, VA: Society for Human Resource Management.

Hawk, R. H. (1967). *The recruitment function.* New York: The American Management Association.

Hollmann, R. W. (2002). *Absenteeism: Analyzing work absences* (SHRM White Paper). Alexandria, VA: Society for Human Resource Management.

Huselid, M. A. (1995). The impact of human resource management on turnover, productivity, and corporate performance. *Academy of Management Journal, 38,* 635–672.

Kaplan, R. S., & Norton, D. P. (1996). *The balanced score card: Translating strategy into action.* Boston: Harvard Business School Press.

Kuzmits, F. E. (1979). How much is absenteeism costing your organization? *Personnel Administrator, 24*(6), 29–33.

Lermusiaux, Y. (2006). Key metrics drive talent management success. IHRIM.*link,* June/July, 7–10.

Lilly, F. (2001). *Four steps to computing training ROI* (SHRM White Paper). Alexandria, VA: Society for Human Resource Management.

Munsterberg, H. (1913). *Psychology and industrial efficiency.* Boston: Houghton Mifflin.

Society for Human Resource Management (SHRM). (2010). *HR metrics toolkit.* Alexandria, VA: Author.

Society for Human Resource Management (SHRM). (2012). Future insights: The top trends for 2012 according to SHRM's subject matter expert panels. Alexandria, VA: Author.

Sullivan, J. (2003). *HR metrics: The world class way.* Peterboro, NH: Kennedy Information, Inc.

Taylor, F. (1911). *The principles of scientific management.* London: Harper Brothers.

CHAPTER 8

Cost Justifying HRIS Investments

Kevin D. Carlson and Michael J. Kavanagh

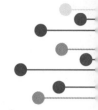

EDITORS' NOTE

Central to the decision to develop and implement a new or improved HRIS will be the costs and benefits of the investment. Like most consumers, HR professionals and managers are frequently awed by the new computer-based HR applications or the entire HRIS and make a purchase decision on the systems features. However, as discussed in this chapter,[1] without a comprehensive cost-benefit analysis (CBA), such purchases may not yield the desired results. As emphasized by several authors (Cascio, 1987, 1991, 2000; Fitz-enz, 2001; Kavanagh, Gueutal, & Tannenbaum, 1990), the language of business is dollars,[2] not just good feelings about an HRIS investment. The CBA for an HRIS investment needs to be made prior to purchase, early in the system's development life cycle. In fact, a preliminary, estimated CBA of an HRIS investment should be presented to senior management before any detailed work on the project is begun. This preliminary estimate should assist senior management in deciding whether or not the HRIS project should continue. A more detailed analysis can then be made as part of the needs analysis. The information in this chapter provides guidance for making CBA estimates as well as practical advice on how to make the CBA palatable to managerial decision makers. Finally, there is an emphasis on the value of the CBA and its documentation for the management of the project and its implementation.

CHAPTER Objectives

After completing this chapter, you should be able to

- Explain why a CBA is critical for a successful HRIS project
- Explain the differences between cost reduction and organizational enhancement as strategies for HRIS investments
- Explain how using guidelines for approaches to investment analysis will lead to a better HRIS project
- Identify the various costs and benefits in a CBA of an HRIS investment
- Explain the differences between direct and indirect benefits and costs
- Describe how to estimate costs and benefits, both direct and indirect
- Explain the difference between average employee contribution (AEC) and variance estimates for estimating values in a CBA, and understand why the difference between these indices is important for investment analysis
- Define and describe utility analysis as being built by alternate CBAs for different outcomes
- Discuss three common problems that can occur in an HRIS CBA

HRIS IN ACTION

An HRIS development and implementation project was being done by FarmforMore,[3] a U.S. manufacturer of farm machinery. FarmforMore has manufacturing operations in the major geographic regions of the United States, although a larger number of plants are situated in the Midwest. Its sales staff is also regionalized with sales offices in all major U.S. cities. FarmforMore currently has approximately 28,000 employees. The HRIS project was designed to have computer applications for 90% of the HR functionality, excluding payroll, which was outsourced to a vendor. The proposal emphasized the benefits of the new HRIS in terms of time saved for HR professionals as well as the timely reports designed for supervisors and managers. According to the project team, the costs, totaling $1.5 million, seemed reasonable considering the potential benefits.

The HRIS project began two years ago with a needs analysis and basic design, approval from the CEO, and the selection of the project team and steering committee.

The project team was led by the vice president of HRM, and steering groups had representatives from all regions of the country as well as from all major departments—finance, IT, HR, production, marketing, and research and development. A cost-benefit analysis was done. The major costs in the proposal were software, implementation costs, and the salaries of the project team's members. However, the project team indicated that time saved by computer-based transactions was the main cost-reduction benefit, estimated to save 14.3 full-time equivalent (FTE) budget lines, which would easily cover the costs of the new HRIS.

About eight months ago, there was information in a project team interim report that indicated the HRIS project was behind schedule and had some minor cost overruns. There did not seem to be much concern at the time since, even though the project was behind schedule, the project team was certain that the delay was due to developing better working relationships among team members. Plus, it had taken more time to transfer the basic employee information from the old system to the new one.

Two weeks later, the CEO sent a memo to the project team leader, the VP of HRM, to meet with her to determine whether the HRIS project was back on schedule and the cost overruns had been resolved. Unfortunately, the HRM VP reported that the project was now running about nine months behind schedule and so would need more funding to complete its tasks. This delay meant that the costs of the project had increased by 147%. The HRM VP could not really explain what had happened since the project team felt it had done a careful cost-benefit analysis. When the CEO looked at the cost-benefit analysis, however, she stated that her college-age son could have done a better job. Since there had been a downturn in national sales as well as profits, the CEO put the HRIS project on "hold."

Alternate HRIS in Action

In its 2012 Business Outcomes Study Report, SHL (2012) reports the results of 66 studies examining talent management strategies and their impact on metrics tied to specific organization goals. Of these, 88% report favorable or very favorable outcomes while 12% of the studies lacked sufficient data to be conclusive. None of the 66 studies reported negative results. The best of these offer evidence of dramatic returns possible from shifting talent management processes. Similar results are reported in other studies examining training, compensation, turnover, and a number of other changes in human resource processes.

The most interesting aspect of the results reported across these studies is that while there are still opportunities in organizations to reduce HRM costs by improving processes, the strongest returns are being generated by interventions that target the organizations' top line—increasing organizational effectiveness and revenue generation. Historically, HRIS cost-benefit analyses have emphasized the capacity of digitizing paper-and-pencil processes, creating online workflow including outsourcing and employee self-service to drive costs down. But in many ways, the larger opportunities in organizations are to be found in increasing effectiveness, rather than reducing costs, and this is not an area in which the HRIS field has historically been able to do well consistently.

The consequence of a cost-centric focus on justifications of HRM functionality is that it can lead to a systematic underinvestment in critical HRIS functionality—not because it does not add value, but because we are simply more comfortable telling and supporting investment decisions that reduce costs. Even without solid justifications for the capacity of HRIS functionality to move the top line, many organizations intuitively recognize the potential for those gains and make those investments anyway when the economy is good. But when things get tight in organizations, these investments, despite their potential, are the first to be cut because we don't have the evidence. Going forward, being able to provide solid evidence-based foundations for the improved effectiveness that results from HRIS investments will be a critical capability.

Introduction

In most organizations today, an HRIS provides the primary infrastructure used to deliver HR programs, ensure HR regulatory compliance, and produce the metrics that are used to evaluate not only the HR function but also the contribution of the organization's human resources to the accomplishment of firm-level strategic objectives. **HRIS functionality** continues to evolve and to expand—we no longer see the simple shifting of paper-and-pencil processes to their electronic equivalents but rather new capabilities that leverage the advantages of **integrated information systems** that are faster and more capable computing technologies. As a result, organizations are faced with new opportunities to extend their investments in HRIS functionality. HRIS functionality refers to the number of programs or functions—such as recruiting, compensation, and job analysis—that are operational using the specific HRIS configuration, as well as to the features of these programs that enhance their usability and capacity to affect outcomes. Thus, HRIS functionality could include all HR programs in a fully integrated system or only a number of the more important programs, for example, compensation and benefits. HRIS functionality typically varies with organizational size, with larger companies having a greater number of programs or functions in their HRIS configurations than smaller companies.

However, as discussed in Chapter 6, statistics measuring the success of HRIS projects are not very encouraging. The failures of the implementation of systems have been well documented (Browne & Rogich, 2001). Delays in projects and budget overruns as well as user dissatisfaction are some of the most common reasons for the failure of HRIS projects. Systems that are completed generally exceed cost estimates by more than 55% and time estimates by a factor of 2. In addition, only 13% of the systems projects that are completed are considered successful by the executives who sponsor them (Lemon, Bowitz, Burn, & Hackney, 2002). Further, there have been significant failure rates for the implementation of human resource information systems in major corporations that indicate HRIS projects need better planning and cost estimates (Bondarouk & Meijerink, 2010; Dery, Hall, & Wiblen, 2010; Dulebohn, 2010; Grant, Newell, & Kavanagh, 2010; Tansley, 2010). Many of these failures occurred because a **cost-benefit analysis (CBA)** was not done as part of the business case for the justification of the HRIS project. Historically, HRISs were justified because of their primary benefit of improving employee transactions, plus their potential to save HR time.

In the 1990s, CBA played only a limited role in HRIS investment decisions. The pending obsolescence of noncompliant systems in Y2K (Year 2000) fueled widespread implementation of new HRIS technology. The result was one of the most concentrated and dramatic shifts in HR practice ever. During this period, purchase decisions were driven by two primary criteria: Did new systems offer the **baseline functionality** required by the organization in a Y2K-compliant form, and could the systems be delivered and implemented on time? It was apparent that something had to be done to meet the potential problems of Y2K, and more fine-grained investment analyses would not have affected purchase decisions. Thus, many organizations chose not to invest the time and effort to complete an investment analysis. However, the business landscape has changed today. Many decision makers, some of whom are still waiting to see returns from past IT purchases in terms of successes and failures, are wary of new HRIS investments. Without an event like Y2K driving change, justifying new investments in HRISs will require strong business cases, that is, cost-benefit analyses (CBAs).

Justification Strategies for HRIS Investments

Strategies for justifying HRIS investments fall into two categories—*risk avoidance* and *organizational enhancement*. A **risk avoidance strategy** is used when investments are believed to eliminate or mitigate significant future risks faced by the organization, for example, generating reports of the gender and racial diversity of employees. The potential obsolescence of **legacy computing systems** was a prototypical risk avoidance scenario. The old system simply needed to be changed to avoid Y2K problems and also because it was out of date. The need to comply with laws and regulations (e.g., the Equal Employment Opportunity Act) and changes to these laws provide other circumstances in which justification based on risk avoidance is popular. Risk avoidance justifications focus on the magnitude and probability of risks and often are not supported by the extensive investment analyses required by a CBA.

Organizational enhancement strategies, on the other hand, highlight how the effectiveness of the firm will be improved by the addition of a new or improved HRIS—as measured by increases in revenues or reductions in costs such as voluntary employee turnover. Organizational enhancement justifications are often more challenging to "sell" to decision makers than risk avoidance ones because enhancements do not carry the threat of real loss if no action is taken. Hence, there is often a reduced sense of urgency. This situation is supported by research on decision making under risk that consistently demonstrates that, when faced with potential losses, decision makers are willing to accept much greater risk; in other words, they become more risk seeking and willing to make investments to avoid losses than when investment alternatives are framed as gains (Kahneman & Tversky, 1979). Investments justified by organizational enhancements typically require more rigorous support and are subjected to more intense scrutiny by decision makers.

Evolution of HRIS Justification

Several factors suggest that the next generation of HRIS functionality will be more difficult to justify. Much of the "low-hanging cost reduction fruit" has already been picked due to the Y2K implementation "scare." HRIS implementations in the past decade have shifted many organizations from administratively intense paper-and-pencil HR processes to electronic transaction processing supported by integrated computer systems. Employee and applicant self-service, online recruitment, electronic payroll processing, and work flow software have dramatically reduced transaction costs. Employee self-service alone is reported to reduce the cost of many HR transactions by 50% or more. These changes were the low-hanging cost reduction fruit mentioned previously. The next wave of HRIS functionality is unlikely to generate comparable reductions in costs, making investment decisions based on further cost reductions more difficult to justify.

Of course, there will be small and medium-size organizations that still have paper-and-pencil systems or HRIS legacy systems that need to be updated. For many of these organizations, the value of reducing costs, such as transactions costs, will still serve as legitimate justification for adopting or upgrading an HRIS. In addition, these firms may also use a risk avoidance approach to justify the new HRIS—for example, the need for accurate and timely employee records in litigation. However, as will be argued in this chapter, the use of an organizational enhancement approach, which incorporates a revenue enhancement and **cost reduction strategy**, may provide a powerful means of determining the cost-benefit analysis (CBA) for investment in a new HRIS.

It is therefore less certain that organizations with an operational HRIS will continue to pursue investments in new HRIS functionality aggressively. In fact, underinvestment in HRIS—that is, failing to approve many worthwhile investments—is likely. This underinvestment will not occur because the benefits of new investments in HRIS functionality are too small—in absolute terms, they are still substantial.

This underinvestment in HR functionality is more likely to result from the use of outdated CBA methodologies that emphasize cost reduction and do not adequately recognize the value of organizational enhancements attributable to important new HRIS functionality. HRIS managers will need tools so they can identify the sources of value to the organization that will result from HRIS investments. The field is maturing, and investment analysis tools must mature with it. This chapter examines HRIS cost-benefit dynamics and provides tools and techniques that can be used to conduct and evaluate HRIS CBAs that incorporate organizational enhancement.

Approaches to Investment Analyses Make a Difference: Some Guidelines

As discussed previously, one *must* conduct an **investment analysis**, frequently referred to as "making the business case" (Mayberry, 2008), for the acquisition of a new or improved HRIS. Usually, there is an HR or HRIS professional with selected team members who form the **HRIS project team**, as described in Chapters 3 and 6. This project team, or usually a subset of it, conducts the analyses and can be referred to as the CBA team. The members of this team include senior professionals from the HR and IT departments as well as representatives from other departments who will be affected by the HRIS project. The CBA is one of the first steps in seeking initial approval from senior management for an HRIS project. It is important to recognize that a proper perspective has as much to do with conducting an effective HRIS investment analysis as do the tools and techniques used. Understanding why the analysis is being conducted and understanding the expectations of what is going to be done with the results will influence the judgments made by both the CBA and the entire HRIS project team during the analysis, as well as increase the value of the results produced. It is important that the CBA team be representative of the project management team to ensure the complete involvement of all operational departments and maintain communications between the two teams. In addition, here are several considerations or guidelines that can help the CBA team approach the analysis with an improved likelihood of making the best decision for the organization. These guidelines are contained in Table 8.1. We will briefly cover each of these **CBA guidelines**.

The objective for conducting a CBA is to improve organizational effectiveness. The primary purpose of each analysis is to make the best decision for the organization. In some instances, the best decision may be not to proceed with an investment. Making an investment should never be the ultimate objective. The desired outcome is to become a more effective organization, not simply *to justify a purchase.*

Be honest with yourself. The CBA team should enter each analysis with an open mind—not with a solution to justify. It is best to think of the analysis as an investigation devoid of any

Table 8.1   Guidelines for Successful HRIS Cost-Benefit Analysis (CBA)

Key	Description
The objective is improving organizational effectiveness.	The objective of any HRIS CBA is not to purchase specific hardware or software. The objective is to improve organizational performance.
Be honest with yourself.	Start each analysis with an open mind, not an investment to justify.
Focus on functionality, not products.	The analysis should focus on the improvement in organizational functionality that is to be achieved. Start with that functionality, and let it lead to the product. Don't start with the product and attempt to identify ways to justify its purchase.
Estimate benefits first.	Examine costs only after you have completed the analysis of benefits.
Know your business.	This means really understanding what your business is and how your current processes allow your organization to accomplish its objectives. Understand the dynamics of your current processes and where potential for improvement can be found. Understand organizational politics.
Develop the best estimate possible.	Don't be overly optimistic or conservative. Develop the best estimate you can with the data available to you. This is the core of making the business case.
Separate the development of CBA estimates from questions of how best to package the analysis to justify a final decision.	The questions involved in developing an accurate CBA and attempting to determine how best to justify a choice to organizational decision makers are two separate processes. The latter involves choices about which sources of value should be included in the business case to be presented to decision makers. These are determined by the relative comparisons of costs with the magnitudes and types of revenue sources. Decisions about how to package the analysis for decision makers should be pursued only after a thorough analysis based on best estimates of all benefits and costs has been accomplished.

personal biases. The team needs to come into the decision process without preconceived notions, willing to approach the analysis objectively and willing to accept whatever results the analysis produces. If members of the team have a vested interest in a particular solution, for example, cloud computing or employee self-service portals, it will cause difficulties in the analysis. CBA techniques can be used to identify investment opportunities and important contingencies that can influence the success of eventual implementation. Developing a reputation as an impartial evaluator will increase management decision makers' confidence in analyses done by the CBA team.

Focus on key functionality rather than on specific hardware or software solutions. Many proposals for a new HRIS have erroneously started by identifying a new software application and then trying to justify how its features and capabilities could benefit the organization. However, it is whether your organization performs more effectively after an HRIS implementation that will determine the success of any HRIS investment. The CBA team must focus on the organization and its process and outcomes (i.e., reduced costs or increased revenues), identify opportunities in order to improve effectiveness, and only then look to identify software solutions that provide the desired capabilities. Centering the analysis on a specific software solution shifts the focus of the analysis to the capabilities that solution offers, not necessarily the capabilities that are most needed by the organization. Therefore, the question to be answered is not just whether the system will increase HR functionality but whether the new HRIS will improve organizational effectiveness and fit with the business strategy of the firm.

Examine benefits before you examine costs. This is often difficult to do, but training the CBA team to examine the benefits of a change in HRIS functionality before estimating costs will produce better analyses. Knowing before you conduct the analysis of benefits how much would need to be spent to acquire new functionality can easily lead to an inaccurate CBA. This "backward" approach makes it almost impossible not to consider what level of benefits will be necessary to justify the investment. This approach can cause the team to abort prematurely the process of identifying and analyzing benefits, especially if a single source of benefits appears to be sufficient to guarantee adoption of the HRIS project. It can also encourage "fishing" for questionable benefits when the initially identified benefits may not be enough to justify the HRIS investment.

Know your business. As stated in Table 8.1, this means really understanding the organization's business and how the current processes in all departments allow the organization to accomplish its objectives. Furthermore, it means that the CBA team must understand the dynamics of the current business processes and where potential for improvement exists. Since the CBA team consists of senior representatives from all staff departments affected by the HRIS project, this business knowledge should exist within the team. Obviously, then, the

CBA team must have cooperative relationships among its members. Further, it is important that the CBA and PM teams understand the internal politics of the firm.

Develop the best estimate possible. Various methods to achieve this goal are discussed in this chapter. It is also critically important, as mentioned in the previous paragraph, that cooperative relationships exist among members of the CBA team as well as within the PM team. The project team leader must try to reduce or eliminate interdepartmental politics, particularly between the HR and IT departments. Finally, note the advice in Table 8.1 not to be overly optimistic or conservative but to develop the best estimate possible with the available data.

Distinguish between the analysis and the packaging of that analysis for decision makers. The primary purpose of analyzing an HRIS investment is to determine whether and to what extent it will improve your organization. The objective of the analysis should be to provide the "best" estimate of the impact of an HRIS investment as is possible. Developing the estimate should be seen as separate and distinct from the process of presenting and "selling" the investment opportunity to management decision makers. Decision makers may choose to rely on specific forms of benefit evidence or to adopt conservative assumptions in order to gain approval for the investment. Inappropriate investment decisions may result if overly conservative assumptions in the HRIS investment analysis conducted by the CBA team are compounded by the conservative bias common among decision makers.

HRIS Cost-Benefit Analysis

A CBA is simply what its name indicates—a comparison of the projected costs and benefits associated with an HRIS investment, which can be presented as a comparison of cost and benefit dollars or presented as a cost-benefit ratio. A **cost-benefit ratio** can be expressed mathematically, with the benefits of the project as the numerator and the costs as the denominator. Therefore, values greater than one indicate a positive ratio. A cost is any new outlay of cash required for the initial purchase, implementation, or ongoing maintenance of the investment. A benefit is any financial gain resulting from the investment that occurs at any time during the investment's useful life. Benefits include both revenue enhancements and cost reductions.

At its core, the CBA is an analysis of change in the cost-benefit ratio—a comparison of current existing circumstances with new conditions that are projected to exist after the HRIS investment. This comparison means the cost-benefit ratio for the current HRIS must be calculated first. Then the cost-benefit ratio is estimated for the projected HRIS. The *size of the gap between these two cost-benefit ratios* is what will have an effect on the decision to implement a new HRIS or new HR functionality

A common misconception is that conducting a meaningful CBA (and utility analysis) requires financial expertise. Knowing some financial basics, such as discounting, cost of capital, cash flow, **return on investment (ROI)**, **payback period**, net present value, and **internal rate of return (IRR)**, is useful but not required. Organizations differ in the specific financial measures they use to evaluate investments. Organizations may use ROI, IRR, payback period, or other measures alone or in combination. Therefore, it can be useful to seek out an internal adviser to help you package your analysis for the managerial decision-making process used in the organization. Typically, this internal adviser will be someone in the finance or accounting department. However, regardless of the specific financial measures used in the organization, investment analyses, that is, CBAs, are based on **three basic pieces of information**: (1) sources of costs and benefits, (2) an estimated dollar value for each cost and benefit item, and (3) the time when the organization will incur each cost and receive each benefit. These are the core data on which any investment analysis is based, including one for a new HRIS. The remainder of this chapter will cover how these three basic pieces of information are obtained and used in a CBA.

Identifying Sources of Value for Benefits and Costs

Investments in HRIS functionality differ from more traditional investments because HR is commonly perceived as a source of costs rather than a direct source of revenue (Cascio, 2000). Any impact that HR department activities have on revenues occurs *indirectly* through the effect of HR programs and practices on other units of the organization. For example, a program focused on training retail employees to provide quality customer service is typically a cost ascribed to the HR department; however, its indirect effect of increased sales is classified as revenue for the operations department. Thus, the effects of many HR programs or practices are often described as "soft" or, more appropriately, indirect. As a result, managerial decision makers are justifiably concerned about using "soft" benefits to justify spending "hard" dollars, particularly when considering large investments such as a new HRIS. Approving an investment only to find that the expected benefits never materialize is something all decision makers fear. In the absence of obvious risk avoidance justifications and significant reductions in costs from previous HRIS investments, developing expertise in identifying and valuing the direct and indirect benefits derived from HRIS investments is one of the critical challenges that HRIS managers face.

Failing to recognize important sources of costs or benefits is a common problem in HRIS CBA. The HRIS CBA matrix shown in Figure 8.1 can be used to help uncover all reasonable benefit and cost components in HRIS investment analyses. The HRIS CBA matrix consists of six cells.

The four upper cells (1–4) represent sources of benefits (i.e., direct revenue enhancements, indirect revenue enhancements, direct cost reductions, and indirect cost reductions).

The two cells of the bottom row capture costs of implementation (i.e., direct and indirect costs). A simple evaluation of each cell of the HRIS CBA matrix can ensure that important sources of benefits or costs are not overlooked.

Direct Benefits

The four "benefit" cells of the HRIS CBA matrix (Figure 8.1) represent the crossing of two dimensions. The first dimension is the type of benefit—revenue enhancements versus cost reductions. Organizations can enhance revenues by changing employees' job performance. These changes could result in *new revenue* in terms of new sales due to more efficient procedures, for example, those instituted because of a better training program for new employees. Organizations can also reduce costs by changing the locations of HR functions to make them more effective. For example, an organization with a new HRIS could decide to outsource programs (such as employee recruiting) to vendors. HRIS investments often involve both types of effects. HRIS investments can also permit the offering of new products and services that can increase revenues and enhance profit margins. Thinking about opportunities for cost reductions and revenue enhancements separately allows each to be explored more fully.

Figure 8.1 HRIS Cost-Benefit Analysis Matrix

		Direct (Hard)	Indirect (Soft)
Benefits	Revenue enhancement	1 New revenue (new sales)	2 Improvement potential (better decision making)
	Cost reduction	3 Direct costs (canceled vendor contracts)	4 Potential costs (saved staff time)
Costs	New implementation costs	5 Out-of-pocket costs (software, service agreements)	6 Indirect costs (increased technical support needs)

The terms *direct* and *indirect* are used here to refer to benefits and costs that might be described elsewhere as "hard" and "soft," respectively. Hard or direct outcomes generally refer to benefits (and costs) (a) that are very likely to occur and (b) whose values are easily estimated. Some examples of **direct benefits** can be seen in Table 8.2, which shows an example of a CBA for an e-learning investment. As can be seen, the organization is considering having e-learning modules created by an external vendor to replace in-house training programs. Direct revenue enhancements include the additional revenue the organization can earn by selling the e-learning modules. Direct cost reductions include expected reductions in the costs associated with delivering training programs, as seen in Table 8.2, for example, reduced travel expenses and reduced facilities costs.

Indirect Benefits

Soft or **indirect benefits**, on the other hand, are often less easily quantified because their occurrence may be less certain or because their value is more difficult to establish. After the HRIS functionality is introduced, indirect revenue enhancements result from improvements in intermediate outcomes that could position the organization to be able to increase revenues. For example, in Table 8.2, e-learning training modules can be used to improve customer service, and potentially sales, by improving the skills of sales employees. Improving managerial leadership could also have an impact on the indirect benefits at the top of Table 8.2 by encouraging employee engagement in the activities that most directly influence organizational effectiveness. Thus, in this example, the intermediate outcomes are the effects of the e-learning training modules that then may lead to the revenue increases. As listed in Table 8.2, these are "Better customer service leading to increase in repeat sales" and "A more agile organization able to respond rapidly to market changes." The e-learning training modules may also affect revenue increase outcomes, by, for example, improving the organization's capacity to attract and retain high-quality employees, achieving a reduction in turnover and absenteeism (see Table 8.2), improving employees' capacity to make decisions, or freeing up time for employees to engage in activities that more directly support the strategic objectives of the organization (see Figure 8.1). Indirect revenue enhancements occur through one or more intermediate outcomes that require some additional activity or condition exists before an increase in revenues is realized. For example, before managers can work on leadership responsibilities and activities that are directly related to strategic company goals, it may be necessary to restructure several departments and provide some in-service training.

Since these benefits are not reported in a dollar metric, current CBAs typically do not include these items in the numeric analysis but will often address them in the narrative discussion supporting the investment. In the e-learning example, better customer service (i.e., service that can lead to increased customer retention and repeat sales) and a more agile organization (i.e., one that can retrain or retool its employees more quickly to respond to rapidly changing markets) are examples of indirect or contingent sources of revenues.

Table 8.2 **Example of an e-Learning CBA Matrix**

	Direct (Hard)	Indirect/Contingent (Soft)
Revenue enhancements	Conducting custom e-learning training module development for other organizations Sales of locally developed learning modules or programs	Better customer service leading to increase in repeat sales A more agile organization able to respond rapidly to market changes
Cost reductions	Reduced travel expenses Reduced facilities costs (e.g., for room and equipment rentals and refreshments) Reduced requirements for paper-based training materials and teaching aids Reduced expenses for instructor fees or salary and benefits costs (if internal) Reduced costs for replacement workers if trainees are required to be away from their work	Improved training effectiveness through customization and just-in-time delivery = faster learning curve, less lost productivity while waiting for training, and right amount and type of content More agility, able to disseminate new cost-reducing best practices more quickly Reduction in turnover (41% of employees will look for another job within 12 months due to poor training and education; with good training and education, this percentage drops to 12%) and in absenteeism Improved safety (fewer injuries, less lost time, fewer insurance claims, lower workers' compensation costs) Employee time saved
Costs of implementation	Installation support Software fee/license Software support Analyst/administrator Training administrator Courseware development Courseware purchase Bandwidth fees	Increased use of end-user help desk Courseware redevelopment Lost productivity during conversion to new system

Indirect cost reductions involve those changes that are expected to lead to reduced costs. If we reexamine Figure 8.1, these benefits would fall in box number 4, potential cost reductions through saved staff time, and would include (a) staff time saved, but not those reductions that lead to direct reductions in payroll (i.e., not ones tied directly to reductions in overtime or **employee headcount**); (b) expected reductions in the amount of or requirements for technical support; (c) expected reductions in absenteeism and turnover; and (d) expected reductions in the time required to bring trainees up to the status of fully functioning employees.

In many instances, time-saving applications are incorrectly projected to result in reductions in employee headcount or FTEs—a direct savings in payroll expenses. More often, though, the deployment of new HRIS functionality results in a new structuring of work that enables the elimination of parts of jobs rather than whole jobs. As a result, the benefit is indirect—a saving of time that can be deployed in other activities rather than a direct saving of the costs of salary and benefits. In the e-learning example, enhancements in training effectiveness are expected to lead to faster learning curves and less time to proficiency. This benefit is expected to result in fewer errors and less rework. Reductions in turnover costs are also anticipated because better-trained employees are expected to have higher satisfaction and remain in their jobs longer. Lower turnover rates for valued employees would have a strong positive effect, allowing the firm to reduce the costs of hiring new employees (see Cascio, 2000). Furthermore, improved access to safety training is also expected to result in less time lost as a result of injuries and reduced insurance claims and workers' compensation costs.

Consequently, because the effects are indirect, analyses of indirect benefits can be challenging. But, in many instances, these indirect effects are the real source of benefits for new HRIS functionality. Being able to identify the indirect effects and understand how they are expected to affect costs and revenues is critical to understanding how to justify HRIS investments. An important advantage of understanding how and where indirect benefits are expected to occur is that it allows the organization to plan and manage HRIS implementations specifically, in ways that make it more likely for indirect benefits to actually occur. Because these benefits are often contingent on other events, knowing what those events are and managing them as a part of the implementation will likely result in greater organizational impact.

Implementation Costs

Once benefits have been estimated, the analysis can proceed to estimating the costs of implementation (Table 8.2). In contrast to estimating benefits, cost estimation is often easier to complete because cost information is readily available and already offered in a dollar metric.

In most cases, many sources of **implementation costs** will be direct. **Direct costs** will include but are not limited to (a) costs for the initial purchase and updates of software and any additional hardware and (b) ongoing costs for internal or external systems support. In the e-learning example (Table 8.2), direct costs include the purchase of any new software, hardware, and licenses required to implement the system as well as the cost of the expertise necessary to develop and manage training on this new HRIS platform.

Indirect costs comprise those areas of cost that cannot be known specifically up front but may arise in the process of implementing the system. These include the impact of the implementation on the organization, such as lost productivity while the organization completes implementation. This impact includes lost productivity for rank-and-file employees as well as for the HR staff involved in implementation. The e-learning example includes increased use of end-user help desks or other support functions, costs necessary to revamp existing courseware while the organization learns how to use the new system most effectively, and the lost productivity that will occur for any current employees who will be required to take on additional responsibilities associated with the adoption of the new system.

It is important to be thorough in attempting to identify all the sources of cost. If your analysis recognizes some benefit without incorporating an offsetting change in cost, you likely have missed a source of cost in your analysis. For example, organizations that projected significant reductions in employee headcounts due to converting paper-and-pencil transactions to electronic systems, as was erroneously done in the opening vignette, often failed to recognize the full additional costs that would be required in technical support, training on the new system, or transitioning large numbers of employees out of the organization.

Also, the total costs of implementation will depend on the current state of information system development in the organization. The components of organizational information systems evolve at different speeds across organizations. Knowing the current level of technological evolution of the organization's total information architecture and systems is quite important. These components would include those that are operational within departments concerned with finance, operations, marketing, and information systems, as well as HR. Assessment of these departments' systems should include evaluations of (a) the current state of their computer hardware, software, data, and processes; (b) user sophistication and networking; and (c) telecommunications technology. New HRIS investments may affect all these information systems (IS) components. In any one of these areas, the greater the change required supporting the implementation of the new HR functionality, the more expensive the implementation will be. Total cost will be driven by (a) the scope or size of the HRIS implementation; (b) the amount of customization required; (c) the maturity of the HRIS functionality being considered—the less mature the functionality, the greater the costs of implementation and upgrades are likely to be; and (d) the experience levels of the implementers.

Although early attempts at CBA often grossly underestimated or ignored significant sources of costs, the experiences of organizations over the past decade have provided insights that can be used to do a much better job of recognizing what cost items need to be included in cost analyses. Several sources for determining cost of implementation are available, including organizations that have previously implemented specific packages or functionality, vendors in the HRIS field, and implementation consultant.

Estimating the Value of Indirect Benefits

Most HRIS cost-benefit analyses will include some indirect benefits. One of the more difficult tasks in producing an HRIS CBA is estimating the value of these indirect benefits. The difficulty of converting indirect benefit estimates to a dollar metric has limited their role in HR technology investment decisions. To this point, it has not been uncommon for soft benefits to be relegated to the narrative supporting an investment analysis that is otherwise based solely on estimates of direct cost reductions. For good reason, many managers consider these indirect savings cautiously. That does not mean, though, that these benefits are any less important than direct benefits to the organization. In fact, as noted earlier, ignoring them in HRIS investment analysis could result in incorrect or misleading analyses. As a result, we need to adapt the general techniques used to analyze HR technology investments to meet these new requirements.

Estimating Indirect Benefit Magnitude

Constructing dollar estimates of indirect benefits is challenging, but it can be done. To simplify estimation of the dollar value of indirect benefits and provide a basis for justification, one should break this task into the following three steps: (1) estimating benefit magnitude, (2) mapping benefits to cost or revenue changes, and (3) converting magnitude estimates to dollar values. By separating these steps, we can begin to understand better the factors that influence the value of indirect benefits and, perhaps more important, when these benefits are likely to occur during the HRIS project. Also, since magnitude and value are often driven by different factors, separating these decisions provides a better framework for post-implementation evaluations. Both benefit and value estimates are then open to objective review.

An objective of HRIS CBA is to develop the best-possible estimates of the likely effect of the new HRIS functionality. Therefore, using a metric that is familiar or comfortable to those developing the estimate of this impact is likely to improve accuracy and, ultimately, make the project easier to manage. For instance, if the new functionality is predicted to reduce turnover (see Figure 8.2), the magnitude of the expected change in "turnover rates" would be estimated first. Then, the determination of the dollar value of the differences between the current rate and the expected rate is likely to produce better estimates than if decision makers attempted to estimate the dollar impact of the expected reductions in turnover in a single step. The objective is to choose the metric and measurement procedure that will result in the most accurate estimate possible of the size of the benefit.

Once that metric has been chosen, there are three approaches for estimating **benefit magnitude**: (1) direct estimation, (2) benchmarking, and (3) internal assessment. Which method is the most appropriate depends on the amount of specific information that is available to the organization and the CBA team.

Direct Estimation

Direct estimation is the simplest of the three methods. It is quick and easy to perform. It relies solely on the expertise of analysts or subject matter experts in the CBA team to "estimate" the expected magnitude of the benefit. **Direct estimation** is most appropriate when the scope of the project is small, compliance or risk avoidance is a primary investment justification, other substantial sources of direct cost reduction or direct revenue enhancement exist, or no other method for estimating benefit magnitude is available. The primary limitation of direct estimation is that the accuracy of the analysis depends on the expertise of the estimator.

When several equally qualified subject matter experts are available, collecting independent estimates from each expert and using the average of these estimates is recommended. In addition, it can be useful to require that experts articulate the rationale for their estimates. Requiring this step not only ensures that experts are thoughtful in the preparation of their estimates but also provides the organization with an analysis of the assumptions or expectations contained in these rationales, which can be used to help improve the accuracy of future estimates.

Benchmarking

Benchmark data on the magnitude of indirect benefits achieved in other firms can be used. The advantage of **benchmarking** is that it allows an organization to build on the experiences of others. These data can provide evidence that a specific outcome can occur as well as evidence of its potential magnitude. Howes (2002) offers an insightful example of how benchmarking data can be used to estimate how much reduction in turnover an organization might expect. In this example, benchmark data about industry-wide levels of turnover are used to construct estimates of the potential for improvement in turnover that might be possible for a given organization. If an organization has high turnover relative to industry standards, it has the potential for greater improvement than might be expected for other firms in that industry.

Benchmarking information of various types is becoming more widely available from a number of sources (e.g., Gartner, Inc., The Hackett Group, the Saratoga Institute, the Society of Human Resource Management, and Harris Associates—see the websites provided in the Appendix). Chapter 7 contains a reference to HR metrics that can be used in benchmarking (Society of Human Resource Management [SHRM], 2010). Organizations can also conduct their own benchmarking studies to gather specific data from targeted firms, data that may not be readily available from third-party sources. Benchmarking is preferred over direct estimation for larger, more costly projects for which investment risks are greater. Benchmarking is also useful when organizations have limited experience with the targeted functionality of the HRIS project or when there is no access to local data. The primary disadvantage of benchmark data is that the experiences of other organizations may not completely generalize to your firm or business unit. A good recent source of information on benchmarking is the *SHRM Human Capital Benchmarking Study: 2009 Executive Summary* (Dooney, Blackmon, & Williams, 2009).

Internal Assessment

Internal assessment involves the use of a firm's own internal metrics (see Table 8.1) or other forms of the firm's specific data as the basis for estimates. Use of this method requires that the organization has maintained historic records on previous information system projects. Internal assessment is best done when investment scopes are large and direct estimation or benchmarking suggests that benefits may not be dramatically higher or lower than costs (e.g., less than ± 30%). Internal assessment requires that the organization possesses the capability of gathering data about its own processes, as these data are necessary to support this kind of analysis. An advantage of integrated information systems—systems built on common platforms that permit single instances of data to be used in several applications and the seamless transfer of data between applications—is that the marginal costs of assessments are greatly reduced, permitting cost-effective assessments of a wide range of organizational outcomes. Internal assessments offer the most precise estimates of the costs and performance of existing or newly implemented processes. Internal assessments, though, may be able to provide only a portion of the needed data. That is, an organization may be able to gather accurate data about the outcomes of current processes, but, in order to complete the analysis, it may need to rely on benchmark data from other organizations or obtain direct estimates of the outcomes for new processes.

Even though possessing integrated information systems can reduce the marginal costs of assessments, conducting internal assessments and evaluating the data they produce are not costless activities. As described in Table 8.3, internal assessment provides the most precise estimates of the baseline costs and current performance of existing processes against which to compare potential improvements. However, internal assessments will result in higher costs than direct estimation and, depending on the nature of the assessment, could result in higher decision-support costs than benchmarking. As noted, internal assessment is only possible when the organization has experience with a given form of functionality. It is not possible to assess the effects of new functionality that has not been previously implemented anywhere in the organization.

Each of these three approaches is recapped in Table 8.3. The ideal method for estimating the magnitudes of indirect benefits in most HRIS analyses is to use a combination of these three approaches. This permits each benefit to be estimated using the method that is most appropriate given the availability of data and the investment's cost, risk, and opportunity characteristics. For high-stakes investment decisions, using multiple methods to develop estimates can provide additional insight and increased confidence in the final decision.

Table 8.3   Different Approaches to Estimating Benefit Magnitude

Approach	Description	When to Use It	Advantages/Limitations
Direct estimation	Direct ("gut level") estimates of the relationship of the potential benefits to the estimated costs of engaging in an investment	Best when costs are not large Appropriate when attempting to gain compliance or mitigating extreme risks When substantial direct cost reduction or revenue enhancements exist	Quick and low cost to perform May not provide data that contain sufficient detail for use in monitoring implementation effectiveness or to perform follow-up analyses Highly dependent on the expertise of the decision maker
Benchmarking	Using benchmark data from other firms to estimate the potential	Superior to direct estimation when costs are large When the organization	Allows the organization to develop more precise estimates than direct estimation based on the

Approach	Description	When to Use It	Advantages/Limitations
	benefits and costs that are likely to result from the purchase of HRIS functionality	either has limited experience or no data concerning the area of functionality	collective experience of other organizations Average estimates of outcomes may not generalize to the target organization
Internal assessment	Analysis based on specific internal assessments of actual costs and likely benefits (e.g., activity-based costing)	When costs are high and benefits are not obviously dramatically larger than costs When the organization has the assessment capabilities in place to gather the appropriate data	Provides the most precise estimates of the baseline costs and current performance of existing processes against which to compare potential improvements May increase both costs and time required to make decisions
Mix and match	Using combinations of these approaches	When different amounts or sources of information are available for different types of costs and benefits (e.g., most likely scenario)	Permits the organization to use the best methods available

Mapping Indirect Benefits to Revenues and Costs

In some instances, the metric of choice may not be one that is easily or unambiguously tied to reductions in costs or increases in revenues. That is, estimating the value of indirect benefits requires that the analyst first be able to articulate how the indirect benefit is linked to an actual reduction in costs or increase in revenues.

Then a Miracle Occurred! The challenge of linking indirect benefits to revenues and costs is not a step that should be taken lightly. In many instances, it can be challenging to articulate exactly the change of events that leads from an investment to changes in the organization's bottom line. This can lead to causal language in investments that identify the initial links in the sequence, and then jump immediately to argue for the benefits to the organization. These analyses are of the form A causes B which causes C . . . then a miracle occurs . . . and the organization is more profitable. While articulating hypotheses about exactly how the causal change is expected to unfold can be difficult, doing so allows the organization to plan more effectively for success—by adding new metrics at critical junctures to track progress and to identify potential contingencies that must be managed to assure success.

To examine this idea further, let's assume that an indirect benefit of a proposed investment is reduced turnover; and we predict that implementing a new HRIS functionality will result in a reduction in voluntary turnover from 10% to 5% for a targeted group of jobs. Since the effect of turnover on costs and benefits is indirect, we need to understand how reducing turnover is expected to affect an organization's revenues or costs in order to translate our 5% reduction in turnover to other metrics that are more closely associated with changes in costs and revenues.

Employee turnover is a good example because it affects costs and revenues in several ways, some of which are depicted graphically in Figure 8.2. The departure of an employee can increase costs because it may require the organization to engage in a new recruitment and hiring cycle, and the new employee is likely to require training. But there are other effects as well. For instance, the loss of an employee in a position critical to the day-to-day functioning of the organization will require that efforts be made to cover the work responsibilities in that employee's absence. How an organization chooses to cover those responsibilities will influence the magnitude of the net loss of contribution that results from the vacancy. There will be salary savings for the vacant position, but the cost of temporary hires or of shifting other employees off their primary assignments, not to mention the opportunity costs that result from using less than fully effective temporary or overextended employees, also must be considered. The total loss added by this vacancy is represented in Figure 8.2 by the region $A * B$—the value of the daily loss of contribution multiplied by the number of days the position remains vacant. Also, as noted in Table 8.2, turnover affects the contribution the organization derives from a position. Perhaps the departing employee was a poor performer and replacing him or her will actually result in a net gain in average long-term effectiveness for that position (i.e., C in Figure 8.2). Even with training, new hires will most likely require some time on the job before they can become fully effective; their effectiveness will increase as they gain expertise. But, during this time, contribution will be less than would have been experienced had there been no turnover in the position (i.e., E in Figure 8.2). Each of these intermediate outcomes can be tied to a specific cost or revenue effect through one or more links.

In this example, a comprehensive estimate of the impact of the expected reduction in turnover is represented by the sum of the estimates of each of these components in Figure 8.2. In some

Figure 8.2 Conceptualizing the Effects of Turnover

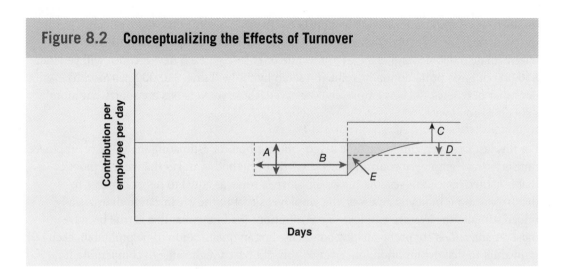

Note: A is the average value (contribution) that is lost per day that a given position is left unfilled. B is the number of days that a position remains unfilled. C and D represent the increase or decrease in contribution that occurs if a new hire is more or less effective, respectively, than the employee who left. The gray area noted as E represents the loss of contribution that occurs during the time when a new employee is learning the job.

cases, and for specific types of benefits, these relationships may seem quite complex. Do not be discouraged or dissuaded from being thorough. Understanding exactly how these changes are projected to affect the organization may yield important new insights about intermediate outcomes and contingent factors, insights that may put managers in a position to ensure the success of HRIS investments. Understanding which factors are affected by the investment can also aid in further refining magnitude estimates and is essential for estimating value. Cascio (2000) provides a complete list of the costs of voluntary turnover. In addition, there are several metrics important for measuring the effects of turnover, such as "time to fill," "turnover costs," "vacancy costs," and "vacancy rate."

Methods for Estimating the Value of Indirect Benefits
••

Direct revenue enhancements or direct cost reductions are typically estimated in dollars, so their value is provided by the total estimate. Estimates that are developed in other metrics, such as total absenteeism in days lost, must also be converted to dollars. For indirect benefits that can be tied more directly to cost reductions or revenue enhancements (i.e., new products developed or market share increased), the task is somewhat more difficult, but it can be done. It requires estimating the strength of the relationship between the change in intermediate outcomes and changes in revenue or cost (e.g., each new account will generate $50,000 in gross profit annually; reducing scrap by 5% will save $10,000 per month). For other outcomes, such as employee time saved, these conversions are somewhat more difficult to conduct.

For this last category, employee time saved, one method for estimating the value of employee time is average employee contribution (AEC). This method is an alternative to a practice that is *not recommended*—estimating an employee's value as equal to his or her cost to the organization. In nearly all cases, the employee's cost to the organization dramatically underestimates the average employee's contribution. We know that this is true because most organizations are profit-making concerns. For an organization to be profitable, each individual in that organization, on average, contributes enough value to compensate for the cost of his or her wages and benefits and for the outlay on the equipment and facilities employed on the job, in addition to covering taxes and accounting for profit. This scenario helps explain why downsizing does not always improve financial results. Downsizing only makes sense when the contribution of the employees eliminated is less than their cost in salary and benefits to the organization.

Average Employee Contribution

In the turnover example discussed earlier, estimating the value lost while a position remains open (i.e., the region represented by the area $A * B$ in Figure 8.2) requires an estimate of the value of the average daily contribution made by an employee. The average contribution approach argues that the **average employee contribution (AEC)** in an organization is equal to total gross profit divided by the number of employees or full-time equivalents (FTEs). FTEs are the budgeted number of positions for each job in an organization. AEC is not a metric that most organizations track, although a measure of average daily gross margin (i.e., net revenue – cost of goods sold) generated per salesperson would be an example of this type of measure. This is one of the simplest metrics that captures AEC as accurately as is needed for estimating the value of indirect benefits.

$$AEC = (\text{Net revenues} - \text{Cost of goods sold})/\text{No. of employees}$$

By definition, in a profitable organization, this number will be substantially higher than labor costs, which is the sum of total employee pay and benefits. Dividing this number by the number of workdays in a year (i.e., 252) produces an estimate of average daily contribution. Note that this method, as indicated in the previous equation, does not reduce contributions attributable to employees by the amount of capital expenditures and other nonemployee-related expenses—the equipment and tools that aid employees in doing their jobs. The reason is that these tools are used to enhance employee contribution. The tools enhance what employees can do, but they do not generate contribution on their own. That is, if you take away the employees who use the tools and equipment, the contribution goes with them. The tools provide no independent and unique contribution to the organization in the absence of the employee.

AEC can be used to estimate the average annual contribution of an organization's employees. Obviously, average contribution can and does differ across jobs. Thus, organizations may want to adjust this number up or down for specific jobs to recognize differences in contribution potential. Jobs that more closely support the organization's mission and offer jobholders broader authority to influence the work of others, and greater autonomy for choosing how and when work will be accomplished, are likely to offer above-average levels of contribution. The advantage of this method is that it establishes a baseline contribution value for each of the different jobs, one that is consistent with the actual financial performance of the organization.

Average contribution estimates, though, provide little guidance in estimating differences in contribution between employees holding the same or similar jobs. This calculation is represented in the turnover example in Figure 8.2 by the difference between the values C and D—the differences in contribution for two different employees who might hold the same position. Differences in contribution can be developed using internal assessment by examining directly the individual employee differences (variance) in the work outcomes produced by a large number of individuals holding equivalent positions. This assessment can be accomplished more readily for jobs when individual production rates can be monitored (i.e., sales, transaction processing, and some manufacturing settings). It is important to understand the difference between AEC and the variance of work outcomes by employees. AEC is the average contribution of work outcomes, and it can be estimated for entire organizations or for individual jobs. So it would be fairly easy to calculate the AEC for sales representatives by week by adding the sales for all representatives and dividing by the number of representatives. However, this does not tell us the range or variance in the weekly sales for the representatives. Some individuals could have done poorly in terms of weekly sales whereas others could have done quite well. This variance in productivity is very important in the calculation of utility analysis (Boudreau, 1991; Cascio, 1987, 2000; Schmidt & Hunter, 1983), which is beyond the scope of this book.

Numerical Example for Figure 8.2

Cascio (1991, 2000) devotes an entire chapter to "The High Cost of Employee Turnover," and provides some numerical examples for the calculations of employee loss. Cascio also provides the both general and specific categories, similar to the ones already discussed, for the costs involved in employee turnover. By using Cascio's categories and numbers, the calculations required in Figure 8.2 will be done. The first general category in Cascio's list, Measuring Separation Costs, measures the following cost items: *the exit interview,* the administrative functions related to termination,[1] and *the cost of replacing employees.*

The interview combines the cost of the interviewer's time both prior to the interview and the time for the interview. This interview also has two other cost factors—the cost of terminating the employee, which is measured by the time required for the interview multiplied by the average daily pay rate for the terminated employee. This value is part of the separation costs, but the time (in days) to replace the employee multiplied by the average daily pay rate for the terminated employee must be added to the interview costs to have a better total costs. Looking at Figure 8.2, this total cost represents a part of A. This total cost can also be calculated for a month or a year. If the exit interview process takes one hour, 15 minutes for preparation and 45 minutes for the interview, then multiplying by the interviewer's pay rate at $15/hour is one part of determining the value of A. The second part of the cost for the exit interview is the cost of the terminating employee's time. If the employee earns $11.80/hour, that is multiplied by .75 (approximate time for the interview) to get costs incurred by the exit interview by the employee. If we add these two costs—$15.00 plus $8.85 ($11.80 times .75), we can calculate the *total costs of the exit interview to be $23.85,* i. e., part of the value for A in the figure. If there are 100 turnovers in one year, then the total cost for the exit interviews for the year would be $2,385.00.

The second specific cost category identified by Cascio is the Administrative Functions Related to Termination. This category involves the time required by the HR department in completing the administrative functions multiplied by the average HR employee's pay rate. If the HR employee's average hourly pay is $15.75 and the administrative functions meeting takes two hours, *the total cost for this category is $31.50.* Adding the total cost for the exit interview to this cost means the total cost of terminating one employee is $55.35—$23.85 plus $31.50. This value is another part of A in Figure 8.2.

The final specific category identified by Cascio is the separation pay for the terminated employee. If the average daily amount of separation pay by employee, the total in this example *would be $472.00 as the average separation pay per employee terminated*—calculated by multiplying 40 hours/week by $11.80/hour. This value would be the last part of A in Figure 8.2. Adding the three costs would be $23.85 + $31.50 + $472.00 = $527.35. The total of Separation Costs would be $527.35. This means the total costs of separation of terminated employees by year would be $52,735 (100 turnovers × $527.35 = $52,735).

The general costs incurred by an organization in replacing a terminated employee are defined as replacement costs. These costs represent B in Figure 8.2. The specific cost categories include the following:

1. communication of job availability

2. pre-employment administrative functions

3. entrance interviews

4. testing

5. staff meetings

6. travel/moving expenses

7. employment medical exams

8. dissemination of information after hired

As expected, many of these costs involve personnel time by time spent on the activity, both from the HR department as well as managerial time.

Most of the measures of these specific cost categories are common sense, for example, advertising and employment agency fees, costs of tests as well as cost of time for test administration by HR department, and pre-employment administrative functions multiplied by a HR professional's time to complete the tasks involved. Thus, it seems that examining most of these costs would not be fruitful. The interested student can check Cascio (1991, 2000) for details from the chapter on the high cost of employee turnover. However, remember that these costs are shown as B in Figure 8.2 and represent the number of days that a position is filled.

In addition, new employees can either increase or decrease separation costs due to their effectiveness in their job performance after being hired. Thus, from Figure 8.2, C represents a new hire that is more effective in fulfilling the requirements and tasks of his new position than the employee who left; whereas D represents a new hire that is less effective in fulfilling the requirements and tasks of the new position than the employee who left. The gray area E in Figure 8.2 represents the loss of contribution by the new employee who is learning the job and can be quite variable depending on the individual. That is, some people learn to perform the requirements and tasks of the job faster than others and this cost would be positive, thus, reducing total cost of the termination and replacement. Of course, the slow learner on the job requirements might be terminated and thus the organization would incur additional termination and replacement costs.

Estimating the Timing of Benefits and Costs

Once you have identified and valued the sources of benefits and costs associated with an investment in HRIS functionality, the next step of the analysis is to determine when in time each benefit and cost will be incurred during the entire HRIS project. Organizations use this information to estimate the cash outflow and inflows associated with investments. The **timing of cash flows** is particularly important when costs and benefits occur in different time periods and when the organization's cost of capital is relatively high. This information is critically important in the management of the entire HRIS project, which was discussed in Chapter 6.

The task of assigning the benefits and costs to time periods can be accomplished by constructing a simple grid that lists benefit or cost items along one axis and future time periods on the other axis. The number of time periods required will depend on the expected useful life of the investment and the relevant length of time periods (usually years, but months or quarters may be used in some instances). The critical period for most HRIS investments is the first five years. Few organizations are likely to approve HRIS investments with longer payback periods. Furthermore, current rates of development of HRIS functionality and computing systems suggest that most HRIS investments may be functionally obsolete after five years.

The Role of Variance in Estimates

Since the estimates produced for cost-benefit analyses are necessarily based on forecasting future events and may also depend on events outside the control of management, actual outcomes are likely to deviate from those estimated. For example, one may expect an average reduction of 2 hours in transaction processing time. However, the actual amount of reduction will vary depending on the mix of transaction types, operator expertise, and other job requirements, and could range from 105 to 135 minutes. *The primary estimate of interest is the overall average expectation.* However, particularly for indirect benefits, it is useful to develop expectations about the range and potential distribution of possible outcomes. Lower- and upper-bound estimates as well as deviations from the average (variance) for magnitude and value estimates are useful auxiliary information that can help convey expectations about potential variability in outcomes.

Variance estimates can be developed by each of the estimation methods described in Table 8.3. For direct estimation, HR and IT professionals could produce estimates of the range and likelihood of various outcome levels. In addition, multiple estimators could be used if two or more equally knowledgeable individuals exist. Each could be instructed to estimate a target value and upper- and lower-bounds for the estimated expectations, and these could then be averaged to develop overall estimates. Variance estimates for benchmark data from other organizations in the same industry are more difficult to acquire, since most sources only report averages and do not report variance data. In some instances, it may be possible to request the standard deviations associated with each benchmark value from other organizations. However, with internal analysis, variance estimates can be calculated from the archival records of existing HR or IT processes before and after implementation. In all instances, an estimate of the variance of outcomes could then be used to provide a range of the most likely outcomes. However, remember that, in the absence of compelling evidence to the contrary, the best estimate is the one you developed, and that should be the focus of your analysis.

Avoiding Common Problems

It is not uncommon for HRIS CBA to include an extensive analysis of costs matched with a single source of benefits—typically, an estimate of direct cost reductions. Recognizing only direct cost reductions is problematic for two reasons. First, it ignores HR's more strategic role in improving organizational effectiveness. Online recruitment that results in hiring employees with higher potential and in developing and administering training programs through online tools, for example, is designed to enhance employee job performance and organizational effectiveness—not necessarily to reduce employee headcount. Ignoring these benefits can lead people to dramatically understate the actual value of HRIS investments.

A second problem is that, in many instances, items listed as direct cost reductions are actually indirect cost reductions. Time saved is a prime example. An HRIS will reduce the amount of time required to complete typical HR transactions, but these time savings do not result in actual reductions in overtime or headcount. In these instances, time saved is actually an indirect benefit. Its value depends on how individuals spend the extra time made available to them. As noted in Chapter 1, transactional activities deal mostly with day-to-day record keeping—for example, entering payroll information or employee status changes—and the administration of employee benefits. An HRIS that reduces the time on transactional activities would allow the HR employee to spend more time on traditional or transformational activities (see Chapter 1), both of which can assist the organization in meeting its strategic goals.

Incorrectly recognizing time saved as a direct cost reduction creates the wrong expectation among decision makers. This false expectation can lead to the incorrect perception that an investment did not succeed—no reduction in payroll expenses occurred—when, in fact, the benefits to the organization actually occurred in other forms. This point is illustrated in a CBA completed by the National Institute for Health's Center for Information Technology.

This analysis, which does an exceptional job of cost analysis, includes only one source of benefit—employee time saved. In this example, investing in the new system was projected to reduce staff time required by 75%, resulting in a 53% ROI.

Admirably, this organization was required to conduct a post-implementation review within 18 months to examine actual versus estimated costs and benefits and to determine whether use of the new system should be continued. The post-implementation analysis revealed that time saved was only 50%, not 75%. As a result, instead of the expected 53% ROI, the revised ROI was only 6%. One can only wonder what might have happened if the post-implementation review indicated the amount of time saved had been only 45%. In that case the CBA formulas would have shown a negative ROI. Would this organization have been forced to abandon this new system? Interestingly, in the post-implementation analysis, the evaluators pointed to other benefits to justify the continued use of the new system. However, since they were not included in the original analysis, bringing them into the post-implementation review may have been seen by some as inappropriate. Nevertheless, an indirect benefit, such as the improved employee morale that analysts found in the post-implementation evaluation, would be a powerful indication that the HRIS investment was worthwhile. In addition, employee morale has been directly linked to voluntary turnover, for which costs can be measured.

Third, be sure that value estimates assigned to time saved are reasonable. Many HRIS investments purport to save employee time, making it a common component of an HR technology CBA. When new HRIS functionality will save enough time to make it feasible to reduce the number of employees or reduce overtime expenses, time saved is a source of direct cost reduction. However, more often HR technology saves time in smaller increments that do not permit direct savings. That is, the amount of time saved does not permit whole positions to be eliminated. In these circumstances, time saved is an indirect benefit. The value of the time saved actually depends on what value-generating activities employees engage in during the time made available to them. For example, if the implementation of self-service functionality reduces workload but does not lead to headcount reductions, the new functionality might still have tremendous organizational value if those saved hours are used to improve the effectiveness of recruitment efforts or some other value-generating activity, such as the development of a team-training program.

Time saved, though, may not always have value. Consider a situation in which an individual engages in an activity that requires five minutes every day, but the application of new HRIS functionality is estimated to cut this time from five minutes to one minute. What is the value of the four minutes saved each day? Generally, larger blocks of time are more easily employed in value-enhancing activities. Consider your own use of time during the day. Could you constructively employ an additional minute of time each day? In most cases, we already have several of these minutes in our schedule that, because of the ebb and flow of daily events, are difficult to use productively. Therefore, it is questionable whether most employees can consistently use short periods of time (i.e., blocks of less than five minutes, for instance) productively. Thus, it may be very difficult to generate value for HR technology that is expected to save time but does so in many small increments.

Obviously, knowledge of your organization's business, as noted earlier in this chapter, will be important in identifying potential benefits. Use your own knowledge, but enlist other knowledgeable professionals and managers in this process as well. Individuals in your organization who are currently responsible for HR functionality prior to implementation of the HRIS (i.e., staff engaged in recruiting) or who are downstream customers of these HR products or services are good resources to enlist to identify benefits. They can help fill in the gaps and highlight other sources of benefits that might not be readily apparent to others. Vendors are a second resource. A review of the features and benefits cited by vendors in the relevant HRIS product space can also be used to identify potential sources of benefits. Vendors may also provide case studies that describe the experiences of companies that have implemented their products and the outcomes that were affected in those organizations. Using a combination of these sources can ensure a comprehensive list of the benefits to be gained when new HRIS functionality is developed.

Packaging the Analysis for Decision Makers

When you have completed your analysis, you should have (1) data that identify each benefit and cost component examined; (2) estimates of the dollar magnitude of each, including upper and lower bounds; (3) estimates of when the organization will incur each cost and receive each benefit; and (4) documentation justifying each decision you made in developing these values. The importance of documentation has been emphasized in all previous chapters, especially Chapter 6, and will be reemphasized in Chapter 9. After steps 1 to 4 are completed, the next step is to package the analysis for decision makers in your organization. Obviously, this process involves "selling" the analysis to senior management so that it will not be overlooked or minimized. Managerial decision makers prefer well-organized and clear CBAs to help them make their investment decisions.

Packaging the analysis for consideration by decision makers includes deciding what data to include and how the data should be organized. This process should be done with the entire project management (PM) team since the report must cover the entire HRIS project, not just the investment analysis. A table outlining the value and timing of costs and revenues is likely to be the central focus of the analysis. Some experts encourage limiting the number of sources of benefits presented to decision makers to simplify the presentation and the required justifications. This approach is satisfactory for small projects, which is, for a stand-alone HRIS application such as applicant tracking, but would be inappropriate for a complex HRIS project.

Although being able to make your case on a single page is beneficial, there are several advantages in including all the cost and benefit components that influence the likely outcomes of the investment decision. First, this offers the most complete, best estimate of the value of the investment, thereby giving decision makers the best information to make an appropriate investment decision. Second, it provides the decision maker with a fuller understanding of the investment and of the impact of the investment on the organization. Particularly with respect to indirect benefits, contingent actions taken by managers are likely to influence the extent to which the estimated benefits will be achieved. Making decision makers aware of these contingencies can help enlist their assistance in ensuring each investment's future success.

Conclusion

Accurately identifying and estimating the value of the benefits and costs of new HRIS functionality will play a critical role in HRIS investment decisions in the foreseeable future. A renewed interest in detailed investment analysis is healthy and should be embraced by analysts and decision makers. In addition to supporting improved investment decisions, detailed CBAs of HRIS investments are also likely to identify implementation contingencies and opportunities that can increase the chances for successful implementations. These analyses also provide the desired organizational targets against which to judge the effectiveness of an investment after implementation.

SUMMARY

The central focus of this chapter has been estimating and understanding the cost effectiveness dynamics of new investments in HRIS, which are assessed by the completion of a cost-benefit analysis (CBA). The calculation of a CBA has become critical for any new investment by an organization, as CBAs are closely linked with strategic goals such as profitability and the survival of the organization. Without a well-done CBA, managerial decision makers will be much less likely to approve expenditures for new HRIS investments, especially today. In the past, investments in an HRIS were primarily driven by a risk avoidance strategy or by cost reductions made possible by replacing paper-and-pencil or out-of-date systems. Today, organizations frequently rely on organizational enhancement strategies to justify the investment in new HRIS functionality. Organizational enhancement strategies highlight how a firm's effectiveness will be improved by the addition of a new or improved HRIS, as measured in a formal CBA by estimated increases in benefits (e.g., revenues) compared with estimated costs. This requires that we change our approach of cost justifying HRIS to account for these new types of benefits.

This chapter also addressed the importance of adopting an appropriate perspective on the CBA before any numbers are analyzed, and it provided guidelines for successful HRIS CBA (Table 8.1). An organizational enhancement strategy, one that examines both revenue enhancement as well as cost reduction, was shown to be the appropriate approach for conducting a CBA to justify an HRIS investment in today's organizations. Instructions on how to estimate direct and indirect costs and benefits were covered in detail, with a focus on creating a palatable CBA report for managerial decision makers. The various direct and indirect costs and benefits of an HRIS that go into the CBA have been discussed throughout the chapter, and several are listed in Table 8.2. Identifying the direct and indirect costs and benefits for a CBA must be extensive and complete. Without a comprehensive listing of direct and indirect costs and benefits, it will be impossible to calculate a correct CBA. After this comprehensive list is complete, the next step is to estimate the value of direct and indirect

costs and benefits. AEC was examined as one method to assess the indirect benefits of employee time saved by an HRIS investment. This estimating task is done by the HRIS project team, and therefore it is critical that the project team have individuals who can provide significant input to the estimates. Finally, it was argued that in addition to a best estimate of the CBA, potential estimates of the variance in estimates should be used to gain insight into best and worst case scenarios. This chapter has provided examples of how to enumerate and then define the value of these estimates (Table 8.2 and Figure 8.1).

Also, the approaches used in the estimation of indirect benefits, as well as the other methods discussed in this chapter for estimating costs and benefits, should be used for the post-implementation evaluation of the HRIS. The three common problems that can occur in a CBA were covered: (1) an extensive analysis of costs matched with a single source of benefits, which typically, is an estimate of direct cost reductions; (2) the listing of items as direct cost reductions that are actually indirect cost reductions (which is a very frequent occurrence); and (3) an unreasonable estimate of the value assigned to time saved or of the effects of time saved on the organization, probably the most common error in developing a CBA. In addition, as recommended in the earlier chapters, the CBA should be documented carefully and completely, as it will be useful in both HRIS project management and HRIS implementation.

KEY TERMS

DISCUSSION QUESTIONS

1. How has the use of HRIS evolved over the past 10 years in organizations, and how might this influence an organization's evaluations of additional investments in new or updated HRIS functionality?

2. Why is it important to estimate the benefits to be derived from new HRIS functionality before you estimate the costs? If costs were estimated first, how might this change the analysis?

3. Develop an argument for the implementation of an HRIS using a risk reduction strategy and an organizational enhancement strategy.

4. Organizations have traditionally used "employee time saved" as the primary source of benefits to justify HRIS and other types of information system investments. Why can this be problematic? Give several reasons and relate them to conducting a CBA.

5. How might an organization estimate the direct and indirect benefits of a new HRIS that decreases the time required by employees to complete transactions of the HR department through the implementation of employee self-service by creating employee portals (see Chapter 10) and allows HR employees to work on other projects such as talent management or online recruiting?

6. What makes indirect benefits so difficult to include in a CBA? What techniques might be used?

7. When should benchmarking be preferred to direct estimates of the magnitudes of benefits? When should direct estimates be preferred? Is it appropriate to use both?

8. Why does average employee contribution offer a better estimate of the contribution of individuals to an organization than total compensation (wages, incentives, and benefits)?

9. What are the factors you would have to use in calculating a cost-benefit ratio to support a decision to purchase a new HRIS when the organization already has an HRIS that was acquired 10 years ago? Be sure to mention the factors that would comprise the costs, direct and indirect, and the benefits, direct and indirect, of the current system versus the proposed system.

CASE STUDY

Investment Associates, Inc. (IA)[4] started as a small firm in 2001 with four employees plus its owner, Jim Tower. The company specialized in providing financial investment and tax advice to its clients. Jim had brought a substantial number of clients from his private practice, which had become too large for him to handle by himself. His four employees included three colleagues who had some experience in financial investment advice and a secretary/administrative assistant. Jim and his three colleagues were all certified public accountants (CPAs), and a considerable portion of the company's business was in tax consultation and the completion of individual and corporate tax returns.

IA was quite successful and, by 2007, had added 42 new employees—financial and tax advisers and additional administrative staff, including an office manager, Marian Sweet. In addition to the office manager's supervisory tasks, Marian had to complete federal and state reports on the employees as required by law.[5] However, Marian was not trained in HRM, and she suggested to Jim that the company needed to hire someone with a background in HRM before they "got into trouble" with the government. Marian was particularly concerned about gender and racial discrimination but did not understand how to apply the provisions of the appropriate laws and guidelines.

In November 2007, IA hired Sylvia Wong, who had an undergraduate degree in psychology and four years' experience in HR. In addition, in December 2007, Jim was negotiating to purchase the financial consulting business of an old friend who was retiring. This purchase would mean the addition of 17 new employees in February or March 2008. Sylvia met with Jim in mid-January 2008 to discuss the growing burden of employee reports and payroll processing, all of which were currently being done using a paper-based HR system. She advised Jim that the company needed an HRIS to process employee records and complete the required government reports. As an example, she stated that, because she had to search through paper copies of all employee files, it took her a full week to complete the Equal Employment Opportunity Report (EEO-1)[6] required by the federal government. Furthermore, based on this report, it appeared that the company could have problems in terms of compliance with several federal laws. She suggested that the company purchase an HRIS to assist with company record keeping and the production of required reports.

Since the company had been using computer-based applications for financial analysis and tax reporting, Jim thought that Sylvia's suggestion to computerize employee records was a good one. However, given his financial background, he wanted Sylvia to develop a business case, including a cost-benefit analysis, for the purchase of an HRIS.

Your task is to help Sylvia justify the purchase of an HRIS.

Case Study Questions

1. What approaches to justifying this investment might Sylvia consider?

2. What are some of the costs and benefits involved in this investment in an HRIS? Which would you be sure to include in your CBA of this project and why?

3. Explain how to estimate costs and benefits, both direct and indirect, in terms that Jim will understand. (Remember, Jim always has his eye on the "bottom line.")

4. Explain how to calculate a CBA to justify the HRIS project. Would you use cost reduction or organizational enhancement (or both) as a strategy for justifying the purchase?

5. What are the three common problems that could occur in your CBA for an HRIS? How would you avoid them?

6. What are some of the ways you can use the HR metrics that would be available after the implementation of an HRIS to justify its purchase?

7. Finally, and most important, explain how variance estimates that can be generated for a CBA would be useful to Jim in the management of his company.

STUDENT STUDY SITE _____

Visit the Student Study Site at **http://www.sagepub.com/kavanagh3e** for additional learning tools such as access to SAGE journal articles and related web resources.

NOTES

1. The content of this chapter was based in part on two articles published in the *IHRIM Journal* (Carlson, 2004a, 2004b).

2. Dollars will be used as an example of currency throughout this chapter. When used so, it implies that other currencies such as the euro, yen, or peso could be substituted for it.

3. The company name is fictitious to protect the confidentiality of the actual company.

4. The names of the company and employees are fictional to protect confidentiality.

5. See Chapter 10 for a discussion of some of these reports.

6. See Chapter 10.

REFERENCES

Bondarouk, T., & Meijerink, J. (2010, August). *Implementation of an HR portal: Results of a qualitative study from a public sector organization*. Paper presented at the annual meeting of the Academy of Management, Montreal.

Boudreau, J. (1991). Utility analysis for decisions in human resource management. In M. D. Dunnette & L. M. Hough (Eds.), *Handbook of industrial and organizational psychology* (Vol. 2, pp. 621–752). Palo Alto, CA: Consulting Psychologists Press.

Browne, G. J., & Rogich, M. B. (2001). An empirical investigation of user requirements elicitation: Comparing the effectiveness of prompting techniques. *Journal of Management Information Systems, 17*(4), 223–249.

Carlson, K. D. (2004a). Estimating the value of the indirect benefits of new HR technology. *IHRIM Journal, 8*(4), 22–28.

Carlson, K. D. (2004b). Justifying HRIS investments post Y2K: Identifying sources of value. *IHRIM Journal, 8*(1), 21–27.

Cascio, W. F. (1987). *Costing human resources: The financial impact of behavior in organizations* (2nd ed.). Boston: Kent.

Cascio, W. F. (1991). *Costing human resources: The financial impact of behavior in organizations* (3rd ed.). Boston: Kent.

Cascio, W. F. (2000). *Costing human resources: The financial impact of behavior in organizations* (4th ed.). Boston: Kent.

Dery, K., Hall, R., & Wiblen, S. (2010, August). *HRISs and the constraint of human agency: The implications for HR skills*. Paper presented at the annual meeting of the Academy of Management, Montreal.

Dooney, J., Blackmon, O., & Williams, S. (2009). *SHRM Human capital benchmarking study: 2009 executive summary*. Washington, DC: Society of Human Resource Management.

Dulebohn, J. (2010, August). *Assessing cross-functional teams in ERP/eHR implementation projects*. Paper presented at the annual meeting of the Academy of Management, Montreal.

Fitz-enz, J. (2001). *How to measure human resources management* (3rd ed.). New York: McGraw-Hill.

Grant, D., Newell, S., & Kavanagh, M. J. (2010, August). *Realizing the potential of an HRIS: Unintended consequences, human agency, and the HR function.* Symposium presented at the annual meeting of the Academy of Management, Montreal.

Howes, P. (2002, February/March). Calculating the ROI for an HRIS business plan. IHRIM. *link,* 12–15.

Kahneman, D., & Tversky, A. (1979). Prospect theory: An analysis of decisions under risk. *Econometrica, 47,* 313–327.

Kavanagh, M. J., Gueutal, H. G., & Tannenbaum, S. I. (1990). *Human resource information systems.* Boston: PWS-Kent.

Lemon, W. F., Bowitz, J., Burn, J., & Hackney, R. (2002). Information systems project failures: A comparative study of two countries. *Journal of Global Management, 10*(2), 28–39.

Mayberry, E. (2008). *How to build an HR business case* (SHRM White Paper). Alexandria, VA: Society for Human Resource Management.

Schmidt, F. L., & Hunter, J. E. (1983). Individual differences in productivity: An empirical test of estimates derived from studies of selection procedure utility. *Journal of Applied Psychology, 68,* 407–414.

SHL. (2012). *2012 Business Outcomes Study Report: People intelligence driving business results.* Alpharetta, GA: SHL.

Society of Human Resource Management (SHRM). (2010). *HR metrics toolkit.* Alexandria, VA: Author.

Tansley, C. (2010, August). *Project team branding on global human resources information systems projects.* Paper presented at the annual meeting of the Academy of Management, Montreal.

Change Management

Implementation, Integration, and Maintenance of the Human Resource Information System

Romuald A. Stone and Richard D. Johnson

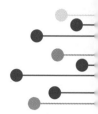

EDITORS' NOTE

Perhaps one of the major obstacles in the use of an HRIS is its implementation. The IT as well as the HR literature is filled with stories about the failure to implement well-designed and well-developed computer technology. This failure has occurred not only in HRIS implementation but also in operations, marketing, and financial computer-based systems. Although technical challenges will always remain in implementing an HRIS, the major challenge to successful implementation is often more behavioral than technical. Lack of employee and user involvement has been one of the central problems with the reported failures. In this chapter, we will examine various approaches to organizational and technology change and apply them to the problem of implementing a new or re-automated HRIS.

After completing this chapter, you should be able to

- Understand the management of change through the perspectives of various change models
- Understand the factors that contribute to HRIS implementation failure
- Discuss the elements important to successful HRIS implementation
- Discuss the importance of integration of the HRIS with the other systems in the organization
- Discuss the importance of continual maintenance of the HRIS
- Understand the differences and similarities between organizational development (OD) and change management (CM)

HRIS IN ACTION

The Arizona Department of Administration, Human Resources Division manages the largest human resources system in Arizona. The department administers the state's Human Resources Information Solution (HRIS). The customer base includes every state agency, with the exception of the universities, that relies on HRIS to accurately pay state employees and manage health insurance coverage. Currently, HRIS processes information for over 40,000 employees and calculates the state's annual payroll of $2.5 billion. HRIS is the system that all state employees use to access their pay, leave balances, and W-2 information.[1] The HR Division's early experience with implementing an HRIS provides a good backdrop to the topical coverage in this chapter.

The HR Division initiated a program in 2002 to update its HRIS system. According to department estimates, the new HRIS system would "produce more than $100 million in cost savings over the next 10 years by automating functions previously performed by administrative staff and [by] reducing turnover due to increased employee satisfaction" (Office of the Auditor General, 2005). The implementation of the new system proceeded in phases: Phase 1 was completed in December 2003 and Phase 2 was supposed to be completed in 2004.

The implementation plan failed to meet planned milestones by a wide margin, and in fact exhausted most of the project budget early into Phase 2.

With the loss of funding, the HRIS project staff was reduced from 60 to 18 positions. As a result, some state agencies had to rely on in-house systems or manual processes to ensure they had the necessary personnel information processing capabilities.

Compounding this situation was the fact that the implementation team had been slow to address some of the user requests for Phase 1 modifications, some of which are needed to correct programs that do not function properly. The net result of this poor management of the HRIS implementation project was that state agencies had not realized the anticipated efficiency savings from the new system (Office of the Auditor General, 2005).

In 2005, the HR Division considered a new plan to restart the project. Some of the questions the change leadership team was thinking about included: Did they have the right change management competencies to manage this project? What were the likely obstacles that they would face during this next phase of the project—and could they prepare for them in advance? Could they deal with the resistance from some agency managers and users? What mistakes made in the earlier effort could they avoid going forward? And finally, they wondered if the HR Division was ready for this new implementation project—that is, what other steps are needed to ensure that the HRIS project was successful?

We hope to answer many of these questions in this chapter.

Introduction to the Management of Change

> It's not the progress I mind, it's the change I don't like.
>
> —Mark Twain

Most managers face change management issues every day; managing change is now a permanent part of every manager's job. It's clear that HR departments and leaders are in the middle of this climate of seemingly endless change, change that involves not only the functioning of the HR department, but also its role within the enterprise and the HR technology used to provide strategic value to the business (Fletcher, 2005).

The evidence is clear that successfully introducing major HRISs into organizations requires an effective blend of good technical and good organizational skills. As Lorenzi and Riley (2000) remind us,

> A "technically best" system can be brought to its knees by people who have low psychological ownership in the system and who vigorously

resist its implementation. The leader who knows how to manage the organizational impact of information systems can sharply reduce the behavioral resistance to change, including to new technology, to achieve a more rapid and productive introduction of information technology. (p. 116)

Effective management of change represents a critical core competence that all organizations and HR leaders must master. By better understanding the field of knowledge and competencies related to managing change, HR professionals can better manage change in organizations and reap the rewards that accrue to successful change initiatives. However, as the HRIS literature suggests, the track record of most change initiatives—be they restructuring, introduction of new technology, mergers, **process improvement**, or **reengineering**—is poor. One expert in the field noted that at best only one third of these kinds of initiatives achieve any success at all (Beer & Nohria, 2000). In addition, a 2007 federal IT project study identified approximately 227 projects totaling at least $10.4 billion as being poorly planned or performing (U.S. Government Accountability Office, 2007). Clearly, learning to effectively manage technology change is an important managerial competency and competitive advantage. Broadly speaking, there are two broad ways of assessing and implementing organizational change: organizational development and change management. Because organizational development is the more comprehensive change project, we will describe it first.

Organizational Development

Organization development (OD) is a planned system of change. Porras and Robertson (1992) define OD as "a set of behavioral science-based theories, values, strategies, and techniques aimed at the planned change of the organizational work setting for the purpose of enhancing individual development and improving organizational performance, through the alteration of organizational members' on-the-job-behaviors (p. 722)." Another aspect of OD is that it is "organization-wide." The goal is to continually transform the organization to remain competitive and remain effective at meeting the needs of the various stakeholders. OD initiatives encompass the entire organization and affect major organizational systems. For example, acquiring new machinery for an assembly line would affect a number of systems. Thus, it is important to recognize the difference between OD and change management. OD is a more general approach that encompasses the complete organization. Change management is one of the processes or procedures that are a part of OD and is based on Change Process Theory. Change Process Theory describes the underlying dynamics of the planned change process within an organization by specifying variables or factors that can be manipulated by the OD intervention.

Change Management

Change management (CM) is the systematic process of applying the knowledge, tools, and resources needed to effect change by transforming an organization from its current state to some future desired state (Potts & LaMarsh, 2004, p. 16). Although this sounds similar to the definition of organizational development, change management is focused more on changing employees' attitudes and behavior than OD, which is also interested in changing employees' attitudes and behaviors; but CM is only one part of an OD intervention. Change management can be used on projects that can be either larger or smaller in scope because it is only focused on changing the attitudes and behaviors of the individuals in that organization, which are important in any OD project. Change management must consider altering the mindset and behavior patterns of the people within that organization. Change in organizations is not something that happens instantaneously. Change is a process that fundamentally involves three elements: the current state, a transition, and a future state. As such, any change model chosen must address the important content, people, and process issues at each phase of the change initiative. At its core, change management is focused on moving organizations from a current state to a desired future state.

If the change is planned, the process typically involves the use of a systematic approach that includes both a vision and a plan to ensure the change activities are on course, and on target with respect to cost, time, and expected results. One of the ways in which this process is controlled is by the use of project management concepts and tools as discussed in Chapter 6.

Consider this example. When the catalog retailer Lillian Vernon Corporation undertook a major transformation of its IT infrastructure, the initial results proved dismal. What happened was that the change management team—which included the president and the chief information officer (CIO)—failed to take change management seriously. In particular, they overlooked the importance of assessing and managing readiness for change. "Employees resisted mightily, avoiding training and blaming new applications for their frustration. . . . The employees had already made up their minds that the system was not going to work, and they didn't want any part of it" (Paul, 2004, p. 80). The net result was that the company fell short of its ambitious timeline for implementation and missed an opportunity to use the new information system to improve overall performance.

The lesson here is that implementing change goes beyond just installing the physical equipment and system. What Lillian Vernon failed to do was create a sense of urgency and help the employees understand how the new IT system would be better than the current system. Very few people like changes in their lives, particularly as it affects their jobs. Effective communication is critical to the change process, as discussed later in this chapter. Successful change requires a "critical mass of people who are committed, are willing to change and will sustain their new behavior to align with the needs of the change" (Miller, 2004, p. 10).

The Change Management Process: Science and Art

Organizations are in a constant state of change, which enables them to remain competitive in the marketplace. Some of the forces for change are external, such as the appearance of new technology, while others are internal, for example, downsizing the workforce. Regardless of the reason for change, it must be effectively managed or chaos will exist. The person who is in charge of the change is referred to as a **change agent** or a **change leader**. This change agent can be internal to the organization, for example, the director of HR, or external to the organization, for example, a consultant. The process of managing change typically begins with a gap analysis. A **gap analysis** indicates the differences between the current state of affairs in the organization and the desired future state. Sometimes this analysis is done by senior management or the HRIS project team and sometimes it is done through questionnaires distributed to employees. This procedure is frequently termed the survey feedback approach. After the gap analysis has been completed and plans for the change process have been made, the next stage is to begin the implementation of the change.

At this point, a major consideration is the **employee resistance to change** from members of the organization. Change is never easy. When faced with change, a natural reaction by employees is to express fear, concerns, struggle, and opposition. The basic employee reaction that leads to fear is the idea that employees were not performing adequately, and perhaps there will be lay-offs in the company. As Pinder (1998) notes in a major book on work motivation: "The nature of the work that people do (or do not have to do) has long been a principal basis for the determination and definition of one's social class—of one's comparable status within society as a whole (p. 148)."

There is no magic formula or easily prescribed processes to guarantee success to overcome this resistance. The reality is that change is "messy, complicated, and its outcomes are easily swayed by a host of factors that only complicate our ability to ensure success" (Herold & Fedor, 2008, p. xiii). One axiom in studying organizational change is that change is the only constant in an organization. There is both art and science to managing change. The science of managing change is the framework for diagnosing, planning, and executing change projects. The art of managing change is what distinguishes the great from not so great change agent in making a real difference through the application of the science of change management. Consequently, we know that any change process requires both the application of art and of science to any change initiative in order to maximize the likelihood of success. We begin by discussing several frameworks or models of change in the following section.

Models of the Change Process

In this section, we introduce and describe a general model of the change process and then four specific models of organizational change that have received considerable attention in the change management literature: Lewin's change model, Gleicher's change equation formula, Nadler's congruence model, and **Kotter's eight-stage change model**. Lawler and Worley (2006) make a very interesting observation regarding change models that is worth highlighting: "we have been intrigued by the various change models . . . most of them suggest that with the right interventions, most, if not all, organizations can make significant changes. We are not at all sure that this is true" (p. xv). The authors go on to suggest that if this were true, then more companies would be successful in executing change initiatives. Notwithstanding the authors' caution, the fate of many change efforts will be worse without a change model to guide change leaders in the process. Some of these models are focused at the individual employee or group level, what is referred to as the micro level, while others are focused at the organizational or macro level. These models help draw our attention to the elements important in the successful management of any HRIS implementation project.

Overview of Organizational Change

Anderson and Anderson (2001) suggest that all change models fall into two categories: frameworks and process models. Frameworks focus mainly on topical areas that change leaders need to pay attention to when executing a change initiative. These models are good planning and diagnostic tools to help in understanding the complexities inherent in organizations and the interdependencies associated with change. Process models are more robust in that they provide more direct guidance on what should be accomplished and in generally what order (Anderson & Anderson, 2001). Just as a roadmap is useful in getting a driver from point A to point B, likewise process models serve as a roadmap and action plan for any transformation effort. "Given the complexity of change, and how to actually get to a new state, a process roadmap is essential" (Anderson & Anderson, 2010, p. 20). Finally, some models can be classified as hybrid, with characteristics of both a framework and process model.

Burke (2008) outlines five reasons why the use of change models is helpful to change leaders:

1. *Categorize information.* With literally thousands of bits of information related to a change initiative, models help categorize the information into manageable compartments.

2. *Enhance understanding.* Given that a change model has a beginning, middle, and end, if problems arise in any of these areas, we can use this information to help diagnose the problem and where action is required.

3. *Interpret data about the organization.* There is much interdependence with any change effort. As such, a model helps us in recognizing these linkages and in taking appropriate action to remedy any problem areas (e.g., structure and strategy).

4. *Provide common language.* A model helps provide a common language and vocabulary to discuss the change with stakeholders and the change team.

5. *Guide action.* Most importantly, a model helps provide the roadmap mentioned earlier. The sequence of actions and potentially the priority of those actions (depending on the robustness of the model) helps guide the change journey and enhances the potential for success.

There is no silver bullet with change. Leading any change initiative is a complex activity, and one model of change cannot be viewed as superior for all organizations. As Schaffer and McCreight (2004) remind us, "because each firm has its own work processes, culture, and competencies, a given change formula may work well in one but fail miserably in the next" (p. 33). The choice of change model to adopt will most likely flow from prior experience or trial and error and be consistent with the culture of the company. In many cases, the adopted model will be a hybrid, with elements taken from more than one of the existing models.

Selected Change Models

Action-Research Model

We begin this section of the chapter with an introduction to a process model of the management of change in organizations. The **action-research model** can best be seen as a general perspective to use in any planned change effort. Examination of the use of any successful change effort used will reveal some, if not all, of the components of the action-research model. Thus, although we use the term *model* to describe the prescriptions of action research, it is better viewed as an approach to the management of change. Careful reading of the change management literature reveals that the action-research model appears in, or is part of, most change management projects.

The term *action research* is not new. It can be traced to the work of Collier (1945), of Lewin (1946), and of Lewin's student (Lippitt, 1950), while others (Corey, 1953; French & Bell, 1973) have provided excellent descriptions of the action-research model as it relates to organizational development and change. French and Bell (1969) defined organization development (OD) at one point as "organization improvement through action research." If one idea can be said to summarize OD's underlying philosophy, it would be that *action research as it was conceptualized by Kurt Lewin is the basis for a successful OD project.* Concerned with social change and, more particularly, with effective, permanent social change, Lewin believed that the motivation to change was strongly related to action: If people are active in decisions affecting them, they are more likely to adopt new ways. "Rational social management," he said, "proceeds in a spiral of steps, each of which is composed of a circle of planning, action and fact-finding about the result of action" (Lewin, 1946, p. 38).

Frohman, Sashkin, and Kavanagh (1976) provided the following definition:

> Action-research describes a particular process-model whereby behavioral science knowledge is applied to help a client (usually a group or social system) solve real problems and not incidentally learn the processes involved in problem-solving, while generating further knowledge with respect to the field of applied behavioral science. (p. 130)

The basis of the action-research model is the interaction of managerial or organizational action and research that both evaluates the action taken and provides data for future planning of the change effort. Thus, using this model involves the interlocking of the research processes of data collection, analysis, and evaluation and the management action processes of planning, directing, and implementing change. As seen in Figure 9.1, a cycle in the action-research model would include the following: (1) initial data collection and gap analysis, (2) feedback of results to the HRIS project team, (3) action planning for the next phase of the HRIS project, (4) directing and implementing changes during the next phase, (5) data collection and analysis to evaluate the changes, and (6) feedback of results to the project team and action planning for the HRIS project.

Lewin's Change Model

One of the earliest and key contributions to organizational change is Kurt **Lewin's three-step change model** (see Figure 9.2). Lewin's (1946) framework serves as a general model for understanding planned change. The model has been used to explain how information systems can be implemented more effectively (Benjamin & Levinson, 1993).

Lewin's change model evolved from his interest in resolving social conflict and in improving the human condition through behavioral change. In his study of group behavior, Lewin argued that behavior was a complex interaction of what the individual brought to the situation and the environment (or *field,* as he called it). We can express this relationship as $B = f(P, E)$, where behavior is defined as a function of the person and the environment. In the main, Lewin believed that the existing condition (or status quo) was maintained by a set

Figure 9.1   The Action-Research Cycle

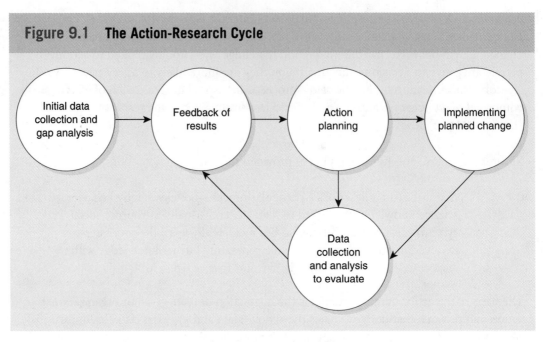

Source: Reprinted with permission from Kavanagh, Gueutal, and Tannenbaum (1990).

of forces affecting the situation, and only by identifying and plotting the potency of these forces is significant change possible.

Lewin's change model conceived of change in terms of a modification of the forces that stabilize a system's behavior. In particular, he envisioned a dynamic in which there are two sets of opposing forces—those that are focused on maintaining stability and the status quo and those driving change. When we have a balance between these two opposing forces, we have what Lewin called a state of "quasi-stationary equilibrium." To alter that state to enhance the probability of change, we must decrease the forces that oppose the change while simultaneously increasing the forces for change. The reader should recognize that the first

Figure 9.2   Lewin's Three-Step Change Model

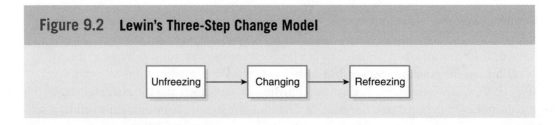

step in the action-research model has to have occurred before this force-field analysis can be done. In fact, as we go through the models in this chapter, they all use the first step in the action-research model, or else, with no information, why would they need to change?

To better understand these forces, we can use a procedure called **force-field analysis**. To develop a force-field analysis, create two columns on a sheet of paper. In one column, list the forces that drive or support a change in an HRIS, and in the other column, list the forces that will inhibit the change. It is helpful to also assign a relative potency or strength to each force listed. By plotting the forces, we can better understand which forces need to be strengthened or diminished to bring about change. Lewin suggested that the path of least resistance, that is, modifying those forces maintaining the status quo, would produce less tension and resistance than would increasing the forces for change; thus, the former is a more effective change strategy than the latter.

The key to understanding this approach, at the individual level, is to see change as a profound, dynamic psychological process (Schein, 1996). This psychological process involves painful unlearning and difficult relearning as one cognitively attempts to restructure one's thoughts, perceptions, feelings, and attitudes. Lewin viewed these three steps as follows:

Unfreezing

At the outset, every change project requires getting people to change their minds and behavior regarding the old way of doing things and to embrace the new state. This means that people need to "see the purpose of the change, agree with it, be supported by rewards and recognition, have the skills to perform the new activities, and see key people modeling the new behavior" (Warhaftig, 2005). This means that the quasi-stationary equilibrium (or status quo) supported by the complex set of driving and restraining forces needs to be destabilized (unfrozen) before the old way of doing things can be discarded (unlearned) and new behavior successfully adopted (Burnes, 2004). **Unfreezing** is sometimes accomplished through a process of "psychological disconfirmation." By introducing information that shows discrepancies between behavior desired by organization members and those behaviors currently exhibited, managers can motivate individuals to engage in change activities.

However, the unfreezing process is not that easy to accomplish. Edgar Schein, in his excellent reflection on Lewin's impact on his own thinking and work, argues that three processes are necessary to ready people for and motivate them to change: (1) disconfirmation of the validity of the status quo, (2) the induction of guilt or survival anxiety, and (3) creating psychological safety (Schein, 1996). Schein suggests that, for any change to occur, some form of dissatisfaction or frustration with the status quo must be presented. People need to know what drives the need for change, why they should change, and where they are headed. In addition, they should know what will and will not change. They should also know the business case or rationale for change. Further, the emotional and motivational needs of those impacted by the change should also be addressed. For example, managers should help people understand what's in it for them if they change. Finally, managers should address the rewards or consequences of changing or not changing.

Here, Schein's "survival anxiety" comes into play. Providing a reason for change is not always enough. We also need to convince people that, if they do not change, individual and organizational goals will be frustrated. This is what Kotter (1996) calls creating a **sense of urgency**. Without a sense of urgency, "people won't give that extra effort . . . they won't make needed sacrifices. Instead they will cling to the status quo and resist initiatives from above" (p. 5).

Psychological safety refers to mitigating the anxiety that people feel whenever they are asked to do something different or new. People are concerned about losing their identities, looking dumb, and losing their effectiveness or self-esteem. This anxiety can be a significant restraining force to change. Without sufficient psychological safety present, change leaders will find the road to change filled with more obstacles than they planned on. We can address psychological safety by addressing employee needs: What must I do differently? What are the new ways I will have to work? How do I learn the new things that I'm going to have to do? Who's going to teach me? Am I capable of making the changes that I will need to make?

Transition

Whereas unfreezing creates the motivation to change, the changing or transition stage focuses on helping change the behavior of organization members to the new state of affairs. William Bridges (2003) defines this stage as "psychological; it is a three-phase process that people go through as they internalize and come to terms with the details of the new situation that the change brings about" (p. 3). Not getting everyone through the **transition** phase puts the outcome of the change project in jeopardy. The transition phase consists of three key stages: ending →neutral zone→ new beginnings (pp. 4–5):

> 1. *Ending:* "Before you can begin something new, you have to end what used to be. You need to identify who is losing what, expect a reaction, and acknowledge the losses openly. Repeat information about what is changing—it will take time to sink in" (Cameron & Green, 2004, p. 108).

> 2. *Neutral zone:* The step between the old and new way of doing things is a "neutral zone," where people need to make the psychological adjustments necessary to say goodbye to the old and begin to welcome the new. In the neutral zone, people feel disoriented, motivation falls, and anxiety rises. Consensus may break down as attitudes become polarized.

3. *New beginnings:* This final step is about coming out of the transition and making a new beginning. In this stage, people develop new identities, experience new energy, and discover a new sense of purpose that makes the change begin to work.

As Bridges (2003) reminds us, if change agents

> don't help people through these three steps in the transition process, even the most wonderful training programs often fall flat. The leaders forget endings and neutral zones (Steps 1 and 2); they try to start with the final stage of the transition. And they can't see what went wrong! (p. 6)

Refreezing

This final step seeks to stabilize the organization at a new state of equilibrium and to ensure that the new behaviors are relatively safe from regression (Burnes, 2004, p. 986). **Refreezing** often requires changes in the organization's culture and norms, policies, and practices. We address culture in a later section.

Change Equation Formula

When initiating an organizational change project, it's important early on to determine how ready people are to accept and implement the change (Burke, 2002, p. 150). Gleicher's **change equation formula**, as modified by Dannemiller and Jacobs (1992), helps us assess this degree of readiness as follows (Beckhard & Harris, 1987):

$$C = (D \times V \times F) > R,$$

where C is the change, D the dissatisfaction with the status quo, V the vision, F the first steps (feasibility), and R the resistance to change (costs).

If we refer to Lewin's (1946) force-field analysis discussed earlier, D, V, and F are all "forces for change," while R represents the "forces against change." Gleicher's change equation formula provides a simple and straightforward perspective that reveals the possibilities and conditions at work in organizational change. Note that all three forces for change must be active to offset the forces against the change, which are usually manifested as resistance to change from organizational members. The change program must address *dissatisfaction* with the present situation, present a clear *vision* of the future and what is possible, and demonstrate knowledge of the *first steps* necessary to reach the vision. If any one of the three is missing, the product of the equation will tend toward zero and *resistance to change* will dominate.

In sum, this "change formula is deceptively simple but extremely useful. It can be brought into play at any point in a change process to analyze how things are going. When the formula is shared with all parties involved in the change, it helps to illuminate what various parties need to do to make progress" (Beckhard & Harris, 1987, p. 104).

Process reengineering is a critical component in HRIS implementation. One of the reasons organizations do not realize their full ROI from new technology is that they simply automate existing processes rather than using the implementation as an opportunity to reengineer them.

According to David Nadler (1998), one of the key steps in understanding and managing change is to first fully understand the dynamics and performance of the organization. Without this understanding of the varied issues affecting performance, accomplished by an initial data collection step, successful change may be misdirected by focusing on the symptoms rather than the true causes of a problem. A useful tool that helps change leaders understand the interplay of forces that shape the performance of each organization is **Nadler's congruence model** (p. 41). The model is based on many years of academic research and practical application in a wide range of companies and industries (see Figure 9.3).

There are several benefits in using the congruence model (Mercer Delta Consulting, 2003, pp. 10–12).

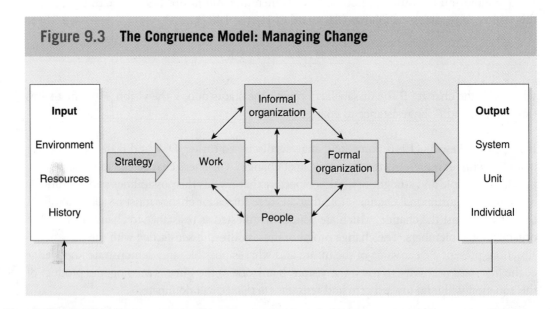

Figure 9.3   The Congruence Model: Managing Change

1. If we use a computer metaphor, at its core, the model depicts both the "hardware" and "software" dimensions of an organization. The hardware represents the strategy, work, and formal organization—how the firm is organized to coordinate, communicate, and motivate the workforce in accomplishing its vision and goals. The software side of the model makes up the social dimension of the organization—its people and the informal processes (e.g., shared values) that shape the behavior and performance of an organization's employees.

2. The model helps us understand the dynamics of change by allowing us to predict the impact of change throughout the organizational system. When leaders conduct a gap analysis to compare results with expectations, it may trigger a review of strategy and a reassessment of what change is needed to achieve stated goals and objectives. This reevaluation may lead to changes in work and formal organization, after which too many change leaders stop without undertaking the difficult but critical task of reshaping the firm's culture to align it with the new strategy.

3. Finally, the model helps change leaders see organizations not as inflexible, static structures that produce outputs but as organic, dynamic sets of people and processes that are interdependent. It helps us recognize that managing real change is a function of several complex dimensions. It provides a useful "mental model" for understanding organizational problems and for enhancing our ability to pinpoint a solution.

Nadler's congruence model is an organizational performance model that is built on the view that organizations are systems and that only if there is congruence ("fit") between the various organizational subsystems can we expect changed and improved performance. As reflected in the model, the basic components of any organizational system include *input, strategy, output, and the operating organization.*

> The transformation process of any organization is composed of four components: (1) work activities, (2) the people that do the work, (3) the formal organization and (4) the informal organization.

This model proposes that effective management of change means paying attention to the alignment of all four components. You can't assume that changing one element will cause the other elements to fall into place (Nadler, 1998, p. 42). Cameron and Green (2004) use an apt metaphor to highlight this important point:

> Imagine tugging only one part of a child's mobile. The whole mobile wobbles and oscillates for a bit, but eventually all the different

components settle down to where they were originally. So it is with organizations. They easily revert to the original mode of operation unless you attend to all four components. (p. 104)

If alignment of each of the components—work, people, structure, and culture—with the others is deficient, then performance will suffer. The greater the fit or congruence, the greater will be the organization's ability to manage a change process.

Kotter's Process of Leading Change

Kotter's (1996) eight-stage model was developed after studying more than 100 organizations undergoing change. The model offers a process to manage change successfully and avoid the common pitfalls that have beset failed change programs (see Figure 9.4). We can view his approach as a vision for the change process, one that calls attention to its key phases.

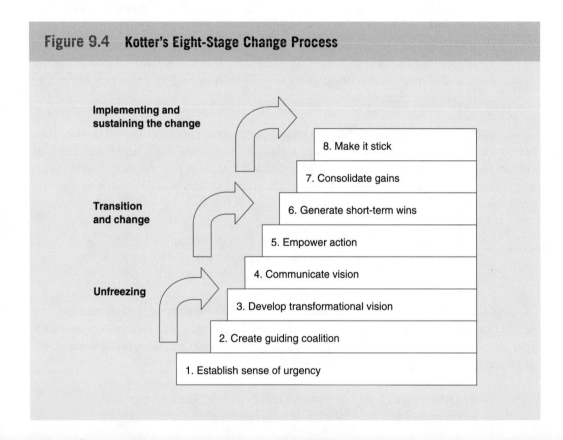

Figure 9.4   Kotter's Eight-Stage Change Process

Implementing and sustaining the change

8. Make it stick

7. Consolidate gains

Transition and change

6. Generate short-term wins

5. Empower action

4. Communicate vision

3. Develop transformational vision

Unfreezing

2. Create guiding coalition

1. Establish sense of urgency

The model provides two key lessons, first that the change process goes through a series of phases, *each lasting a considerable period of time,* and, second, that critical mistakes in any of the phases can have a devastating impact on the momentum of the change process. As can be seen in Figure 9.4, the first four stages coincide with Lewin's "unfreezing" first stage. The next three stages focus on introducing new practices into the organization. Finally, the last stage focuses on grounding the changes in the corporate culture, which coincides with Lewin's third stage, "refreezing."

The model indicates that all the stages should be worked through in order to effect successful change. Skipping a step or getting too far ahead in the change process without a solid base may create problems. Without the follow-through that takes place in the final step, you may not be able to make any changes.

Important Reminders Regarding Change Models

The change models described above fall under the umbrella of traditional philosophy of change models. The traditional approaches to organizational change generally follow a linear, rational model in which the focus is on controllability under the stewardship of a strong leader or "guiding coalition." This approach assumes that change involves a number of predictable, reducible steps that can be planned and managed. In other words, the change agent can choose from a menu of formulaic approaches that supposes that organizational change can and should be a controlled and orderly affair. As such these models appear seductively simple and imply that success is guaranteed if they are followed to the letter. But, as Graetz and Smith (2010) note, there are several shortcomings worth noting to these models.

1. Managers and change agents cannot control organizations the same way that an operator can control a machine made of moving, but inanimate parts.

2. The process models ignore the human factor—treating individuals as automatons rather than active partners in the change process.

3. The models presuppose that employees will respond enthusiastically and uniformly to their leaders' call to arms.

Because the traditional approach to change is concerned with stability and control, what is emphasized in these models is management's singular story about why the change is necessary and ignores the many other distinctive stories unfolding around them in the organization narrative. As a result, the risk is that the principal response by managers may be to *not* listen to, but to silence, dissident voices. These risks should be kept in mind as the organization implements any change initiative.

Next, we turn our attention to the factors that contribute to HRIS implementation failures.

Why Do System Failures Occur?

Increasingly, the failure to successfully implement information systems has less to do with the hardware or software aspects of the new system but instead has more to do with the skills of the change leader, and the people and organizational issues related to the change. A review of the change literature has identified a number of key factors that contribute to IT system implementation failures (see Figure 9.5). Although no one single factor is the culprit, Lorenzi and Riley (2000) suggest that "a snowball effect is often seen, with a shortcoming in one area leading to subsequent shortcomings in other areas" (p. 117). We have grouped the key causal factors related to HRIS implementation failures into five main categories: leadership, planning, change management, communication, and training (Blanchard, 2007, pp. 203–204; Kandel, 2007; Lorenzi & Riley, 2000).

Figure 9.5   Reasons for IT System Failure

Leadership	• Lack of executive support • Lack of strong leadership and change management skills in project manager • Lack of recognition for team's efforts • Lack of accountability for implementing the change
Planning	• No clear vision for the change • Failure to define a clear and comprehensive project scope • Lack of a comprehensive project plan • Failure to define fully the functionality of the system • Insufficient project staffing; staff turnover and complacency • Insufficient project funding • Roles and responsibilities not clearly defined or understood by everyone • Failure to meet budget and deadlines • The change leadership team doesn't include early adopters, resisters, or informal leader • Inadequate testing of the system
Change management	• Culture and level of readiness for change are not assessed prior to the start of the project • Change leaders fail to respect the power of the culture to kill the change

	• No strategies to nurture or grow a new culture
	• The change isn't piloted, so the organization doesn't learn what's needed to support the change
	• Organizational systems and other initiatives aren't aligned with the change
	• End users are not involved in the process
	• Lack of a plan for user resistance/rejection
	• Processes are not reengineered
Communication	• Lack of a comprehensive communication plan
	• Ineffective ongoing communication with all affected stakeholders
	• Failure to customize communications to different audiences
	• People leading the change think that announcing the change is the same as implementing it
Training	• Inadequate or poor-quality training
	• Poor timing of training—too early or too late
	• People are not enabled or encouraged to build new skills
	• Lack of ongoing training

Leadership

Major change is almost impossible without top leadership support. "Leadership must set the direction, pace, and tone and provide a clear consistent rationale that brings everyone together behind a single mission" (U.S. General Accounting Office, 2003, p. 2).

Lack of executive support is one of the main reasons that HRIS implementations fail. Without this support, organizations lack the funding, approvals, and leadership necessary to implement, integrate, and maintain the system. Effective praise and rewards are very powerful tools for maintaining momentum and morale in any transformation effort. To be effective, a rewards system must enforce the desired behavior.

Project managers lacking in leadership skills have also contributed to project failure (see Chapter 6). Those individuals given the responsibility to manage the HRIS project are often very knowledgeable in HR or IT. However, they cannot lead a major change project effectively unless they possess strong **leadership** and communication skills. They must be able to communicate clearly, prioritize projects, make tough decisions, manage people effectively, and navigate the political environment (Kandel, 2007).

Any successful major change initiative must also be driven by a strong and stable project management team. It would take a superhuman individual to lead a successful change initiative by himself or herself. What is needed for successful change is a team of individuals: key executives, department heads, managers, and frontline employees who are committed to the change and who can work together as a team. With respect to leader role and behavior, Higgs and Rowland (2011) identified five broad areas of leadership competency needed in the change process:

1. Creating the case for change

2. Creating structural change

3. Engaging others in the process and building commitment

4. Implementing and sustaining change

5. Facilitating and developing capability

It is also important to highlight that the literature on leadership clearly shows that teams with effective leadership will have significant performance advantages over those that do not (B. Anderson, 2010; Thomas, 1988). Generally, HRIS project leaders should adopt a leadership style suitable for the situation (Fisher, 2010). One area that has received some attention in the leadership literature as an important leadership trait is emotional intelligence (EI). The $64,000 question (or should we adjust for inflation to $1 million?) is whether EI is related to leader performance. The answer appears to be "yes." Research has shown that EI can have a positive effect on employee performance (O'Boyle, Humphrey, Pollack, Hawver, & Story, 2011) and on project management (Clarke & Howell, 2010)

Mersino (2007) believes that a project leader's success with large and complex projects "depends largely on the level of emotional intelligence" and that project managers "who master emotional intelligence will see themselves apart from other managers" (p. 6). So how do you apply EI to HRIS project change management? Mersino offers this list of ways EI can help:

1. Develop stakeholder relationships that support project success.

2. Anticipate and avoid emotional breakdowns.

3. Deal with difficult team members and manage conflict.

4. Use emotional information to make better decisions.

5. Communicate more effectively.

6. Create a positive work environment and team morale.

7. Create a vision for shared project objectives that will attract, inspire, and motivate the project team.

The biggest challenge with leading any HRIS transformation effort is the planning and implementation of change. Change is not a process that can be simply managed. Change needs to be led, and leadership makes a significant difference to chances of achieving change goals (Battilana, Gilmartin, Sengul, Pache, & Alexander, 2010).

Planning

Effective **planning** is essential to change management. Each successful project has a clearly identified project scope and strategy that outline key business requirements and project goals. It is important to keep team members on the same page and working toward the same outcome. Additionally, a clearly defined project scope will prevent "project creep" from occurring—an enlargement of the project as it progresses.

Often, organizations begin HRIS implementation projects without a clear definition of the scope of the project. The project scope must be defined in advance and should identify the project objectives, priorities, goals, and tasks—these serve as the guiding principles for the team throughout the project's life cycle (Kandel, 2007).

Inadequate funding and staffing further contribute to project failure. Organizations often consider the initial start-up costs for an HRIS project but fail to consider fully the costs of the change management process, of ongoing training, and of the support and **maintenance** of new systems. Change leaders must look at the big picture and the resources that will be required to implement and maintain the system successfully.

One key resource relates to adequate staffing to manage the project. Change leaders make the mistake of thinking that employees can implement a new system by working on this implementation part time, while continuing to perform all their regular duties. The time requirements needed to manage a project are often severely underestimated. Although, in smaller organizations, individuals may need to continue with their regular duties, all efforts should be made to have at least some team members dedicated full time to the project. If team members are not fully dedicated, their regular responsibilities will almost always take priority over the project, causing delays and lack of focus.

Change Management

Without question, change management is an ongoing challenge for HR leaders and organizations. Prager and Overholt (1994) argue that a failed effort to implement new technology is always a failure to understand and manage the change process adequately. They indicate that projects often fail not because of technical flaws but because the people in the organization reject them (p. 64). In fact, research shows that the critical factor in achieving rapid and complete adoption of new technology is effective change management (Correll, 2005, p. 12). Unfortunately, too many change initiatives fail to deliver their promised value.

Likewise, a review of the research literature on change suggests that a large percentage of change efforts end in discouraging results. Experts suggest that the figure may be as high as 70% (Mourier & Smith, 2001; Pascale & Millemann, 1997). If only 30% of change efforts are successful, consider then the cost in terms of economic and human resources: "In too many situations the improvements have been disappointing and the carnage has been appalling, with wasted resources and burned-out, scared, or frustrated employees" (Kotter, 1996, p. 4). In a world where the only constant is change, this poor track record is disappointing to say the least, and it suggests that there is considerable room for improvement in successfully managing change.

Eric Abrahamson offers an excellent suggestion to help mitigate the twin problems of forgetting about and perpetuating the failures of past change initiatives. He says that we should not ignore the memory of employees who have been involved in change programs in the past. To this end, we can learn about "whether a proposed change was attempted previously and what its outcome was and why" (Abrahamson, 2004b, p. 4).

Margaret Wheatley (1997) offers an equally compelling insight, which is applicable when organizations consider whether a change effort has been successful. She suggests that change leaders need to ask the following questions:

1. Are people in the organization more committed to being here now than at the beginning of this effort?
2. Do people feel more prepared for the next wave of change?
3. Did we develop capacity [for change] or just stage an event?
4. Do people feel that their creativity and expertise contributed to the changes? (p. 28)

When we pay attention to these kinds of questions as indicators, Wheatley (1997) argues, "we can create organizations [cultures] that know how to respond continuously" to the driving forces in their operating environment. Why? Because we tap what she calls "the intelligence that lives everywhere" in organizations and, in the process, we succeed in engaging people and their capacity to deal with change (p. 28).

In a world where the only constant is change, this poor track record is disappointing to say the least and suggests that there is a lot of room for improvement in managing change successfully. Given its high potential for failure, we next review some of the key change management issues affecting HRIS implementation.

Communication

Effective change **communication** can make the difference between success and failure of an HRIS implementation project. Employee communication is especially critical when we're "trying to get others to see and do things differently" (Duck, 2001, p. 27).

Armenakis and Harris (2002, p. 169) suggest that change leaders who overlook the importance of communicating a consistent change message and vision fuel some of the negative responses (resistance) encountered in managing change. It is the communication process that starts to unfreeze and predispose people to change (Eccles, 1994, p. 158). As Duck (2001) reminds us,

> If leaders want to change the thinking and actions of others, they must be transparent about their own. If people within the organization don't understand the new thinking or don't agree with it, they will not change their beliefs or make decisions that are aligned with what is desired. (p. 28)

No matter what kind of change initiative an organization's leadership may desire, the change won't be successful without the support and commitment of a majority of its managers and employees. Getting people "unstuck"—that is, getting them to not only embrace the vision but also change their beliefs and thinking to move in the new direction—is a huge communication challenge.

For example, the catalog retailer Lillian Vernon encountered huge problems with its IT transformation project when change leaders failed to communicate effectively to employees why the project was necessary and how it would affect each employee specifically. In discussing the end-user training for the new system, the CIO's comments are particularly poignant:

> Before the classes began, "we should have put everyone in a room and said, here is how you fit into this new picture." . . . Instead, the project team fell back on blanket statements that everyone's job would be "better." Once rollout began, however, they were angry when their jobs were harder instead. Since most had not taken the training seriously, they did not know how to use the application. And many were uncertain as to how their jobs had changed. "People were blaming the system for everything." (Paul, 2004, p. 84)

We should recognize too that there are many rationalizations for not communicating. Figure 9.6 highlights some common reasons that change leaders do not communicate (Bridges, 1991, pp. 27–28). In the Lillian Vernon example, when the CIO began work

Figure 9.6 Common Reasons Change Leaders Don't Communicate

1. ***They don't need to know yet. We'll tell them when the time comes. It'll just upset them now***. For every week of upset that you avoid by hiding the truth, you gain a month of bitterness and mistrust. Besides, the grapevine already has the news, so don't imagine that your information is a secret.

2. ***They already know. We announced it. OK, you told them, but it didn't sink in***. Threatening information is absorbed remarkably slowly. Say it again. And find different ways to say it and different media (large meetings, one-on-ones, memos, a story in the company paper) to say it.

3. ***I told the supervisors. It's their job to tell the rank and file***. The supervisors are likely to be in transition themselves, and they may not even sufficiently understand the information to convey it accurately. Maybe they're still in denial. Information is poor, so they may not want to share it yet. Don't assume that information trickles down through the organizational strata reliably or in a timely fashion.

4. ***We don't know the details ourselves, so there's no point in saying anything until everything has been decided***. In the meantime, people can get more and more frightened and resentful. Much better to say what you do know, say that you don't know more, and tell what kind of schedule exists.

on the IT transformation project, he expressed his rationalization for not communicating this way:

> We're bringing in vendors who will bring change management expertise to the table. We have capable, gung-ho teams. Giddyap, let's go. . . . In other words, launch the projects and fix problems later. [The CIO] learned that far from being a frill, basic communication creates the underpinning for a successful implementation. The essence of change management . . . is a few well-placed, well-delivered conversations to the right audience. And then you follow up, again and again. (Paul, 2004, p. 86)

The lesson the CIO learned from this experience is that it is crucial for leaders to develop and widely communicate a compelling case for change. Mercer Delta Consulting (2000) suggests that five key elements (see Figure 9.7) make up a persuasive case for change:

> *Reason for the change:* Answers the question "Why change?" and creates motivation for change. Simply saying that one's job will be better is not sufficient. Employees need to know the business case for the change and how change affects the bottom line.

Figure 9.7 Defining the Case for Change

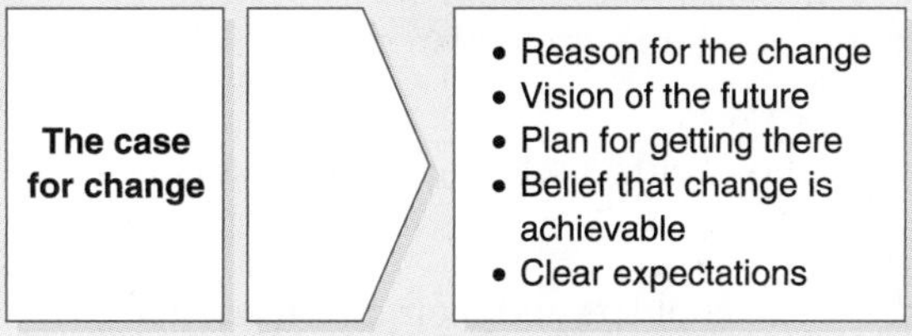

The case for change:
- Reason for the change
- Vision of the future
- Plan for getting there
- Belief that change is achievable
- Clear expectations

Vision of the future: Serves as a starting point and anchor for what we do; answers the question "Change to what?" by providing leadership's vision of the new organization; and creates energy and excitement about the future. We address this factor more deeply later in the chapter.

Plan for getting there: Answers the question "How are we going to change?" and mobilizes people in a common direction. Here, we want to provide the big picture—the agenda, key strategies, and implementation plans.

Believe change is achievable: Answers the question "Is this really possible?" and encourages interest, engagement, and optimism.

Expectations: Answers the question "What can I expect of you and what is expected of me?" and helps people prepare for the change while reducing their uncertainty.

It is vital that HRIS change leaders develop a communication plan to build awareness and enable understanding throughout the development and implementation process. Having a plan helps mitigate potential barriers by meeting the following objectives (Austin, Adkins, Fox, & Mency, 2010):

- Building awareness and mindshare of the HRIS project, its benefits, importance, and priority

- Creating interest in, and energy around, participating in the transition to the new HRIS

- Creating confidence that the HRIS project will be marked by open communication and knowledge

- Sustaining interest in the HRIS project throughout the many phases of the project

- Delivering updates on the progress of the project so that employees can contribute to the success of the project and be recognized for it.

It is beyond the scope of this chapter to get into details on how to create a communication plan. But at a minimum, the communication plan should include the following elements:

- Provide project stakeholders relevant information on the status and direction of the project.

- Identify project stakeholders and their information needs.

- Determine communication tools and communication frequency.

- Assign resources to develop and disseminate communications to project stakeholders.

- Create a process for communication feedback from project stakeholders.

In sum, communication plays a vital role in the success of change programs. It is difficult to engage everyone based on communication alone, however. Ideally, people must participate in the process from beginning to end. If the sentiment is that the change is imposed from the top, then gaining commitment will be tough.

Training

Ongoing, effective **training** is essential in any change management initiative, particularly when new technology and work processes are involved. Successful companies typically offer training in the early stages of the project to reduce uncertainty about the new technology by providing information about its characteristics and to generate user acceptance (Ruta, 2005, p. 38). Training is also used in the final stage of "refreezing" since employees obtain a better idea of how to handle the changes. A targeted training plan is one of several change management components that need to be developed as part of any HRIS implementation project. The training plan identifies the key elements and steps necessary for training the various staff on the use of the functionality and different components of the HRIS. The plan should include a post-assessment tool to measure users' knowledge following the training. A key design feature of the training curriculum will be to ensure employees using the system feel that the learning is valuable to them. Otherwise, the training may not achieve the desired outcomes.

The value of training cannot be underestimated:

> At E&P, the budget for training was cut in the midst of an implementation project. One site was able to do more training with their staff because

they had some additional resources they could use. Even though it wasn't much more, there was a difference in how much better the users were able to take advantage of the new system than those from other locations. (Jones & Price, 2004, p. 32)

The use of training during the technology implementation can impact the "transition" and "refreezing" stages. At the beginning of the project, a training plan should be developed. This plan should include a complete assessment of the current skills and future requirements for all who will be affected by the change. The plan must also include the following:

- What training will be provided

- When training will be provided for implementation team members and user groups

- Who will provide the training—vendors, consultants, staff, or others

- A plan for training new users and addressing turnover issues

- A plan for ongoing training, including advanced skills and refresher training

- A plan for training users in the event of system upgrades or procedural changes

- The resources needed—financial and human—to provide the training

Although some training early in the process is recommended, full training should not be offered until just before the system will be used. One common error is providing too detailed training too early in the learning process. If training is provided too early, users will not retain the material. A person may learn how to perform 10 new tasks on the system. Of those, the user may encounter only 5 in a normal workday, 3 over the next year, and 2 in exceptional circumstances, by which time the training will have been forgotten. Additionally, advanced training should be provided in phases, as users become accustomed to performing routine tasks. On-the-job training, coupled with self-paced e-learning and personalized assistance as required, is a more effective way of ensuring that staff gets training that is relevant to their jobs (Dawson & Jones, 2003).

We should not overlook training for employee self-service applications. If training is not provided, employees will be less likely to use and accept the system. Training should also be provided in new-employee orientation programs.

At Chevron, training in self-service is backed up with supplementary material, including online guides and laminated cards to guide employees through the process of scheduling a vacation or changing their address. Employees can refer to them if they run into problems, and in most cases, they find them useful as memory aids in the first weeks following formal training. (Twentyman, 2006, p. 24)

Involving "**power users**" can be an effective training technique. Organizations may use individuals who adapt to the new technology quickly to provide one-on-one, on-the-job training to those who do not learn the system as rapidly.

USWhole used a power user concept for changing users. They identified users in each of the business units that were influential in their units and interested in the new technology and trained them extensively to do transaction processing as well as in how processes were changing and being integrated. As power users shared their knowledge with other users, knowledge about how to use the system began to permeate the organization. (Jones & Price, 2004, p. 29)

Organizational and Individual Issues in HRIS Implementation

Cultural Issues

One of the challenges of implementing any new or updated HRIS is getting people to use the technology. Simply introducing the new system does not automatically lead to successful implementation. Successful implementation is more than putting in new technology; it often requires a change in the organization's culture. A wide variety of people and cultural issues play a huge role in any change effort or transformation.

Culture can "not only stop a change effort dead in its tracks; it can also propel it to great heights. Wisdom during organizational change understands the power of culture and how to get it to work for you instead of against you" (Senn & Childress, 2000, p. 1). How do you get employees suddenly to change their most basic assumptions about their company? This is the challenge for change leaders—often the need is to create a new organizational culture that is congruent with the realities of its changing environment and that supports the implementation of the new system.

Culture, as defined by Hofstede (1991), "is the collective programming of the mind which distinguishes the members of one group or category of people from another" (p. 6).

Organizational culture is defined as a complex set of shared beliefs, guiding values, behavioral norms, and basic assumptions acquired over time that shape our thinking and behavior; they are part of the social fabric of the organization—its genetic code. As such, culture drives the organization and guides the behavior of everyone in that organization—how they think, feel, and act. In other words, the culture forms a behavior template.

Not understanding a firm's culture in implementing an HRIS project can be fatal. The change literature is clear: Any change initiative is unlikely to be successful—that is, implemented and sustained—unless there is an appropriate organizational culture in place to support the plan. So it's critical that change leaders fully understand the organization's cultural profile before undertaking the change. How then can we go about getting an accurate picture of an organization's culture so that leaders can transition its current value set to a new value set?

An assessment of a firm's culture (sometimes called a gap analysis) is a useful tool in ensuring that the correct cultural elements are in place and aligned to support the strategy or vision, resources, and systems required to follow the roadmap to change. For each change initiative, change leaders must align all four elements to ensure lasting transformation. This alignment is conveyed by the arrows in Figure 9.8. All the arrows should be pointing in the same direction—that is, aligned with one another.

Figure 9.8 Elements of Change Aligned

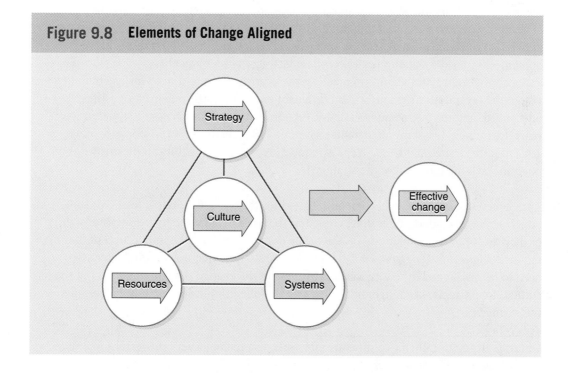

Whenever there is an incongruity between the current culture and the goals of the change initiative, the culture always wins (Conner, 1998, p. 207). For this reason, many change initiatives are ultimately unsuccessful due to lack of the appropriate cultural support needed to get people to embrace and implement the change. So, in effect, what is done to assess the cultural infrastructure is to define the existing organizational culture. Organizations must find the target culture needed to support the change, define what gaps exist between the current culture and the desired culture, and then devise a way to bridge that gap.

Perhaps Lou Gerstner (2005), former CEO of IBM, puts this all in perspective with his apposite observation:

> Leading cultural change is not just one of the things you do when you change an enterprise—it's a totality of what you have to work on if you are going to do a true, transformational change. At the end of the day, you do not change an institution, fundamentally altering how it thinks and behaves, without a deep understanding of the cultural bearings that exist. (p. 18)

As we discussed previously, many organizational change initiatives fail to meet planned expectations. When the elements of change are not in alignment, the picture looks more like the one shown in Figure 9.9. This figure portrays an organization with nonaligned elements of change, with its arrows pointing in all sorts of directions. That the arrows are pointing in different directions may reflect the impacts of previous leadership on these dimensions or failure to consider the implication of these factors on executing change. For example, although the strategy for change may reflect the change vision and steps for reaching that vision, the organization's resources could remain inadequate, the organization's systems unchanged, and the organization's behavioral norms fixed, as has been the situation for years. It's these kinds of misalignments that put a HRIS change effort in jeopardy of not achieving the desired outcome. What is required is alignment, getting all the arrows to all point in the same direction as the strategy for change.

The elements of change can become misaligned for many reasons, but at least two stand out: The change leaders either don't recognize the need to align the four dimensions, or they do so "only perfunctorily because they don't understand the implication of the required alignment" (Higgins, 2005, p. 7). We should note that not all four elements need to be misaligned to reduce the effectiveness of the change. The misalignment of the culture, for example, is enough in itself to lead to difficulties in successfully executing the transformation.

Culture, although difficult to measure precisely, is a real and very powerful force in organizations. Change leaders can use the information gained through the assessment of a firm's culture to help guide each phase of the change process, from the unfreezing phase and determining readiness for change to implementing the transformation and then consolidating and institutionalizing the new state. Through careful planning and using effective change techniques and processes, change leaders can shape and develop organizational cultures that are in alignment with, and supportive of, the desired changes.

Resistance to Change

At a basic level, when we ask employees to totally change the way they have been working, it's like asking a basketball team to switch to playing golf. People cannot change their behaviors overnight, "get smarter over the weekend, or 'grow' skills they do not have" (Williams, 2003). Lou Gerstner (2002), former CEO of IBM, aptly noted why employees resist change: "Nobody likes change. Whether you are a senior executive or an entry-level employee, change represents uncertainly and, potentially, pain" (p. 77). It's natural for individuals to resist change because they are comfortable with the status quo.

Another barrier to change is the tendency for many organizations to develop a comfort level based on their current performance, especially successful organizations. It is easy for

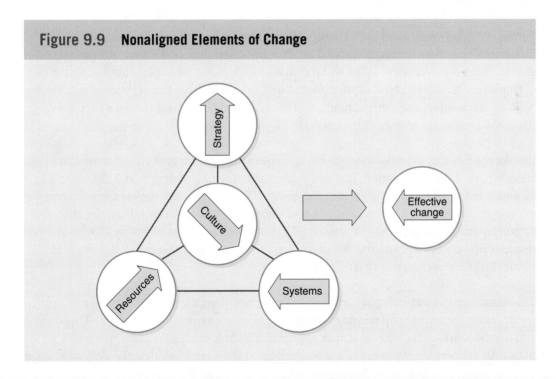

Figure 9.9 Nonaligned Elements of Change

successful organizations to become overconfident, complacent, and even a bit arrogant about the organization's success. Managers can develop a myopic view of their company as the center of the competitive universe. It is much easier to hang onto what made you great than to change, which can be costly.

Further, if an organization accumulates a series of failed change initiatives, employees can become burned out and cynical about the change process. When this happens, it's hard to create a feeling of enthusiasm and zeal for the next change as employees can feel a sense of "initiative overload, change-related chaos, and employee anxiety, cynicism, and burnout" (Abrahamson, 2004a, p. 2–3). Before one change program can be brought to fruition and institutionalized, there comes another wave. Soon people become so overwhelmed that they lose track of which change initiative they are working on and why. Employees are no longer motivated to participate in the change, nor do they exhibit the level of commitment necessary for the change program to be a success.

The barriers and pitfalls to change notwithstanding, change leaders must find a way to move beyond the status quo to overcome **employee resistance to change**, and motivate employees to make the changes necessary to ensure the successful implementation of the new or upgraded HRIS. This can be made more difficult because every employee may have concerns that can lead him or her to act in a way that undermines the change effort (Baum, 2000).

Employees must understand both emotionally and intellectually why they need to change. Employees' responses to change depend on their understanding of the basic purpose of the change. Why is it necessary? What will the change look like? One expert suggests that 20% of employees buy-in and tend to support and drive a change from the beginning, another 50% are fence-sitters and don't commit, and the remaining 30% tend to take a hard-core stand and oppose the change (Kirschner, 1997).

Despite the fact that the new system is being implemented to improve the efficiency and effectiveness of the HR function, fear and resistance to the new system from HR staff will be common and must be anticipated and addressed. HR employees may be concerned about job loss or the new roles, responsibilities, and uncertainty that will result from the change. Organizational employees may be concerned about how the new system may change the relationship between HR and the rest of the organization. Employees may feel that HR is eliminating customer service to cut costs.

This resistance to a technology change can take many different forms. Employees can overtly resist the changes by refusing to make the change or use the new system. They can also overtly sabotage the new system or engage in a passive-aggressive fashion, where they outwardly support the system, while working behind the scenes to defeat the systems change

(Marakas & Hornik, 1996). Despite the negative connotations of resistance to change, resistance can provide important feedback to change leaders.

1. Resistance can represent critical feedback about potential problems associated with the change. For example, those who are providing the resistance may possess vital details of problems that will arise if the change is made.

2. Those resisting the change often care passionately about the organization and this passion ignites the resistance. Change leaders may be able to work with these individuals to refine the change, harnessing their energy to redesign the portion of the plan that could have ultimately derailed the change.

3. Resistance can help narrow the focus and hone the change manager's ability to return to the original focus of the change and help hold them more accountable to the change initiative.

4. Resistance may serve as a conduit for increased communication, participation, and engagement. This increased engagement can potentially deliver greater acceptance and success for the change initiative.

5. Resistance can heighten the awareness of change and can raise its prominence in the organization, extending its life.

Critical to these five benefits of resistance is the importance of getting the users involved in the change process. **Employee participation and involvement** has a long history in the behavioral sciences, and information systems research has generally demonstrated that employee involvement is related to increases in job satisfaction, job performance, systems acceptance, and systems success (cf. Cotton, 1993; Harris & Weistroffer, 2009). It is to this idea of user acceptance that the chapter next discusses.

User Acceptance

Ultimately, acceptance of the new technology and new processes represents project success. Although the technical challenges of implementing any system can be great, it is the people "challenges that cannot be overlooked (although often are) during the implementation phase" of an HRIS (Ruta, 2005, p. 36). Organizations cannot simply rely on the strategy of "if you build it, they will come." Change leaders must use appropriate change management techniques to create **user acceptance**—otherwise, they risk failure as users choose not to utilize the new system. For example, research has shown that up to 70% of the functions of new HR systems go untapped because users make the new system do only what the old system did (Roberts, 1998, p. 40). A strong focus on communication, ongoing training, and process reengineering will help prevent this underuse. One framework for understanding user acceptance of technology is depicted in Figure 9.10.

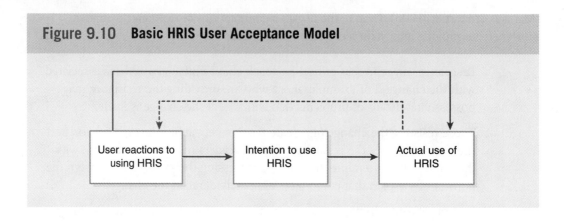

Figure 9.10   Basic HRIS User Acceptance Model

Venkatesh, Morris, Davis, and Davis (2003, p. 427) reviewed the user acceptance literature and, from their study, defined the Unified Theory of the Acceptance and Use of Technology. Their model contains four main elements considered prerequisites of user acceptance: effort expectancy, performance expectancy, social or subjective norms, and facilitating conditions. User perception related to the ease of use of the HRIS (effort expectancy) is an important determinant of user acceptance. The extent to which a user perceives that the HRIS will enhance his or her job performance (performance expectancy) is considered the strongest predictor of intention. These expectancies are obviously important to consider in the early stages of the implementation of the project. Social influence (subjective norms) is defined as the degree to which users perceive others in the organization to feel that the system is important and, consequently, how they think their behavior as users will be viewed by others. In other words, users are more likely to accept the HRIS if they think doing so will help them fit in and conform to the behavior of others (Ruta, 2005). Facilitating conditions relate to the extent to which users believe that the organization is committed and resources are in place to support implementation and use of the system.

To increase the likelihood of employee acceptance of the HRIS, it is important for end users to be involved with and feel ownership of the new system. Ideally, end users should be brought into the project as early as possible, even as early as defining system requirements. It is also important that users feel that their involvement is providing real value to the system change and that their ideas and opinions are recognized (Greenberg, Fauscette, & Fletcher, 2000). By helping shape the real requirements, users begin to take ownership and a personal stake in the system throughout the development process. The challenge facing organizations is how to involve users without expecting them to add additional hours to their already full schedule.

Not everyone will accept the changes at the same time. User acceptance can be influenced by culture and demographics. Younger employees may accept the new technology more quickly because of their higher comfort level with technology and personal computers (Morgan, 2000, p. 20). Those who have been working in the same capacity or who have been using the old system extensively will naturally compare the new one to the old system and may take more time to accept the change than someone who has only recently joined the company. To ensure successful acceptance and adoption of the new system means that managers must use different approaches for different groups of employees, for example, younger vs. older, lower computer experience vs. higher computer experience, etc.

Informal ambassadors, identified as gatekeepers, or professional change agents can help influence the rest of the organization and can make or break the acceptance of a new system. Implementation teams should identify influential individuals and those who have shown an interest in the new HRIS and engage them as informal ambassadors for the change (Prager & Overholt, 1994, p. 67; Ruta, 2005, p. 46). It is also a good idea to identify the most resistant users and involve them right from the beginning to gain their buy-in (Keener & Fletcher, 2004). Otherwise, they may influence others negatively toward the change.

One of the major obstacles to gaining user acceptance is user reluctance to try out the new system. Some companies have used pilot implementation in one part of the organization to get early reactions and suggestions for modifications. One of the authors was involved in a software change across multiple counties within a single state, and the pilot implementation in two counties resulted in significant suggestions before going live across the state. By including the use of new technology and revised procedures in performance goals and linking those goals to compensation, we can reinforce the importance of the change. Of course, this tactic is only applicable when the new technology is required for an individual's job. Ensuring that employees use the system when it is not a requirement of their job is more challenging. Offering rewards to encourage user participation in new systems can be very effective. Some examples follow:

- The State of Kentucky offered those who completed an online survey providing feedback on the new system a chance to win a weekend stay at a Kentucky state park (Anheier & Doherty, 2001).

- One organization awarded gift certificates to the first 50 employees who used the system to update their personal information.

- One organization gave employees a $100 bonus for completing their annual benefits enrollment online.

A small investment in rewards such as these can result in increased user comfort and acceptance.

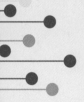

SUMMARY

The aim of this chapter is to deepen your understanding of change management, and the behaviors and organizational factors required for success in implementing an HRIS. To help illuminate the challenges in this effort, this chapter defines change management and the important role effective change management plays in the implementation of any HRIS. The chapter introduces several change models and explains why these are important concepts for today's HR leaders.

The evidence is clear that successfully introducing a major HRIS into an organization requires the effective blend of good technical and good organizational skills. Effective management of change is a critical core competence that management and HR leaders must master. By better understanding the competencies needed to manage change, HR professionals can help in process of change in organizations.

It is interesting for the student to note that Lewin's three-step change model (1946) and the action-research model are quite similar since both are process models. Process models of change look for emotional, attitudinal, and behavioral changes in employees during the implementation of change. Both Nadler's congruence model (1998) and Kotter's (1996) eight-stage change model are more structural and describe how change occurs, but they do not explain the processes required for congruence or, in the case of Kotter there is no explanation of the processes that enter into the eight steps. Basically, the easiest change effort is the one that involves the employee early in the planned change.

Research has identified a number of key factors that contribute to IT system implementation failures, including lack of leadership, communication, planning, change management, and training.

Finally, change leaders must prepare for the inevitable resistance to change and plan to gain user acceptance. A plan must also be created for ongoing post-implementation review and maintenance of the new system.

KEY TERMS

action-research model   244

change agent   242

change equation formula   249

change leader   242

communication   259

culture   264

employee participation and involvement   269

employee resistance to change   242

force-field analysis   247

gap analysis   242

Kotter's eight-stage change model   243

leadership   255

DISCUSSION QUESTIONS

1. Discuss each of the theoretical change models introduced in this chapter. How can we use them when planning an HRIS implementation to increase our chances of success?

2. Analyze the main reasons for HRIS implementation failure. How can we prevent these from affecting us?

3. Discuss the importance of communication in managing a technology change. What roadblocks might an organization face if it fails to create a good communication plan?

4. If you were asked to develop a training plan for an HRIS implementation, what kinds of things would you include? Why?

5. Discuss the role of culture in HRIS implementation. How might two different organizations with very different cultures approach the same HRIS implementation differently?

6. Create recommendations for an organization that is facing resistance to change from its own HR department. What are some of the likely causes of this resistance? How can they be overcome?

7. Discuss how informal leaders within the organization might be used to increase user acceptance.

CASE STUDY: THE GRANT CORPORATION

The Grant Corporation is a financial services firm based in Chicago, Illinois. Its revenue exceeded $1 billion last year, producing a net income of $530 million. It has just over 1,000 employees. Although the organization has been in business for almost 10 years, it has experienced rapid expansion in the past 2 years due to tremendous business growth and a merger with the Enelrad Group, another local firm. Managers have had difficulty keeping up with this growth, especially in the HR department, which has been stretched thin to keep up with staffing needs and other, mainly administrative, duties.

Six months ago, the CEO, Todd Jackson, recognized the need to expand the size and functionality of the HR department and hired Julia Woodland to be its director, reporting directly to him. This was a newly created position, and its incumbent would replace the HR administrator, who had previously reported to the VP of Finance and who decided to retire when the new HR position was announced.

When Woodland was hired, Jackson told her that she would have "full reign" to create a more strategically focused HR department that would be better equipped to handle the organization's needs. She had quite a bit of experience at her previous company and was eager to take on the task.

Although the organization used advanced technology for its business applications, HR was still using a basic payroll processing software program and Excel spreadsheets to track various categories of employee information, including personal data, benefits enrollments, performance evaluation schedules, and compensation. All payroll and benefit information was manually entered into these respective systems, and much of the information had to be entered into multiple spreadsheets when there was a change. The department could not keep up with the information needs—new hires were getting paid incorrectly, or not at all. Benefits enrollments were delayed or contained mistakes, and performance evaluations and pay raises were late. The printed employee handbook, benefits binder, and orientation materials were in serious need of updating. In addition, the company had 16 open positions and stacks of resumes everywhere. It was no wonder that the HR administrator had decided to retire!

Julia Woodland spent long hours trying to determine what she could do to address the immediate and long-term concerns of her new department. She brought in a temporary employee to help her staff file, process paperwork, and enter data. She focused on hiring two higher-level HR representatives and a payroll clerk. She turned to a staffing agency to help the firm identify candidates for open positions, including those in HR. Finally, she proposed the purchase of an integrated payroll/HRIS that was capable of integrating with the finance department's system as well as with the organization's benefit and 401(k) providers' systems. The proposed software solution also offered the option of a Web-based employee portal, which would allow employees to view information online and change their personal data. Jackson responded favorably and told her to "go ahead and do whatever she needed to do to fix the mess." The next day, Woodland contracted with the HRIS provider.

Woodland spent the next week meeting with her new HRIS vendor representative to discuss the installation and implementation of the system. Because she was so overwhelmed and wanted to get the new system in as quickly as possible, she didn't have time to discuss the project with her staff right away, but she knew that employees would be excited about the new system and the opportunities it would open up for them as the burden of administrative tasks eased. She closed her door during the meetings, so participants could concentrate. She wanted to be able to implement the system by January 1, so that the company's year-end payroll data were accurate and managers could track other data on an annual basis with a full year of data. Since she had been through the process in the past and was familiar with such systems, she figured that she could manage the implementation with the help of IT and her staff as needed. She would make all key decisions to move the project along and meet her deadline.

The current HR staff consisted of an HR assistant and two generalists who seemed to function as clerks and recruiters. They had all been hired at the same time more than 5 years ago, when the HR administrator was the sole member of the department. They were very proud of how they had worked so hard together to build HR and keep up with the increasing demand. They were just getting used to working with Woodland but thought that she was very nice and had high hopes for the improvements and new strategic focus that she would help them implement.

Day by day, the staff watched the vendor representative come and go, along with a parade of candidates sent over by the staffing agency to apply for the new HR positions. They soon began to wonder about all the changes that their new boss was making and what these changes would mean for them. They started making assumptions that had them very concerned.

Woodland contacted the IT director to tell him about the project. He expressed concern over the ability of the server to handle the new system and wondered how they would address firewall issues with the portal. Furthermore, all his staff members were tied up with a critical upgrade to the customer service system, which had caused more than its share of problems. He demanded to know why he and his staff had not been involved sooner and told her that it would be unlikely that they would be able to participate in the implementation or help her meet her deadline. Upset, she called Todd Jackson, who advised her not to worry about it— he would tell them to get it done.

When she contacted Finance to obtain information that the HRIS vendor needed to link the HRIS to that department's system, the finance manager was more than willing to help—but she did not know where to get the system information from and did not understand how the information would flow from one system to another. She asked why they couldn't just keep the systems separate and enter the necessary data into the finance system from reports provided by HR. "That's the way we've always done it," she said. "It doesn't take long, and it will be much simpler that way."

In the meantime, morale was declining in HR. Whenever Woodland asked HR employees for information about payroll or their Excel spreadsheets, they seemed uneasy and never provided her with exactly what she was looking for. She didn't understand their antiquated forms or their backward processes but decided she could fix those after the new system was in. Also, it felt like the rest of the company was suddenly treating her differently. They had all made her feel so welcome six months ago when she came on board. Now, employees approached her with caution, and managers always seemed abrupt.

Julia Woodland began to wonder if this was the right role for her. Why were things so difficult? She thought that everyone would be thrilled about the new system and its efficiencies and would be eager to help. Was it her problem or theirs?

She thought that perhaps people didn't realize the impact she was making in the organization. She decided to make an announcement about the exciting new system that would help make things more effective and efficient in HR and help the employees simplify their lives as well. She sent out a company-wide e-mail announcing the new payroll/HRIS and outlining its ability to interface with other systems and its Web-portal capabilities. To her disappointment, no one seemed to understand the significance or even pay attention. A few employees asked her if their paychecks would be delayed as a result.

She wondered how she would ever get through this project and what she needed to do to get everyone on board.

Case Study Questions

1. Overall, what did Julia Woodland do right? What could she have done differently?

2. Were the correct people involved in the process? Whom would you have included and why?

3. What errors did Woodland make with her own staff? What impact might these errors have had on the success of the implementation? What should have been done?

4. Discuss the cultural issues involved in this case. Are there things Julia Woodland should have taken into consideration prior to starting the

implementation? Why are they important?

5. If you were in Julia Woodland's position, what would you include in your communication plan for the implementation?

6. How can training be used in this case to make the implementation more successful?

7. How can the Grant Corporation increase user acceptance of the system?

8. Discuss the potential benefits of process reengineering in this implementation. What impact might it have had?

9. After the implementation, what steps should the HR department take to ensure proper maintenance and support of the system?

10. What can Julia Woodland do now to "get everyone on board" and increase the likelihood that this implementation will be successful?

STUDENT STUDY SITE

Visit the Student Study Site at **http://www.sagepub.com/kavanagh3e** for additional learning tools such as access to SAGE journal articles and related web resources.

NOTE

1. See Arizona Department of Administration, Human Resources website at http://www .hr.az.gov/HRIS/HRIS_About_Us.asp.

REFERENCES

Abrahamson, E. (2004a). *Change without pain.* Boston: Harvard Business School Press.

Abrahamson, E. (2004b, February). The road to better recombination. *Harvard Management Update, 9*(2), 1–4.

Anderson, B. (2010, March). Project leadership and the art of managing relationships. *T&D, 64*(3), 58–63.

Anderson, D., & Anderson, L. A. (2001). *Beyond change management. Advanced strategies for today's transformational leaders.* San Francisco: Jossey-Bass/ Pfeiffer.

Anderson, D., & Anderson, L. (2010). *The change leader's roadmap: How to navigate your organization's transformation (2e).* San Francisco: Pfeiffer.

Anheier, N. & Doherty, S. (2001, October). *Employee self-service: Tips to ensure a successful implementation.* Retrieved from http://www .shrm.org/hrdisciplines/technology/Articles/ Pages/CMS_000210.aspx

Armenakis, A. A., & Harris, S. G. (2002). Crafting a change message to create transformational readiness. *Journal of Organizational Change Management, 15*(2), 169–183.

Austin, D., Adkins, V., Fox, R., & Mency, Y. (2010). *HRMS implementation project: Communication plan.* Richmond, VA: Virginia Community College System.

Battilana, J., Gilmartin, M., Sengul, M., Pache, A., & Alexander, J. A. (2010). Leadership competencies for implementing planned organizational change. *The Leadership Quarterly, 21,* 422–438.

Baum, D. (2000). *Lightning in a bottle.* Chicago: Dearborn.

Beckhard, R., & Harris, R. (1987). *Organizational transitions: Managing complex change.* (2nd ed.). Reading, MA: Addison-Wesley.

Beer, M., & Nohria, N. (2000). Resolving the tension between theories E and O of change. In M. Beer & N. Nohria (Eds.), *Breaking the code of change* (p. 1). Boston: Harvard Business School Press.

Benjamin, R., & Levinson, E. (1993, Summer). A framework for managing IT-enabled change. *Sloan Management Review, 34*(4), 23–33.

Blanchard, K. (2007). *Leading at a higher level.* Upper Saddle River, NJ: Prentice Hall.

Bridges, W. (1991). *Managing transitions: Making the most of change.* Reading, MA: Addison-Wesley.

Bridges, W. (2003). *Managing transitions* (2nd ed.). Cambridge, MA: Perseus Books.

Burke, W. W. (2002). *Organizational change.* Thousand Oaks, CA: Sage.

Burke, W. W. (2008). *Organization change: Theory and practice.* Thousand Oaks, CA: Sage.

Burnes, B. (2004). Kurt Lewin and the planned approach to change: A re-appraisal. *Journal of Management Studies, 41*(6), 977–1002.

Cameron, E., & Green, M. (2004). *Making sense of change.* London: Kogan Page.

Clarke, N., & Howell, R. (2010). *Emotional intelligence and projects.* Newtown Square, PA: Project Management Institute.

Collier, J. (1945). United States Indian administration as a laboratory of ethnic relations. *Social Research, 12,* 275–276.

Conner, D. R. (1998). *Leading at the edge of chaos: How to create the nimble organization.* New York: Wiley.

Corey, M. (1953). *Action research to improve school practices.* New York: Columbia University, Teachers College, Bureau of Publications.

Correll, B. (2005, February/March). Change management: Using the right techniques and technologies to ensure success. IHRIM. *link, 10*(1), 12.

Cotton, J. L. (1993). *Employee involvement: Methods for improving performance and work attitudes.* Thousand Oaks, CA: Sage.

Dannemiller, D., & Jacobs, R. W. (1992). Changing the way organizations change: A revolution of common sense. *The Journal of Applied Behavioral Science, 28*(4), 480–498.

Dawson, M. J., & Jones, M. L. (2003). Human change management: Herding cats. In PriceWaterhouseCoopers (Ed.), *Risky business: The art and science of risk management* (pp. 21–25). New York: Author.

Duck, J. D. (2001). *The change monster.* New York: Crown Business.

Eccles, T. (1994). *Succeeding with change.* London: McGraw-Hill.

Fisher, E. (2010). What practitioners consider to be the skills and behaviours of an effective people project manager. *International Journal of Project Management* (Article in Press).

Fletcher, P. A. K. (2005). Personnel administration to business-driven human capital management. In H. G. Gueutal & D. L. Stone (Eds.), *The brave new world of eHR* (pp. 1–21). San Francisco: Jossey-Bass.

French, W. L., & Bell, C. H., Jr. (1973). *Organization development.* Englewood Cliffs, NJ: Prentice Hall.

Frohman, M. A., Sashkin, M., & Kavanagh, M. J. (1976). Action-research as an organization development approach. *Organization and Administrative Sciences, 7,* 129–161.

Gerstner, L. V. (2002). *Who says elephants can't dance? Inside IBM's historic turnaround.* New York: HarperCollins.

Gerstner, L. V. (2005). Lou Gerstner on change. *Leadership Excellence, 22*(6), 18.

Graetz, F., & Smith, A. C. T. (2010). Managing organizational change: A philosophies of change approach. *Journal of Change Management, 1*(2), 135–154.

Greenberg, P., Fauscette, M., & Fletcher, S. (2000). *Special edition using PeopleSoft.* Indianapolis, IN: Que.

Harris, M. A., & Weistroffer, H. R. (2009). A new look at the relationship between user involvement in systems development and system success. *Communications of the Association for Information Systems, 24*(42), 739–756.

Herold, D. M., & Fedor, D. B. (2008). *Change the way you lead change: Leadership strategies that really work.* Stanford, CA: Stanford University Press.

Higgins, J. M. (2005, March). The eight S's of successful strategy execution. *Journal of Change Management, 5*(1), 3–13.

Higgs, M., & Rowland, D. (2011). What does it take to implement change successfully? A study of the behaviours of successful change leaders. *Journal of Applied Behavioural Science, 47*(3), 309–355.

Hofstede, G. (1991). *Cultures and organizations.* New York: McGraw-Hill.

Jones, M., & Price, L. (2004). Organizational knowledge sharing in ERP implementation: Lessons from industry. *Journal of Organizational and End User Computing, 16*(1), 21–40.

Kandel, A. (2007). *The eight fatal flaws of HR system implementations and how to avoid them* (SHRM HRTX Forum Library). Retrieved from http://www .shrm.org/hrtx/library_published/nonIC/ CMS_006586.asp

Kavanagh M.J., Gueutal, H. & Tannenbaum, S. I. (1990). *Human resource information systems.* Boston: PWS-Kent.

Keener, D. & Fletcher, R. (2004, January). *Good planning, realistic scope and executive sponsorship important in HRIS projects.* Retrieved from http://www.shrm.org/ hrdisciplines/technology/Articles/Pages/ CMS_006631.aspx

Kirschner, E. M. (1997, November 3). In times of change, managers should forget noisemakers and focus on fence-sitters. *Chemical and Engineering News, 75*(44), 44–48.

Kotter, J. P. (1996). *Leading change.* Boston: Harvard Business School Press.

Lawler, E. E., & Worley, C. G. (2006). *Built to change.* San Francisco: Jossey-Bass.

Lewin, K. (1946). Action research and minority problems. *Journal of Social Issues, 2,* 34–46.

Lippitt, R. (1950, September). *Value-judgment problems of the social scientist participating in action-research.* Paper presented at the annual meeting of the American Psychological Association.

Lorenzi, N. M., & Riley, R. T. (2000). Managing change: An overview. *Journal of the American Medical Informatics Association, 7*(2), 116–124.

Marakas, G. M., & Hornik, S. (1996). Passive resistance misuse: Overt support and covert recalcitrance in IS implementation. *European Journal of Information Systems, 5*(3), 208–219.

Mercer Delta Consulting. (2000). *Transition leadership: A guide to leading change initiatives.* Retrieved from http://www .biasca.com/archivos/for_downloading/ management_ surveys/Mgmt_Change_and_ TransitionLeadership.pdf

Mercer Delta Consulting. (2003). *The congruence model.* Retrieved from http://www. mercerdelta.com/organizational_consulting/ help_change_metrics.html

Mersino, A. C. (2007). *Emotional intelligence for project managers: The people skills you need to achieve outstanding results.* New York: AMACOM.

Miller, D. (2004). Building sustainable change capability. *Industrial and Commercial Training, 36*(1), 9–12.

Morgan, L. (2000). Technology changing the role of human resources. *Workspan, 43*(3), 16–22.

Mourier, P., & Smith, M. (2001). Conquering *organizational change.* Atlanta, GA: CEP Press.

Nadler, D. A. (1998). *Champions of change: How CEOs and their companies are mastering the skills of radical change.* San Francisco: Jossey-Bass.

O'Boyle, E. H., Humphrey, R. H., Pollack, J. M., Hawver, T. H., & Story, P. A. (2011). The relation between emotional intelligence and job performance: A meta-analysis. *Journal of Organizational Behavior, 32*(5), 788–818.

Office of the Auditor General. (2005). *Performance audit* (Department of Administration, Report No. 05–02).

Retrieved from http://www.auditorgen.state.az.us/Reports/State_Agencies/Agencies/Administration_Department_of/Performance/05–02/ 05–02.pdf

Pascale, R., & Millemann, M. (1997, December). Changing the way we change. *Harvard Business Review, 75*(6), 126–139.

Paul, L. G. (2004, December 1). Time to change. *CIO Magazine, 18*(5), 78–86. Retrieved from http://www.cio.com/archive/120104/change.html

Pinder C. C. (1998). *Work motivation in organizational behavior.* Upper Saddle River, NJ: Prentice Hall.

Porras, J. I. & Robertson, P. J. (1992). Organizational development: Theory, practice, and research. In M. D. Dunnette & L. M. Hough (Ed.), *Handbook of industrial and organizational psychology* (3rd ed., Vol. 3, pp. 719–823). Palo Alto, CA: Consulting Psychologists Press.

Potts, R., & LaMarsh, J. (2004). *Master change, maximize success.* San Francisco: Chronicle Books.

Prager, K. P., & Overholt, M. H. (1994). How to create a changed organization. *Information Systems Management, 11*(3), 64–70.

Roberts, B. (1998, February). The new HRIS: Good deal or $6 million paperweight? *HR Magazine, 43,* 40–48.

Ruta, C. (2005). The application of change management theory to HR portal implementation in subsidiaries of multinational corporations. *Human Resource Management, 44*(1), 35–53.

Schaffer, R. H., & McCreight, M. K. (2004). Build your own change model. *Business Horizons, 33*–38.

Schein, E. H. (1996). Kurt Lewin's change theory in the field and in the classroom: Notes toward a model of managed learning. *Systems Practice, 9*(1), 27–47.

Senn, L. E., & Childress, J. R. (2000). *Why change initiatives fail: It's the culture dummy!* London: Senn-Delaney Leadership Consulting Group.

Thomas, A. B. (1988). Does leadership make a difference to organizational performance? *Administrative Science Quarterly, 33,* 388–400.

Twain, M. (2007). *Personal recollections of Joan of Arc.* Stilwell, KS: Digireads. (Original work published 1896)

Twentyman, J. (2006, May 30). Teams before technology. *Personnel Today,* 24–25.

U.S. General Accounting Office. (2003, July). Results-oriented cultures: Implementation steps to assist mergers and organizational transformations (Publication No. GAO-03–669). Washington, DC: Author. Retrieved from http://www.gao.gov/new.items/d03669.pdf

U.S. Government Accountability Office. (2007). Further improvements needed to identify and oversee poorly planned and performing projects (Publication No GAO-07-1211T). Washington, DC: Author.

Venkatesh, V., Morris, M. G., Davis, G. B., & Davis, F. D. (2003). User acceptance of information technology: Toward a unified view. *MIS Quarterly, 27*(3), 425–478.

Warhaftig, W. (2005). Flight to the future: Managing change in financial services for sustainable growth. *LIMRA International.* Retrieved from http://www.limra.com/abstracts/abstract.aspx?fid=5184

Wheatley, M. (1997, Summer). Goodbye, command and control. *Leader to Leader, 5.* Retrieved from http://www.leadertoleader.org/knowledgecenter/journal.aspx?ArticleID=147

Williams, W. (2003). Why almost all organizational change efforts fail. *CEO Refresher.* Retrieved from http://www.refresher.com/!wwfail.html

Human Resource Information Systems Applications

CHAPTER 10

HR Administration and Human Resource Information Systems

Linda C. Isenhour

EDITORS' NOTE

This chapter begins the examination and discussion of the HRM applications enabled by the successful development and implementation of an HRIS. It is appropriate to begin the applications chapters with an introduction to HR administration. The first nine chapters of this book explained how to build an HRIS, so, in a sense, these chapters were the building blocks for the HRIS "house." Now the filling of the house begins. One of the crucial outcomes of following the advice from the first nine chapters is that the employee database, frequently referred to as the employee master file,[1] will be accurate and up to date. This characteristic of the module allows HR professionals to use the software in the HRIS to develop HR programs, such as recruitment and compensation, with confidence. The use of human resource information systems for compliance with government laws and guidelines, which is discussed in this chapter, absolutely requires an accurate and timely database. In addition, benchmark data for use in cost-benefit analyses of HR programs demand accuracy in the employee master file, or serious and costly mistakes could be made in decisions to continue or expand an HR program such as e-learning. Finally, as explained in this chapter, the accuracy of the employee master file is doubly important because of the use of the data and results to build the HR balanced scorecard, which is used in assessing strategic alignment with organizational goals.

CHAPTER Objectives

After completing this chapter, you should be able to

- Understand the basic role of job analysis in human resources, and explain the role of HRIS in supporting job analysis
- Discuss the complexity of HR administration and the advantages of an HRIS over a "paper-and-pencil" HR operation
- Discuss the advantages of having a service-oriented architecture (SOA) for the HRIS
- Differentiate among the four structural approaches to HR administration service delivery (e.g., self-service portals, shared-service centers, human resource outsourcing, and offshoring)
- Discuss the advantages and disadvantages of each of the four structural approaches to HR administration
- Understand how legal compliance with government mandates is an important part of HRIS functionality and how these mandates add to the complexity of an HRIS in both domestic and multinational organizations
- Discuss the various privacy laws, particularly as they relate to an HRIS
- Discuss the elements important to successful measurement of the strategic alignment of the HR balanced scorecard and how this alignment is related to the strategic alignment of an organization

HRIS IN ACTION

In 2011, Procter & Gamble (P&G) had more than 135,000 employees in 80 countries. Identifying common measures, improving employee service, and reducing HR administrative costs continued to be strategic imperatives for this global consumer products company committed to ensuring its principles: "Everyone Valued, Everyone Included, Everyone Performing at Their Peak" (Procter & Gamble, 2011).

Today, the human resource managers at P&G continue to consider a variety of solutions to meet their strategic goals. Should they maintain their decentralized global operation in HRM and use technology such as Internet service portals to improve efficiency? Would the trend toward shared-services centers (SSCs) be better for centralizing operations? How will decisions about outsourcing selected human resource functions be affected by cloud and mobile computing advances? With so many countries and governmental regulations involved, how can P&G achieve sufficient standardization through an HRIS to gain increased savings and still meet its varied responsibilities to such diverse entities? Will its internal customers view the move from decentralized to centralized shared services as meeting their needs? How will such changes be measured from an internal customer satisfaction perspective? Which measures for the various administrative approaches will best align the HR functions with the P&G balanced scorecard strategic goals and objectives?

These are common HRM problems faced by businesses today. This chapter provides a framework to help answer such questions.

Introduction

Human resource management (HRM) administration deals with the efficient performance of the transactional activities introduced in Chapter 1. Record keeping, updating policy and informational materials for a self-service portal, generating and disseminating internal reports, complying with governmentally mandated external reporting, and administering labor contracts are all examples of HRM administration associated with managing an organization's workforce. Approximately 65% to 75% of all HR activities are transactional (Wright, McMahan, Snell, & Gerhart, 1998). Human resource information systems (HRIS) are vital tools in managing these increasingly complex transactional requirements. For this reason, it is absolutely crucial that the employee database, frequently referred to as the **employee master file**, be carefully constructed so that the information is *accurate and timely* (Kavanagh, Gueutal, & Tannenbaum, 1990; Walker, 1982). The employee master file is a record and repository for all relevant employee information and must be created prior to any other modules for programs, such as recruiting and applicant tracking. The approaches and technological techniques described in this chapter ensure that the employee master file, once initially built, remains accurate and up to date. Before this module can be developed, though, an analysis of the jobs in the firm must be conducted, and specific job descriptions for each position in the organization must be developed. As will be discussed in the next chapter, job analysis is crucial to the development of talent management, which is one of the most important HRM programs since it is used in all of the functional HRM programs.

Technical Support for Job Analysis

A primary goal of an effective HR department is to ensure that the organization has the best available people working in the proper jobs at the appropriate time to maximize the organization's productive capacity. To do this, however, the organization must know not only what each job entails but also what **knowledge, skills, and abilities (KSA)** are necessary to perform the job successfully. Job analysis provides both types of information. Specifically, **job analysis** is the process of systematically obtaining information about jobs by determining the duties, tasks, or activities of jobs, from which KSA can be estimated. From this analysis, job descriptions can be developed. **Job descriptions** define the working contract between the employee and the organization. Job descriptions uses include: (1) evidence for any litigation involving unfair discrimination in hiring, promoting, or terminating employees; (2) development of all the HRM programs, especially talent management in organizations, and other important HRM programs including recruitment, selection, training and performance appraisal; (3) development of compensation structures; and (4) employee disciplinary programs and union grievances. In fact, job descriptions are often termed the "heart" of the HRM system. Given the importance of job descriptions, it is *critically important that they be accurate and timely*. Effectively managed HR departments capture and store the results of all job analysis and job descriptions within the HRIS to facilitate future changes in jobs required by reorganizations, mergers/acquisitions, technology, and market-driven customer expectations.

Approaches and Techniques

A variety of approaches to job analysis are covered in detail in other sources (Ghorpade, 1988); thus, only a general approach to conducting job analyses will be discussed in this chapter. Job analysis involves the following phases or considerations:

1. Identify the sources of information about the job. The best sources are usually job incumbents and their supervisors; however, professional job analysts can be used for newly created or complex jobs. Company records and the Internet, specifically the U.S. Department of Labor's **O*Net database (http://onetonline.org)**, are also good sources of information about jobs.

2. Identify the types of job information needed. This information can include tasks, duties, responsibilities, the knowledge required, performance standards, job context, and the equipment used. A determination of what specific information will be used for the analysis of all jobs must be made to maintain consistency across the final job descriptions.

3. Determine the appropriate methods of collecting the job data. Techniques include interviews, questionnaires, observation, and focus groups. The choice of technique(s) depends on the number of jobs to be analyzed and the funding available.

4. Consider using one or more of the standardized techniques for conducting job analysis to enhance the final job description, for example, functional job analysis, the **position analysis questionnaire (PAQ)**, task inventory analysis, or the critical incident method (see Ghorpade, 1988).

Regardless of the approach or technique used to analyze the jobs in an organization, the outcome must obtain accurate and timely job descriptions. Thus, a key question facing HR professionals is, how can technology assist HR in establishing and maintaining the accuracy of job descriptions?

HRIS Applications

The utilization of technology, including Web-based job analysis tools, has increased the availability of information supporting job analysis, reduced costs of collecting information, and enhanced convenience of collect and analyzing information. For example, O*Net, an online repository of information on 1,000 broad occupations, can be used to help guide in the development of job descriptions. Consider, for example, the occupation of professor. O*Net contains generic descriptions for professors of physics, architecture, sociology, forestry, business (e.g., see http://www.onetonline.org/link/summary/25-1011.00 for the summary description of the position "business teachers, postsecondary"). To ensure that the KSA list is accurate for a specific position in a specific discipline (e.g., human resources) at a specific university, additional information and reviews of this job description would need to be conducted. As another example, HR-Guide.com (http://www.hr-guide.com) provides a simple, free job analysis tool for HR professionals (http://www.hr-software.net/cgi/JobEvaluation.cgi). Finally, there are many different vendors who offer these tools as stand-alone products or components of a larger product offering.

Completing job analyses and deriving job descriptions can be accomplished through online survey techniques. Job analysis questionnaires can be administered online to job incumbents and supervisors, and the resulting job descriptions can be analyzed statistically to finalize job descriptions. This online questionnaire capability can be part of an integrated HRIS software package covering multiple programs (e.g., SAP, PeopleSoft) or purchased as stand-alone software. The position analysis questionnaire, for example, has its own software package (see www.paq.com/?FuseAction=home.main), and the Economic Research Institute (ERI) has **Occupational Assessor® software** (www.erieri.com/index.cfm?fuseaction=EDOT.Main) to aid in completing job analysis.

Maintaining accurate job descriptions can also be aided by an HRIS. Later in this chapter, service-oriented architecture (SOA) with self-service portals for employees (ESS) and managers (MSS) will be discussed. These portals can be used to make sure that job descriptions remain accurate and timely. For example, if work procedures or new equipment are introduced, it would be easy to request that the persons affected by the change, both employees and supervisors, access their current job descriptions via portals to make necessary updates to the job descriptions. In addition, it is a good idea to establish an annual review of all job descriptions to maintain their timeliness. If a company requires annual reviews of employee performance, and these forms are generated by the HRIS, it would be quite easy to generate a copy of the current job description to accompany each request for a job performance evaluation. The employees and the supervisors could then review the accuracy of the job descriptions and submit any changes necessary through portals. With accurate and timely job descriptions, human resources planning (HRP) is now possible.

The HRIS Environment and Other Aspects of HR Administration

HRIS can assist managers charged with improving the efficiency of HR administration by reducing costs, enhancing the reliability of reporting, and improving service to internal customers. Information technology facilitates administration in multiple ways. First, an HRIS can help improve data accuracy by (1) reducing the need for multiple inputs, (2) eliminating redundancies in data, and (3) reducing the opportunity for human input errors and associated corrections. In addition, an HRIS, through *relational databases* (see Chapter 2), speeds the process of building reports with simple query capabilities. Moreover, an HRIS, if properly designed for flexibility, can support differences in reporting mandated by global governmental jurisdictions. Finally, a properly designed HRIS permits secure global distribution of data while providing the desired privacy for employee data, facilitating consideration of alternative methods of consolidating, and improving services to internal customers (Ceriello, 1991; Gueutal & Stone, 2005; Kavanagh, Gueutal, & Tannenbaum, 1990; Osle & Cooper, 2003; Walker, 1982, 1993, 2001).

Administrative issues associated with specific HRM functions as part of the development and implementation of an HRIS have been briefly mentioned in earlier chapters (e.g., recruiting, training, compensating) and will be discussed in more detail in later chapters. However, HR managers face a variety of other administrative requirements in the rapidly evolving HRIS era. The HRM administrative issues highlighted in this chapter include (1) organizational approaches for providing HR in a global economy (i.e., self-service portals, SSCs, outsourcing, offshoring); (2) compliance mandates for record maintenance and report requirements (e.g., **Employer Information Report EEO-1**), which are associated both with government laws in the United States (e.g., **Occupational Safety and Health Act [OSHA]**) and with the labor laws of other countries; and (3) the measurement of HRM contributions to an organization's strategic goals via a balanced scorecard.

HRM Administration
and Organizing Approaches

Historically, HR managers operated as adjunct staff to organizations, overseeing the daily transactions associated with hiring, paying, or training employees and reporting on employee issues as required by managers in organizations. As organizations grew more complex, administering these daily transactions also grew more complex. The introduction of mechanization to handle payroll signaled the changing future of HR administration; technology would play an increasingly important role in managing daily employee transactions (Walker, 1982, 1993, 2001).

Today, computer hardware and the accompanying software packages offer considerable support for daily HR transactions and make it possible to move beyond the limited administrative approaches available to the HR managers of the 1950s (PricewaterhouseCoopers, 2006). Modern HR professionals use technology to more effectively support administrative activities and reduce organizational costs while improving data accuracy, employee productivity, and customer service (Bender, 2001; Ulrich, 1997). Indeed, 92% of the companies worldwide included in the 2012–13 CedarCrestone HR technology survey indicated the use of some type of HR administrative technology (CedarCrestone, 2012). Moreover, global companies reported that, even with challenging economic conditions, they anticipated growing their technology commitment for strategic human capital talent management, as well as for workforce management, service delivery, and business intelligence. The next section briefly describes the enabling architecture that allows HR administrators to leverage technology.

Service-Oriented Architecture
and eXtensible Markup Language

Service-oriented architecture (SOA) "is a paradigm for organizing and utilizing distributed [computing] capabilities that may be under the control of different ownership domains . . . providing a uniform means to offer, discover, interact with, and use capabilities to produce desired [business] effects" (Organization for the Advancement of Structured Information Systems [OASIS], 2006, p. 8). It is focused on providing overall service that is well defined, self-contained, and context and platform independent; in other words, it is focused on adding value to the organization's business purpose rather than simply adding technological value. In effect, SOA is a collection of internal and external services that can communicate with each other by point-to-point data exchange or through coordination among different services to achieve a business purpose. Figure 10.1 demonstrates the business-driven SOA process (Marks & Bell, 2006).

Figure 10.1 SOA Business-Modeling Process

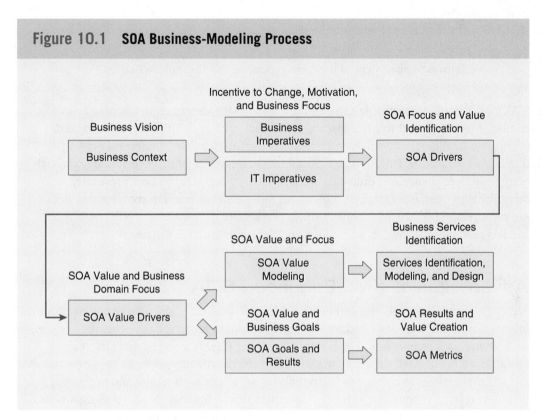

Source: Marks and Bell (2006, chap. 3).

For example, an HR administration manager in the United States who needs to generate the government-mandated, annual EEO-1 cares little about where the information is stored or which applications, servers, communications technologies, or programming languages are used. Rather, the manager wants easy access to the myriad data necessary to complete the report in a timely manner. SOA focuses on fulfilling that need, moving away from a point-to-point perspective (e.g., HR linked to a single EEO database) to a market perspective of services, reusing data and applications from multiple sources as long as the required service is provided. The principles of SOA include loose coupling, flexibility, autonomy, standards-based computing, reusability, modularity, and services discoverability and optimization. The architectural benefits of SOA include (Campbell & Mohun, 2007)

- IT consolidation opportunities and standards-based integration, using a standards-based approach to integration for IT systems that are very complex and heterogeneous to reduce both cost and complexity over time;

- faster implementation and change management through reuse, modeling, and composite development; and

- improved alignment of business processes and IT implementation.

SOA is enhanced by eXtensible Markup Language (XML), described in Chapter 3. XML combines text and other information about the text, such as its structure, allowing data sharing across different information systems via the Internet. XML underpins SOA such that SOA is ineffective without it. Specifically, XML improves interface technology through platform independence and protocols, such as security and transactions, previously unavailable in interfaces (Erl, 2005). Platform independence refers to software that does not rely on any special features of any single platform (e.g., Windows, UNIX) or, if it does, handles those special features such that it can deal with multiple platforms.

Advantages of XML-Enhanced SOA

Although HR professionals engaged in administration may not make final decisions about the information technology described previously, they need to recognize the benefits associated with having such architecture. For example, Schwartz (2003) reported that Oracle's introduction of HR-XML standards would reduce the requirement to input applicant resumes manually. Therefore, today's use of HR portals for job application receipt and processing, including resume submission, is related directly to this technology. Thus, HRIS capabilities are leveraged dramatically by SOA and XML such that (Lublinsky, 2007; Walker, 2001)

- security is improved—this is especially important because of the privacy protection issues associated with HR data and applications;

- performance is enhanced—this aids in reducing transaction costs and increasing customer satisfaction;

- auditing capabilities are added—this supports the growing demand to demonstrate compliance with corporate quality and policy mandates;

- change capabilities are enhanced—this improves reaction time to better meet business-driven change requirements; and

- alternative HR administration structures (e.g., self-service portals, SSCs, outsourcing) are facilitated—this encourages HR managers to consider multiple approaches to meeting the HR administration goals of cost reduction and service improvement.

The remainder of this section will focus on the four structural approaches to HR administration facilitated by technology. Each has opened paths to increased efficiency and effectiveness, improved service, and cost controls, possibilities unimagined by HR professionals a decade ago. The four HR administrative approaches—self-service portals, shared-service centers, outsourcing, and offshoring—presented in this chapter are shown in Figure 10.2.

- The **self-service portal** is an electronic access point to an organization's HRM information, such as company policies, benefits schedules, an individual's payroll data, or other records; access may be via the organization's computers and intranet or remotely from other locations via the Internet.

- A **shared-service center (SSC)** is a technology-enabled HRM group focused on value creation by providing excellent service to internal customers while reducing costs through increased efficiency and continuous improvement.

- **Human resources outsourcing (HRO)** is the practice of contracting with vendors to perform HR services and activities.

- **Offshoring** is an extension of outsourcing that involves contracting with vendors outside a nation's boundaries to effect additional cost savings or gain other benefits over domestic outsourcing alone.

Following a discussion of the theories underpinning these approaches to HR administration, the purpose, advantages, and disadvantages of each will be highlighted. Next, the chapter will examine the different ways in which each alternative approach facilitates the HR administrative reporting mandated by government entities. The chapter concludes with a discussion of how each administrative alternative can be measured to demonstrate the

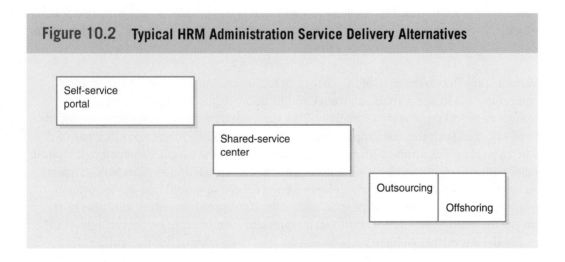

Figure 10.2 Typical HRM Administration Service Delivery Alternatives

Self-service portal

Shared-service center

Outsourcing

Offshoring

value-added nature of efficient, effective HR administrative functions in support of an organization's strategic goals.

Theory and HR Administration

The first theory that explains alternative approaches to HR administration is the **resource-based view** of the firm (Barney, 1991, 2001). Barney, in delineating the resource-based view of organizations, argued that organizations are bundles of resources, identified as physical capital, organizational capital, and human capital. *Physical capital* includes an organization's technology, geographic locations, physical assets (e.g., plants, money), and access to raw material. *Organizational capital* includes its formal reporting structure; its coordinating, planning, and organizing systems; and its internal and external group relationships. *Human capital* includes the experience, capabilities, relationships, and insights of individual employees. Taken together, these resources are combined and managed to determine an organization's *opportunity* to win sustainable competitive advantage in the marketplace.

To achieve **sustainable competitive advantage**, a firm's resources, when compared with those of its competitors, must be *valuable, rare, difficult to imitate, and invulnerable to substitutes*. Based on this theory, then, it is likely that innovative combinations of technology (physical capital), organizing systems (organizational capital), and strategic individual knowledge, skills, and abilities may serve to give an organization a strategic position in its marketplace. Thus, alternative HR administrative approaches seek to combine HR technology (e.g., HRIS and Internet) with organizing systems (e.g., self-service portals) and strategic HR knowledge, skills, and abilities (e.g., compensation expertise) to leverage a specific firm's competitive position. It is important to note that this theory suggests that *each* firm in an industry is likely to acquire resources such as human talent to support its *unique* combinations based on its strategic choices; it is this unique combination that leads to sustainable competitive advantage. *Merely benchmarking or following trends is unlikely to lead to sustainable competitive positioning for a firm!*

Walmart provides an example of this theory. In the 1990s, Walmart gained a substantial competitive advantage with its innovative combination of "just-in-time" supply chain management and proprietary technology. This approach linked each Walmart store directly to its suppliers such that the supplier was notified electronically when a product was sold; when a store's predetermined inventory level was reached, the supplier shipped replacement items without any interaction with store managers. This resulted in significant cost savings and improved service with fewer employees. For a time, it appeared that this innovation might lead to a sustainable competitive advantage. However, competitors were able to imitate the management supply chain techniques and even improve on the technology to negate the advantage. Walmart's innovation did lead to an advance for the entire industry but did not provide a sustainable advantage for the firm because the innovation could be imitated. Thus, organizations looking to achieve sustainable competitive advantage are more likely to reach that goal through *strategic and unique* combinations of physical, organizational, and human capital than by relying on any one resource.

A second theory that explains alternative approaches to HR administration is **transaction cost theory** (Coase, 1937; Williamson, 1975). Transaction cost theory suggests that organizations can choose to purchase the goods and services they need in the competitive marketplace or make those goods and services internally. Transaction costs are the expenses associated with an economic transaction, whether internal or external. Managers can compare the "transaction costs" required to purchase products or services, such as contract administration, licenses, and delivery services, from external providers with those incurred in providing the same product or service internally by, for example, using additional personnel, retraining employees, or purchasing hardware and software. Thus, managers can make optimum economic decisions for their organizations. This decision is the classic "make or buy" economic choice facing rational economic actors. Behaving rationally, organizations would make such decisions based on total costs, choosing to "buy" from external providers when total costs were lower and products or services were readily available and choosing to "make" what was needed internally when total costs from external sources were higher or products or services were not readily available. Of course, this example assumes that the make or buy benefits of either choice are straightforward and equal. Typically, however, such decisions are more complex; thus, a cost-benefit analysis (CBA; described in Chapter 7) should be completed to determine if the organization should make or buy. For example, a small business might elect to buy HR compensation and payroll services from an external provider rather than decide to make its own HR compensation program, which would require purchasing hardware and HRIS software and adding compensation specialists.

General Motors (GM) provides an example of this theory. In the 1990s, amid market pressure to reduce costs as competitors increased their market share at GM's expense, GM elected to divest itself of its fully integrated parts manufacturing functions. GM managers found that "transaction costs" would be reduced if the company standardized automobile parts and purchased them from multiple external providers rather than continuing to manufacture them internally. Transaction costs associated with internal parts production were increasing rapidly in terms of employees' wages, salaries, and benefits and the ongoing maintenance of aging production plants. Thus, GM spun off its Delphi unit as an independent company in 1999. Although Delphi continued to sell to GM, GM no longer relied exclusively on the newly independent company for parts, helping reduce GM's overall corporate costs. Increasing internal transaction costs coupled with a robust external parts production market determined GM's strategic "make or buy" choice.

Both resource-based and transaction cost theories can explain the different choices organizations make in their preferences for HR administration approaches. For example, the increasing internal transaction costs of recruiting and hiring employees may lead to the search for an external vendor who specializes in the recruitment and selection of new employees. Organizations may then decide to compare those internal transaction costs and benefits with external transaction costs and benefits from the specialized recruitment and selection providers, leading to outsourcing. Alternatively, strategic concerns about the security of having external providers inadvertently "share" crucial talent-positioning information with competitors, coupled with the decreasing costs of technology, might lead an organization to focus on internal innovation involving physical and organizational resources (e.g., self-service portals coupled with SSCs) to reduce transaction costs, while increasing spending on strategic talent management issues (e.g., hiring, development) to achieve a sustainable competitive position in its industry. Keep these theoretical perspectives in mind as we examine each of the HR administration approaches.

Self-Service Portals and HRIS

The first structural approach to HR administration (Figure 10.2), **employee self-service (ESS)** HR portals, provides an electronic means for a company's employees to access its HR services and information. Such portals provide a single sign-on capability for employees, who can individually complete transactions for their personal data. ESS portals can range from simple intranet websites that allow employees to access static HR policies, such as safety requirements, to sophisticated Internet websites that allow employees to access and change their individual records. For example, adding a new child to an employee's medical benefits, from any computer location on a 24-hour, 7-days-a-week basis, would be possible with ESS portals. A sample screenshot of an ESS screen for an address change is found in Figure 10.3 and a partial list of information and services commonly available via ESS portals is given in Table 10.1.

In addition to providing an interface for current employees, ESS portals are also available to prospective employees. For example, individuals who have applied for jobs online through an employer's Internet website have accessed the HR portal to complete the application and forward their resumes (Anheier & Doherty, 2001; Gueutal & Falbe, 2005; Walker, 2001). CedarCrestone (2012) reported that 67% of the responding global companies used ESS portals, with 23% planning to add the capability within 36 months. Chapter 12 discusses Web recruiting in more detail.

Manager self-service (MSS) portals are becoming more prevalent in organizations as well. CedarCrestone (2012) reported that 49% of responding companies used MSS portals, with an additional 18% planning to add the capability within 36 months. MSS portals are

Figure 10.3 Sample Employee Self-Service Screen

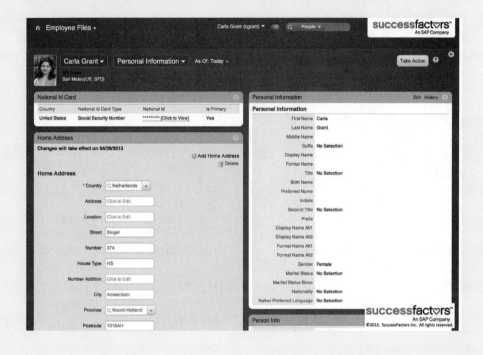

specialized versions of ESS portals designed to allow managers to view extensive information about their subordinates and perform many administrative tasks electronically, including traditional HR functions. For example, in typical MSS applications, managers can complete job requisitions and view resumes of prospective applicants. In addition, managers can view **performance appraisals**, subordinate salaries, productivity, and training histories, and model annual salary increases. However, MSS is not limited to HR functions and may also include budgeting and tracking, reporting, and staff policy and procedure development (Gueutal & Falbe, 2005; Walker, 2001).

Advantages of Self-Service Portals for HR Administration

Self-service portals provide several advantages for achieving HR administration goals, including (1) improved speed and quality of service to employees and managers, and (2) simplified routine inquiries and changes. Reducing the number of inquiry transactions

Table 10.1   Sample Employee Self-Service (ESS) Functionality

Communications	Benefits Services	Personal Data	Development
Review company communications	Research and view plan rules and requirements	Update emergency contact, address, telephone information	Enroll in training courses
Access company policies or procedures	Enroll in cafeteria-style programs (medical, dental, insurance)	Correct errors in personal data (degree, graduation date)	View completed training
Access HR policy manuals and e-mail inquiry or help request	Add or delete dependents	Change W-4 withholding forms	Access internal or external e-learning courses
Complete employee surveys or 360-degree feedback data	Model retirement or access 401(k) savings investment records	View previous or current pay and performance information	View or apply for internal job vacancies
View/respond to personal information requests from HR	Model health plan alternatives' costs (e.g., HMO, PPO)	Enter time reports, vacation or sick days, and travel expense reports	Complete employment tests for new jobs

requiring direct HR staff involvement helps keep information current. For example, with self-service, changes in the doctors and hospitals allowed for each medical plan or status reports on the hiring of a new employee are more likely to be entered into the system as required. Self-service portals also enhance employee satisfaction by permitting employees to control when and where such access activities occur, empowering employees, increasing their productivity, especially for those who travel frequently, and offering privacy for those who prefer to handle such matters without the presence of coworkers. In addition, self-service portals facilitate easy, increased access to HR information, helping employees ensure that important personal data (such as individual job performance appraisals used by managers in making decisions about salary increases, promotions, or other employment rewards) are accurate and current.

Executives believe that having managers use more accurate, timely information contributes to improved managerial decision making (Gueutal & Falbe, 2005; Walker, 2001). Finally, self-service portals help reduce the number of transactions for HR employees and, correspondingly, overall HR costs. For example, CedarCrestone's (2012) survey showed that companies with 500 to 10,000+ employees reported that those firms with minimal HR technology served an average of 93 employees per HR staff member. By comparison, organizations with ESS portals served an average of 99 employees per HR staff member, whereas those with MSS portals served an average of 118 employees per HR staff member. Organizations can realize cost savings of 67% to 99% on tasks such as changing employee information, providing current pay and benefit statements, and posting of jobs (Gueutal & Falbe, 2005). Such savings relieve HR specialists of routine transactional work and allow them to focus more on both the traditional and transformational strategic activities described in Chapter 1.

Disadvantages of Self-Service Portals for HR Administration

Although HR administrators can gain advantages from deploying self-service portals, they are also faced with multiple disadvantages. Permitting employees to access company data through self-service portals may increase the possibility of security breaches and the associated negative outcomes, like identity theft, for affected employees. Employees are concerned that even having their data in a company's HRIS can lead to misuse of such information by others in the organization and may feel their privacy is invaded when organizations fail to limit access to personal data housed in HRIS (Phillips, Isenhour, & Stone, 2008). For example, managers may learn negative information (e.g., that employees have medical disabilities) through MSS portal access that would have been unavailable in a paper record system. Even the inadvertent use or sharing of such information may preclude training or promotional opportunities for employees. Misuse of this personal information in this manner can constitute a violation of labor laws such as the **Americans with Disabilities Act (ADA)** in the United States. Privacy and security issues will be discussed in more detail later in this chapter, as well as in Chapter 16.

In addition to security issues, HR administrators may find that unions and managers resist using the self-service portals. In particular, unions may argue that employees are "doing HR work" when they enter data and make changes online via an ESS portal. Union members who perform such transactions on their own time may request overtime pay for completing such functions or may choose to do such functions at work, thus reducing productivity. Managers may also resent having to do work that previously was handled completely by

HR staff, particularly when such work involved calling the staff members rather than completing forms. For example, managers may have had relationships with HR staff that permitted the managers to bypass established procedures for requesting a new hire. Thus, using MSS portals would not only require more actual work for the managers but also enforce standardized interfaces that might lead managers to perceive a reduction in their status and power in the organization. Accordingly, HR managers should recognize and take action to ameliorate such perceptions and concerns as part of the project management planning and implementation process for an HRIS.

Shared-Service Centers and HRIS

The second structural approach to HR administration, SSCs, generally appeared in response to the increasing globalization of competitive markets occasioned by the proliferation of multinational enterprises (MNEs). To compete successfully, organizations were pressured to reduce costs through the consolidation of administrative transactions while still providing excellent service. Such a challenge involved balancing the desire for control inherent in centralized administrative structures and the desire for flexibility inherent in decentralized administrative structures—a constant organizational conflict within large and expanding corporations (Lucenko, 1998; Quinn, Cooke, & Kris, 2000; von Simson, 1990). Over time, many organizations have chosen SSCs as the structural solution to that pressure.

> **Shared services** is a collaborative strategy whereby [one or more] staff functions of a firm are concentrated in a semi-autonomous organization and managed like a business unit . . . to promote greater efficiency, value generation and improved service for internal customers. (Goh, Prakash, & Yeo, 2007, p. 252)

To emphasize this aspect of SSCs, some organizations have described them as "centers of excellence" (Bender, 2001). Figure 10.4 illustrates that SSCs include HR in 66% of manufacturing and 53% of service companies (Powell, 2004).

Powell (2004, p. 6) identified the following common elements of SSCs:

- Centralizing or decentralizing of business processes
- Using economies of scale to reduce unit costs
- Developing customer relationship models (CRMs) to better meet the needs of customers
- Concentrating on cost reduction to enhance competitive positioning
- Deploying quality tools to ensure continuous process improvement

Figure 10.4 Functions in Shared Services

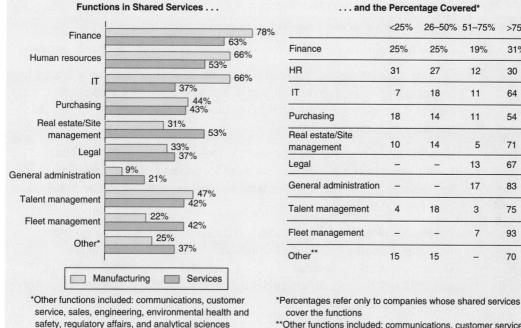

Functions in Shared Services . . .

Function	Manufacturing	Services
Finance	78%	63%
Human resources	66%	53%
IT	66%	37%
Purchasing	44%	43%
Real estate/Site management	31%	53%
Legal	33%	37%
General administration	9%	21%
Talent management	47%	42%
Fleet management	22%	42%
Other*	25%	37%

Legend: ☐ Manufacturing ▨ Services

. . . and the Percentage Covered*

	<25%	26–50%	51–75%	>75%
Finance	25%	25%	19%	31%
HR	31	27	12	30
IT	7	18	11	64
Purchasing	18	14	11	54
Real estate/Site management	10	14	5	71
Legal	–	–	13	67
General administration	–	–	17	83
Talent management	4	18	3	75
Fleet management	–	–	7	93
Other**	15	15	–	70

*Other functions included: communications, customer service, sales, engineering, environmental health and safety, regulatory affairs, and analytical sciences

*Percentages refer only to companies whose shared services cover the functions

**Other functions included: communications, customer service, sales, engineering, environmental health and safety, regulatory affairs, and analytical sciences

Source: Powell (2004).

To be successful, a shared-service center involving HR, for example, must view itself as an independent business unit offering products (e.g., HR reports), which it must "sell" to its customers at a price (internal transaction cost) they are willing to pay. These internal customers are managers in different business units such as operations and marketing. If the HR function is unsuccessful in reducing costs, providing desirable services, and adding value, it may find itself "outsourced" by business unit managers who perceive that they can get better service and value from an external provider. To demonstrate added value to the organization, the SSC should establish measures that demonstrate customer satisfaction levels, productivity, cost controls, and quality. Such measures are necessary to allow internal customers to assess the value of the consolidated unit and to facilitate continuous improvement by SSC managers.

Accenture (2007) outlined several principles to embrace when considering the use of SSCs:

- Establish a "global good" vision for the SSC that includes its definition and benefits to ensure that business units "losing" functions are willing to make the commitment to transfer their work.

- Identify leaders, in all the affected groups, to sponsor the SSC vision, promote the center's value to the organization, and serve as responsible change agents.

- Support transparency regarding who (e.g., affected employees), what (e.g., which functions), when (e.g., transition plans), and where (e.g., location of the new center). This openness is essential to building the trust needed to initiate and maintain the center's effectiveness.

- Conduct initial and ongoing customer "values and requirements" meetings to build trust, establish performance and service expectations, and solve problems. Implementing jointly acceptable measures facilitates SSC success and internal customer satisfaction.

- Focus on viewing the SSC's processes in the context of the overall business functions. Examine the process behind each function from "end to end." Understanding the context of all processes in each function encourages the recognition of the interdependencies inherent in the SSC concept and bolsters the value-creating goal of SSCs.

Advantages of Shared-Service Centers for HR Administration

Advantages of SSCs for HR administration (Robinson & Robinson, 2005; Ulrich, 1997; Walker, 2001) include (1) permitting HR administration managers to focus on delivering the timely, high-quality transactions necessary to fulfill corporate requirements, such as mandated governmental reporting, and (2) removing the artificial barriers inherent in the generalist-specialist continuum common in HR organizations, smoothing work and communication processes. This is particularly important for multinationals, which have to respond to the labor laws of multiple countries.

Combining such transactional responsibilities into a single business unit encourages the unit to focus on customer satisfaction with specific user interactions, such as responses to employee questions or requests for assistance. This frees specialists to focus on more strategic activities. SSCs also encourage the efficiency and standardization necessary to support strategic cost-control goals by consolidating individuals responsible for transactions, providing organizations with greater motivation to redesign procedures and create more effective ones. Finally, such centers facilitate development of the measures of efficiency, quality, and customer responsiveness that are necessary to demonstrate appropriate contributions to strategic goals. However, there are several potential pitfalls associated with SSCs.

Disadvantages of Shared-Service Centers for HR Managers

Frequently, organizations combine multiple, unrelated shared services into a combined business unit. Depending on the nature of such functions, the synergies needed to consolidate and improve processes may be less prevalent. For example, combining vehicle fleet management and HR transactions may offer few synergies. Leaders of such units may be stretched as they seek to unify and manage diverse functions. However, careful development of the mission and appropriate selection of the leaders of such units can overcome this problem by establishing a shared mindset among those involved (Walker, 2001).

In addition, creating SSCs may lead to unanticipated power shifts in organizations. For example, combining financial and HR transactions in a single center may lead to reduced emphasis on HR transactions since business managers are especially concerned with the budget reporting associated with financial transactions. Again, establishing an effective mission and overarching goals for the center can forestall such power shifts (Ulrich, 1997).

Finally, SSCs can lead to depersonalization. For example, line managers, accustomed to personal contact with HR professionals, may feel isolated when handling transactions through self-service portals. Similarly, they may feel abandoned when traditional communication patterns are disrupted because specialists have been consolidated in SSCs. Because such units are concerned with efficiency and cost controls, individuals working in them can become more involved with the technology with which they work and less involved with others who are engaged in the day-to-day aspects of the business (Ulrich, 1997).

Outsourcing and HRIS

The third approach to HR administration, outsourcing, is the practice of contracting with vendors to perform HR services and activities. Outsourcing is not new in HR administration. For example, Automatic Data Processing, Inc. (ADP) moved quickly in 1945 to offer its expertise in payroll and tax calculations to businesses facing increasingly complex employee income tax and withholding calculations (Dominguez, 2006). Nonetheless, few would have predicted the recent explosion in specialized organizations capable of providing a few or all of an organization's HR functions (Hewitt, 2005). According to the 2012 KPMG Institutes' outsourcing survey, 31% of participating global firms viewed HR as a top functional area for outsourcing. In addition, 40% of those surveyed were in the process of coordinating new global sources for outsourcing some HR functions (KPMG Institutes, 2012).

HR outsourcing (HRO) firms are hardly uniform. There are many different types of providers, reflecting the diverse needs of organizations. HRO firms provided HR services for 3.3 million employees in North America (Everest Research Institute, 2007). Moreover, for firms that had more than 1,000 employees and revenues of greater than $100 million and that participated in comprehensive outsourcing (defined as more than five human resource functions outsourced), satisfaction with HRO levels increased over time. Of the 310 firms surveyed, HRO satisfaction (on a scale of 1 [*not at all satisfied*] to 5 [*very satisfied*]) improved from an average of 2.9 in the first two years to 3.4 after two or more years (EquaTerra, 2007).

Outsourcing contracts should include specific pricing agreements (e.g., flat or fixed fee per process or per employee served, unit prices per transaction levels, hourly and overtime rates, revenue sharing, risk-reward sharing, failure penalties), expected performance and associated measures (e.g., transaction quality standards, error rates, system availability and downtime, customer satisfaction levels, hours of operation), and terms and conditions (e.g., start and end dates, extensions permitted, termination agreements, dispute resolution procedures, audit procedures). Obviously, HR administration managers would require significant assistance from multiple groups such as the legal, operations, and information systems departments within the organization to establish and monitor the contract, ensuring that the organization is adequately protected from incompetent or unethical outsourcing providers.

Reasons to Pursue HR Outsourcing

HR administration managers elect to pursue HRO for multiple reasons (Keebler, 2001). Weatherly (2005) suggests that managers may pursue discrete, multiprocess, or total-process HRO.

Some organizations outsource only discrete or selected functions, pursuing **discrete HRO** through niche third-party providers. This outsourcing involves having specialized external firms deal only with a particular HR function. External HR recruiting firms, for example, fall into this category. Such an approach is common in smaller organizations with limited numbers of HR professionals or in larger organizations with few, sporadic recruiting requirements. Also included in this category is the outsourcing of parts of various HR functions. For example, even organizations with large, effective recruiting staffs may elect to outsource executive or specialty recruitment functions (e.g., recruiting for multilingual positions) to external search firms that have unique expertise. Similarly, organizations may outsource only annual benefits enrollment, flexible spending accounts (FSA) administration, or payroll administration.

Generally, the outsourcing of discrete HR functions is attractive for two reasons. First, discrete HRO can achieve cost savings by eliminating the company's need to hire highly specialized HR professionals (e.g., executive recruiters) or those with the HRIS expertise necessary to perform infrequent functions (e.g., FSA administration). In addition, discrete HRO can reduce the HR administration costs associated with frequent, high-volume transactions such as payroll. In both cases, discrete HRO serves to reduce HRIS expenses and the number of HR employees while ensuring the desired strategic outcome of hiring the right executive or paying employees correctly on schedule. Although discrete tactical HRO has existed for many years, it still remains a popular HR administration approach for achieving strategic goals.

HR administration managers may also pursue **multiprocess HRO**, also known as *comprehensive* or *blended services outsourcing*. This approach involves outsourcing to niche, third-party providers all of one or more related HR functions, for example, recruitment and selection or defined and 401(k) retirement plan administration. Multiprocess outsourcing has become more popular with the increase in the number of specialized vendors providing such services and the spread of enabling Internet portal capabilities. With an HR portal and HRIS employees can model their pension decisions independently (to determine pension amounts associated with different retirement dates, for example) and then change 401(k) investment directions by speaking to pension specialists at the third-party vendor when questions arise. This outsourcing of sets of functions reduces the number of specialized HR employees, improves service levels to employees, and reduces HRIS hardware and software upgrades and ongoing maintenance costs. Overall, such an HR administration approach can provide significant cost reductions and simultaneously maintain or enhance service levels.

Total HRO is the third type of outsourcing approach and involves having all, or nearly all, HR functions handled by one or more external vendors. All traditional HR administrative and functional activities would be managed through third-party vendors. For example, Johnson & Johnson Inc. contracted with Convergys to provide full HR administrative and transactional services for its global workforce for $1 billion (CBR, 2007). Under such arrangements, employees would contact the vendor for assistance or inquiries directly, without any company HR employee involvement or knowledge. Certainly, such a plan would reduce internal HR employee expenses, HRIS expenditures, and administration costs dramatically; however, such savings would be offset by costs for vendor contract administration, quality controls, and oversight. In addition, the HR strategic functions, such as long-term force planning and strategic business unit support, should not be outsourced because third-party vendors frequently deal with multiple clients, one or more of whom might be competitors. It is not hard to imagine how even the most sincere vendor efforts to secure strategic HR plans might be inadvertently compromised, leading to disclosure of these plans and severe strategic disadvantages. Although this HR administration approach is not as prevalent as either discrete or multiprocess outsourcing, it is gaining in popularity. Organizations might opt for such a total HRO solution to deal with the myriad HR requirements associated with the global workforce of an MNE, to focus on HR strategic issues, or to reduce costs. That this strategy is gaining support is demonstrated in Hewitt's HRO survey (2010): 82% of surveyed companies rated their outsourcing as effective or highly effective in meeting strategic goals.

Advantages of HR Outsourcing

The advantages of HR administration outsourcing can be both financial and strategic (Keebler, 2001; Weatherly, 2005). For example, organizations seeking to increase financial profitability and enhance shareowner value might employ HRO to reduce ongoing expenses for employees and software, forestalling capital expenditures for new buildings and equipment. This decision would entail a careful "make-buy" assessment of the total costs and benefits of continuing internal operations versus contracting for them in the external market. Benefits of such an approach might include redesigned processes, improved quality, centralized or consolidated operations, access to technology, and enhanced employee satisfaction. The cost-benefit analysis (CBA) approach covered in Chapter 7 would be essential in this situation.

The strategic advantages of HRO might include the ability of the organization to better focus on its core business by transforming the HR function. By outsourcing the simpler, transaction-based function, the HR department can move from its historical focus on administrative activities to a new position as strategic business partner. Organizations recognize that, more than ever, effective talent management may be the source of sustainable strategic advantage in a knowledge-based, global economy. However, many HR professionals are mired in day-to-day transactional administrative tasks that preclude the value-added consulting, planning, and visioning activities required from them to achieve strategic goals (Fletcher, 2005; Lawler, 2005). HRO could free HR professionals to focus on strategic issues, such as talent management, while providing the firm with skilled transactional and professional services in HR functional areas such as compensation and in administrative areas such as governmental compliance and regulations. Moreover, these services would be powered by the up-to-date technology provided by the external vendor.

Disadvantages of HR Outsourcing

Although there are a number of financial and strategic reasons for considering HR administration outsourcing, there are also serious potential problems for firms that use the approach without fully understanding how to manage it to achieve desired goals. For example, firms that used HRO to achieve HR transformation and cost savings rated their success at an average of 3 on a 5-point scale, (1 equaling *benefits not at all achieved* and 5 equaling *benefits fully achieved*) (EquaTerra, 2007). Thus, one big disadvantage of HRO is the likelihood that the organization will *not* achieve its strategic goals. Such a failure could have a significant, negative impact on the organization's ability to survive. Steps to minimize such a failure include realistic cost-benefit analyses (see Chapter 7), successful project planning and implementation (see Chapter 8), unambiguous goals and measures of HRO success, rigorous vendor assessment and selection processes, and skilled vendor contract negotiation, management, and auditing (Weatherly, 2005). Indeed, one of the primary responsibilities of

HR administration managers in an outsourcing environment is to ensure that the contract terms are fulfilled on a daily basis and that corrective actions are immediately taken when failures occur.

Another disadvantage of HRO includes the loss of institutional expertise in the outsourced functions, making an HRO decision reversal difficult or impossible. Frequently, when outsourcing is undertaken, HR subject matter experts are reassigned or released. This restructuring can be a serious strategic error if the vendor is unable to fulfill its contractual obligations. As noted above, an organization would be unwise to outsource core or strategic HR planning functions because of the possibility that competitors might learn its plans from vendors. In addition, loss of internal strategic HR expertise may be devastating to an organization over time. Unfortunately, these outsourcing organizations may lack the contract management expertise to oversee the vendor and hold it accountable for contract terms. Other potential problems include security risks in multivendor outsourcing, internal employee and manager resistance, compliance failures, and cultural clashes between the organization and its vendors.

As outsourcing arrangements continue to increase, evidence from information technology (IT) outsourcing can provide a cautionary tale for those considering HRO. For example, in a recent study, approximately one-third of organizations reported that they had canceled an IT outsourcing contract (Lacity & Willcocks, 2001). In addition, when these contracts are canceled, the functionality is often brought back in-house instead of shifted to a new outsourcing partner (Lacity & Willcocks, 2000). The effort to bring functionality back in-house, also known as **backsourcing**, can be expensive, as firms pay to reorganize twice: first when outsourcing a function and again when backsourcing it.

In summary, HRO is another approach to HR administration that offers potential for cost reduction, process improvement, and employee satisfaction. However, managers of HR administrative functions must be highly skilled at using HRO strategically to achieve organizational goals.

Offshoring and HRIS

The final approach to HR administration, offshoring, is an expansion of HR outsourcing that includes sending work outside the United States to vendors located in other countries. Technological capabilities and global competition have combined to make HRO a global business, and offshoring for MNEs is quite complex. For example, if an Australian airline has call centers in India to obtain improved cost performance, why not have its SSC for HR there as well? Based on responses from 5,231 executives in North America and Europe, Hatch (2004) reported that 19% of all companies and 95% of the *Fortune* 1000 companies considered offshore outsourcing. Moreover, there are now more than 10,000 offshore vendors in 175 countries competing for the business. Figure 10.5 shows the various reasons organizations consider offshoring.

Esen's (2004) survey of HR managers reported that organizations consider offshoring primarily for financial reasons, including lower labor costs (76%), increased profits (50%), and reduced health care costs (23%). For example, researchers found that labor costs for a software developer in India were $6 per hour as opposed to the $60 per hour earned for doing the same job in the United States (Chiamsiri, Bulusu, & Agarwal, 2005). In addition, some firms were seeking skilled employees (16%) or productivity (10%) and service improvement (7%). Only 7% considered offshoring for strategic reasons. In fact, 40% of HR managers reported that their organizations would not consider offshoring because it was inconsistent with strategic direction.

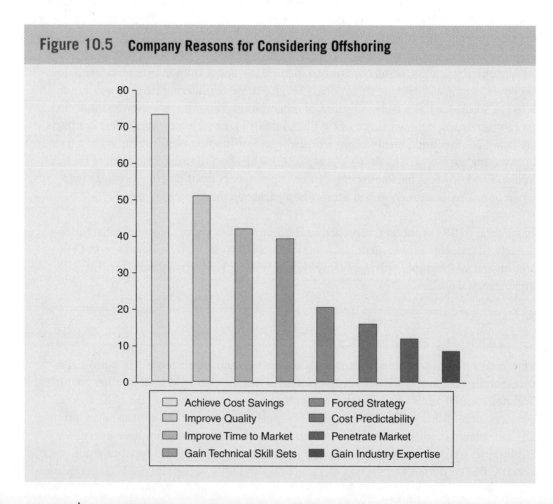

Figure 10.5   Company Reasons for Considering Offshoring

Achieve Cost Savings
Improve Quality
Improve Time to Market
Gain Technical Skill Sets
Forced Strategy
Cost Predictability
Penetrate Market
Gain Industry Expertise

Types of HR Offshoring

When their organizations pursued offshoring, HR managers reported that manufacturing functions were most common (43%), followed by IT (29%) and computer programming (22%), customer call centers (29%), and HR functions (16%). Such organizations used both offshore ownership and offshore outsourcing (Esen, 2004). **Offshore ownership** may include opening a new subsidiary in the foreign country, entering into a joint venture with an existing firm in that country, or purchasing an existing firm. By comparison, offshore outsourcing is a traditional contractual relationship with an existing firm.

Offshore ownership is riskier than simple offshore outsourcing. In addition to appropriate strategic and financial due diligence, organizations considering offshore ownership must pay particular attention to

- ready availability of necessary employee knowledge, skills, and abilities such as language;

- information and communication systems compatibility with HRIS;

- governmental regulations and legal employment requirements such as wage laws;

- political stability of the country for facility and employee security; and

- cultural differences such as expectations about participative versus directive supervision.

Although an offshore outsourcing strategy is less risky than offshore ownership, organizations would still face more risk than they would had they outsourced domestically. HR managers should always perform due diligence in assessing the reputation and business capabilities of an outsourcing partner. However, such processes are more complex when dealing with organizations located halfway across the globe. For example, concerns about electrical power availability, which might determine whether HRIS processing can occur as scheduled, are rarely discussed with outsourcing firms in the United States but might be a significant issue in parts of Indonesia. In addition, worker availability to meet a 24/7 service center requirement is less of a problem in the United States than in countries where overtime is limited to a few hours per month, as it is in the European Union (EU). Finally, oversight and audit functions may be less onerous and expensive when U.S. companies establish offshore outsourcing agreements in nearby countries such as Canada or Mexico rather than in more distant nations such as India or China.

Summary of HR Administration Approaches

Based on the previous discussion, it is clear that HR administration managers have a number of approaches that can contribute to the goals of reducing costs, improving efficiency, and increasing service levels for internal customers. It is also important that such alternatives be pursued consistent with each organization's strategic plan to achieve sustainable competitive advantage in its industry. Multiple approaches may be appropriate based on those strategic goals. For example, HR portals may be combined with SSCs and selective outsourcing or offshoring to achieve the optimum solution for a particular firm.

In assessing whether one or more approaches is best, HR administration managers must understand the impact of their decisions on the specific administrative functions to be accomplished. Therefore, the next section describes two specific U.S. governmental reporting mandates (i.e., to the Equal Employment Opportunity Commission [EEOC] and OSHA) that are included among the many HR transactions for which HR administration is responsible. Following a discussion of the governmental mandates, their legal underpinnings, and the actual reports and records maintenance required, we explore how HR administration approaches can facilitate improved accuracy, reduced costs, and increased organizational value during the process of successfully completing such HR transactions.

Legal Compliance and HR Administration

As noted in Chapter 1 (Figure 1.2), the country and its general environment constitute a major effect on HRM and on the development and implementation of HRIS (Beaman, 2002). Whether the organization pursues a "domestic only" strategy (i.e., doing business in only one country) or an MNE approach, countries' government and labor laws are important external forces in establishing the context for business (Hersch, 1991). In particular, the labor laws provide the foundation of employee protections in the workplace. For example, in the United States, the Constitution and its Amendments establish the rights of citizens in general. In addition, multiple employment laws have been passed by the U.S. Congress to complement those rights. Some of the more important of these U.S. employment laws are identified in the glossary provided at the end of the book. For a more detailed discussion of the employment laws in the United States, see Ledvinka (1982).

It is important to recognize that U.S. employment laws underpin the *general principles* used in the practice of HRM. There are a number of laws in the United States prohibiting unfair discrimination on the basis of employee sex, race, age, and disability. There are similar laws and regulations in other industrialized nations that prohibit unfair discrimination (Briscoe & Schuler, 2004). The general principle underlying these unfair discrimination laws and regulations is that job performance should be the primary basis for employment decisions that change the employment status of an individual. When hiring new employees, for example, a company should base its hiring decision primarily on expected job performance, which might be assessed through employment tests and interviews. Whether applicants are male or female is irrelevant in all but a few cases (e.g., restroom attendant). Similarly, decisions to award a pay raise, or to promote or terminate an employee, should be based on the employee's job performance. As noted, the general principles underlying employment laws in the United States bear significant similarities to the general principles underlying employment laws or regulations in other countries, such as those specified in the EU directives (Briscoe & Schuler, 2004; Dowling & Welch, 2005; Paskoff, 2003). Since compliance with employment laws and regulations is a critical part of HR administration, provisions for handling the employment laws of multiple countries need to be considered in the development of an HRIS for a multinational firm.

What complicates U.S. employment laws for HR professionals is that the 50 states frequently expand on, adopt rules and regulations that differ from, or add additional protections not covered by federal law. For example, a partial comparison of elements of the **Family and Medical Leave Act (FMLA)** with the federal and state legislation of California and Oregon demonstrates these variations. Both California and Oregon deviate from the federal FMLA statute, but do so in different ways. The federal law specifies that its provisions apply to private employers with 50 or more employees in at least 20 weeks of the current or preceding year (U.S. Department of Labor, 2007). California law applies the provisions of the FMLA to *all* employers with 50 or more employees. In contrast, Oregon applies the provisions of the FMLA to employers with 25 or more employees in at least 20 weeks of the year. In this case, HR managers operating in both California and Oregon would be required to provide annual reports demonstrating that they have complied with both the federal and the state laws that are applicable. Since country-level and local laws can differ for all nations, administrative expenses to comply with employment laws can mushroom for firms with national and international exposure, even when an HRIS is used to support such compliance requirements. Indeed, this example reinforces the need for flexibility in HRIS software to accommodate such reporting differences.

This is, of course, just one example among many that demonstrates how governments affect HR administration. There are many laws and regulations in the United States that require organizations to report to government agencies (Ledvinka, 1982). All these manual reports are tedious and time-consuming, and they account for a significant amount of the transactional activity of the HR department. The processing for these activities was affected significantly by the introduction of computer technology and has always been a part of any integrated HR software package. The next sections take an in-depth look at two U.S. governmental mandates associated with equal employment opportunity (EEO) and employee safety. Specifically, HR administration and related concerns associated with EEO records and reporting (EEO-1 report) and OSHA record keeping and reporting will be highlighted. As you read about the reporting requirements of these laws, just imagine the tremendous amount of time it would take to complete an EEO-1 report manually for a medium-sized company of 1,000 employees; that is a considerable amount of "paper shuffling." Again, it is important to recognize that the following discussion is illustrative of HR administration, employment laws, and the use of an HRIS and, thus, could be applied to any country in the world.

HR Administration and Equal Employment Opportunity

U.S. Civil Rights Act of 1964, Title VII, and the EEO-1 Report

Figure 10.6 displays the broad categories of HRM administration associated with governmental mandates for meeting the requirements of **equal employment opportunity (EEO)** and affirmative action laws and guidelines. That all individuals should be considered for employment based on knowledge, skills, and abilities rather than irrelevant factors (e.g., sex, race, religion) is the *general principle* of EEO. Title VII of the Civil Rights Act of 1964 provides the requirements for such EEO. Under Section 703 of Title VII (42 U.S.C. §2000e-2), it is illegal for employers with 15 or more employees working 20 or more weeks per year

(1) to fail or refuse to hire or discharge any individual with respect to his compensation, terms, conditions, or privileges of employment because of such individual's race, color, religion, sex, or national origin, or

(2) to limit, segregate, or classify his employees or applicants for employment in any way that would deprive or tend to deprive any individual of employment opportunities or otherwise adversely affect his status as an employee because of such individual's race, color, religion, sex, or national origin. (U.S. EEOC, 1964)

In addition, employers who engage in business with the federal government and have contracts valued at $50,000 or more must comply with additional requirements that include providing a written **affirmative action plan (AAP)** to the Office of Federal Contract Compliance Procedures (OFCCP). This report details how the employer is actively seeking to hire and promote individuals in protected classes. Specifically, the AAP must (1) provide a detailed comparison of the available labor force with the employer's workforce by race, color, religion, national origin, and sex; (2) specify goals and timetables for achieving workforce balance if underutilization exists; and (3) indicate the specific steps to be taken to attain the goals in order to erase underutilization. In 1967, Congress expanded protection against illegal discrimination in employment by including the age criterion (i.e., persons aged 40 or older) with the passage of the **Age Discrimination in Employment Act (ADEA)**, and, in

Figure 10.6   EEO/Affirmative Action Plan (AAP) Administrative Functions

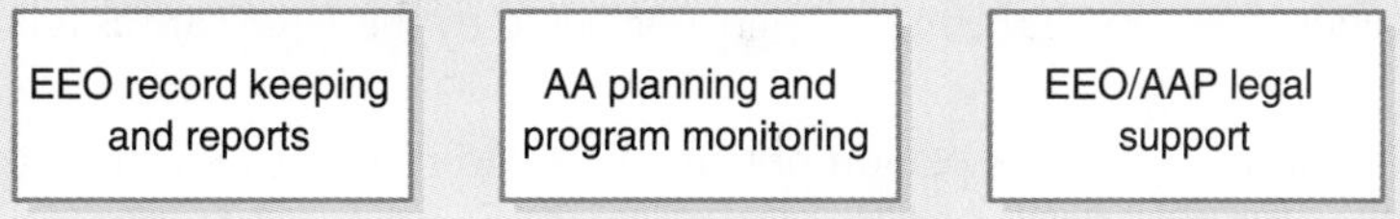

EEO record keeping and reports	AA planning and program monitoring	EEO/AAP legal support

1990, it provided protection to individuals with disabilities with its passage of the Americans with Disabilities Act (ADA). One example of the many mandated government reports is the EEO-1 report.

EEO-1 Report (Standard Form 100)

To monitor and assess equal employment opportunity practices, the EEOC was charged with gathering data, investigating alleged violations, and bringing legal charges against employers who failed to comply with Title VII requirements. Accordingly, all employers with 15 or more employees must keep records regarding their compliance with the law based on occupational category (i.e., professional, technical, managerial, craft) and sex and race/ethnicity. Although the records historically included six EEO categories (i.e., white, black, Hispanic, Asian or Pacific Islander, Native American), changes in the number and designation of categories were made based on the 2000 U.S. Census, with reporting by the revised categories beginning in 2007.

A sample of the "Employment Data" section of the EEO-1 report (Standard Form 100) with its revised categories is shown in Figure 10.7. Substantial changes in the report include expanding occupational categories from 4 to 10 and, more important, allowing individuals to specify more than one race/ethnicity category. Previously, individuals were limited to a single designation. The EEO-1 report must be prepared each September 30 by

> all private employers . . . with 100 or more employees. . . . [M]ulti-establishment employers doing business at more than one establishment, must complete online: (1) a report covering the principal or headquarters office; (2) a separate report for each establishment employing 50 or more persons; and (3) a separate report . . . for each establishment employing fewer than 50 employees . . . showing the name, address and total employment for each establishment employing fewer than 50 persons . . . by race, sex, and job category. (U.S. EEOC, 2006)

Revised reporting instructions include definitions of the revised designated racial/ethnic categories shown below, columns for reporting individuals who specify more than one race/ethnicity, and strong encouragement to have employees "self-identify" rather than relying on the employer's visual categorization. The race and ethnic designations used by the EEOC are as follows:

- *Hispanic or Latino*—A person of Cuban, Mexican, Puerto Rican, South or Central American, or other Spanish culture or origin regardless of race.

- *White (not Hispanic or Latino)*—A person having origins in any of the original peoples of Europe, the Middle East, or North Africa.

- *Black or African American (not Hispanic or Latino)*—A person having origins in any of the black racial groups of Africa.

- *Native Hawaiian or Other Pacific Islander (not Hispanic or Latino)*—A person having origins in any of the peoples of Hawaii, Guam, Samoa, or other Pacific Islands.

- *Asian (not Hispanic or Latino)*—A person having origins in any of the original peoples of the Far East, Southeast Asia, or the Indian subcontinent, including, for example, Cambodia, China, India, Japan, Korea, Malaysia, Pakistan, the Philippine Islands, Thailand, and Vietnam.

- *American Indian or Alaska Native (not Hispanic or Latino)*—A person having origins in any of the original peoples of North and South America (including Central America) and who maintain tribal affiliation or community attachment. (U.S. EEOC, 2006, Appendix 4)

EEO-1 and HRIS

Smith (2006) suggests that the recent changes to the EEOC guidelines will be the most sweeping change in the history of the EEOC, as workers reclassify themselves based on the new EEO designations and organizations pore through job descriptions to classify individuals into the new work categories. For example, individuals who classify themselves as white could also classify themselves as Asian under the new plan. Even small firms without an HRIS have a large amount of work to do. However, HRIS changes will be significant as well (Jossi, 2004). For example, human resource information systems and enterprise resource planning (ERP) systems have generally used a single field letter or number to represent race/ethnicity categories. Potential system changes required by the updated EEO-1 report include the following:

- Track race separately from ethnicity (e.g., Hispanic or not Hispanic).

- Provide separate codes for Asian and Native Hawaiian or Other Pacific Islander.

- Modify limitations on reporting only one race (e.g., individual may be black and Asian).

- Ensure that queries can identify all individuals in a particular category (e.g., American Indian), even when individuals self-identify as two or more race categories.

Moreover, the EEOC is encouraging online reporting of the EEO-1 and, simultaneously, discouraging manual reporting (U.S. EEOC, 2006). Thus, in addition to generating direct costs associated with software modification, employee self-designation, and job reclassification, these policy changes also affect, albeit in a more subtle way, HRM administration. For example, if firms choose to use electronic reporting, they may also find that the costs associated with complying with legislation will be reduced. This detailed description of EEO-1 reporting is provided to facilitate an understanding of how complex HR administration can be. The point is that the amount of paperwork required for compliance with all federal and local employment laws and regulations would be overwhelming without an HRIS. The HRIS applications software helps greatly reduce this complexity. Nevertheless, no matter how sophisticated the HRIS and its reporting software, the employee and organizational data must *be entered accurately* into the system. To understand the complexity of governmental reporting requirements, let us examine a second example of how these affect HRM administration. Specifically, consider the necessity of reporting data to show compliance with the Occupational Safety and Health Act (OSHA).

Occupational Safety and Health Act Record Keeping

Figure 10.8 displays the broad categories of HRM administration associated with governmental mandates for safety requirements in OSHA. In 1970, with work-related fatalities reaching 15,000 annually, Congress charged the U.S. Department of Labor with responsibility for establishing, monitoring, and enforcing occupational safety and health standards and practices for firms engaged in interstate commerce. OSHA primarily established, in the general duty clause of the law, that employers must provide a workplace free of known hazards likely to cause death or serious injury. The National Institute for Occupational Safety and Health (NIOSH) researches and publishes safety and health standards under the law. To ensure that all businesses with 11 or more employees fulfill their occupational safety and health obligations, OSHA compliance officers typically arrive unannounced for an OSHA inspection. The inspector then proceeds to

- review employer records of workplace deaths, injuries, and illnesses;
- conduct on-site inspections of the work premise and note observed violations;
- conduct employee interviews to elicit any safety concerns; and
- discuss findings and violations or issue citations to the employer (Noe, Hollenbeck, Gerhart, & Wright, 2004).

Figure 10.7 EEO-1 Report

Section D – EMPLOYMENT DATA

Employment at this establishment—Report all permanent full- and part-time employees including apprentices and on-the-job trainees unless specifically excluded as set forth in the instructions. Enter the appropriate figures on all lines and in all columns. Blank spaces will be considered as zeros.

Number of Employees (Report employees in only one category)

Job Categories	Hispanic or Latino		Not-Hispanic or Latino												Total Col A-N
			Male						Female						
	Male	Female	White	Black or African American	Native Hawaiian or Other Pacific Islander	Asian	American Indian or Alaska Native	Two or more races	White	Black or African American	Native Hawaiian or Other Pacific Islander	Asian	American Indian or Alaska Native	Two or more races	Total Col A-N
	A	B	C	D	E	F	G	H	I	J	K	L	M	N	O
Executive/Senior Level Officials and Managers 1.1															
First/Mid-Level Officials and Managers 1.2															
Professionals 2															
Technicians 3															
Sales Workers 4															
Administrative Support Workers 5															
Craft Workers 6															
Operatives 7															
Laborers and Helpers 8															
Service Workers 9															
TOTAL 10															
PREVIOUS YEAR TOTAL 11															

1. Date(s) of payroll period used: _____ (Omit on the Consolidated Report.)

O.M.B. No. 3046-0007
Revised 00/2006
Approval Expires 1/2009

Source: U.S. EEOC (2006).

Figure 10.8   Occupational Health and Safety Administrative Functions

| Accident reporting and record keeping | Safety and health training records | Workers' compensation claims |

Failing to correct violations or maintain required records could result in substantial fines and jail sentences for employers.

OSHA Form 300 (Log of Work-Related Injuries and Illnesses) and HRIS

All covered employers are required to notify OSHA within eight hours of any accident involving either a fatality or an in-patient hospitalization of three or more employees. In addition, all covered employers must complete an annual **OSHA Form 300** recording all reportable work-related injuries and illnesses. **OSHA Form 301** (Injury and Illness Incidence Report) is used to record supplementary information about reportable cases. Finally, **OSHA Form 300A** (Summary of Work-Related Injuries and Illnesses), which displays total injuries and illnesses for the year, must be posted for all employees to view. A sample of the Form 300 is shown in Figure 10.9.

HR administration managers must be aware daily of any safety problems in order to meet OSHA Form 300 regulations and ensure that up-to-date records are available for OSHA inspections. Generally, details for the report must be obtained from the reporting supervisor involved in the reportable accident/illness investigation and recorded on OSHA Form 301. However, in smaller organizations, HR managers may be directly involved in accident/illness investigations. Reportable incidents are defined as work-related injuries and illnesses resulting in "death, days away from work, restricted work, transfer to another job, medical treatment beyond first aid, loss of consciousness, or diagnosis of a significant injury or illness" (U.S. Department of Labor, 2004). Because safety issues differ for different types of businesses, the HRIS may not have a standard safety module. More likely, limited fields are added to permit tracking and facilitate federal and state reporting (Ceriello, 1991). However, including safety modules in HRIS can be beneficial. Desirable functions would include HR portal access at remote locations so that supervisors could enter accident/illness data, linkages to safety training and equipment records, and interfaces with required workers' compensation claims, in addition to record keeping and report generation. Such functionality can be an important part of an overall safety program as well as a means of increasing HRM administrative efficiency (O'Connell, 1995).

Figure 10.9 OSHA Form 300

OSHA's Form 300 (Rev. 01/2004)
Log of Work-Related Injuries and Illnesses

Attention: This form contains information relating to employee health and must be used in a manner that protects the confidentiality of employees to the extent possible while the information is being used for occupational safety and health purposes.

Year 20__

U.S. Department of Labor
Occupational Safety and Health Administration

Form approved OMB no. 1218-0176

You must record information about every work-related death and about every work-related injury or illness that involves loss of consciousness, restricted work activity or job transfer, days away from work, or medical treatment beyond first aid. You must also record significant work-related injuries and illnesses that are diagnosed by a physician or licensed health care professional. You must also record work-related injuries and illnesses that meet any of the specific recording criteria listed in 29 CFR Part 1904.8 through 1904.12. Feel free to use two lines for a single case if you need to. You must complete an Injury and Illness Incident Report (OSHA Form 301) or equivalent form for each injury or illness recorded on this form. If you're not sure whether a case is recordable, call your local OSHA office for help.

Establishment name _____
City _____ State _____

Identify the person			Describe the case			Classify the case							
(A) Case no.	(B) Employee's name	(C) Job title (e.g. Welder)	(D) Date of injury or onset of illness	(E) Where the event occurred (e.g. Loading dock north end)	(F) Describe injury or illness, parts of body affected, and object/substance that directly injured or made person ill (e.g. Second degree burns on right forearm from acetylene torch)	CHECK ONLY ONE box for each case based on the most serious outcome for that case:				Enter the number of days the injured or ill worker was:		Check the "Injury" column or choose one type of illness:	
						Death (G)	Days away from work (H)	Job transfer or restriction (I)	Other recordable cases (J)	Away from work (K)	On job transfer or restriction (L)	(M) (1)(2)(3)(4)(5)(6)	

Source: U.S. Department of Labor (2004).

Technology, HR Administration, and Mandated Governmental Reporting

Within the context of these complex legal requirements, what role can technology-enabled HR administration approaches have in increasing efficiency, quality, and cost reduction while enabling the fulfillment of mandated reporting? The answer to this question is especially important in the area of equal employment opportunities and safety and health. Certainly, the increasing use of HRIS is essential for accurate, timely record keeping and reporting that facilitates the performance of both EEO and OSHA mandates. For example, accurate, timely completion of the EEO-1 reports presupposes ready access to employee records, where such information is maintained. For a smaller employer, paper records may suffice. For larger national or international employers with multiple locations, however, paper records are inadequate. Paper record keeping would require that each location search the records of each employee, manually record the appropriate information, and forward it to a centralized location for consolidation into the company report. For organizations with centralized HRM, either operations employees or managers would be required to do the report at each remote location. However, this waste of productive time is substantially reduced by the presence of an HRIS in the following ways:

- HRIS records can be established coincident with the employee application, including optional self-reporting of EEO race/ethnicity and sex data. No separate input functions are required unless corrections are needed. Self-reported data are likely to be more accurate and are preferred for compliance reporting.

- Simple queries of the HRIS database can secure required data, categorized by employee job classification, sex, and race/ethnicity in the EEO-1 format if desired.

- Required information for either EEO or OSHA reporting can be secured in minutes, with minimal HR employee involvement, rather than having staff take days or weeks to manually review records, compile the information, and forward it to a centralized location for further compilation.

- HR employees can handle the complete reporting function without interrupting productive time in operational units.

- Changes in mandated reporting requirements (e.g., an increase in the number of job classifications) can be handled mechanically by HR, without the involvement of field employees.

- Electronic reporting (i.e., computer to computer) can ensure timely receipt of reports.

If an ESS portal is available, government-mandated changes can be accomplished more easily, even when individual employees must be involved. For example, HR administration managers can communicate directly with employees, explaining the changes in EEO categories and requesting that each employee update his or her information directly via the ESS portal. Supervisors can be notified via the MSS portal of individual employees who have not updated their information, precluding meetings with all employees to introduce and monitor this type of change. Finally, if the employee refuses to update the information, the supervisor can use the MSS portal to enter the updated data directly.

If an SSC is added to the HR portal capabilities, individual employees with questions about the reporting requirements can contact the center directly for assistance. The supervisor need not be involved, and employees will receive rapid responses, which will allow them to complete the update more quickly and accurately. Thus, an HRIS, augmented by HR portals (i.e., ESS and MSS portals) and SSCs, can substantially improve the accuracy and timeliness of mandated governmental reporting while reducing the hours wasted on routine administrative work, hours that could be spent more productively.

Similarly, HR portals, SSCs, and even outsourcing can facilitate OSHA record keeping and reporting, reducing costs and enhancing timely reporting. For example, HRIS records and MSS portals permit supervisors to complete the required record of a reportable accident electronically, filling out the 300A Form via computer terminal immediately after an accident occurs. In addition, updates can be handled with minimal effort. With appropriate linkages, workers' compensation reporting to state agencies can be generated by the system. If an employee files a workers' compensation claim and the company disagrees, HR administration managers can access the data and provide the rationale for disallowing the claim. If an organization outsources either workers' compensation reporting or accident investigation to third-party vendors, electronic linkages can notify those groups immediately so that appropriate procedures can be instituted. Finally, HR administration managers, without involving productive employees, can generate an accurate, up-to-date Form 300 whenever one is required for inspection, posting, or safety performance analysis.

Summary of Government-Mandated Reports and Privacy Requirements

The EEO-1 report and the OSHA Form 300 are only two of the many required administrative transactions for which HR managers are responsible. In addition, privacy laws add more complexity to the administration of the HR function via an HRIS. As noted, HRIS capabilities can be enhanced by the use of one or more HR administration approaches to improve accurate and timely reporting while reducing costs and increasing productivity. These examples demonstrate how effective HR administration can help organizations comply with government mandates while supporting strategic goals. The final HR administration issue included in this chapter is how, by using a balanced scorecard approach, HR managers can measure their activities in ways that demonstrate their contribution to an organization's strategic goals. Following a brief introduction of the use of a balanced scorecard in strategic management, we will examine which HR measures that are part of an HR administration can contribute to the balanced scorecard for an organization.

HR Strategic Goal Achievement and the Balanced Scorecard

As should be obvious from the topics covered thus far in this chapter, HR administration is crucial to effective HRM functioning. As discussed in Chapter 1, the HR department has historically been seen as performing a "paper-pusher" function in organizations and has been thought of as a cost-only operation. One of the major reasons for this situation was that the HR department could not easily or accurately generate metrics describing its operations and programs. The paper system existed, but it was exceedingly difficult to extract HR metrics (especially the metrics described in Chapter 6). Advances in computer technology, particularly those applicable to the HR function and its programs, made the calculation of these metrics possible. As a result, CBAs could also be calculated to evaluate the effectiveness of the HR department and its programs. The next step for HR was to become a part of the strategic management system in the organization.

The historic sequence and outcomes described in the previous paragraph depend on building an accurate, up-to-date database that is easy to access and manipulate. This is critical for all HR programs, and it all begins with a correctly designed HRIS that supports HR administration. The data from HR administration, particularly HR metrics (Chapter 6), are also used to support strategic goals, and one of the best examples of their use is in the balanced scorecard. Kaplan and Norton (1992, 1996, 2006), recognizing that an organization can no longer rely solely on a simple financial measure to assess its ability to achieve sustainable competitive advantage, devised the balanced scorecard to facilitate the organization's efforts to measure its success in achieving the strategic goals required to meet the needs of its stakeholder groups. A **balanced scorecard** is both a management and a measurement system that "enables organizations to clarify their vision and strategy and translate them into action, . . . [providing] feedback around both the internal business processes and external outcomes to continuously improve strategic performance and results" (Arveson, 1998).

Kaplan and Norton (1996) define the four components of the balanced scorecard as financial, customer, internal business processes, and learning and growth. Inclusion of these components represents an organization's commitment to balancing its strategic goals and reflects the expectations of its multiple stakeholders. An overview of all four components can be seen in Figure 10.10 along with the key question associated with each of the four.

HRM and the Balanced Scorecard

HRM is often not viewed as a strategic function in organizations primarily because its managers fail to develop measures demonstrating its strategic business value (Lawler, 2005; Ulrich, 1997). For example, successful HR administration efforts that ensure compliance with governmental mandates (e.g., EEO and OSHA reporting) are often viewed as simple administrative transactions rather than as strategic imperatives. However, failing to hire and retain the diverse workforce documented in EEO compliance reports can result in expensive lawsuits and reduced stock prices (Hersch, 1991), as well as in diminished firm credibility (Pomerenke, 1998) and decreased long-term innovation (Florida, 2002, 2005; Page, 2007). Each of these items is directly related to the balanced scorecard categories. Specifically, lawsuits and stock price are associated with financial success, reputation is associated with the customer

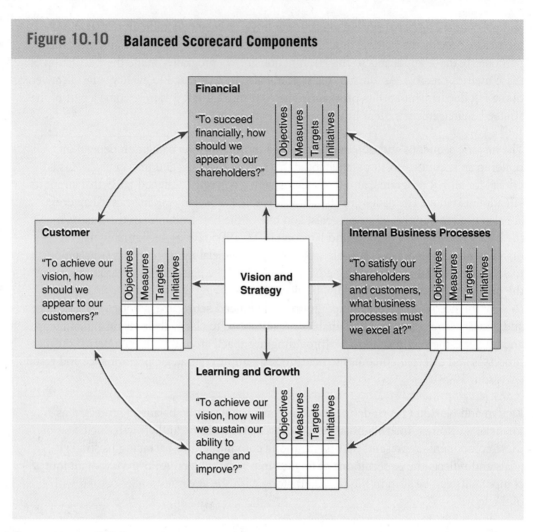

Figure 10.10 Balanced Scorecard Components

Financial

"To succeed financially, how should we appear to our shareholders?"

Objectives | Measures | Targets | Initiatives

Customer

"To achieve our vision, how should we appear to our customers?"

Objectives | Measures | Targets | Initiatives

Vision and Strategy

Internal Business Processes

"To satisfy our shareholders and customers, what business processes must we excel at?"

Objectives | Measures | Targets | Initiatives

Learning and Growth

"To achieve our vision, how will we sustain our ability to change and improve?"

Objectives | Measures | Targets | Initiatives

Source: Arveson (1998).

category, and innovation is part of the learning and growth category. Certainly, HR professionals understand the impact effective human capital management has on an organization. However, unless measures to reflect the value-added nature of HRM in leveraging human capital are developed and linked to the strategic goals reflected in a firm's balanced scorecard, it is unlikely that organizations will view such HRM-linked activities as strategic.

Figure 10.11 provides a simple example of the linkage between HR functions and an organization's balanced scorecard. The next section will highlight the development of an HR scorecard.

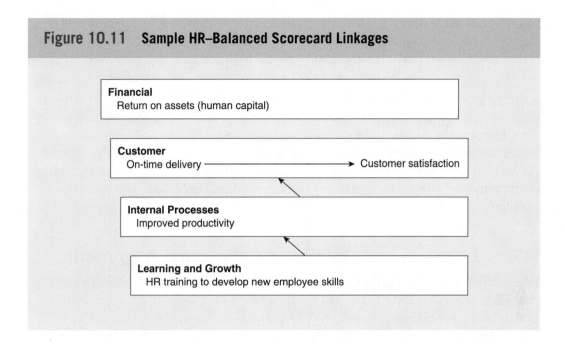

Figure 10.11   Sample HR–Balanced Scorecard Linkages

Financial
  Return on assets (human capital)

Customer
  On-time delivery ⟶ Customer satisfaction

Internal Processes
  Improved productivity

Learning and Growth
  HR training to develop new employee skills

HR Scorecard, Its Measures, and Its Alignment With the Organization's Balanced Scorecard

Suppose that the company is losing some customers, and analysis indicates that customer complaints spiked and on-time product delivery and new orders declined just before these losses. HR professionals want to identify the processes and measures that support the strategic goal of customer retention. The steps they might take are as follows:

1. Specify the business strategy to be supported (e.g., customer retention).

2. Identify leading (e.g., on-time order delivery) and lagging (e.g., customer satisfaction level) indicators.

3. Identify associated internal processes (e.g., worker productivity, product quality).

4. Identify HR linkages (e.g., training, rewards).

5. Specify the HR strategy (e.g., offer enhanced productivity training for workers to reduce product time to market and ensure on-time order delivery).

6. Measure worker productivity increase, on-time deliveries, and reduction in customer complaints to demonstrate the strategic value of HR training in the "Customer" and "Learning and Growth" balanced scorecard categories.

A leading indicator is a predictor of future outcomes (e.g., on-time order delivery), whereas a lagging indicator shows what has already occurred (e.g., customer satisfaction level). Thus, to ensure the on-time order delivery required to retain customers, HR professionals must understand the internal business processes involved in this retention and identify the HR function (training) that can be employed to improve these processes (i.e., to improve productivity) and increase the probability of the desired strategic outcome (customer retention).

HR Scorecard and Balanced Scorecard Alignment

Researchers have long recognized the need to ensure goal alignment in organizations (Beatty, Huselid, & Schneider, 2003; Becker & Gerhart, 1996; Becker, Huselid, & Ulrich, 2001; Lawler, 2005). For example, Boswell (2006) reported that employees who did not have "line of sight" between their work and the strategic goals of the organization were more likely to have poor work attitudes and consider leaving the organization. In addition, Decoene and Bruggerman (2006) reported that failure to implement the business scorecard properly (i.e., by neglecting to cascade strategic goals to all levels in the organization) reduced middle managers' motivation to support strategic goals such that the organization failed to achieve its strategic financial objectives.

In recognition of the importance of alignment between the organization's balanced scorecard and HRM strategic initiatives, researchers (Becker et al., 2001) have suggested that HR professionals develop an HR scorecard as a means of establishing measures for HR that reflect this alignment. HR measures should reflect a balance of cost controls (e.g., improved productivity) and value creation (e.g., increased innovation) consistent with the business's balanced scorecard and strategic goals. Figure 10.12 identifies sample HR measures that might be included in an HR scorecard (Becker et al., 2001).

From the previous discussion, we can see multiple opportunities for HR administration managers to align with the strategic goals covered by the balanced scorecard. For example, deploying HR portals (i.e., ESS and MSS portals) can provide simultaneous support for financial goals (e.g., cost control through reduced employee expense) and learning and growth (e.g., e-learning courses). Similarly, strategic use of outsourcing can support financial goals (e.g., cost reductions) and internal processes (e.g., improved time from vacancy request to hiring). Thus, HR administration managers can make decisions that support the strategic goals contained in the balanced scorecard.

HR Functions to support Learning and Growth category (e.g., employee development)	• Backup talent ratio—Value Creation • Competency development expense per employee—Cost Control • No. of "special projects" for employee development—Value Creation • No. of employees with development plans—Cost Control
HR Internal Efficiency measures to support Financial category	• HR departmental expense/$ of sales revenue—Cost Control • HR sales training expense/$ of sales revenue—Value Creation • HR recruitment expense/R&D hires—Cost Control • No. of patents per R&D hire—Value Creation

SUMMARY

One of the most basic features within an HRIS is the HR administration module. HR administration allows organizations to streamline processes, increase service levels, and reduce costs. This chapter discussed the relative value of the HR administration module versus a traditional, "paper-and-pencil" approach to HR administration. In addition, the chapter discussed the various options available in the implementation of an HR administration module, including HR portals, shared services, outsourcing, and offshoring. Each of these approaches was considered in detail, and its advantages and disadvantages were outlined. The chapter also briefly discussed the flexibility that organizations have in implementing the HRIS. For example, HR portals may be combined with SSCs and selective

outsourcing or offshoring to achieve the optimum solution for a particular firm.

Before developing and implementing the HR administration module, the organization must have conducted a basic job analysis to determine the appropriate knowledge, skills, and abilities for each job. In addition, basic job descriptions for each job should be developed. The data from this analysis form the basis for the data that are eventually entered into the HRIS. The chapter further discussed how human resource information systems can support organizations as they conduct a job analysis.

One of the key issues in implementing the HR administration module is to ensure that it meets legal and compliance requirements. This chapter discussed two specific U.S.

governmental reporting mandates (i.e., EEO and OSHA reporting) as well as how an HRIS can facilitate improved accuracy, reduced costs, and increased organizational value by successfully completing such HR transactions. Even though the topic was a theme throughout the chapter, privacy, as this requirement relates to legislation and data security, was discussed in a separate section, which also presented a discussion of privacy laws and their consideration when one develops an HRIS. Finally, the chapter closed with a brief investigation of the elements important to the successful measurement of the strategic alignment of the HR balanced scorecard.

KEY TERMS

affirmative action plan (AAP) 310

Age Discrimination in Employment Act (ADEA) 310

Americans with Disabilities Act (ADA) 297

backsourcing 305

balanced scorecard 319

discrete HRO 302

employee master file 284

employee self-service (ESS) 294

Employer Information Report EEO-1 (EEO-1 report) 287

equal employment opportunity (EEO) 310

Family and Medical Leave Act (FMLA) 309

human resources outsourcing (HRO) 291

job analysis 285

job description 285

knowledge, skills, and abilities (KSA) 285

manager self-service (MSS) 294

multiprocess HRO 303

Occupational Assessor® software 286

Occupational Safety and Health Act (OSHA) 287

offshore ownership 307

offshoring 291

O*Net database 285

OSHA Form 300 315

OSHA Form 300A 315

OSHA Form 301 315

performance appraisals 295

position analysis questionnaire (PAQ) 285

resource-based view 292

self-service portal 291

service-oriented architecture (SOA) 288

shared-service center (SSC) 291

sustainable competitive advantage 292

total HRO 303

transaction cost theory 293

DISCUSSION QUESTIONS

1. Discuss the theoretical bases for the four HR administrative approaches introduced in this chapter. Are such theories useful to HR professionals in their efforts to improve transactional performance? Why or why not?

2. Why is service-oriented architecture enhanced by XML important to HR administration? Choose two HR administrative approaches, and discuss how each is facilitated by this architecture.

3. What are the primary advantages of HR portals and shared-services centers? Give examples of how HR professionals might use each to better achieve cost controls and service enhancement.

4. What are the primary purposes of ESS and MSS? What are the advantages and disadvantages of each?

5. Define outsourcing and offshoring. Compare and contrast the two as HR administrative tools. Give examples of the decision factors to consider when choosing one over the other.

6. Using the EEO-1 report as an example, discuss the purpose of government mandates. Give examples of penalties

that organizations incur when they fail to comply with government mandates such as EEO and OSHA reporting.

7. Based on information in this chapter, recommend the most effective HR administrative approach or approaches for the owner of a small business with fewer than 50 employees and infrequent staffing needs. Would what you recommend work for a business with 5,000 employees and high turnover? Why or why not? Defend your position with information from the chapter.

8. Identify and explain the purpose of each of the four perspectives included in the balanced scorecard. Give two examples of HR measures for each of the four areas that would demonstrate the value of HR in achieving the strategic goals of organizations.

9. Return to the vignette that opened this chapter and answer the questions posed there.

CASE STUDY: THE CALLEETA CORPORATION _____

Jan Samson, CEO at CalleetaCO, sat staring at the now-empty boardroom. Her board of directors had reacted negatively to Jan's growth proposals for expanding CalleetaCO globally, leaving Jan with a big problem. Shareholders, who had bought its stock as the radio frequency identification (RFID) manufacturer led the boom in new uses for its products, were restless as financial returns slowed. In addition, board members expressed concern that CalleetaCO plants in Mexico and Vietnam were becoming the targets of activists who advocated that organizations ensure that the humane working conditions common in the United States be established in American-owned offshore facilities. Finally, board members demanded that Jan move immediately to rein in the employee costs of the U.S. operation. Those costs were growing at a rate of 12% annually, compared with an industry average of 4%. HR Vice President John Nosmas defended his practice of hiring the best, paying them well, and providing them with expensive benefit programs to keep them developing the innovative products the market demanded. However, board members were adamant and demanded a plan at the next meeting, only six weeks away.

CalleetaCO, with its current 1,900 employees spread across three countries (i.e., the United States—1,000, Mexico—200, Vietnam—700), had grown rapidly over its eight-year existence. Although it started as a small entrepreneurial company, CalleetaCO was now challenging the top providers in its industry as it pursued its goal—to become the global leader in RFID products. RFID use exploded after the introduction of memory for passive radio transponders, which led to the production of RFID tags, microchip field radios embedded in products and used for electronic inventory. These tags were replacing traditional bar codes and manual scanning.

Electronic product coding associated with RFID has been embraced by retailers and consumers alike. Retailers such as Gillette, Hewlett-Packard, and Walmart benefit through more rapid restocking, less likelihood of out-of-stock items, and the electronic identification of product expiration dates. In addition, consumers can more easily return purchases. Applications seem unending. Members of Congress have introduced legislation to track sales of tobacco products using RFID technology, for example. New U.S. passports contain RFID tags. "Swipe-less" checkouts, RFID medical alert bracelets, and security identification wristbands are on the horizon. In addition, California is likely to use RFID to comply with the 2005 Real ID Act mandated by Congress (Billingsley, 2007). However, some groups are concerned that RFID proliferation could lead to the surreptitious tracking of an individual's purchases and other privacy violations, especially since individuals may be unaware that their purchases include RFID devices. In addition, hackers may be able to steal identity information by remotely scanning an individual's passport, credit card, or driver's license.

Jan's company had grown rapidly by perfecting several of these products. To keep the innovations coming, Jan and John Nosmas devised a human capital talent acquisition and retention plan to attract the most highly skilled individuals in the industry. The company had 25 HR recruiters focused solely on identifying potential employees, 17 selection specialists to test and interview them, and above-market compensation and benefits at its U.S. location to retain them: health, dental, and life insurance at no cost to the employee; six weeks of paid vacation annually; elder care; child care; onsite pet boarding; liberal performance bonuses; 401(k) matching at 10%; stock options; and onsite spa and exercise facilities. The programs had been incredibly successful in finding the right people to fuel the company's innovative products.

With the company's success had come an even larger HR department. For example, employees regularly stopped by the HR office to chat with their designated HR support representatives (there was one HR support representative for every 10 employees). The employees were thrilled with the personal service and responsiveness to inquiries on everything from health questions to veterinary referrals. Managers had access to their own HR support specialists, who handled everything from performance appraisals and salary increases to filling vacancy requests and overseeing employee discipline. When the company had formed an SSC for information technology and financial services, the HR department had balked at participating because employees were so satisfied with service levels, even though departmental costs were 20% higher than those of counterparts at competitor firms. The firm's HRIS remained under the control of HR information technology specialists in the department, and there seemed few reasons to pursue portals. However, employees who traveled to Mexico and Vietnam had begun to complain about their inability to access HR support specialists for needed information because of time differences. U.S. expatriate managers from CalleetaCO controlled employees from Mexico and Vietnam at the offshore locations. HRO firms had recently approached John about the possibility of purchasing or managing those locations, but John had not yet explored such a possibility.

Jan picked up the telephone to call John. She explained the problem and asked him to prepare a list of ideas that could help them both demonstrate how successful CalleetaCO's talent programs had been and meet the board's requirements for cost controls. Jan knew that she would need to get John to work miracles to help meet the board's demands. She didn't want to stop talent searches or above-average total compensation, but board members were unyielding. Unless Jan could develop a successful plan to slow employee expense growth, control the activist stakeholder groups, and ultimately improve earnings, she could easily become the ex-CEO.

Case Study Questions

1. What are the key business issues facing Jan?

2. In what ways are CalleetaCO's HR operations contributing to the company's success? How do these contributions support the company's strategic goals? What changes can John make in his HR operations to meet the board's demands?

3. Describe whether each of John's proposed changes will hinder or help CalleetaCO achieve sustainable competitive advantage? Which ones would you choose if you were in John's position? Defend your choices.

4. How would a balanced scorecard help Jan explain the value of her HR talent approach? Provide sample measures for each of the four categories that would support Jan in her presentation to the board.

STUDENT STUDY SITE

Visit the Student Study Site at **http://www.sagepub.com/kavanagh3e** for additional learning tools such as access to SAGE journal articles and related web resources.

NOTE

1. This electronic record has also been called the master file for compensation or, simply, the employee master file, in general usage.

REFERENCES

Accenture. (2007). *Managing shared services change: Beyond communications and training.* New York: Author. Retrieved from http://www.accenture.com/us-en/Pages/insight-managing-shared-services-change-beyond-communications-training-summary.aspx

Anheier, N., & Doherty, S. (2001, October). *Employee self-service: Tips to ensure a successful implementation* (SHRM White Paper). Alexandria, VA: Society for Human Resource Management. Retrieved from http://www.shrm.org/hrdisciplines/technology/Articles/Pages/CMS_000210.aspx

Arveson, P. (1998). What is the balanced scorecard? *Balanced Scorecard Institute.* Retrieved from http://www.balancedscorecard.org/BSCResources/AbouttheBalancedScorecard/tabid/55/Default.aspx

Barney, J. (1991). Firm resources and sustained competitive advantage. *Journal of Management, 17,* 99–120.

Barney, J. (2001). Resource-based theories of competitive advantage: A 10-year retrospective on the resource-based view. *Journal of Management, 27,* 643–650.

Beaman, K. (Ed.). (2002). *Boundaryless HR: Human capital management in the global economy.* Austin, TX: IHRIM Press Book.

Beatty, R., Huselid, M., & Schneider, C. (2003). New HR metrics: Scoring on the business scorecard. *Organizational Dynamics, 32,* 107–121.

Becker, B., & Gerhart, B. (1996). The impact of human resource management on organizational performance: Progress and prospects. *Academy of Management Journal, 39,* 779–801.

Becker, B., Huselid, M., & Ulrich, D. (2001). *The HR scorecard: Linking people, strategy, and performance.* Boston: Harvard Business School Press.

Bender, J. (2001). HR service centers: The human element behind the technology. In A. J. Walker (Ed.), *Web-based human resources* (pp. 212–225). New York: McGraw-Hill.

Billingsley, K. (2007). *Playing tag: An RFID primer.* San Francisco: Pacific Research Institute. Retrieved from http://www.pacificresearch.org/docLib/20070706_RFID.pdf

Boswell, W. (2006). Aligning employees with the organization's strategic objective: Out of "line of sight," out of mind. *International Journal of Human Resource Management, 17,* 1489–1511.

Briscoe, D. R., & Schuler, R. S. (2004). *International human resource management* (2nd ed.). New York: Routledge.

Campbell, S., & Mohun, V. (2007). *Mastering enterprise SOA with SAP Netweaver and my SAP.* Indianapolis, IN: Wiley & Sons.

CBR. (2007, May 29). Convergys wins $1bn Johnson & Johnson HR deal. *Computer Business Review.* Retrieved from http://www.cbronline.com/news/convergys_wins_1bn_johnson_johnson_hr_deal

CedarCrestone. (2012). *CedarCrestone 2012–2013 HR systems survey.* Alpharetta, GA: Author.

Ceriello, V. (1991). *Human resource management systems.* San Francisco: Jossey-Bass.

Chiamsiri, S., Bulusu, S., & Agarwal, M. (2005). Information technology offshore outsourcing in India: A human resource management perspective. *Research and Practice in Human Resource Management, 13,* 105–114.

Coase, R. (1937). The nature of the firm. *Economica, 4,* 386–405.

Decoene, V., & Bruggerman, W. (2006). Strategic alignment and middle-level managers' motivation in a balanced scorecard setting. *International Journal of Operations & Production Management, 26,* 429–449.

Dominguez, L. (2006). *The manager's step-by-step guide to outsourcing.* New York: McGraw-Hill.

Dowling, P. J., & Welch, D. E. (2005). *International human resource management: Managing people in a multinational context* (4th ed.). Mason, OH: Thomson/South-Western.

EquaTerra. (2007). *Taking the pulse of today's human resources outsourcing market.* Retrieved May 18, 2007, from www.equaterra.com/KR/download.aspx?fn=EquaTerra-HRO-Buyer-Pulse-Results-April-2007.pdf

Erl, T. (2005). *Service-oriented architecture (SOA): Concepts, technology, and design.* New York: Prentice Hall PTR.

Esen, E. (2004). *SHRM human resource management outsourcing survey report.* Alexandria, VA: Society for Human Resource Management.

Everest Research Institute. (2007). *Human resources outsourcing (HRO) market update: May 2007.* Retrieved from http://www.outsourcing-requests.com/common/sponsors/ 60629/Human_Resources_Outsourcing_HRO_Market_Update.pdf

Fletcher, P. (2005). Personnel administration to business-driven human capital management. In H. Gueutal & D. Stone (Eds.), *The brave new world of eHR* (pp. 1–21). San Francisco: Jossey-Bass.

Florida, R. (2002). *The rise of the creative class: And how it's transforming work, leisure, community and everyday life.* New York: Basic Books.

Florida, R. (2005). *The flight of the creative class: The new global competition for talent.* New York: HarperCollins.

Ghorpade, J.V. (1988). *Job analysis.* Englewood Cliffs, NJ: Prentice Hall.

Goh, M., Prakash, S., & Yeo, R. (2007). Resource-based approach to IT in a shared services manufacturing firm. *Industrial Management & Data Systems, 107,* 251–270.

Gueutal, H., & Falbe, C. (2005). eHR trends in delivery methods. In H. Gueutal & D. Stone (Eds.), *The brave new world of eHR* (pp. 190–225). San Francisco: Jossey-Bass.

Gueutal, H., & Stone, D. (Eds.). (2005). *The brave new world of eHR.* San Francisco: Jossey-Bass.

Hatch, P. (2004). *Offshore outsourcing 2005 research: Preliminary findings and conclusions*

(Ventoro Report, January 22, 2005, version). Retrieved from http://itonews.eu/files/f1222430088.pdf

Hersch, J. (1991). Equal employment opportunity law and firm profitability. *Journal of Human Resources, 26,* 139–153.

Hewitt. (2005). *A fresh look at the logic of HR outsourcing.* Lincolnshire, IL: Hewitt Associates LLC. Retrieved from http://www.outsourcing-requests.com/common/sponsors/54934/A_Fresh_ Look_at_the_Logic_of_HR_Outsourcing.pdf

Hewitt. (2010). *HR outsourcing trends and insights 2009.* Lincolnshire, IL: Hewitt Associates LLC. Retrieved from http://www.aon.com/human-capital-consulting/thought-leadership/outsourcing/surveys_2009_outsourcing_trends.jsp

Jossi, F. (2004). Reporting race. *SHRM.* Retrieved from www.shrm.org/hrtx/library_published/nonIC/CMS_006477.asp

Kaplan, R., & Norton, D. (1992). The balanced scorecard: Measures that drive performance. *Harvard Business Review, 70,* 71–80.

Kaplan, R., & Norton, D. (1996). *The balanced scorecard: Translating strategy into action.* Boston: Harvard Business School Press.

Kaplan, R., & Norton, D. (2006). *Alignment: Using the balanced scorecard to create corporate synergies.* Boston: Harvard Business School Press.

Kavanagh, M., Gueutal, H., & Tannenbaum, S. (1990). *Human resource information systems: Development and application.* Boston: PWS.

Keebler, T. (2001). HR outsourcing in the Internet era. In A. Walker (Ed.), *Web-based human resources* (pp. 259–276). New York: McGraw-Hill.

KPMG Institutes. (2012). *3Q12 Global pulse survey.* Retrieved from http://kpmginstitutes.com/shared-services-outsourcing-institute/insights/2012/pdf/3Q12-sourcing-advisory-global-pulse-report.pdf

Lacity, M., & Willcocks, L. (2000). Relationships in IT outsourcing: A stakeholder perspective. In R. Zmud (Ed.), *Framing the domains of IT management: Projecting the future through the past* (pp. 355–384). Cincinnati, OH: Pinnaflex.

Lacity, M., & Willcocks, L. (2001). *Global information technology outsourcing: In search of business advantage* (1st ed.). West Sussex, England: Wiley.

Lawler, E. (2005). Making strategic partnership a reality. *Strategic HR Review, 4,* 3.

Ledvinka, J. (1982). *Federal regulation of personnel and human resource management.* Boston: Kent.

Lublinsky, B. (2007, May). Versioning in SOA. *Architecture Journal, 11.* Retrieved from http://msdn2.microsoft.com/en-us/arcjournal/bb491124.aspx

Lucenko, K. (1998, March). *Shared services: Achieving higher levels of performance* (The Conference Board Report R-1210–98-CH). New York: The Conference Board. Retrieved from http://www.conference-board.org/publications/publicationdetail.cfm?publicationid=396

Marks, E., & Bell, M. (2006). *Service-oriented architecture: A business planning and implementation guide for business and technology.* Indianapolis, IN: Wiley.

Noe, R., Hollenbeck, J., Gerhart, B., & Wright, P. (2004). *Fundamentals of human resource management.* New York: McGraw-Hill.

O'Connell, S. (1995, June). Safety first: Computers to the rescue. *HR Magazine, 40*(6). Retrieved February 22, 2007, from http://findarticles.com/p/articles/mi_m3495/is_n6_v40/ai_17191250

Organization for the Advancement of Structured Information Systems (OASIS). (2006). *OASIS reference model for service oriented architecture 1.0.* Burlington, MA: Author. Retrieved April 7, 2007, from

www.oasis-open.org/committees/download.
php/18486/pr-2changes.pdf

Osle, H., & Cooper, J. (2003). Structuring HR
for maximum value. IHRIM.*link, 8,* 4.

Page, S. (2007). *The difference: How the power of
diversity creates better groups, firms, schools,
and societies.* Princeton, NJ: Princeton
University Press.

Paskoff, S. M. (2003, September). *Around the world
without the daze: Communicating international
codes of conduct.* Paper presented at the fourth
annual program on International Labor and
Employment Law, Dallas, TX.

Phillips, T., Isenhour, L., & Stone, D. (2008).
The potential for privacy violations in
electronic human resource practices. In
G. Martin, M. Reddington, & H. Alexander
(Eds.), *Technology, outsourcing, and
transforming HR* (pp. 193–230). Oxford:
Butterworth Heinemann.

Pomerenke, P. (1998). Class action sexual
harassment lawsuit: A study in crisis
communication. *Human Resource
Management, 37,* 207–219.

Powell, A. (2004). *Shared services and CRM*
(Conference Board Technical Report
E-0005–004RR). New York: The
Conference Board. Retrieved from http://
www.conference-board.org/publications/
publicationdetail.cfm?publicationid=786

PricewaterhouseCoopers. (2006). *Key trends in
human capital: A global perspective—2006.*
London, UK: Author. Retrieved from
http://www.pwchk.com/webmedia/
doc/633077569676719728_hra_
keytrends_mar06.pdf

Procter & Gamble. (2011). Diversity and inclusion:
Fulfilling our potential. *P&G.* Retrieved
from http://www.pg.com/en_US/company/
purpose_people/diversity_inclusion.shtml

Quinn, B., Cooke, R., & Kris, A. (2000). *Shared
services: Mining for corporate gold.* London:
Pearson Education.

Robinson, D., & Robinson, J. (2005). *Strategic
business partner: Aligning people strategies
with business goals.* New York: Berrett-
Hoehler.

Schwartz, E. (2003, December 8). Oracle
launches HR-XML product: Will Microsoft
Word follow? *InfoWorld.com.* Retrieved
from http://www.infoworld.com/t/
platforms/oracle-launches-hr-xml-
product-390

Smith, A. (2006). New EEO-1 report kicks in
for 2007 survey. *HR News.* Retrieved from
http://www.shrm.org/hrnews_published/
archives/CMS_015698.asp

Ulrich, D. (1997). *Human resource champions.*
Boston: Harvard Business School Press.

U.S. Department of Labor. (2004). *OSHA
instruction* (Directive No. CPL 02–00–135).
Washington, DC: Author. Retrieved from
http://www.osha.gov/pls/oshaweb/owadisp
.show_document?p_
table=DIRECTIVES&p_id=3205

U.S. Department of Labor. (2007). *Federal
vs. state family and medical leave laws.*
Washington, DC: Author. Retrieved from
http://www.dol.gov/whd/state/fmla/index
.htm

U.S. Equal Employment Opportunity
Commission. (1964). *Title VII of the Civil
Rights Act of 1964.* Washington, DC: Author.
Retrieved from http://www.eeoc.gov/laws/
statutes/titlevii.cfm

U.S. Equal Employment Opportunity
Commission. (2006). *EEOC instruction
booklet.* Washington, DC: Author.
Retrieved from http://www.eeoc.gov/
employers/eeo1survey/2007instructions
.cfm

von Simson, E. (1990). The "centrally"
decentralized IS organization. *Harvard
Business Review, 68*(4), 158–162.

Walker, A. (1982). *HRIS development: A project
team approach to building an effective*

personnel information system. New York: Van Nostrand Reinhold.

Walker, A. (1993). *Handbook of human resource information systems.* New York: McGraw-Hill.

Walker, A. (Ed.). (2001). *Web-based human resources.* New York: McGraw-Hill.

Weatherly, L. (2005). HR outsourcing: Reaping strategic value for your organization. *SHRM Research Quarterly.* Retrieved from http:// www.shrm.org/research/articles/articles/pages/0805rquart_essay.aspx

Williamson, O. (1975). *Markets and hierarchies.* New York: Free Press.

Wright, P., McMahan, G., Snell, S., & Gerhart, B. (1998). *Strategic HRM: Building human capital and organizational capability* (Technical report). Ithaca, NY: Cornell University.

CHAPTER 11

Talent Management

Kevin M. Johns and Michael J. Kavanagh

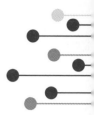

EDITORS' NOTE

This chapter is the first of four on topics that are related to talent management (TM). Talent management has become an extremely important strategic goal for organizations, both domestic and global ones. Talent management has also been called human capital management (HCM), which recognizes that TM involves the effective management of the human capital of any organization. Talent management has multiple meanings. However, all of these definitions recognize that, to gain competitive advantage in the marketplace, an organization's talent (i.e., its people) must be managed effectively. This management of people includes attracting, selecting, training, compensating, and retaining employees. However, the underlying requirement for talent management is forecasting the need for talented employees in terms of both numbers and skills, particularly the need for employees in leadership positions. In order to forecast these needs, the organization must have accurate information about the knowledge, skills, and abilities (KSA) necessary for effective job performance, and these are identified through job analysis, as discussed thoroughly in Chapter 10. Thus, this chapter is focused on (1) managing talent, (2) forecasting future demand and supply of employees through human resource planning (HRP), and (3) understanding how an HRIS can assist both talent management and HRP. Chapter 12 will focus on recruiting and selecting employees with desired talent, Chapter 13 is concerned with improving talent through training and developing employees, Chapter 14 deals with managing employees' talent through performance management and compensation practices, and Chapter 15 covers the management of employees in international organizations.

CHAPTER Objectives

After completing this chapter, you should be able to

- Understand the origin of talent management and how it fits within human resources planning (HRP), human capital management, workforce management, strategic HRM, and corporate strategy

- Discuss the evidence for the importance of TM in general and, specifically, in terms of the talent management life cycle

- Discuss the common attributes of talented individuals

- Discuss the steps in the development and use of an HRP program

- Explain the use of HRP in forecasting supply and demand of new employees

- Explain the importance of job analysis and job descriptions to talent management programs

- Identify and discuss the important HR metrics for the HRP program of a company

- Explain the difference between a long and short strategy for TM and why it is important

- Explain the contribution of a TM program to corporate strategy as well as the importance of an adaptable workforce

- Discuss the effects of corporate culture on the talent management program

- Discuss how the use of computer applications in an HRIS support the components of talent management as well as their use in setting performance goals and evaluating job performance

- Discuss how companies are using social networks to recruit talented individuals

- Explain the relationship between talent management and performance management and the need to show measurable results on a balanced scorecard

- Explain how workforce analytics are used in a TM program

- Explain how to measure the success of a TM program

HRIS IN ACTION

Rudiger is sitting at his desk in his seventh-floor corner office in the City, gazing out over London and reflecting on life. At 43 he is at the top of his game. He has everything he could wish for—a lovely partner, a 4-year-old in a private nursery, a new executive house in the suburbs, a holiday home in southern Italy, and a remuneration package that's the envy of his peers and beyond anything his German immigrant parents could have imagined. But it hasn't been easy, oh no! Hard work, long hours, geographical moves every two or three years, and sacrifices in terms of his personal life.

But now he has a problem. Rudiger has just been appointed global head of People and Talent responsible for the future of 35,000 people worldwide, the bulk of whom are based in the United States, the United Kingdom, and Europe, and manufacturing is likely to relocate to China in the next two years, adding to his responsibilities. In his previous role, he was responsible for the United Kingdom and Northern Europe and had operational oversight for 11,000 people. An initial consideration of his responsibilities has identified a number of people issues for the next five years:

- recruiting and placing new employees in appropriate jobs as vacancies occur,

- developing the skills of current and new employees in training programs, and

- retaining unique specialists in highly skilled roles.

In addition, several other issues have been brought to his attention by the outgoing global head of People and Talent:

- some of the brightest high performers and the most experienced midlevel managers appear to be leaving the company;

- the general employee population is aging, and there will be a significant number of retirements over the next decade, which will require extensive replacements; and

- there is an aging senior directorship, most of who are looking toward early retirement.

Although he knows he has a problem, the main problem is that he does not have enough detailed information about the employees to know the scale of the problem. He wishes he could find a general framework in which to address these problems and issues, and he wants to be able to show how the framework and programs he implements will impact on the "bottom line" of the organization.

Introduction

When looking for a new job, don't expect to get calls from "headhunters," because that title is no longer appropriate. Today, recruiters identify themselves as either the executive director of People Talent or more simply, talent manager.

Talent management (TM) is not just a new title for the HR professional who is the manager of new hiring at a company. The field of TM brings with it a new perspective that unifies recruiting, hiring, training, promoting, and retaining talented individuals who can contribute to the overall growth and competitive advantage of a company. Historically, the management of a company's talent was primarily focused on hiring individuals who had good experience along with appropriate educational credentials—and then hoping they would fit. The concept of TM has transformed this approach. Just matching individual skills to specific job requirements is insufficient; TM requires an HRM plan that is a comprehensive program of using and developing the person's knowledge, skills, and abilities. The outcome of a TM program nested within the HRM function is that individuals can become high-performing employees who can contribute to the effectiveness and profitability of the company.

Defining Talent Management

For the past 15 or 20 years, talent management has been defined in a number of ways. In general, TM refers to the process of hiring, socializing, developing, and retaining employees, while at the same time attracting highly skilled individuals from the labor market. A detailed approach to defining talent management comes from an article by Lockwood (2006) that appeared in *HR Magazine:* "Talent management is the implementation of integrated strategies or systems designed to increase workplace productivity by developing improved processes for attracting, developing, retaining and utilizing people with the required skills and aptitude to meet current and future business needs" (p. 17). Take note that TM can be used on all job levels in a company, from unskilled workers to CEOs. For example, if there is a labor demand (e.g., skills, quantity) for lathe machine operators due to high turnover in this job, then the general process and software used to hire new lathe machine operators would be the same as for hiring senior management. Thus, no matter if a company is looking for operators of a lathe or a CEO, the steps in the TM life cycle are the same. However, even though the steps are the same, the actual processes, for example, recruiting, interviewing, selecting, etc., of finding the CEO vs. operators of a lathe would be quite different. More recently, Larry Dunivan (2010) notes that, "talent management has become the call to action for a more consultative, knowledge-based role for Human Resources in overall business management. In other words, talent management from a technological perspective provides companies the opportunity to collect and leverage rich data about people to respond to business needs" (p. 14). From an information systems perspective, the door has been opened to utilize technology to manage the employee life cycle from recruitment to retirement.

Importance of Talent Management

In a poll conducted by the **Society for Human Resource Management (SHRM)** and entitled "Challenges Facing Organizations and HR in the Next Ten Years," 449 HR professionals responded to questions asking them to describe the "top challenges that their organization and the HR profession will face during the next decade." Of these survey respondents, 72% were from U.S.-based companies and 28% from multinational organizations (SHRM, 2010).

Responses to this question yielded the following results: "Nearly half the respondents (47 percent) said that obtaining human capital and optimizing on human capital investments was the top investment challenge for businesses over the next 10 years. Slightly less than a third (29 percent) of the respondents listed 'obtaining financial capital and optimizing capital investments' and 12 percent answered 'obtaining intellectual capital and optimizing intellectual capital investments' as the top challenges" (p. 1).

Another question on the poll asked the respondents to list the tactics that they thought would be effective in meeting the HR challenges they would face over the next 10 years: "58 percent of the respondents listed providing flexibility to balance life and work as the top tactic to meet the challenge of attracting, retaining and rewarding the best people" (p. 1).

In another survey conducted by CedarCrestone (2010), respondents were asked what HR computer-based application categories would have increased adoption and usage in the near future. The results indicate that "three application categories will grow 90% or more: talent management, social media, and workforce optimization, the latter of which includes workforce planning and workforce analytics [see Chapter 6]" (p. 9). In addition, respondents thought that more talent management automation was related to net income growth, sales growth, and more sales per employee for organizations with talent management applications.

The Talent Management Life Cycle

Today, organizations recognize that an important workforce issue is the lack of leadership capability. The most significant example of a lack of leadership comes from the 2008 financial crisis that has continued to cause global ripple effects. Greed and the pressures to show quarterly growth to investors led to risky investments, and over-leveraging based upon the boom in housing.

But lack of leadership in companies today is not just tied to lack of experience or training. It also comes from (1) expanding too quickly into new markets or geographies, (2) the changing needs of the employees, and (3) the ongoing retirement of the "baby boomers." A report by McKinsey and Company (2001) stated that the United States was facing a long-term talent shortage as a result of retiring baby boomers. Since this report appeared, little has been done to solve this mass retirement problem. Thus, the first step in the talent management life cycle is to estimate the leadership demand for labor, that is, the number of new leaders needed to replace the retiring baby boomers. The second step is to estimate the supply of leaders available in both the labor market and internal to the company. Then the *difference* between the estimated supply and demand for new and potential leaders can be calculated. The final step is to use HR programs to change the *difference* so that *supply* and *demand* are equalized (e.g., hiring new leaders when needed). When the estimated supply and demand become different, the life cycle begins again.

It is interesting to note that the McKinsey report could not predict what would happen if there were a severe economic downturn. The economic downturn of 2008–2009 kept many baby boomers in the workforce. However, it is still inevitable: baby boomers will eventually leave. Figure 11.1 contains the results of a survey by Beaman (2011) that demonstrates the growth in computer applications among global companies. Beaman notes:

> However, when the demand for leaders exceeds the supply for leaders, it will be necessary for the company to either recruit new leaders from the labor market or promote current company employees to leadership positions.
>
> Talent Management technologies are globalizing at the fastest rate [of all HR technologies], 46% over the last four years, whereas Core HR and Payroll technologies are going global more slowly, at the rate of 23%. The fact that Talent Management software is more readily adopted globally can be attributed to the 'low impact' legislative requirements with talent management functionality than are typically found with Core and Payroll processes (p. 21).

In relation to the TM life cycle, an important aspect of Figure 11.1 is that each HR application represents an important part of the progression through TM process. For example, workforce planning, succession planning, and recruiting management comprise the early stages of selecting individuals. The remaining four applications would occur while the individuals are going through the phases of the TM program.

Criticisms have come from unions and former employees who have lost their jobs; they claim that companies are replacing an aging workforce with less expensive overseas workers, that is, through outsourcing. As opposed to the claim made by critics of outsourcing, it is not a new idea, but questions must arise as to whether leadership skills are being substituted for something that costs less but may be producing questionable results. Attracting less talented and less expensive employees to replace departing employees who have leadership

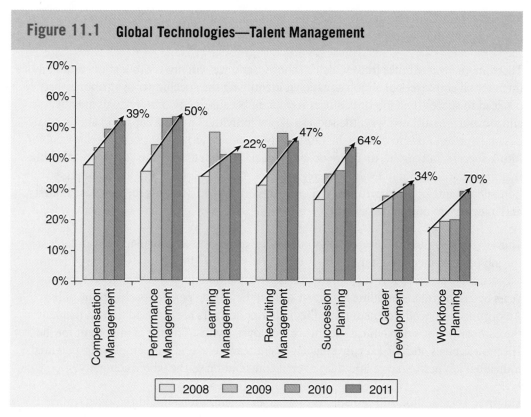

Figure 11.1 **Global Technologies—Talent Management**

Source: Beaman (2012, p. 26). Reprinted with permission.

skills can erode an organization's future revenues. So it is very important to ensure that key leadership skills are being replaced either from within the company or from outside sources. Acquiring and growing a talented human capital workforce that adapts to the new challenges occasioned by changes in the marketplace is key to the **talent management life cycle** and, subsequently, to finding the leadership capabilities necessary to compete in the global economy.

Attributes for Talent

The McKinsey report stated that talented employees who were "high performers" were 50–100% more productive than employees who were "average performers" (McKinsey and Company, 2001). During the downturn in the economy when forced layoffs have occurred, it is the talented performer that needs to be retained in the company. Job performance evaluations are a good method to determine employees' efforts to be effective in their jobs, but evaluations are sometimes narrow and do not measure the employees' potential for long-term success in an organization. The real measure for the long-term success of a talented individual is to evaluate the underlying attributes necessary for achievements.

There are many attributes from which to choose, and we will not try to identify and evaluate them for all employees in all job situations. Identifying the specific set of attributes that can lead to success in a job or business is difficult because no two individuals are alike, and attributes associated with the success of one individual may not apply to another. The best anyone can do is to choose the most likely attributes to measure people's potential for future success, but, again, there are no guarantees. However, there are some core attributes that organizations should evaluate in regard to current employees or potential hires, such as honesty and integrity. Unfortunately, there are executives in business today whose honesty and integrity are questionable.

One effective method to measure what it takes to succeed in a particular job is to look at the job performance of past individuals who have succeeded in that position and identify the attributes possessed by those individuals. This methodology has been used for many years by HR recruiters and line managers to find the "right" person for the "right" job. An organization needs to ensure that the higher performers are retained to help maintain the company's operations in case there are employee layoffs. Thus, it is important for the HR professionals and the executive management team to assess both employees' potential individual job performance and their overall contribution to the whole company.

However, the question still remains as to what an organization should try to determine beyond core values or particular job skills for current employees or new hires. Although a complete list of the characteristics that make for success is impossible, the following appear to be the **common attributes of talented individuals**:

- **Ability to communicate with others using multiple media**; for example, communication could be by phone, presentation, or e-mail. An individual's ideas may be the best, but if she or he cannot communicate those ideas with clarity, then those ideas have no impact.

- **Drive**; motivation plays a big role in determining who succeeds in any venture in life. Look at examples of people who constantly "reinvent" themselves, such as Governor Schwarzenegger—bodybuilder to Hollywood actor to California governor.

- **Ability and willingness to listen to the ideas of others**; listening is one of the most important ways of establishing good personal and business relationships.

- **Problem-solving skills**; many tasks today in business deal with solving problems, whether that involves handling a small request by a client over the phone or closing the biggest acquisition deal in a company's history.

- **Imagination**; the closest version of the word "imagination" from a business perspective is when we are asked to think "outside the box."

The usefulness of the above attributes can be seen in numerous examples. If you have the ability to communicate and listen to others, you may be more likely to be a better team player and work effectively within teams. One reason to hire potentially talented employees may be based on their experience, for example, of running their own business—a venture for which initiative and drive are key success attributes. Being able to solve problems also relates to being willing to learn new things.

Imagination is an important attribute for people in business today. Albert Einstein once stated that the true sign of intelligence is not knowledge but imagination. How many companies today, in developing their talent, allow for a sabbatical from work so an employee can just take a break and think? Use of one's imagination is the mechanism for building a vision for a business. Imagination is a key attribute for differentiating between talented individuals who can become future business leaders and those who will have difficulty succeeding.

Job Analysis and Human Resource Planning: Part of TM

Job Analysis

The introduction to this chapter discussed acquiring the most talented employees, such as skilled professionals and experienced managers; however, talent management comprises more than recruiting and so will be built on a program of **human resource planning (HRP)**,[1] which is sometimes referred to as workforce management. HRP is closely related to **strategic HRM** (Chapman, 2009). The aim of an effective HRP program is to have the best available people working in the proper jobs at the appropriate time so that the organization maximizes its productive capacity. Fulfilling this goal means that future employee needs are forecasted accurately based on annual employee turnover and expected strategic directions. For example, if a strategic goal for a company is to increase market share by 3% over the next two years, this will affect the number of needed new employees in multiple job categories. With accurate estimates of employee turnover in those job categories added to the forecasted employee needs based on the strategic goal, the company can begin planning to recruit new employees as well as train current ones. In order to make these forecasts accurate, however, it is *crucial* that the **knowledge, skills, and abilities (KSA)** required in the forecasted jobs be known. As was covered in Chapter 10, job analysis provides this information by producing **job descriptions**. **Job analysis** is the process of systematically obtaining information about jobs by determining the duties, tasks, or activities of jobs from which KSA requirements can be estimated.

Human Resource Planning (HRP)

HRP begins with the identification of the strategic goals of the company and of how an HRP program can assist in achieving the effective use of the human capital of the company. Organizations know that change is a constant in their business. It could be a change in competition, new markets, environmental concerns, or economic conditions. For example, a company may want to succeed under new competitive conditions by expanding its business into new geographic markets. A company may need to change its strategic vision, organizational values and structure, or corporate culture. When these types of changes occur, there must be corresponding changes in HRM programs, and one of the most important ones is the HRP program.

Changes in organizational strategy and business objectives focus attention on the use of the HRP program to estimate three factors related to an organization's employees:

- number of employees needed for growth or decline,

- required competencies and behaviors of these employees, and

- required levels of productivity expected from these employees.

This information is the primary input that starts the process of an HRP program. An HRP program involves three major processes and a number of actions within each process.

HRP Process Model

There have been a number of conceptual and descriptive models of the stages and processes involved in an HRP program. However, because of its simplicity, we favor the general three-phase model developed by Dyer (1982). In addition to being simple, this model can be used to implement the HRP program for all employees, sales associates to senior managers. In this model, the HRP program involves three major phases: (1) **setting HRP objectives**, (2) **planning personnel programs**, and (3) **evaluation and control** (Dyer, 1982). Figure 11.2 depicts an expansion and modification of Dyer's model, and it provides greater specificity in terms of the activities that occur within the three phases. It is important to understand that HRP refers to all levels of jobs in a company, from janitor to CEO—these employees comprise the human resources of the company. The phase-specific activities in Figure 11.2 will be discussed in the following sections.

Phase 1: Setting HRP Objectives

Estimating Demand. As can be seen in Figure 11.2, one of the first activities in phase 1 of the HRP process involves estimating demand for the total number of employees in a future business scenario. As an example, we will use a fictitious company that manufactures brake assemblies. The company has just had a very profitable year and currently has approximately 21% of the market for its products. The company's strategic planning committee has decided that a 2.5% increase in market share for the next fiscal year seems reasonable. This strategic statement comprises the "Strategic Future Business Plan," as seen in the lower left box in Figure 11.2, and is the first element in "estimating the human capital demand" for this company. The estimation of demand involves an examination of the history of the changes in numbers of employees by job when the company changed production levels in the past. This forecasted demand, then, is an estimate of the number of employees, by job category, needed to handle the 2.5% increase in market share, and it must be calculated by the HR department based on these historical records. Note the two-headed arrow from "Estimating Demand" to the HRIS box. With the data from the historical records available in the HRIS, the company, using simple statistical tools, should be able to calculate the needed number of new employees.

In addition to using historical records, HR professionals can use a number of forecasting techniques, both statistical and judgmental, that are available in the literature (see Noe, Hollenbeck, Gerhart, & Wright, 2010). These techniques will all produce a list of the estimated number of *employees by job* needed to accomplish the increased workload necessary to meet production changes based on a projected 2.5% market share increase. However, note from Figure 11.2 that these estimates comprise only one part of the estimated demand. The other part of this demand estimate comes from the annual average employee turnover, again, *by job*. Adding the forecasted need for employees based on the strategic objective, a 2.5% market share gain, to the average employee turnover rate by job provides an estimate of the total demand for human capital.

Estimating Supply. As indicated in the box in Figure 11.2, estimation of the supply of available labor involves two components, external and internal. The external component is obtained from recent estimates of the potential availability of new employees by experience and skills in the company's geographic labor market. These estimates are available from state and national labor departments, local unemployment agencies, and employee referral agencies. These availability figures can be categorized by company jobs in terms of potential new employees with the necessary KSA sets to fill jobs. The second source of data for the supply estimate is internal and concerns the historic movement of employees within the company by job, for example, the number of promotions and lateral transfers of employees between jobs. Again, there are both sophisticated mathematical and judgmental techniques

Figure 11.2 Model of the HRP Process With Use of an HRIS (as Modified From Dyer, 1982)

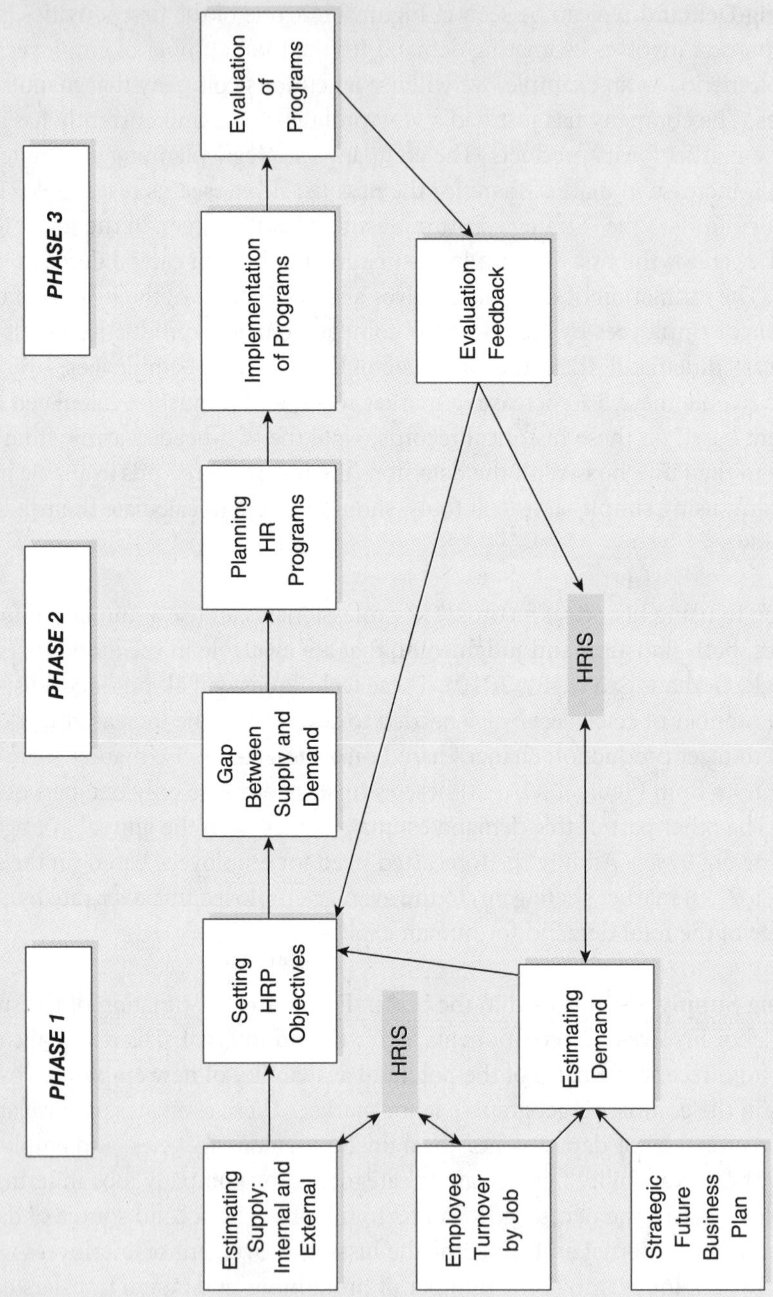

PHASE 1

PHASE 2

PHASE 3

Estimating Supply: Internal and External

Employee Turnover by Job

Strategic Future Business Plan

HRIS

Setting HRP Objectives

Estimating Demand

Gap Between Supply and Demand

Planning HR Programs

Implementation of Programs

Evaluation of Programs

Evaluation Feedback

HRIS

to estimate the internal supply of employees. Note again that most of the data necessary for estimating internal supply will be available in an HRIS. These two estimates of supply are combined to provide an estimate of the total supply.

Phase 2: Planning HR Programs

Phase 2 in Figure 11.2 involves calculating the gap between the estimated *demand for employees* and the estimated *supply* of current and potential employees. Subtracting the supply from the demand figures can result in a negative or positive gap. Returning to our case of the brake assembly manufacturing company, we would expect the gap to be positive, thus indicating a need to add new employees and promote some current employees to open job positions. Of course, the gap could be negative (more supply than demand), indicating a decrease in the need for future employees. This situation could occur, for example, in a company downsizing its workforce due to weak annual sales.

The important point is that there will be a gap, and, as a result, planning for HR programs to close the gap must be done. In the case of the company estimating a 2.5% market share increase, a variety of programs tied to the HRM functions could be initiated. For example, recruiting for new employees could be expanded beyond the current method of using only newspaper ads to include the use of television and radio advertising. The company might also want to start recruiting on college campuses or to develop Internet recruiting, which will be discussed in Chapter 12. Internally, the company could begin training programs to facilitate the promotion of current employees. For example; it might offer a first-level supervisory training program for line workers that could have both formal classroom and on-the-job aspects (to be discussed in Chapter 13). Such programs would be expected to produce employees to fill the jobs that the HR department has predicted will become available.

Phase 3: Evaluation and Control

As indicated in Figure 11.2, this final phase involves the implementation of the planned HRM programs from phase 2. There are some choices to be made at this point regarding HRM programs, for example whether they will involve Internet recruiting and training. Will these programs be implemented by internal HR staff or by an outside vendor? Another aspect to consider is the expected cost-benefit ratio estimated for the new programs. Regardless of the programs that are implemented, one of the most important aspects of the HRP program is the evaluation of these new programs to determine if they have actually closed the gap between supply and demand. For the HRP program to be complete, the HR department must send the results of this evaluation to the HRIS, so they can be used in "Setting HRP Objectives" in future HRP programs. Particularly important is the evaluation of how useful the new HRM programs were in closing the demand-supply gap. This section covered the basics of HRP programs, which can be applied to planning the utilization of human capital, whether entry level or senior management. Having established the "nuts and bolts" of HRP, we will now examine the relationship between talent management and corporate strategy.

Workforce Management/Human Resource Planning With an HRIS

As expected, **Workforce Planning Systems (WPSs)** are available from a number of vendors. Their capabilities can be found in a variety of enterprise applications and standalone tools. The primary purpose of a WPS is to get the right people with the right skill sets in the right place at the right time to meet customer demand. A good example of a WPS is offered by Towers Watson (http://www.towerswatson.com/en/Insights/IC-Types/Survey-Research-Results/2012/11/workforce-planning-translating-the-business-plan-into-the-people-plan). You may want to examine this website since it will provide excellent information on WPSs and what they can do for a company. Other vendors who have WPSs include SuccessFactors (www.successfactors.com), WorkForce Planning Associates, Inc. (www.workforceplanning .com), and WorkForce Software (http://www.workforcesoftware.com/). Each of these websites provides information on WPSs/HRP as well as discussing its uses and benefits. Having established the "nuts and bolts" of HRP, we will now examine the relationship between workforce and talent management with the development of corporate strategy.

Long- and Short-Term Strategic Importance of Talent Management

There needs to be both a **long-term talent management strategy** and a **short-term tactical strategy** since the dynamics in the marketplace can change easily. In the long term, organizations need to invest now in employee talent to sustain a competitive advantage over time. When a new competitor enters the market with a substitute product or when the economy goes sour, investment in human capital may be suspended for a short period of time. Then, short-term tactics must be put in place to get past the economic downturn and keep employees motivated until the market improves. When conditions do improve, then the short-term talent management (TM) strategy—the *tactical strategy*—is halted, and the long-term investment in talented individuals—the *management strategy*—returns.

Population characteristics and labor market diversity will also have an effect on the deployment of a talent management strategy in both domestic and multinational enterprises. Regional differences in work ethic, age, gender, education, and culture will affect how talent management will be implemented and tied to the business model deployed for a particular geographic area within a country. More important, organizations need to consider sources of potential labor when building new plants in other countries as a result of going global. In Figure 11.3 we see the impact of globalizing a company on the "Inability to retain key employees" as a workforce problem because of differences in labor markets in different countries. It could also impact on the "Inability to attract qualified candidates" because there may be no potential new hires in specific countries who have the knowledge and skill for open positions.

Long-term talent management strategies also need to be linked to corporate strategy. One very important strategy that must be maintained despite the state of the marketplace is **corporate brand management**. It has been confirmed repeatedly that the best labor talent is linked to highly regarded corporations that have excellent brand images

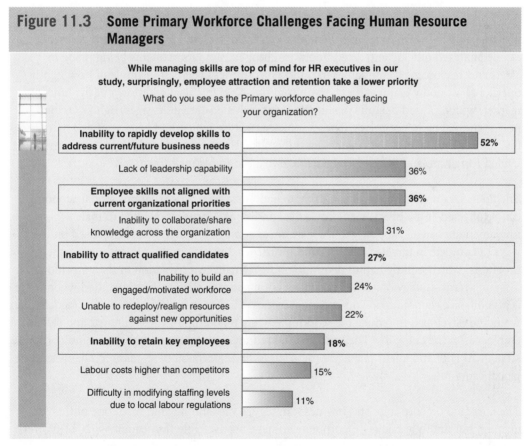

Figure 11.3   Some Primary Workforce Challenges Facing Human Resource Managers

While managing skills are top of mind for HR executives in our study, surprisingly, employee attraction and retention take a lower priority

What do you see as the Primary workforce challenges facing your organization?

Challenge	Percent
Inability to rapidly develop skills to address current/future business needs	52%
Lack of leadership capability	36%
Employee skills not aligned with current organizational priorities	36%
Inability to collaborate/share knowledge across the organization	31%
Inability to attract qualified candidates	27%
Inability to build an engaged/motivated workforce	24%
Unable to redeploy/realign resources against new opportunities	22%
Inability to retain key employees	18%
Labour costs higher than competitors	15%
Difficulty in modifying staffing levels due to local labour regulations	11%

Source: Adapted from the *IBM Global Human Capital Study 2008* (IBM Global Business Services, 2008, p. 20).

(Burmann, Schaefer, & Maloney, 2008). Google, for example, is considered the number one brand in the world—over $100 billion worth in value. As a result of this brand image, the company receives over 1,000 resumes each day.

Maintaining the brand image, whether its excellence is derived from the company's products, services, or corporate leadership, is a key factor in attracting and keeping the best and the brightest employees in the workforce. Customer satisfaction, quality control, and promoting good corporate citizenship and a culture of learning and innovation help build a company-wide brand image. A good talent management strategy needs to be tied to that brand image.

Talent Management and Corporate Strategy

There is little question today that our world is linked together in a global economy. One of the primary reasons for that link is the amount of information available almost instantaneously to everyone. Information about industries, stock markets, and governments can be analyzed quickly and acted upon, resulting in more investments being made in assets and resources by companies in multiple countries. The best example of how tightly our global economy is integrated comes from the 2008 financial meltdown of the housing market, which caused defaults in subprime and adjusted-rate mortgages, tighter credit policy, and falling house prices. These "junk" securities, which had been seen as a lucrative investment by financial institutions not only in the United States but also in China, the United Kingdom, and Europe, triggered a global economic meltdown.

The financial crises led to layoffs, corporate bailouts, and a sense that our global economy can be affected easily by shifts in economic conditions. Corporations had to make fundamental changes, not only to their business strategies, which became focused on the ways to compete in targeted markets and industries, but also to their talent management programs, which rapidly had to determine how to manage a reduction in their workforce. The long-term strategy of growing talent in an organization has to be suspended when there is a significant economic downturn, and a tactical plan must be introduced. The tactical plan would be developed to reduce the workforce while retaining the most talented and skilled employees in the company. The fundamental requirement to connect business and corporate strategy to HRP and talent management is based on the capability to adapt to changes in the global economy.

The literature on corporate and business strategy is vast and beyond the scope of this chapter, but multiple books on corporate strategy are available (Mascarenhas, 2011; Porter, 1998). However, an organization's strategic direction does have a significant impact on human resource planning and subsequently on its talent management strategy. Corporate strategy answers the question of what businesses to pursue to maximize the long-term profitability and growth of an organization or of how to enter particular markets. Once the decision is made concerning which market or industries to enter, a business-level strategy defines how to compete effectively against other companies in that same market. In order to compete effectively, HR must play a key role by ensuring that employees have the right skills and tools to guarantee the success of that strategy.

But how can HR make a substantial contribution to executing a firm's business strategy when many executives at corporations still treat HR as a line of business focused on transactions and compliance? According to Becker, Huselid, and Ulrich (2001), for decades, HR professionals have struggled for credibility while achieving little or no impact on company strategy and only limited recognition of their contributions to corporate success. CEOs and top executives understand the importance of human resources—the number one asset within their companies. But how can human capital be linked to the success of the corporation? HR departments need to take on a **value creation role** to support corporate and business-level strategy. Becker et al. (2001) argue that the HR function has to become a **high-performance system**, "where every element of the HR system (selection, rewards, performance management, career development, etc.) is designed to maximize the quality of human capital in the organization" (p. 3). The research reported in their paper suggests that firms that have aligned HR systems with company strategy have seen an increase in dollar market value per employee.

Despite the suggestion that HR should be a source of value creation for an organization, immediately investing heavily in new HRP systems is not recommended. The key is to understand what areas of an HRP program will make the most impact on a firm's strategy. Even more important is the idea that corporate and business strategies are not things to be kept inside an executive boardroom. Every aspect of a business operation, including marketing, sales, manufacturing, and HR, must be aligned to support the overall goals and strategies of the business.

An example of aligning HR with corporate strategy was the decision by Walmart to enter the overseas market in China in the mid-1990s. Walmart's success occurred primarily because the company took a successful infrastructure, including an HRP best practices program and information systems used in the United States, and implemented it overseas. Trunick (2006) noted that Walmart brought its internal Walton Educational Institute to China when managers discovered that many of the Chinese employees were not fluent enough in English to come to the United States. Today, in comparison with its U.S. counterpart, Walmart China has a higher percentage of employees with university degrees and a much lower turnover rate, 16% as compared with 40% (Trunick, 2006).

Another key to Walmart's success in China was hiring qualified managers locally who knew the culture and buying habits of the local customers. Walking into a Walmart is a different experience in China than it is in the United States. Not only can you buy fresh produce in China, but items such as fish, turtles, clams, and eels are cleaned at the store and handed to the shopper in a plastic bag. The Chinese tend to shop at Walmart more often for fresh items because of their small-sized refrigerators and smaller living spaces, so the company fills a different need in China than it does in the U.S. market (Naughton, 2006).

This example illustrates how HR departments must make changes in their programs based on future corporate and business strategy. The marketplace for companies is changing constantly, and a sound business strategy that works today may not work tomorrow. Companies entering the consumer market compete for the same human resources available in the labor market. The only axiom with merit about the future business of a company is that things change, and any business that is successful today may not be successful tomorrow. If the HR function is going to be aligned closely with changing corporate and business strategy, then it must be able to anticipate change and develop new HRP programs and talent management practices based on forecasted future corporate strategy. Using business intelligence systems that model competitors' business processes is a good start to anticipating the future direction of a company.

Anticipating Change and Creating an Adaptable Workforce

Change is given as a constant within any business, so companies need a workforce that can adapt to changes. In a study done by IBM Global Business Services (2008), three key capabilities were found to influence a workforce's ability to adapt to change. "*First,* organizations must be capable of predicting their future skill requirements. *Second,* they need to effectively identify and locate experts, and *lastly* they must be able to collaborate across their organizations, connecting individuals and groups that are separated by organizations' boundaries, time zones and cultures" (p. 2). Boundaries that exist today between the lines of business, geographies, and cultures of merged or acquired companies put a tremendous strain on an organization. If executive leadership is not involved to meld the workforce together under a unified vision, goal, or strategy, this strain will have negative consequences for the effective operation of the company.

The HR department needs to establish programs to assess the existing skills of employees, to develop new skills through training, and to create job conditions that help retain valued employees. Talent can be nurtured from within an organization by training. When the necessary skills are still not available from a workforce adaptable to change, then an organization must look to hire from the outside. It is interesting to note that, according to the IBM study (2008), almost 60% of the 400 executives interviewed believed they did a better job of attracting and retaining talent than their competitors. But, as seen in Figure 11.3, attracting employees or retaining them was still considered a high priority when the same executives were asked about the primary workforce-related issues facing their organizations. The inability to develop skills rapidly to address current and future business needs and the lack of leadership capability were, respectively, the number one and two workforce-related issues reported in this study.

In planning for the future needs of a company, traditional HR managers need to recommend changes in their programs to attract, hire, train, and retain employees effectively. Developing an employee's talent is a driving force that enables a company to enhance employees' skills to adapt to future business needs. If HR executives are aligning HRM programs with corporate and business strategy, then unlocking and assessing employees' talent will give the employees the capability to adapt to change more easily. Some companies develop these capabilities by ensuring key individuals are rotated in job assignments every two years so that they learn multiple aspects of the company's business. Other companies use mentoring programs that partner long-term, experienced employees with newly hired employees. Still other companies have formal education programs for employees at various career development stages. Just as the marketplace for doing business is in constant change, so too are the HRM programs to develop talent within an organization and create an **adaptable workforce**. Mentoring, formal education, and job rotation have been available for years and have been used effectively by many companies. When the business climate changes, some long-term HR programs specific to talent management may get shelved or substituted for something else. It may be cheaper to acquire existing talented professionals from outside the company rather than to hire university graduates and spend time and money on extensive training programs. However, it may also be more difficult for newly hired and talented individuals to assimilate to the organization's culture, which might clash with the values and culture they experienced at their previous jobs.

Talent Management and Corporate Culture

Choosing the right knowledge, skills, and abilities (KSA) to require of job applicants is important for an organization looking to hire talented individuals. But what are the organizational factors that a prospective applicant seeks when choosing an employer? Personal factors such as the applicant's age, family status, health, and financial condition can have a significant impact on what the applicant is seeking when he or she is considering joining an organization. For example, a young applicant who has a spouse with a good job at a *Fortune* 500 corporation may feel it would be more important to have a high income and forgo having the potential for promotion. There are a myriad of situations that could change what applicants are seeking in their next job; thus, there is not one set of organizational attributes that apply in all situations. But there seems to be one attribute of an organization that is considered important and valued by almost all applicants—the culture of the organization. As was discussed in Chapter 1 (Figure 1.2), the internal culture of an organization determines the manner in which HR programs and an HRIS are adopted.

Corporate culture is an interesting phenomenon. Corporate culture is based on the values that are seen as important to all members of a company. Corporate culture is developed as part of social networking and the creation of social norms when individuals work together as a group. Schein (1985), in an early definition of corporate culture, describes it as involving an understanding of what constitutes correct attitudes and perceptions, one that is shared by coworkers. Specifically, this culture is a pattern of basic assumptions—invented, discovered, or developed [by a firm's members] to cope with problems of external adaptation and internal integration—that has worked well enough to be considered valid and, therefore, to be taught to new members as the correct way to perceive, think, and feel in relation to those problems (Schein, 1985, p. 9).

Corporate culture has a strong effect on employees' beliefs and actions since it is based on a set of fundamental norms and values. Thus, there are many attributes of corporate culture, including ethics, dress codes, working at home or in the office, planned or unplanned vacation schedules, brand image, goals, and vision for the future. Corporate culture is not just defined but rather described to a potential applicant. The role of company executives and HR professionals is to foster culture and cultivate it to support the vision of how to conduct business within the organization. In addition, potential applicants need to know if the culture of the company matches their own attitudes and values about appropriate behavior in an organizational setting. High-potential employees need to understand the fit between their work patterns and the way an organization goes about doing business; they need to be able to envision themselves as being a part of the way in which the organization operates.

It is important for the organization to project a positive and accurate image to the applicant. As with its creation of a positive brand image, the corporation has to create a positive employment image, and recruiters should include a description of this image when introducing the company's culture to potential applicants. A study done by the Aberdeen Group (Saba, 2009) indicated that *organizational fit,* also known as *cultural fit,* surpassed other organizational attributes for first-time applicants. If the company culture does not match the values, interests, work habits, and personality of the applicant, then that applicant either will not take the job or will only stay for a short while.

Keep in mind that cultural fit between the company and applicant is an important consideration, but it is not the only one. There is no guarantee that, if the applicant fits well with the company's culture, high performance will be the end result. Current skills, past experience, previous job references, and educational history are all important ways to determine if there is a good employee-organization fit. Cultural fit is an additional factor that is of high importance for both the employer and the potential applicant. Determining whether or not there is employee-organization fit is a critical component of a talent management program.

Talent Management and Information Systems

The Link Between Talent Management and Human Resource Information Systems

Investing in human capital is one of the most significant expenditures for corporations. Measuring the return on investment (ROI) for human capital, as described in Chapter 7, has to be reflected in the HR **balanced scorecard** program to justify its acquisition and use (see Chapter 10). Talent management (TM) is just one of many components involving the investment in human capital. The importance of using an HRIS is to ensure that the HR programs of attracting, hiring, educating, and nurturing employees are executed well and consistently over time because this is the heart of the talent management program. The numeric results of the components of the HRM program that comprise the criteria for the TM program are (1) the number of talented individuals hired, (2) the training of these talented individuals, (3) the job performance of the individuals, and (4) the retention of these individuals. The HRIS can capture these results based on performance criteria, so it is possible to measure how well HR programs, as part of the overall talent management program, are meeting the expectations of HR executives and senior management. As discussed in Chapter 8, these numeric results can also be used to calculate cost-benefit ratios to determine the contribution of these HR programs to the profitability of the organization. Details on the criteria measures needed as well as on the calculation of the cost-benefit ratios can also be found in Cascio (2000).

Not only can an HRIS assist in the implementation of best of breed programs and processes, but it can also be used to help ensure adoption of these processes by the user community. Building consistency and setting standards are the key drivers for an HRIS—every process implemented should be done in a similar manner. An HRIS can also assist in developing those processes (see Chapter 5) and help to establish the best talent management programs. For example, an HRIS can also be used to help develop and administer education programs for all employees, regardless of job level.

Since talent management is only one component of **human capital management (HCM)**, there are many questions that need to be answered when one initiates a general HRP program that includes TM and considers how to best use the HRIS to support this program. Is there an existing HRIS in use today that has software that can support talent management? If not, should you build the new system in-house, buy an out-of-the-box application, or outsource all of the processes to a vendor who specializes in TM? How will critical, secure data be protected for prospective applicants across multiple systems and, for MNEs, across multiple geographic regions?

Information systems can be found in every aspect of talent management, from conducting job analysis to focusing on the human capital demand and supply for current and future jobs, attracting the right talent in a specific location, hiring based on desired attributes, and retaining high-performing employees. Ultimately, the HR department of an organization would use an HRIS to monitor and measure the overall contributions of talented employees with other results on a balanced scorecard, and these results could affect the design of other HRM programs. As with the other parts of an organization's HRIS, today's talent management software applications are increasingly deployed using a **software as a service (SaaS)** approach. As can been seen in Figure 11.4, SaaS/hosted applications have grown in most of the HRM programs that support a talent management strategy. Beaman (2012) further notes:

> SaaS deployments for Talent Management functions show steady growth, particularly in the areas of Compensation (44%), Succession (219%), and Career Development (185%), which also can be attributed to the 'unified talent management' approach of vendors such as SuccessFactors and Workday. (p. 24)

Also as noted in Chapter 10, Kaplan and Norton (1992, 1996, 2006) recognized that an organization cannot use only financial measures such as ROI on a balanced scorecard as an indication of its ability to survive and maintain a competitive advantage. Kaplan and Norton (2006) further identified the four components of the balanced scorecard as financial, customer, internal business processes, and learning and growth. As discussed in Chapter 10 and depicted in Figure 10.12, these components reflect a commitment to balance the organization's strategic goals, which are important to the expectations of its multiple stakeholders. An overview of all four components can be seen in Figure 10.12 along with the key question associated with each of the four. Particularly relevant to the results from a talent management program is the "Learning and Growth" box in Figure 10.12. Note the requirement in this box for *objectives* to be set, *measures* to be developed, *targets* to be achieved, and *initiatives* to be implemented. These categories represent the results that would be entered into the balanced scorecard for an organization.

However, no matter how an HRIS is used to support talent management or other functional business areas, accurate and timely data are the key to successful program operations.

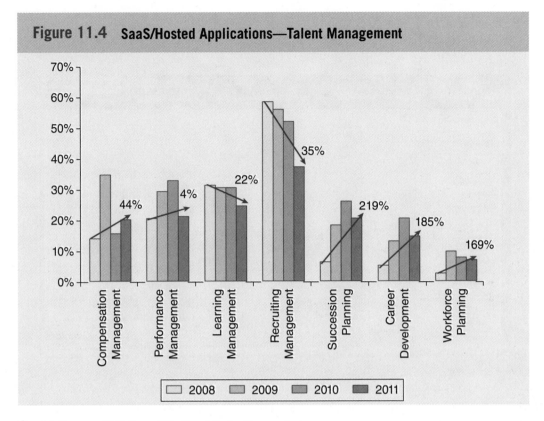

Figure 11.4 SaaS/Hosted Applications—Talent Management

Source: Beaman (2012, p. 23). Reprinted with permission.

An organization needs not only to collect data about potential job applicants but also to know the skills of the current employee resource pool. Before planning new HR programs to resolve the gap between forecasted demand and supply of human capital, a company needs to know what skills exist in the current workforce and what skills are needed based on the future strategy, and it needs a systematic approach to acquiring this information. An HRIS can be of great assistance in providing information on current employee skills, succession relationships, and leadership readiness (see Figure 11.5).

If the organization does not have the capability to develop the necessary HR business programs and processes, this is probably the time to use outside HRIS consulting companies as detailed in Chapters 10 and 5. HRIS consulting and management consulting companies are able to define future business strategies, and they can also help the organization implement those strategies. IT consulting companies, in particular, specialize in improvements to business processes in areas such as enterprise resource planning, supply chain management, and product life cycle management. HRIS consulting firms can also

Figure 11.5 Employee Skill Assessment and Succession Planning With an HRIS

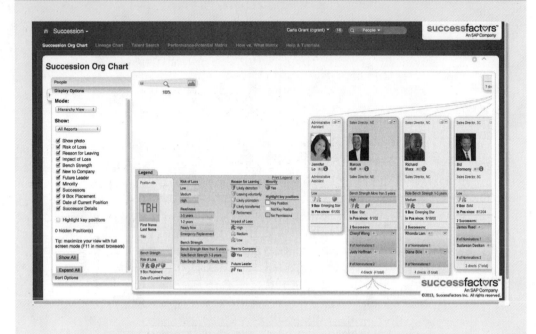

make recommendations to use business process management systems, and they can support the implementation and integration of those systems.

The key starting point for any consulting group is performing a business strategy assessment for an organization, and the organization should not proceed with a vendor until this project is finished. No information system, whether it is an application package recommended by a consulting firm or homegrown software, will fix, enhance, or salvage a poorly defined business strategy plan. For example, in the mid-1990s, Kodak was trying to transition from film-based to digital photography and then to focus its business on digital sharing. Kodak's business strategy shifted from the need to have employees skilled in the manufacturing of film to a need for employees skilled in the manufacture of digital cameras (Nossbaum, 2006). The age of digital equipment advanced so quickly that Kodak almost missed the revenue growth area of writing the software to support the sharing of digital photos across the Internet. But the company did finally shift its business strategy to offer digital sharing services.

The talent management functional areas offered by application software products include many of the topics that we have already covered in this chapter, such as skills assessment, succession planning, recruiting management, career development, and employee life cycle. There are also a number of consulting firms that can help tailor an application package for a company and help to implement it. The International Association for Human Resource Information Management (IHRIM) has a list of consulting companies and routinely evaluates HRIS software applications. Additionally, IHRIM is a good source for finding HRIS vendors.

Many of the applications covering the above topics are usually categorized as cross-industry packages. This label means that the application functionality and the processes are similar and can be applicable for all industries. Many of the functions and processes within HR tend to be the same and can be handled by the same application. Thus, the application companies can keep software development and ongoing maintenance costs low by supporting the concept of one version fits all. Today, HR processes supporting talent management are becoming more intricate, and application software vendors are now offering solutions by specific industry. An HR recruiter seeking to hire former doctors and nurses for a biotech or large pharmaceutical firm will get a different industry view of the recruiting software package than someone hiring drivers or dispatchers for a trucking company.

Application packages are also divided into offerings for small, medium, or large firms. There is a tendency today to offer scaled-down applications for small companies, which may not need all the features of a large-enterprise version. In addition, as discussed above, software companies will also offer a hosted, subscription-based version of the application to various customers as part of a SaaS solution. By using the hosted software, clients save on investing in licensing and maintenance fees; instead, they pay a low monthly rate to use the software. A hosted offering allows a customer to try the software using Web access without making a large investment in hardware and other computer infrastructure.

Recruiting Top Talent Using Social Networking Sites (SNSs)

Social networking using the Web has become popular with recruiters and potential applicants. Print ads in newspapers are still being used but at a considerably lower rate than 10 years ago. **Social networking sites**, such as Facebook, LinkedIn, and Twitter, are just media to increase the flow of information for making social connections. It is accurate to remember that many employees hired by a given company were referred to the HR department by a friend already working in the company. Contacting the people you know is sometimes the quickest way to get an interview. There are no guarantees that you will be hired, but personal referrals generally give you an advantage over those applicants just submitting a resume to a company. On the flip side, HR professionals network in support of talent recruitment. So social networking to support both HR and career development is not new—only the tools have changed.

Using SNSs to recruit top talent can be effective, but there are some limitations. Social network demography indicates that social networks are primarily used by a younger audience. Therefore, recruiters have to be aware of the difficulty of matching potential applicants to the required skills. If recent college graduates comprise the target audience for your recruiting effort, then social networks can usually provide a direct link to potential applicants. But if a company is looking to hire individuals to work in IT jobs, then the age of the audience and the way you reach it may change due to the necessity of hiring experienced IT professionals.

Recruiters searching for top talent also must be aware of their own company's website and ask themselves if it has enough information for applicants to be interested in envisioning working for the company. A company website needs to target not only potential customers but also high-potential applicants. Here are some questions to keep in mind when you are looking to recruit top talent:

> Does the website make it difficult to find the link to career paths?
>
> Does the link use the word "careers" or the phrase "job opportunities"?
>
> Are there employee testimonial videos or videos from senior-level executives discussing the company's culture and mission?
>
> Is it easy to use the search engine to find specific jobs?
>
> Are there too many steps for an applicant trying to submit a resume and apply for a job?
>
> What is the process to contact the applicant after he or she has applied for a job?
>
> Is there any follow-up contact over a period of time?

See Chapter 12 for more information related to these questions and for a broader discussion of e-recruiting.

Using Information Systems to Set Goals and Evaluate Performance

Tying measurable goals to company strategy is important. Studies have found that overall employee productivity increases along with company morale when employee goals are aligned with company strategy. Before employee goals can be set, the company strategy needs to be well defined, outlined, and communicated throughout the company. Large multinational enterprises (MNEs) are typically in global businesses and have to ensure that the strategy is passed down from the CEO to first-line managers and all employees—and then to all subsidiaries of the parent company. If goal setting at any level in the organization is done poorly, it can hurt overall employee morale and cause confusion in the company's operations. In order to develop and retain highly motivated employees, the company must link employees' job responsibilities to the overall company strategy, and this link must be visible to other employees.

There are many packaged goal alignment software tools available in the market to help show the value of an employee's contribution to an organization. SuccessFactors (2010) is a company that specializes in business alignment and performance management software that assists in managing the employee's life cycle in an organization. This package and integrated offering automates the creation of goals that are reviewed and agreed to by both the manager and the employee. This process allows the employee to develop a career path within the organization, and the manager can help by cooperatively aligning the employee's measurable goals to the company strategy. The software package speeds up the task of setting goals, and it helps define how to measure results and provide feedback to the employee.

Subjectivity, however, will never be removed from any manager-employee relationship or from any performance review, but HRIS package tools provide a basis from which to monitor performance results that are recorded throughout the course of the performance measurement cycle. Many performance tools utilize the SMART acronym for goal setting. SMART has gone through various interpretations over the years since it was first introduced by Doran (1981). In the article, Doran established the acronym SMART to describe how to write performance goals. The acronym SMART stands for (1) *specific*, (2) *measurable*, (3) *attainable* or *acceptable*, (4) *reasonable* or *results* oriented, and (5) *timely*.

Using Analytics for Talent Management

Much has been said about **workforce analytics** (Chapter 7) and **business intelligence** (Chapter 2) in this book. Analytics is a part of the business intelligence (BI) tool set, and workforce analytics is specific to BI as it relates to HRM. Although the focus of this section is using analytics for talent management, it may be good to first dispel some of the assumptions about using analytics in general. Analytics is an interesting area within information systems and the HRIS literature. It is one of the most frequently discussed topics between IT professionals and line managers. Analytics have a tendency to be seen as a panacea for many problems associated with the inability of getting the correct information to the end users, managers, and HR professionals—the information they need so they can make better decisions. Whether it is in the HR, IT, or another department, most people know enough about analytics to use it to solve problems or make forecasts, for example, predicting future workforce needs or trying to discover why their organization has a high employee turnover rate. Unfortunately, analytics does not solve the problem of inaccurate data entry since garbage in, garbage out (GIGO) will prevail. They also cannot predict the future with 100% accuracy. Instead, analytics can build a model of what the future may hold, but businesses cannot rely solely on strategic decision making based solely on the results of predictive analysis. Other factors must be taken into consideration, such as the competition, government compliance, or the current state of the economy. That is, analytics, by themselves, cannot solve everything, but they constitute a very powerful tool to analyze data and to provide the fuel for intelligent decision making—good information. In short, analytics can be used to gain a competitive advantage in the marketplace.

Today, there are software packages from HRIS and IT solution vendors that can build front-end dashboards and queries that anyone can use. These packages have taken the complicated world of business intelligence and its components, which were quite difficult to use in the past, and made it easier for business professionals to leverage BI tools more quickly. Deploying an analytic software package, however, does not tell you what specific kind of data you should be analyzing or what questions need to be asked. The skill of knowing the right questions still has to come from the business professional. When questions become complicated and linked to other areas of the business or the amount of data that needs to be analyzed is huge, then a skilled BI person is a necessary resource; you need someone able to get the most out of the software package.

Workforce Analytics and Talent Management

Using workforce analytics to manage talent can involve asking many questions about an individual person or a group of employees. Typically, a simple question about an individual employee's history is answered by using a query program against the **employee data warehouse**. This is not a really complicated environment as long as your organization has the query tools that can get the answer from a data warehouse. The real purpose of analytics for talent management is to use the analytics to model characteristics of success, in terms of the skills and abilities of employees who were successful in the company versus employees who were not successful. This empirical analytics model could then be used for a pool of existing employees or new potential hires to determine their possibility of success in the organization.

For new hires, an employer may like to know the demographics of existing, successful employees to see if the company image and recruiting programs are attracting the right individuals to the company. This is an important use of analytics because recruiting programs vary from Internet-based recruitment using social networking to programs focused on local media advertising through newspapers or television or participation in recruiting fairs. All of these recruiting programs cost money, and it is important to know where to spend the money to attract the best talent. By successfully using analytics, a company can also better train its managers on hiring tactics, and resources can be better funneled to the right recruitment channel.

For existing employees, analytics can be used to understand the personal characteristics of successful employees. Data such as previous work experiences and education and training both within and outside the company can be collected and analyzed to determine what helps prepare these employees for success. Also, data about performance objectives can be compared with actual business results. This information can be collected and stored in an employee's electronic career jacket, which also contains a record of current job responsibilities, previous promotions, and the length of time between promotions. Analyzing all of this data is the reason that models need to be designed and the right data must to be loaded into the data warehouse. It is better to understand the type of information that you need for decisions prior to building a data warehouse. Without this, data warehouses have a tendency to multiply across organizations until there are too many to manage. Generating reports and answering simple queries is the primary baseline for analytics within business intelligence systems. Being able to turn data into intelligent information and draw conclusions about the employee population is where sophisticated analytics come to the forefront of business intelligence systems. The newer generation of BI systems with HR-specific algorithms can now give what senior executives have desired for many years—an accurate description of the employee population and the means to make intelligent decisions regarding the company's human capital.

Mapping employee success to business results is not an easy task. The dilemma is that, although employees are the largest capital cost of any organization, not enough information is known about this most expensive asset. This problem leads one back to the HR balanced scorecard and the importance of using analytics to draw the right conclusions about the demographics of successful employees. This information on the HR balanced scorecard offers so much more than a simple monitoring of performance results. It helps to answer an important question: What characteristics make a talented employee successful?

Measuring the Success of Talent Management

As baby boomers retire and leave the workforce, both the competition to attract and the costs of acquiring new, highly talented individuals are only going to increase. Many boomers may delay retirement due to the 2008 economic crisis and the lack of stability associated with pensions, but, at some point, there will be a labor shortage that needs to be addressed by HR executives (Kavanagh, 2008). The HR organization will also be under heavy pressure to provide a succession plan for key executive roles, as well as a succession plan for the company's board of directors. All of the costs associated with acquiring the best applicants will have to be justified and approved by financial management using an ROI calculation no matter if the job is for a senior executive or a new sales representative. So given that the costs of developing succession plans and acquiring talented workers will increase in the future, it is important to measure the success of these programs over a period of time. Performance management and its use within the balanced scorecard will be critical in justifying the extra expenditures needed to acquire the most talented individuals in the market.

Performance management is not simply evaluating an employee at the end of a given business cycle; it is not just a year-to-year appraisal. There are critical success factors that are evaluated by management: for example, leadership, skill development, creativity, and knowledge about the industry and sales results. The key to performance management is to ensure there are measurable performance criteria that an employee can realistically achieve over a period of time.

Measuring performance results is critical in today's workplace. This results-oriented perspective is not just limited to the sales department, where results can be measured against quota objectives. It now exists in all departments from marketing, which measures campaign results by tracking new customers, to procurement, which accepts a new purchase order application that saves double the cost. This results-oriented perspective is also expected in the HR department (see Chapters 6 and 7). That is, the HR organization needs to compare the costs of current or proposed programs to the financial benefits produced. Then, the overall result can be expressed as a cost-benefit ratio, and this information can be reflected on the balanced scorecard.

SUMMARY

The primary purpose of this chapter on talent management (TM) was to investigate how an HRIS and other information systems can be used to support a talent management program. The importance of talent management was illustrated by examining the results of two comprehensive surveys. The origin of talent management and its fit with human resources planning (HRP) and human capital management (HCM) were discussed in detail.

In addition, strategic HRM was covered, and its relation to corporate strategy was discussed.

The relationship between TM and performance management was explained as being critical to the effectiveness of the entire TM program. In addition, the chapter emphasized that the metrics from both the performance management and the TM programs could be entered on the balanced scorecard, which, in turn, contributes to the strategic HRM function. In order to understand a TM program, it is necessary to realize that the program reacts to labor and consumer market changes, producing a life cycle for TM. In developing and implementing a TM program, HR specialists must identify talented individuals by assessing the important personal attributes of employees and new hires.

A talent management program is part of the human resources planning (HRP) function of an organization. One of the important ingredients for an effective HR plan is to have *accurate and timely* job descriptions based on job analysis. An HRP program consists of three phases, (1) estimation of the demand and supply of human capital to set HRP objectives, (2) planning HR programs, and (3) evaluation of HR programs and control through feedback on program outcomes. The HRP program will generate HR metrics that are useful for the organization in going through these three phases.

Long- and short-term strategies for TM were covered. When an external event occurs unexpectedly, such as the recent recession, a short-term strategy should be available. Conversely, the company should have a long-term strategy for TM, usually

one looking 5 to 10 years into the future; this long-term talent management strategy is part of the overall corporate strategy. In this way, the TM program can make a major contribution to the immediate and future strategic positions of the corporation. A major aspect of a successful TM strategy, short or long, is to have an adaptable workforce. For example, cross-training employees on jobs are a way to increase the adaptability of the workforce. Finally, the value of a positive corporate culture in attracting talented individuals was discussed.

The link between TM and HRIS was also covered in this chapter. There are quite a few quality TM computer applications available to companies, and most have been used successfully. Recruiting talented individuals by using social networks has been increasing too, but companies should be aware of the limitations of this approach. Some questions were posed that people should keep in mind when using social networks for recruiting talent. The use of analytics in TM was described, particularly the use of business intelligence to produce TM analytics. The success of TM was covered and emphasized the use of metrics generated by the performance management program and entered on the HR balanced scorecard.

KEY TERMS

adaptable workforce 351

balanced scorecard 353

business intelligence 359

common attributes of
talented individuals 340

corporate brand
management 347

corporate culture 352

employee data
warehouse 360

estimating demand 343

estimating supply 343

evaluation and control 342

high-performance
system 349

DISCUSSION QUESTIONS

1. Why is it important to establish the meaning of talent and talent management in a particular organizational setting?

2. How does the strategic direction of the organization influence human resource planning activities?

3. Given the different needs of the HRP/ workforce planning process discussed in this chapter, what types of data would you expect the HRIS data warehouse to contain?

4. What would be the most effective "bundles" of metrics for talent management?

5. How would one justify the purchase of software for an HRP program?

6. What are the uses and benefits of workforce management systems/HRP systems? Check one of the websites mentioned in this chapter to obtain this information.

7. Discuss the pros and cons of using social networks to recruit top talent.

8. What are some potential disadvantages of using a packaged application to help automate the employee goal-setting process?

9. How would you use workforce analytics to support talent programs such as recruiting, retention, and employee development?

10. Why is it important to have an adaptable workforce in a global economy?

11. Discuss the underlying attributes necessary to support high achievers.

12. How might the attributes of a highly motivated employee change for different job descriptions?

13. Discuss corporate tactics that can be used in a down economy to keep top talent.

14. Discuss how you would use information systems (IS) to support succession planning.

15. How would a company benefit from using a social networking site to assist in the recruitment process?

CASE STUDY: VIGNETTE CASE CONTINUED

18 months later . . .

Once again Rudiger is sitting at his desk in his seventh-floor office in central London reflecting on life. The move from Barcelona to England went smoothly with the last crate arriving only two months later than the rest. He is still working hard, but the hours are slightly better since the introduction of the work-life balance policy last year, and his family has settled well into the idyllic English countryside.

As the global head of People and Talent, he still has problems though—just different ones. The talent strategy "Our People—Our Talent—Our Future," which he presented to the board in his third month, identified the need for robust HRP information and analyses that required a new version of HRP software. It is in its early stages, but the intensive data-cleansing and updating activity has been straightforward so far. More concerning are the metrics responsible for producing the information needed to develop far-reaching HRP policies and practices for the future. The metrics are relatively easy to construct, but it is proving tricky to find the right "bundles" of predictive metrics—this is holding up progress with the analysis application package. In addition, there have been cost overruns in the implementation of the HRP software, and some senior managers are wondering if the new software should be abandoned.

At least 3 of the 12 board members will retire in the next two years, and they are looking to groom their successors. At least one will have to be hired from outside the organization, and the HR department is not sure what the CEO wants for this position. In addition, employee turnover and an aggressive growth strategy mean hiring new employees as well as training transferring current employees. The work that is involved in defining competences (KSA sets) at skill levels within jobs is progressing well, with hard-won support from the unions. However, job descriptions that can be found are at least three to five years old, and some jobs have no descriptions. The new apprenticeship scheme is about to be launched, and the international graduate student package and development program has been completely revised. Overall things are progressing OK, but there is much to be done.

Case Study Questions

1. How would you recommend that Rudiger begin to develop an HRP program? What are the steps that he needs to take?

2. How should the problem with the job descriptions be handled? Should the unions be involved?

3. What are some of the problems in the past that have led this current situation to occur?

4. Why do you think there are cost overruns? How could this have been avoided?

5. Why are there problems with implementation of the new software?

6. How will job descriptions be developed for the positions of board member and international student intern?

STUDENT STUDY SITE

Visit the Student Study Site at **http://www.sagepub.com/kavanagh3e** for additional learning tools such as access to SAGE journal articles and related web resources.

NOTE

1. Human resource planning (HRP) is also referred to as workforce planning. The two terms are synonymous.

REFERENCES

Beaman, K. (2011). *2011–2012 going global report: HCM trends in globalization.* New York: Jeitosa Group International & IHRIM.

Beaman, K. (2012). *2011–2012 global readiness report* (Figure 26, p. 21). New York: Jeitosa Group International & IHRIM.

Becker, B., Huselid, M., & Ulrich, D. (2001). *The HR scorecard: Linking people, strategy, and performance.* Boston: Harvard Business School Press.

Burmann, C., Schaefer, K., & Maloney, P. (2008). Industry image: Its impact on the brand image of potential employees. *Journal of Brand Management, 15,* 157–176.

Cascio, W. F. (2000). Costing human resources: The financial impact of behavior in organizations (4th ed.). Boston: Kent.

CedarCrestone. (2010). *CedarCrestone 2010–2011 HR systems survey* (13th ed.). Alpharetta, GA: Author.

Chapman, S. (2009). Strategic workforce planning—the foundation of talent management. IHRIM.*link, 14*(5), 9–12.

Doran, G. T. (1981). There's a S.M.A.R.T. way to write management goals and objectives. *Management Review, 70*(11), 35–36.

Dunivan, L. (2010). Talent management: Changing demands, changing technology. *Workforce Solutions Review, 1*(3), 14–17.

Dyer, L. (1982). Human resource planning. In K. M. Rowland & G. R. Ferris (Eds.), *Personnel management* (pp. 31–47). Boston: Allyn & Bacon.

IBM Global Business Services. (2008). *Unlocking the DNA of the adaptable workforce: The global human capital study.* Somers, NY: Author.

Kaplan, R., & Norton, D. (1992). The balanced scorecard: Measures that drive performance. *Harvard Business Review, 70,* 71–80.

Kaplan, R., & Norton, D. (1996). *The balanced scorecard: Translating strategy into action.* Boston: Harvard Business School Press.

Kaplan, R., & Norton, D. (2006). *Alignment: Using the balanced scorecard to create corporate synergies.* Boston: Harvard Business School Press.

Kavanagh, M. J. (2008, February). *Global challenge: Managing the exodus of older workers.* Paper presented at the 17th Annual Zurich MBA Forum, Zurich, Switzerland.

Lockwood, N. (2006, June). Talent management: Driver for organizational success. *HR Magazine,* (SHRM White Paper). Alexandria, VA: Society for Human Resource Management.

Mascarenhas, O. A. (2011). *Business transformation strategies: The strategic leader as innovation leader.* Thousand Oaks, CA: Sage.

McKinsey and Company. (2001). *The war for talent.* New York: Author.

Naughton, K. (2006, October 30). The great Wal-Mart of China. *Newsweek, 148,* 1.

Noe, R., Hollenbeck, J., Gerhart, B., & Wright, P. (2010). *Fundamentals of human resource management.* New York: McGraw-Hill.

Nossbaum, B. (2006, August 1). Kodak struggles with innovating its business model. *Bloomberg Business Week,* 1.

Porter, M. (1998). *Competitive strategy: Techniques for analyzing industries and competitors.* New York: The Free Press.

Saba, J. (2009). *Assessments in talent management: Strategies to improve pre- and post-hire performance.* Boston: Aberdeen Group. Retrieved from http://www.aberdeen.com/aberdeen-library/5790/RA-assessment-talent-management.aspx

Schein, E. H. (1985). *Organizational culture and leadership.* San Francisco: Jossey-Bass.

Society for Human Resource Management (SHRM). (2010, September 21). SHRM poll identifies top HR challenges for next 10 years. *HR News.* (SHRM White Paper). Alexandria, VA: Society for Human Resource Management.

SuccessFactors. (2010). *Driving success: The incredible power of company-wide goal management.* San Mateo, CA: Author.

Trunick, P. (2006, January 1). Wal-Mart reinvents itself in China. *Logistics Today,* 1.

Recruitment and Selection in an Internet Context

Kimberly M. Lukaszewski, David N. Dickter,
Brian D. Lyons, and Jerard F. Kehoe

EDITORS' NOTE

This chapter is the second one that is concerned with the talent management of employees. As noted in previous chapters, talent management is an extremely important strategic goal for organizations, both domestic and global, and relates directly to the HR balanced scorecard discussed in Chapter 10. After the need for external hiring of new employees has been identified via HR planning (Chapter 11), the next step is to design recruitment and selection programs that will result in the successful hiring of needed talent. Successful recruiting and hiring of new talent is an early step following the identification of job requirements, in the talent management process, which concludes with the retention of high-performance and committed employees. This chapter will cover the concepts of recruitment and selection and the use of the Internet and an HRIS to improve the operation of these HR programs.

CHAPTER Objectives

After completing this chapter, you should be able to

- Understand the relationship between the Internet and organizational recruiting objectives
- Discuss the potential advantages and disadvantages of online recruitment in the framework of recruiting objectives
- Discuss recruitment strategies and social networking
- Understand the relationship between e-recruitment and HRIS
- Understand the relationship between selection and assessment with HRIS
- Discuss the technological issues that influence selection and the solutions that have been reached
- Understand the value of HRIS selection applications through the use of utility analysis

HRIS IN ACTION

Bank of America looked for a computer-based solution for its problem of merging selection tests with the firm's applicant-tracking software application and found that this could be done. The company wanted to improve the quality of the applicant pool it obtained through Internet recruiting by adding selection tests to the process. It was thought that adding valid selection tests would improve the quality of candidates such that those assessed by tests would be much more likely to be successful on the job than those who simply applied through the Internet. Also, the company, by increasing applicant quality through testing, could reduce applicant-processing time.

Bank of America contracted with a test vendor to improve its selection system first. The vendor created competency profiles for jobs by interviewing about 50 current job incumbents and managers to ascertain that the competency profile for each job had the correct skills listed for the job. A "set of inventories was then identified to map onto the confirmed competencies and serve to identify the candidates who had the greatest potential for success in the job and would be the right candidates scheduled for final interviews" (Society for Human Resource Management [SHRM], 2004, p. 1).

The next aspect of the project was to change the interface on the Web page for Bank of America so that recruiters could get the applicant information they needed to manage applicant information for 100 hiring sites.

Next, the promising applicants were asked to visit a Bank of America staffing facility, where they completed three tests and inventories on a computer terminal. Once there, candidates watched a job preview video and then were directed to a computer terminal to key in basic contact information and complete three more tests. Candidates who were not comfortable with computers were able to access a built-in tutorial. After candidates had completed this procedure on the computer, the site administrator had just-in-time access to the test results. This enabled the administrator to conduct on-the-spot interviews with the candidates or schedule just-in-time interviews for a later time. Thus, Bank of America was able to introduce technology in one area of the selection process rather than trying to automate the entire process. In addition, this procedure allowed human contact with the candidates and maintained system security, particularly for the selection tests.

By combining online testing with its applicant-tracking system, Bank of America netted some significant results:

Improved ability to identify successful performers. Of those who passed the test phase and were hired, 84% were rated as successful performers by their supervisors. In fact, passing candidates were 5 times more likely to be successful on the job.

Significant return on investment. The estimated annual return on investment from using the system in selecting for the Operations job family was more than 2,000%.

Favorable reactions from candidates. Ninety-seven percent of respondents expressed overall satisfaction with the selection process and agreed that the answers they were asked to provide represented their abilities.

Valid and fair assessment of candidates. The inventories included in the system were able to distinguish between high and low performers and increase the probability of selecting the best candidates. In addition, analyses broken out by race, gender, and age showed that the inventories treated all groups fairly. (SHRM, 2004, p. 2)

Introduction

To remain competitive in today's global environment, organizations are searching for more efficient and effective means of acquiring and maintaining a highly qualified workforce. One popular and highly productive strategy for meeting this goal has been the use of technology, especially the Internet. Thus, the focus of this chapter is to consider the impact of technology on the recruitment and selection processes in organizations. In the paragraphs that follow, we will discuss the effects of technology on these two key processes. In the recruitment section, we address the objectives of the recruitment process and whether or not online recruitment is helping to achieve these objectives. The recruitment objectives, which are based on the model of Breaugh and Starke (2000), include cost of filling a job opening, speed of filling a job opening, psychological contract fulfillment, employee satisfaction, retention rates, quality of applicants, quantity of applicants, and diversity of applicants. We also discuss the impact of the attributes of the organizational website on applications and the use of social networking. In addition, the relationship between e-recruitment and HRIS is explained. In the selection section, we address the importance of assessment and its role in HRIS. Technology issues surrounding selection, such as validity, computerized assessment, security, and proctoring, are also discussed. We then present the ways in which the HRIS has been integrated with the function of selection and assessment to address the issues mentioned previously. Finally, we demonstrate the value of selection with HRIS selection applications through the use of utility analysis.

Recruitment and Technology

The goal of the **recruitment** function is to identify, attract, and hire the most qualified people (Cascio, 2013). However, this task has become quite challenging because there is a growing competition for talent in the labor market (Towers Watson, 2012). Companies are increasingly being required to expand their search for applicants beyond local and domestic borders in order to find qualified talent. As a result, they have begun using the Internet as a means of attracting job applicants. In the United States, over 90% of large companies use the Internet to recruit applicants for job openings (Cappelli, 2001, Lee, 2005, Taleo Research, as cited in MacMillan, 2007). With more than 46 million people looking for job openings online (PewInternet, 2006), it is no surprise that many organizations, both large and small, are turning to online recruitment. Organizations are utilizing the Web as a way of attracting candidates, and they are also using Web-based HRIS to support the recruiting process (Figure 12.1).

Although there are certainly a number of benefits associated with using online recruitment, there are also several issues that need to be considered before organizations adopt this strategy. For instance, is online recruitment a win-win situation for both job applicants and organizations? A good way to answer this question is to step back and examine the degree to which online recruitment (a) enables organizations to meet their recruiting objectives and (b) provides applicants with the means of obtaining jobs. We discuss these issues in the following sections.

Figure 12.1 Screen Shot of Current Applicants Form

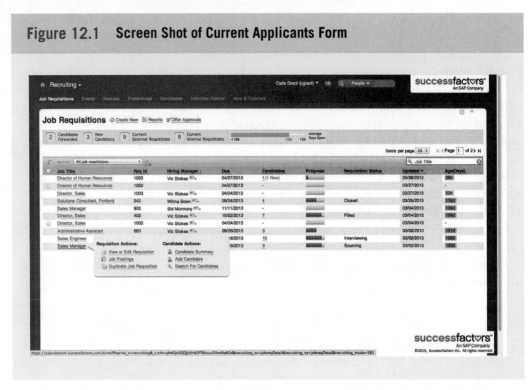

Source: © SuccessFactors, Inc. All Rights Reserved.

The Impact of Online Recruitment on Recruitment Objectives

Research by Breaugh and Starke (2000) has identified a number of objectives for the recruitment process, including (a) cost, (b) speed of filling job vacancies, (c) psychological contract fulfillment, (d) satisfaction and retention rates, (e) quality and quantity of applicants, and (f) diversity of applicants. To what extent does online recruitment help organizations meet each of these objectives?

Recruitment Objective: Cost of Filling the Job Opening

One important recruitment objective that organizations constantly strive for is to minimize the cost of filling job openings (Breaugh & Starke, 2000). Research has consistently shown that online recruitment does reduce costs (Buckley, Minette, Joy, & Michaels, 2004; Cappelli, 2001; Chapman & Webster, 2003; Galanaki, 2002; Lee 2005). For example, one study shows that organizations saved 95% of recruitment costs when they used online recruitment as opposed to more traditional methods (e.g., newspaper ads). Other estimates reveal that the cost of traditional systems of recruitment was $8,000 to $10,000 per position compared with $900 for online recruitment (Cober, Brown, Blumental, Doverspike, & Levy, 2000). This cost difference has prompted many organizations to replace or supplement more traditional systems with online recruitment systems. So it appears that online recruitment can save companies money when compared with traditional methods, but do these cost savings apply to all organizations? The answer is, not necessarily.

The evidence just presented is quite enticing and would probably persuade most organizations to jump into the online recruitment arena; however, before doing so, decision makers should examine the specifics of their recruitment situation and not just assume that online recruitment saves money for all organizations. First, HR professionals need to consider whether or not online recruitment is appropriate for their company. More specifically, organizations need to plan how to process resumes and screen out those applicants who do not possess the qualifications needed. Failure to think through the entire process may generate greater administrative burdens for the HR department or departmental managers (Chapman & Webster, 2003; Russell 2007). These burdens would definitely cut into any cost savings produced by online recruiting. A good example is found in an article written by Seminerio (2001), which profiles the **online recruiting** efforts of Sutter Health, a nonprofit health care network. Sutter Health decided to post jobs online to facilitate its recruitment process. The use of online recruitment generated an enormous number of resumes—more than 300,000—for fewer than 10,000 open positions. In most situations, this is something an organization would desire; however, Sutter Health failed to think past the generation of applicants. Managers had not planned how they would accommodate such a large volume of resumes in terms of processing and screening of applicants. Although, in this case, resumes were received quickly, they often sat for weeks on end before processing and selection occurred. Sutter Health quickly realized its error in planning and that the organization needed to revamp the use of online recruitment to serve its needs better.

In addition, organizations also need to track the effectiveness of the online recruitment method through the assessment of yield ratios and placements made. When dealing with a website for recruiting, you may find it useful to monitor the numbers of hits your company's websites are receiving on career pages. However, the number of hits on a website is only one small component in measuring effectiveness (Cober et al., 2000). For example, a recent study examined the sources job seekers were currently using for new opportunities and how they actually found their present positions (Stevens, 2007). The results showed that over 90% would use or were actively using online sources to find work. The study further reported that only 30% found their present positions through online means. In an additional study, conducted in the United Kingdom, large organizations with 5,000 employees or more were surveyed about the effectiveness of online recruitment (Reed Company, 2003). The results of the study show that about 40% of the organizations consider online recruitment to be a more effective means than any other traditional method of recruitment. These results imply that organizations need to track the outcomes (e.g., successful placements) of using online recruitment and compare these outcomes with those achieved by other recruiting methods.

Thus, although some research shows that online recruiting may result in cost savings, other research shows that the use of online recruiting may generate a large number of applications, which may result in quite an administrative burden for organizations. As a result, organizations need to consider the overall costs associated with the entire recruitment process before implementing these new systems.

Recruitment Objective: Speed of Filling Job Vacancies

Another recruitment objective for assessing the effectiveness of recruitment is the speed of filling the job vacancy (Breaugh & Starke, 2000). Research has shown that online recruitment can decrease cycle time and increase the efficiency of the process by allowing organizations to spend less time gathering and sorting data (Cardy & Miller, 2003; Chapman & Webster, 2003; Cober, Brown, Levy, Keeping, & Cober, 2003; Lee, 2005; Web Recruiting Advantages, 2001, as cited in Braddy, Thompson, Wuensch, & Grossnickle, 2003). One estimate indicated that online recruitment can decrease hiring cycle time by 25% (Cober et al., 2000). Another study using data from 50 *Fortune* 500 companies showed that the use of online recruitment reduced their average hiring cycle time of 43 days by 6 days and allowed them to cut 4 days off the application process (Recruitsoft/iLogos, cited in Cappelli, 2001). Another study at Cisco Systems found that online recruitment allowed the company to fill job openings quickly. When Cisco Systems adopted online recruitment, the company attracted more than 500,000 individuals in one month, which enabled them to hire 1,200 people in just three months (Cober et al., 2000).

It is evident from this brief review that online recruiting can decrease the cycle time and enhance the speed with which vacancies are filled, but this leads to other questions that need to be answered. Does this speediness enable organizations to hire the most qualified employees? Do these hires remain with the organizations? What is the diversity of these new hires? These questions and others need to be examined further to determine whether certain disadvantages of online recruiting may offset the benefits of the shortened hiring cycle.

Recruitment Objective: Psychological Contract Fulfillment, Employee Satisfaction, and Retention Rates

Psychological contract fulfillment, employee satisfaction, and retention rates are three other important goals of the recruitment process. These three goals have a close relationship. The psychological contract refers to the employees' beliefs about the reciprocal obligations and promises between them and their organizations (Morrison & Robinson, 1997). Not surprisingly, when employees believe that their psychological contracts with the organization have been breached, they are more dissatisfied and more likely to leave the organization (Rousseau, 1990). Thus, it is important to explore the extent to which online recruitment can help ensure that employees' psychological contracts are fulfilled.

The information gathered and disseminated during the recruitment process shapes the expectations that lead to psychological contract fulfillment, which directly affects employee satisfaction and retention rates (Breaugh & Starke, 2000). There are numerous types of expectations that shape the psychological contract. These expectations include the work role (skills use, job performance), social relations (coworker and customer interactions), economic rewards (raises, monetary incentives), and company culture (Baker, 1985). So let's look at one factor, such as corporate culture, to provide an example. Chen, Lin, and Chen (2012) found that online applicants' perceptions of organizational culture positively influence the perception of their fit with the organization and the choice of organization to work. In addition, Braddy, Meade, Michael, and Fleenor (2009) found websites that incorporated culture-specific, or relevant, testimonials would more strongly convey culture perceptions to viewers than would websites containing null testimonials and policies. The use of online recruitment can truly impact the psychological contract. Therefore, it is critical during the recruitment phase that both the potential employee and the employer communicate what these expectations are and recognize whether this employment relationship will be able to meet the expectations of both parties (Baker, 1985).

Information that is provided by the applicant and by the recruiting company is a crucial part of the recruitment process. Oftentimes, the recruitment process is rushed by the recruiters, who want to complete the task of filling job openings. When a process is rushed, job seekers may find incomplete or vague information regarding job openings and company expectations. Furthermore, when job seekers receive sugarcoated information from recruiters that exaggerates the opportunities and provides unrealistic expectations about the company, then the expectations of employees are incongruent with those of the organization. Inaccurate, overly optimistic, or vague information is something organizations need to minimize or avoid. The use of such information can often lead to unrealistic expectations about the psychological contract between the organization and the individual. This circumstance is problematic for organizations because the new hires may begin to see the inconsistencies between their actual experiences and their expectations, which were formed throughout the recruitment process, and feel that their psychological contracts have been breached by their employer. Violations of the psychological contract can often result in negative attitudes and behaviors and higher levels of employee dissatisfaction and, eventually, will lead to greater turnover (Morrison & Robinson, 1997). Therefore, organizations really need to monitor and distribute accurate and timely information to potential job seekers to avoid such problems in the workplace.

Given that numerous companies now have their own websites, which contain a job page and endless space to provide information, more realistic information can be offered to job seekers. In addition, since the information is posted in real time, changes in content can be made at a moment's notice so that information is up to date and accurate. Therefore, it is no surprise that applicants rely more on posted information to form their expectations about the job and the company. Allen, Mahto, and Otondo (2007) found the amount of company information found on their website is positively related to job seekers' attraction to the organization. They also found the amount of job and company information provided on the company website is positively related to attitude toward the website.

Thus, employers can use websites to help provide realistic expectations about their companies and form psychological contracts. Companies really need to make sure that the message being conveyed on their websites is producing the psychological contract that can be fulfilled for both the employees and the employer. Once again, because the fulfillment of the psychological contract affects satisfaction and turnover levels, it is worthwhile for companies to convey realistic information about what new hires should expect and what will be expected of them—these expectations form the basis of the psychological contract. The use of a realistic recruitment message and the employment brand message should be the focus.

Realistic Recruitment Message

A realistic recruitment message is one that describes the organization and the job as they truly are without sugarcoating (Heneman & Judge, 2006). One important tool many organizations use is the realistic job preview. A **realistic job preview** shows applicants the positive and negative attributes of a job they are applying for to see if this job is truly what they desire or thought it was (Wanous, 1992). Realistic job previews can be communicated through written information that is posted on the employers' websites, but more and more companies are using video clips or Webcams that allow candidates to view what it is like to work for the organization in real time. One example is found at Target, a large retail organization, which posts video clips on its website, so you can see what working there is like (http://sites.target.com/site/en/company/page.jsp?ref=nav_footer_careers&contentId=WCMP04–030796). Some companies are taking this a step further by allowing some kind of interaction with current employees so applicants can gain realistic information about what it is like to work for the company. One example of a company that uses this feature is Cisco Systems, which offers online applicants a chance to "Make a Friend at Cisco." This allows the applicant to communicate with someone inside Cisco, who can describe what it is like to work for the organization (Cascio, 1998). Another interesting example is found at McKinsey & Company. On their website they provide an in-depth look at what you will do on the job by showing various employees with various job titles and their typical week activities in great detail (McKinsey, 2012).

In addition to realistic job previews, organizations are also using the unlimited space on their company websites to provide a **realistic culture preview** (Cober et al., 2003; McCourt-Mooney, 2000). A realistic culture preview allows an organization to expand beyond the traditional job information and provide information about the company philosophy, value systems, history, diversity, salary structure, and benefits. This information could be vital for constructing realistic expectations in forming the psychological contract. An interesting example can be found at Accenture's website in the career section (www.careers.accenture .com/us-en/working/overview/pages/index.aspx). Accenture provides detailed information about their core values, focus on teamwork, investing in training and development, providing a supportive work environment, and sharing their skills in the community. This company definitely provided information beyond the basic job and company information and would help to gauge if one should apply to such a place.

Research has shown that the availability of particular information (i.e., advancement opportunities, salary) can have a positive impact on applicants' attraction to an organization (Cober et al., 2003; Mohamed, Orife, & Wibowo, 2002). The use of a realistic culture preview is also helpful since often applicants seek out jobs and organizations that best fit their own personal values and beliefs (Dineen, Ash, & Noe, 2002). Providing this information about corporate culture could help develop a better relationship between the organization and the applicant and could lead to the building of trust between the applicant and the organization, which is key in the psychological contract. In addition, if the company fits the applicants' values and beliefs, they may experience higher satisfaction and stay with the company longer. Since research has shown that applicants feel that they have a better chance of collecting realistic information from websites than from traditional sources (Rozelle & Landis, 2002), online recruitment is a critical recruitment tool.

Overall, the use of realistic recruitment messages in online recruitment should enable organizations to increase the degree to which employees perceive that their psychological contracts are fulfilled and should also enhance satisfaction and retention levels. Realistic recruitment messages should not only help organizations attract applicants who possess the skills and values that are aligned with those of the company but also communicate what employers are looking for in candidates applying for job openings. This communication could potentially help applicants construct realistic expectations, which could lead to a well-developed psychological contract that could be fulfilled in the future on the job if candidates are selected for positions. The fulfillment of the psychological contract could lead to a long and productive relationship for both the employee and the employer, so satisfaction and retention rates could be increased.

Employment Brand Messages

A company's **employment brand** can be a powerful tool to attract applicants to its website. A company's employment brand is often based on the organization's well-known values or distinctive image and culture (think Southwest Airlines or Apple). A company often sets itself apart from competitors by means of its employment brand (Stone, Stone-Romero, & Lukaszewski, 2003; Ulrich, 2001) or uses the brand to help create a particular image in hopes of attracting job applicants (Galanaki, 2002). For example, Cisco Systems uses its image of being technologically advanced and, therefore, relies only on recruitment through the Internet to fill openings (Cascio, 1998).

Research shows that the use of online recruitment can help some organizations create a specific brand identity in the labor market (Chapman & Webster, 2003; Ulrich, 2001). One unique example is found on the Johnson & Johnson website (http://careers.jnj.com/home). The firm brands itself as having a "small-company environment, big-company impact philosophy"—to attract individuals who are familiar with the Johnson & Johnson brand but don't want to get lost among numerous employees. In addition, the current brand or reputation is another way that companies can lure applicants to their job pages, by simply linking employment opportunities to their products and services. Doing this is quite helpful in attracting applicants who are familiar with the company's products but possibly never thought about the company's employment opportunities.

Overall, the employment brand may be an important determinant of applicants' attraction to organizations and of subsequent satisfaction and retention rates. If a person believes in and identifies with a particular company, he or she may find fulfillment and satisfaction and stay there if extended a job opportunity. However, more research is needed in this area to examine the direct impact of this type of message.

Recruitment Objective: Quantity, Quality, and Diversity of Applicants

The quantity, quality, and diversity of applicants are three other important recruitment objectives (Breaugh & Starke, 2000). Each topic will be discussed in greater detail.

Quantity of Applicants

Online recruitment is extremely convenient for applicants and is available to them 24 hours per day and seven days a week. It also allows them to fill out an online application or upload a resume for various positions in a matter of seconds. Although this convenience can be very beneficial, it may encourage applicants to apply for jobs without assessing their own qualifications for each job, which can result in a large number of applicants for every job opening (Chapman & Webster, 2003). To offset this volume, organizations need to put into place methods to screen out applicants who are not qualified. Many organizations are using resume management systems that allow for keyword searches (i.e., of specific degrees or skills) to scale down the large volume of applications. However, some caution needs to be taken when using keyword searches. Applicants may tailor the content of their resumes to the words in the job descriptions to enhance their chances of passing through the resume-screening systems (MacMillan, 2007; Mohamed et al., 2002), which may result in the selection of those who use the right words but are not necessarily the most qualified for the job. Therefore, organizations using online recruiting need to be concerned with the quality of the numerous applications received.

Quality and Diversity of Applicants

Two other important goals of the recruitment process are to generate highly qualified applicants with diverse backgrounds. The quality and **diversity of the applicant pool** are determined by the users of online recruitment. Some research indicates that online recruitment systems place artificial limits on the applicant pool. Most applicants who typically use online recruitment are computer-literate, well-educated, driven individuals with a high need for achievement, seeking relatively high-level jobs (McManus & Ferguson, 2003). However, research also shows that these applicants are more likely to be job hoppers than those who do not use online recruitment (McManus & Ferguson, 2003). In addition, online recruitment users often have low levels of computer anxiety or high levels of computer self-efficacy (Marakas, Yi, & Johnson, 1998). Research has also found that college students preferred online recruitment methods as compared with other recruitment methods such as newspapers or television (Zusman & Landis, 2002).

Although online recruitment appeals to fairly well-educated applicants, research shows that there are also ethnic differences in the use of online recruiting, with these initiatives attracting 7% of Hispanics, 9% of blacks, and 16% of whites (Kuhn & Skuterud, 2000). However, the research findings on ethnicity and online recruitment usage have been somewhat contradictory. For example, one study found that African Americans often react quite favorably to online recruiting and use it to self-select themselves out of the application process for a poor fit job or organization (McManus & Ferguson, 2003). Some possible explanations for the low Internet usage of various groups include lack of access to computers, lack of computer skills, and poverty (Kuhn & Skuterud, 2000). Others have argued that cultural differences in relationship orientation may affect Hispanics' use of online recruiting systems (Stone, Lukaszewski, & Isenhour, 2005).

There are also gender and age differences in responses to online recruitment. Employed men are more likely to search for jobs on the Internet than employed women (Kuhn & Skuterud, 2000). The reason for this may be that females generally have more computer anxiety and lower computer self-efficacy than males (Jackson, Ervin, Gardner, & Schmitt, 2001). Research has also shown that older individuals (55 or above) tend to have lower computer self-efficacy (Reed, Doty, & May, 2005) than younger adults, which may inhibit older applicants' ability and perceived ability to use online recruiting. Given these findings, it is clear that the use of online recruitment may limit the extent to which an organization attracts qualified women, Hispanic Americans, and older workers.

Thus, if an organization relies only on Web-based recruitment, the system will indirectly influence the overall composition of the workforce and decrease the level of diversity within the organization (Stone et al., 2005). Therefore, online recruiting may facilitate workforce homogeneity and, as a result, hinder innovative and creative decision making (Schneider, Goldstein, & Smith, 1995). Organizations must be aware of the potential biases created by their recruiting practices and align their recruiting strategies with their overall business strategies to create competitive advantage (Becker & Gerhart, 1996; Wright & Snell, 1998). For example, if an organization wants to hire an individual for an HRIS-related job, the organization may find Web recruiting to be a cost-efficient and effective source of recruitment because members of the applicant pool are technologically proficient and would most likely use the Web in their job searches. Conversely, if the organization is looking for a person in a nontechnical position (e.g., staff writer, creative consultant), then the use of traditional recruitment sources may be more effective than the use of online recruitment alone.

Overall, it is apparent that online recruitment may help organizations meet the objective of increasing the number of job applicants (Chapman & Webster, 2003; Galanaki, 2002). However, it is not clear whether the use of online recruitment will help organizations attract high-quality applicants. If an organization is looking for job applicants with particular skills (e.g., computer skills), then it may be able to find and attract such applicants with online recruitment. However, the use of online recruitment may also result in some dysfunctional consequences. For instance, online recruiting may attract job hoppers and may be less likely to attract those with low levels of computer self-efficacy. Furthermore, online recruitment may have a negative impact on the extent to which organizations are able to attract women, older workers, and some minorities (e.g., Hispanic Americans). However, research is not clear about the extent to which online recruitment helps organizations attract African Americans. Further research is needed on this topic.

Organizations need to be very cautious about using only online recruitment, especially since this recruitment method may not help organizations meet their diversity-related goals. There is clearly potential for an adverse impact on the number of applications received from women, minorities, and older workers, which may pose potential legal problems for organizations (Hogler, Henle, & Bemus, 1998). Therefore, it is important that organizations consider the potential legal issues associated with the use of online recruitment and ensure that all qualified applicants are given the opportunity to apply for jobs (Stone et al., 2003). Furthermore, organizations may want to use online recruitment in conjunction with other recruitment sources (e.g., newspaper ads, job fairs) to ensure that their recruitment processes are fair.

Attributes of the Recruiting Website

Another factor that may affect the acceptance and effectiveness of online recruiting is the design of the website. In general, the best website design is user-friendly in that users can easily navigate and browse through multiple Web pages to find information. The extent to which the website is usable or not has been referred to as "website usability" in the empirical literature (Cober et al., 2003; Karat, 1997; Nielsen, 2000). The construct of website usability has been conceptualized as encompassing a number of dimensions, including navigability, content information, and aesthetic features. Each dimension and its use in recruitment are further discussed in this section.

First, **navigability** can be defined as the overall ease with which a user can browse through multiple Web pages to locate topics of interest. Hosting a website that displays current information and includes active hyperlinks to retrieve information is essential in maintaining user interest within the site. To achieve this goal, organizations should follow the "three-click" rule for users to locate information of interest. For instance, users who wish to browse job opportunities on the organization's website should be able to reach the desired Web page by the third hyperlink from the home Web page. Accordingly, research has shown that applicants have more favorable impressions of an organization when its website is easy to navigate as opposed to being difficult to navigate (Braddy, Meade, & Kroustalis, 2008). Such favorable impressions are important to elicit within applicants because they may lead to greater organizational attraction (e.g., Allen et al., 2007; Lyons & Marler, 2011).

Next, **content** information refers to the degree to which the website hosts relevant information that the user deems valuable and informative in nature. Providing information that the user desires is another mechanism by which organizations can sustain user interest and satisfaction with the website. The **media richness** theory (Daft & Lengel, 1986) has been frequently applied to explain why hosting relevant content information is beneficial to applicants. Specifically, this theory contends that communication effectiveness is a function of the degree to which media sources reduce user uncertainty and equivocality (Daft & Lengel, 1986). Rich media sources (a website) contain enough relevant and accessible information to reduce user uncertainty and subsequent anxiety toward the target source (an organization). Conversely, when a source has a low degree of richness, inadequate information fails to reduce users' uncertainty about the organization, which may then lead to ambivalence and anxiety toward the target source. The result of this process may stimulate positive or negative attitudes toward the organization, such as more favorable impressions of an organization's image (Cable & Yu, 2006). Thus, an organization would be advised to host a website that includes information about the organization and its products, available job opportunities, developmental opportunities, compensation, and culture (Barber & Roehling, 1993; Cable, Aiman-Smith, Mulvey, & Edwards, 2000; Cable & Graham, 2000; Judge & Cable, 1997). For example, Walker, Field, Giles, Armenakis, and Bernerth (2009) found when organizations posted employee testimonials on their employment Web pages, their sites generated greater organizational attraction than other websites that did not have such testimonials. Consequently, hosting information that applicants value will most likely facilitate person-job (P-J) and person-organization (P-O) "fit"-related decisions.

Specifically, when applicants perceive similarity between their qualifications and what is required by the job (P-J) and between their personality and the organization's values (P-O), it is more likely that they will pursue employment with the organization (e.g., Kristof-Brown, Zimmerman, & Johnson, 2005). Indeed, perceived fit has been found to be one of the strongest predictors of organizational attraction (Uggerslev, Fassina, & Kraichy, 2012). Overall, these applicant-evaluative processes cannot be formed if the organization does not include useful information on its website. For example, many organizations (e.g., Texas Instruments) provide a list of cultural values on their employment Web pages. It is important to note, however, that the more customizable information an organization provides on its Web page, the more likely an applicant will engage in appropriate **self-selection** behavior (to apply or not apply for a job within the organization). In other words, if the website provides direct feedback to applicants regarding their P-O or P-J fit, the online recruiting effort will likely attract a more qualified applicant pool (Dineen et al., 2002; Dineen, Ling, Ash, & DelVecchio, 2007; Dineen & Noe, 2009). Therefore, in order to avoid the "dark side" of Web recruitment, an organization must first determine and maximize the information that is most likely going to influence fit perceptions and then engage the user to seek and understand this information. For example, professional sports teams who advertise job openings on a third-party website, www.teamworkonline.com, frequently have potential applicants respond to a few P-J fit-related questions before they are allowed to apply for the job in question.

Finally, companies should consider how the **aesthetic features** of their websites engage user interest and attention. These features encompass the overall stylistic or innovative aspects of a website, such as contrasting colors, pictures, animation, and playfulness, which keep the user engaged while he or she navigates through multiple Web pages (Cober, Brown, Keeping, & Levy, 2004). When a user is engaged, it is more likely that he or she will maintain interest in the organization and browse for more information about the organization (Cober et al., 2003). Ultimately, an applicant may perceive these innovative features of a website as "signals" about broader organizational attributes, such as the organization's culture and image (Lyons & Marler, 2011). For example, if a website has attractive stylistic features (e.g., the Goldman Sachs's website, www.gs.com), it may stimulate more favorable perceptions of organizational image, which has been found to be positively related to organizational attraction (Lyons & Marler, 2011). These results are especially important for entrepreneurial or smaller firms that wish to attract qualified applicants to their organizations. That is, when an organization invests in the latest Web design, a user or applicant will be more likely to perceive that organization as reputable. Similarly, an information technology (IT) firm would be wise to invest in the latest Web design software to generate applicant or even customer perceptions that the organization values innovation and creativity. This investment is especially prudent from the perspective that this firm's potential applicants will most likely be attracted to an organization that values innovation and creativity.

Integrating these attributes together, a website's **usability** has been found to affect applicant perceptions and attitudes toward the organization. A recent meta-analytic study by Uggerslev et al. (2012) found a corrected correlation coefficient of .41 between website usability and organizational attraction—in other words, the more usable the website was perceived, the more likely the applicant was attracted to the organization. A study by Allen et al. (2007) found that website **attributes** were positively related to applicants' intentions to pursue employment, which is the immediate precursor to the actual behavior of applying for a job within an organization. Toward this end, in a sample of U.S. state government recruitment websites, Selden and Orenstein (2011) determined that website usability was positively related to applicant pool quantity (i.e., total number of applicants). All these studies converge on the finding that website usability perceptions influence applicant attitudes toward an organization. As a result, organizations should be attuned to how their websites influence applicant perceptions and be prepared to update their Web design to embody high navigability, content fidelity, and engaging aesthetic features. HR and IT employees should monitor the usability of their firm's website by surveying applicant perceptions of and reactions to the Web recruiting process, especially in situations where the Web recruiting function entails gathering applicant data and preliminary online ability testing.

The decision to host job openings on organizational websites and to have the capability of screening job applicants for positions should be based on the firm's resources and strategy. With this statement in mind, we can see that the purpose of an organization's recruitment website can be classified as either recruiting and screening oriented or as just recruitment oriented (Williamson, Lepak, & King, 2003). A **recruiting- and screening-oriented website** has the capability to list job openings and accept applications through a secure server. Conversely, a website that focuses only on recruiting just hosts a list of job openings with the option of submitting an application via mail, e-mail, or fax to an organizational representative. Williamson et al. (2003) articulated that both recruitment orientations can be effective in attracting applicants; however, it could be contended that applicants may prefer submitting personal information through websites that they perceive to be secure and trustworthy (Stone et al., 2003). Therefore, if an organization does not have the financial resources to invest in building a secure server to accept applications, an alternative would be to still offer information about the organization and its culture on the website's employment Web page and then have a hyperlink that connects interested applicants to jobs that are hosted by a third-party vendor, such as Monster.com. A more logical alternative would be to host an organization's job opportunities on a third-party vendor's website (e.g., Monster.com, Careerbuilder.com) and include a hyperlink on each announcement that connects the applicant to the organization's home Web page. These alternatives would allow the organization to achieve the benefits associated with Web recruiting and provide the applicant an opportunity to learn more about the organization by browsing the firm's home Web page. Also, from the applicant's perspective, these options would reduce any anxiety or adverse perceptions about lack of privacy or about Web security concerning those organizations that the applicant does not know well or does not entirely trust.

Recruitment Strategies and Social Networking

Organizations have always used social relationships and networking, including employee referrals, to attract talent. Increasingly, social networking sites such as Facebook, Twitter, and LinkedIn are gaining in use and popularity, and they now provide a unique method of allowing recruitment professionals to source, contact, and screen both active and passive job candidates. For example, domestically in the United States, the United Parcel Service (UPS) uses Facebook, Twitter, LinkedIn, and Google Plus to post job openings and host relevant information about the company and its culture (Zielinski, 2012). Internationally, the Hard Rock Café solely used Facebook as a recruiting source to hire 120 employees for a new restaurant in Florence, Italy (Colao, 2012). Although there are benefits to using **social networking websites** (SNWs) for recruitment and selection purposes, there are also concerns regarding its proliferation, targeted applicant pool, use in selection, saliency of more negative profile information than positive, and merit as a worthwhile recruiting source.

- First, SNWs and online search engines are being used more frequently now as an HR tool (SHRM, 2008). For example, a recent Society for Human Resource Management (SHRM) survey determined that more than half of responding organizations were going to increase their use of SNWs for recruiting purposes (Zielinski, 2012). In addition, a few organizations may use SNWs to evaluate and infer an applicant's personality and/or integrity (e.g., Kluemper, Rosen, & Mossholder, 2012). However, most organizations do not have a formal policy on its use as an HR tool (SHRM, 2008).

- During recruitment, SNWs are primarily used to search for passive applicants, particularly at the middle-management levels, who might not otherwise apply or be contacted by an organization (SHRM, 2008). Similar to the benefits of Web recruiting, organizations can potentially expand the sheer number of potential applicants by examining the profiles of their followers on Twitter, Facebook, and LinkedIn and sending job openings to those followers who are perceived as qualified. However, they may also be used to recruit active applicants, especially at the full-time, entry-level rank and even hourly or part-time positions (Colao, 2012). For example, Ben & Jerry's has a Facebook page that hosts job openings and allows applicants to begin the application process by clicking the "Join Our Talent Pool" tab (Colao, 2012). Further, this page also allows applicants to examine how their Facebook profile information matches or fits any current job openings.

- Next, organizations may be reluctant to use SNWs for employee selection purposes because of potential legal issues associated with using SNWs in this way and the inability to verify with confidence the profile information on these sites. In regard to the former issue, by viewing profiles on SNWs, organizations may be discriminating, either explicitly or implicitly, applicants belonging to a protected class. For instance, an applicant profile picture can reveal the applicant's gender, perceived age, ethnicity, and/or disability. Organizations who view and judge applicant profiles on SNWs likely increase the probability of engaging in disparate treatment (i.e., intentional discrimination) or even disparate/adverse impact (Davison, Maraist, & Bing, 2011), leaving the organization susceptible to litigation. In terms of the latter issue, organizations may be unable to infer, with relative validity, the qualifications, personality, and/or integrity-related information on an applicant's profile. In turn, the inability to evaluate this information validly will create error in the selection process. With that said, however, the ability to evaluate this information validly likely depends on how "public" the information is available to the organization. Toward this end, relatively new research using Facebook profiles suggests that outside "raters" (e.g., HR recruiters) can, to a degree, validly and reliably assess a "target's" (e.g., applicant's) personality if the profile information is publicly available (Kluemper & Rosen, 2009; Kluemper et al., 2012). Additionally, personality ratings from outside sources have been shown to be significantly related to the target's job performance, hirability, and academic performance (Kluemper et al., 2012). Taken together, although research is starting to shed new light on the issue of evaluating the credibility of profile information, organizations should use this information with extreme caution due to the likelihood of discriminating against applicants belonging to a protected class.

- The saliency of negative information on SNW profiles seems to have a greater influence on selection decisions than positive information (SHRM, 2008). In general, people tend to recall more negative events than positive events (Baumeister, Bratslavsky, Finkenauer, & Vohs, 2001). Applicants who reveal confidential information about former or current employers, post slanderous discussions of the applicant's friends, peers, or coworkers, and/or display profile information that contradicts their resume will likely be viewed as unethical by organizational representatives, which damages the applicant's perceived integrity or reputation and likelihood of receiving a job offer. As noted by Baumeister et al. (2001), ". . . bad reputations are easy to acquire but difficult to lose, whereas good reputations are difficult to acquire but easy to lose" (p. 344).

- Finally, considering the legal implications, many question whether SNWs are a worthwhile recruitment source and screening device (Davison et al., 2011). For instance, do SNWs yield higher-quality applicants and are they more economical in terms of cost per hire than traditional sources such as employee referrals? Unfortunately, very few organizations calculate the return-on-investment (ROI) of their SNW usage in recruitment (Zielinski, 2012). However, a few organizations are indeed evaluating SNWs's ROI. In particular,

UPS tracks how many candidates are transferred from the SNWs (e.g., Facebook, Twitter) to their careers web page (www.UPSjobs.com) and examines how many candidates complete an application. This estimate is then compared to how many are considered during the selection process and then eventually hired. Ultimately, returns are evaluated against the cost of developing the SNW (estimated to be $7,500 per site) and the labor costs involved with updating the site (Zielinski, 2012). In an example mentioned before, Hard Rock Café in Florence, Italy, solely used Facebook to recruit a staff of 120 employees, which resulted in a recruitment cost of $2,000. Hard Rock Café representatives, however, concluded that the cost of solely using Facebook as a recruitment source was less than a tenth of what they usually spend on recruiting staff for a new restaurant (Colao, 2012). Although success stories exist involving the value of SNWs for recruitment, more research is needed to determine whether the reward (e.g., faster hiring/time-to-fill) offsets risk (e.g., increased probability of litigation) when compared to other recruitment sources.

The Relationship of e-Recruiting and HRIS

The applicant's information acquired through the company's online recruitment can be funneled into the company's HRIS. The use of the HRIS in the recruitment process can make the process more efficient and effective by having information readily available and usable at a moment's notice. Many of the suggestions made in the above sections are illustrated here. One important function the HRIS provides is applicant tracking. Applicant tracking allows for the generation of applicants' profiles, which are compiled through application blanks and/or resumes. These profiles can aid the hiring manager in their employment decisions. Recruiters or the hiring managers can perform key word searches to find qualified applicants for available jobs. Applicant tracking also allows recruiters, hiring managers, and sometimes the applicant themselves, to see where they are in the recruitment process. The HRIS can provide information about the yield ratios for each recruiting source, cost effectiveness of the recruitment process as a whole or by recruitment source, and to support EEO/AA analyses. Applicant data can be also stored and searched for future vacancies. Lastly, when applicants become new hires the HRIS provides the data to populate the core HR system and other HR purposes, such as payroll and benefits.

Online Recruitment Guidelines

Stone et al. (2005) offer the following research-based guidelines on the effective design and use of online recruitment strategies:

- Online recruiting is more suitable for well-known firms with excellent employer branding.

- It should be used as one of many sources of recruitment.

- It is more suitable when many candidates are needed for high-level jobs requiring high levels of education.

- Organizations should be aware of the limitations of this method, such as its limited ability to attract highly qualified candidates and minority candidates. It may in fact attract job hoppers.

- The websites should be easy to use and navigate and designed to attract, not screen, candidates.

- Online screening systems should be based on job analyses.

- E-recruiting systems should provide realistic previews of jobs and of the firm.

- Effectiveness should be regularly reviewed and continuously improved based on feedback from job applicants.

- Online recruiting should be culturally sensitive and suit people from diverse backgrounds, including those with low education levels and low computer self-efficacy.

- Online recruiting must incorporate privacy protection policies, including those limiting the collection of information to only employment-specific data and those restricting access to and distribution of such data.

In summary, organizations should consider the extent to which online recruitment enables them to meet their recruitment objectives. Our previous discussion provides evidence that online recruitment can help organizations reduce the costs of recruiting, decrease the cycle time of filling job vacancies, and generate large quantities of applicants. However, organizations must remember that these are not the only recruitment objectives and must focus on finding the impact of online recruitment on the other recruitment objectives (quality and diversity of applicants, psychological contract fulfillment, employee satisfaction, retention rates). In addition, the attributes of the website can affect the acceptance and effectiveness of online recruiting. The best website design is user-friendly in that users can easily navigate and browse through multiple Web pages to find information that is valuable and conveys whether or not the applicants fit not only the job requirements but also the organization's value system. Last, the aesthetic features of a website, combined with the content presented, may shape the attributions of job seekers toward the organization in a positive manner. However, the attraction of applicants to job openings is only the beginning—organizations now have to focus on assessing the applicants who constitute their applicant pools. Therefore, we now need to switch our focus to a discussion of selection.

Selection and Technology

This section focuses on tests and assessments of individual employees and candidates, which are at the heart of the evaluation processes that enable organizations to manage their talent. These tools are used for selecting employees, placing them in positions in the organization, training and developing them, promoting them, and evaluating them. Tests and assessments are important for HRIS because they provide data that are used for making organizational decisions. To explore the data-based decision-making process in further detail, we focus our discussion on the use of tests and assessments to make a critical decision—whether or not to hire a particular candidate.

What Are Selection Tests and Assessments, and Why Are They Used?

Most organizations that seek HRIS expertise on selection will likely consider the term *test* to refer to traditional multiple-choice examinations that can be used to measure ability, personality, or knowledge, as well as to skills tests, such as typing tests. Organizations seeking assessments may be referring to these same tests, or, alternatively, they may be thinking of different types of **selection procedures** and tools, such as reference checks or work samples. Whatever the label, tests and assessments are job-related decision-making tools that provide information about candidates, information that organizations can use in selection. Figure 12.2 contains examples of the major tests and assessment instruments. For this section of the chapter, we use the terms *test, assessment, selection tool,* and *selection procedure* interchangeably to refer to any tool designed to measure attributes of individuals for the purpose of selecting employees.

Figure 12.2 **Specific Examples of Tests and Assessments**

Knowledge test: A multiple-choice training posttest of knowledge of the tools, machines, and equipment used in a factory and designed to measure how well the new hire has learned essential job information taught in classroom training.

Skill test: A practical exercise or simulation that tests the candidate's effectiveness in using Microsoft Word software.

Ability test: The Watson-Glaser Critical Thinking Appraisal, a multiple-choice reasoning test, in which the examinee reads a short or medium-length passage and draws logical conclusions about the statements, choosing the answer that makes the best logical sense. Many other ability tests are similar in appearance and format to educational tests that are familiar to students (e.g., the Scholastic Aptitude Test [SAT], the Miller Analogies Test [MAT], and the Graduate Record Examination [GRE]).

Personal attributes test: A multiple-choice personality assessment in which the examinee reads statements such as "I enjoy making presentations in front of large groups of people" and indicates the extent to which she or he agrees or disagrees with these statements. Results are scored on several scales or dimensions.

Work simulation: An in-basket exercise in which the examinee must examine the variety of types of information (correspondence, reports, and other information) and also interact with simulated coworkers, employees, or other business associates (whether computer simulated or role-played by actors over the telephone or in person). The examinee is evaluated on a variety of dimensions, from accuracy and the quality of decisions to work-related competencies, interpersonal skills, and other personal attributes.

Here is a more comprehensive list of assessments, as provided by the Society for Industrial and Organizational Psychology (SIOP):

> Selection procedures refer to any procedure used singly or in combination to make a personnel decision, including, but not limited to, paper-and-pencil tests, computer-administered tests, performance tests, work samples, inventories (e.g., personality, interest), projective techniques [ambiguous stimuli such as inkblots or pictures, often used for personality assessment], polygraph [lie detector] examinations, individual assessments, assessment center evaluations [summaries of multiple assessments, as evaluated by multiple raters], biographical data forms or scored application blanks, interviews, educational requirements, experience requirements, reference checks, background investigations, physical requirements (e.g., height or weight), physical ability tests, appraisals of job performance, computer-based test interpretations, and estimates of advancement potential. (SIOP, 2003, p. 3)

While this chapter will address a variety of important concepts about selection and assessment for personnel decision making, a full discussion is beyond the chapter's scope. Interested readers are encouraged to consult additional sources, including the SIOP document. We also recommend the text by Guion (1998), one of the essential references on the topic. The U.S. Department of Labor (1999) offers a less technical summary white paper, and the SIOP website (www.siop.org) provides links to many useful websites and papers.

Why Is Assessment Important for HRIS?

When used for employee selection, assessments have value because they assist organizations in identifying those individuals who are more likely to succeed on the job and prevent the hire of those who are less likely to succeed. The following paragraphs provide several reasons that it is important for HR managers to understand the purpose and use of assessments.

All Organizations Use Assessments

Resumes are assessment tools, and so are interviews. Every company that has ever had more than one candidate for a job opening has assessed in some way, whether or not it used structured, professionally developed assessments to make hiring decisions. Increasingly, human resource information systems are supporting organizations' selection processes: how firms identify the most qualified candidates and determine whom to choose for internal positions and promotions. The reason is that many organizations are using some type of selection instrument or tool in addition to the employment interview, and, in most cases, the tools involve HRIS. In 40% of the *Fortune* 100 companies, for example, there is some form of individual assessment of job candidates (Shaffer & Schmidt, 2006). In 2005, *Newsweek* estimated that the business of testing and assessing job candidates, including both the development and administration of tests, was a $400 million industry, growing at 8% per year.

Organization Leaders Know That Employees' Abilities, Skills, and Personal Attributes Are Critical for Success

To see the evidence, pick up a book by a business leader, such as former General Electric CEO Jack Welch, or a popular-press book on successful businesses, such as *Good to Great* (Collins, 2001). If, as leaders often say, an organization's greatest asset is its people, then selection determines the value of the company's most important advantage.

Some Selection Systems Work Better Than Others

Better-designed selection systems are more likely than poorly designed systems to select successful employees. In fact, many company-grown and commercially available assessments are of little value. The most frequent problems that occur include the following: (a) they assess attributes that are not relevant to job performance, (b) they are not used consistently or as intended, and (c) they are unreliable indicators of job-relevant attributes. HR departments must learn how to distinguish between effective and ineffective selection systems and how to choose or improve selection systems.

To be effective, assessments must be valid, they must provide information that is clearly related to their intended use, and the information must be related to the job's requirements in a manner that can be demonstrated by research. For instance, the research might show that the assessment mirrors the content of the job, such as a typing test or work sample that duplicates or simulates the actual job duties that are essential for employees to perform. Another aspect of validity involves the ability to predict important criteria: measures of work performance or behavior such as productivity, accident rate, absenteeism, tenure, reject rate, training score, and supervisory ratings of job-relevant behaviors, tasks, or activities (SIOP, 2003). For instance, an **ability test** can be shown to be valid if scores on the test are statistically correlated with scores on a post-hire training evaluation that measures the knowledge individuals have acquired that is critical for successful job performance. Unfortunately, many commercially available assessments are poorly designed and researched, and their creators make unjustifiable claims about their effectiveness. When deciding whether to purchase assessment tools and systems from vendors, the organization should always obtain validation documentation that follows professional and legal guidelines, including the federal government's *Uniform Guidelines on Employee Selection Procedures* (U.S. Equal Employment Opportunity Commission, 1978; see also www.uniformguidelines.com) and the SIOP *Principles* publication (2003).

Importantly, validity involves not only research but also proper use. It would be irresponsible to use a test for a purpose other than that for which it was validated, such as installing a typing test to predict training success if there is no reason to believe the two would be related. Thus, the selection system and the methods, procedures, and policies concerning the use of selection tools matter as much as the tools themselves.

Employee Selection Is Regulated by Antidiscrimination Laws

Many laws, such as the Civil Rights Act of 1991 and the Americans with Disabilities Act, regulate companies' employee selection decisions. HRIS experts can contribute to their organizations by being aware of these **antidiscrimination laws**. The primary intent of these laws is to prohibit employment practices that unfairly discriminate against people in various protected groups, such as racial/ethnic minorities, women, and older candidates. In general, these federal, state, and local laws require that selection decisions must be valid and fair if they differentially affect protected group members. Selection decisions that differentially affect protected group members must provide equal treatment and be equally predictive of success for minorities and other protected groups in order to be fair and legal. The most commonly used term, but only part of the story, in an evaluation of fairness is *adverse impact,* which describes the circumstance of candidates from a protected group, *A* (e.g., women and minorities), being proportionately less likely to be hired than candidates in group *B*, which has the highest selection rate (for good discussions on the topic, see Guion, 1998; SIOP, 2003). Often, but not always, the group with the highest selection rate is the nonminority group. A guideline that federal and state enforcement agencies and courts use is the 80% rule. By this rule of thumb, adverse impact may be judged to exist if protected group *A*'s selection rate is less than .80 of group *B*'s selection rate. Importantly, having adverse impact does not, by itself, make a selection system illegal. A selection system that causes adverse impact may be legal if it can be shown to be job relevant (i.e., valid) and consistent with business necessity (i.e., important for business success). Interested readers should consult the U.S. Equal Employment Opportunity Commission (1978) and SIOP (2003) for more details.

The Value of Selection Is Quantifiable

HR departments and HRIS experts, in particular, should understand how to use selection-related data in order to (a) provide strategic information to the company and (b) demonstrate the return on the company's investment in assessments.

Being able to provide important strategic information about the company, such as the expected skill levels of new employees who have been tested and the implications of these skills for business unit performance, can help transform the HRIS manager's role from a supporting, transactional one to that of valued partner with key insight into the company's strategic directions. And, of course, being able to show a return on investment is essential for the survival of HRIS projects. A good system improves the quality of hires in a way that can be measured and verified. Although no selection system is perfect (not all individuals who are selected can be guaranteed to succeed and not necessarily all who are rejected would have been unsuccessful on the job), HRIS can measure the dollar value of selection to demonstrate its economic value as a company investment. This topic is discussed in more detail later in this chapter.

Technology Issues in Selection

The most common use of technology for selection systems is the use of computers to administer and score tests. HRIS experts need to be aware of several general concerns about the computer administration of selection procedures. First, if traditional **paper-and-pencil assessments** are computerized, does the computer version have different measurement properties? Second, as the capabilities of microprocessors increase, it is possible to make assessments that more closely simulate the job, that is, ones that closely approximate the work that would be done once the candidate is hired. What are the benefits and risks of high-fidelity work simulations? Third, how does online testing affect the validity of selection systems? Does the technology that allows candidates to take tests anywhere, and organizations' increasing interest in using that technology, compromise the test security that is present in traditional settings with proctored examinations?

Equivalence Between Conventional and Computerized Assessments

Most of the first **computerized assessments** were meant to look like their paper-and-pencil, low-tech counterparts, except that they were delivered on a computer and required candidates to answer questions (generally multiple choice) via a keyboard or a mouse or to take a computerized skill test (e.g., a typing test). Interestingly, although today there are also simulations that mirror the job, traditional multiple-choice tests still abound, in part because the format is easy to administer and score and in part because there are many good multiple-choice tests in use that predate the availability of inexpensive stand-alone computers and online testing.

Organizations tend to think that the paper-and-pencil and computerized forms (versions) of a test are interchangeable, assuming that the test items and instructions are the same. (Often, particularly in large organizations, both types are used, depending on the availability of computer facilities at different offices and whether or not large test sessions are conducted at recruiting events and at other locations where there are not enough computers available at once.) However, the assumption of equivalence may not be justified, and the HRIS expert must know when the assumption is warranted. The primary concern is that the mode of administration (paper or computer) will affect the measurement properties of the test. For assessments that do not include ability, such as **personality tests** and career interest inventories, most researchers have little concern that giving the test on paper will result in a different measure than would occur with a computerized test. However, there is clear evidence that the mode of administration matters for ability tests that are speeded, those for which there is time pressure and the possibility that candidates will not finish all the items in the allotted time (e.g., see Mead & Drasgow, 1993; Potosky & Bobko, 2004). For such tests, the physical or virtual materials and test administration methods affect the time (in seconds) it takes to complete a test item and, thus, the results. For instance, think of a paper test form that requires a candidate to match questions printed in booklets to an answer sheet; now imagine a computer screen on which the examinee sees one item at a time and uses a mouse to click on the answers. Total scores, average scores, and performance on individual test items are affected. The more speeded a test is, the more likely that there will be differences between the paper and computer results. In contrast, **power tests**, tests in which there is no designated time limit to create time pressure or in which the time limit is set such that most candidates will complete the test without working hastily, typically do not show differences between paper and computerized testing modes. To understand the differences, an industrial/organizational psychologist or some other expert in tests and measurements will conduct a study of the equivalence between the two. The study entails administering both types of tests, ideally to the same individuals, with the order of administration counterbalanced across participants, and examining and comparing the overall results and the statistical results for each item. Then, when necessary, a formula equating the two can be developed to adjust for differences. The result is a method of ensuring that, irrespective of whether the candidate takes the paper test or the computerized test, he or she will have the same opportunity to perform well.

Bandwidth Versus Fidelity: How Closely Should We Simulate the Job?

Technology has enabled organizations to create work sample simulations that represent the job with high fidelity. Company leaders may want this because they believe that no assessment could be nearly as good as a simulation that closely matches the work that will be performed on the job. However, as Figure 12.3 illustrates, an analysis of decades of assessment research has found that general cognitive ability tests can, on average, predict success virtually as well as simulations, and, when combined with other types of assessments, they can exceed the predictive ability of simulations. The bar chart in Figure 12.3 displays statistical correlations between assessment scores and job performance data. Schmidt and Hunter (1998) provided these data in a comprehensive meta-analysis, research that quantitatively summarizes the data from many studies on a particular topic—in this case, the personnel selection research literature. The research is most supportive of **work simulations**, ability tests, structured interviews, and personality testing. Higher scores on these types of assessments are predictive of higher job performance. For comparison, less valid assessments are also shown, such as education and training ratings and graphology (handwriting analysis), which has been shown to have little or no validity.

It is also important to be aware of the trade-off between **fidelity** and **bandwidth**, the range of settings to which the simulation might apply. For example, suppose that a management simulation is designed to closely represent a particular line of business in the actual organization chart and reporting structure, as well as the unique subject matter that is addressed in the management job from day to day. If the company then wants to use the simulation for a different business unit or job, the details that made the simulation highly appropriate in the first setting may interfere with its use in the other setting. The same problem applies to jobs and settings that change over time, as most do. Therefore, although as the HRIS expert you may be adept at creating an assessment that looks just like the job,

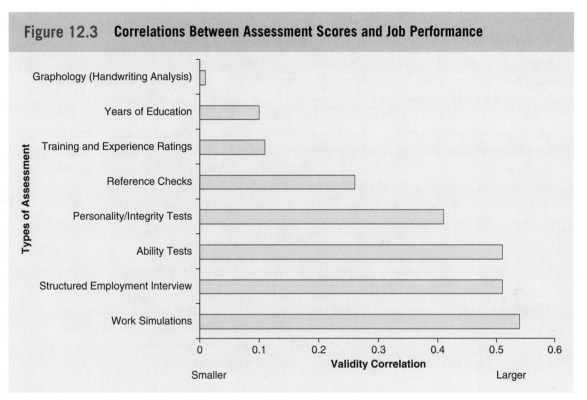

Figure 12.3   Correlations Between Assessment Scores and Job Performance

Source: Schmidt and Hunter (1998).

such a tool might have a narrow range of uses. Also, simulations generally require that the job candidate already knows how to do the job, at least at some basic level, or that the job is simple enough that the candidate can learn the job tasks quickly to perform the simulation. In general, HRIS managers should keep in mind that, depending on the effort and expense one is willing to expend on assessment development and installation, lower-fidelity simulations or combinations of other types of assessments might be preferable to a simulation that is highly job specific. For example, Schmidt and Hunter (1998) argue that an ability test might be the most efficient general assessment method:

> Of all procedures that can be used for all jobs, whether entry level or advanced, it has the highest validity and lowest application cost. Work sample measures are slightly more valid, but they are much more costly and can be used only with applicants who already know the job or have been trained for the occupation or job. (p. 264)

Validity and Security Issues
Created by Unproctored Online Testing

Numerous consulting companies offer online tests. These tests may be administered in the same way as paper-and-pencil or stand-alone computer tests, that is, they may be conducted in an office by a proctor who gives instructions, checks identification, and monitors the test session. **Online testing** also allows for the possibility of unproctored (unsupervised) administration, with tests taken anywhere at any time. (Note that this could also be said for other types of technology-enabled tests that are available, such as those administered by telephone keypad or telephone-based interactive voice response systems. Others that involve fixed facilities, in-store kiosks in particular, are similarly unproctored and convenient.) Such testing can be attractive to organizations because of its convenience for both the candidate and the hiring organization.

However, this convenience may come at a cost. A panel of industrial/organizational psychologists convened at the annual SIOP conference in 2006 and published an article that summarizes the issues well and describes the opinions of the various members of the panel. These individuals are employed by a range of different types of organizations: a university, several test-publishing firms, the U.S. government, and a publicly held company in the finance industry (Tippins et al., 2006). The issues they identified include candidate identity, test security and cheating, and fair access to testing for minorities.

Establishing candidate identity is a straightforward problem, currently without a straightforward solution. There is no failsafe method to verify who the test taker is. In contrast to in-office testing requiring identification, when testing is unproctored, anyone might be taking the test in the candidate's place. Perhaps a live video feed or a biometric method of verifying the candidate's identity would provide more assurance. Alternatively, the organization might choose to retest all the candidates who qualify, using a proctored setting. However, there are technical problems with evaluating and acting on score differences, and retesting diminishes the convenience and cost savings that were the original reasons for **unproctored testing** (Tippins et al., 2006).

A related issue is **test security**. One facet of this is keeping the test content under lock and key for future use. The HRIS manager must take precautions to prevent the test content from being copied and compromised. Another facet is preventing cheating. In addition to having someone else take the test or assist the candidate, the candidate might use resources that are not permitted (e.g., Internet search engines, offline dictionaries, calculators). Cheating is of particular concern when the tests have right answers (e.g., ability tests) or require skills that the candidate can have others perform (e.g., typing tests). Common sense tells us that the higher the stakes in a testing situation, the higher the likelihood of cheating.

HRIS experts also must be aware of a third issue, equal and fair access. In particular, tests must be fair to legally protected groups, yet unproctored testing and, indeed, Internet recruitment and candidate processing in general run the risk of having a chilling effect on minorities, who, because of the so-called "digital divide," might have greater difficulty accessing the Internet to apply for jobs. Organizations must provide for multiple ways to gain entry.

These problems do not have easy solutions for organizations that wish to rely on unproctored Internet testing. Tippins et al. (2006) discussed the pros and cons of unproctored Internet testing but did not come to a consensus about the ethics of administering unproctored tests and keeping the process fair. A practice commonly suggested by test providers is to follow up unproctored testing with proctored testing of applicants who "pass" the unproctored test and who satisfy other job qualification requirements.

Applying HRIS to Selection and Assessment

Selection systems are information management systems for organizational decision making and administration. Therefore, human resource information systems play an important part in their development and use. One uniquely HRIS-centered role is database design. Selection systems require the careful design of databases to store and keep track of selection data, both before and after individuals are hired, and the ability to link information in interrelated systems, such as candidate test data and demographics, employment data for those who are hired, and job movement and position histories within the company. Increasingly, HRIS experts will be called on to assist in integrating the organization's various HR systems. At a minimum, integration involves linking data in two or more systems, such as the candidate and employee identification data, so that one may conduct database queries and follow individuals as their information passes through the different systems. Integration often also involves linking transactional operations in a system such that, after the first system has conducted a transaction that requires follow-up in the next system, the first system contacts the next system to launch the required transaction. For instance, once a candidate has completed an online application, he or she may be automatically sent to another Web-based application to complete an assessment. The HRIS manager must have a conceptual understanding of what it means to link a test delivery system with other systems, such as applicant-tracking systems. In addition, organizations frequently wish to integrate a homegrown system with a vendor system or to integrate multiple systems, many or most of which are Internet based. Therefore, HRIS experts must have a technical knowledge of protocols and programming languages for sharing data between Web-based systems, such as eXtensible Markup Language (XML).

Another general HRIS role in selection systems is the development of **scoring and decision rules** and of the administrative functions of the system. Whether the output of the completed assessment is simple to interpret (e.g., pass/fail) or complicated (e.g., multiple sources of information, levels of performance, and data from various screening events that could follow), the HRIS expert who participates in the creation of scoring or decision rules must be sure that they are easy for the HR department and others to understand and apply consistently throughout the organization. Another key HRIS role is helping to design and apply the administrative functions of the system, the features permitting access to assessments results and the right to distribute candidate information. Below are some more specific considerations for designing a computerized or Web-based selection system (Kehoe, Dickter, Russell, & Sacco, 2005):

- *Test access and security:* The HR department must decide how candidates will gain access to the test (By permission? Will there be prescreening? Is testing open to anyone?) and how the test content will be kept secure.

- *Test inventory and administrative privileges:* The HRIS expert must consider how the computerized tests will be purchased and inventoried (if accessed from a vendor) and the **administrative privileges** that determine

    1. who should be assigned the right to work with particular types of test data,

    2. whether there will be multiple levels of access, and

    3. whether individuals will be able to delegate record-viewing rights to others.

- *Options for scoring:* Will there be multiple ways to score an assessment, with a variety of possible scoring rules? How might examinees' scores be compared with those of reference groups to make these scores more meaningful?

- *Accessing results:* In what data format and by what methods will test results be stored, transmitted, and interpreted?

- *Applying test policies:* What organizational requirements will affect the testing methods (e.g., systems that allow accommodations for disabilities) and the data that are kept and used (e.g., mandatory waiting periods before retests)?

For additional discussion on psychological testing on the Internet, the interested reader may wish to consult an article published by the American Psychological Association (Naglieri et al., 2004).

Demonstrating the HRM's Value With HRIS Selection Applications

As mentioned earlier, the HRIS manager plays a key role in proving the value of a selection system, through knowledge of how to obtain and use the right data on individual and organizational outcomes, data that will demonstrate a return on investment in the system. This expertise is also critical for defending the selection system, which is generally a high-stakes event: The use of the selection information determines individual careers and the company's ultimate success.

Demonstrating the value of selection requires that we know how well the employees who were assessed eventually perform on the job. For instance, if we measure their productivity (e.g., more products assembled or repaired, customers served, or products sold), we may find that people who score higher on the tests also are more productive. As another example, suppose the assessed individuals are supervisors. Among this group, we may find that the higher the supervisors' assessment scores, the better they supervise their subordinates, who have higher skill levels (perhaps as measured with a **knowledge test**) and lower turnover than the subordinates of people whose assessment results were not as high. Testing experts refer to this value or return on investment as utility: the extent to which a selection system results in the selection of better candidates than would have been possible if the system had not been used (Blum & Naylor, 1968). The quality of the candidates may be defined in terms of one or more of the following (Cascio, 1991):

1. The proportion of candidates who are successful on the job

2. The average numeric value of an outcome of interest (such as number of products sold or customers served)

3. The dollar amount of benefit resulting to the organization (such as the annual increase in revenue)

If a selection system produces a higher proportion of successful candidates (e.g., a 10% increase in the number of new financial advisers who, once hired, can pass a government-mandated licensure exam), then that system has clear value to the company. The same can be said of a selection system that results in an increase in some **performance criterion** (e.g., cable service technicians who are able to complete an average of 20% more installations per day as a result of testing). And the same can be said for a benefit that can be measured in dollars (e.g., for every 10 points higher a salesperson scored on a sales skill assessment, annual sales increased by $1,000).

There are many approaches to estimating utility. Apart from an anecdotal approach (Does it seem like more people are successful on the job now?), perhaps one of the simplest approaches is to conduct pre- and post-comparisons of measurable performance to see if the selection system has coincided with a change in performance. As a more precise alternative, industrial/organizational psychologists frequently use a **utility formula** that takes several factors into account: the **selection ratio**; the **validity coefficient**, expressed as the correlation between assessment scores and criteria (outcomes); and information about the dollar value of performance. The utility formula and related concepts are described here in some detail.

The selection ratio is the number of candidates who, based on the assessment, are chosen for the job, divided by the number of candidates who are assessed. The validity coefficient is a statistical correlation that indicates the correspondence between test scores and job performance or some other important work outcomes. When validity is high, there is a close correspondence between assessment performance and work results. In general, a high-validity, low-selection-ratio system produces the greatest benefit of selection but also incurs the highest cost of selection, all else being the same. When the selection ratio is low, the bar is set high on the assessment, and more rarified, higher-performing candidates will be chosen. (This generalization works as long as the selection ratio is not so high or so low that nearly everyone is hired or no one is hired, respectively; in those cases, the assessment has little value as a decision-making tool.) Information about the process used to estimate the dollar value of job performance follows. The value can be obtained from job experts at the organization. Alternatively, published research may be used to estimate this value, and, in many cases, the published value is used for utility estimates.

The result of the **utility calculation** is the dollar value of the selection system per individual, or group of individuals, hired. (Note that here utility refers to the dollar benefit of selection, without consideration of the cost. Certainly, it is important to compare this benefit with its corresponding cost to make good business decisions about selection systems.) The formula for utility is $\Delta U = r_{xy} * SD_y * N * \Phi/\rho$, and the elements of the calculation are as follows:

1. ΔU is the utility or annual change in the dollar value of productivity. Items 2 through 5 will be multiplied to calculate this number.

2. r_{xy} is the validity coefficient of the assessment, quantified as a correlation that falls between −1 and +1 and notated as a correlation between x (the assessment score) and y (the performance criterion score). Positive values indicate that the assessment (also called the predictor) and the criterion (work outcome) increase together; for instance, looking at the range of candidate data, as ability test scores increase, so might evaluations of ability to learn on the job. Negative values indicate that as one increases, the other decreases. For instance, as scores on an assessment of conscientiousness and work ethic increase, the frequency of absence and tardiness might decrease.

3. SD_y is the standard deviation (*SD*) of performance (*y*), that is, the difference, in dollar terms, between an average and a superior performer, which on a normal curve would be estimated as a 1 standard deviation difference. Estimated at 40% of salary based on published research across the spectrum of jobs in the U.S. economy, this value has consistently been shown to approximate the difference in the value of productivity between average and above-average employees (Hunter & Schmidt, 1982).

4. *N* is the number of employees hired.

5. Φ/ρ refers to the test score of applicants who are selected by the organization and is expressed in a statistically standardized form (the standard deviation units in this value and the standard deviation of performance in Item 3 cancel out, leaving a dollar value for the utility estimate).

For example, suppose an employer tests 2,500 clerical job candidates on an assessment with a validity of 0.43 and hires the top 1,000 scorers at an annual salary of $20,000. Therefore, $r_{xy} = 0.43$. The standard deviation of job performance (SD_y or 40% of salary) is estimated to be $8,000. One thousand employees are hired ($N = 1,000$). The selection ratio is 40% (4 out of 10 qualify); for this ratio, Φ/ρ can be determined from statistical tables of the normal curve; this value is 0.64. Therefore, $\Delta U = (0.43) * (8000) * (1000) * (0.64) = \$2,201,600$, meaning that the average increase in utility per person hired is $2,202 per year. If all 1,000 employees were to stay three years, we would estimate the utility over that period at approximately $6.6 million. Supposing that the testing program expenses were $300,000 per year, the return on investment for a three-year period would still be about $5.7 million. This example serves to illustrate a method of estimating utility and also shows that, when many people are hired, the total value of the assessment quickly yields high numbers. Although organizational stakeholders occasionally are skeptical because of the extremely high utility values that are possible, the principles behind the numbers are sound.

After reading this section, you should reasonably conclude that there are a variety of technical concepts related to selection and assessment with which HRIS experts should familiarize themselves. Our intent has been to provide an overview of these topics and of the trends that are currently taking place in organizations, in the testing industry, and in research programs. By becoming familiar with this work, the HRIS student will gain awareness of the major issues he or she is likely to face when implementing database-based decision-making systems.

SUMMARY

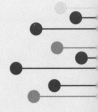

In summary, this chapter explained the intersection between the use of technology in the recruitment and selection process and the use of HRIS in organizations. This highlighted the need for HRIS experts to understand how to use the Internet for recruitment as well as selection-related data in order to provide strategic information to the company and demonstrate the return on the company's investment in assessments. In addition, technology issues surrounding the selection process were addressed. Measurement properties of paper-and-pencil assessments and their computer versions were discussed. The mode of assessments that do not include measurements of ability is of little concern for researchers since giving these tests on paper will not result in a different measure from that obtained with a computerized test. However, there is clear evidence that the mode of administration (paper vs. computer) matters for ability tests that are speeded. The more speeded a test is, the more likely that there will be differences between the paper and computer test results. A second issue focused on in this chapter is the trade-off between fidelity and bandwidth. Technology has enabled organizations to create work sample simulations that represent the job with high fidelity. However, if the company then wants to use the simulation for a different business unit or job, the details that made the simulation highly appropriate in the first setting may interfere with its use in the other setting. In general, HRIS managers should keep in mind that, depending on the effort and expense one is willing to expend on assessment development and installation, lower-fidelity simulations or combinations of other types of assessments might be preferable. One of the final issues dealt with was unproctored testing, which can be convenient to both the applicant and the organization. Unfortunately, this means of delivering assessment gives way to a floodgate of concerns such as how to verify candidate identity, provide test security and eliminate cheating, and ensure fair access to testing for minorities. The chapter further examined the role that HRIS experts have to play in solving these problems through the use of technology and the decision to develop and use an HRIS.

KEY TERMS

DISCUSSION QUESTIONS

1. What recruiting objectives are being met through the use of online recruitment?

2. What are some of the advantages and disadvantages of using online recruitment?

3. Should organizations rely solely on recruiting through the Internet? Why or why not?

4. What are some of the technological issues that arise through the use of technology in the function of selection?

5. Describe how the use of technology in the selection process is adding value to organizations.

CASE STUDY

The case from Chapter 11 will be used here, since recruitment and selection are the next step in the operationalization of a talent management strategy. The background for this chapter case is the case material from Chapter 11; at the end of this background material, more details relevant to the recruitment and selection of new employees will be presented.

Rudiger is sitting at his desk in his seventh-floor corner office in the City, gazing out over London and reflecting on life. At 43 he is at the top of his game. He has everything he could wish for—a lovely partner, a 4-year-old in a private nursery, a new executive house in the suburbs, a holiday home in southern Italy, and a remuneration package that's the envy of his peers and beyond anything his German immigrant parents could have imagined. But it hasn't been easy, oh no! Hard work, long hours, geographical moves every two or three years, and sacrifices in terms of his personal life.

But now he has a problem. Rudiger has just been appointed global head of People and Talent responsible for the future of 35,000 people worldwide, the bulk of whom are based in the United States, the United Kingdom, and Europe, and manufacturing is likely to relocate to China in the next two years, adding to his responsibilities. In his previous role, he was responsible for the United Kingdom and Northern Europe and had operational oversight for 11,000 people. An initial consideration of his responsibilities has identified a number of people issues for the next five years: the company needs to recruit and retain particular specialist and skilled personnel; some of the brightest and most experienced midlevel managers are leaving; an aging senior directorship is looking toward early retirement. But the main difficulty is that, although he knows he has a problem, he doesn't have enough detailed information to know the scale of the problem.

18 months later . . .

Once again Rudiger is sitting at his desk in his seventh-floor office in central London reflecting on life. The move from Barcelona to England went smoothly with the last crate arriving only two months later than the rest. He is still working hard, but the hours are slightly better since the introduction of the work-life balance policy last year, and his family has settled well into the idyllic English countryside.

As the global head of People and Talent, he still has problems though—just different ones. The talent strategy "Our People—Our Talent—Our Future," which he presented to the board in his third month, identified the need for robust HRP information and analyses that required a new version of HRP software. It is in its early stages, but the intensive data-cleansing and updating activity has been straightforward so far. More concerning are the metrics responsible for producing the information needed to develop far-reaching HRP policies and practices for the future. The metrics are relatively easy to construct, but it is proving tricky to find the right "bundles" of predictive metrics—this is holding up progress with the analysis application package. In addition, there have been cost overruns in the implementation of the HRP software, and some senior managers are wondering if the new software should be abandoned.

At least 3 of the 12 board members will retire in the next two years, and they are looking to groom their successors. At least one will have to be hired from outside the organization, and the HR department is not sure what the CEO wants for this position. In addition, employee turnover and an aggressive growth strategy mean hiring new employees as well as training transferring current employees. The work that is involved in defining competences (KSA sets) at skill levels within jobs is progressing well, with hard-won support from the unions. However, job descriptions that can be found are at least three to five years old, and some jobs have no descriptions. The new apprenticeship scheme is about to be launched, and the international graduate student package and development program has been completely revised. Overall things are progressing reasonably well, but there is much to be done.

Case Supplemental Material

On the basis of your analyses and answers completed for Chapter 11, assume that Rudiger has completed an acceptable HRP program and his staff members have completed current and accurate job descriptions for all positions in the talent management project. These job descriptions all contain the specific duties, tasks, and responsibilities as well as the KSA sets needed for each job.

Rudiger's next task is to recruit and select individuals for jobs. He wants to use the new HRIS software applications that the company has purchased and implemented for recruiting and selecting new employees. Fortunately, he can get assistance on this task from the IT department, which has built and maintains the company's website. In addition, he has several staff members with doctorates in industrial/organizational psychology who can work with the IT professionals to develop recruitment and selection materials. However, Rudiger must provide the guidelines for the selection and recruitment of individuals who can fit into the talent management project.

Case Study Questions

1. What guidelines would you establish as part of Rudiger's plan that emphasized the use of the Internet via the company's website to communicate the recruiting objectives of the talent management project?

   a. What are the potential advantages and disadvantages of online recruitment to communicate recruiting objectives?

2. What guidelines would you establish for the use of an HRIS for the selection and assessment of potential employees?

   a. What selection and assessment tools could be used on the Internet, and which ones would need to be done on a face-to-face basis?

   b. What are the technological problems that affect selection via the Internet and the solutions that have been suggested?

   c. What guidelines would you develop to make sure that a utility analysis was done for all HRIS selection applications?

STUDENT STUDY SITE

Visit the Student Study Site at **http://www.sagepub.com/kavanagh3e** for additional learning tools such as access to SAGE journal articles and related web resources.

REFERENCES

Allen, D. G., Mahto, R. V., & Otondo, R. F. (2007). Web-based recruitment: Effects of information, organizational brand, and attitudes toward a Web site on applicant attraction. *Journal of Applied Psychology, 92,* 1696–1708.

Baker, H. G. (1985). The unwritten contract: Job perceptions. *Personnel Journal, 64,* 36–41.

Barber, A. E., & Roehling, M. V. (1993). Job postings and the decision to interview: A verbal protocol analysis. *Journal of Applied Psychology, 78,* 845–856.

Baumeister, R. F., Bratslavsky, E., Finkenauer, C., & Vohs, K. D. (2001). Bad is stronger than good. *Review of General Psychology, 5,* 323–370.

Becker, B., & Gerhart, B. (1996). The impact of human resource management on organizational performance: Progress and prospects. *Academy of Management Journal, 39,* 779–801.

Blum, M. L., & Naylor, J. C. (1968). *Industrial psychology: Its theoretical and social foundations* (Rev. ed.). New York: Harper & Row.

Braddy, P. W., Meade, A. W., & Kroustalis, C. M. (2008). Online recruiting: The effects of organizational familiarity, website usability, and website attractiveness on viewers' impressions of organizations. *Computers in Human Behavior, 24,* 2992–3001.

Braddy, P. W., Meade, A. W., Michael, J. J., & Fleenor, J. W. (2009). Internet recruiting: Effects of website content features on viewers' perceptions of organizational culture. *International Journal of Selection and Assessment, 17,* 19–34.

Braddy, P. W., Thompson, L. F., Wuensch, K. L., & Grossnickle, W. F. (2003). Internet recruiting: The effects of Web page design features. *Social Science Computer Review, 21,* 374–385.

Breaugh, J. A., & Starke, M. (2000). Research on employee recruitment: So many studies, so many remaining questions. *Journal of Management, 26,* 405–434.

Buckley, P., Minette, K., Joy, D., & Michaels, J. (2004). The use of an automated employment recruiting and screening system for temporary professional employees: A case study. *Human Resource Management, 43,* 233–241.

Cable, D. M., Aiman-Smith, L., Mulvey, P. W., & Edwards, J. R. (2000). The sources of accuracy and job applicants' beliefs about organizational culture. *Academy of Management Journal, 43,* 1076–1085.

Cable, D. M., & Graham, M. E. (2000). The determinants of job seekers' reputation perceptions. *Journal of Organizational Behavior, 21,* 929–947.

Cable, D. M., & Yu, K. Y. T. (2006). Managing job seekers' organizational image beliefs: The role of media richness and media credibility. *Journal of Applied Psychology, 91,* 828–840.

Cappelli, P. (2001). Making the most of on-line recruiting. *Harvard Business Review, 79,* 139–146.

Cardy, R. L., & Miller, J. S. (2003). Technology: Implications for HRM. In D. Stone (Ed.), *Advances in human performance and cognitive engineering research* (pp. 99–118). Greenwich, CT: JAI Press.

Cascio, W. F. (1991). *Applied psychology in personnel management* (4th ed.). Englewood Cliffs, NJ: Prentice Hall.

Cascio, W. F. (1998). *Managing human resources: Productivity, quality of work life, and profits* (5th ed.). New York: Irwin/McGraw-Hill.

Cascio, W. F. (2013). *Managing human resources: Productivity, quality of work life, and profits* (9th ed.). New York: Irwin/McGraw-Hill.

Chapman, D. S., & Webster, J. (2003). The use of technologies in the recruiting, screening, and selection processes for job candidates. *International Journal of Selection and Assessment, 11,* 113–120.

Chen, C., Lin, M., & Chen, C. (2012). Exploring the mechanisms of the relationship between website characteristics and organizational attraction. *The international Journal of Human Resource Management, 23,* 867–885.

Cober, R. T., Brown, D. J., Blumental, A. J., Doverspike, D., & Levy, P. (2000). The quest for the qualified job surfer: It's time the public sector catches the wave. *Public Personnel Management, 29*(4), 479–494.

Cober, R. T., Brown, D. J., Keeping, L. M., & Levy, P. E. (2004). Recruitment on the Net: How do organizational Web site characteristics influence applicant attraction? *Journal of Management, 30,* 623–646.

Cober, R. T., Brown, D. J., Levy, P. E., Keeping, L. M., & Cober, A. B. (2003). Organizational websites: Website content and style as determinants of organizational attraction. *International Journal of Selection and Assessment, 11,* 158–169.

Colao, J. J. (2012, September 12). *With Facebook, your recruitment pool is one billion people.* Retrieved from http://www .forbes.com/sites/jjcolao/2012/09/12/with-facebook-your-recruitment-pool-is-one-billion-people/

Collins, J. C. (2001). *Good to great: Why some companies make the leap . . . and others don't.* New York: HarperCollins.

Daft, R. L., & Lengel, R. H. (1986). Organizational information requirements, media richness and structural design. *Management Science, 32,* 554–571.

Davison, H. K., Maraist, C., & Bing, M. N. (2011). Friend or foe? The promise and pitfalls of using social networking sites for HR decisions. *Journal of Business and Psychology, 26,* 153–159.

Dineen, B. R., Ash, S. R., & Noe, R. A. (2002). A web of applicant attraction: Person-organization fit in the context of Web-based recruitment. *Journal of Applied Psychology, 87,* 723–734.

Dineen, B. R., Ling, J., Ash, S. R., & DelVecchio, D. (2007). Aesthetic properties and message customization: Navigating the dark side of web recruitment. *Journal of Applied Psychology, 92,* 356–372.

Dineen, B. R., & Noe, R. A. (2009). Effects of customization on application decisions and applicant pool characteristics in a web-based recruitment context. *Journal of Applied Psychology, 94,* 224–234.

Galanaki, E. (2002). The decision to recruit online: A descriptive study. *Career Development International, 7,* 243–251.

Guion, R. M. (1998). *Assessment, measurement, and prediction for personnel decisions.* Mahwah, NJ: Lawrence Erlbaum.

Heneman, H. G., & Judge, T. A. (2006). *Staffing organizations* (5th ed.). Boston: McGraw-Hill.

Hogler, R. L., Henle, C., & Bemus, C. (1998). Internet recruiting and employment discrimination: A legal perspective. *Human Resource Management Review, 8*(2), 149–164.

Hunter, J. E., & Schmidt, F. L. (1982). *Personnel selection programs based on cumulative knowledge.* Presentation at the PTC fall conference on validity generalization, Newport Beach, CA.

Jackson, L. A., Ervin, K. S., Gardner, P. D., & Schmitt, N. (2001). Gender and the Internet: Women communicating and men searching. *Sex Roles, 44,* 363–379.

Judge, T. A., & Cable, D. M. (1997). Applicant personality, organizational culture, and organizational attraction. *Personnel Psychology, 50,* 359–394.

Karat, J. (1997). Evolving the scope of user-centered design. *Communications of the ACM, 40,* 33–38.

Kehoe, J. F., Dickter, D. N., Russell, D. P., & Sacco, J. M. (2005). e-Selection. In H. G. Guental & D. L. Stone (Eds.), *The brave new world of eHR* (pp. 54–103). San Francisco: Jossey-Bass.

Kluemper, D. H., & Rosen, P. A. (2009). Future employment selection methods: Evaluating social networking web sites. *Journal of Managerial Psychology, 24,* 567–580.

Kluemper, D. H., Rosen, P. A., & Mossholder, K. W. (2012). Social networking websites, personality ratings, and the organizational context: More than meets the eye? *Journal of Applied Social Psychology, 42,* 1143–1172.

Kristof-Brown, A. L., Zimmerman, R. D., & Johnson, E. C. (2005). Consequences of individuals' fit at work: A meta-analysis of person-job, person-organization, person-group, and person-supervisor fit. *Personnel Psychology, 58,* 281–342.

Kuhn, P., & Skuterud, M. (2000). Job search methods: Internet versus traditional. *Monthly Labor Review, 123,* 3–11.

Lee, I. (2005). The evolution of e-recruiting: A content analysis of Fortune 100 career web sites. *Journal of Electronic Commerce in Organizations, 3*(3), 57–68.

Lyons, B. D., & Marler, J. H. (2011). Got image? Examining organizational image in Web recruitment. *Journal of Managerial Psychology, 26*(1), 58–76.

MacMillan, D. (2007, May 7). The art of the online resume. *BusinessWeek,* 86.

Marakas, G., Yi, M., & Johnson, R. (1998). The multilevel and multifaceted character of computer self-efficacy: Toward clarification of the construct and an integrative framework for research. *Information Systems Research, 9,* 126–163.

McCourt-Mooney, M. (2000). Internet briefing: Recruitment and selection—R&D using the Internet—Part III. *Journal of Managerial Psychology, 15,* 737–740.

McKinsey. (2012). Careers: A week in the life. Retrieved from www.mckinsey.com/careers/what_youll_do/a_week_in the_life

McManus, M. A., & Ferguson, M. W. (2003). Biodata, personality, and demographic differences of recruits from three sources. *International Journal of Selection and Assessment, 11,* 175–183.

Mead, A., & Drasgow, F. (1993). Equivalence of computerized and paper-and-pencil cognitive ability tests: A meta-analysis. *Psychological Bulletin, 114,* 449–458.

Mohamed, A. A., Orife, J. N., & Wibowo, K. (2002). The legality of key word search as a personnel selection tool. *Employee Relations, 24,* 516–522.

Morrison, E. W., & Robinson, S. L. (1997). When employees feel betrayed: A model of how psychological contract violation develops. *Academy of Management Review, 22,* 226–256.

Naglieri, J. A., Drasgow, F., Schmit, M., Handler, L., Prifitera, A., Margolis, A., & Velasquez, R. (2004). Psychological testing on the Internet. *American Psychologist, 59,* 150–162.

Nielsen, J. (2000). *Designing Web usability.* Indianapolis, IN: New Riders.

PewInternet. (2006). *Internet activities.* Retrieved from http://www.pewinternet.org/trends/Internet_Activities_1.11.07.htm

Potosky, D., & Bobko, P. (2004). Selection testing via the Internet: Practical considerations and exploratory empirical findings. *Personnel Psychology, 57,* 1003–1004.

Reed, K., Doty, H. D., & May, D. R. (2005). The impact of aging on self-efficacy and computer skill acquisition. *Journal of Managerial Issues, 17,* 212–228.

Reed Company. (2003). *The Reed Recruitment Index report.* Retrieved from http://www.onrec.com/content2/news.asp?ID=1981

Rousseau, D. M. (1990). New hire perceptions of their own and their employer's obligations: A study of psychological contracts. *Journal of Organizational Behavior, 11,* 389–400.

Rozelle, A. L., & Landis, R. S. (2002). An examination of the relationship between use of the Internet as a recruitment source and student attitudes. *Computers in Human Behavior, 18,* 593–604.

Russell, D. P. (2007). Recruiting and staffing in the electronic age: A research-based perspective. *Consulting Psychology Journal: Practice and Research, 59,* 91–101.

Schmidt, F. L., & Hunter, J. E. (1998). The validity and utility of selection methods in personnel psychology: Practical and theoretical implications of 85 years of research findings. *Psychological Bulletin, 124,* 262–274.

Schneider, B., Goldstein, H. W., & Smith, D. B. (1995). The ASA framework: An update. *Personnel Psychology, 48,* 747–773.

Selden, S., & Orenstein, J. (2011). Government e-recruiting web sites: The influence of e-recruitment content and usability on recruiting and hiring outcomes in US state governments. *International Journal of Selection and Assessment, 19,* 31–40.

Seminerio, M. (2001, April 24). E-recruiting takes next step. *eWeek, 18,* 16, 51–54.

Shaffer, D. J., & Schmidt, R. A. (2006). Personality testing in employment. In *Society of Human Resources Management legal report.* Retrieved from http://www.shrm.org/hrresources/lrpt_published/CMS_000991.asp

Society for Human Resource Management (SHRM). (2004). *Merging tests with applicant tracking systems.* Retrieved from http://www.shrm.org/hrdisciplines/staffingmanagement/articles/pages/cms_006199.aspx

Society for Human Resource Management (SHRM). (2008). *Online technologies and their impact on recruitment strategies: Using social networking websites to attract talent.* Alexandria, VA: Author. Retrieved from http://www.shrm.org/Research/SurveyFindings/Articles/Documents/SNS%20PresentationFinal.ppt

Society for Industrial and Organizational Psychology (SIOP). (2003). *Principles for the validation and use of personnel selection procedures* (4th ed.). Bowling Green, OH: Author.

Stevens, L. (2007). *Where people are looking for jobs.* Retrieved from http://www.ere.net/2007/12/13/where-people-are-looking-for-jobs/

Stone, D. L., Lukaszewski, K. M., & Isenhour, L. C. (2005). e-Recruiting: Online strategies for attracting talent. In H. G. Gueutal & D. L. Stone (Eds.), *The brave new world of eHR* (pp. 22–53). San Francisco: Jossey-Bass.

Stone, D. L., Stone-Romero, E. F., & Lukaszewski, K. (2003). The functional and dysfunctional consequences of human resource information technology for organizations and their employees. In D. L. Stone (Ed.), *Advances in human performance and cognitive engineering research* (pp. 37–68). Greenwich, CT: JAI Press.

Tippins, N. T., Beaty, J., Drasgow, F., Gibson, W. M., Pearlman, K., Segall, D. O., & Shepherd, W. (2006). Unproctored Internet testing in employment settings. *Personnel Psychology, 59,* 189–225.

Towers Watson. (2012). *Emerging choices, enduring changes: Creating service delivery success in an era of new opportunity.* Retrieved from http://www.towerswatson.com/united-states/research/7805

Uggerslev, K. L, Fassina, N. E., & Kraichy, D. (2012). Recruiting through the stages: A meta-analytic test of predictors of applicant attraction at different stages of the recruiting process. *Personnel Psychology, 65,* 597–660.

Ulrich, D. (2001). From e-business to e-HR. *International Human Resources Information Management Journal, 5,* 90–97.

U.S. Department of Labor. (1999). *Testing and assessment: An employer's guide to good practices.* Washington, DC: Author.

U.S. Equal Employment Opportunity Commission, U.S. Civil Service Commission, U.S. Department of Labor, & U.S. Department of Justice. (1978). Uniform guidelines on employee selection procedures. *Federal Register, 43*(166), 38295–38309.

Walker, H. J., Field, H. S., Giles, W. F., Armenakis, A. A., & Bernerth, J. B. (2009). Displaying employee testimonials on recruitment Web sites: Effects of communication media, employee race, and job seeker race on organizational attraction and information credibility. *Journal of Applied Psychology, 94,* 1354–1364.

Wanous, J. P. (1992). *Organizational entry.* Reading, MA: Addison-Wesley.

Williamson, I. O., Lepak, D. P., & King, J. (2003). The effect of company recruitment Web site orientation on individuals' perceptions of organizational attractiveness. *Journal of Vocational Behavior, 63,* 242–263.

Wright, P. M., & Snell, S. A. (1998). Toward a unifying framework for exploring fit and flexibility in strategic human resource management. *Academy of Management Review, 23,* 756–772.

Zielinski, D. (2012, August). Find social media's value: The platform's return on investment often eludes measurement. *HR Magazine, 57,* 53–55.

Zusman, R. R., & Landis, R. S. (2002). Applicant preferences for Web-based versus traditional job postings. *Computers in Human Behavior, 18,* 285–296.

CHAPTER 13

Training and Development

Issues and Human Resource Information Systems Applications

Ralf Burbach

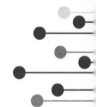

EDITORS' NOTE

Training is one of the major programs offered by HR departments and is an important aspect of an organization's talent management program. Organizations use training not only for skill and knowledge learning but also to develop employees for future positions. In addition, training plays an important role in the motivation of employees. It shows that the organization is concerned about the development of its employees and would like to retain them. However, training generally captures the largest portion of the HR departmental budget. Due to these heavy costs, the application of an HRIS to save money is very important. In the applications section of this chapter, you will learn how training can be made to be cost-effective through an HRIS that serves both as a more efficient transaction processor and as an aid to managerial decision making.

CHAPTER Objectives

After completing this chapter, you should be able to

- Discuss how training can be used as a source of competitive advantage
- Differentiate between training and development (T&D)
- Understand how training and development affect both learning and motivation
- Explain the steps in a systems model of training
- Understand the essential features of the culture of a learning organization
- Explain the factors that influence transfer of training
- Understand both the costs and the benefits metrics associated with training
- Discuss the critical importance of the evaluation of training
- Understand MIS, HRMS, and DSS (see Chapter 1) training applications
- Explain the advantages and disadvantages of Web-based learning
- Develop a practical application, using EXCEL, in the evaluation of training

HRIS IN ACTION

Midwestern Mighty Markets (Triple M)[1] is one of the largest supermarket chains in five states, with 275 store locations. The corporate director of training, June Grady, was hired externally and has been on the job for two months. She has inherited the job with little information about what had been happening in the past relative to training and the use of any computer-based technology to manage the training activities and programs. She has begun a careful examination of the training activities, particularly supervisory training since that is where the next higher-level managers will be identified. The annual budget for training has been $2.2 million, of which $1.1 million is devoted to supervisory training.

Supervisory training is one week in length and occurs on a monthly basis in each state at a central location. It is focused on training assistant department managers (e.g., produce, meat, and grocery) in the supervisory skills needed to be a department manager. Based on department managers' recommendations, assistant managers are sent to training at a central location in their state. However, all assistant managers across the states have the same training content and training activities.

At the conclusion of the training, all trainees complete an evaluation of the training program based on their experiences.

The company has an HRIS software application developed by PeopleSoft and implemented three years ago. It is used for the management of all the training in the company. There are a number of reports that can be generated from the software, including attendance by states, stores, and departments within the stores. This information is useful for June, so she can make sure that training is occurring evenly across departments, stores, and states. Other reports are also available that can be sent to department and store managers as well as to the regional managers of Triple M.

June has been examining all these reports available from the HRIS software to determine if anything is missing. During her examination, she notices that no one has been accessing the reports summarizing the trainees' evaluations of the training programs. On further examination, she finds that some store managers receive these summary reports but rarely use them. Also, she discovers that there is an additional report that has been designed to be generated by the software. This report is based on evaluation data that are to be collected from department managers three months after the trainees have returned to their jobs. This report appears quite important since it asks the department managers to rate the trainees' job performance after they have completed training to determine any effects of the training.

June sees a serious problem with this lack of training-evaluation data collection and assessment; the trainees' post-training evaluations are not being analyzed by the available software, and, more important, the department managers' ratings of trainee job performance are not being completed. Therefore, even though the company owns sophisticated (and costly) software, it is not being used to evaluate the supervisory training programs. More seriously, June has no idea if the $1.1 million being spent on supervisory training has had any effect on the job performance of the trainees.

Introduction

The nature of work and the structure of organizations are rapidly changing. Internationalization, globalization, and changing customer expectations of service and quality standards require firms to improve and transform themselves perpetually to remain competitive. Emerging concepts such as the global marketplace, knowledge economy, knowledge worker, information age, and digital revolution underscore that an organization's ability to survive in a constantly changing business environment is founded on its capacity to generate new knowledge, to share knowledge, and to innovate continuously (Nonaka & Takeuchi, 1995; Porter, 1990; Senge, 1990). In the new global economy, knowledge is now the new lever for success, since knowledge potentially adds more value than the traditional factors of production—capital, raw material, and labor (Harrison, 2005). This new knowledge-based economy is

> directly based on production, distribution and use of knowledge and information. Knowledge is now recognised as the driver of productivity and economic growth, leading to a new focus on the role of information, technology, and learning in economic performance. . . . Employment in the knowledge-based economy is characterized by increasing demand for more highly skilled workers. . . . The knowledge-based economy is characterized by the need for continuous learning of both codified information and the competencies to use this information. (Organisation for Economic Co-operation and Development [OECD], 1996, pp. 3, 7, 13)

Knowledge is created by a firm's knowledge assets, that is, its **human capital**[2] (see OECD, 2001, p. 18), which has long been recognized as one of the key sources of competitive advantage (Grant, 1996; Prahalad & Hamel, 1990; Wright, Dunford, & Snell, 2001). Hence, the **learning, training, and development (LT&D)** of employees is now center stage in today's organizations to ensure long-term competitiveness, excellence, quality, flexibility, and adaptability. Changing work practices and new services and products necessitate new knowledge, competences, and skills. It may also be argued that today's organizations ought to learn faster and more effectively than their rivals in order to remain competitive. However, a range of other reasons exists as to why organizations train and develop their workforces— for instance, to enable employees to cope with daily workloads. T&D activities can also alleviate possible future skill shortages and play a fundamental role in talent management. High-commitment organizations train and develop their employees to foster employee motivation and satisfaction (Pfeffer, 1996, 1998). In a time when job security is diminishing and employability is of increasing value, employees place much greater emphasis on career prospects and career development in their choice of employer. This point is of particular relevance for specialist knowledge workers who are in short supply in a tight labor market. The strategic importance of individual and organizational learning and development is mirrored in the continued interest in the concepts of the **learning organization** and **organizational learning**. These terms are often used interchangeably. However, the learning organization is the ultimate state of organizational learning at which the organization is able to facilitate the learning of all its members and can continuously transform itself (Argyris & Schon, 1978; Pedler, Burgoyne, & Boydell, 1991). "It is the potential of organizational learning to enable organizations to reinvent themselves in order to compete in the changing and increasingly uncertain and competitive environment that is making it such an attractive proposition for many managers" (Burnes, 2004, p. 129).

Yet it has been argued that few firms, if any, have actually achieved this aim. Nonetheless, the notion of the learning organization illustrates that organizational learning is inextricably linked to individual LT&D. It is also closely linked to the notion of lifelong learning and continuous professional development. Employees at all levels of the organization will have to demonstrate their commitment to these, especially when they seek a new employer, pay increases, or promotions. T&D activities are thus closely allied with **performance management** and talent management. Most large organizations use human resource information systems (HRIS) to collect, store, and analyze T&D information. This information is generally contained in specialist talent management modules, T&D modules, and learning management systems to reflect the strategic importance of LT&D in the organization. This chapter examines the strategic implications of T&D before it covers the **systems model of training and development**. The section on the systems model will look in detail at its four stages—identifying T&D needs, designing T&D solutions, implementing T&D, and evaluating T&D. Then, training metrics and benefit analysis will be discussed. The next section investigates some HRIS applications in training and some implementation issues. The chapter concludes with a summary of the key issues.

Training and Development: Strategic Implications and Learning Organizations

The introduction to this chapter has already alluded to a number of key terms associated with T&D. Some of the terms, such as *learning, training, development,* and *education,* are frequently used in combination and sometimes even, incorrectly, as substitutes. To comprehend the processes involved in LT&D, we must differentiate these key concepts. *Education* is aimed at developing, usually as part of a formal program of study, general knowledge, understanding, and moral values. *Training* refers to the planned acquisition of the knowledge, skills, and abilities (KSA) to carry out a specific task or job in a vocational setting. The purpose of training interventions is to attain a positive change in performance. *Development* is a continuous process of systematic advancement, of "becoming increasingly more complex, more elaborate and differentiated, by virtue of learning and maturation" (Collin, 2007, p. 266). Development in an organizational context ensures that employees possess the KSA required to fulfill future roles in the organization. Hence, development may be conceived as a lever for career development, succession planning, performance management, and talent management (Gunnigle, Heraty, & Morley, 2002). Training focuses on immediate job performance, whereas development centers on long-term, continuous changes of an individual's potential. Learning is defined as the process of assimilating new knowledge and skills in consequence of experience or practice that will bring about relatively permanent changes in behavior. Effective learning necessitates a capacity to integrate new knowledge with existing knowledge (Learning, 2007). However, the manner in which adults learn and are motivated to learn differs fundamentally from the ways in which children and adolescents learn. Andragogy, or the study of adult learning, purports that adults learn best when

1. They know the reasons for learning a new concept or skill

2. They are actively involved in creating or setting the learning activity

3. They can connect new learning to the knowledge and experience they have developed over time

4. Learning is problem centered

5. They believe a learning activity is immediately relevant to their job

6. They are internally rather than externally motivated to learn; in other words, they learn when they can see a benefit (Knowles, Holton, & Swanson, 2005)

Learning at an individual or organizational level is ineluctably linked to the creation and management of knowledge. Learning is the basis for any T&D activity. The outcomes of learning include skills, competencies, know-how or tacit knowledge, and higher-level cognitive and other skills (Collin, 2007). Skills are directly related to performance and the ability to carry out a task. It has been argued that new organizational realities require higher levels of cognitive skills. Bloom's taxonomy of learning, for example, identifies six increasingly higher levels of thinking—knowledge, comprehension, application, analysis, synthesis, and evaluation (Bloom, Engelhart, Furst, Hill, & Krathwohl, 1956). Competencies consist of KSA and the underlying characteristics of a person that allow the jobholder to perform a task effectively. The knowledge of employees is a tacit commodity, an intangible asset. It is associated with an understanding of and a constructive application of information (Grant, 1996). In a knowledge-based economy, organizations must become knowledge productive, and employees, knowledge workers and knowledge assets. Knowledge-intensive organizations are those that heavily depend on knowledge creation and knowledge sharing, such as firms with a significant research and development focus or consultancy firms. **Knowledge management (KM)** essentially consists of five separate activities, which are the acquisition, documentation, transfer, creation, and application of knowledge (Yahya & Goh, 2002). Whereas knowledge is generated by individuals, organizational knowledge and learning are the result of the combined learning of everybody in the organization and the acquisition of knowledgeable individuals (Grant, 1996).

Hence, if a firm's organizational culture rewards learning, it facilitates KM and the transformation of the firm into a knowledge organization (Mayo, 1998; Soliman & Spooner, 2000). The sharing, codifying, storing, and replicating of knowledge within the organization is greatly facilitated by information and communication technology (ICT). Consequently, KM focuses on the interaction of human beings and ICT and the subsequent creation of knowledge and, in addition, on the alignment of technology with people systems within a firm. The HR department plays a vital role in determining where, among employees, tacit knowledge exists, what type of knowledge is present, and whether and to what degree this knowledge is conducive to attaining present and future organizational goals (Soliman & Spooner, 2000). Should the HR function detect a gap between existing knowledge and the knowledge necessary to pursue strategic objectives, it can initiate procedures to remedy this shortfall through recruitment, socialization, and T&D initiatives. It is evident that the concepts of KM and organizational learning are closely related. Organizational learning is by no means a new concept. Argyris and Schon (1978) suggested a three-level model of organizational learning, consisting of single-loop, double-loop, and triple-loop learning. Single-loop learning is adaptive and focuses on the detection of deviations in performance from established organizational norms, practices, policies, and procedures. Double-loop learning questions the suitability of norms, practices, policies, and procedures that define performance standards. Triple-loop learning challenges the rationale of the organization with the aim of completely transforming it (Burnes, 2004). One of the most influential proponents of the learning organization is Peter Senge. In his book *The Fifth Discipline*, he puts forward five interrelated disciplines that an organization should cultivate among its employees to engender learning and success (Senge, 1990):

1. *Personal mastery:* individual growth and learning

2. *Mental models:* deep-rooted assumptions that affect the way in which employees perceive people, situations, and organizations

3. *Shared visions:* a shared view of the organization's future

4. *Team learning:* a shift from individual learning to collective learning

5. *Systems thinking:* or the "Fifth Discipline," which connects the previous disciplines (Burnes, 2004)

Other writers promote generic organizational characteristics that stimulate organizational learning. Cummings and Worley (2001), for instance, advocate a flat teamwork-based organizational structure to facilitate networking; the use of information systems to collect, process, and share information; human resource practices such as appraisals and rewards that reinforce learning; effective leadership that is supportive of organizational learning; and an organizational culture that encourages openness, creativity, and experimentation among members of the firm. A learning culture is one of the key levers for organizational learning, training, and development. Transfer of training is far more likely to occur in an environment where the basic assumptions, shared values, norms, and artifacts of an organization espouse successful LT&D, and where employees are encouraged to create, process, and share information and knowledge (Cummings & Worley, 2001). A T&D intervention can only be considered successful if transfer of training has occurred and a permanent change in behavior has taken place.

HRIS training and development applications play a fundamental role in fostering organizational learning. These applications provide organizations with a mechanism to assess, measure, facilitate, manage, and record systematically the LT&D of each employee and thus the entire organization. In that way, HRIS LT&D applications also support HRIS Talent Management and Performance Management applications. For instance, LT&D applications may be utilized to manage the training and development of high potential employees. In addition, employees' training records could feed into their performance evaluations.

Systems Model of Training and Development

The approaches to T&D adopted by organizations are quite possibly as diverse as the organizations that employ them. The literature is teeming with different, sometimes competing, models, which mirror the approaches to T&D found in practice. One of the most frequently cited models is the systems or systematic approach. This formal or planned approach to workforce T&D consists of four interrelated and connected steps, which are illustrated in Figure 13.1. The steps are arranged as a cycle to highlight the cyclical and continuous nature of the process; the systems model, then, is conceptualized as an ongoing

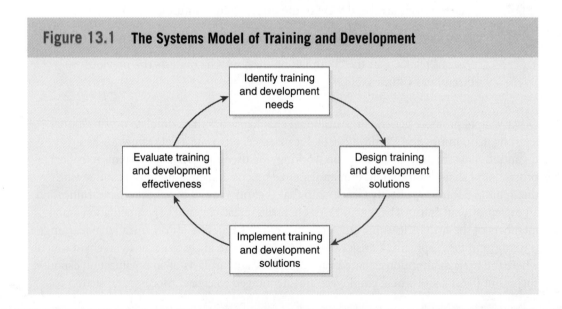

Figure 13.1   The Systems Model of Training and Development

- Identify training and development needs
- Design training and development solutions
- Implement training and development solutions
- Evaluate training and development effectiveness

activity, in much the same way as is employee development. Thus, the model is applicable to both training and development. Its simplicity and clear structure make it ideally suited in the context of HRIS applications in this area. In addition, the model provides a rational foundation for the allocation of resources throughout the T&D process. However, the systematic model has also received some criticism *because* of its simplicity, because of the fact that it is a closed system, and because it does not take account of individual differences among the learners. Notwithstanding these criticisms, the model continues to find broad application, for instance, in the development of national training standards and, indeed, in many IT-based T&D applications that are designed based on the four steps (Stewart, 1999).

Identifying T&D Needs

The first step of the systems model is concerned with the identification of the learning and development needs of organizational members. The **training needs analysis (TNA)** is the key activity of the systematic approach and essentially serves to identify any discrepancies, the T&D "gap," between existing KSA and those required in the present and in the future. Thus, it ensures the integration of employee T&D activities with the business needs of the firm. Hence, the TNA must assess the validity of initiatives, it ought to assist in prioritizing T&D objectives and initiatives, and it has to be able to determine the actual training needs. Training needs may arise at three distinct levels (Boydell, 1983):

- At an organizational level (current and future employee T&D requirements that an organization has to fulfill in order to attain its strategic long-term objectives)

- At a job level (relevant KSA that are part of specific jobs)

- At a personal level (the competences required)

Because of the crucial importance and comprehensive nature of the TNA, many organizations employ an HRIS to collect, store, and analyze training needs data, thus ensuring that the resulting information is both timely and accurate. Data sources range from business objectives and statistics, at the organizational level, to job descriptions and output levels, at the job level, and staff appraisals, biographical data, and individual training records, at the personal level. Most HRIS can be configured to gather data from these and other sources. However, a host of specialist T&D software (discussed further on in this chapter) exists that will aid a firm in accomplishing its T&D activities. In the event, however, that the TNA highlights a considerable gap between existing and desired KSA, an organization may decide on external recruitment to hire individuals who already possess the required competencies. In that case, it will be of vital importance that the organization has access to skilled personnel and demographic data, which might provide some indication regarding the skill levels of the wider population and the environment in which the firm operates.

Developing T&D Initiatives

The second stage of the cycle focuses on the development of T&D initiatives, objectives, and methods that should be capable of meeting the three levels of needs identified during the first phase, the TNA. Organizations have a wide array of T&D methods at their disposal, and advances in and access to ICT and mobile technologies will further increase the number of methods and ways of content delivery available. Faced with an apparent overabundance of methods, how should organizations choose the ones most appropriate for their needs? A number of criteria will guide the decision-making process.

The effectiveness of individual learning plans and events ultimately hinges on the design of these T&D interventions. A learning activity can be considered successful if it leads to transfer of learning as well as a noticeable and permanent change in behavior in the trainees. The aim of the HRIS in this context is to compare employee training data with subsequent performance data. Successful learning events must achieve a "best fit" between

- the content of what is to be learned,

- the media through which content is delivered, and

- the method used to facilitate learning (see Figure 13.2).

With regard to individual learning, it is important to note that every individual has his or her preferred learning style and that these learning styles must be taken into consideration when one designs a training event to encourage learning transfer (explained below). Based on Kolb's (1984) learning cycle, which involves a concrete experience, reflective observation, abstract conceptualization, and active experimentation, Honey and Mumford (1992) developed four preferred learning styles—activist, reflector, theorist, and pragmatist.

In today's highly regulated working environments, it is also essential to attain internal and external consistency. Internal consistency is achieved if learning interventions are mutually supportive of one another and of the business objectives. External consistency is attained if T&D activities are aligned with external regulations (e.g., health and safety legislation), best practices in the industry, and the stipulations and standards of external training award bodies. The conditions for a successful learning event are illustrated in the **best-fit learning event model** in Figure 13.2.

T&D methods essentially fall into two broad categories—on the job and off the job, albeit the emergence of e-learning has somewhat diluted this distinction, as it can be either. **On-the-job training** usually involves peer observation and can be informal, structured, or unstructured, although successful learning outcomes are more likely to occur in a structured rather than an unstructured environment. Compared with **off-the-job training**, on-the-job

Figure 13.2 **Best-Fit Learning Event Model**

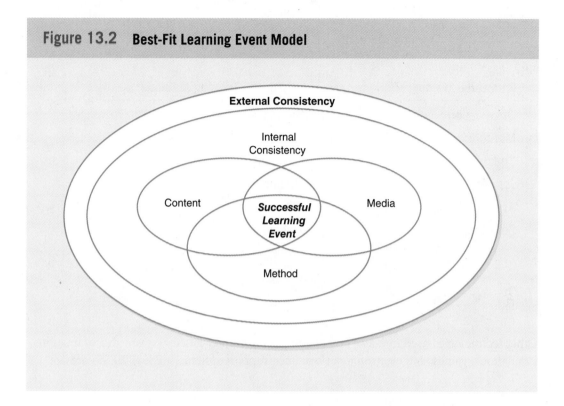

training is relatively inexpensive. While off-the-job methods may provide greater exposure to expert knowledge, they may also be more time-consuming and may not encourage knowledge transfer. Table 13.1 lists a number of examples of T&D methods in each category.

e-Learning

e-Learning (also elearning, Elearning, or eLearning) is an umbrella term and broadly refers to any learning facilitated using electronic means. Recent reports by the Chartered Institute of Personnel and Development (CIPD, 2012), the Society for Human Resource Management (2011) and American Society for Training & Development (2011) indicate that as the number of people accessing the Internet using a mobile device surpasses the number of people doing so using ordinary desktop computers, mobile learning and social media are rapidly replacing traditional forms of learning and early forms of e-Learning, such as computer-based training. **e-Learning** can capitalize on a variety of different technologies that have emerged as a result of rapid developments in information technology and the World Wide Web. The technologies can be commonly categorized as **Web 1.0, Web 2.0, and Web 3.0**. These are explained in Table 13.2.

Table 13.1 Training Methods

On-the-Job Training Methods	Off-the-Job Training Methods
Observation	Simulation
Mentoring	Role play
Coaching	Case study
Job rotation	Business games
Apprenticeship	External course or workshop
Self-directed learning	Behavior modeling
	Placement
	Open, distance, or blended learning

Other technologies used in e-learning encompass computer-aided assessments, animations, simulations, games, and electronic performance support systems (EPSSs). EPSSs are not

Table 13.2 Web Technologies

Technology	Explanation
Web 1.0	The first-generation web, including CD-ROMs, interactive videos, DVDs, video streaming, web pages, and software programs
Web 2.0	Web-based file sharing and user-generated interaction using discussion forums, e-mails, blogs, wikis and/or social media websites such as Yammer, MySpace, YouTube, Twitter, Facebook, Renren, LinkedIn, etc.
Web 3.0	The "intelligent web" based on a number of developments such as the semantic web, open access, augmented reality, and intelligent applications (e.g., speech recognition). Web 3.0 focuses on the use of software as a service, cloud computing, multiple technologies, and mobile devices. This is often associated with mobile learning.

learning technologies per se. However, they provide an electronic support infrastructure that allows employees to carry out their work. An EPSS would typically include assistants (e.g., Microsoft Office Assistant), wizards, knowledge bases, help, and advice functions. A number of Web 1.0 e-learning methods to address different training needs are identified in Table 13.3.

The e-learning methods explained in Table 13.3 are arranged according to the extent to which they use the Internet, the degree to which they facilitate interaction between peer learners and instructors, and the degree to which computers are networked or not networked. They are arranged in increasingly complex order; **mobile learning** shows the highest level of interaction and networking. However, this does not imply that methods that rely on greater student interaction or that allow greater access to external resources are necessarily the best options for all situations—the choice of e-learning method will depend on the best fit with the training needs that ought to be addressed (see Figure 13.2).

However, rapid developments in ICT also imply that many methods and approaches have a relatively short shelf life; that is, they quickly become obsolete (e.g., computer-based training). In addition, the distinction between some of these e-learning methods has become blurred, and the terminology can be confusing as terms are often used interchangeably. Increasingly the media employed in e-learning is interactive; that is, the learner interacts with the media. Using Web 2.0 and Web 3.0 technologies the e-learning content is generated by the users themselves and learning occurs "socially"; that is, the learner interacts with other learners and media to create their own learning environment.

Thus, online learning relies on digital collaboration. The term *digital collaboration* denotes networking and communication via the Internet using a variety of mobile devices. Although digital collaboration is of vital importance in the effectiveness of virtual teams in the business world, online collaboration between learners also tends to increase learning and learning transfer. Intranet-based **collaborative technologies**, such as groupware (electronic meeting software), provide a company forum for tracking, sharing, and organizing information. Groupware combines e-mail, document management, and electronic bulletin boards and allows users to collaborate on projects and documents simultaneously. The most common groupware is Lotus Notes (Noe, 2002). However, Google Mail combined with Google Docs, or Outlook combined with Office 365, represent free alternatives. Internet-based collaborative Web 2.0 technology, or **social networking technology** (e.g., blogs, wikis, or podcasts), play an increasingly important role in informal peer-to-peer learning, which is much faster, more flexible, and more responsive than formal modes of training (Frauenheim, 2007). Collaboration and communication in this context may be synchronous or asynchronous. **Synchronous communication** refers to "real-time" or live communication using tools such as messenger services or videoconferencing. Smartphones have become the device of choice for this type of communication and various apps are available for the

Table 13.3   Web 1.0-Based e-Learning Methods

e-Learning Methods	Explanation
Computer-based training (CBT) or technology-based training, computer-managed instruction (CMI), computer-aided (assisted) instruction (CAI), computer-based learning (CBL)	Interactive training experience using a stand-alone computer, when no collaboration and access to external resources is necessary; media used include CD-ROMs, DVDs, interactive video
Multimedia-based training (MBT)	Training experience that combines text, colors, graphics, audio, and video to engage the learner; MBT can range from a simple graphical presentation of text to a complex flight simulation
Distance learning (or education)	Learner and tutor are in different locations; the approach uses both synchronous and asynchronous communication; the course provider usually provides online support and supplies students with a course pack, including printed and audiovisual materials; courses follow a predetermined curriculum and schedule
Open learning (or education)	Learner has complete control over how, what, when, where, and at what pace learning occurs; any type and combination of media may be used
Open distance learning (ODL)	Umbrella term that covers both open and distance learning
Virtual learning environment (VLE) or virtual classroom	Online environment in which learning takes place
Web-based training (WBT) or online learning (or education), **Internet-based training (IBT)**	Any training and learning that takes place online, that is, via the World Wide Web
Mobile learning	Any T&D offering that involves mobile technologies; mobile technologies include notebooks, pads, smartphones, MP3 players

various mobile platforms such as iOS and Android. Web 2.0 and Web 3.0 technologies thus create virtual classrooms that can be accessed anytime, anyplace and which have the potential to be far more interactive than traditional classrooms could be.

However, not all collaboration can occur in real time, especially if learners are geographically dispersed across different time zones. While **asynchronous communication** still makes use of the Internet, communication is delayed, and learners access the learning spaces at their own convenience. Table 13.4 provides some examples of synchronous and asynchronous methods of e-learning.

Although it is important to make a distinction between different forms of collaboration, most e-learning combines various types of communication, collaboration, e-learning methods, and, in some cases, more traditional approaches to maximize learning transfer. Testing and assessment of e-learning may rely on traditional paper-based methods, the electronic submission of files, or interactive assignments (including online discussions). The combination of e-learning methods with traditional face-to-face methods is referred to as **blended learning**. According to industry reports, the use of blended learning in workplace training is rapidly increasing (Rossett & Frazee, 2006; Shaw & Igneri, 2006; Sparrow, 2004). This hybrid approach promises to combine the advantages of both traditional and e-learning approaches to training. For instance, one of the key issues in workplace training is the ability

---

Table 13.4   e-Learning Communication Typology

Synchronous	• Virtual learning environments (VLEs)
	• Instant messaging services
	• Audio- and videoconferencing
	• Digital chat rooms
	• Shared whiteboard applications
	• Application sharing
Asynchronous	• E-mail
	• Discussion forums or blogs
	• Threaded discussions
	• Self-paced learning

to apply new skills to the actual job. However, most online training does not provide for the application of new knowledge and skills, which is one of the key elements of Kolb's learning cycle. Blended learning, thus, allows the learner to apply new skills in a real-life situation, either in a classroom or on the job.

The development of e-learning programs and resources requires significant investments of time and money. However, the volatile nature of the global marketplace and the rapidly changing information needs of firms necessitate a different approach to e-learning. While standard e-learning solutions can take months to develop, **rapid e-learning (REL)** or just-in-time learning solutions may be developed in weeks, days, or even hours, depending on the complexity of materials to be created. Essentially, REL allows companies to produce a large amount of content, using limited resources, in a short time interval, and deliver this content in real time to a large number of people. Therefore, it is not surprising that industry observers predict significant increases in the REL market in years to come (Archibald, 2005; van Dam, 2005). REL has a number of key characteristics:

- It has a short development time.
- Subject matter experts (SMEs) act as the key source of content development.
- It can be created using standard presentation software.
- It allows for easy assessment and tracking of training.
- Auxiliary multimedia tools (including flash applications) can be used to enhance training experiences.
- Training units can be undertaken in minutes rather than hours.
- It can be synchronous as well as asynchronous (Bersin, 2005).

REL should ideally be used to deal with

- urgent necessary business and training needs,
- short shelf life of training,
- critical information needs and standard information broadcasts,
- training that is purely informational in nature,
- training that does not require mastery,
- prerequisite and introductory training, and
- training updates

but finds limited application for training in new skills and competencies (Bersin, 2005).

Although e-learning methods diverge on a number of levels, for instance, the level of interaction between learners, e-learning, in general, offers a range of advantages and disadvantages to the learner and to the organization. These are shown in Table 13.5. The key advantage of e-learning is flexibility; that is, it affords learners the choice of what, when, where, and how much is learned. The key disadvantages center on the lack of human contact and technological issues.

Table 13.5   Advantages and Disadvantages of e-Learning

Advantages	Disadvantages
Cost advantages compared with traditional methods	Basic computer skills necessary
Improves computer skills	Use of computers might cause apprehension
Self-paced	
High degree of learner control	Not suitable for certain content
Choice of learning environment	Privacy concerns if based online
Interactive	
Easy tracking of learner progress and engagement	Requires self-motivation to learn
Real-time feedback	Learners may feel isolated from instructors and peers
Consistent delivery method	
Variety of formats and methods available	Lack of human contact in general
Consistent content	Technical difficulties impede access
Unlimited access in terms of time and locale	
Better support, help functions, knowledge base than other methods	
Appeals to several senses simultaneously	
Increased benefits through the combination with traditional training methods	
Can be both synchronous and asynchronous	
Accommodates different learning styles	

Despite the increasing global popularity of e-learning initiatives, they suffer from several shortcomings. Nunes, McPherson, Annasingh, Bashir, and Patterson (2009) identify several of these:

- Some of the most advertized advantages of e-learning, such as reductions in the travel and accommodation costs associated with face-to-face training, are not well accepted by learners. Often, trainees have to undergo e-learning in addition to their normal workloads, in the office, and subject to their usual daily work pressures.

- Another source of dissatisfaction with e-learning is its lack of human touch: the lack of interaction with knowledgeable trainers and the lack of socialization with fellow learners.

- Generic multimedia simulations without an organizational and work-specific focus tend to alienate learners.

- Organizations still tend to rely on the conservative "drill-and-practice" model and "force-fed instruction" and, in the process, ignore the social, informal, and collaborative aspects of learning.

- There is also less emphasis on learner-centered approaches that take advantage of social negotiation, on-the-job learning, on-demand learning, and peer support. New learning models are moving in the direction of "casual, instant, and informal" learning facilitated by Web 2.0 technologies, such as blogs, Webcasts, online conferencing, and mobile learning using mobile devices.

- There is little research that links e-learning to employee creativity, innovation, and adaptability—all of which are essential to any workforce in the 21st-century knowledge economy.

- Often, learners are pushed into e-learning without being properly equipped with the basic skills required for being successful in a networked learning environment. e-Learning may also ignore diversity considerations, as certain groups of employees, such as ethnic minorities, women, and older people, may not have the aptitude and confidence to learn in a computer-mediated environment.

- Finally, e-learning is currently serving the needs of mainly large organizations and has yet to address the learning needs of small and medium-sized enterprises.

Salas, DeRouin, and Littrell (2005) offer several research-based guidelines for designing e-learning packages. Even though these guidelines pertain to **distance learning**, they are relevant and useful for other e-learning methods as well:

- Only provide e-learning when you are sure it meets the organization's specific learning and development needs.

- Train learners on computer basics before offering computer-based training.

- Take into consideration human cognitive processes when designing e-learning programs.

- Enhance the learning experience by including graphics, texts, and learning games in the presentation of learning topics.

- Keep learners "engaged" by offering blended learning and allowing interaction among trainees and between trainees and facilitators.

- Offer trainees control over certain aspects of instruction, and guide them through the learning process by using tools, such as cognitive maps.

Implementing T&D

The third stage of the systems model of T&D involves the implementation of training. Although this stage is depicted as a separate phase of the training process, it is closely linked with the preceding stage, the design stage. Indeed, many book chapters on T&D consider both stages in unison. The reason for this is that the design of a training solution ultimately determines its implementation, as any issues and factors that could arise during the implementation phase should be anticipated at the design stage (Stewart, 1999). For instance, if an organization wanted to roll out e-learning to its entire workforce via the company intranet, the firm would have to ensure that every employee had access to the intranet. To ensure that the implementation phase runs smoothly, organizations ought to formulate an implementation plan that should specify

- the resources required,

- how the training should be carried out,

- who should facilitate the training, and

- the period within which the training should occur.

The requisite resources vary with the training method chosen. While traditional face-to-face training necessitates physical training rooms and equipment, e-learning requires initial investments in ICT. Available resources are normally set out in predetermined annual training budgets. The training design will provide answers to the questions of how, by whom, and when training should be implemented. The implementation of a T&D initiative can only be considered successful if transfer of learning has occurred.

Training Transfer

Positive and long-lasting changes in employee behavior and, ultimately, increased shareholder value can only be attained if training (or learning) transfer occurs. **Training transfer** is the continuous application of the KSA acquired during the training exercise. Various classifications of transfer of training exist depending on the context:

- Near versus far (how close the training task is to the actual job task)
- Specific versus general (transfer of skills versus transfer of principles)
- Positive versus negative (linked to the perception of the training experience)
- Lateral versus vertical (Hayashi, Chen, & Terase, 2005)

Lateral transfer is about the application of training to similar tasks at the same level of complexity, while vertical transfer implies analysis and synthesis, that is, the ability to apply training to more complex tasks (Gagné, 1985). Training transfer depends on a number of variables, which can be summarized under five headings (Baldwin & Ford, 1988):

1. Trainee characteristics (the trainee's predisposition to training)
2. Training design (the organization of the learning environment)
3. Work environment (the immediate factors at work that affect transfer)
4. Learning and retention
5. Generalization and maintenance (ensuring that the trainee is given the opportunity to continuously use the acquired KSA)

Only if the trainee possesses the necessary characteristics, the training design and workplace environment foster learning transfer, and the trainee is given ample opportunity to apply the training will learning and retention take place. In addition, it has been demonstrated that transfer of training is *critically* dependent on the organizational climate that supports the training transfer (Lance, Kavanagh, & Brink, 2002; Rouiller & Goldstein, 1993; Tracey, Tannenbaum, & Kavanagh, 1995; Velada, Caetano, Michel, Lyons, & Kavanagh, 2007).

Evaluating T&D

To assess whether a particular training initiative, method, or solution has met the training needs and objectives of the firm and whether transfer of learning has taken place, organizations must evaluate their T&D efforts. Training evaluation is not an isolated activity. It is part of the T&D cycle and must be considered alongside and aligned with **needs analysis**, design, and implementation to provide a holistic picture of the entire T&D process. Similar to the T&D cycle, the evaluation process should be viewed as cyclical. The steps in the evaluation process are illustrated in Figure 13.3.

The evaluation process commences with the needs analysis. Training needs must then be translated into measurable learning outcomes. Appropriate metrics must be identified against

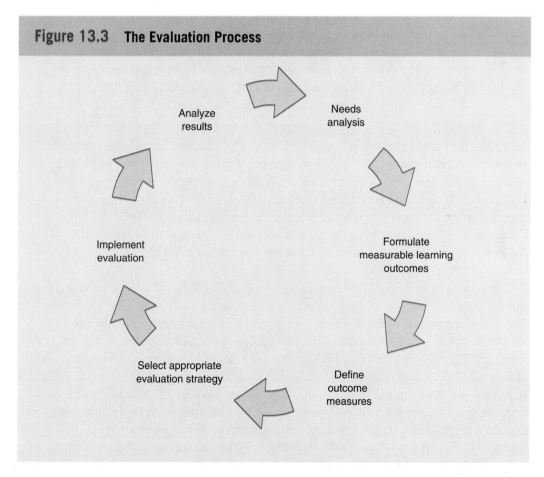

Figure 13.3   The Evaluation Process

Analyze results

Needs analysis

Implement evaluation

Formulate measurable learning outcomes

Select appropriate evaluation strategy

Define outcome measures

Source: Developed from Noe (2002).

which outcomes can be measured. The next step involves the selection of an appropriate evaluation strategy. Not all training can be assessed in the same manner because of the diversity in training methods. Once an evaluation has been carried out, the results must be analyzed and fed back into the training process. This final step is omitted in many evaluation models, even though it is crucially important to use evaluation data to make decisions about future training initiatives. An HRIS can be invaluable in supporting this process as it contains a vast amount of data related to training and performance that can form the basis of any T&D decision.

However, many organizations pay lip service to evaluation without having a clear concept of what evaluation means and what purpose it serves.

> People often confuse the process of monitoring, validation and evaluation. The purpose of monitoring is to take the temperature of a learning event from time to time, picking up any problems or emerging needs. Validation measures the achievement of learning objectives set for a learning initiative or process. Evaluation looks at the total value of that event or process, thereby placing it into its organizational context and aiding future planning. Faced with an evaluation task, there are four crucial questions to answer: why, who, when and how? (Harrison, 2005, p. 143)

Hence, the purpose of evaluation is manifold. Figure 13.2 shows that training initiatives must attain internal and external consistency to be effective. Thus, training is frequently validated under these aspects. Internal and external validations assess the degree to which stipulated T&D objectives are attained (Stewart, 1999). The purposes of evaluation discussed in the literature are plentiful (see, for example, Bramley, 1991; Gibb, 2002; Thomson, 2008) and range from the "very vague" to the "very specific" (Marsden, 1991). The primary purposes of evaluation could be summarized as in Table 13.6.

So what should be evaluated? As a rule, criteria for evaluation should be based on the training objectives (see Figure 13.3). In addition, the criteria ought to be relevant; that is, they should not be contaminated (biased) or deficient. However, criteria should also be reliable, practical, and discriminative. Training outcomes fall into a number of distinct categories. The number of training evaluation models in the literature seems almost infinite. Kirkpatrick (1960) suggests four levels of outcomes: reaction, learning, behavior, and results. Warr, Bird, and Rackham's (1970) CIRO framework also has four levels: context, inputs, reactions, and outcomes (immediate, intermediate, and ultimate). Easterby-Smith (1986) suggests a CAPIO framework comprising context, administration, process, inputs, and outputs. Finally, individual outcomes of training programs have been identified as falling within **Bloom's taxonomy** of learning domains (cognitive, psychomotor, and affective), which is one of the most widely used models to describe learning outcomes (Bloom et al., 1956;

Table 13.6 Purposes of Evaluation

Summative	Quantitative in nature; establishes whether T&D program was effective, was efficient, has added value, and has met its objectives
Formative	Qualitative in nature; assesses how training, learning, and development can be improved, that is, how they could be made more efficient and effective
Learning	Quantitative and qualitative assessment of learner's post-training performance to evaluate whether learning transfer has occurred
Power and Politics	Subjective in nature; is used to serve the interests of specific stakeholders within the organization

Source: Based on Easterby-Smith (1986).

Bloom, Masia, & Krathwohl, 1964). A comparison of these and other frameworks reveals a significant overlap between these evaluation models, as well as between a number of the key learning outcomes contained within them.

The key objective of any evaluation process will be to assess the broad range of individual and organizational outcomes as well as return on investment (ROI). Hence, one of the key considerations will be whether a T&D program has had any measurable impact on the firm's bottom line, so as to justify training expenditure and training budgets. The following section will consider some of the complexities involved in establishing the costs and the actual benefits of T&D initiatives.

Training Metrics and Cost-Benefit Analysis

The costs involved in training can be established relatively easily. These overheads can be substantial and involve direct costs and indirect costs (Noe, 2002). (See Chapter 7 for information on cost-benefit analysis.) A considerable direct cost is the loss of production sustained through the absence of trainees from work for the duration of the training. e-Learning significantly reduces this element of direct costs, as trainees generally do not have to leave their place of work to participate in online training (provided they have access to a computer).

Online courses may also be taken outside of work. In many cases, employees can avail themselves of online training through an intranet, which can be accessed from work and from home, thus allowing for greater flexibility at a reduced cost.

However, the actual benefits to the firm may be much more difficult to ascertain, as many of the benefits take a long time to materialize or can often be of an intangible nature. Moreover, it may prove almost impossible to isolate completely from other organizational variables the effects of training on performance. Ascertaining these effects is of great significance, though. In fact, this preoccupation with the quantification of the business benefits of training has frequently been described as the search for the "Holy Grail," and those organizations that evaluate training employ a number of different models and approaches to pursue this quest, including the balanced scorecard (Kaplan & Norton, 1992, 1993) and ROI (Phillips, 1996b). Russ-Eft and Preskill (2005) highlight three critical factors in HR development evaluation that complicate the assessment of training outcomes:

1. Evaluation occurs within a complex, dynamic, and variable environment.

2. Evaluation is essentially a political activity.

3. Evaluation ought to be purposeful, planned, and systematic.

Notwithstanding these factors, Phillips (1996a) advocates that any available post-training data should be analyzed and converted into monetary values to establish ROI. Phillips's (1996c, 2005) ROI methodology (or ROI process) produces six types of data, which are based on **Kirkpatrick's** (1960) **evaluation taxonomy**:

1. Reaction, satisfaction, and planned action

2. Learning and application

3. Implementation

4. Business impact (see Table 13.6)

5. ROI

6. Intangibles

The ROI method advocates five useful steps for converting hard (tangible) data and soft (intangible) data into monetary values:

1. Focus on a single unit of improvement in output, quality, or time.

2. Determine a value for each data unit.

3. Calculate the change in output performance directly attributable to training.

4. Obtain the annual amount of the monetary value of the change in performance.

5. Determine the annual value (the annual performance change times the unit value).

Having identified relevant data sources and applying these best practices, firms can use a number of approaches to quantify the relationship between training costs and benefits. These approaches are shown in Table 13.7. Organizations may use one or more of these ratios to determine the costs and benefits of planned and existing learning technology projects.

It is possible to enter basic values into a spread sheet application to calculate the ratios listed in Table 13.6. However, the variety of possible outcomes from training, the variety of factors that affect these outcomes, and the variety of data to be collected to produce any meaningful results appear to make the evaluation process a rather tedious task that would be next to impossible to complete efficiently and effectively without the help of a computerized system. Most commercial HRIS can be customized to record, analyze, and report on the training metrics that have been identified by a firm. For instance, the system could be configured to collect information on the monetary benefits of T&D projects, such as increased production output or a reduced number of complaints, and compare this information with data

Table 13.7 Cost-Benefit Approaches

Approach	Explanation
Benefit-cost ratio (BCR)	Monetary benefits of T&D projects
	Costs of T&D projects
Cost-benefit ratio (CBR)	Costs of T&D projects
	Monetary benefits of T&D projects
Payback period	Costs of T&D projects
	Annual savings
Return on investment (ROI)	Monetary benefits of T&D projects
	Costs of T&D projects

Source: Sadler-Smith (2006).

collected on the costs of T&D projects. In addition, the satisfaction with or the success of particular training interventions could be assessed. T&D data will usually be stored in the T&D module of the HRIS. The human capital management (HRM) modules included in the HRIS of the largest ERP systems, for example SAP or Oracle, incorporate functionalities for creating employee development plans, competency management tools, and online learning environments, as well as numerous training metrics. In addition, many dedicated T&D systems are commercially available. The following section will discuss the data elements and various HRIS applications used in the training function.

HRIS Applications in Training

Traditionally, training software applications have been employed to record information associated purely with training administration purposes (Noe, 2002). Today, firms place much greater demands on training applications in terms of compatibility with existing systems, analytical functionality, and accessibility to meet business needs. The primary demand on any system, however, must be that it furnishes usable information to key decision makers to achieve both administrative and strategic advantages (Kovach, Hughes, Fagan, & Maggitti, 2002).

Hence, useful HRIS information should possess three key characteristics:

1. It must be presented in a user-friendly manner and must be easy to use.

2. It must be meaningful and appropriate (Keebler & Rhodes, 2002).

3. It must be used effectively in the decision-making process to support an organization's overall business strategy (Kovach & Cathcart, 1999).

According to the Society for Human Resource Management (2011), HRIS training and development applications need to:

Be easy to use

Be customizable

Be integrated with other HR systems and functions

Offer a fully digital experience

Provide mobile access to all users

Be integrated with social media platforms

Be available as software as a service

However, Kovach and Cathcart (1999) argue that an HRIS does not need to be intricate or even computerized to serve the information needs of a business. Elementary HRIS training databases are easily set up using commercial or open-source desktop software (see Figures 13.4 and 13.5). These databases may then be used to collect, store, and analyze training-related HR information. The amount of data that can be stored, the manner in which it is collected, and the level of analysis possible will depend on the application used. Table 13.7 shows the basic data elements an electronic T&D database should contain. The first column, "Data Element," shows the main categories of data elements, while "Subcategory 1" and "Subcategory 2" provide examples of the type of information these data elements could include.

Using these essential data elements, we could create a spreadsheet (see Figure 13.4). This basic database contains relevant training information and possesses limited search and reporting capabilities. Should a firm decide to upgrade to commercial training software, data stored in a spreadsheet can be imported into most training applications.

Clearly, both the amount of information that can be collected and stored using a spreadsheet and the level of analysis that this application permits are limited. Therefore, many organizations create bespoke databases, which offer greater possibilities regarding the collection and presentation of training data. These database applications allow users to run queries using customizable search criteria; they provide greater reporting options; and information on different screens can be linked to avoid multiple entry of data. An example of such a database, one that includes the data elements and subcategories of Table 13.7, is shown in Figure 13.5. As more functionality is desired, organizations can also use a more sophisticated learning management system (LMS) to collect and manage training data (see Figure 13.6).

Figure 13.4　Example of an HRIS T&D Database in Spreadsheet Format

HRIS Training & Development Application.xls

	A	B	C	D	E	F
1	Employee ID	Employee name	Training history	Certified skills & competencies	Professional memberships	Educational Qualifications
2	001	Joe Soap				
3	002					
4	003					
5	004					
6	005					
7						

Sheet1 / Sheet2 / Sheet3 /

Figure 13.5　Example of a Database

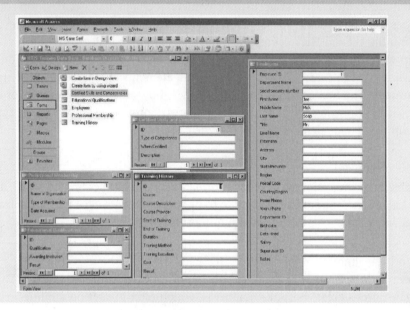

Table 13.8　Basic Data Elements for an HRIS Training Database

Data Element	Subcategory 1	Subcategory 2
Employee information	Employee ID	
	Employee name	Title
		First name
		Middle name
		Second name
	Social Security number	
	Department	
	Position	
	Reporting to	

Training history (training course completed)	Date of training (start and end)	
	Training methods	(see above)
	Course (including description)	List of common courses
	Course provider	List of common providers
	Training location	In-house
		Out-of-house
	Result	
	Duration	
	Cost	
	Notes on performance	
Certified skills and competencies		
Professional memberships		List of professional organizations
Educational qualifications		

As firms grow in size, their need to manage training activities and training data more effectively and efficiently increases accordingly. A host of commercial systems service the broad spectrum of T&D, ranging from stand-alone training administration software to fully integrated expert systems. T&D software is available in many guises. The most common applications are discussed here.

HRIS/Learning Applications: Learning Management Systems

The vast majority of large organizations rely on fully integrated enterprise-wide systems, called enterprise resource planning (ERP) systems, to satisfy their information needs. An ERP system amalgamates the management information systems (MIS) capabilities from all

Figure 13.6   Training Module With OrangeHRM (an Open Source HRIS)

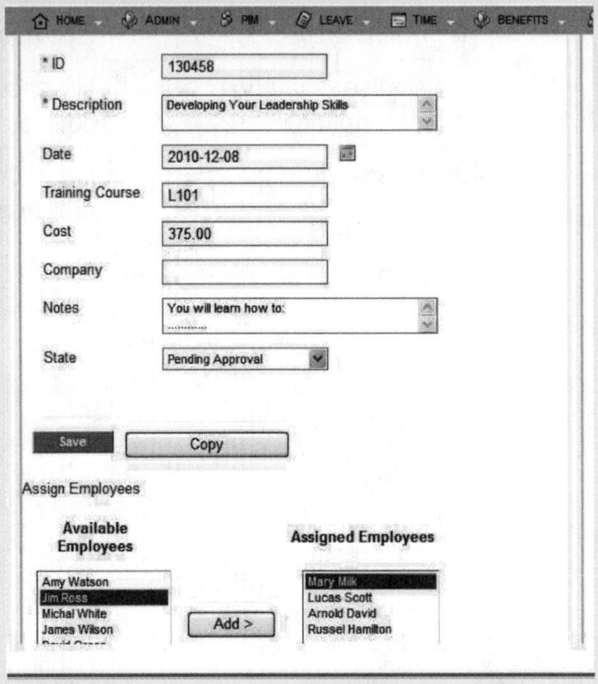

Source: OrangeHRM (www.orangehrm.com). Reproduced with permission.

functional areas in a business, for example, finance, production, marketing, and HRM, into a single integrated system. The ERP component that supports the HR function is commonly referred to as an HRIS. These data repositories for HR-related data typically comprise a number of modules, which in turn can support every area of HR, including T&D. Traditionally, firms used HRIS T&D applications and modules for administrative purposes only. The capabilities of today's HRIS T&D applications—learning management software that is usually bundled into a **learning management system (LMS)**—range from training administration to training and talent management. The uses and capabilities of an LMS are shown in the LMS classification presented in Table 13.8.

The use of administrative systems is restricted to transaction processing, including the calculation of training costs. Training management systems can facilitate the entire T&D

Table 13.9 Learning Management System Classification

Classification	Uses and Capabilities
Administration	Basic employee and T&D records
	Calculation of training costs
	Administrative permissions (who has data access, who can enter data)
Training management (including learning content management)	Scheduling and access to training courses
	Setup of training courses and initiatives
	Assignment of training based on skills and certification requirements
	Authoring of training courses and initiatives
	Online access to courses
	Training evaluation
	Tracking of training attendance and results
	ROI measurement
Talent management	KSA assessment
	Performance reviews and appraisals
	Recruiting
	Succession planning
	Career planning
	Management development

Source: Adapted from e-Learning Consulting (2007).

process (see the systems model of T&D described previously) from TNA to training evaluation. A **learning content management system (LCMS)**, as the name implies, can be used to store and develop T&D content, such as multimedia files, templates for training courses, or assignments. It may also be employed to track training attendance and completion records or for quality assurance purposes. LCMS is frequently used in combination with REL. A **talent management system (TMS)**, sometimes referred to as a human capital management system, is an integrated software suite that can comprise a range of applications, such as applicant tracking, succession and career planning, performance management, compensation and benefits management, and learning management. Talent management systems allow employees to create personal electronic *talent profiles,* which can be updated and usually reflect their KSA and goals. Organizations can use these data to generate information on the talent profile of the organization and to develop macro- and micro-level employee development plans. A large number of commercial learning management systems exist (see list of vendor websites in the appendix). These range from off-the-shelf products to server and Web-based enterprise solutions. The choice of system will be determined principally by an organization's LT&D needs, LT&D budget, and ICT capabilities. The reporting, analytical, and strategic potential of these systems will diverge accordingly. The degree to which learning management systems can assist strategic decision making may be assessed using Beckers and Bsat's (2002) decision support system (DSS) classification. Their model consists of five levels:

1. Management information systems (MIS)

2. Decision support systems (DSS)

3. Group decision support systems (GDSS)

4. Expert systems (ES)

5. Artificial intelligence (AI)

Each consecutive category offers the users more extensive reporting and analytical capabilities that can support strategic T&D decision making. MIS can be used to support T&D decision making at the operational, functional level of the organization. DSS and GDSS are designed to facilitate senior management decision making in the long term and relate to the overall mission and objectives of an organization. They are based on "what if" scenarios. Expert systems consist of a knowledge base, a decision-making function, and an interface. They replicate the decision-making capabilities of human experts. An example of a system that uses AI is an intelligent tutoring system (ITS). An ITS can be employed to tutor, coach, or empower employees. The advantages of these systems are that instruction can be aligned with learner needs, the system can respond to learner actions, and learner progress can be modeled (Noe, 2002). ES and AI aid strategic T&D decision making at the board level of the organization. However, capital investments in sophisticated HRIS T&D applications alone will not necessarily improve LT&D in the organization, nor will they lead to knowledge creation or organizational learning. Any HRIS project requires careful planning and ample resources (time, money, and expertise). Bonadio (2009) puts forward five key issues that could enhance the effectiveness of an LMS:

1. Employee development should be linked to learning delivery.

2. Learning activities ought to be aligned with business objectives.

3. Regulatory compliance must be maintained.

4. Learning effectiveness must be measured throughout the organization.

5. An integrated approach to employee onboarding (employee orientation) should be established.

HRIS T&D Applications: Implementation Issues

Many HRIS T&D projects fail to meet the expectations of key decision makers. The reasons for these failures are manifold. Some firms introduce a new TMS only because competitors have done so; yet, these companies may not have the necessary expertise to operate the system. Frequently, decision makers have false expectations of ROI or apply training metrics that merely focus on cost savings and fail to take note of intangible gains derived from T&D (see the section "Training Metrics and Cost-Benefit Analysis"). In other cases, the HRIS T&D application strategy is not aligned with training needs and the overall T&D, HR, and business strategies. Few organizations involve employees during the implementation stage of the HRIS, which can lead to underutilization and dissatisfaction with the system (Burbach & Dundon, 2005). For a variety of reasons (see "Disadvantages" in Table 13.4), many employees never actually complete the e-learning programs in which they are enrolled. Sometimes, disenchantment is simply the result of poor planning and the consequent incompatibility of various disjointed HR systems, albeit an increasing number of organizations purchase one or more items of their training management system from a single vendor to prevent these problems (Frauenheim, 2006). A number of authors have suggested success factors for the introduction of HRIS T&D applications (Gascó, Llopis, & González, 2004; Noe, 2002; Sadler-Smith, 2006) and for increasing e-learning completion rates (Frankola, 2001):

- Align e-learning strategy with T&D strategy, HR strategy, and overall business strategy.

- Create a corporate learning culture that fosters e-learning and the use of HRIS T&D applications.

- Assess HRIS T&D projects based on their suitability to meet the T&D strategy of the organization rather than the technical sophistication and elegant features of the system.

- Carefully plan HRIS T&D projects to guarantee compatibility with legacy systems, affordability in terms of budget allocations, and the existence of expertise to use the system.

- Involve line managers and employees in HRIS T&D projects to ensure greater buy-in.

- Match HRIS T&D applications and e-learning initiatives with their ability to meet training needs to encourage learning transfer.

- Establish a suitable evaluation strategy to assess the extent to which training technology meets training needs, and evaluate this fit regularly.

- Identify suitable T&D metrics that take account of all direct and indirect training outcomes.

- Promote the use of HRIS T&D applications and e-learning.

- Make managers accountable for the uptake of e-learning and for HRIS T&D utilization.

- Reward employees for their use of e-learning.

- Ensure that e-learning and T&D systems are user-friendly and provide quality information.

- Develop a data security policy for the T&D system and applications.

- Do not focus on only financial gains from HRIS T&D projects.

- Train managers and employees in the use of T&D technologies.

SUMMARY

This chapter highlighted the strategic importance of LT&D in an increasingly knowledge-intensive global economy. The discussion showed that it is important to distinguish between learning, training, and development to understand the processes that lead to the acquisition of knowledge, skills, and abilities (KSA). Other key concepts, such as knowledge management (KM) and the learning organization, were also explained. Knowledge creation, innovation, and organizational learning are inextricably linked to an organization's capacity to remain competitive. This chapter identified and explained various e-learning methods, their role in knowledge acquisition, and their advantages and disadvantages. Nonetheless, traditional face-to-face methods still carry considerable credence, which is reflected in the increasing use of blended learning, an approach that combines both traditional and online methods of learning. Notwithstanding the effect of face-to-face learning, emerging Web 2.0 and Web 3.0 technologies, such as social media and mobile learning, furnish organizations with a multitude of exciting new ways in which LT&D can be delivered and measured. The key differences to early e-Learning options are that the learners actively participate in creating the learning materials and that learning increasingly occurs in an informal virtual and social setting amongst peers rather than in the training rooms of a corporation. A careful analysis of training needs, various LT&D methods, and individual learning styles is necessary to ensure that transfer of learning occurs and that, ultimately, the strategic objectives of the organization can be attained. HRIS T&D applications are vitally important tools in pursuing a systematic approach to LT&D, which necessitates identifying training needs, designing LT&D solutions and methods, implementing these initiatives, and evaluating the effectiveness of training (including completing an assessment of ROI on training). As many LT&D outcomes are of an intangible nature or take a long time to materialize (note the definition of development in this context), it is inherently intricate to determine appropriate training metrics that may be employed to perform any meaningful CBA. The key is to analyze any available data. Notwithstanding these difficulties, a number of approaches to ascertain ROI using HRIS T&D applications were offered. This chapter also expounded on how an elementary T&D system can be created using a spreadsheet or database desktop application. A variety of HRIS T&D applications exist. Learning management systems may be embedded in an HRIS or ERP. These learning management systems vary considerably in their capacity to manage the training process, generate reports, or assist in strategic decision making. Talent management suites integrate a range of applications, including succession planning and learning management. Learning management systems with DSS and ES capabilities offer the greatest strategic value. However, the choice of system is contingent on the T&D needs of an organization, its budget, and its ICT capabilities. This chapter concluded with a discussion of the implementation of HRIS T&D applications.

KEY TERMS

DISCUSSION QUESTIONS

1. What is the systems model of T&D? Discuss how HRIS T&D applications can assist in carrying out the steps in the systems model.

2. Explain synchronous and asynchronous communication in relation to e-learning.

3. What are the advantages and disadvantages of e-learning?

4. How can HRIS T&D applications help firms foster organizational learning?

5. Explain how organizations should choose appropriate T&D methods.

6. What is transfer of training? What role does transfer of learning play in e-learning?

7. Explain the issues involved in establishing ROI for T&D initiatives. What role do HRIS T&D applications play in establishing ROI?

8. Outline how standard desktop applications such as a spreadsheet or database can be used to set up a basic T&D system.

9. Discuss the different types of HRIS T&D applications and their reporting and decision-support capabilities.

10. What issues might arise during and as a result of the implementation of HRIS T&D applications?

CASE STUDY

Meddevco (name changed) is a large multinational corporation that operates in the medical devices sector. The firm employs around 33,000 people in five divisions and has operations in 120 countries. A total of 66% of the multinational's revenue is generated from products that are less than two years old, and 80% of employees are working on products that are less than two years old. These figures illustrate the highly competitive and fast-paced nature of the medical devices sector. This sector is also characterized by high levels of regulatory control and a need to comply with industry norms. Meddevco is headquartered in the United States and Switzerland. The information needs of a firm of this size are substantial, and it would be next to impossible to collect, store, and analyze HR-related information without the use of a fully integrated global HRIS. Moreover, the diversity of the workforce, the multiplicity of skills required in the different divisions and to support the various product lines, and the pressure of compliance necessitate a perfectly orchestrated T&D effort. Needless to say, HRIS T&D applications play a major role in managing the T&D function. Meddevco uses an HRIS by PeopleSoft (now Oracle) to manage the majority of its global HR processes, including e-recruitment and performance appraisals. With regard to data entry into the system, the corporation operates a strict "no customization unless legally required" policy to ensure data compatibility across the system. In the United States, most HR services are centralized in an HR shared services center. The corporation has a dedicated HRIS center in Europe, and negotiations are ongoing to implement a European HR shared services model. The company uses a number of different payroll systems in Europe for compliance reasons. All employees in the corporation have access to a company intranet called My Meddevco, which also includes a learning portal that provides access to online training programs, which employees can use at work and at home. The intranet also includes a knowledge base and detailed company information, including a full listing of all employees and their job titles and locations. Employee transfers and promotions are also listed. A number of years ago, the corporation made the decision not to use the training module included in PeopleSoft and opted for a training management system called SABA to coordinate and manage training initiatives; for example, the recent rollout and training for the use of SAP (an ERP system) for production facilities was managed through SABA. In addition, Meddevco has recently commenced using the talent management module included in PeopleSoft to identify and track high-performing employees for promotion. Every employee is required to complete an online talent profile, which is similar to an online CV and which can be updated by the employee. The combination of systems and applications and the careful analysis of HR information contained therein allow the organization to develop and implement a global T&D strategy. However, the firm also faces some challenges arising from the use of these systems. As the organization largely grew through acquisition, a number of legacy systems still coexist with the global HRIS at some of its subsidiaries. Data compatibility issues also derive from the use of SABA, which is not part of PeopleSoft. In addition, the firm is also using SAP, and it is questionable whether Oracle (the owner of PeopleSoft) will support data exchanges with a system supplied by its chief competitor. Furthermore, because Meddevco did not involve the workforce in the implementation process of the TMS, employees are reluctant to complete their talent profiles. Moreover, the need to customize the HRIS locally to comply with the national legislation affecting Meddevco subsidiaries further complicates the collection and transfer of data within the global HRIS.

The example of Meddevco illustrates how large organizations employ HRIS to manage their workforces and how they leverage HR development through the use of HRIS T&D applications, learning portals, and specialized learning management systems. However, it is also apparent that careful planning is essential to avoid compatibility issues and to ensure a consistent global flow of HR- and T&D-related information.

Case Study Questions

1. What should Meddevco have done to avoid some of its problems?

2. How could Meddevco now solve the problems created by not involving employees during the implementation of the HRIS?

3. What else should Meddevco do now to improve the operation of its system?

Practical Exercise

Try to set up an interview with someone from a company such as FedEx, UPS, or Amazon with a view to discussing corporate training initiatives and the effects of these on employee retention, development, and performance. In particular, try to establish the role and integration of HRIS in the organization's training programs and how HRIS is being used to increase the efficiency and effectiveness of training initiatives.

STUDENT STUDY SITE

Visit the Student Study Site at **http://www.sagepub.com/kavanagh3e** for additional learning tools such as access to SAGE journal articles and related web resources.

NOTES

1. The company's name must remain confidential.

2. The bold terms in this chapter are included in the list of key terms. These terms cannot and do not purport to provide an exhaustive list of HRIS T&D applications. However, they furnish explanations of the key concepts discussed in this chapter. More extensive e-learning glossaries are available on the World Wide Web, for instance, from the American Society for Training and Development, or ASTD (www.learningcircuits.org/glossary), and from WorldWideLearn (www.worldwidelearn.com/elearning-essentials/elearning-glossary.htm).

REFERENCES

American Society for Training & Development (2011), *Mobile Learning—Learning in the Palm of your hand,* Whitepaper, 3(1), Alexandria, VA: ASTD.

Archibald, D. (2005). *Rapid e-learning: A growing trend.* Retrieved from http://www.learningcircuits.org/2005/jan2005/archibald.htm

Argyris, C., & Schon, D. A. (1978). *Organization learning II: Theory, method and practice.* Reading, MA: Addison-Wesley.

Baldwin, T. T., & Ford, J. K. (1988). Transfer of training: A review and directions for future research. *Personnel Psychology, 41*(1), 63–105.

Beckers, A. M., & Bsat, M. Z. (2002). A DSS classification model for research in HRIS. *Information Systems Management, 19*(3), 41–50.

Bersin, J. (2005). Making rapid e-learning work. *Chief Learning Officer, 4*(7), 20–24.

Bloom, B. S., Engelhart, M., Furst, E. J., Hill, W., & Krathwohl, D. (1956). *Taxonomy of educational objectives: Vol. 1. The cognitive domain.* New York: McKay.

Bloom, B. S., Masia, B. B., & Krathwohl, D. (1964). *Taxonomy of educational objectives: Vol. 2. The affective domain.* New York: McKay.

Bonadio, S. (2009). *HR field guide—5 tips to effective learning management.* Wayland, MA: Softscape.

Boydell, T. H. (1983). *A guide to the identification of training needs.* London: British Association for Commercial and Industrial Education.

Bramley, P. (1991). *Evaluating training effectiveness: Translating theory into practice.* London: McGraw-Hill.

Burbach, R., & Dundon, T. (2005). The strategic potential of human resource information systems: Evidence from the Republic of Ireland. *International Employment Relations Review, 11*(1/2), 97–118.

Burnes, B. (2004). *Managing change: A strategic approach to organisational dynamics.* Harrow, UK: Prentice Hall/Financial Times.

Chartered Institute of Personnel and Development (2012), *From e-learning to 'gameful' employment, Research Insight, April 2012,* London, UK: CIPD.

Collin, A. (2007). Learning and development. In J. Beardwell & T. Claydon (Eds.), *Human resource management: A contemporary approach* (5th ed.). Harlow, UK: Prentice Hall, Financial Times.

Cummings, T. G., & Worley, C. G. (2001). *Organization development and change* (7th ed.). Cincinnati, OH: South-Western College Publishing.

Easterby-Smith, M. (1986). *Evaluation of management, training, and development.* Aldershot, UK: Gower.

e-Learning Consulting. (2007). *Learning management systems.* Retrieved from http://www.e-learningconsulting.com/consulting/what/learning-management.html

Frankola, K. (2001). Tips for increasing e-learning completion rates. *Workforce, 80*(10), 56.

Frauenheim, E. (2006). Talent management software is bundling up. *Workforce Management, 85*(19), 35.

Frauenheim, E. (2007). Your co-worker, your teacher: Collaborative technology speeds peer-peer learning. *Workforce Management, 86*(2), 19–23.

Gagné, R. M. (1985). *The conditions of learning and theory of instruction* (4th ed.). New York: Holt, Rinehart & Winston.

Gascó, J. L., Llopis, J., & González, M. R. (2004). The use of information technology in training human resources: An e-learning case study. *Journal of European Industrial Training, 28*(5), 370–382.

Gibb, S. (2002). *Learning and development: Process, practices, and perspectives at work.* Basingstoke: Palgrave Macmillan.

Grant, R. M. (1996). Toward a knowledge-based theory of the firm. *Strategic Management Journal, 17*(10), 109–122.

Gunnigle, P., Heraty, N., & Morley, M. (2002). *Human resource management in Ireland* (2nd ed.). Dublin, Ireland: Gill & Macmillan.

Harrison, R. (2005). *Learning and development.* London: Chartered Institute of Personnel and Development.

Hayashi, A., Chen, C. C., & Terase, H. (2005). Aligning IT skills training with online asynchronous learning multimedia technologies. *Information Systems Education Journal, 3*(26), 3–10.

Honey, P., & Mumford, A. (1992). *Manual of learning styles* (3rd ed.). London: Peter Honey.

Kaplan, R. S., & Norton, D. P. (1992). The balanced scorecard: Measures that drive performance. *Harvard Business Review, 70*(1), 71–79.

Kaplan, R. S., & Norton, D. P. (1993). Putting the balanced scorecard to work. *Harvard Business Review, 71*(5), 134–140.

Keebler, T. J., & Rhodes, D. W. (2002). e-HR: Becoming the "path of least resistance." *Employment Relations Today, 29*(2), 57–66.

Kirkpatrick, D. L. (1960). Techniques for evaluating training programmes. *Journal of the American Society for Training and Development, 14,* 13–18, 25–32.

Knowles, M. S., Holton, E. F., III, & Swanson, R. A. (2005). *The adult learner: The definitive classic in adult education and human resource development* (6th ed.). San Diego: Elsevier.

Kolb, D. A. (1984). *Experiential learning: Experience as a source of learning and development.* Englewood Cliffs, NJ: Prentice Hall.

Kovach, K. A., & Cathcart, C. E. (1999). Human resources information systems (HRIS): Providing business with rapid data access. *Public Personnel Management, 28*(2), 274–282.

Kovach, K. A., Hughes, A. A., Fagan, P., & Maggitti, P. G. (2002). Administrative and strategic advantages of HRIS. *Employment Relations Today, 29*(2), 43–48.

Lance, C. E., Kavanagh, M. J., & Brink, K. E. (2002). Retraining climate as a predictor of retraining success and as a moderator of the relationship between cross-job retraining time estimates and time to proficiency

in the new job. *Group and Organization Management, 27,* 294–317.

Learning. (2007). In *Encyclopædia Britannica.* Retrieved from http://www.britannica.com/eb/article-9369902

Marsden, J. (1991). Evaluation: Towards a definition and statement of purpose [Electronic Version]. *Australian Journal of Educational Technology, 7,* 21–28. Retrieved from http://www.ascilite.org.au/ajet/ajet7/marsden.html

Mayo, A. (1998). Memory bankers. *People Management, 4*(2), 34–38.

Noe, R. A. (2002). *Employee training and development* (2nd ed.). New York: McGraw-Hill.

Nonaka, I., & Takeuchi, H. (1995). *The knowledge-creating company.* New York: Oxford University Press.

Nunes, J. M., McPherson, M. A., Annasingh, F., Bashir, I., & Patterson, D. C. (2009). The use of e-learning in the workplace: A systematic literature review. *Impact: Journal of Applied Research in Workplace E-learning, 1*(1), 97–112.

Organisation for Economic Co-operation and Development. (1996). *The knowledge based economy.* Paris: Author.

Organisation for Economic Co-operation and Development. (2001). *The well-being of nations: The role of human and social capital.* Paris: Author.

Pedler, M., Burgoyne, J., & Boydell, T. (1991). *The learning company: A strategy for sustainable development.* Maidenhead, UK: McGraw-Hill.

Pfeffer, J. (1996). *Competitive advantage through people: Unleashing the power of the work force.* Boston: Harvard Business School Press.

Pfeffer, J. (1998). *The human equation: Building profits by putting people first.* Boston: Harvard Business School Press.

Phillips, J. J. (1996a). How much is the training worth? *Training & Development, 50*(4), 20.

Phillips, J. J. (1996b). ROI: The search for best practices. *Training & Development, 50*(2), 42.

Phillips, J. J. (1996c). Was it the training? *Training & Development, 50*(3), 28.

Phillips, J. J. (2005). The value of human capital: Macro-level research. *Chief Learning Officer, 4*(10), 60–62.

Porter, M. (1990). *The competitive advantage of nations.* New York: Free Press.

Prahalad, C. K., & Hamel, G. (1990). The core competencies of the corporation. *Harvard Business Review, 6*(3), 79–91.

Rossett, A., & Frazee, V. (2006). *Blended learning opportunities.* New York: American Management Association.

Rouiller, J. Z., & Goldstein, I. L. (1993). The relationship between organizational transfer climate and positive transfer of training. *Human Resource Development Quarterly, 4,* 377–390.

Russ-Eft, D., & Preskill, H. (2005). In search of the Holy Grail: Return on investment evaluation in human resource development. *Advances in Developing Human Resources, 7*(1), 71–85.

Sadler-Smith, E. (2006). *Learning and development for managers: Perspectives from research and practice.* Oxford, UK: Blackwell.

Salas, E., DeRouin, R. E., & Littrell, L. N. (2005). Research-based guidelines for designing distance learning. In H. G. Gueutal & D. L. Stone (Eds.), *The brave new world of eHR* (pp. 104–136). San Francisco: Jossey-Bass.

Senge, P. (1990). *The fifth discipline.* New York: Doubleday.

Shaw, S., & Igneri, N. (2006). *Effectively implementing a blended learning approach* (Eedo Knowledgeware White Paper). New York: American Management Association.

Society for Human Resource Management. (2011). *Future Insights—The top trends for 2012 according to SHRM's HR subject matter expert panels.* Alexandria, VA: SHRM.

Soliman, F., & Spooner, K. (2000). Strategies for implementing knowledge management: Role of human resources management. *Journal of Knowledge Management, 4*(4), 337–345.

Sparrow, S. (2004). Blended is better. *Training & Development, 58*(11), 52–55.

Stewart, J. (1999). *Employee development practice.* London: Financial Times/Pitman.

Thomson, I. (2008). Evaluation of training. *Chartered Institute of Personnel and Development (CIPD).* Retrieved from http://www.cipd.co.uk/subjects/lrnanddev/evaluation/evatrain.htm

Tracey, J. B., Tannenbaum, S. I., & Kavanagh, M. J. (1995). Applying trained skills on the job: The importance of the work environment. *Journal of Applied Psychology, 80,* 239–252.

van Dam, N. (2005, January 28). e-Learning development at the speed of business. *Chief Learning Officer.* Retrieved from http://clomedia.com/articles/view/e_learning_development_at_the_speed_of_business

Velada, R., Caetano, A., Michel, J. W., Lyons, B. D., & Kavanagh, M. J. (2007, December). The effects of training design, individual characteristics, and work environment on transfer of training. *International Journal of Training and Development, 11*(4), 282–294.

Warr, P., Bird, M., & Rackham, N. (1970). *Evaluation of management training.* Aldershot, UK: Gower.

Wright, P. M., Dunford, B. B., & Snell, S. A. (2001). Human resources and the resource based view of the firm. *Journal of Management, 27*(6), 701–720.

Yahya, S., & Goh, W.-K. (2002). Managing human resources toward achieving knowledge management. *Journal of Knowledge Management, 6*(5), 457–468.

Performance Management, Compensation, Benefits, Payroll, and the Human Resource Information System

Charles H. Fay and Renato E. Nardoni

EDITORS' NOTE

This chapter is the fourth one involving an organization's talent management program and its utilization as aided by an HRIS. This chapter completes our look at the cycle of activities involved in talent management—planning and forecasting the need for talent (Chapter 11), recruitment and selection of talent (Chapter 12), and training for talent management (Chapter 13). The purpose of talent management is to achieve the organization's strategic goal of remaining competitive in its market. This chapter describes the HR programs used in talent management and performance management, and how in concert they maintain market competiveness for the organization. The focus of this chapter is on management of employee performance in a systematic manner. This performance management system involves evaluation of both individual job performance and the reward system of the organization that supports the evaluation. The reward system of the organization involves the design, decision making, and administration of both compensation and benefits practices. To understand why this performance management system works we will cover the meaning of work and how it affects the motivation of employees. The uniqueness of this chapter is its description of the design and operation of typical HRIS applications in the performance management, compensation, and benefits programs.

CHAPTER Objectives

After completing this chapter, you should be able to

- Understand the performance management (PM) cycle and the role of the HRIS in PM design, decision making, and administration
- Understand typical compensation practices and the role of the HRIS in compensation design, decision making, and administration
- Understand typical benefits practices and the role of the HRIS in benefits design, decision making, and administration
- Understand payroll systems and the role of the HRIS in payroll administration
- Be able to discuss the meaning of work to employees in terms of their identities and self-esteem
- Discuss a motivation theory that helps to understand why work is so important to employees and how the HR programs in talent and performance management affect employee motivation.

HRIS IN ACTION

As Mark walked into his work area, he was fuming. "Those idiots in HR and payroll are really the gang that couldn't shoot straight," he announced to everyone in the vicinity. "What did they do now?" asked Marsha. "Don't tell me they got it wrong again!"

"They sure did," said Mark. "After I complained last month you'd think they would at least check to make sure they corrected their mistake. If I treated a customer this way I'd get fired!"

Mark's paycheck is wrong once again, and the story is a complicated one. It started with the performance review Mark had received from his boss the previous month. The review was good, and Mark had earned an "Exceeds standards" summary rating. Somehow, when an HR data-entry clerk entered the approved rating into the system an error was made, and "Does not meet standards" went into the compensation review system. The error snowballed, and Mark received no merit increase or bonus for the year. In fact, because of increased deductions for health coverage, his check was actually smaller than the one he had received two weeks earlier. Apart from the financial costs, Mark was psychologically shattered because his boss had discussed in their performance review meeting how good his performance was.

After his boss intervened, HR and payroll corrected the error and noted that Mark would receive the expected increase and a one-time adjustment for back pay. On the strength of that, Mark made additional financial commitments. When the latest check was direct deposited into Mark's bank account, the mistake had not been corrected, and a check Mark had written was returned for insufficient funds. Payroll's excuse? HR had not received the approved changes at least one week prior to check issuance—payroll's deadline for changes.

How can errors like this be avoided? They are not uncommon. A large state university in the Northeast makes salary adjustments to faculty who receive performance increases in two stages: The adjustment becomes part of the biweekly paycheck in late spring, and the adjustment for January 1 through late spring is paid out as a lump sum in summer. Last summer, the back-pay adjustment was considerably higher than it should have been because of a data-entry error in the adjustment formula. No one caught the error until this year, when the university had to notify all faculty members that the back-pay adjustment for this year would be reduced by the excess adjustment received the previous year.

PM, compensation, benefits, and payroll are sensitive areas for most employees. The typical employee tends to "keep score" on his or her relationship with an employer through these systems. It is critical that information technology (IT) systems in these areas be flawlessly executed from the employee's perspective because getting the wrong (or no) paycheck sends a very bad message to the employee. Given the amounts of money involved, it is critical that IT systems in these areas be flawlessly executed from the employer's perspective as well.

In this chapter, we will provide an overview of PM, compensation, benefits, and payroll, so that you have an idea of the complexity that must be captured if the HRIS is to work well.

Introduction

Performance, rewards, and payroll systems focus on the basic exchange of inputs and outcomes between employees and employers. Employees provide performance, and, in exchange, employers provide rewards, which are distributed via payroll systems. These systems also serve as good examples of several IT issues in human resources management (HRM). **Performance management (PM)** systems are usually entirely internal to the organization, but data must be linked to several other systems, including rewards, staffing, training and development, and career development. PM systems are used as working tools by managers to motivate employees to perform well in their jobs and must, therefore, be inherently self-explanatory. Often, data are specific to the individual, although various summary measures must be comparable across subsets of employees or all employees.

Since job performance is a function of individuals' knowledge, skills, and abilities (KSAs) and their motivation to work, a good starting point to understand how a PM program works is to examine the meaning of work.

The Meaning of Work

For most of us, work takes up a large part of our time and effort and is our major source of income. It shapes our identity, is critically important in how we perceive ourselves, and affects our self-esteem and self-worth. Each is an important part of the meaning of work, and strongly affects our motivation to work and perform effectively. The employee-employer exchange is the basis of a work motivation theory called **Equity Theory** (Adams, 1963, 1965). Basing our discussion of PM in motivation theory is necessary since the primary purpose of a PM program is to both help align employee performance with organizational outcomes and to motivate employees to perform well. Due to the importance of effective employee performance, we will cover the major tenets of equity theory.

How does the theory apply to work and management? All employees seek a fair balance between what they put into their jobs and what they get out of it. But how do we decide what is a *fair balance*? The answer lies in Equity Theory. Importantly, we arrive at our measure of fairness, or equity, by comparing our balance of effort and reward, that is, the ratio of input and output, with the balance enjoyed by other employees whom we deem to be relevant reference points. None of us like to feel that we are placing more effort into our work and receiving fewer rewards (e.g., salary, bonuses, benefits, etc.) than those around us. Equity Theory can therefore help explain why people can be happy and motivated by their situation one day, and yet with no change to their terms and working conditions can be made very unhappy and demotivated, if they learn for example, that a colleague (or worse an entire group) is enjoying a better reward-to-effort ratio. Use of this theory can help us understand why people select one job over another, or seek a raise because one's coworker has gotten a raise. Thus, the effectiveness of the PM system in motivating employees' performance has its basis in Equity Theory.

In contrast to performance management systems, which are entirely internal to an organization, reward systems have both internal and external ties to multiple other information systems. Both pay and benefits must be linked (or linkable) to external survey data, legal requirement data, and internal systems such as budgeting and planning systems. Usage of parts of reward systems must be restricted to HR professionals, while other parts must be widely available to employees for self-queries. Most organizations consider rewards data to be highly confidential, so system security is critical. Reward systems data focus on the individual, small-group, unit, and organization levels for different purposes, and the same variable (e.g., value of a specific benefit, seniority, option value) may have to be defined, calculated, stored, and reported in multiple ways depending on the need.

In the case of payroll systems, flawless data integrity and even more flawless execution are critical. Anyone who has ever received an inaccurate paycheck will understand the frustration and anger that occur; a payroll system that is not flawless is an administrator's nightmare. Payroll systems must be linked to external data (e.g., federal and state requirements for minimum wage) and internal data (e.g., general ledger, benefit choices) and must be capable of incorporating constant change. The payroll system is generally used only by payroll specialists, but every employee "audits" his or her own results. One final aspect of payroll is that some summaries of payroll data are not likely to match summaries of the same variables used in compensation or other HR systems. Even in a question as seemingly simple as number of employees, there will be discrepancies in these data summaries. For example, the compensation system is likely to contain only currently active employees; benefits might also include employees on leave, retired employees, and those former employees who have elected continuation of benefits under the **Consolidated Omnibus Budget Reduction Act (COBRA)** of 1986; and payroll files will contain everyone for whom a check is cut.

Although the interrelationships between performance management, rewards, benefits, and payroll are clear, and it is obvious that the HRIS applications for these four functions need to interface seamlessly, it would be a mistake to assume that these four functions can be considered independently of other HR applications or, indeed, of any of the information systems operated by the organization. The HRIS must allow for all aspects of the employment relationship (including relationships with prospective and past employees that affect equity perceptions) to be considered, analyzed, and acted on. Neither managers nor employees see the relationship between the organization and the employee through a single lens. In turbulent times, it is difficult to predict how information may need to be used. The potential must be there for any data sets currently collected by the organization to be retrieved and analyzed based on the requirements of the problems faced, not on the bin in which the data currently reside.

This chapter focuses on the data inputs, the typical reports that are generated, data outflows to other systems, and the ways that the IT system can provide decision support to organizations and managers in the areas of PM, rewards, and payroll. Before that discussion can be meaningful, however, a brief overview of each of the areas is necessary.

Performance Management

Overview

Until recently, most discussion in organizations focused on the performance appraisal process. The emphasis was on getting the "best" appraisal format and training managers to "rate" employees using the format. Most research, whether by scholars or professionals, was on rating formats, rater error, and the training of raters. The assumption was that, if the correct format could be developed and managers were trained to use it, the resulting ratings would be accurate.

During the 1980s, professionals and some scholars became interested in a different goal: improving performance (Banks & May, 1999; Bernardin, Hagan, Kane, & Villanova, 1998). This interest led to a reconsideration of the whole performance process, and attention shifted to PM. The PM process consists of three parts: performance planning, **performance observation**, and providing **positive feedback** and/or **corrective feedback**. In support of this process, periodic performance summaries are developed to serve as a basis for performance planning for the next period while providing data for a variety of HR decisions, including rewards, staffing, training, and other decisions affecting the employee's relationship with the organization. This description of the process of performance management is based on the motivational theory of goal setting (Locke & Latham, 1984, 1990a, 1990b).

The fundamental tenet of **Goal-Setting Theory** is that goals and intentions are responsible for human behavior. After years of research on this theory, the evidence for this tenant was strong (Locke, Shaw, Saari, & Latham, 1981). On the basis of this extensive research, several other tenants of the theory were verified. First, it was found that if goals determine human behavior, higher or more difficult goals result in higher levels of performance than those resulting from easy goals. Second, it was found that specific goals (such as reducing employee absences by 25%) result in higher levels of effort than vague goals such as "Why don't we reduce absenteeism by 15%. Third, it was found that incentives such as money, feedback, and competition will have no effect on behavior unless they lead to the setting and acceptance of specific, hard goals. It is clear that the whole performance process described above was based in some part on this theory since the theory and PM work.

PM is now considered within the framework of "talent management," which encompasses all areas of HR that have to do with onboarding, developing, evaluating, and managing the workforce through all the normal cycles (see Chapter 11 for more complete coverage of talent management and HRIS). PM is just one of the areas connected to others such as

- recruiting (external),
- staffing (internal),
- career management,
- 360° assessment,
- development management/training,
- retention management, and
- workforce planning.

The model of contemporary talent management is shown in Figure 14.1.

Note that many organizations today, although having installed expensive and expansive enterprise resource planning (ERP) systems, which were supposed to provide a single platform for all these integrated applications, found that it was necessary to add specialized talent management solutions from third-party vendors to achieve the necessary functionality.

The link from the resulting performance and compensation processes to the core payroll systems, however, still remains as an integral link between the ERP systems and the specialized talent management solutions. This link would also be consistent with the findings from goal-setting theory. In the example given in the opening vignette, if there were an integrated talent management system linking the performance module and compensation,

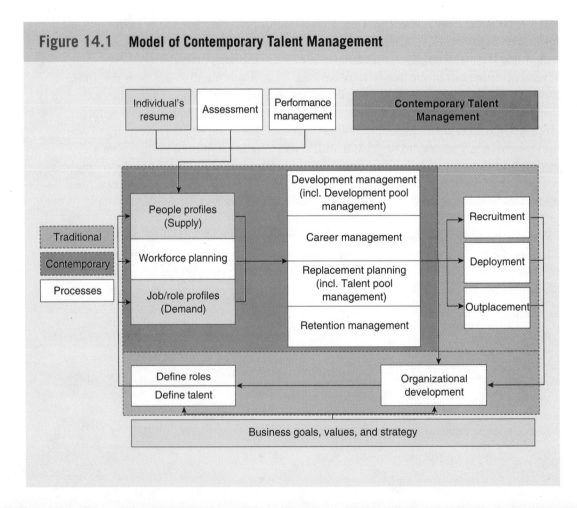

Figure 14.1   Model of Contemporary Talent Management

there would be no need for anyone to enter the performance rating into the compensation system since the performance rating would have already been there as a result of the approved employee review.

Performance Planning

Performance planning, like most management processes, must be constructed in such a way that any manager can do it, regardless of management style or skills. Better managers involve the employee collaboratively in all phases of the PM process, but the system is designed so that even directive managers can follow the process. This discussion assumes that the manager is more directive than collaborative.

The manager must first define what performance means in the case of a specific **direct report** (i.e., the employee whose job performance is being evaluated). At the broadest level, this definition of performance would encompass any employee who fills the job position. Remember that the job position is described in terms of duties and tasks outlined in the job description. Another way to conceive the definition of performance is that it is the performance expected of a new employee in the position if the direct report were terminated. Ideally, this definition is developed by a cascade of goals, fitting the research findings on goal-setting theory, beginning with the organizational strategy and operating plan, with the immediate source being what the manager is expected to accomplish during the period and ending with the direct report's expected part of that accomplishment (Evans, 2001). The manager must then move from the general to the specific, usually expressed in terms of desired outcomes. This constitutes the performance dimensions for the direct report and is consistent with the findings from goal-setting theory.

When outcomes are difficult to observe or measure, behaviors that are expected to lead to desired outcomes are added. For each performance dimension, the manager must develop specific outcomes and behaviors that will be used to measure the direct report's performance. For a performance dimension of budget management, an outcome might be "Stays close to budget for each budget category." A behavior on the same dimension might be "Checks expenditures against budget." After the measures are determined, the manager must set appropriate standards for each measure. The standard for "Checks expenditures against budget" might be "Checks expenditures against budget weekly." After defining standard performance, "Exceeds standards" and "Fails to meet standards" would be defined. The "Exceeds standards" level for "Checks expenditures against budget" might be "Checks expenditures against budget weekly; where discrepancies exceed 2%, checks those categories daily until discrepancies disappear." The "Fails to meet standards" level might be "Misses weekly check of expenditures against budget; allows discrepancies to continue without any follow-up." It should be noted that performance dimensions, measures, and standards are unique to each position, although attempts should be made to develop common standards for employees with identical job titles.

When performance dimensions, measures, and standards have been developed, the manager must communicate them to the direct report. The manager must make certain that the direct report understands measures and standards. The manager then gets the direct report to set goals for performance for the coming year. Note that goals and standards are not the same thing. The standard is what is expected of a fully job-knowledgeable employee who exerts normal effort. One purpose of PM is to get employees to set stretch goals, to be better than the standard. At the end of the goal-setting discussion, the direct report has agreed on some performance level as a goal. The set of performance measures, with standards and goals, becomes the **performance contract** for a defined performance period, typically a year.

Formats

Most organizations define the performance instrument differently depending on the type or level of the employee. For example, a nonmanagement or clerical position may have a relatively standard set of criteria that requires little or no change year after year. On the other hand, management employees tend to use a format that combines both goals and objectives together with a competency evaluation. A well-designed performance application can automatically map the correct "format" based on the employee who has logged into the performance website.

For the management "format," the performance evaluation can reflect a weighting of a goal portion and the competency portion (e.g., 60% of the overall rating will be based on the goals results, while 40% will reflect the competency ratings). Also, within each of these sections, a specific performance level for each goal or competency might be rated. Therefore, the overall result could reflect a weighted calculation of each goal, competency, and section. Web-based performance systems can easily perform these calculations for the user. Even if the organization prefers that the employee and/or the manager actually determine the overall rating, the system can provide "advice" as to the reasonableness of the entered rating versus the underlying ratings.

Performance Period

During the performance period, the manager uses the performance contract as a benchmark for observing the direct report. When performance above standard is observed, the standard becomes the basis of positive feedback. When performance is below standard or below the goal set by the direct report, corrective feedback is used, again relying on the standard and on the goal set as the benchmarks for the performance observed. When discussion about performance is couched in terms of known measures, standards, and performance goals, feedback can be much more objective, and it is less likely to be seen as criticism of character. The direct report is not bad per se, but is simply not performing at the agreed-on level on one or more measures.

Periodic Performance Summary

At some point, a summary of performance during the period is provided to the direct report. In most organizations, this is an annual event, but some organizations have quarterly or semiannual performance summaries. At this point, the manager provides a summary of how the direct report has done on each performance measure and whether standards and goals have been met. In performance systems that offer both the employee and the manager Web-based input capabilities, periodic review of the employee's progress toward achieving goals is much easier. Once the employee self-assesses her or his own performance, the manager can also review each goal while viewing the employee's comments (see Figure 14.2 for an example).

Figure 14.2   Performance Planning and Rating Module Screen

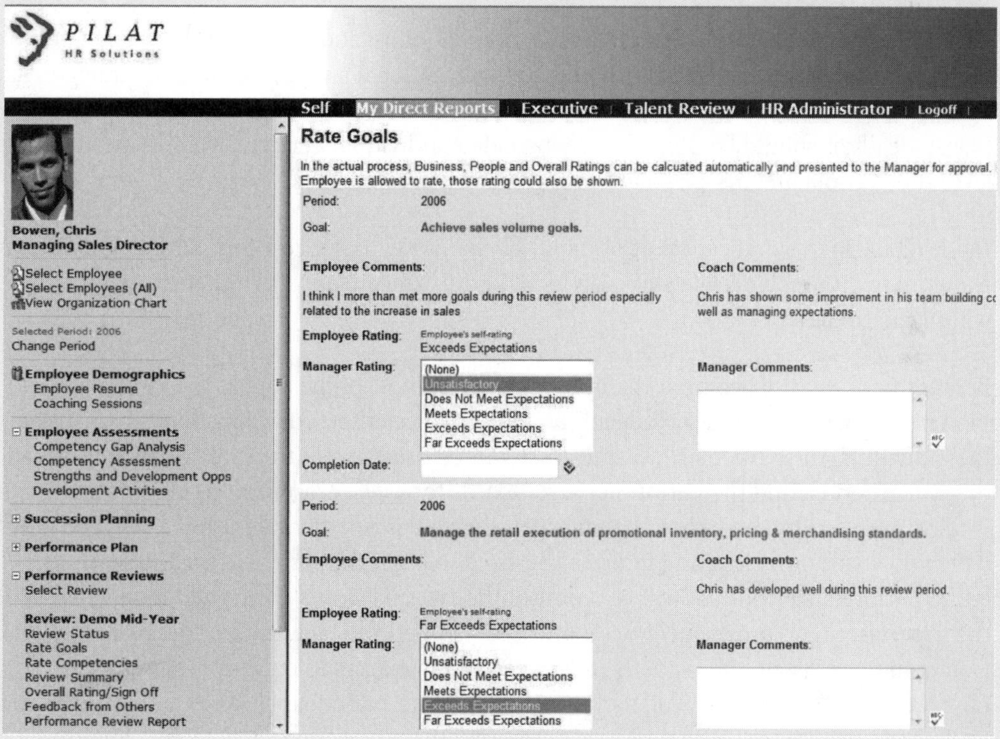

Consequences of achieving various performance levels are communicated, and planning for the next period's performance begins. If PM has been done correctly, the summary appraisal should have no surprises for the direct report. As shown in Figure 14.1, development is a critical component. One of the more important outputs of the performance process is an **individual development plan (IDP)** that is used to document any steps necessary to improve employee performance. Each employee should have an IDP.

The process described above applies to PM at the individual level. Yet most employees today work as an integrated part of one or more teams. The PM process does not change significantly for a team. It is usually easier to get outcome performance measures for a team than for an individual, and it is more difficult to get individual performance measures for a team member (Bing, 2004). Some organizations have elected to use team output as the primary outcome measure of performance for all team members and then develop a "team citizenship measure" for each team member.

Typical Data Inputs

Data inputs for PM systems include organizational-, job-, and individual-level data. Organizational-level data consist of links to organizational and unit goals and strategies and business plans. Performance plans should be able to tie back to unit and organizational plans; ideally, it should be possible to consolidate individual performance plans to the unit level and consolidate unit plans to the organizational level.

Job-level data is a significant part of the PM system. Key tasks, responsibilities, and outcomes should flow from job data sets to individual performance plans. Performance exists only within the context of the job.

Because performance begins at the individual level, most of the data in the PM system are individual-level data. Data include all the performance criteria developed by the manager for the individual, the particular measures that will be used to rate the individual's performance on each criterion, and the performance standards for each measure. If rating information is to be provided by more than the manager, the names of other raters and the criteria for which they will provide rating information need to be in the system as well. Usually, the entire performance contract will be a part of the system. Most systems will include space for the supervisor (and other raters) to enter observed performance and performance incidents. Contemporary systems allow both employees and managers to enter comments and observations at any time during the review period and provide the option of having all those comments swept into the final review, presenting them in a concatenated area for editing by users. There should also be space for documentation of positive and corrective feedback. While creating an IDP, many systems can recommend and provide a library of development activities that can be used to correct specific problems.

Performance management systems must interface with staffing and training applications. As an example, if certain jobs are hard to staff, the PM system will want to add the competencies required for that job so that more internal candidates can be surfaced. Similarly, training applications need to be coordinated with the PM system so that evaluation of training (and development) programs will be possible.

Typical Reports

The most important standardized reports produced by the HRIS are the performance contract and the annual summary appraisal for each employee. Other reports include aggregate performance data by unit and reports comparing aggregated unit performance with unit output (Cohen & Hall, 2005, p. 64). The HRIS needs to have the capability of archiving data so long-term performance trends for individuals and groups can be tracked. If competency assessments are used as a part of the review, the HR department can monitor systemic developmental requirements based on the aggregated competency results (e.g., those for business unit, location, or level).

Data Outflows

Performance data are used in many HRM decisions and will flow automatically into some processes or be available for others as needed. One automatic flow will be into compensation. Organizations with merit pay need performance distributions to construct a merit matrix. (Note that many performance applications are capable of having compensation functionality built in.) The performance measure used is the summary performance level for each employee. Performance data on various performance dimensions are used in decisions relating to promotion, layoffs, assignment to training programs, and developmental assignments. Performance data are also central to HR planning. Other applications that make use of performance data are training and development (so that training needs can be analyzed based on current weaknesses in employee performance) and staffing, where aggregated strengths and weaknesses of currently needed skills and competencies can trigger recruitment and staffing goals. In addition, performance processes utilizing competency assessment can be used by manpower planning applications to assist in forecasting future deficiencies based on required skill profiles.

Decision Support

The basic decision support system in the area of PM is the entire system. Having performance criteria, performance measures, performance standards, goal-setting results, and recent performance documentation in a single place allows managers to keep track of how each direct report is doing and what interventions need to be made to improve performance (Evans, 2001). This self-service feature for managers makes the performance management module a management tool for daily use. All performance management documentation activities required of the manager can be dealt with through the system. Performance planning, documented observation of performance, feedback documentation, and the formal appraisal can all be developed on the system itself and stored there for future reference by managers. Similarly, the system can provide self-service for employees by allowing them to view the same data and use those data as a basis for deciding on areas where improvement is needed. For example, were performance "specific" goals set at a high enough level to motivate employees to perform at higher levels on their jobs? Appropriate interfaces between the performance management module and training and development modules can lead either the manager or the direct report to training programs or other developmental activities based on the specific performance problems noted. Indeed, PM software can be categorized as either preformatted appraisal systems—systems that allow the development of customized appraisals—or systems that diagnose performance problems (Forrer & Leibowitz, 1991, pp. 104–106).

Flowers, Tudor, and Trumble (1997) note that such systems should allow managers to update information, serve as a support in conducting the appraisal interview, allow the creation of effective appraisal forms, and support all legal mandates relevant to performance appraisals. In some systems, a copy of the current job description for the position is available to the manager so that it can be reviewed for accuracy on an annual basis. A system supporting multisource feedback appraisals such as **360° appraisals** is described by Meyer (1998).

Group performance can also be tracked and the data used for performance improvement; because most employees work as part of teams, there has been increased interest in measuring and managing team performance (e.g., Jones & Schilling, 2000). Stegner and Kofahl (2004) provide a case study of a process for group performance improvement that could not exist without heavy input from the HRIS. In some cases, systems tie closely with marketing and management information systems; Charles, Kurlander, and Savage (2000) describe a sales performance tracking system that keeps home office and sales personnel aware of results against quotas and suggests where efforts need to be made to enhance sales performance.

Finally, automated PM systems allow managers and HR managers to track the administrative aspects of PM: Have all managers completed performance contracts with their direct reports? Are summary appraisals done on time? Do ratings by a manager and the performance of the manager's unit jibe? These are questions that can be answered by the system. Additionally, performance ratings can be checked for possible bias against protected groups. This checking can include not only the ratings themselves but also their use in HR decisions.

Under the *Uniform Guidelines on Employee Selection Procedures* (U.S. Department of Labor & U.S. Department of Justice, 1978), performance appraisals are considered "tests" when used for HR decisions, such as promotions, and are subject to the same validity and reliability requirements as other tests when they are found to have an adverse impact on protected groups.

Web-based systems can also provide a calibration tool for employee performance ratings that allows for a visual inspection of the distribution of ratings for a population. This calibration is often essential as a tie-in to the compensation process since performance ratings often dictate how much employees may receive for their annual merit review. The example of performance calibration presented in Figure 14.3 is part of a succession planning system being used by a large utility organization, a system that allows managers to view the distribution and even drag-and-drop employees within the ratings to adjust for any discrepancies.

Figure 14.3 **Example of Relating Performance to Compensation**

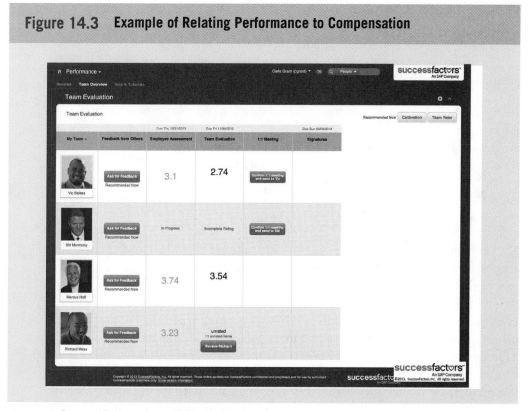

Source: © SuccessFactors, Inc. All Rights Reserved.

Compensation

Overview

Compensation is one of the most complex topics in HRM, and attempting to present an overview is ambitious. The central motivational issue for compensation is whether or not it is seen as equitable or inequitable to employees as defined by Equity Theory. Since compensation is the primary outcome for most employees, a great deal of dissatisfaction could result when it is viewed as unfair. Organizations faced with the complexities of creating and administering compensation systems are increasingly turning to technology for help. Wright (2003, p. 55) estimates that a 12,000-person firm can save as much as $850,000 per year in administrative costs by automating compensation planning alone. Brink and McDonnell (2003) point out that nearly all processes used to design, communicate, and manage pay are moving toward Web applications.

The basic compensation system includes **base pay**, merit pay, short-term and long-term incentives, perquisites, recognition awards, and attraction or retention awards. There are many processes associated with each of these, all of which must be coordinated. If that were not enough, there are also special populations that have unique pay processes: executives, sales personnel, scientists and engineers, expatriates, unionized workers, and the whole panoply of temporary, contract, or part-time workers.

Base pay is built around two processes: **job evaluation** and market benchmarking. Job evaluation creates an internal hierarchy of value. In the most common form of job evaluation, a set of factors is developed that reflects characteristics that add value to work in the specific organization (e.g., the education required). Each factor is weighted by importance, and scales are developed. Every job that will be in the base pay system is evaluated on the set of scales, and a point score is calculated. Jobs are arranged by total points, and this forms the basis for a salary structure.

Market benchmarking is used to price the structure (or individual jobs). Market data are collected for as many jobs as possible. In most organizations, one or more surveys may be developed in-house to collect market benchmarks; but the bulk of benchmark data come from commercial and association surveys. Many of these surveys are now available electronically (either on disk or through a website) and can be integrated into the compensation information system. Entering data can be done through a website with a format that maximizes ease of data entry (Tobin, 2002). However, websites with salary data are not without problems; employees frequently access websites that may have unrepresentative data and argue that they are underpaid based on bad data (Menefee, 2000).

An employee is placed in the salary grade appropriate for her or his job. Each grade has a midpoint that serves as a proxy for all the jobs in that grade, and a range is built around that midpoint. (This range defines the minimum and maximum salary for jobs in that grade, usually ±20% from the midpoint.) Exact placement in the range is usually a function of performance and individual characteristics (quality of degree, job seniority, and experience).

The structure is adjusted each year based on market movements. If the market were to increase by 3%, for example, the midpoints would increase by 3% as well. However, not all employees receive a 3% increase if the organization uses a merit pay system. In a merit pay system, the size of the increase is a function of performance level and of where an employee is in the range: the higher the performance, the larger the increase and, generally, the lower the place in the range, the higher the increase. A merit matrix, developed to provide guidelines based on performance and place in the range, ensures that the total amount spent by the organization is no more than the specified percentage of payroll.

There are many forms of short-term **incentive pay**. Unlike merit pay, short-term incentive pay is rarely added to base pay and must be re-earned every year. Typical short-term incentive programs include bonuses, gain sharing, goal sharing, small-group incentives, and profit sharing. Short-term incentive programs usually have specific measures, set up prior to the beginning of the program that will drive payout (profit sharing as an incentive is not typically covered by these measures). Gain sharing, for example, bases payouts on reductions in production costs due to more efficient use of labor. Specific preplanned formulas based on past production costs drive payouts. Bonus systems can be driven by preplanned criteria related to manufacturing, customer service, safety, or anything else that the company wishes to motivate employees to achieve. Profit sharing is usually retrospective, however; the board decides after the books have closed for the fiscal year that some percentage of profits will be shared with employees. In all cases, the measures driving short-term incentive payouts must be collected, either through existing measurement systems or through special systems designed for the purpose.

Long-term incentives are primarily based on organization stock, options to buy organization stock, or phantom (make-believe) stock. The goal of long-term incentives is twofold: to align the interests of employees with those of shareholders and to motivate aligned performance over periods of more than one year.

Perquisites are rewards that are a function of organizational status. Executive dining rooms, first-class or corporate jet air travel, and club memberships are examples. Perquisites frequently have tax consequences to the employee receiving them and, thus, must be included as part of the pay system. In the past several years, some organizations have transformed perquisites into incentive rewards based on performance; go to any Disney property, and you will see parking spaces near the employee entrance that are reserved for high performers.

Recognition awards are low-cost or no-cost awards that are retrospective: When an employee does something of note, he or she receives an award that may have little financial value but is psychologically rewarding. The use of websites in recognition programs, so that every employee can go online and find where he or she stands in comparison with other eligible employees, can greatly enhance the motivational impact of such programs (Perlmutter, 2002). **Attraction** or **retention awards** are one-time awards that are used to attract prospective employees to the organization or persuade them to remain with the organization. These awards may take the form of cash, stock options, benefits, or adjustments to benefits rules. The goal is to incur a one-time cost that does not drive up base pay.

Although the types of compensation already described are made up of multiple programs, it is critical that all compensation programs be integrated, so employees receive a single message about what adds value in the organization and the type of behavior and culture that is desired.

Compensation programs must also meet federal and state statutory and regulatory requirements. The **Fair Labor Standards Act (FLSA)** differentiates **exempt workers** and **nonexempt workers**; the organization must pay nonexempt workers at least the minimum wage, must pay for time worked in excess of 40 hours a week at an overtime rate of 1.5 times the normal pay, and must provide records to the federal government on hours worked and regular and overtime pay for all nonexempt workers. The **Office of Federal Contract Compliance Programs (OFCCP)** requires annual evidence of no unfair bias with respect to race and gender for similarly situated employee groups (SSEGs) and requires multiple linear regression analyses as evidence.

Typical Data Inputs

Compensation data inputs include internal, external, and generated data. Internal data include information about jobs (descriptions, specifications), people (performance, salary history), and organizational units (salary budget, job evaluation system). External data would include market survey data and information on rewards practices. Internal and external data would be combined and used to generate job evaluation results, salary structures, merit matrices, and a variety of reward guidelines. Incentive programs will require input data on whatever behavior or outcome is being encouraged; such data might include customer survey results, accident data, time-to-market data, or product quality data. Data from the staffing function can highlight problem areas, for example, jobs for which compensation may be too low.

Compensation for a special employee group usually requires data specific to that group. Executive compensation is likely to require organization-wide sales, productivity, profit, share price, market share, and other financial, market, and production data indicative of organizational success. Sales compensation systems may require data on quotas, sales, bonus or commission rates, and competitive market data. Gain-sharing programs require historical averaged data on labor costs as a proportion of value of production. Bargaining unit employee pay systems require data on contract specifics. For nonexempt employees, hourly rates and hours worked per week are required.

In short, there are very few data within the organization that might not be required by some part of the compensation system. As an example, a company that market-prices jobs will collect as much market data on wages as possible. Even so, it is unlikely that market data can be found for all jobs. The "market rate" for these jobs must be estimated. It is common to use multiple linear regressions for this purpose. As much information about all jobs is collected as possible, using either job specification data or aggregate information from job incumbents. Some specific information that might be collected from the HRIS includes the average education level of job incumbents in each job, the average amount of training incumbents in each job have had, the average number of direct reports each incumbent in a job has, and so forth. Although logic guides the choice of which independent variables to use in the regression equation to predict market rates, the goal is to get the best prediction, so whatever variables end up providing the best prediction are the ones that will be used. Similarly, incentive programs may make use of any financial, market, or production data to determine whether bonuses should be paid and, if so, how much and to whom.

Typical Reports

There are a number of standard reports in the compensation arena; however, because of the sensitive nature of compensation information, they are not widely circulated. The most common reports include budget reports to managers showing how their actual compensation costs compare with the projected costs. Most organizations provide each employee with an "Annual Compensation Report" showing the total amount of money spent by the organization on the employee, including money spent on wage or salary, incentive pay, and the cost of benefits paid for by the organization. Similar reports, such as incentive reports that tell people how they are doing with respect to earning a specific incentive award, become much more effective when a website is used for communication (Stiffler, 2001).

Companies participating in wage surveys produce reports for use by surveying organizations. In some cases, a compensation analyst draws the data from the HRIS and enters them into the survey, but, in other cases, an automated application gathers data from the HRIS and enters them into the survey program.

A new report on the analysis of possible "systemic compensation bias" among "similarly situated employee groups" is now required by the U.S. OFCCP. This report will be due annually, along with the organization's EEO-1 Report.

Data Outflows

The primary data outflow from compensation modules is to payroll. Compensation analysts draw on the data for additional analyses, however. Managers preparing budgets draw on compensation data as they project costs over the next budget period. Benefits analysts draw on compensation data as they analyze probable future costs of wage-based benefits (pensions are usually a function of salary level while health benefits are largely independent of salary level).

Data are sent to federal, state, and local agencies, including taxing agencies, labor departments, and other units tracking wage data. Many organizations also provide data to firms conducting reward surveys.

Decision Support

The major rewards decision that has to be made about every employee is how much to pay that individual to be seen as fair by the employee. Decision support systems in compensation are all aimed at that decision. Because of the complexity of compensation, though, a series of decisions must be made before a final compensation decision is made. Thus, there are decision support systems dealing with job evaluation, the use of market data, market pricing, building a salary structure, developing a merit matrix, and running incentive programs. Although much of this activity is carried out by compensation and other HR managers, other managers can do much of the work themselves if the system is set up correctly as a self-serve system. The most common areas that managers would handle themselves include salary budget planning, merit, promotional and other increases, and most incentive programs. Using Web-based compensation modules, managers can perform salary-planning functions much easier than was possible with paper-based processes. Data such as current salary, compa-ratio, and salary ranges can be viewed for all their employees at once; for international organizations, such systems can handle multicurrency requirements; and these systems can ensure that the total of the projected salary increases recommended by each manager does not exceed budgeting guidelines. Figure 14.4 depicts the work area of a Web-based application that enables managers to do compensation planning for their employees.

Koski (2003) describes a project that automated a worldwide employee bonus system; executives and managers got a self-service system, and compensation executives could keep track (in real time) of award amounts and payouts. Supported by computer and Web-based products, these processes generally offer advantages to the organizations using those (Zingheim & Schuster, 2005). Indeed, Zingheim and Schuster (2004) argue that Web management of pay and rewards is one of two great innovations in the rewards field.

Employees do not make many compensation decisions themselves, so self-service functions are largely restricted to providing information. Most companies now make salary structures available on the company intranet, and job postings typically provide either structure information or the salary grade of a job, so employees can look up what the range of pay for any job would be. The merit matrix, average salary increases, average bonuses of various kinds, and other reward information are all posted by some companies. Most public sector salaries are publicly available under state and local "freedom of information" acts, and, in these cases, salaries (and total earnings) of specific employees are available; private organizations almost never post such information.

There can be difficulties with Web management of pay. Van De Voort and McDonnell (2003) point out that working "live" can create problems when numbers change during the process. As an example, if a manager is calculating merit pay and is working off a specific budget number, changes to that number by a senior manager can create confusion and bad decisions. The use of a frozen or static database ensures that everyone is working with the same data, formulae, and figures.

Other decision support systems deal with sales compensation. Cocks and Gould (2001) note that compensation software is critical in defining commission levels, designing compensation plans, and managing compensation, since all three areas require on-the-fly complex calculations on a repeated basis. Weeks (2000) notes that virtual sales teams in widely separated areas can be much more effective in maintaining customer satisfaction; only the Web allows the coordination between team members required to pull off this strategy, and it also allows sales compensation experts to audit and fine-tune the sales compensation system to maintain high motivation levels.

A whole set of applications relate to executive pay. Since the Enron scandal and the subsequent passage of the **Sarbanes-Oxley Act (SOX)**, compliance reports, including those dealing with executive pay, are required. SOX compliance is greatly supported by data from the HRIS ("How HRIS Can Help with SOX Compliance," 2005; Sherman, 2005). Additional regulations covering executive pay have come about as a result of the **Troubled Asset Relief Program (TARP)** of 2009 and the financial bailout of troubled financial services firms and automakers. More financial regulations are expected in the future. The HRIS must be flexible enough to add any new fields required by these regulations and capable of running the audits required.

Benefits

Overview

A full discussion of benefits programs is beyond the scope of this chapter. There are five broad types of benefits programs in most U.S. organizations. Because some company-provided

Figure 14.4 Screen of Salary Review Module for Department Manager

Salary Review - USA

Budget Figures

Total Budget for United States: 14674
Budget Used: 13500.7
Budget Remaining: 1173.29

USA Merit Increase Matrix

The following table is used to determine the merit increase percentage based on the employee's Consolidated Rating and RSP scores.

Rating	RSP 70 - 100 (From)	RSP 70 - 100 (To)	RSP >100 - 130 (From)	RSP >100 - 130 (To)
10 - 24.9 Points 0	0	0	0	
25 - 34.9 Points 0	0	0	0	
35 - 44.9 Points 3	5	0	3	
45 - 54.9 Points 5.5	7.5	3.5	5.5	
55 - 70 Points 8	10	6	8	

Employee Merit Increase

The local currency is: US Dollar. The Euro exchange rate is: 0.830220.

Employee	Rating	Consolidated Rating	Range %	Current Salary Local	Current Salary	Merit Range From	Merit Range To	Merit Increase %	Merit Increase Amount	Salary with Merit	Adjustment Increase %	Adjustment Increase Amount	Salary with Adjustment	New RSP
Blasi, Charles	60	20	90.00	27,000.00	22,416.00	0.00	0.00	3.00	672.48	23,088.48	0.00	0.00	23,088.48	90.00
Flint, Fred	38	38	108.00	35,000.00	29,058.00	0.00	3.00	4.00	1,162.32	30,220.32	0.00	0.00	30,220.32	111.00
Rossi, David	43	43	101.00	36,500.00	30,303.00	0.00	3.00	5.00	1,515.15	31,818.15	0.00	0.00	31,818.15	104.00
Bowen, Chris	45	50	79.00	36,000.00	29,888.00	5.50	7.50	5.50	1,643.84	31,531.84	2.00	630.64	32,162.48	89.00
Steinberg, Maureen	56	56	85.00	45,000.00	37,360.00	8.00	10.00	8.00	2,988.80	40,348.80	0.00	0.00	40,348.80	92.00
Innocenti, Cynthia	59	70	90.00	73,000.00	60,606.00	8.00	10.00	8.00	4,848.48	65,454.48	0.00	0.00	65,454.48	98.00
				252,500.00	209,631.00				12,831.07	222,462.07		630.64	223,092.71	

benefits in this country are government provided in other countries, a different typology would be required for organizations abroad. As might be expected by Equity Theory, benefits are becoming important outcomes from the organization and could affect employee turnover.

The first set of benefits programs common in U.S. companies includes **pension plans** (both defined benefit and defined contribution), individual savings plans (such as Keoghs, **simplified employee pensions [SEPs]**, and **individual retirement accounts [IRAs]** and Social Security. Although few Americans think of Social Security as a benefit, the organization must fund contributions to Social Security just as an employee does. The goal of all these benefits programs is to ensure that the employee will have continuing income after retirement. The second set of benefits programs includes workers' compensation, unemployment insurance, long- and short-term disability insurance, and life insurance. The goal of these programs is to ensure that employees who cannot work (through no fault of their own) have some income until they can work again and to provide income protection to employees' families.

The third set of benefits programs includes medical and other health benefits, such as hospitalization and medical care insurance; surgical and major medical care insurance; long-term care; dental, vision, and hearing care insurance; and prescription drug coverage insurance. These benefits are designed to make sure that employees and their families are not bankrupted by illness or accident and can obtain preventative and curative care. The fourth area of benefits is paid time off and includes vacation, holidays, personal days, special purpose days (because of jury duty, bereavement, or military service, for example), and family leave. The purpose of paid time off is to allow employees to recharge their batteries, spend time with their families for celebrations, and participate in other significant life events.

The fifth and final category of benefits includes miscellaneous benefits such as dependent care, flexible working benefits (telecommuting, job sharing, and compressed workweek), employee assistance programs, professional memberships, tuition reimbursement, holiday parties and gifts, subsidized cafeterias and gyms, legal advice benefits, and employee discounts. These benefits round out the benefits package and are typical of organizations found in the "best companies to work for" lists.

Benefits programs differ from compensation in two major ways. First, in the majority of organizations, employees pay part (or all) of the costs for most benefits. (Even when benefit costs are borne entirely by employees, group purchasing reduces the cost that the employee would pay for an equivalent self-purchased benefit.) Second, most organizations offer some flexibility in their benefits programs. All employees receive a core benefits package but then choose additional coverage or additional benefits, or both, up to the level of the total benefits package. (**Flex plans** also allow the employee to purchase additional coverage or benefits, or both, at cost.) These two characteristics of benefits programs make them relatively complex to administer; each employee in the organization may have a slightly different benefits package with a unique salary deduction profile. Things even get complicated with paid time off. Not only may different employee groups (e.g., bargaining units, executives) have different configurations for paid time off, but these configurations may also differ within groups based on seniority. In addition, many organizations have what is called a paid time off bank, through which employees can trade paid time off for cash or other benefits, can buy additional paid time off, or can donate paid time off to other employees (e.g., in cases of long-term illness). All this makes benefits programs extremely complex and difficult to administer.

Another major difference between benefits and compensation programs, one that strongly affects HRIS configuration, is the growing trend to outsource benefits programs and administration. Few parts of the typical compensation program are outsourced. The most common is the outsourcing of wage benchmarking. Although consultants are frequently used in compensation, they tend to work offline. In benefits, however, program design, benefit delivery, and program administration (including employee communications) are increasingly outsourced. As a result, the HRIS must interface not only with other internal systems, such as rewards and payroll, but also with the IT systems of other organizations. The necessity of establishing these interorganizational linkages introduces problems such as how to define fields, which fields can be included, what protocols for interaction to establish, and how to maintain security.

Legal requirements for benefits programs are also more stringent than those for compensation programs. Most benefits programs are influenced by the **Employee Retirement Income Security Act (ERISA)**, which grants benefits a tax-favored status. However, to qualify for favorable tax treatment, the benefit must meet stringent requirements. These include reporting to recipients of benefits and to the federal government, demonstrating that requirements for qualified status are met. In addition, many organizations offer nonqualified benefits to some employee groups, particularly to executives.

Typical Data Inputs

There are HRIS benefits modules with different purposes, and each requires a different type of data input. One set of functions focuses on the organization's relationship with current and prospective benefits vendors (of health insurance, for example). Inputs, in this case, will include aggregate data about the people to be covered, data outlining the relevant demographics for the covered groups, and data specifying the program coverage desired and cost limitations.

A second set of functions focuses on the internal management of benefits programs and will be used to track usage, employee choices (in the case of flex plans), and costs. Experience, usage, and costs will be fed into this program.

A third (and the most common) set of programs focuses on employee input about enrollment and other coverage choices, changes in coverage desired, and changes in employee status (e.g., addition of a dependent, change in marital status) that may affect coverage and employee costs. These programs may also allow employees to file claims with the organization. In these programs, many of which are Web based, employees feed in personal data, coverage choices, and other data relevant to their use of the benefit.

The fourth set of data placed into the system consists of the myriad federal, state, and local laws and regulations governing benefits practice. These laws and regulations provide decision support system "rules" for managers using the system.

Typical Reports

There are dozens of reports required by federal and state government units, including the IRS, units of the U.S. Department of Labor, other federal agencies, and similar units at the state level. The most common report is the annual benefits report to employees required for tax-qualified plans under ERISA. This report requires organizations to report to employees annually about certain benefit facts, such as vested pension levels. Most organizations have gone beyond the ERISA requirements and provide a report to each employee showing the total value of all compensation and benefits received by the employee during the year. This annual compensation report is the "rewards scorecard" for the employee. Ceccon (2004) estimates that putting this annual report online rather than distributing printed copies can save a company with 30,000 employees $678,000 in actual costs over five years and that productivity savings from reducing the amount of time employees use to find benefit account balances, pay information, and other rewards information on multiple sites or via phone calls to the HR department can save $625,000 per year. HR productivity increases net an annual savings of $30,000, and increased employee retention would reduce costs by $150,000 per year. With a five-year savings of $678,000 and an annual productivity savings totaling $805,000, Web reporting is clearly advantageous.

With Web-based access to benefits and other employee information, staff can view summary reports at any time, which, in many cases, eliminates the need for a company to produce expensive paper versions. With a Web-based system, an employee can, at his or her convenience, view his or her current benefits, salary, and other information directly (as shown in Figure 14.5) and decide to print a paper copy if one is needed. For an international company that distributes benefits or pay in multiple currencies, the system could normalize that data into a single currency.

Data Outflows

Data generated by benefits programs have to be transferred to payroll and accounting internally. Data are sent externally to benefits providers, outsourced benefits administrators, and a variety of federal, state, and local agencies. Aggregate data are provided to benefits survey firms.

The real-time transfer of data can result in large cost savings. Moynihan (2000) notes that AT&T saved $15 million when it switched to providing updated enrollment information to all its various health plans. Previously, tardy data transfer resulted in health plans denying coverage to employees who were in fact eligible and in claims being paid out to people who no longer worked for AT&T.

Decision Support

Decision support tools overlap to some extent with reports in the benefits arena because, frequently, these reports trigger the need to make changes to comply with federal, state,

Figure 14.5 Compensation and Benefits Planning Screen

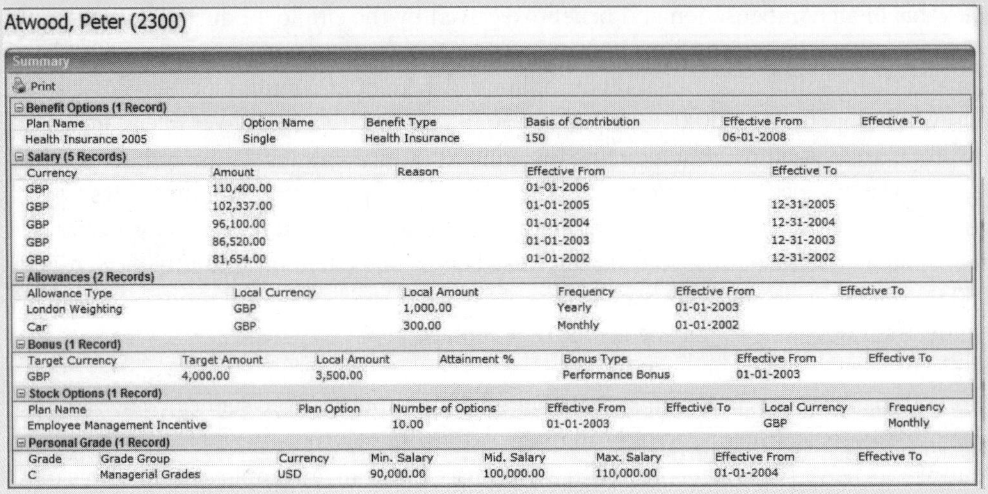

Atwood, Peter (2300)

Summary

🖶 Print

Benefit Options (1 Record)

Plan Name	Option Name	Benefit Type	Basis of Contribution	Effective From	Effective To
Health Insurance 2005	Single	Health Insurance	150	06-01-2008	

Salary (5 Records)

Currency	Amount	Reason	Effective From	Effective To
GBP	110,400.00		01-01-2006	
GBP	102,337.00		01-01-2005	12-31-2005
GBP	96,100.00		01-01-2004	12-31-2004
GBP	86,520.00		01-01-2003	12-31-2003
GBP	81,654.00		01-01-2002	12-31-2002

Allowances (2 Records)

Allowance Type	Local Currency	Local Amount	Frequency	Effective From	Effective To
London Weighting	GBP	1,000.00	Yearly	01-01-2003	
Car	GBP	300.00	Monthly	01-01-2002	

Bonus (1 Record)

Target Currency	Target Amount	Local Amount	Attainment %	Bonus Type	Effective From	Effective To
GBP	4,000.00	3,500.00		Performance Bonus	01-01-2003	

Stock Options (1 Record)

Plan Name	Plan Option	Number of Options	Effective From	Effective To	Local Currency	Frequency
Employee Management Incentive		10.00	01-01-2003		GBP	Monthly

Personal Grade (1 Record)

Grade	Grade Group	Currency	Min. Salary	Mid. Salary	Max. Salary	Effective From	Effective To
C	Managerial Grades	USD	90,000.00	100,000.00	110,000.00	01-01-2004	

or local requirements. As an example, McCormack (2004) notes that the Family and Medical Leave Act (FMLA) has complicated the administration of employee leave. Many states have more stringent leave requirements than FMLA or the 40 other federal leave laws. A system that tracks these laws and can tell the HR manager exactly what the leave requirements are in a specific locality ensures compliance and minimizes the risk of lawsuits and fines.

Similarly, tax-qualified benefit plans are subject to federal bias regulations. In this case, "bias" refers to income level rather than protected group status. Federal policy is that tax laws should not underwrite benefits that are available only to highly paid employees. If an organization is to have a qualified 401(k) retirement plan, for example, the plan must be available to both low- and high-paid employees, and, in addition, it must be used by both. Tracking enrollments against those eligible for participation can trigger efforts to get more low-paid employees to participate in the plan.

When organizations offer flexible benefit plans, it is common to track the choices made by employees to guide plan development. A few organizations have looked at benefits choices made by high performers to see if they differ from the choices made by low performers.

Others look at the choices made by protected groups. Recruitment literature can then be tailored to specific groups to ensure a better yield of desirable applicants.

Web-based services also offer decision support to employees deciding what levels of coverage to sign up for (Dawson, 1997). Employees can readily compare the cost of various levels of benefits service and more readily understand the cost-benefit trade-off that they are going to make. Similarly, transferring the enrollment process to the employees themselves can save the organization money (Teer, 1997). However, such savings are not likely to occur unless the system is easy to use for all employees, not just the technologically savvy (Ashley, 2006).

Self-service systems for managerial use in the benefits area are not frequent, as few managers have a role in benefits decisions concerning their direct reports. However, self-service systems for employees are increasingly relied on by employers to lessen the burden of benefits transactional administration. Employees typically make and change selections in flexible benefits plans through the company intranet. They can change beneficiaries or dependents as births, deaths, and divorces occur. They can increase tax-deferred or pretax contributions to various benefits categories such as 401(k) plans, health spending accounts, and similar programs. They may buy or sell vacation days from the paid time off (PTO) bank. They may transfer PTO days into their 401(k). (There are timing and contribution limits and other rules that must be observed, but these can be built into the application.) Employees can also find out the status of various benefits through self-service approaches. At least one organization allows employees to do "what-if" scenarios with respect to retirement: for example, "If I retired tomorrow, what would my pension be?"

The outsourcing of benefits creates additional issues for the HRIS. Some major corporations have outsourced all benefits. An extensive interface must be built connecting the organization's HRIS with the outsource firm's system. The benefits advisers at the outsource firm must have current, accurate data on the benefits status of every organizational employee to be able to answer questions and provide advice. Outside access raises security issues to a greater level of concern; benefits data (including hospital and other medical billing and psychiatric care and employee assistance program billing) are the most sensitive employee data held by the organization, and privacy standards (including Health Insurance Portability and Accountability Act [HIPAA] requirements) must be met.

A whole range of decisions concerning benefits is made outside the HR department. Benefits costs are the most rapidly increasing part of labor costs, particularly costs for health care benefits and defined benefit pension plans. Consequently, senior executives (especially the CFO) are interested in the aggregate costs of the various benefits packages offered by the organization. However, determining these costs is complicated. For many benefits, such as workers' compensation, cost is a function of experience; for others, such as insurance, cost depends on usage; and for others, such as health insurance and pensions, employee demographics are particularly significant. Therefore, the organization needs to be able to price current benefits packages and project costs based on expected demographic changes. It also needs to be able to run "what if" scenarios based on alternate benefit packages: What would we save over the next five years if we switched from a defined benefit pension to a cash balance plan? How would that compare to switching to a 401(k) with match?

Payroll

Overview

Payroll is the transactional process through which compensation is transferred to employees and federal, state, and local income and payroll taxes are withheld from employees' checks. It is also through payroll that any benefits costs borne by employees are withheld. Although some employees receive actual checks for net pay, it is more common, especially among large organizations, for direct deposits to be made to employees' bank accounts. Companies that outsource need to make sure that the compensation and benefits modules of the HRIS interface flawlessly with the provider's payroll input. Even when companies do payroll in-house, the payroll module is usually part of the accounting system rather than the HRIS, so it is critical that the interface between the HRIS and the payroll software work flawlessly (Walker, 1987).

In the majority of organizations, payroll is a function administered by finance or accounting rather than the HR department. HR departments feed compensation data and benefits coverage (and employees' coverage choices) to payroll, which makes sure that all appropriate federal, state, and local income and payroll taxes are withheld at the correct rate and that any deductions for benefits are also withheld at the correct rate. Payroll usually has the responsibility for keeping track of income and payroll tax rates and applicable salary levels. Payroll results are fed back into the general accounting system by payroll. Because labor costs are the largest variable cost for most organizations, it is critical for the organizations' financial well-being that payroll records be accurate and timely. Because the paycheck is a signal of the employment relationship and because many employees rely on their paychecks to meet bills that are due, it is critical that the payroll system deliver accurate and timely paychecks or bank transfers. Little will anger or demoralize an employee more than a missing or an inaccurate paycheck or transfer. In short, payroll is a transactional task that must be flawless.

Payroll is the most heavily outsourced HRM function. Great economies of scale can be achieved by a payroll processor with respect to keeping up with the intricate requirements of income and payroll tax deductibles or maintaining (and upgrading) software that ensures that payroll is accurate and completed in a timely manner. However, outsourcing companies do not work in a vacuum, and compensation and benefits functions must deliver data to the outsourcer, and the accounting and finance functions must receive data back from the outsourcer. Also, some companies argue that integrating the HR and payroll functions makes sense and saves data entry and labor costs while providing greater accuracy and timeliness (Gale, 2002).

Typical Data Inputs

Data entered into the payroll system from inside the organization include compensation data, benefits data, and other payroll addition data (e.g., special awards) and deductions data (e.g., union dues, wage garnishments for child support, credit union repayment installments). Time and attendance data are usually handled in a special module, and data from this module are also fed into payroll (Robb, 2004). Data external to the organization include federal, state, and local income and payroll tax rules that allow the organization to withhold appropriate amounts from each employee's paycheck. There may be payments made to individuals who are not active employees. Although these are usually taken care of in a separate COBRA module, there may even be payments from ex-employees for the continuation of benefits. The most frequent data input are change data. Every time a new employee goes on the payroll, an employee changes status, an employee makes benefits elections changes, governments change tax or withholding rates, or the organization makes changes such as pay increases, data reflecting the changes have to go into the payroll system. Many of these elections can be performed by employees themselves using the self-service capability of a Web-based payroll system. Through a direct entry screen (shown in Figure 14.6), the employee can enter or update any data that he or she controls, such as the number of exemptions or extra withholding, without the need for HR intervention. For an international company, the system could automatically present any financial data in whatever currency the employee requested.

In addition to internal and external data, the system generates data that it stores and uses over time. For example, in 2010, FICA (**Federal Insurance Contributions Act**, i.e., Social Security) taxes were withheld on the first $106,800 of income and the maximum tax withheld for any employee was $6,621. Payroll must keep a running total of FICA paid to date so that it does not deduct too much from the employee's paycheck.

Typical Reports

There are a number of standard payroll reports. These show—for the organization as a whole (or for subunits)—the actual amount paid to employees for a period (and cumulatively) and the amounts deducted for various purposes. Reports go to federal, state, and local agencies, including taxing authorities, and to benefits providers. Employees receive reports with their

Figure 14.6   Screen Used for Entering Data for a Paycheck

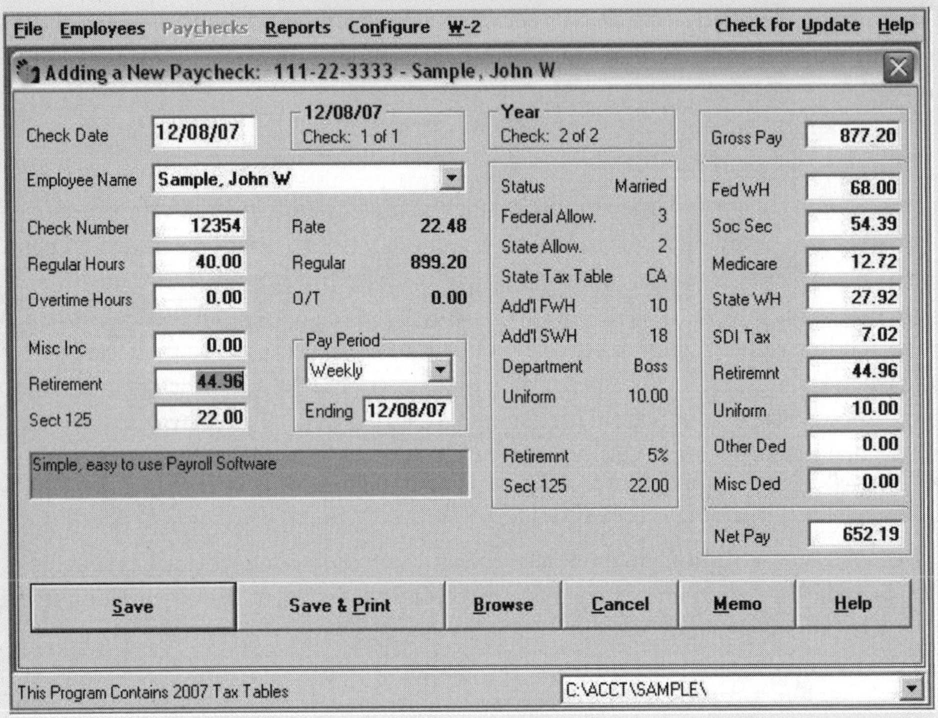

paychecks or notices of deposit; the report shows gross pay and all deductions. Usually year-to-date accumulations are also provided.

Data Outflows

Payroll data go to accounting; federal, state, and local agencies; benefits outsourcing firms; and individual benefit program providers. These payroll data are the input for a variety of processes in those units, so it is critical that systems interface flawlessly. Interface becomes even more complicated as external systems communicate not only with payroll but also with compensation, benefits, and other HR systems.

Decision Support

Payroll data are not usually used by HR departments or line managers for decision-making purposes. They are used extensively for audit purposes. Employees, on the other hand, like to know from time to time how much money they have earned in a given year, how much income and payroll taxes have been paid, and the level of pretax and deferred tax contributions made for various benefits. This information can be made available through a self-service system. Similarly, a self-service system can allow employees to increase withholding or make other (limited) changes in their pay.

SUMMARY

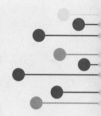

The overall goal of this chapter was to provide the reader with a broad understanding of the role and focus of HRIS in supporting performance management, compensation, benefits, and payroll processes. The combined PM, compensation, benefits, and payroll systems constitute some of the most important parts of the HRIS. Money may not be at the forefront of how people talk about the organization and their linkages to it, but, if performance ratings result in lower than expected salary increases, bonuses are miscalculated, benefits elections are not implemented, or a paycheck is wrong or (worse still) not delivered, employees become vocal. Because pay and benefits constitute the largest variable cost to any organization and the largest cost overall to many organizations, it is critical that managers plan, track, and audit outlays on a real-time basis. A significant proportion of the data and reports owed to federal, state, and local agencies come from the compensation, benefits, and payroll modules. The consequences of inaccurate, misleading, or missing data and reports include embarrassment, fines, and even jail time. And these are the risks associated with poor data from just the transactional part of these modules. The additional fallout would be the negative

effects on the motivation of the employees to work at higher levels and/or to leave the company for a company that does not have these problems. Thus, one of the major purposes of an HRIS is to help organizations administer their performance management, compensation, benefits, and payroll systems.

The role of motivation in work performance was covered, with a specific discussion of Equity Theory. It is easy to see that employees who perceive their job situation in terms of the ratio of their inputs to the company's outputs as inequitable will not be highly motivated to perform adequately on their jobs. A key part of strategic HR is aligning employee behaviors with the strategic intent of the organization. As seen in the discussion of goal-setting theory, the process of the PM system needs to follow the research findings on goal setting. It is important to hire the best people and provide them with the training and development needed. Without PM, the success of hiring strategies is unknown, and, similarly, the need for training and development interventions is unknown. PM systems support the translation of corporate strategy into individual performance plans. Compensation and benefits systems can be used to hire the right people, retain the high performers, and motivate all employees to perform at a higher level.

Compensation can also be used to motivate poor performers out of the organization. As systems technology has progressed, managers have become better able to enhance the performance of their direct reports and to tailor compensation and benefits programs to attract, retain, and motivate the best. Thus, the importance of understanding the central role of an HRIS in assisting managers in making key decisions regarding performance, compensation, benefits, and payroll cannot be underestimated.

KEY TERMS

DISCUSSION QUESTIONS

1. Discuss how a manager might make sure that the performance plan for each of her direct reports was driven by organizational strategy and the business plan. How can information systems support this goal?

2. Merit increases require a single "performance" number, while most incentive plans have multiple and varying performance measures. How can the PM system meet both needs?

3. Compensation strategy includes how competitive the organization wants to be, the number of different compensation systems the organization

wants to have, the mix of various reward and benefit components, and the basis of increases. Discuss the data inflows required if an organization wanted to automate its compensation design and administration processes.

4. Both PM and benefits information systems make provisions for employee access and input. What access would you provide in each of these systems, and what leeway would you provide employees in reading, entering, and changing data?

5. A lot of compensation information is available to employees today on the Web (e.g., www.salary.com), and much of it is inaccurate. How can an organization assure employees that they are fairly compensated (assume they are) when public data suggest otherwise?

6. Flexible benefit plans are common today. Discuss ways in which employers can ensure that employees make good choices about the benefits and benefit levels that they choose within the benefits information system itself.

7. Payroll and benefits are commonly outsourced. Discuss which parts of PM, compensation, benefits, and payroll you would consider outsourcing; justifying your views.

CASE STUDY: GRANDVIEW GLOBAL FINANCIAL SERVICES, INC. _____

Grandview Global Financial Services is an international corporation providing multiple financial services. Although it is one of the smaller players in the field, the firm has about 20,000 employees worldwide. Corporate strategy has focused on serving a niche market comprised of high net worth individuals, providing them with all the wealth management services they require. These services include investments, insurance, banking, real estate, financial planning, and related services.

The linchpin making all these services work well is the quality of the employees—the degree to which they are motivated to provide "over-the-top" attention to clients' needs. Clients have come to expect this level of service regardless of where they might happen to be and regardless of the time. Because of clients' high expectations, every employee is expected to provide flawless service.

As it has expanded globally, Grandview has hired employees from all the countries in which it does business. While all employees are expected to speak English, business is conducted in nine different languages in 45 locations. Grandview has invested heavily in developing a uniform corporate culture but has not succeeded in doing so in all locations.

One difficulty has been the PM and reward systems. Each geographic area developed its own PM tools, which reflect the national culture and the past experiences of local employees. There are a variety of systems using different performance criteria. Most of the PM materials are in Microsoft Word. Some of the systems seem to work all right, while others do not.

None of the systems are coordinated, except to the extent those final performance ratings are sent to the Grandview corporate HR department. There has been enormous push back and noncompliance with PM policies from the employees because of the difficulty of the paper performance process as well as the nine different languages being used worldwide.

Rewards systems are similarly localized. Base pay, incentive systems, and benefits have grown up in each geographic location in accord with local market practices, laws, and customs. The complexity and number of Excel spreadsheets needed to manage the financial targets and the resulting compensation plans for that many employees have created perceived and actual inequities. It is difficult to transfer employees across geographic areas because of the different systems in place, and awareness that employees in different locations have very different terms and conditions has created morale problems.

Corporate HR has PM and rewards modules in its HRIS covering U.S. employees, but this takes care of only about 60% of Grandview's employee population. An executive rewards module does cover about 2,000 senior executives worldwide, but all foreign data are sent from different locations and entered into the module at headquarters. Part of the historic reason for this process involves the legal requirements concerning privacy of information in the EU and some other locales; it is easier to get executives to grant permission for the transmission of specific data when those data are used to calculate stock option awards and other executive incentive payments granted by the corporation.

Corporate HR would like to move away from local systems and institute a corporate-wide system that relies neither on Word documents for performance reviews nor on Excel spreadsheets for the resulting compensation plans that result from the overall performance ratings. It was thought that common systems for PM and rewards would support a more unified culture and help translate Grandview's corporate strategy into individual performance plans worldwide.

The ideal system would be a Web-based, multilingual, integrated PM and compensation system. The PM system would be accessible by managers and their direct reports and would be tied to corporate strategy and the current business plan. Managers and their direct reports could access the system at any time to see performance criteria, measures, and standards and to look at current progress against standards. The rewards and benefits modules, while based on local law and customs, would be standardized with respect to process, fostering a more uniform rewards culture. It is critical to HR managers that the technology selected is flexible enough so that yearly changes to the application could be made efficiently and legal requirements in different locations could be accommodated, as well as changes in those requirements.

Because the performance goals are based on financial targets, and employees' merit and incentive payments are directly related to employee performance as well as Grandview's overall results, all necessary functionality for the compensation process should be built into the performance system. At year end, results should be able to be imported directly from corporate financial systems and used to generate performance reviews and compensation plans for the employees. The resultant pay increases and bonus payments would be fed directly into the payroll system already in use by Grandview in the United States and abroad. The system administrators should be able to ensure worldwide compliance with the performance process directly from the system through a variety of reports.

Case Study Questions

1. What is the role of PM in establishing and maintaining corporate culture?

2. What is the role of compensation and benefits in establishing and maintaining corporate culture?

3. Since laws, labor markets, and customs relevant to PM, compensation, and benefits differ from country to country, does it make sense to try to maintain a common global process for managing each of these areas?

4. Given all the cross-country differences, why would a global organization want to have a common HRIS?

5. How should Grandview go about implementing a global PM system?

6. How should Grandview go about implementing a global rewards system?

7. How should Grandview go about implementing a global benefits system?

8. How should Grandview go about implementing a global HRIS to manage these functions?

STUDENT STUDY SITE

Visit the Student Study Site at **http://www.sagepub.com/kavanagh3e** for additional learning tools such as access to SAGE journal articles and related web resources.

REFERENCES

Adams, J. S. (1963). Toward an understanding of inequity. *Journal of Abnormal and Social Psychology, 67*, 422–436.

Adams, J. S. (1965). Inequity in social exchange. In L. Berkowitz (Ed.), *Advances in experimental social psychology*, 267–299. New York: Academic Press.

Ashley, D. (2006). Intuitive technologies increase employee adoption of human resource solutions. *Compensation & Benefits Review, 38*(1), 62–68.

Banks, C. G., & May, K. E. (1999). Performance management: The real glue in organizations. In A. I. Kraut & A. K. Korman (Eds.),

Evolving practices in human resource management: Responses to a changing world of work (pp. 118–145). San Francisco: Jossey-Bass.

Bernardin, H. J., Hagan, C. M., Kane, J. S., & Villanova, P. (1998). Effective performance management: A focus on precision, customers, and situational constraints. In J. W. Smither (Ed.), *Performance appraisal: State of the art in practice* (pp. 3–48). San Francisco: Jossey-Bass.

Bing, J. W. (2004). Metrics for assessing human process on work teams. *IHRIM Journal, 8*(6), 26–31.

Brink, S., & McDonnell, S. (2003). e-Compensation. In *The e-merging technologies series go-to-guide* (pp. 4.1–4.18). Burlington, MA: IHRIM Press.

Ceccon, A. (2004). The real value statement: Aggregating pay and benefits on the Internet. *Compensation & Benefits Review, 36*(6), 53–58.

Charles, E. W., Kurlander, P., & Savage, B. (2000). Tracking sales performance. *ACA News, 43*(3), 38–41.

Cocks, D. J., & Gould, D. (2001). Sales compensation: A new technology-enabled strategy. *Compensation & Benefits Review, 33*(1), 27–31.

Cohen, A. J., & Hall, M. E. (2005). Automating your performance and competency evaluation process. *WorldatWork Journal, 14*(3), 64–70.

Dawson, S. (1997). Leveraging an intranet for employee self-service: A Q & A with Unisys corporation. IHRIM.*link, 2*(3), 54–65.

Evans, E. M. (2001). Internet-age performance management: Lessons from high-performing organizations. In A. J. Walker (Ed.), *Web-based human resources: The technologies and trends that are transforming HR* (pp. 65–82). New York: McGraw-Hill.

Flowers, L. A., Tudor, T. R., & Trumble, R. R. (1997). Computer-assisted performance appraisal systems. *Journal of Compensation and Benefits, 12*(6), 34–35.

Forrer, S. E., & Leibowitz, Z. B. (1991). *Using computers in human resources: How to select and make the best use of automated HR systems.* San Francisco: Jossey-Bass.

Gale, S. F. (2002). How three companies merged HR and payroll. *Workforce, 81*(1), 64–67.

How HRIS can help with SOX compliance. (2005). *HR Focus, 82*(10), 7, 10.

Jones, S. D., & Schilling, D. J. (2000). *Measuring team performance: A step-by-step, customizable approach for managers, facilitators, and team leaders.* San Francisco: Jossey-Bass.

Koski, L. (2003). Executive/manager self-service: Stat Street Corporation's annual incentive program. *Compensation & Benefits Review, 35*(2), 21–25.

Locke, E. A., & Latham, G. P. (1984). *Goal setting: A motivational theory that works.* Englewoods Cliffs, N. J.: Prentice Hall.

Locke, E. A., & Latham, G. P. (1990a). *A theory of goal-setting and task performance.* Englewoods Cliffs, N. J.: Prentice Hall.

Locke, E. A. & Latham, G. P. (1990b). Work motivation and satisfaction: Light at the end of the tunnel. *Psychological Science, 1,* 240–246.

Locke, E. A., Shaw, K. M., Saari, L. M. & Latham, G. P. (1981). Goal-setting and task performance: 1969–1980. *Psychological Bulletin, 90,* 125–152.

McCormack, J. (2004). Compliance tools: Technology can help HR stay on the right side of the law. *HR Magazine, 49*(3), 95–98.

Menefee, J. A. (2000). The value of pay data on the Web: Nominal or real? *Workspan, 43*(9), 25–28.

Meyer, G. (1998). 360 on the net: A computer toolkit for multirater performance feedback. *HR Magazine, 43*(11), 46–50.

Moynihan, J. J. (2000). HIPPA compliance offers human resource department savings. *Healthcare Financial Management, 54*(3), 82–83.

Perlmutter, A. L. (2002). Taking motivation and recognition online. *Compensation & Benefits Review, 34*(2), 70–74.

Robb, D. (2004). Marking time. *HR Magazine, 49*(7), 111–115.

Sherman, E. (2005). Use technology to stay in SOX compliance. *HR Magazine, 50*(5), 95–99.

Stegner, R., & Kofahl, B. (2004). Case study: Human performance improvement model at work. *IHRIM Journal, 8*(6), 18–20.

Stiffler, M. A. (2001). Incentive compensation and the Web. *Compensation & Benefits Review, 33*(1), 15–19.

Teer, M. S. (1997). Surfing for benefits. IHRIM. *link, 2*(3), 66–74.

Tobin, N. (2002). Can technology ease the pain of salary surveys? *Public Personnel Management, 31*(1), 65–77.

U.S. Department of Labor & U.S. Department of Justice. (1978). Uniform guidelines on employee selection procedures. (1978). *Federal Register, 43*(166), 38290–39309.

Van De Voort, D. M., & McDonnell, S. W. (2003). Computers and compensation. In W. A. Caldwell (Ed.), *The compensation guide* (pp. 21–32). Minneapolis, MN: Thomson/West.

Walker, A. J. (1987). *HRIS development: A project team guide to building an effective personnel information system.* New York: Van Nostrand Reinhold.

Weeks, B. (2000). Setting sales force compensation in the Internet age. *Compensation & Benefits Review, 32*(2), 25–42.

Wright, A. (2003). Tools for automating complex compensation programs. *Compensation & Benefits Review, 35*(6), 53–61.

Zingheim, P. K., & Schuster, J. R. (2004). What's the next great pay and reward innovation? Business value, paying for skill, and the Internet! *IHRIM Journal, 8*(5), 47–50.

Zingheim, P. K., & Schuster, J. R. (2005). Evaluating human resource pay and reward computer and Web products. *Compensation & Benefits Review, 37*(5), 42–45.

CHAPTER 15

Human Resource Information Systems and International Human Resource Management

Michael J. Kavanagh and John W. Michel

EDITORS' NOTE

Chapter 1 emphasized the emergence of the global marketplace as one of the most important trends in the field of HRM. In particular, Figure 1.2 in Chapter 1 indicates that the system model of organizational functioning centered on an HRIS exists within each country's national cultural environment. The influence of the national culture may raise some of the most important issues for HRM, and there are frequent conflicts between the culture of the country and the culture of both the organization's and HR's environments. The cultural differences between countries will influence HR programs and practices. In this chapter, some of the significant differences between **domestic HRM[1]** *and* **international human resource management (IHRM)** *in* **multinational enterprises (MNEs)** *are covered, and some of the additional HRM issues involved in an international organization are also described. To understand the operation of multiple companies in the global marketplace, we identify the different organizational structures that exist. The importance of the influence of national culture on the external environment in which the firm competes for market share is highlighted. The external environment also has a major impact on the IHRM department's activities and program—that is, the human capital management (HCM) of a firm. This impact, in terms of six factors listed in Figure 1.2 and their effects on IHRM programs, is discussed. Naturally, these added international issues and additional complexities pose significant challenges for the design, development, implementation, and use of an HRIS in a global company, and the ways in which these challenges are met will be covered.*

CHAPTER *Objectives*

After completing this chapter, you should be able to

- Understand the differences between domestic HRM and international HRM
- Identify the types of organizational forms used while competing internationally
- Understand the different types of employees who work in MNEs
- Discuss the staffing process for individuals working in MNEs
- Understand the problems that handling expatriates poses for the IHRM department
- Describe the training needs of and programs for international assignees
- Reconcile the difficulties of home-country and host-country performance appraisals
- Identify the characteristics of a good international compensation plan
- Understand the modifications necessary for using HRIS applications in an IHRM

HRIS IN ACTION

Skylor Electronics,[2] an MNE with headquarters in Seattle, Washington, was having considerable difficulty with expatriate failure in its overseas subsidiaries. Although there were a number of failures in the European Union (EU) countries, the largest failure rate was in its subsidiary in China. The vice president for HR, Marvin Russell, was deeply concerned since the costs of expatriate failure were very high, from $145,000 in the EU to over $400,000 in China. These comprised the direct costs, that is, dollars lost. The indirect costs of having the expatriate return early from the assignment were also quite heavy in terms of the negative image it created for the company in the local economy. In fact, the plant manager for one of the subsidiaries in China refused to accept any more American expatriates until they "could function in the Chinese culture."

Marvin was looking for answers to this problem, and he called a meeting with Director of Overseas Operations Elaine Peterson and Director of Career Development Bill Seamon. Elaine was also quite upset with this expatriate failure because it was very disruptive in terms of meeting production deadlines and maintaining quality.

Bill did not understand why there was a problem since he, along with Director of Training Dawn Fisher, had expatriates attend a three-hour orientation meeting that provided information on their destination countries. As Bill noted, each expatriate saw a 45-minute film, which was followed by a question-and-answer period. Then, the expatriate was given written material on the country.

Marvin indicated that he had spoken directly to several expatriates who returned early to determine the reason for the high failure rate. In general, each former expatriate had mentioned "not being prepared" for the new country and its culture. This experience of "culture shock" was most severe for the failed expatriates from China. After some discussion, it was clear that no one really knew what all the problems were with the expatriate failure problem and that no systematic data existed to help understand the problem. Marvin directed Bill and Dawn to investigate this problem and to provide a report in two weeks. Elaine indicated that she would provide a member of her staff to help with this investigation.

Two weeks later, Bill and Dawn presented their report to Marvin and Elaine. The gist of the report was that the predeparture training for the expatriates and their families was completely inadequate. In fact, there was no training for expatriates' families, and one of the most common problems that led to the premature return of the expatriate was that the spouse was extremely unhappy. Bill and Dawn proposed a predeparture, two-week training program for potential expatriates and their families as well as a trip, paid by the company, to the country where the expatriate was to be assigned. When Marvin objected to the costs of this program, Bill and Dawn were able to show by completing a cost-benefit analysis (CBA), as described in Chapter 7, that the costs saved by reducing expatriate failure exceeded the costs of the predeparture training program.

Introduction: Increasing Importance of International Human Resource Management (IHRM)

As noted in Chapter 1, the **globalization of business** is one of the major changes in the world of work. Tsui (2007) notes that exports as a percentage of world gross domestic products (GDP) increased from 11.6% in 1970 to 30.7% in 2006. Further illustrating this change, the competitive environment for businesses is the topic of a recent executive action report from The Conference Board (Iyer, 2005), which raised this question: "Globalization: Will Your Company Be Left Standing?" This question provides evidence for the impact that globalization is having worldwide.

Perhaps one of the major changes in the world's business economy has been the formation of regional free-trade zones. The passage of the **North American Free Trade Agreement (NAFTA)** in 1994 established the world's largest free market, increasing trade between Mexico, the United States, and Canada. Subsequently, the EU was formed and includes more than 25 member countries (a membership that's still growing) engaged in free trade. Other trade agreements, such as the **Association of Southeast Asian Nations (ASEAN)**, the **East Asia Economic Caucus (EAEC)**, the **Asia-Pacific Economic Cooperation (APEC)**, and the **South Asian Association for Regional Cooperation (SAARC)**, have improved trading relationships in Asia. One can only expect that there may be an African, and perhaps a Middle Eastern, free-trade zone in the future.

As illustrated in the diagram in Chapter 1 (see Figure 1.2), organizational functioning is contained *within* a **national culture envelope**. There is little doubt that the external environment for global business is significantly affected by the country in which it occurs, that is, the host country. The host country and its culture will affect all the factors in the **external environment**: government regulations, labor market, societal concerns, technology, HRM research, and competition. As noted by Bartlett (2002),

> The most important corporate transformation in 75 years is taking place right now. It will radically change human resource management and its role in the organization. . . . Behind this transformation are numerous forces, such as privatization, deregulation, the information revolution, and above all, globalization. (p. xi)

Many of the issues that were caused by the globalization of business and, in turn, by changes in the IHRM function are clearly caused by factors in the external environment. However, there are still **internal issues** to consider in the effective globalization of an MNE. As noted by Beaman (2002), "The heritage of the industrial age prevents many organizations from creating the organizational structures, operational infrastructures, HR policies, and company cultures required to effectively function in the global economy" (p. v). As will be covered in this chapter, there has been considerable progress in handling these internal issues, and much of it has come from the implementation of an HRIS in these MNEs.

There are a variety of factors that have led to the increased globalization of business and the increased importance of the IHRM function. These factors include the following: (1) a dramatic increase in global competition; (2) deregulation in the United States, Germany, and other industrialized countries, which has changed the domestic business environment in those countries; (3) an increase in international mergers and acquisitions; and (4) an increased awareness of the existence of talented human capital throughout the world. Globalization means managing human resources worldwide.

One cannot overlook that one of the major factors related to a firm's choosing to have an international presence is the availability and cost-effectiveness of computer technology. Computer technology has had a major influence on the acquisition and use of physical and financial resources, as well as greatly enhancing the marketing capabilities of MNEs. However, the most important impact of computer technology has been in HRM. Improved communications, worldwide recruiting and selecting, and better talent and performance management programs tied to career planning are only a few of the HR programs in MNEs that have been improved by the use of computer technology. In this chapter, we will examine the characteristics of MNEs and the management of people within these enterprises. In addition, we will be covering the various ways in which computer technology and a well-developed HRIS have affected the field of IHRM.[3]

Types of International Business Operations

In today's global economy, organizations tend to compete based on different levels of participation in international markets (Noe, Hollenbeck, Gerhart, & Wright, 2006). International business operations differ primarily by their level of global participation on a continuum from an international corporation to a global corporation. Although many organizations have only limited global scope, a growing number, such as Dell and Microsoft, have a large number of personnel and facilities throughout the world (Bohlander & Snell, 2007). The following section provides a brief description of the four types as identified by Beaman (2012) and are based on the types of international business operations described by their level of global participation (Bartlett & Ghoshal, 1998).

International Corporation

An **international corporation** uses its existing core competencies to expand operations into foreign markets (Bohlander & Snell, 2007). These organizations' approach is centralized and focused on learning and sharing. This type of organization competes in the global marketplace by exporting existing products and eventually opening facilities in other countries. While their corporate headquarters typically reside in the parent country, international corporations have foreign operations in one or more host countries. Companies operating as international corporations include Honda, General Electric, and Procter & Gamble (see Bohlander & Snell, 2007).

This type of international business operation presents various unique challenges for the HRM function of the organization. Two issues particularly relevant to international corporations are the host country's legal system and the host country's national culture. A legal issue might arise because of a country's minimum wage, for example. In some countries, the minimum wage is relatively high, driving up labor costs (Noe et al., 2006).

Examples of cultural differences affecting international corporations are communications and morale problems.

Multinational Corporation

A **multinational corporation** is a more complex international business operation. In an attempt to capitalize on lower production and distribution costs, multinational corporations' HR role is highly decentralized, locally responsive, and operates as fully autonomous units in multiple countries, (Bohlander & Snell, 2007; Noe et al., 2006). An example of a multinational corporation is General Motors (GM). While GM's headquarters and some of its operations are located in the United States, many of its manufacturing facilities have been relocated to places such as Mexico and China with the goal of reducing production costs by paying lower employee wages. Locating facilities to China has allowed GM to sell to the Asian markets with reduced distribution costs. The HRM issues experienced by multinational corporations are similar to those encountered by international corporations, but exacerbated.

One approach taken by multinational corporations has been to hire expatriates from countries other than the parent country to help with staffing and management issues (Noe et al., 2006). However, according to Noe and others (2006), although hiring expatriates from other countries has its disadvantages, such issues can be overcome by requiring greater cross-training of cultural and managerial skills.

Global Corporation

Global corporations are similar to international corporations in that their HR functions are highly centralized and focused on efficiency; however, the **global corporation** also integrates its worldwide operations through a centralized home office (Bohlander & Snell, 2007). Multinational corporations produce and distribute identical products and services worldwide. Global corporations, on the other hand, emphasize flexibility and mass customization to meet the needs of differing customer groups worldwide (Noe et al., 2006). Ford represents an example of a global corporation. Ford offers two different lines of automobiles, one to its American consumers and the other to its European consumers. For example, it meets the need of European consumers for smaller, more fuel-efficient cars by offering the Ka—a car similar to Daimler's smart car.

Because of this integrative international focus, global corporations must manage their human resources through a multicountry HRM system. This type of system is characterized by three attributes: (1) it is essential that HR decisions be made from a global rather than a national perspective, (2) it is important that the company's management be composed of people from all over the world, and (3) it is imperative that decision making and planning processes include people from a variety of cultures and backgrounds (Noe et al., 2006).

Transnational Corporation

A **transnational corporation** uses an HR approach that is locally responsible to its country location and is focused on being highly efficient plus emphasizing learning and sharing. The type of international business operation chosen by the corporation will inevitably influence the way in which the organization manages its human resources. It is feasible to conceptualize organizations on a continuum based on their level of global participation, from the domestic corporation representing the lowest level of global participation to the global corporation representing the highest level of global participation. With this in mind, we provide in the following sections of this chapter a discussion of issues surrounding the management of human resources internationally. Although these distinctions among MNEs are important, the actual structure of the MNE determines its effectiveness. There is no "best structure" that fits the distribution and marketing needs of all MNEs. Perhaps having a flexible approach to structure is the best way to manage an MNE. Use an HR approach that is locally responsive to its country location and is focused on being highly efficient plus being focused on learning and sharing.

Going Global

For domestic and international firms, becoming a global corporation is a desirable and important step due to potential sales in international markets. Since going global requires a significant investment, most companies that go global are fairly large and have products or services that would appeal to an international market. However, there are specialty companies for which the international market is also desirable due to country by country market niches. We will cover some of the important aspects of going global in this section of the chapter. Since this topic is important, we will cover some of the problems and successes in the process of going global for companies. Briefly, in order to go global, it requires considerable planning and learning how global companies operate. The first step in going global for most companies is to establish a sales office in the countries being considered as potential subsidiaries. This initial action of establishing sales offices enables the company to gain important knowledge of the local culture, regulations, and living conditions. When it is possible, companies also will calculate an initial cost-benefit analysis to determine if the potential ROI indicates they should continue to explore the establishment of a subsidiary in the country. In this section we will cover some of the problems that HR researchers and writers have discovered when companies make the switch to global expansion. We will then cover some of the results of a survey sent to existing global companies to determine the top challenges and top successes experienced by going global. Finally, we will discuss the results of this survey in terms of "Key Competencies for Successful Global Work."

With the realization that going global could be a positive path for a company, researchers and writers in the HRM field began to address this topic in terms of both problems and advice for companies going global. Many companies were reluctant to start the process of going global, so the articles written by HR professionals were invaluable for advice on the difficulties in transforming a domestic company into a global one. Roberts (2000) raised four issues that companies should consider before deciding to go global: (1) understanding the power of the people, (2) technical issues, (3) cultural clashes, and (4) privacy law hurdles. An example of understanding the power of the people cited by Roberts was that of an electrical component manufacturer in Tennessee that needed 83 faxes just to get a worldwide head count. The company had more than 26,000 employees at 163 sites in 24 countries so getting an accurate head count was difficult but quite important. Often companies feel that globalization will surely be able to solve this problem. Related to the power of the people was that a company needs more than monetary resources to go global. It also needs the willing participation of all parties involved. This process of globalization was a major organizational step and it needed to be implemented carefully (see Chapter 9). The second problem, according to Roberts, that most people assume to be solved easily involves the technical issues and changes needed to globalize. First, it is important to ensure that the network, desktops, and users are ready for the global HRIS. The second major technical issue is the choice of a database model (Chapter 2). Options are a single database on one server or several regional databases. The issue of culture clashes may be the most important for any company going global. Some of the attempts to go global by companies have failed because the employees from the home country location have difficulties with the cultural diversity in other countries. The fourth issue of the varying, country by country, privacy laws is the most difficult to handle. For example, the privacy laws in the United States are more liberal than the ones in the **European Union (EU)**. Further, the privacy laws in EU differ significantly from country to country.

Similar issues are raised by Batyski (2008) in an article titled "Global HRIS: It's Just a Matter of Turning It On, Right?" This article discusses several impediments to going global. The first impediment mentioned is the privacy issue that was raised by Roberts (2000), but Batyski also adds that people in any country handling personal data must be well trained in the privacy laws for that country. *Well-trained in the privacy laws for that country.* The second area of complexity covered is the existence of country-specific regulatory reporting and requirements. Since the HR department is the keeper of employee data elements, the HRIS must be aware of these country requirements surrounding the tracking of employee data. One example of this difficulty involves the tracking of union memberships—allowed in some countries but forbidden in others. The primary way to handle these country-specific requirements is by extensive training in the use of HRIS manuals. The manuals serve as a reference material providing the documentation needed for the new HRIS. Good documentation is the key and it must be made available so that these small, but important items are remembered. The third area of complexity when going global covered in this article is the payroll interface landscape. Countries have a variety of payroll systems, from homegrown applications to outsourced solutions. In order to achieve data integrity, payroll interfaces frequently must be built for each payroll system that exists in the subsidiary companies. The final difficult issue, echoing Roberts above, raised by Batyski is the cultural factor. Working styles in countries may be entirely different, with strict levels of hierarchy and formalities expected in some countries while others may not have this structure. These differences in cultural values and practices in countries, because of their critical importance to successful globalization, will be discussed in more detail later in this chapter.

In another article on going global, "Streamlining HRMS for a Global Business," Mason (2009) covers more challenges when companies decide to go global. The companies need to make sure there is an effective and efficient strategy in place for cross-country and cross-cultural collaboration. The only way to develop cohesiveness across global operations is to be successful in moving HR from the local country level to global business lines. Mason also raises the issues surrounding the regulatory environment across different geographic regions and countries. These differing regulations and reporting requirements make it very difficult to implement an HRMS that spans multiple countries. Regardless of these difficulties, Mason indicates that most multinationals proceed to globalize their companies since a global HRMS creates significant cost savings through standardization for new implementations as well as creating greater efficiency, effectiveness, and improved work performance. By having consistent global HR processes, organizations can strengthen cultural cohesiveness across countries of operation. The factors for success in implementing a global HRMS, according to Mason, depend on three factors: (1) choosing the right vendor for technology, (2) choosing the right platform for HRIS implementation, and (3) ensuring a smooth company rollout.

In the *2011–2012 Going Global Report: HCM Trends in Globalization,* Beaman (2012) describes the decision of "**going global**" as quite difficult and time-consuming. Jeitosa Group International, in collaboration with the **International Association for Human Resource Information Management (IHRIM)**, completed a survey of 130 multinational organizations from diverse industry sectors that focused on the factors that lead a corporation to "go global." The sample represents a balanced cross-section of global organizations, ranging from very small (fewer than 500 employees) to very large (more than 50,000). Two-thirds (65%) of the respondents have more than 5,000 employees globally, and 72% have more than 1,000 international employees. The respondents cover a broad range of industries, ranging from technology, manufacturing, services, and trade to health care, government, and nonprofits. The majority of respondents come from middle management (55%), with another sizable group represented by executive management (20%). Of the respondents, 40% come from the HR/Payroll field and 47% from the HRIT field. The survey was designed to answer these questions:

1. How does an organization decide when it should go global?

2. How does it determine whether or not its HR department and HRIS[4] are ready?

3. Are its business and HR functions capable of supporting a move to a global level for the organization?

Figure 15.1 lists a number of challenges that organizations face when going global. The figure presents the percentage of survey respondents who felt a particular factor was challenging. The top four—time zone differences (39%), lack of resources (36%), cultural differences (33%), and international compliance (33%)—are among the top IHRM-related challenges facing global organizations (Adler, 2002; Briscoe & Schuler, 2004; Dowling & Welch, 2005; Evans, Pucik, & Barsoux, 2002). It is interesting to contrast these challenging factors from the earlier 2009–2010 survey report (Beaman, 2010) with the 2012 survey results. In the 2010 survey, the top four challenges were—cultural differences (47%), lack of resources (36%), technology/systems issues (39%), and time zone differences (35%). Before leaving Figure 15.1, it is important to note that the remaining issues in Figure 15.1 are also quite significant for organizations moving to a global status. Many of them are the result of organizations being established in countries whose circumstances and cultures are different from those of the home country. For example, data quality, data privacy, international

Figure 15.1   Top Challenges Organizations Face in Going Global

Source: Beaman (2012, p. 5). Reprinted with permission.

compliance, the legal environment and economic situation of host countries, and risk avoidance are all factors that have been, or will be, covered in this chapter to describe the complexity and managerial issues that MNEs face when they expand to a global status.

In addition to asking about the challenges faced by organizations going global, the survey also queried the respondents about the successes they experienced during the transition. Figure 15.2 contains the percentage of respondents in terms of the top successes they experienced. The top four successes were: time zone differences (39%), lack of resources (36%), cultural differences (33%), and international compliance (33%). The results for organizational success in the 2009 survey show that three of four top successes are the same from the 2009 survey to the 2011 survey. One could conclude that organizations anticipating going global recognize the challenges of these factors and thus put more resources and time into handling the issues. The other successes in Figure 15.2, in general, could reflect an understanding by management that organizational support, data quality/ integrity, the legal environment, and the lack of global leadership are quite important for the transition to a global status and thus have received increased attention.

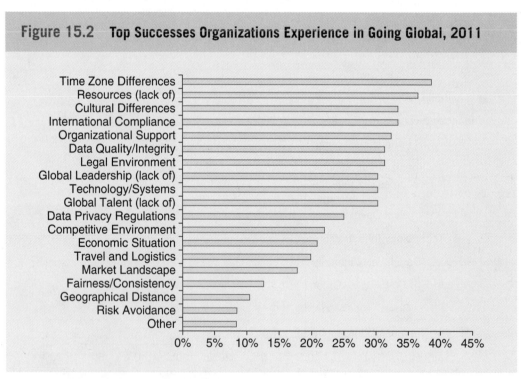

Figure 15.2 Top Successes Organizations Experience in Going Global, 2011

Source: Beaman (2012, p. 5). Reprinted with permission.

A third question in the survey asked the respondents what are the key competencies for successful global work, and the results of that survey question are contained in Figure 15.3. As seen in Figure 15.3, the top five are a global mindset (67%), cultural intelligence (64%), strategic thinking (64%), adaptability to change (47%), and accommodation/flexibility (38%). The next five key competencies are all focused on management: leadership skills, decision-making ability, analytic thinking, interpersonal skills and business acumen. As a set, these 10 competences indicate that professionals and managers working in global companies need to develop these competencies through training and experience in order for the global company to be successful.

One clear conclusion is that becoming a global organization is complex and challenging. Beaman (2009)[5] concludes the report as follows:

> The world of globalization is complex, but comprehensible; it is daunting, yet exciting; it is challenging and achievable! Studying the leading practices of others who have "gone global" before is an effective way to avoid the traps and to develop a path forward. Globalization is a journey, not a destination. (p. 19)

The difficulties involved in managing the workforce of any MNE, including a global one, are covered in the remainder of this chapter.

Differences in HRM in MNEs

Even though there were a number of different types of international business operations described in the previous section, for convenience, these types will all be referred to as multinational enterprises (MNEs). As one might expect, there are significant differences in HRM programs and practices between a domestic enterprise and an MNE. Most organizations start out as domestic corporations (Noe et al., 2006). Because the domestic organization only operates in one labor market, managing its human resources is much easier than is the case for organizations operating in multiple countries. MNEs operate in multiple countries and must have information on the labor markets in all the countries in which they do business.

Another obvious difference is that there are three types of employees in a typical MNE, as opposed to one type in a domestic firm. These MNE employees include **parent-country nationals (PCNs)**, **host-country nationals (HCNs)**, and **third-country nationals (TCNs)**. PCNs are from the country in which the corporate headquarters of the MNE is located, while HCNs are from the countries where subsidiaries are located. Obviously, TCNs are employees from countries other than the parent or host countries. In spite of these differences in

Figure 15.3 Key Competencies for Successful Global Work, 2011

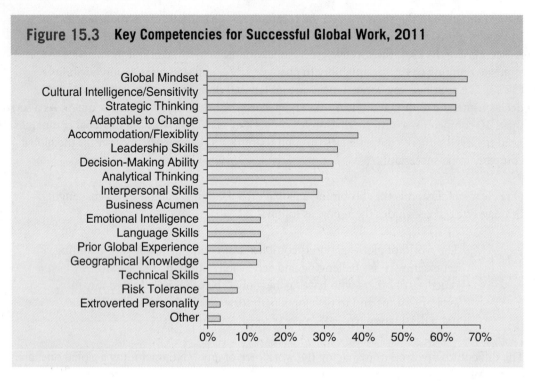

Source: Beaman (2012, p. 13). Reprinted with permission.

the types of employees hired by a domestic enterprise and an MNE, the major programs of HRM, for example, talent management and compensation, exist in both domestic and international organizations. However, the fact that an MNE competes in multiple countries versus the single-country orientation of a domestic company contributes to the complexity of IHRM.

An example of this complexity for the IHRM function is that, although operating in multiple countries provides a larger labor pool for the organization, it makes the talent management process multifaceted since applicants from different countries will have very different levels of education and experience. In particular, applicants from third-world countries likely have very little formal education and less experience with technology. While these applicants can work in entry-level or less technical positions, they will require greater training and preparation if the organization wants to promote them. In a similar fashion, compensation levels and policies will differ between home country and other MNE employees. It is likely that home-country employees will demand higher salaries and more benefits than other employees. MNEs will have to use IHRM systems to manage these different compensation policies. Other factors affect the complexity of IHRM. Dowling and Welch (2005) argue that the complexity of international HR management can be attributed to six factors:

- More HR activities: An HR department in an international firm must be concerned with activities that would not be part of an HR department in a domestic firm, for example, relations with host governments; differences in labor laws and guidelines in the host country; and administrative details of the employees, such as international taxation, international relocation, orientation, and language training.

- The need for a broader perspective: The HR department and managers in MNEs need a broader worldview in dealing with PCNs, HCNs, and TCNs, and recognition of both the cultural differences among employees and the differences in work ethic and practices in the employees' home countries.

- More involvement in employees' personal lives: The IHRM department is more involved in the lives of employees in the areas of taxation, education, and even banking services. It also has to address the issue of visas and housing arrangements for PCNs (expatriates) and TCNs.

- Changes in emphasis of HR programs, such as compensation, managerial style, and tolerance of employee diversity, as the workforce mix of expatriates and locals varies. The immense pool of talent available to MNEs means a varying mix of PCNs, HCNs, and TCNs in the workforce. Consequently, a number of different languages will often be spoken. This situation would dictate language training to support a common language for employees and to improve communication in the working environment.

- Risk exposure: The IHRM department must be aware of the risks to its employees and keep them apprised of any significant problems (e.g., terrorist threats, impending war, and environmental disasters). It must be prepared for any necessary evacuation of employees.

- Broader external influences: Many factors can affect the operation and activities of IHRM in multiple countries, such as government regulations and relations, the labor market, societal concerns, and the level of technology.

Managing Different Types of Employees in MNEs

Managing in the global business environment creates unique complexities for managers—especially expatriate managers. These complexities have been created due to the mix of PCNs, HCNs, and TCNs. In the past, organizations have relied on expatriates as a major source of staffing for their overseas operations (Schuler & Tarique, 2007). Although the diversity of its workforce will depend on the type of international business operation adopted by the MNE, more and more, MNEs are shifting from an expatriate-focused workforce to a global workforce. Beaman (2008), discussing the organization of IHRM in MNEs, centralized versus decentralized, argues that "it is only by first 'thinking locally' to truly understand the needs of our local business communities, and then 'acting globally' to seamlessly knit together diverse business functions and (HR) systems into a holistic, global approach that we can build an effective, efficient and competitive organization" (p. 6).

In addition, it is important for management to understand the cultural differences between expatriates and the host- and third-country workforce. A study conducted by Inform Group of 79 international companies found that only 14% reported they were ready for the future use of this mixed group of potential employees in terms of their workforce planning (Babcock, 2007; see Chapter 11 for HRP). Understanding cultural differences can make it easier for managers to relate to and manage their global workforce. Some of the most important cultural factors include education, politics and law, and economics (see Bohlander & Snell, 2007).

Global Diversity and Inclusion

As previously noted, the globalization of business and corporations has been one of the major changes in the world of work. MNEs, in their search for human talent, are focused on a worldwide labor market. Organizations are recognizing the importance of having a global approach to the management of employees in order to remain competitive in the global marketplace, particularly when the MNEs are in need of additional employees to meet business needs. This search for new employees must take account of cultural differences in multiple countries by recognizing the importance of developing greater cross-cultural competence in their employees. In order to survive, organizations must manage differences so that employees from all backgrounds can be heard, be understood, and be able to work together productively. This organizational program and effort is known as managing diversity and inclusion of employees.

In a study measuring the degree of **global diversity and inclusion** within countries of the world, 546 senior executives of MNEs were surveyed and 40 senior executives in North America, Europe, Asia, and Latin America were interviewed to determine the extent to which various countries support diversity and inclusion in their organizations (Society for Human Resource Management [SHRM], 2009). The entire survey had questions focused on the opinions of the executives about the support for diversity and inclusion in the organizations in various countries of the world, reflecting the need for locating the human talent that is critical to the survival of MNEs. SHRM commissioned the Economist Intelligence Unit (EIU), a subsidiary of The Economist Group, to conduct this international study on diversity and inclusion (SHRM, 2009). As noted in the introduction to the report, "Driven by a need to compensate for talent shortages—and compete in an increasingly diverse marketplace— companies are extending their recruiting and promotion efforts to groups that traditionally were under-represented or not present at all" (p. 5). According to the report, "This study was launched to provide a deeper understanding of Diversity and Inclusion issues on a global scale, and to offer insight into Diversity and Inclusion best practices worldwide" (p. 3).

The arguments for increased diversity and inclusion have their basis in equal employment legislation. However, two additional reasons for increasing diversity and inclusion in an MNE are (1) the moral issue of discrimination in hiring and promotion on the basis of gender and race and (2) the business case that increasing diversity and inclusion will improve the financial position of the MNE. The business case simply states that, if the consumer population is diverse, then it behooves an MNE to have a diverse workforce.

The EIU also researched the diversity readiness of 47 countries to create the **Global Diversity Readiness Index (DRI)**, an online spreadsheet tool that is available on the SHRM website (www.shrm.org/diversity). The DRI is used to rank the 47 countries on 39 separate indicators, which combine to create diversity scores on five categories. Using this tool, we can see the overall rankings in these five categories on a single page. A high ranking on the DRI indicates a higher degree of readiness to manage diversity and foster inclusion for that country. Individual country profiles show all the indicators of diversity and inclusion for each surveyed country on all of the diversity and inclusion indices. The importance of this tool is obvious for an MNE seeking to enter a new country by establishing a sales office or a production plant; if a country has a reputation (or cultural value) to support workplace diversity and inclusion, it is likely that it will be easier for MNEs to find available talent within the country. Finally, the DRI can help global managers understand the prevailing attitudes and values of the countries in which their companies are located.

Education

Having a workforce of PCNs, HCNs, and TCNs means the educational level of the workforce will be highly varied. It is important for managers to understand and deal with the human capital needs of a highly diverse workforce made up of individuals (1) coming from different cultural backgrounds, (2) possibly speaking different languages, and (3) having different educational experiences. These education differences require that managers provide a supportive work environment for their employees. One important aspect of support is training on (1) cultural differences, (2) verbal and nonverbal communication, and (3) specific skill sets particular to the employee's job.

Political and Legal Systems

The political and legal systems within the host country will affect the type of HR practices that can be used (Noe et al., 2006). The laws and regulations of the host country are determined in part by the societal norms of that country. For example, the United States has created laws governing issues such as equal employment opportunities and fair pay standards (Noe et al., 2006). However, these laws are specific to the United States and do not exist in other countries. In addition, free speech is a **cultural norm** in the United States and is protected by law. It is acceptable for organizations and individuals to speak out against the government if they do not like certain government regulations or taxes or if they think they are being unfairly treated. However, in other parts of the world, it may be highly inappropriate, and possibly dangerous, for organizations to speak out against the government.

Economic System

The economic system of the host country is one determinant of the way in which HR programs and practices are used. This economic system affects human capital primarily through its compensation system (Noe et al., 2006). Countries such as Germany, Switzerland, and Japan have strong educational systems and provide employees with good wages. In comparison, third-world countries such as Sri Lanka, Afghanistan, and Haiti have poorer educational systems and provide substantially lower compensation to their workforces. A study by the U.S. Department of Labor (2002) indicates that the average compensation for employees in the manufacturing sector in Sri Lanka was $0.42 per hour, compared with $21.33 per hour for manufacturing employees in the United States. If the workforce of an MNE in Sri Lanka were composed of employees from both Sri Lanka and the United States, an equity issue might arise and must be managed effectively.

HR Programs in Global Organizations

International Staffing

The complexities inherent in managing a global organization make staffing an especially important part of the IHRM system. When staffing for managerial and nonmanagerial positions, the MNE needs to determine if personnel will be selected from the home-country, host-country, or third-country talent pool.

As described by Bohlander and Snell (2007), each of these employee groups provides a different advantage for the MNE. A common issue for all of these employee groups, however, is the underutilization of and lower pay for female employees (Adlung, 2010). Adlung found that, in a number of European countries, females received approximately 25% less salary than their male counterparts. This point suggests that MNEs should emphasize hiring female employees and paying them fairly. Adlung suggests that companies could utilize an integrated talent management system such as PeopleSoft, TalentSoft, or SuccessFactors to leverage this untapped talent pool and reduce the salary gap between male and female employees.

Selecting Global Managers: Managing Expatriates

One of the most difficult, but important, responsibilities of the IHRM function is the selection of managers from the parent country for assignments in host countries. Most of the literature on this topic is focused on the selection of expatriates, whether they are PCNs, HCNs, or TCNs. The reason expatriates can be from any of these three categories is that, at the managerial level in an MNE, these individuals will move from country to country. Thus, the term **expatriate** will be used to designate global managers, regardless of the home country. To understand the difficulty in selecting expatriates, we will discuss in this section (1) the **cultural environment of countries**, (2) expatriate failure and its causes, and (3) selection criteria and procedures for expatriates.

The Cultural Environment of Countries

One of the most important aspects of an expatriate's job that will significantly affect performance is his or her interaction with the local government and people of a country. Because of this interaction, most expatriates will experience **culture shock** as they move from country to country within an MNE. Culture shock can be mild, for example, for a German manager who relocates to a subsidiary plant in France, or quite severe, for example, for an Australian manager who moves to a subsidiary in Egypt. Thus, one of the most important tasks of the IHRM department is to gather information about the culture of countries where the MNE does business to try to estimate the cultural differences between the home countries of employees and the countries where they may be assigned. An HRIS can be very useful in that it can serve as a repository of this information, and, thus, **cultural profiles of countries** can be quickly generated.

Further emphasizing the importance of a country's culture, Briscoe and Schuler (2004) state,

> Knowledge about and competency in working with country and company cultures is the most important issue impacting the success of international business activity. And possibly the area of business that is most impacted by cultural differences is the human resource function. (p. 114)

Culture, as defined by Hofstede (1991), "is the collective programming of the mind which distinguishes the members of one group or category of people from another" (p. 6). Hofstede's research was the first systematic study of the dimensions of national culture, and he identified five dimensions on which the cultures of countries differ. In addition to Hofstede's work, other studies have examined differences in national culture (GLOBE Research Team, 2002; Trompenaars, 1992). Trompenaars, like Hofstede, found five distinct cultural factors that differentiated country cultures, while the Global Leadership and Organizational Behavior Effectiveness (GLOBE) research project categorized countries on nine cultural dimensions. Regardless of which study we examine, all authors agree that the cultural environment of a country has a strong effect on the management of employees and should be considered when selecting expatriates.[6]

To define the culture of a country, Bohlander and Snell (2007) list the following elements that will differentiate countries in terms of their cultural environment for international business: (1) education/human capital, (2) values/ideologies, (3) social structure, (4) religious beliefs, and (5) communication. Information gathered in these five categories could be used to create profiles of the cultural environment of countries in which the MNE does business. It is most important to emphasize that this information could be stored electronically in the HRIS and maintained by the IHRM department. Both of the major IT platforms, Oracle PeopleSoft (www.peoplesoft.com/corp/en/public_index.jsp) and SAP (www.sap.com/usa/index.epx), have this capability, or it can be customized by the MNE.

A final note on country culture: It will have an *effect on all the activities and programs* of the IHRM function, including selection, training, compensation, and performance management.

Expatriate Failure and Causes

Expatriate failure is defined as the return of an expatriate to the home country before the period of the assignment has been completed. Thus, expatriate failure represents an error in a selection decision. There is such an emphasis on expatriate failure because of its costs to the MNE. These costs are both direct and indirect. Direct costs include the actual money spent on selecting and training, relocation costs for the expatriate (and family), and salary. These costs can be quite substantial. However, indirect costs can frequently be higher than direct costs. Indirect costs are harder to quantify, but they could include loss of market share in the country, negative reactions from the host country's government, and possible negative effects on local employee morale. For example, expatriate failure could lead a local host government to insist that, in the future, only an HCN fill the position. Finally, there will be the indirect costs experienced by the returning expatriate in terms of personal failure, loss of respect by peers, and possibly negative influences on future promotions.

What are the causes of expatriate failure? Although there has been considerable research on this topic, the answer is not completely clear. It is safe to say that one cannot generalize from the research results to every expatriate situation; however, the results do provide a guide to the information that should be collected during the selection of expatriates. In general, one could state that the major factor affecting expatriate failure is the *inability to adjust to the new situation and culture* by the expatriate and her or his family.

In terms of specific reasons for expatriate failure, Dowling and Welch (2005) cite the global surveys of the Organizational Research Counselors (ORC) (2002) and the GMAC Global Relocation Services and Windham International (2002). The problems reported by expatriates and companies in these surveys were

- spouse/partner dissatisfaction,

- inability to adapt,

- difficulties with family adjustment in the new location,

- difficulties associated with different management styles,

- culture and language difficulties, and

- issues associated with the accompanying partner's career development.

Similarly, Briscoe and Schuler (2004) indicate that "a number of surveys and studies have found that the most important factors in the early return of expatriates . . . lie in the inability of their families (and/or themselves) to adjust to the foreign environment" (p. 242). The clear implication of these findings is that the expatriate's family or partner must be considered in the selection decision process.

Selection Criteria and Procedures for Expatriates

In selecting expatriates, IHRM professionals should remember that the selection process is an exchange between the organization and the employee. Furthermore, the prospective expatriate's family must be involved in the exchange. In terms of the utility of selection, that is its cost-effectiveness (covered in Chapter 12), making a mistake is extremely costly. IHRM professionals must be cognizant of the causes of expatriate failure when developing the selection procedures, for example, tests or interviews, and also have an understanding of the cross-cultural issues in the evaluation and recommendation of employees for an expatriate assignment.

The factors involved in the selection of expatriates can be divided into two general categories—individual and situational (Dowling & Welch, 2005). In the individual category are technical ability, **cross-cultural suitability**, and family requirements. Technical ability is quite clear and would include both managerial and technical skills. The person selected must be technically proficient in his or her field (e.g., electrical engineering) and also must have a good performance record as a manager. Technical ability is very important to the selection process, as indicated by the results of the ORC worldwide survey (2002), in that 72% of responding firms used it as the first screening criterion in their selection procedure. In selection terms, technical ability would be the *absolute minimum* requirement for the first screening of prospective employees for the assignment. Note that technical incompetence or poor performance is not mentioned as a cause of expatriate failure; however, job-related factors could possibly cause premature departure—for example, the nature of the job not being as described or the expatriate being unable to transfer technical or managerial skills to the new assignment.

The second individual factor, cross-cultural suitability, has several aspects. It could include language ability, cultural empathy, adaptability, and a positive attitude toward the assignment in the specific country being considered. Although technical ability is very important for success in the assignment, cross-cultural suitability is equally important since a number of the causes of expatriate failure are directly related to this factor.

The third individual factor, family requirements, has a great deal to do with the success of the expatriate's assignment. In all the research and surveys on causes for expatriate failure, the poor adjustment of the accompanying spouse or partner and children has been well documented as one of the major causes of expatriate failure. Although it is appropriate to use standard testing and interview techniques to assess the technical ability and cross-cultural suitability of potential expatriates, evaluation of these factors means the involvement of the family. Interviewing the candidate's spouse or partner and children regarding the assignment is frequently done. In addition, most MNEs have learned to build in a pre-assignment visit for the expatriate candidate and his or her family as part of the selection process. This involvement of the entire family in the selection process has become a common practice for MNEs. In fact, if there are two possible locations for the assignment, companies may encourage a pre-assignment visit to both countries.

With regard to the general factors that affect the assignment situation, Dowling and Welch (2005) list country and cultural requirements, language, and MNE requirements. Country and cultural requirements could include work permits and visas. Generally, the work permit is given to the expatriate, and the accompanying spouse or partner may not be permitted to work. As for the children, there may not be schools that would be acceptable, particularly if the children do not speak the language of the host country. In some expatriate assignments, the children either receive language training or there is a school in which their native language is spoken. The opportunity for the spouse or partner and the children to learn another language is sometimes seen as a benefit of the international assignment. Of course, this relates to the second factor of language. Difficulties in language are a major barrier to cross-cultural communication; thus, this is a very important factor for the expatriate and the family. Fortunately, many companies offer language training to the entire family prior to departure for the assignment. The final factor, MNE requirements, could involve getting permission from the host country for the selection of any expatriate. This is common in joint international ventures. Other factors could be the duration and type of assignment. When the duration of the assignment is for only two to three months or the assignment is in a "high-risk" country, the family members usually would not accompany the expatriate.

Selection of expatriates is a critical function of IHRM, particularly in MNEs where expatriate assignments are used to "groom" managers for higher levels of management. Many of the factors to consider in selecting expatriates and the factors causing expatriate failure are handled by training. However, the software applications available can greatly reduce the time required to make this process work. The next section focuses on training in the MNE, primarily the training of expatriates.

Training and Development of Expatriates

This section will focus primarily on training and career development for expatriates. As was done in the previous section, all managers in an MNE will be considered as expatriates since their career assignments and development typically mean that they will move from country to country. Training and development activities and programs in MNEs also include nonmanagerial employees of all types—PCNs, HCNs, and TCNs. Because traditional training and development were covered in detail in Chapter 13, most kinds of typical organizational training (e.g., orientation or technical training) will not be discussed. However, the use of an HRIS and its applications (covered in Chapter 13) will still be discussed. In fact, the training applications that are a part of the HRIS will be very useful for training expatriates. Not only will the expatriates' personal, work experience, and skills information stored on the HRIS be easily accessible but also the results of the training in terms of expatriate success or failure can be recorded. This information should be useful for future expatriate selection.

The corporate IHRM department has responsibility for all training; however, this responsibility is usually decentralized by delegating it to the MNE's subsidiaries. There may be training programs developed at the headquarters of the MNE, but it is unusual for these IHRM professionals at headquarters to deliver programs to the subsidiaries when it can be done more economically by the local IHRM professionals. Most of this local training for nonmanagerial employees will vary by different geographic locations of the MNE. Therefore, some cross-cultural training for nonmanagerial employees who are not HCNs will be necessary, for example, language training; but again, Chapter 13 covers the approach and design of these training programs.

This section will cover expatriate training in detail and will be divided into the following subsections: (1) the purpose of expatriate training, (2) **predeparture training** and the repatriation of expatriates, and (3) **transfer of training**.

Purpose of Expatriate Training

The dual purpose of any training program is to inform and motivate employees. Even training that is focused on learning a manual skill, for example, keyboarding, has both knowledge and motivational aspects. Clearly, the employee is learning a new skill, but with the proper training method, the employee can be encouraged to be more productive; and with the improved skill, the employee may be happier in the job. In addition to these two purposes of training, the first specific purpose of expatriate training is to supplement the selection process and assist the expatriate and her or his family in adjusting to the new situation. It must be emphasized that selection of expatriates is never perfect. Why else would there be expatriate failure? Thus, the training program content for expatriates is based on both the selection criteria identified above and the causes of expatriate failure.

The second specific **purpose of expatriate training** is economic. Recall that the expatriate brings both technical and managerial expertise to the subsidiary when there are no HCNs ready to fill the positions. In addition, the expatriate assignment is used by MNEs as a career development process for managers. Thus, the MNE has significant economic reasons for using expatriates. When one calculates the potential **direct and indirect costs of expatriate failure**, the amount of the investment increases. The MNE makes a major investment in selecting employees for placement in its subsidiaries, and training programs are another IHRM element used to protect that investment.

Predeparture Training

It should be noted that predeparture training programs do not focus on the technical ability of the expatriate, unless there are new technical or managerial skills necessary for the assignment, for example, the introduction of new technology. Because one of the major causes of expatriate failure is the dissatisfaction of or the lack of adjustment by the employee's spouse, partner, or family, the inclusion of these people in predeparture training is very important. To assist the adjustment of the expatriate and his or her family to a new culture, predeparture training typically includes training in cultural awareness, language, and practical matters regarding daily living in the new culture. Most MNEs will also include preliminary visits as a part of predeparture training.

Another element in predeparture training that is highly recommended is **repatriation** training. Formal repatriation is the process that occurs as the expatriate and family return to their homeland. However, recent research and literature has indicated that the repatriation process should begin before the person leaves the home country. The expatriate may find on return that the situation that was expected in the home country (e.g., a promotion to a new position) is not available; and thus, the expatriate will seek other employment. This problem of losing expatriates during the repatriation process has been well documented in the literature (Black, 2000; Feldman & Tompson, 1993; Poe, 2000; Solomon, 1995). There is considerable discussion in the recent literature on the design and implementation of repatriation programs that suggests that companies need to begin repatriation training prior to the expatriate leaving the home country—in predeparture training—rather than waiting for the return of the expatriate (Briscoe & Schuler, 2004; Dowling & Welch, 2005; Evans et al., 2002), and most companies consider repatriation as part of the career development program of the MNE.

Training in cultural awareness, language, and practical matters regarding daily living in the new culture constitutes the predeparture training that the expatriate and family will attend. It is important to recall that expatriate selection is a two-way street. The expatriate still has the right to decline the assignment. Thus, the predeparture training both informs and attracts, which are the two purposes of training. There are a large number of topics that can be included in predeparture training. The topics listed in Table 15.1 make up a possible content for the predeparture program. Note that this list could change depending on the host and parent countries involved.

Transfer of Training

The idea that the predeparture training program could change as a function of the two countries involved has been recognized by scholars, and several models have been proposed to provide guidelines on predeparture training programs (Mendenhall, Dunbar, & Oddou, 1987; Tung, 1981, 1998). These researchers argue that predeparture training should not be viewed as "one size fits all" but rather that the training design and program should be contingent on other factors in the expatriate assignment. According to Tung (1981, 1998), the two factors that most affect predeparture training design are (1) the dissimilarity between the expatriate's native country and the host culture—low to high— and (2) the expected amount of interaction between the expatriate and members of the host country—low to high. Based on an analysis of these two factors, Black and Mendenhall (1989) argue that the design of the training program can then vary on three dimensions: (1) the training methods used, (2) the level of training rigor, and (3) the duration of the training program. For example, if both the dissimilarity between the expatriate's native country and the host culture and the expected amount of interaction between the expatriate and members of the host country are quite high, then the predeparture training should be rigorous and the length of training should be one to two months. In this situation, the training methods would attempt to immerse the expatriate in the host country's culture through assessment centers, simulations, sensitivity training, and extensive language training. As mentioned earlier, the use of the HRIS to analyze the success or failure of these training programs will enable the MNE to make more effective decisions about expatriates and their training in the future.

Table 15.1   Topics for Predeparture Training

1. Cultural values and religions

2. Websites for country information

3. Country history, recommended readings, videos,* and achievements in the country

4. Classical literature describing the country's history, its folkways, and heroes and heroines

5. Information about other HCN expatriates in the country

6. Information on job opportunities for spouses and partners

7. Descriptions of the educational facilities and opportunities for families

8. Current news about the country, particularly its relationship to the parent country

9. Traditional family roles of father, mother, and children

10. Locations for shopping and shopping hours

11. Dominant language of country; extent of bilingualism in country

12. Nonverbal gestures and their meanings

13. Political structure, particularly as it affects the operation of the MNE

14. Descriptions of currency, temperature variations, transportation, hours of business

15. Sightseeing, including historic, artistic, and important cultural locations that would appeal to all the family

Note: This is a very general list, which will vary from country to country.

*Videos should be made available to expatriates and their families, either to review or to keep.

Performance Appraisal in MNEs

Performance appraisal is an important process for documenting the performance of employees, determining areas for development, deciding on pay increases and promotional opportunities, and giving employees the opportunity to express their views (Von Glinow,

Drost, & Teagarden, 2002). The type of performance appraisal conducted and its content depend on the specific job requirements and personal attributes of the person being appraised (Schuler, Budhwar, & Florkowski, 2002). This is particularly true when we compare the appraisal of expatriates with that of HCN and TCN employees. The section in Chapter 14 on performance evaluation and performance planning covers a number of HRIS applications that could be used for performance appraisal in an MNE. Naturally, the inclusion of plants with a diverse employee population in multiple countries creates considerable complexity, particularly when the results of the appraisals are being used to move managers from country to country. However, most vendors of HRIS products have packaged software applications available that can be modified for local conditions in each specific country.[7]

Appraising Expatriate Performance

Important considerations in the appraisal of an expatriate's performance are who should conduct the appraisal and what performance criteria are specific to the expatriate's situation (Bohlander & Snell, 2007). The first question is who should complete the performance appraisal. Typically, the performance of employees is appraised by their supervisors. Expatriate managers are geographically distanced from their parent-country supervisors, and, as a result, supervisors who are located in the parent country cannot observe the day-to-day activities of these employees (Dowling & Welch, 2005). Therefore, managers of expatriates tend to base their evaluations of the person on the objective criteria used for other employees in similar positions located in the parent country. A potential problem with this type of assessment is that the parent-country manager does not have direct information or observational data about the more subjective performance criteria, such as the expatriate manager's leadership skills or performance within the context of the subsidiary (Borman & Motowidlo, 1993). Moreover, the supervisor located in the parent country may not be aware of culturally bound biases that constrain the job performance of the expatriate manager.

Because of these complexities, it may be most appropriate to obtain multiple ratings of the expatriate's performance through the use of a 360° feedback system (Dowling & Welch, 2005). Ratings of the expatriate manager's performance could be garnered from his or her superiors, peers, and subordinates in the expatriate assignment, as well as from the expatriate himself or herself. This would provide a clearer picture of the expatriate's total job performance. In fact, in a study of 58 U.S. multinational firms, Gregersen, Hite, and Black (1996) found that 81% of the companies used more than one rater when assessing the job performance of expatriate employees.

What Performance Criteria Should Be Appraised?

As with managers in domestic assignments, it is important to evaluate the specific job-related competencies of the expatriate manager. However, assessing the competence of an expatriate is somewhat more complex in that there are qualities unrelated to their jobs that they need to possess to perform their roles effectively (Schuler et al., 2002). In addition to typical task and contextual performance behaviors, expatriates should be assessed on other criteria, such as cross-cultural interpersonal skills; sensitivity to differences in the norms, laws, and cultures of various countries; and the ability to adapt to uncertain and unpredictable circumstances. Since expatriates are working in a new culture, they will face new experiences that may be vastly different from their experiences in their home countries. As a result, it is important that the HR department of the parent country recognize the impact of these aspects of the expatriates' experience in their performance appraisals.

Appraising Host- and Third-Country Nationals' Performance

Appraising the performance of HCNs and TCNs is somewhat different from appraising the performance of domestic employees in the United States. It is important for PCNs to be sensitive to cultural differences when appraising performance. For example, in Japan, discussing the negative aspects of an employee's performance may be taken as an insult (Dowling & Welch, 2005). Because "saving face" is so important in Japan, discussing the negative attributes of an employee may cause that employee to distrust the manager. To deal with these cultural differences, organizations should employ HCNs to assist in the development and administration of performance appraisals (Dowling & Welch, 2005). HCNs know what type of information is culturally sensitive. Unlike expatriates, they are less likely to be perceived as outsiders. This perception is important since performance evaluations are used to determine pay increases and promotional decisions, training opportunities, and dismissal decisions. Finally, these appraisals can help identify individual performance problems that can be solved by training.

Managing International Compensation

The management of compensation[8] in an MNE is one of the most complex but critically important functions of the IHRM department. Its complexity comes from having a mix of PCNs, HCNs, and TCNs within one company and, thus, having to handle wage, salary, and benefits information that differs across countries. As a result, the IHRM compensation manager must be aware of differences in taxation, labor laws affecting compensation and benefits, currency fluctuations, and cost-of-living differences within and between countries where the MNE has a presence. The criticality of compensation and benefits management by the IHRM rests, in part, on the effects that salary and benefits have on employee motivation. In spite of differences across countries regarding the motivational factors in the workplace, money seems to be consistently at the top of the list.

The other reason for the critical importance of compensation management in subsidiaries is its link to the strategy of the MNE. To help us understand some of the important elements and dynamics of compensation in an MNE, this section will cover (1) the objectives of international compensation, (2) the components of international compensation, and (3) two approaches to international compensation.

The Objectives of International Compensation Policy

Actually, the objectives of a compensation policy in an MNE are similar to those in a domestic company. It has been fairly well established in the management research literature that compensation administration is closely related to the strategy of the firm. For example, if the company has forecasted increased sales in the next year and thus has determined a need for new employees with specialized skills, it may be necessary to pay above the labor market's "going salary rate" in order to get the best available individuals. This necessity would be especially true when information from the labor market indicates that there is a shortage of people in a particular country having the skills needed for the target job—for example, computer programmers. Similarly, when the labor market statistics indicate that there is an abundance of people with the skills necessary for a specific job, it would be recommended that the compensation level match the labor market values.

As in a domestic firm, the *first objective* for an MNE is to align its compensation administration with the strategy of the firm. Of course, compared with the domestic firm, this alignment is much more complex for the MNE. It requires the MNE to have accurate and up-to-date labor market compensation information for all the countries in which it has a presence. This requirement is one of the most powerful advantages of having an HRIS with labor market information for the IHRM department. Labor market statistics, such as average compensation as well as forecasted shortages and surpluses for jobs, are available for most countries and can be stored in the HRIS. The applications in the computer software that produce analyses of these data would be quite similar to those described in Chapter 14. However, it is clear that the reports generated from the HRIS would be much more complex in an MNE since multiple countries would be involved.

The *second objective* of compensation administration in an MNE, as in a domestic firm, is to affect employee motivation in several ways. It must motivate employees to (1) join the firm, (2) be productive while members of the firm, and (3) stay with the firm. Employee motivation, then, is an important objective of an MNE's international compensation policy, which is complicated since multiple cultures are involved. Although most cultures see monetary rewards as motivational, there are clear differences across world cultures in terms of the other factors that motivate employee behaviors. For example, the meaningfulness of the work may be very important in some cultures, whereas the opportunity for promotion would be most important in other cultures.

The *final objective* of compensation policy for an MNE is that it must be perceived as fair by the employees. This notion of fairness or equity has been shown to be a powerful motivator of human behavior (Colquitt, Conlon, Wesson, Porter, & Ng, 2001), and it may be the most important objective of an international compensation policy. Given the mix of employees from different companies (PCNs, HCNs, TCNs), *perceived or real* differences in wages or benefits between groups of employees could lead to considerable dissatisfaction among the less privileged groups and consequently affect the retention of employees.

The Components of International Compensation

The components of an international compensation system are very similar to those of a domestic program. The major components are a base salary and a set of benefits. However, extra pay premiums would be much more complex for an MNE. For example, there may be a foreign-service or hardship premium for expatriates, whether they are from the parent or a third country. Other premiums could be based on the "risk level" of the assignment in the country. Although most domestic companies give cost-of-living allowances (COLAs) based on where one works (e.g., rural vs. urban locations), MNEs must also use between- and within-country COLAs to have an equitable compensation system. These considerations, along with the other compensation issues discussed, make managing the compensation system a "nightmare" for the IHRM department. Having the employee, country, and compensation/benefits data in an HRIS means that IHRM professionals have the ability to access important information quickly for making both policy and operational decisions about compensation in an MNE.

Two Approaches to International Compensation

The IHRM textbooks mentioned earlier in this chapter (Briscoe & Schuler, 2004; Dowling & Welch, 2005; Evans et al., 2002) all discuss two approaches to international compensation—the **going-rate** and the **balance-sheet approaches**. In the going-rate or **host-country approach** (Bohlander & Snell, 2007), the base salary for international employees is tied to the salary levels in the host country. For example, an expatriate would earn pay that is comparable with the salaries of employees in the host country. Thus, the compensation levels for employees would depend on wage surveys of (1) local nationals (HCNs), (2) expatriates of the same nationality, and (3) expatriates of all nationalities (Dowling & Welch, 2005). For low-pay countries, the base pay and benefits could be supplemented with additional payments. It should be obvious that HRIS applications for compensation based on the going rate would be useful for establishing initial compensation levels, particularly for expatriates. Having this database would also be quite useful for handling complaints by any MNE employee regarding the equity of his or her compensation. Computer-based compensation applications are available from the major providers of software platforms such as Oracle PeopleSoft or SAP.

The second approach to compensation policy, the balance-sheet approach, has as its goal the maintenance of a home-country living standard plus a financial inducement for accepting an international assignment. As Dowling and Welch (2005) note, "The home-country pay and benefits are the foundation of this approach; adjustments to home package to balance additional expenditure in the host country and financial incentives (expatriate/hardship premium) are added to make the package attractive." Although this approach would appear to be more attractive to the expatriate, it has a disadvantage for the IHRM department—it can be very complex to administer. Software applications and reports from an HRIS can assist in untangling these objectives, and probably perceived, inequalities, but IHRM professional and line managers are still required to explain these programs to employees.

In sum, compensation is probably the most difficult and complex of the HR programs to implement and administer in an MNE. However, it is critically important to the equity exchange (or psychological contract) between the company and its employees. Ergo, it can affect employee motivation. Interactions between employees and their immediate supervisors in a domestic enterprise or an MNE regarding compensation have the greatest impact on motivation of the employees. Having an HRIS produce the needed data and information on the equity of compensation among employees is a tremendous boon to employee relations.

HRIS Applications in IHRM

Introduction

It should be apparent from the previous sections of this chapter that management, and HRM in particular, in an MNE is exceedingly more complex than in a domestic firm. As business becomes more global, ignoring its international aspects would be foolish. International companies functioning in the 1970s through the 1990s were hampered by the lack of sources for, and the slowness of transmission of, important HR information for effective management decisions. However, with the current technologies and applications discussed earlier in the "Going Global" section, difficulties in executing the basic HR functions of planning, recruiting, selecting, training, and managing performance in MNEs have been reduced.

Specific HRIS applications for MNEs have been noted previously, mostly in concert with two software platforms, Oracle PeopleSoft and SAP. These two platforms have all HR applications needed for a global corporation. Not only are these the only software providers available for software applications in the IHRM field, but they are also good starting points for the student interested in examining the variety of software that can be used in an HRIS. Thus, this last section of this chapter will focus on broader issues in the application and use of an HRIS in IHRM. Problems and potential solutions will be examined[9] and discussed briefly under three topics: (1) organizational structure for effectiveness, (2) IHRM-HRIS administrative issues, and (3) HRIS applications in MNEs.

Organizational Structure for Effectiveness

The issue of the *most effective* structure for the operation of an HRIS in an MNE has been a "moving target." The most common advice regarding the management of an MNE has been to "**think global, act local**." This advice applies to the total management process of an MNE—its strategy, operations, finance, marketing, and HR—and has been followed religiously for many years in international management. However, Beaman (2008) has provided arguments for a different approach, at least in terms of the development and use of an HRIS in international organizations. As she states,

> I maintain that we have been going about globalization the wrong way. The slogan, "Think Global, Act Local" . . . is completely the inverse of what we should be doing with our HRIT [synonym for HRIS] organizations. Rather, it is only by first "thinking locally" to truly understand the needs of our local business communities, and then "acting globally" to seamlessly knit together diverse business functions and systems into a holistic, global approach that we can build an effective, efficient and competitive organization. (p. 6)

A well-established piece of advice in the management literature has been that "structure does not drive success—people do." So to build an organizational structure for an HRIS in an MNE, we should consider Beaman's very reasonable suggestion.

IHRM-HRIS Administrative Issues

Service-Oriented Architecture (SOA)

It may be repetitive, but it is important to reexamine some of the HRIS approaches covered in Chapter 10 in terms of HRIS applications in an MNE. These applications can be much more useful in an international firm than in a domestic one. One of the most important approaches for handling administrative issues in an MNE is the use of a service-oriented architecture (SOA). As discussed in Chapter 10, an SOA "is a paradigm for organizing and utilizing distributed [computing] capabilities that may be under the control of different ownership domains . . . providing a uniform means to offer, discover, interact with and use capabilities to produce desired [business] effects" (OASIS, 2006, p. 8). SOA is focused on providing a service for a function that is well-defined, self-contained, and context and platform independent, a function that adds value to the organization's business purpose rather than simply being focused on the technology itself. In effect, SOA is a collection of internal and external services that can communicate with each other by point-to-point data exchange or through coordination among different services to achieve a business purpose. As a result, an SOA can combine multiple business functions from different organizational departments, for example, production, marketing, and HR, that have similar electronic transactions (such as change of address or salary level) into a central procession unit. SOAs were created when it was discovered that the various departments of organizations (marketing, finance, operations, R&D, and HR) were storing the same basic information on employees. Creating an SOA was a way to use the IT capabilities of an organization more efficiently.

Outsourcing, Offshoring, and Insourcing

MNEs were the first organizations to outsource many of their jobs that required low levels of skills (e.g., call centers). Outsourcing in HR had been done for years, for example, using Automatic Data Processing, Inc. (www.adp.com/corporateLanding) for payroll administration. However, the HR departments in the 1990s were looking to outsource other programs (recruiting and selection) to supposedly save money for their operations. Thus, using the Internet for outsourcing HR programs became a reality (Gueutal & Stone, 2005; Walker, 2001). Most of these approaches failed for a variety of reasons; the major one had to do with the privacy and confidentiality of employees' personal data. Still, because of the tremendous financial benefits if the MNE could use outsourcing or offshoring, these practices continued. Another major problem, however, was that many companies outsourced or offshored HR functions that were a critical part of the primary business of the organization, for example, talent management. Thus, many companies reverted to insourcing certain business processes, particularly those in the HR department.

Data Privacy and Security

The general cautions and guidelines for maintaining data privacy and security given in Chapters 3, 10, and 16 also apply to MNEs. In addition to the normal safeguards used in a domestic company, the MNE has to create additional ones to be in compliance with security and privacy laws and regulations in different countries. As noted by Harris (2002), 36 countries in the world have legislation governing the manner in which personal information can be collected and handled. The Safe Harbor program, negotiated by the European Commission and the U.S. Department of Commerce, is an attempt to create a single set of privacy regulations regarding the use and transfer of personal information. These regulations represent a compromise between the American and European approaches to privacy issues with personal data. Regarding privacy and security in an MNE, Harris (2002) suggests the following:

> Adopting a global approach to employee privacy issues, and building an internal culture of respect for privacy, is the best course of action open to a multinational corporation that wants to act as a global employer in the current regulatory environment surrounding the collection and use of personal information. (p. 198)

HRIS Applications in MNEs

As discussed in this chapter, most of the HRIS applications available for a domestic company can be used for MNEs. However, some modifications are necessary due to the complexity of the database in an MNE. In today's global environment, access to data from any physical location in the world is increasingly important. Teams of employees may be stationed in Thailand, India, and the United States. As covered in Chapter 2, two issues arise when data are shared across wide geographic locations. These are (1) managing the day and time of a transaction and (2) determining where to store the various components of the business application, DBMS, and database.

To deal with the date and time issue, developers of DBMS such as Oracle, MS SQL Server, and IBM DB2 are building the capability to deal with recording dates and times according to the time zone in which the data originated. So, for example, if a database is stored in London and an employee records a transaction while sitting at a terminal in Los Angeles, in addition to the time (say 1 P.M. in Los Angeles), the time zone (–08:00 from Greenwich Mean Time) is also stored with the transaction.

As part of a global information system design, organizations have chosen to break their business applications and DBMS into components, often called "tiers." More detail on tiers was covered in Chapter 3. Traditional client-server architectures broke an application into two tiers, typically with the **user interface** and some business logic on the user's computer, such as a PC (the client), and the database and mainstream parts of the application stored on a server. In today's global environment with high-speed data networks, **N-tier architectures** exist with databases and applications being distributed among many different computers around the world. So if, for example, you are in an Internet café in Bangkok trying to get information about your benefit election, the hosting computer may be in London and the data may be located on a computer in Chicago. In sum, computer networks are created that provide instant access to these operational data, allowing real-time decision-making capabilities regardless of one's physical location.

A centralized database allows a company to confine its data to a single location and, therefore, to more easily control data integrity, updating, backup, queries, and access. A company with many locations and telecommuters, however, must develop a communications infrastructure to facilitate data sharing over a wide geographical area. The advent of the Internet and a standardized communication protocol made the centralized database structures and geographically dispersed data sharing feasible.

The database structures and system architectures we have discussed would be very useful to a multinational enterprise. Consider the differences between a compensation database for a domestic corporation operating in a single labor market and for an MNE. The multinational's compensation database would include labor market data for all countries in which the MNE has a presence, for example. Also, a great number of the modifications to an HRIS in an MNE would be driven by the different labor laws and regulations of the various host countries. As noted, there is software available for IHRM, but the use of this software demands that the database be accurate and timely. Being able to create and access reports based on employee data, and do it quickly, requires that the data be accurate and up to date—an axiom that has been emphasized throughout this book.

SUMMARY

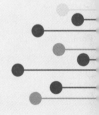

Globalization is a reality. Twenty-five years ago it was the reality primarily for major corporations such as GE and IBM. Now, it has become increasingly important for midsize firms—the fastest-growing group in all countries. This chapter has examined the implications of this globalization on the HRM function in MNEs and has documented the explosion of the HRM function into a separate field, IHRM. How IHRM has become increasingly complex by expanding on the traditional HR functions of selection, training, and compensation was also covered. The complexity of having diversity of employees (PCNs, HCNs, and TCNs) and of contending with the varying laws and practices of host countries dictated that MNEs abandon the paper-and-pencil system for computer technology.

The advantages of having employee information stored, manipulated, and reported using computer technology were discussed relative to the use of these capabilities in multiple IHRM programs. However, some of the more critical information that an HRIS can store, analyze, and produce reports on is contained in the cultural and legal profiles of countries. This information is valuable in all the activities and programs of the IHRM department and significantly influences the management of the many parts of an MNE.

KEY TERMS

DISCUSSION QUESTIONS

1. Describe the differences between domestic and international HRM.

2. What are the different types of organizational forms that corporations use for international operations?

3. What are the three types of employees who work in MNEs? Explain how an HCN could change to become a TCN in an MNE.

4. Describe the staffing process in an MNE. How does it differ from that of a domestic-only corporation?

5. What are the causes of expatriate failure?

6. Describe a training program for expatriates. Why is it recommended that the family of the expatriate also receive training?

7. Which method is best for completing performance appraisals for each of the three different types of employees in an MNE?

8. What are the objectives of an international compensation plan?

9. What are the modifications necessary for using HRIS software applications that are designed for domestic companies in an MNE?

CASE STUDY

A large MNE in the cookware industry was having difficulties maintaining its market share due to a number of mergers among other competing firms in the industry. The MNE, with corporate headquarters in Canada, had production plants in 15 countries and a company presence[10] in a total of 29 countries. Although the firm had a number of competitors, its product was considered as having the highest quality—the Mercedes of cookware. The firm was family owned and founded in 1937. The most pressing problem was how the firm could stay competitive in the marketplace and stop decreases in sales. Naturally, it was highly desirable to increase sales beyond annual averages, but, first, the firm had to change something to stabilize its place in the market.

Examining the problem, the CEO and the corporate board, consisting of all the corporate vice presidents as well as the CEOs of all the international locations, concluded that it was necessary to reduce operating costs by 5% to 6% to remain competitive. Thus, it was decided to determine if these cost savings could be achieved in operations, raw materials, finances, or HR.

The MNE managers examined the latest production technology in their industry. The firm discovered that its technology was fairly current and the few technological changes available would only help decrease costs by less than 1%. However, these modifications to their current technology were very expensive and did not appear to have a favorable return on investment (ROI).

Trying to obtain better financing was nearly impossible since the MNE had very favorable financing currently. The same was true for raw materials, since a decision to use cheaper materials would greatly reduce the quality of the company's products.

As a result, the management of the MNE asked the IHRM department for some suggestions as to how personnel costs could be trimmed. However, there was one constraint established by tradition in the company. The MNE had never had a layoff of employees in its history, and the CEO refused to use this option to reduce personnel costs. One of the complicating factors was the different labor legislation as well as the very different cultures in the 29 countries in which the MNE did business.

Case Study Questions

1. How would you approach a solution to this problem for the MNE?

2. Assuming that reducing personnel costs is the best, and probably only, way to reduce overall corporate costs, what specific programs would you suggest to reduce costs? Why?

3. How would an HRIS for the MNE aid in finding HR programs to help solve this problem? What would be the important data to access in the HRIS for all the units and divisions of the MNE to determine feasible HR programs?

4. Are the problems of reducing personnel costs for an MNE different from those for a domestic-only company? Explain.

STUDENT STUDY SITE

Visit the Student Study Site at **http://www.sagepub.com/kavanagh3e** for additional learning tools such as access to SAGE journal articles and related web resources.

NOTES

1. For convenience, domestic-only corporations will be referred to as domestic corporations.

2. The company and individual names used are fictitious.

3. This chapter cannot cover all the literature and issues in the field of IHRM. However, for the interested reader, there are excellent and comprehensive textbooks available on IHRM (Adler, 2002; Briscoe & Schuler, 2004; Dowling & Welch, 2005; Evans et al., 2002).

4. In the paper by Beaman (2010), human resources information technology (HRIT) is used instead of HRIS. However, we feel these two terms are interchangeable.

5. There are 24 more charts and figures in this report (Beaman, 2010), and the interested student can access it by going to the Jeitosa Group International website (http://www .cedarcrestone.com/research.php).

6. Readers interested in more information on the culture of countries can access any of the works cited in this paragraph.

7. Readers are referred to the websites for Oracle PeopleSoft or SAP for information on these applications for international companies.

8. In this chapter, compensation will refer to the entire wages, salaries, benefits, and extra allowances available in an MNE.

9. It is difficult to target exactly where the IT, HR, or HRIS fields are in terms of their development at any specific time. Thus, this section will provide only a snapshot of the field when this chapter was written.

10. A company presence for an MNE means that the firm has at least a sales office in the country.

REFERENCES

Adler, N. J. (2002). *International dimensions of organizational behavior.* Cincinnati, OH: South-Western.

Adlung, I. C. (2010, March). The male-female salary gap. *Regional HR update: Europe, HRinsights.* New York: Jeitosa Group International.

Babcock, P. (2007). Workforce planning remains largely unaddressed global challenge. *SHRM India.* Retrieved from http://www.shrm.org/hrdisciplines/staffingmanagement/Articles/Pages/WorkforcePlanningGlobalChallenge.aspx

Bartlett, C. (2002). Foreword. In K. Beaman (Ed.), *Boundaryless HR: Human capital management in the global economy.* Austin, TX: IHRIM Press.

Bartlett, C., & Ghoshal, S. (1998). *Managing across borders: The transnational solution* (2nd ed.). Harvard Business School Press.

Batyski, H. (December 2007/January 2008). *Global HRIS: It's just a matter of turning it on, right?* IHRIM.*link, 12*(8–6), 38–39.

Beaman, K. (Ed.). (2002). *Boundaryless HR: Human capital management in the global environment.* Boundaryless HR: Human capital management in the global environment. Austin, TX: Rector Duncan & Associates.

Beaman, K. (2008). Think local, act globally: The collaborative transnational HRIT organization. IHRIM.*link, 12*(6), 6, 10.

Beaman, K. (2010). *2009–2010 global readiness report.* New York: Jeitosa Group International & IHRIM.

Beaman, K. (2012). *2011–2012 going global report: HCM trends in globalization.* New York: Jeitosa Group International & IHRIM.

Black, J. S. (2000, January/February). Coming home. *HR World,* 30–32.

Black, J. S., & Mendenhall, M. (1989). A practical but theory-based framework for selecting cross-cultural training methods. *Human Resource Management, 28*(4), 511–539.

Bohlander, G., & Snell, S. (2007). *Managing human resources* (14th ed.). Mason, OH: Thomson South-Western.

Borman, W. C., & Motowidlo, S. J. (1993). Expanding the criterion domain to include elements of contextual performance. In N. Schmitt & W. C. Borman (Eds.), *Personnel* selection in organizations (pp. 71–98). San Francisco: Jossey-Bass.

Briscoe, D. R., & Schuler, R. S. (2004). *International human resource management* (2nd ed.). London: Routledge.

Colquitt, J. A., Conlon, D. E., Wesson, M. J., Porter, C., & Ng, K. Y. (2001). Justice at the millennium: A meta-analytic review of 25 years of organizational justice research. *Journal of Applied Psychology, 86*(3), 425–445.

Dowling, P. J., & Welch, D. E. (2005). *International human resource management: Managing people in a multinational context* (4th ed.). Mason, OH: Thomson South-Western.

Evans, P., Pucik, V., & Barsoux, J. (2002). *The global challenge: Frameworks for international human resource management.* The global challenge: Frameworks for international human resource management. New York: McGraw-Hill.

Feldman, D. C., & Tompson, H. B. (1993). Expatriation, repatriation, and domestic geographical relocation: An empirical investigation of adjustment to new job assignments. *Journal of International Business Studies, 24,* 507–529.

GLOBE Research Team. (2002). *Culture, leadership, and organizational practices: The GLOBE findings.* Culture, leadership, and organizational practices: The GLOBE findings. Thousand Oaks, CA: Sage.

GMAC Global Relocation Services & Windham International. (2002, October). *Global relocation trends 2002 survey report.* New York: Author.

Gregersen, H. B., Hite, J. M., & Black, J. S. (1996). Expatriate performance appraisal in U.S. multinational firms. *Journal of International Business Studies, 27,* 711–738.

Gueutal, H. G., & Stone, D. L. (Eds.). (2005). *The brave new world of e-HR.* San Francisco: Jossey-Bass.

Harris, D. (2002). Managing data privacy in global systems. In K. Beaman (Ed.), *Boundaryless HR: Human capital management in the global environment* (pp. 173–199). Austin, TX: Rector Duncan & Associates.

Hofstede, G. (1991). *Cultures and organizations.* New York: McGraw-Hill.

Iyer, R. (2005, December). *Globalization: Will your company be left standing?* (Report No. A-0171–05-EA). New York: The Conference Board.

Mason, K. (2009). *Streamlining HRMS for a global business.* IHRIM.*link, 13*(6), 34–35.

Mendenhall, M., Dunbar, E., & Oddou, G. (1987). Expatriate selection, training, and career-pathing: A review and critique. *Human Resource Management, 26,* 331–345.

Noe, R. A., Hollenbeck, J. R., Gerhart, B., & Wright, P. M. (2006). *Human resource management: Gaining a competitive advantage* (5th ed.). New York: McGraw-Hill Irwin.

Organizational Research Counselors. (2002, September). *Dual careers and international assignments survey.* Retrieved from https://www.orc-netsafe.com/surveys/dual.cfm (Name changed to ORC Worldwide in 2003 and to Mercer in 2010.)

Organization for the Advancement of Structured Information Systems (OASIS). (2006, May). *OASIS reference model for service oriented architecture 1.0.* Retrieved from http://www.oasis-open.org/committees/download.php/18486/pr-2changes.pdf

Poe, A. C. (2000, March). Focus on international HR: Welcome back. *HR Magazine,* 94–105.

Roberts, W. (2000, August). Going global. *HR Magazine,* 45 (10),

Schuler, R., Budhwar, P. S., & Florkowski, G. W. (2002). International human resource management: Review and critique. *International School of Management Review, 4*(1), 41–70.

Schuler, R., & Tarique, I. (2007). International human resource management: A North American perspective, a thematic update, and suggestions for future research. *International Journal of Human Resource Management, 18,* 717–744.

Society for Human Resource Management (SHRM). (2009). *Global diversity and inclusion: Perceptions, practices and attitudes.* Alexandria, VA: Author.

Solomon, C. M. (1995, January). Repatriation: Up, down, or out. *Personnel Journal,* 21–26.

Trompenaars, F. (1992). *The seven cultures of capitalism.* New York: Currency Doubleday.

Tsui, A. S. (2007). From homogenization to pluralism: International management research in the academy and beyond. *Academy of Management Journal, 50,* 1353–1364.

Tung, R. (1981). Selecting and training of personnel for overseas assignments.

Columbia Journal of World Business, 16, 68–78.

Tung, R. (1998). A contingency framework of selection and training of expatriates revisited. *Human Resource Management Review, 8*(1), 23–37.

U.S. Department of Labor. (2002). *International comparisons of hourly compensation costs for production workers in manufacturing.* Washington, DC: Bureau of Labor Statistics. Retrieved from http://www.bls .gov/

Von Glinow, M. A., Drost, E. A., & Teagarden, M. B. (2002). Converging on IHRM best practices: Lessons learned from a globally distributed consortium on theory and practice. *Human Resource Management, 41,* 123–140.

Walker, A. J. (Ed.). (2001). *Web-based human resources.* New York: McGraw-Hill.

Special Topics in Human Resource Information Systems

HRIS Privacy and Security

Humayun Zafar and Dianna L. Stone

EDITORS' NOTE

This chapter expands on the information security and privacy issues in HRIS described in Chapter 3 (system considerations) and Chapter 10 (HR administration). Many organizations mistakenly believe that the biggest threat to information security is from outside. This chapter explains the importance of employee information privacy, the threats to employee privacy, and the varying privacy protections afforded employees by laws. In addition, the chapter reviews information security focusing on the technical and behavioral practices of strong information security practices. It also highlights how present and past employees can pose a greater threat to employee privacy than outsiders in the light of the emergence of collaborative and convergent technologies. Finally, the chapter describes the importance, legal aspects, and best practices in maintaining and promoting safe information-handling procedures.

HRIS IN ACTION

John, an HR specialist at a multinational firm, routinely visits a Starbucks across from his house on Saturday mornings. It gives him an opportunity to enjoy a latte while logging onto work and going through what he needs to accomplish in the following weeks. He usually leaves his bag with his laptop at an available table to reserve his spot. He then goes to the counter and orders. However, in his most recent trip, he did not realize that another person was at the store waiting to steal something. While John was paying, his bag with the laptop was headed out the door. The worst part was that John had let his daughter Samantha use his laptop the night before, and he had disabled the password protection feature to allow her access. The laptop had sensitive employee information that he had downloaded from the company's servers. By the time John was able to report that his laptop was missing on Monday, Social Security numbers of thousands of employees had been exposed, with many of these already being used for financial gain.

Introduction

Information privacy and security are particularly important issues for HRIS because unlike many other organizational systems, an HRIS includes a great deal of confidential data about employees, such as Social Security numbers, medical data, bank account data, salaries, domestic partner benefits, employment test scores, and performance evaluations (DeSanctis, 1986; Kovach & Cathcart, 1999). Consider the scenario above, which highlights the use of distraction and extraction by thieves. Without a weapon and without attracting notice, a thief may be able to get unlawful access to sensitive employee data. A place with a blend of jazz, leather chairs, and free Wi-Fi is so familiar to customers that no one thinks twice about saving a round blond-wood table with a personal item while they stand in line. Therefore, it is critical for organizations to understand and pay close attention to what employee data is collected, stored, manipulated, used, and distributed—when, why, and by whom. Organizations also need to carefully consider the internal and external threats to this data and develop strong information security plans and procedures to protect this data and comply with legislative mandates.

Doing this is much more complex than it was 30 years ago. Consider that most computers at that time were mainframes that were secured in a central physical location, with very few HR staff having access to them. If an HR staff member had access to the mainframe it was through "dumb" terminals with limited functionalities and access was easily restricted through physical access and passwords. Due to this closed environment, there was little threat of **security breaches** or vulnerabilities being exploited. During those days information security was considered to be a process that was composed mostly of physical security and simple document classification schemes. Physical theft of equipment, espionage, and sabotage were considered as the primary threats. However starting in the 1990s as computer networks became more common, threats to information security became more involved due to the presence of enterprise-wide systems.

There is a growing concern about the extent to which these systems permit users (both inside and outside of the organization) to access a wide array of personal information about employees. As a result, employees may perceive that if these data are accessed by others, the information contained in their employment files may embarrass them or result in negative outcomes (e.g., denial of promotion or challenging job assignment). Recent research suggests that this concern may be well founded. For example, one report indicated that over 500 million organizational records have been breached since 2005, and there has been a rise in the theft of employment data (Privacy Rights Clearinghouse, 2010). For instance, in 2010, a hard drive was stolen from AMR Corporation, the parent company of American Airlines. The hard drive included names, Social Security numbers, health records, and bank account data for many current employees, retirees, and former employees. As a result, some employees and retirees experienced identity theft. Given these problems, AMR took important steps to implement information security practices to secure the confidentiality of all employee records (Privacy Rights Clearinghouse, 2010).

In view of the growing concern about identity theft and the security of employment information in HRISs, a number of states (e.g., AK, CA, FL, HI, IL, LA, MO, NY, SC, WA) passed privacy laws requiring organizations to adopt reasonable security practices to prevent unauthorized access to personal data (Privacy Protections in State Constitutions, 2012). Despite these new laws, results of surveys revealed that 43% of businesses stated that they did not put any new security solutions in place to prevent the inadvertent release or access to employee data, and almost half did not change any internal policies to ensure that data were secure (Ponemon, 2012). The cost of these data breaches can be large. For example, the average cost of a data breach has increased to almost $7 million per firm (Ponemon, 2009). In addition, a study by McAfee estimated that global economic losses due to information security breaches amounted to over $1 trillion (Mills, 2009).

Software vendors such as Oracle are aware of the potential for security breaches and offer multiple security models (e.g., Standard HRIS Security and Security Groups Enabled Security) that enable an administrator to set up HRIS security specifically for an organization. This means that the software allows companies to determine the kind of data access and responsibility each employee has. For example, an HR manager will have higher privileges and access to data than an employee in sales or even an employee in human resources. This would allow him or her to access a wide array of employee data. On the other hand, a sales manager would need limited data for each employee (e.g., performance-based records for their subordinates) and thus would have less access to employee data. As importance of HRIS privacy and security continues to grow in salience to organizations, it provides an interesting avenue for new employment opportunities. A typical entry-level HRIS analyst position now requires knowledge of implementing secure HR information systems.

Therefore this chapter elaborates on various aspects of HRIS privacy and security. The next few sections consider (a) practices that may affect individuals' perceptions of invasion of privacy, (b) the components of information security, and (c) the implications for developing fair information management policies. After this, the chapter elaborates on some of the key security threats faced by organizations and the policies that organizations need to implement to ensure HRIS privacy and security. We discuss privacy issues first because security systems are typically designed to protect employee privacy, and ensure that employment information is not subject to unauthorized access.

Employee Privacy

The **U.S. Fair Labor Standards Act of 1938** requires employers to maintain basic information on all employees including Social Security numbers, address, gender, occupation, pay, and hours worked. However, the increased use of HRISs to store these data has prompted concerns about the degree to which these systems have the potential to invade personal privacy. Information privacy has been defined as the "degree to which individuals have control over the collection, storage, access, and release of personal data"

(E. F. Stone & Stone, 1990). Given the growing concerns about the privacy of information in HRIS, we consider some practices that may be perceived as invasive of privacy in the sections that follow. In particular we discuss concerns about (a) unauthorized access to information, (b) unauthorized disclosure of information, (c) data accuracy issues, and (d) stigmatization of individuals.

Unauthorized Access to Information

One reason that employees are concerned about the storage of data in an HRIS is that they fear that these systems may allow **unauthorized access** to their private information (D. L. Stone, Stone-Romero, & Lukaszewski, 2003). For example, employees may perceive that if users have access to their Social Security numbers or bank data they will experience identity theft. In fact, some reports indicate that identity theft is the primary consequence of the breach of HRIS data (Privacy Rights Clearinghouse, 2010). Similarly, if unauthorized users have access to medical data or domestic partner benefits then employees feel that they will experience embarrassment or loss of job opportunities (e.g., promotions, pay raises, challenging job assignments).

Interestingly, results of some survey research suggested that these concerns may be justifiable. For instance, one study found that 34% of companies collect and store medical and prescription drug information about employees (Society for Human Resource Management [SHRM] & West Group, 2000). In addition, the findings of the same study indicated that employee information is often released to insurance companies and future employers. Furthermore, even though there are laws that restrict the use of health data in the employment process (e.g., Americans with Disabilities Act [ADA], 1990; Health Insurance Portability and Accountability Act [HIPAA]) some employees have been terminated when employers discover they are using prescription drugs for hypertension, diabetes, or pain control (Personnel Policy Service, 2013). For instance, in one case an organization established a policy requiring that employees report all drugs present in the body and prohibited the use of legal prescription drugs unless approved by a supervisor (e.g., Roe v. Cheyenne Mountain Conference Resort, 1997). Not surprisingly, the court ruled that requiring employees to report their legal prescription drug use was an invasion of privacy and in violation of ADA.

Some research also indicated that employees were more likely to perceive an HRIS as invasive of privacy when they were unable to control access to their personal data, and information was accessed by users outside the organization than those inside the organization (Eddy, Stone, & Stone-Romero, 1999). Results of other research revealed that the use of an HRIS was perceived as invasive of privacy when (a) supervisors were able to access information in employee records, (b) the same data were used for employment rather than HR planning decisions, and (c) the employees did not have the ability to check the accuracy of the data before decisions were made (Eddy et al., 1999). Furthermore, findings of another study showed that employees were more likely to perceive that their privacy had been invaded when medical data were collected and stored in an HRIS, and they were required to use a Web-based HRIS to enter personal data than when they were able to reveal the data to HR professionals (Lukaszewski, Stone, & Stone-Romero, 2008).

It merits noting that HIPAA requires that medical data should be stored separately from other employment data, but some HRISs still include medical or health data in employment records. For instance, HIPAA allows a great deal of medical information to be stored in employee records (e.g., data from drug tests, Family Medical Leave Act certifications, OSHA, workers' compensation, and sick leave). Similarly, Affirmative Action data (e.g., race, ethnicity, gender, age, self-reported disability status), which are collected for EEO-1 reports, are not always separated from employment data in these systems. As a result, applicants and employees may be concerned that sensitive data will be accessed by decision makers, and used unfairly against them in the employment process. At present there are very few legal restrictions on access to data in an HRIS. Therefore, we believe that organizations concerned with protecting employee privacy may want to utilize sound security practices to limit the degree to which unauthorized individuals have access to employee data.

Unauthorized Disclosure of Information

Another concern about the use of HRIS is that employees may perceive that these systems allow for the **unauthorized disclosure** of information about them to others (D. L. Stone et al., 2003). For example, research by Linowes (2000) revealed that 70% of employers regularly disclose employment data to creditors, 47% give information to landlords, and 19% disclose employee data to charitable organizations. In addition, some reports indicated that organizations regularly sell data collected on recruiting websites (D. Stone, Lukaszewski, & Isenhour, 2005). Furthermore, 60% of employers do not inform applicants or employees when they disclose information within or outside the organization (Society for Human Resources Management & West Group, 2000).

Thus, the use of an HRIS may make it much easier to disseminate personal information internally and externally to the organization, and there are currently few restrictions on the release of employee data in private sector organizations. However, the disclosure of employee data may result in negative outcomes for employees if data collected for one purpose (e.g., performance appraisals) are used for other purposes (e.g., decisions about an apartment lease or credit). As a result, employees may be understandably concerned that HRISs facilitate the unauthorized release of personal information, and we believe that organizations should develop policies that limit the unauthorized disclosure of employee information.

Data Accuracy Problems

Employees are also troubled about **data accuracy** because HRISs may contain inaccurate or outdated information about them. Not surprisingly, individuals are often unaware that data in these systems are inaccurate, and many organizations do not give them the opportunity to review or correct data stored in an HRIS. For example, studies showed that data from background checks, credit checks, or social media are often inaccurate, and become permanent records in an HRIS (Society for Human Resource Management & West Group, 2000). In addition, survey results indicated that 73% of participants had errors in their background data that resulted in the loss of job opportunities (Society for Human Resource Management & West Group, 2000).

We believe that inaccurate data in HRISs are especially problematic because they may stigmatize individuals unfairly and result in denial of job outcomes (e.g., termination, loss of promotions or training opportunities). For instance, an executive at Hilton Hotels was terminated shortly after he was hired when data in his background check incorrectly noted that he had been convicted of a misdemeanor and served six months in jail (Socorro vs. IMI Data Search and Hilton Hotels, 2003).

Hilton hired a firm, IMI Data, to conduct the background check but did not check the accuracy of their findings. Socorro was not informed of the background check, but his managing director asked if he had ever been convicted of a crime or spent six months in jail. Socorro replied truthfully that he had not. Although the data about Socorro's conviction and jail sentence were incorrect, Hilton terminated Socorro for falsifying information on his job application. After Socorro's termination, Hilton told third parties that Socorro was fired because he lied on his application, and that he was a convict who had spent six months in jail. Subsequently, he had a great deal of difficulty securing new employment because of the false and defamatory statements made by Hilton. Socorro did finally secure new employment, but at a substantially lower rate of compensation than the Hilton position.

It is clear from this example that the storage and use of inaccurate data in an HRIS may have a negative effect on both organizations and individuals. For example, when data in these systems are inaccurate organizations may make erroneous decisions regarding employees and fail to hire or promote highly qualified individuals. In addition, employees may be unfairly denied job outcomes and opportunities to experience gratifying careers. As a result, employees are likely to perceive that HRISs are invasive of privacy if the data stored in them are inaccurate or outdated.

In support of these arguments, Linowes (2000) found that 72% of private sector organizations do not allow employees to review their employment records for inaccurate data, and 24% do not give them the opportunity to correct their records. In addition, research by Stone, Lukaszewski, and Stone-Romero (2001) found that individuals were more likely to perceive that their privacy had been invaded when they were not able to check the accuracy of data in an HRIS than when they were allowed to check the accuracy of data. Thus, employee concerns about the degree to which inaccurate data may unfairly stigmatize them or affect their outcomes in organizations appear quite justified.

Stigmatization Problems

Employees are often uneasy about the use of HRISs especially when they feel that networked data may lead to them to be **stigmatized** or deeply discredited in the employment process (D. L. Stone & Stone-Romero, 1998). For example, HRISs often provide for the permanent storage of employee data (e.g., performance appraisals, credit scores, employment test scores) that are used to make employment decisions over time. For example, an employee who had a below-average performance ratings very early in his or her career may have difficulty purging these data from an HRIS, and the data may negatively affect subsequent decisions about him or her. As a result, the employee's advancement and career development opportunities may be negatively affected by data that have no bearing on his or her present-day job performance.

Use of Data in Social Network Websites

Recently, organizations have started collecting and using data about applicants and employees from social network websites (SNWs; e.g., Facebook, MySpace, Google +) (Black, Johnson, Takach, & Stone, 2012; Roth, Bobko, Van Iddekinge, & Thatcher, 2012). For instance, organizations now use SNWs to collect information about job applicants' lifestyle, family background, friends, sexual orientation, religion, political affiliation, and personal interests. Estimates indicate that between 20% and 40% of employers now scan SNWs to gather data about job applicants (Framingham, 2008; Zeidner, 2007), and 75% of recruiters are currently required to do online research on applicants before making hiring decisions (Preston, 2011).

One consequence of the organizational use of SNWs data is that individuals are likely to perceive that the data in these systems will unfairly stigmatize them and result in the loss of job opportunities (D. L. Stone & Stone-Romero, 1998). For example, a recent court case (e.g., *Snyder v. Millersville University,* cited in Narisi, 2009) indicated that a student-teacher was terminated from a teaching position when a picture was posted of her on MySpace as a "drunken pirate." It merits noting that there was no evidence that she was drinking alcohol or drunk. Her students found the picture and reported it to school administrators and the university, who terminated her student teaching because they thought she would be a poor role model for the students. When she sued, the court ruled in favor of the university, indicating that she did not have the right to any free speech that might damage her employer's reputation (Narisi, 2009). As a consequence, data in SNWs may be used without an individual's knowledge and may result in termination or loss of other employment opportunities. Although the collection of data from an SNW is not illegal, there is a growing concern that the collection of information from these sites may erroneously stigmatize employees and result in an invasion of their rights to privacy.

Lack of Privacy Protection Policies

Despite the widespread use of HRISs and growing concerns about the (a) unauthorized access, (b) unauthorized release, (c) data accuracy, and (d) use of data to stigmatize employees, many companies have not established fair information management policies to control the use and release of employee information (Linowes, 2000). For instance, a study by Linowes (2000) found that 42% of companies do not have privacy protection policies and the same number has not designated an executive-level person to be responsible for privacy and security of employment records. When no policies exist, the person in charge, whether a manager or record clerk, decides for himself or herself what and when sensitive personal information is released to others. Thus, we believe that one strategy for decreasing employees' perceptions of invasion of privacy is to develop fair information management policies with respect to the collection, storage, use, and dissemination of data in an HRIS. These policies will be discussed in greater detail in a section that follows. Prior to considering these policies, we will consider the important issue of information security and the components of information security systems in protecting employee information and privacy.

Components of Information Security

Brief Evolution of Security Models

As noted above, information security is particularly important for an HRIS because of the high degree of automation in these systems and the wealth of private employee data being stored. **Information security** has traditionally been defined as the protection afforded to an automated information system in order to attain the applicable objectives of preserving the confidentiality, integrity, and availability (CIA) of information system resources (Stallings & Brown, 2008). However, the complexity of the networked environment in which HR data is captured, stored, and utilized means that personnel transactions and information processing are increasingly more vulnerable to security threats and risks than ever before. Therefore, the traditional CIA model of information security does not suffice. The National Security Telecommunications and Information Systems Security Committee (NSTISSC) security model, also known as the **McCumber Cube** (See Figure 16.1) provides a more detailed perspective on security.

Figure 16.1 The McCumber Cube

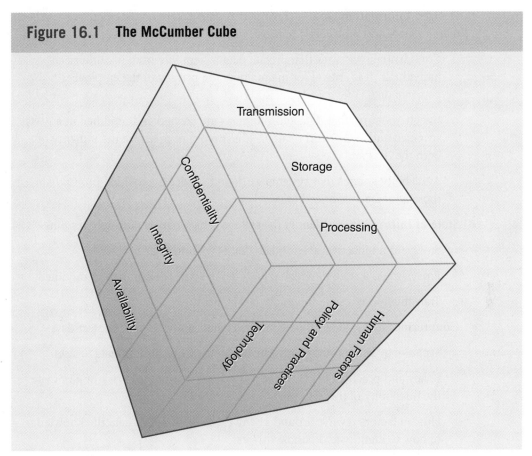

Source: Pohlman (2008).

The McCumber Cube provides a graphical representation of the architectural approach widely used in information security. The McCumber Cube is more granular than the CIA classification because it examines not only the characteristics of the information to be protected, but also the context of the information state. The cube allows an analyst to identify the information flows within an HRIS, view it for important security-relevant factors, and then map the findings to the cube. The cube has three dimensions. If extrapolated, the three dimensions of each axis become a 3 × 3 × 3 cube, with 27 cells representing areas that must be addressed to secure a modern-day information system (Whitman & Mattord, 2011). To ensure system security, each of the 27 areas must be properly addressed during the development and implementation of security processes and policies for the HRIS. The three dimensions and their attributes are categorized as follows:

- **Desired Information Goals**—Ensure that data is kept confidential, has not been manipulated, and is available to those who are authorized to access it.

  o Confidentiality assures that private data is kept safe from unauthorized individuals. It is critical for maintaining the privacy of the employees' personal data (Wong & Thite, 2009).

  o Integrity assures that data and programs are created and modified in a specified and authorized manner. It is important to assure the integrity of both the data and the system.

  o Availability assures that systems work and service is provided promptly to those who are authorized to use them.

- **State of Information**—Identify the state in which data is currently residing.

  o Storage is an inactive state of data that is waiting to be accessed.

  o Processing is a state in which data is being actively examined or modified.

  o Transmission is a state in which data is moving.

- **Countermeasures**—Identify mechanisms that can be used to protect data.

  o Technology is the use of hardware and software to limit threats to data.

  o Policy and practices is the use of procedures that mitigate risk or eliminate the possibility of threats.

  o Human factors revolve around giving each consumer of data the knowledge of how to identify and handle threats.

As an example of the use of the McCumber Cube, consider a 2005 data breach suffered by Ameriprise Financial where data from more than 200,000 clients were stolen off of an unencrypted laptop (Dash, 2006). Ameriprise needed to preempt the data needed to be encrypted (countermeasure) even when it was stored (state of information), and not just when it was being transmitted. This would have ensured confidentiality (desired information goal) of data.

As another example, consider the intersection between the technology countermeasure, the integrity goal, and the storage state. In other words, how do we use technology to ensure that our stored HR data maintains its integrity? One way to do this would be to develop a system for detecting host intrusion (intrusion at the individual workstation level), which protects the integrity of information by alerting the security administrators to the potential modification of a critical file. This is very pertinent to HRIS. An HRIS specialist is asked to perform group data updates and export the results to his or her immediate supervisor for verification. The results are encrypted, and a hash (an algorithm used to ensure that data remains secure and accurate) is computed, and then uploaded to a server via secure FTP, which only specific employees have access to. This example covers multiple cells. For example, only specific employees are allowed access to specific information (*Confidentiality*), and the data is encrypted (*Technology*) before being stored (*Storage*). Also, since a hash is computed after it is encrypted, it ensures that information may not be changed outside of proper processes (*Integrity*). Data is transmitted via secure FTP, whereby maintaining security (*Transmission*). The use of secure transmission protocols is a matter of organizational policy (*Policy*). The examples touch on only a couple of the 27 possible cells in the McCumber Cube. Organizations need to consider the implications of all dimensions and attributes in this cube when designing an HRIS to get a more detailed and accurate representation of threats faced and countermeasures that need to be implemented.

Security Threats

What kind of threats are our organizational security practices protecting us from? In security, it is important to "know your enemy." You have to understand your vulnerabilities. If you do not know what the threat vector (attack method) is, you cannot plan to defend yourself. The following are common security threats:

- Threat Sources
  - *Human error:* When an HRIS is not well designed, developed, and maintained and employees are not adequately trained, there is a high potential threat of security breaches. Research suggests that human errors, such as incorrectly entered data or accidental destruction of existing data, constitute security threats to the availability, accessibility, and integrity of information. The Ameriprise Financial example discussed above showed that an error on the part of an employee can potentially expose private employee or customer data.
  - *Disgruntled employees and ex-employees:* One of the concerns overlooked by HR managers is that information may be damaged by **disgruntled employees**. This is commonly referred to as an insider threat. Employees and ex-employees are dangerous since they have extensive knowledge of systems, have the credentials needed to access sensitive parts of systems, often know how to avoid detection, and can benefit from the trust that usually is accorded to an organization's employees (Boyle & Panko, 2013).
  - *Other "internal" attackers:* Many businesses hire contract workers, who work for the organization for a short period. Contract workers usually gain temporary access to various critical areas of an organization. This creates risks almost identical to those created by employees.

- o *External hackers:* Another significant threat is the penetration of organizational computer systems by hackers. A **hacker** is defined as someone who accesses a computer or computer network unlawfully. Such attacks, often termed "intrusions" (Austin & Darby, 2003), can be particularly dangerous because, once the hacker has successfully bypassed the network security, he or she is free to damage, manipulate, or simply steal data at will.

- o *Natural disasters:* Typical forms of natural disasters are floods, earthquakes, fires, and lightning strikes, which destroy or disrupt computing facilities and information flow. As noted earlier in the chapter, physical threats such as this were once considered the main threats to computing resources. Although they are now less visible do not pose the daily risks that these other security threats pose, each must be nonetheless considered when developing security practices.

- Types of Threats

  - o *Misuse of computer systems:* One of the predominant internal security threats is employees' unauthorized access to or use of information, particularly when it is confidential and sensitive.

  - o *Extortion:* The perpetrator tries to obtain monetary benefits or other goods by threatening to take actions that would be against the victim's interest.

  - o *Theft:* The value of information can be much higher than the price of hardware and software. With contemporary advances in technological developments, a relatively small computer chip (e.g., a USB device) can easily store over 100 GB of data. For example, the State of Hawaii's HR department had medical records stolen when offices of two doctors servicing workers' compensation claims were burglarized (Mangieri, 2013).

  - o *Computer-based fraud:* There is growing evidence that computer-based fraud is widespread. Over 90% of companies have been affected by computer-based fraud, such as data processing or data entry routines that are modified (Garg, Curtis, & Halper, 2003).

  - o *Cyber-terrorism:* **Cyber-terrorism** is the leveraging of an information system that is intended to intimidate or cause physical, real-world harm or severe disruption of a system's infrastructure (Austin & Darby, 2003; Hinde, 2003). In one such scenario, a person with high-level computer and network skills (e.g., a hacker) is hired to break into a specific computer or computer network to steal or delete data and information. Cyber-terrorists often send a threatening e-mail stating that they will release some confidential information, exploit a security leak, or launch an attack that could harm a company's systems or networks.

- *Phishing:* Victims usually receive e-mail messages that appear to come from an authentic source with which the victim does business. The official appearance of the message and the website often fool victims into giving out confidential information. According to Gartner the estimated annual cost of **phishing** is around $2 billion (Moore & Clayton, 2007).

- *Denial-of-service:* A **denial-of-service (DoS)** attempts to make a service unavailable for legitimate users by flooding it with attach packets. The server that is hosting that service is then unable to handle the large number of requests, whereby shutting it down. The financial services sector has been hit particularly hard by this type of attack. For example, Bank of America and JP Morgan Chase have both experienced outages on their public websites due to DoS attacks (Holland, 2012).

- Software Threats

  - *Viruses:* A **computer virus** is a type of malware that works by inserting a copy of itself onto a computer or device (e.g., smartphone) and then becoming part of another program. It can attach itself to files without the user's knowledge and duplicate itself by executing infected files. When successful, a virus can alter data, erase or damage data, create a nuisance, or inflict other damage (Panko, 2003). In a period of five hours in 2000, the "I love you" e-mail virus infected millions of computers, causing damages estimated at $10 billion (Abreu, 2001).

  - *Worms:* **Worms** are in some ways similar to viruses since they can replicate themselves. However, unlike viruses that require the spreading of an infected file, worms such as Code Red, Slammer, and MyDoom can spread by themselves without attaching to files (Panko, 2003).

  - *Spyware:* **Spyware** is software installed on an unknowing user's computer that gathers information about the user's activities on the Web (keystrokes, websites visited, etc.) and transmits it to third parties such as advertisers or attackers (Stafford & Urbaczewski, 2004). Problems associated with spyware include potential privacy invasion, appropriation of personal information, and interference with the user's computer operation (Stafford & Urbaczewski, 2004).

  - *Blended Threats:* These threats propagate both as viruses and worms. They can also post themselves on websites for people to download unwittingly (Boyle & Panko, 2013).

  - *Trojan:* A **Trojan** is another type of malware that usually hides inside e-mail attachments or files and infects a user's computer when attachments are opened or programs are executed. Trojans are named after the Trojan horse of Greek mythology in that they appear to be something positive, but are in reality doing something malicious. Unlike viruses and worms, Trojans do not reproduce by infecting other files nor do they self-replicate. Instead, they must be opened on a computer by a user. Some Trojans can work as spyware, while others can display a login or install screen and collect personal data such as usernames and passwords, or other forms of identification, such as bank account or credit card numbers. They can also copy files, delete files, uninstall applications using remote access programs on the computers, and format disks without alerting the victim. One type of Trojan horse is a **rootkit**. A rootkit takes over a root (administrator) account, and uses its privileges to hide itself. Most rootkits find their way into a system though installation or updating of application software, such as a word-processing program. Rootkits have the capability to modify the behavior of the application so that it can escape detection and do what it was written to do. Therefore rootkits are seldom caught by ordinary antivirus programs, and rootkit detection programs have to be designed to detect a specific rootkit.

Information Policy and Management

As you can see from the above discussion, it is important that organizations have policies and procedures in place to protect employee data. There are two mechanisms though which this can occur: fair information management policies and strong security practices. We believe, as do others (e.g., Privacy Protection Study Commission, 1977; D. L. Stone & Stone-Romero, 1998) that one way to decrease individuals' perceptions of invasion of privacy is to establish fair information management policies for controlling data in HRIS. These policies and organizational strategies for ensuring information security will be considered in the sections below.

Fair Information Management Policies

To date, there has been legislation restricting the collection, storage, use, and dissemination of employee information in the public sector (e.g., Privacy Act of 1974), but there is no comprehensive federal legislation on employee information privacy in private sector organizations. However, one state, California, has recently passed a law that protects the privacy of employee records in private sector organizations (Privacy Protection in State Constitutions, 2012). Space limitations preclude a complete review of all employment-related privacy laws, but we suggest that interested readers see the Privacy Rights Clearinghouse (2013) at https://www.privacyrights.org/background-checks-and-workplace for a complete review of all federal and state laws. In addition, multinational organizations should also consider the privacy practices in the countries in which they operate. The challenge for organizations is that every country takes a different perspective on protecting employee information privacy, and your organization will need to be familiar with all the applicable laws in each country in which you operate. A sample of interactional laws protecting employee privacy across the globe is found in Table 16.1.

Even though there are few laws governing the storage, use, and dissemination of information in HRIS, organizations may decrease the degree to which employees perceive that HRIS invades their privacy by establishing fair information management policies and practices. For example, in 1977 the Privacy Protection Study Commission recommended that private sector organizations proactively establish policies for managing employee information to protect individuals' perceived or actual rights to privacy. For instance, they recommended that organizations limit the collection of information to data which are job related, control unauthorized access to information in HRIS, adopt reasonable procedures for assuring that data are accurate and timely, and limit external disclosures of data without employees' consent. A complete review of these recommendations is provided in Table 16.2.

Table 16.1   Example Privacy Laws in Various Countries

Country	Law	Date
Angola	Da Protecção de Dados Pessoais	2011
Argentina	Personal Data Protection Act	2000
Canada	Personal Information Protection and Electronics Document Act	2000
European Union	The European Union Data Protection Directive	1998
Germany	Bundesdatenschutzgesetz	2001
Japan	Personal Information Protection Act	2003
Mexico	Ley Federal de Protección de Datos Personales en Posesión de los Particulares	2010
New Zealand	The Privacy Act	1993
South Korea	Personal Information Protection Act	2011
United Kingdom	Computer Misuse Act	1998

Table 16.2 Fair Information Management Policies and Practices Based, in Part, on Privacy Protection Study Commission Recommendations (1977)

Organizational Practice	Policy Recommendation
Collection of Employee Data	Limit the collection of information on individual employees, applicants, and former employees to that which is relevant to jobs or specific employment decisions.
Inform Employees About Uses of Data	Inform employees, applicants, and former employees about the uses made of their information and types of records maintained.
Ensure Accuracy of Data	Adopt reasonable procedures to ensure the accuracy, timeliness, and completeness of employment information.
Allow for Correction of Data	Permit employees to see, copy, correct, and amend records maintained about them.
Unauthorized Access to Data	Limit the internal and external use of records maintained about employees, applicants, and former employees. Data are available to users on a "need to know" only basis.
Unauthorized Release of Data	Limit external disclosures of information kept on employees, applicants, and former employees. Require that employees, applicants, and former employees provide authorization for the release of personal information or requests for verification of information.
Ensure That Employees Are Aware of and Understand Fair Information Management Policies	Provide employees with training about fair information management policies to ensure they understand them. Require that employees provide written acknowledgments that they understand these policies.

We believe that the use of these fair information policies and practices may lessen many of the concerns that applicants and employees have about the collection, storage, use, and dissemination of data in an HRIS. However, it is imperative that all users review and clearly understand these policies before HRISs are implemented in organizations.

Effective Information Security Policies

The second way that organizations need to protect employee data is through their security practices. Bruce Schneier once stated that "security is a process, not a product" (Schneier, 2000). This statement alludes to the nature of information security. That is, information security is not predominantly a technical issue; it is more of a management issue. It is easy to see why at times there is a major focus on technology. Technology is visible, and there are many things that we can say about security technologies. Management can seem more abstract. There are fewer general principles to discuss, and most of these cannot be put into practice without well-defined and complex processes (Boyle & Panko, 2013). But the management issues are actually often complex and focused both on behavioral information policies as well as the technical practices.

This lends credence to importance of effective security policies. Security policies identify valuable assets, provide a reference to review when conflicts pertaining to security arise, outline personal responsibility, help prevent unaccounted-for events, outline incident response responsibilities, and outline an organization's response to legal, regulatory, and standards of due care.

For effective implementation of security, organizations usually follow established security standards such as **ISO/IEC 27000** series. This series focuses on areas such as access control, security management, good practices, and protection of health-related information. Almost all aspects of the ISO/IEC 27000 series mesh with HRISs. For example it is standard practice to require HR employees to change their passwords on a quarterly basis to achieve optimal access control. It is also a generally good practice to verify that all HRIS users are properly trained in the secure use and handling of equipment, data, and software. Many breaches occur when users are not consciously aware of what they are doing. Unconscious behavior can defeat the best efforts of security experts, meaning all of the security protocols in the world are powerless in the face of a stressed-out worker. According to Microsoft's Security Intelligence report, 44.8% of vulnerabilities result from user action such as clicking a link, or being tricked into installing malware (Microsoft, 2011).

Several best practices have been proposed to ensure that employee data is secured and employee privacy is protected (Canavan, 2003; David, 2002; Tansley & Watson, 2000). These include the following:

- Adopt a comprehensive information security and privacy policy.
- Store sensitive personal data in a secure HRIS and provide appropriate encryption.

- Dispose of documents properly or restore persistent storage equipment.

- Build document destruction capabilities into the office infrastructure.

- Implement and continuously update technical (firewalls, antivirus, anti-spyware, etc.) and nontechnical (security education, training, and awareness) measures.

- Conduct privacy "walk-throughs" and make spot checks on proper information handling.

Although there is no question that all organizations need to be aware of HRIS security issues and best practices, global organizations need to be particularly diligent. An organization may face specific laws regarding storage, transmission, and transfer of data based on the areas in which it operates. This may limit the flow of employee data across borders and may make the HRIS more complex, or may require the organization to adopt different HRIS in different countries.

SUMMARY

Although it is clear that HRISs have numerous benefits in organizations, this chapter considers some recent issues associated with their use including employee privacy and information security. In particular, the chapter considers (a) practices that may affect individuals' perceptions of invasion of privacy, (b) the components of information security, (c) the security threats faced by organizations, and (d) the implications for developing fair information management policies and security practices. Throughout the chapter, we argued that organizations should take proactive steps to develop fair information management policies that can be used to protect individual privacy, and implement information security practices and policies that safeguard employment data.

KEY TERMS

DISCUSSION QUESTIONS

1. Why are information security and privacy important considerations in the design, development, and maintenance of an HRIS?

2. List and discuss the major information security and privacy threats to organizations.

3. What are the important goals and considerations of information security?

4. Identify the important legal provisions governing information security and privacy in your country.

5. What is the role of HR professionals in information security and privacy management?

6. What are some of the best practices to manage information security and privacy in terms of procedural, technical, and physical controls?

CASE STUDY: PRACTICAL APPLICATIONS OF AN INFORMATION PRIVACY PLAN

XYZ University is a medium-sized tertiary education provider in the state of Queensland, Australia. In undertaking its normal business of teaching, learning, and research, the university collects, stores, and uses "personal information," that is, anything that identifies a person's identity.

With respect to students, this information may include, among other things, records relating to admission, enrollment, course attendance, assessment, and grades; medical records; details of student fees, fines, levies, and payments, including bank details; tax file numbers and declaration forms; student personal history files; qualifications information; completed questionnaire and survey forms; records relating to personal welfare, health, equity, counseling, student and graduate employment, or other support matters; records relating to academic references; and records relating to discipline matters.

The bulk of this information is retained in the student management information systems and in the file registry. Academic and administrative staff, at various levels, have access to these records only as required to carry out their duties. Portions of the information held in university student records are disclosed outside the university to various agencies, such as the Australian Taxation Office; the Department of Education, Employment and Workplace

Relations; other universities; consultant student services providers; the Department of Immigration and Citizenship; and overseas sponsorship agencies.

The university has a well-documented information privacy policy in accordance with the community standard for the collection, storage, use, and disclosure of personal information by public agencies in Queensland. The policy relies on the 11 principles developed in the Commonwealth Privacy Act of 1988. These principles broadly state the following:

- Personal information is collected and used only for a lawful purpose that is directly related to the collector's function.

- Before the information is collected, the individual concerned should be made aware of the purpose, whether it is required by law, and to whom the information will be passed on.

- Files containing personal information should be held securely and protected against loss; unauthorized access, use, modification, or disclosure; or any other misuse.

- Personal information can only be disclosed to another person or agency if the person concerned is aware of it and has consented and the disclosure is authorized or required by law.

- Personal information should not be used without taking reasonable steps to ensure that it is accurate, up to date, and complete.

Presented below are three scenarios in which you need to decide how to apply the privacy policy and principles. The following scenarios were sourced from the Griffith University Privacy Plan (http://www.griffith.edu.au/about-griffith/plans-publications/griffith-university-privacy-plan/pdf/privacy-training-guide.pdf). The link to the privacy plan itself is www.griffith.edu.au/ua/aa/vc/pp. A complete statement of the relevant privacy principles can be found at *www.dva.gov.au/health_and_wellbeing/research/ethics/Documents/ipps.pdf*.

Scenario 1

Roger, a photocopier technician, has been asked to repair an office photocopier that just broke down while someone was copying a grievance matter against an employee of the agency. The officer who was copying the file takes the opportunity to grab a cup of coffee and leaves Roger in the photocopy room while the photocopier cools down. While waiting, Roger flips through the file and realizes that the person against whom the grievance was made lives on the same street as he does.

Scenario 2

Tom telephones a student at home about attending a misconduct hearing. The student is not at home; however, the student's partner, Christine, answers the phone. She states that she knows all about the misconduct hearing but asks for clarification of the allegations. When pressed, Tom provides further details. Tom feels comfortable about providing this information to Christine because she is the student's partner, and she has already told Tom that she knows all about her partner's misconduct hearing.

Scenario 3

Brad works in a student administration center, and Janet is a student. They know each other, as they used to attend the same high school. Occasionally, they get together at the university to have coffee and chat about mutual friends. Brad knows that Janet's birthday is coming up because Janet happened to mention that she'll be another year older in the near future. Brad decides to access the student information system to find out Janet's date of birth and home address. A few weeks later, Janet receives a birthday card from Brad sent to her home address.

Case Study Questions

With regard to the above scenarios, you need to decide

1. what information privacy principles (IPPs) have been breached,

2. how, and

3. what you would do to address the situation.

STUDENT STUDY SITE _____

Visit the Student Study Site at **http://www.sagepub.com/kavanagh3e** for additional learning tools such as access to SAGE journal articles and related web resources.

REFERENCES _____

Abreu, E. (2001). *Computer virus costs reach $10.7 billion this year.* Retrieved from http://www.crn.com/news/channel-programs/18816957/computer-virus-costs-reach-10–7-billion-this-year .htm

Americans with Disabilities Act of 1990. ¶ 602 § 102.

Austin, R. D., & Darby, C. A. R. (2003). The myth of secure computing. *Harvard Business Review, 81*(6), 120–126.

Black, S. L., Johnson A. F., Takach S. E., & Stone, D. M. (2012, August). Factors affecting applicants' reactions to the collection of data in social network websites. Paper accepted at the meeting of the Academy of Management, Boston, MA.

Boyle, R., & Panko, R. (2013). *Corporate computer security* (3rd ed.). Upper Saddle River, NJ: Pearson.

Canavan, S. (2003). *An information security policy: A development guide for large and small companies.* Bethesda, MD: SANS Institute. Retrieved from http://www.sans .org/reading_room/whitepapers/ policyissues/information-security-policy- development-guide- large-small-companies_1331

Dash, E. (2006). *Ameriprise says stolen laptop had data on 230,000 people.* Retrieved from http://www.nytimes.com/2006/01/26/ business/26data.html

David, J. (2002). Policy enforcement in the workplace. *Computers and Security, 27*(6), 506–513.

DeSanctis, G. (1986). Human resource information systems: A current assessment. *MIS Quarterly, 10*(1), 15–27.

Eddy, E., Stone-Romero, E. F., & Stone, D. L. (1999). Effects of information management policies on reactions to human resource information systems: An integration of privacy and procedural justice perspectives. *Personnel Psychology, 52,* 335–358.

Fair Labor Standards Act of 1938 as amended 29 U.S.C. § 201 et seq.

Framingham, H. H. (2008). *Employers use social networks in the hiring process.* Retrieved from news.nsf/care/ 63C6E9BE6E9BE6AD920C C2574C90003ADDD

Garg, A., Curtis, J., & Halper, H. (2003). Quantifying the financial impact of IT security breaches. *Information Management & Computer Security, 11*(2), 74–83.

Health Insurance Portability and Accountability Act of 1996, Public Law No. 104–191.

Hinde, S. (2003). Cyber-terrorism in context. *Computers & Security, 22*(3), 188–192.

Holland, S. (2012). *Bank group warns of heightened risk of cyber attacks.* Retrieved from http://www.nbcnews.com/technology/ technolog/bank-group-warns-heightened- risk-cyber-attacks-1B5995458

Kovach, K., & Cathcart, C. (1999). Human resource information systems (HRIS): Providing business with rapid data access, information exchange and strategic advantage. *Public Personnel Management, 28*(2), 275–282.

Linowes, D. F. (2000). *Many companies fail to protect confidential employee data.* Retrieved from http://epic.org/privacy/workplace/ linowesPR.html

Lukaszewski, K. M., Stone, D. L., & Stone- Romero, E. F. (2008). The effects of the ability to choose the type of human resources system on perceptions of invasion of privacy and system satisfaction. *Journal of Business and Psychology, 23,* 73–86.

Mangieri, G. (2013). *Security breaches by public agencies.* Retrieved from http://www.khon2 .com/content/news/editorschoice/ story/EXCLUSIVE-Security-breaches -by-public-agencies/bbXQ- zolp0SyzE1Cga7zuA.cspx

Microsoft. (2011). *Microsoft security intelligence report.* Retrieved from http://www .microsoft.com/security/sir/default.aspx

Mills, E. (2009). *Cybercrime cost firms $1 trillion globally.* Retrieved from http://news.cnet. com/8301–1009_3–10152246–83.html

Moore, T., & Clayton, R. (2007). *An empirical analysis of the current state of phishing attack and defence.* Paper presented at the Workshop on the Economics of Information Security.

Narisi, S. (2009). MySpace's 'drunken pirate' gets fired, sues employer. *HR Tech News.*

Retrieved from http://www.hrtechnews
.com/myspaces-drunken-pirate-gets-fired-
sues-employer/

Panko, R. (2003). *Corporate computer and
network security.* Upper Saddle River, NJ:
Prentice-Hall, Inc.

Personnel Policy Service, Inc. (2013). *ADA and
prescription drug use at work Q&A.*
Retrieved from http://www.ppsupublishers
.com/ez/html/121608txtb.html

Pohlman, M. B. (2008). *Oracle identity
management: Governance, risk, and
compliance architecture* (3rd ed.). Boca
Raton, FL: Auerbach Publications.

Ponemon. (2009). *2009 annual study: Cost
of a data breach.* Retrieved from http://
www.encryptionreports.com/download/
Ponemon_COB_2009_US.pdf

Ponemon. (2012). *2012 business banking
trust study.* Retrieved from http://info.
guardiananalytics.com/rs/guardiananalytics/
images/2012_Business_Banking_Trust_
Study_Exec_Summary.pdf

Preston, J. (2011, July 20). Social media history
becomes a new job hurdle. *The New York
Times.* Retrieved from http://www.nytimes
.com/2011/07/21/technology/social-media-
history-becomes-a-new-job-hurdle
.html?pagewanted=all&_r=0

Privacy Protection Study Commission. (1977).
The report of the privacy protection
study commission: Personal privacy in an
information society. Washington, DC: U.S.
Government Printing Office.

Privacy Rights Clearinghouse. (2010). *500
million sensitive records breached since 2005.*
Retrieved from http://www.privacyrights.
org/500-million-records-breached

Privacy Rights Clearinghouse. (2013).
Background checks & workplace. Retrieved
from https://www.privacyrights.org/
background-checks-and-workplace

Privacy protections in state constitutions.
(2012). Retrieved from http://www.ncsl.org/
issues-research/telecom/privacy-protections-
in-state-constitutions.aspx

Privacy Act of 1974: Privacy act regulation.
(2010). Lanham, United States. Retrieved
from http://search.proquest.com/
docview/758859747?accountid=7122

Roe v. Cheyenne Mountain Conference
Resort, 124 F.3d 1221 (10th Cir. 1997),
the Tenth Circuit, Retrieved from
http //.www.ppsupublishers.com/ez/
html/121608txtb.

Roth, P. L, Bobko, P., Van Iddekinge, C. H., &
Thatcher, J. B. (2012). *Using social media
information for staffing decisions: Some
unchartered territory in validity research.*
Symposium presented at the Academy of
Management Conference, Boston, MA.

Schneier, B. (2000). Computer security: Will
we ever learn. *Crypto-Gram Newsletter.*
Retrieved from http://www.schneier.com/
crypto-gram-0005.html

Society for Human Resource Management
(SHRM) & West Group. (2000). *Workplace
privacy survey.* Retrieved from http://www
.shrm.org/surveys

Socorro v. IMI Data Search and Hilton Hotels.
(2003). Retrieved from http://il.findacase
.com/research/wfrmDocViewer.aspx/xq/
fac.20030428_0001388.NIL.htm/qx

Stafford, T., & Urbaczewski, A. (2004).
Spyware: The ghost in the machine.
*Communications of the Association for
Information Systems, 14,* 291–306.

Stallings, W., & Brown, L. (2008). *Computer
security: Principles and practice.* Upper Saddle
River, NJ: Pearson Prentice Hall.

Stone, D., Lukaszewski, K., & Isenhour, L.
(2005). E-recruiting: Online strategies for
attracting talent. In H. G. Gueutal & D. Stone
(Eds.), *The brave new world of eHR: Human
resources management in the digital age*
(pp. 22–53). San Francisco: Jossey-Bass.

Stone, D. L., Lukaszewski, K., & Stone-
Romero, E. F. (2001, August). *Privacy and*

human resources information systems. Paper presented at the Annual Meeting of the Society of Industrial and Organizational Psychology, San Diego, CA.

Stone, D. L., & Stone-Romero, E. F. (1998). A multiple stakeholder model of privacy in organizations. In M. Schminke (Ed.) *Managerial ethics: Morally managing people and processes* (pp. 35–60). Mahwah, NJ: Lawrence Erlbaum.

Stone, D. L, Stone-Romero, E. F., & Lukaszewski, K. (2003). The functional and dysfunctional consequences of human resource information technology for organizations and their employees. In D. Stone (Ed.), *Advances in human performance and cognitive engineering research* (pp. 37–68). New York: Elsevier.

Stone, E. F., & Stone, D. L. (1990). Privacy in organizations: Theoretical issues, research findings, and protection strategies. In K. M. Rowland & G. R. Ferris (Eds.), *Research in personnel and human resources management* (pp. 349–411). Greenwich, CT: JAI Press.

Tansley, C., & Watson, T. (2000). Strategic exchange in the development of human resource information systems (HRIS). *New Technology Work and Employment, 15*(2), 108–122.

Whitman, M. E., & Mattord, H. J. (2011). *Principles of information security* (Vol. 4). Boston, MA: Course Technology

Wong, Y., & Thite, M. (2009). Information security and privacy in HRIS. In M. Kavanagh & T. Mohan (Eds.), *Human resource information systems: Basics, applications, and future directions (1st ed.).* Thousand Oaks, CA: Sage.

Zeidner, R. (2007). How deep can you probe? *HR Magazine, 52*(10), 57–62.

CHAPTER 17

The Future of Human Resource Information Systems

Emerging Trends in HRM and IT

Richard D. Johnson and Michael J. Kavanagh

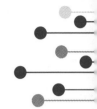

EDITORS' NOTE

In Chapter 1, the history of HRM was discussed along with its eventual merging with the field of IT, thus creating a new field of study and managerial practice—human resource information systems (HRIS). This book has provided information on the development and implementation of an HRIS. Most of the HRIS development and sophistication began in the United States, but these systems have spread rapidly throughout the industrialized countries of the world. The question to be answered here is where the field of HRIS is going in the future. This chapter will discuss some of these trends and provide our thoughts on where the HRIS field will be moving in the next few years.

After completing this chapter, you should be able to

- Discuss the short-term future trends in HRM
- Discuss the long-term future challenges for HRM and tactics to handle them
- Explain the impact of future trends in IT/IS and workforce technologies on the improved operation of an HRIS and HRM programs
- Understand how HR and IT/IS are combining for future HRIS business applications

Introduction

Before we analyze future trends in HRISs, it is appropriate to revisit how we got here. In chapter 1 we noted that, with its changing and expanding role, the typical personnel department started keeping increasing numbers and types of employee paper records. Computing technology began to emerge as a way to store and retrieve employee data. Early advantages of using computing were that (1) the HR departments could obtain the records much faster for managerial reports (e.g., total number of males and females in the company) and (2) the employee records were more accurate than paper-and-pencil records. In the subsequent chapters, we had an in-depth look at the entire system development life cycle (SDLC) of an HRIS that included planning, analysis, design, implementation, and maintenance (Chapters 2–6). We also looked at the specific applications of HRISs in some of the core functions of HRM (Chapters 10–15), for example, talent management, recruiting and selecting, training, compensation, and globalization of HRM.

There is no doubt that technology has radically altered the world of work. Today, one can work anytime and anywhere, using any device—possibilities that have globalized the workplace and given it a 24/7 work cycle. Beyond the early advantages through automating HR processes, technology enables HR processes to be more integrated than ever with other corporate functions (e.g., payroll, finance, supply chain, marketing, etc.) in the pursuit of organizational success. Although HR has evolved from an administrative to a strategic focus, transactional activities, such as HR administration, legal compliance, and benefits management, still consume a major portion of HR resources. With the increasing focus on strategic HRM and developments in technology, HR professionals are deploying innovative technology solutions to address their core challenges, such as talent management and workforce metrics and analytics (Haines & Lafleur, 2008). Multinational enterprises are leveraging HRISs to align their information technology, processes, and people to replicate their HR policies and practices across global operations (Morris et al., 2009). Some enterprises also use HRIS for effective disaster planning and recovery during various crises, such as terrorist attacks and natural disasters (Hurley-Hanson & Giannantonio, 2008).

However, the contribution of technology to Strategic HRM has been limited, and some research indicates that HR professionals view enterprise resource planning (ERP) vendors as "over promising and under delivering" in this area (Dery & Wailes, 2005). In other words, organizations have done a great job at automating basic HR functions and reducing staff, but organization leaders are questioning whether these changes have delivered enough strategic benefits. In answering this question, it is important to remember that technology is only an enabling tool and not a solution or panacea for HR-related problems. Instead, the successful implementation of an HRIS depends on many different factors, such as the organizational culture, leadership and managerial competence, and the fit of the technology with organizational processes. In addition, many organizations fail to implement technology successfully because of their inherent rigidity, inertia, and resistance to change by employees as covered in Chapter 9 (Lengnick-Hall & Lengnick-Hall, 2006). Further, there can be "unintended negative consequences" within the process of realizing the potential of an HRIS; problems "related to the various ways in which different organizational stakeholders and groups engage with, enact, subvert, or avoid the technology or its planned objectives . . . can undermine its anticipated value" (Grant, Newell, & Kavanagh, 2010, p. 4). It is now largely up to HR professionals to exploit technology's potential fully by taking it to the next level of transformational impact. And we're just getting started! The future of e-HR will be driven by changes in both HRM and HRIS. In this chapter, we briefly touch on the trends affecting each.

Future Trends in HRM

Forecasting the future is, in general, quite difficult and even more so in HRM. Although one can examine past trends and extrapolate to the future, there can be unexpected contingencies, such as the financial crisis of 2008–2009. Also, changes in laws, directives, and guidelines from governmental agencies can strongly affect the future of HRM and HRIS. In fact, any significant changes in the environmental factors depicted in Figure 1.2 could cause major changes in the operation of HRM and an HRIS in organizations. To examine any future trends in the HR field, one must look within and between countries, since labor laws differ from country to country and, thus, could have a significant impact on any new developments in HRM for that country (see Chapter 15). Although this chapter focuses on trends that are affecting HRM in the United States, it is important to remember that some of these trends will also be true for other countries, while others may differ somewhat in terms of specific future trends within another country or culture. We briefly discuss five trends that will impact HR in the coming years.

Health Care Questions

For organizations, health care costs are a growing concern. In a recent survey, rising health care costs were identified by nearly 90% of executives surveyed as an important challenge facing their organization in the next two to five years (Society for Human Resource Management [SHRM], 2007), and in another survey, chief financial officers identified health care costs as the number one issue facing their organization (Robert Half, 2012). To address these concerns, organizations are turning to wellness initiatives, others are reconsidering what health plans to offer, and most are passing increased costs on to their employees.

Not only are health care costs increasing in the United States, but with the passage of the Patient Protection and Affordable Care Act (i.e., "Obamacare"), HR departments are facing a number of issues associated with its implementation. For example, some organizations offer multiple health plans, some of which are available only to highly compensated employees. The new law makes some provisions of these plans illegal if they are not available to lower compensated employees as well. In addition, organizations will have to consider the penalty costs of not offering health care to employees, and the makeup of their workforce (e.g., full time, part time, contingent) as they determine how to best comply with the new law, as well as offering plans that best serve their employees. Whatever your opinions on "Obamacare" or the state of health care in the United States, it is safe to say that health care issues will be taking up a lot of time in human resources during the next five years.

Business Intelligence

HR is under increasing pressure to show that its policies and practices add value to the firm (e.g., to show positive ROI as discussed in Chapter 8.). To address these pressures, HR is increasingly turning to the use of business intelligence to support complex metrics. Although covered in greater detail in Chapter 7, we also discuss data analytics and HR metrics here because they are growing in importance to HR departments in most large organizations. Many organizations already have basic reporting capabilities, but they are increasingly looking to incorporate more sophisticated metrics to better support HR programs, for example, training. How important are metrics becoming to HR? Consider that each year

SHRM brings together a panel of experts to address the most important upcoming concerns facing HR, and one of the panels is specifically focused on metrics. Three key predictions from these panels about metrics are (Clark & Schramm, 2012):

1. Organizations will increasingly demand that HR better measure and assess the value of their human capital initiatives.

2. The increasing use of metrics may lead to a standard, and widely accepted set of metrics to "describe, predict and evaluate the quality and impact of HR practices and the productivity of the workforce" (p. 6).

3. Organizations begin to transform their view of HR, from that of a people function to more of one focused on decision science.

Essentially, with the increasing use of metrics and data analytics, organizations are bringing "decision-making tools such as environmental scanning, scenario-based planning, hypothesis formulation, and testing and organizational development tools . . . to improve workforce management decisions" (Clark & Schramm, 2012, p. 7). HR will need to develop metrics for both static statistics to "benchmark" HR progress and programs as well as dynamic measures that assess the effectiveness of HR progress and programs *over time*. During the next several years, this trend to the use of data analytics will only grow as HR seeks to use both their static and dynamic metrics to drive more effective decision making.

Demographic Workforce Changes

The workforce in the United States is undergoing a dramatic transformation on multiple fronts. First, it is becoming more diverse. More women and minorities are entering the workforce than ever before. For example, nearly 60% of working-age women are now in the workforce compared to only 40% in 1970 (Bureau of Labor Statistics, 2011). Also contributing to the diversity of the workforce is the growth in the Hispanic American (Hispanics) population in the United States. Currently, Hispanics make up 15% of the U.S. population and account for more than half (50.5%) of its population growth (Pew Hispanic Center, 2010). They are also expected to comprise at least 25% of the population by 2030 (U.S. Census Bureau, 2009).

Second, there is a major demographic shift occurring in the workforce. Although as recent as a few years ago, there would be upcoming large retirements of baby boomers from the workforce, more recent data suggests that baby boomers are postponing retirement. Data from the Bureau of Labor Statistics suggest that the fastest-growing age groups in the workforce will be those over 65 years old, with projections suggesting that participation of those over 65 will have grown by over 80% between 2006 and 2016 (Bureau of Labor

Statistics, 2008)! At the same time, this same study identified a coming problem. The participation rates of those less than 25 are projected to decrease by 7% over the same time frame. This means that organizations will have a workforce that has much greater age diversity than they are typically used to managing.

What does this mean for human resources in the coming years? Although there are positive aspects to this changing age demographic, there will also be challenges for organizations. Having a workforce that has large ethnic, cultural, and age diversity brings tremendous opportunities for creativity, innovation, and market growth for organizations. But it can also bring challenges for human resources. HR will need to rethink recruiting and retention strategies in light of these changes. Employment factors that are attractive to a married 60-year-old male may be very different that what is attractive for a 24-year-old Hispanic female. In addition, there are a number of critical technological factors that may come into play with a diverse workforce. For example, as briefly discussed in Chapter 12, there are a number of issues with respect to minorities, computer use, and adverse impact.

Second, with multiple generations working together, there will be varied experiences, comfort, and use of technology. As we will discuss in a future section, younger workers have different expectations on the use of technology at work and how they balance their work data and personal data. As one specific example, over 81% of college students get their news from an electronic device (Cisco, 2011) whereas nearly 60% of those over 65 read a physical newspaper (Pew Research Center, 2012).

Ultimately, organizations that are able to most effectively leverage the potential of their workforce diversity will be most successful. "Workforce diversity is not just a competitive advantage. Today it's a competitive necessity" (Cascio, 2013, p. 14).

Growing Complexity of Legal Compliance

One of the most important themes moving forward for HR will be the growing governmental and agency compliance requirements. Human resources has always been affected by legal compliance, but many would say that the pace of regulations continues to grow. For example, the EEOC continues to develop additional guidelines and states continue to pass additional regulations on issues as varied as hiring practices to workplace safety. In addition, the recent negotiations due to the recent "fiscal cliff" has resulted in a change in the Social Security tax rates for all employees, and the raising of taxes for high-earning employees. Human resources will need to be prepared to implement these changes, and additional changes are likely to occur in the coming years. In addition, changes due to the new Patient Protection and Affordable Care Act will require human resources departments in organizations from the very small to the *Fortune* 100 to comply with a myriad of federal requirements and very likely state mandates as well. Consider the comments from SHRM's expert panel (Clark & Schramm, 2012):

1. Firms will increasingly focus on evidence-based hiring to ensure that they remain compliant with federal and state laws as well as EEOC guidelines.

2. Globalization means that labor law will be increasingly affected by trade agreements and global labor standards.

3. Organizations will need to be more actively aware of their compliance environment as the National Labor Relations Board and the Department of Labor are becoming more active in making new rules and attempting to reverse prior decisions.

What will HR departments need to do in response to these changing laws and compliance guidelines? Essentially, they will need to have the information to support adjustments to the way that HR operates. But, they will also have to ensure that the HRIS applications they are using have the ability to handle these changes. Fortunately, there are HRIS applications that assess the legal risk level in terms of unfair discrimination on the basis of race, age, and gender. Results from these analyses can identify the departments where there could be legal problems in complying with laws and legal guidelines. This would enable the company to be proactive in resolving these problems before litigation. Consider the following:

> Firms increasingly will need to adapt their HRIS in order to remain compliant. Pending changes in tax codes, financial reports, equal employment opportunity compliance and health care all suggest that compliance and reporting demands will increase. For example, the new Patient Protection and Affordable Care Act will significantly increase the amount of corporate reporting required by the federal government. It is hard to imagine organizations without a strong HRIS effectively navigating this new environment. (Johnson & Gueutal, 2011, p. 25).

Virtualization of Work

A final trend in HRM on which we briefly touch is the virtualization of work. No longer are employees confined by physical or temporal space. Employees can conduct work anywhere and at any time. "The **virtual workspace** can be defined as an environment where employees work away from company premises and communicate with their respective workplaces via telephone or computer devices" (Lockwood, 2010, p. 1). For example, one of the authors has recently taught a class in which a student was part of a virtual team. His team consisted of six members on four continents, none of whom had physically met.

Together, they were responsible for ensuring that a global corporation's database systems were "constantly up" and free of errors. They had to coordinate global schedules to hold monthly meetings to ensure that the team was meeting targets and schedules. Yet, they had to do this while never working in the same physical space.

Managing in this geographically dispersed environment creates challenges in leadership, in the effectiveness of communication, in technology, and in procedures for conducting virtual meetings and ensuring appropriate HR management. For example, Figure 17.1 lists several keys to managing virtual meetings successfully (Lockwood, 2010). Given the growing use of virtual teams, organizations will increasingly need to be aware of the benefits and pitfalls of managing employees in the virtual workplace.

Future Trends in HRIS[1]

In the first edition of this book, we started this section as follows: "When examining future trends in HRIS, it is impossible to separate the future trends in IT/IS without relating them

Figure 17.1   Tips for Effective Virtual Meetings and Management
Prepare and distribute agendas in advance; ensure agendas reflect input requested from participants.
Initiate meetings with "roll call" of all participants; review agenda, meeting objectives and timeframe.
Identify the key roles of facilitator and scribe.
Position participants in locations "free" of distractions or background noise.
Promote climate of collaboration and inclusion; encourage every attendee to participate and express his or her view.
Encourage participants to effectively use available technology.
Conduct meeting evaluation at the close of the session.
Establish expectation for distribution of the meeting minutes.
Establish "next steps" and make follow-up assignments.

Source: SHRM Interview with Global Dynamics, Inc. (www.global-dynamics.com), as presented in Lockwood (2010).

to the field of HRM" (Kavanagh & Thite, 2009, p. 413). If anything, this statement is more accurate today than when the first edition of this book appeared. The knowledge economy is being profoundly influenced not only by the intensity but also by the speed of technological evolution. Information technologies have been steadily evolving and improving from mainframes to client servers and now to Internet/Web interfaces (Collective HR Solutions, 2010; Macy, 2010; Roberts, 2006). Network communication technologies (broadband and wireless), convergence technologies (e.g., cell phones and PDAs), collaborative tools (e.g., Web 2.0, portals), **service-oriented architecture (SOA)**, rich Internet application (RIA), and business intelligence HR software systems are some of the notable developments that have affected the field of HRIS and its related technologies and in turn the practice of HR. Apart from achieving better coordination and integration of different systems within an enterprise, these technologies are empowering both employers and employees to deploy, share, and use their knowledge for the common benefit of their company. One of the most critical aspects of the emerging technology is a focus on more efficient and accurate decision making, also a primary focus throughout this book. For example, the goal of intelligent HR software is to replace the traditional approach to decision making with an approach that makes a better decision in the most efficient manner. Obviously, this technology can help organizations improve their use of human capital and increase their competiveness in the market. We next briefly discuss the changes in technology that will have a large impact on the HRIS and the delivery of HR functionality.

Bring Your Own Device

The first trend in technology that will affect HR and HRIS is mobile computing and "bring your own device" (BYOD). The change is a dramatic departure from how organizations have previously managed their technological infrastructure, and presents a challenge for organizational IT support. Previously, the most common arrangement by organizations was to manage a centralized and tightly controlled technological platform (e.g., IBM, HP, Dell, Windows, etc.), and anyone who wanted to use another platform (e.g., Mac, Linux, etc.) would potentially have problems receiving adequate support.

But, today, employees are more likely to want to use their own personal mobile devices (e.g., smartphones, tablets, and laptops) to work. In a recent Forrester research survey, nearly 70% of employees noted that they would like to be able to bring their own personal mobile devices and use them at work (Forrester, 2012). Gartner also predicts that by 2013 mobile devices will become the most common technology used to access the Web, even surpassing PCs (Gartner, 2012)! Employees are using these devices to share information, to connect with other employees, to become more responsive, and to increase their productivity. Due to the potential of mobile in the workplace, organizations are increasingly providing support for personal mobile devices, with nearly 50% of firms expanding the breath or depth of support for these devices (Forrester, 2012).

The move to mobile does create some interesting issues for employees and the organization. For example, how do you deal with the privacy issues associated with the storage and use of personal and work data on the same device? In addition, the complexity of managing network and data security dramatically increases when employees bring their personal devices into work, which means that organizations will need to rethink data and network security practices to support these devices. Finally, companies will need to develop policies in regard to the use of these devices and who will pay for these devices. Cisco found that over 70% of younger employees expected companies to pay for their mobile data plans if they used their personal device for work, but less than one third of firms are doing this. Interestingly, though, the extent to which organizations will pay for subscriptions showed great variance by country, with companies in Mexico (72%), Brazil (61%), and China (58%) showing the greatest support (Cisco, 2011).

Along with the growth in the use of mobile devices will be the growth in smartphone apps (e.g., for the iPhone, Blackberry, Android, or Windows). For example, vendors such as Workday and SuccessFactors have built apps where employees can use their mobile devices to access and connect to the corporate HRIS. Because of the rapid growth in the use of apps, Workday has promoted a "mobile first" development model where tablet and smartphone devices are targeted as the primary user interface (Workday, 2012). An example of a mobile app on the iPhone can be seen in Figure 17.2.

Mobile computing increases access to HR data. No longer are employees "chained" to their desks to when working with HRIS data. For example, tablets can be used during the interview process to evaluate applicants in a real-time manner. Employees can fill out expense reports wherever they are located and can capture electronic images of receipts as they incur expenses. If a workers' compensation incident occurs, HR case managers can document issues at the scene of the event—taking photos of the situation for immediate storage in the database. In a BYOD world, as employees become more comfortable with using their personal devices at work, and as younger employees continue to lead, we expect there to be an expansion of organizational support for these devices.

Software as a Service (SaaS) and the Cloud

Traditionally, HRIS implementations were large, time-consuming, and expensive undertakings. Whether implementing a large-scale system such as an enterprise resource planning (ERP) system or a smaller system focused on a single HR function, an organization would often work with vendors and consultants to purchase and install hardware and software on its premises. This "on-premise" approach to acquiring software was the dominant and often the only approach available to organizations. Traditional software development models are being replaced by "on-demand" software plans, which see the

Figure 17.2 SuccessFactors Mobile HRIS App

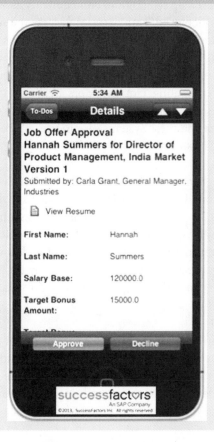

company or customer leasing access to as few or as many HR functions as it wishes to access. This approach to accessing software has been called **software as a service (SaaS)** (Zeidner, 2007). With SaaS, small and medium-sized companies are now able to access HRIS capabilities that were previously only available to large organizations. These companies currently comprise the largest customer pool for new HRIS packages.

The newest trend in delivering software to companies is **cloud computing**. With cloud computing, HRIS functionality is delivered to companies via the Web, without the requirement of purchasing and maintaining hardware and software. Examples of popular cloud-based tools include i-Cloud, Instagram, Facebook, Dropbox, Gmail, and Amazon S3.

For HR, cloud-based software can provide more control over data while reducing reliance on IT staff. As with SaaS, companies are able to adopt only the amount of functionality currently needed and then scale up to additional functionality as their HR needs change. Because the software is Web-deployed, employees can access the software anywhere they have a Web browser. Industry research has shown that companies using cloud-based HR software are more likely to have access to the latest functionality offered by a vendor than those who use an on-premise business model (CedarCrestone, 2011). In addition, because of the rapid growth in mobile computing, cloud vendors are also beginning to deploy apps that can be used on smartphones and tablet computers. Organizations find moving to the cloud attractive because employees find these systems easy to use and because it leads to both lower up-front and ongoing costs.

How big is cloud computing? In the last four years, the market share for the largest three cloud vendors (SuccessFactors, Ultimate Software, and Workday) has increased by 361% (Beaman, 2011). In addition, in a recent survey of companies with IT budgets over $50 million, over 85% of them were exploring ways of getting out of long-term, on-premise contracts and are actively considering cloud vendors to provide a viable option for them (Asay, 2012). These findings are also similar to a recent study by Towers Watson that found that over 50% of firms were planning to implement a cloud- or SaaS-based solution (Towers Watson, 2012a).

These new "rent" versus "buy" decisions should become more common in the next few years (Johnson & Gueutal, 2011) as contracts with large-scale ERP vendors expire and companies are able to consider new options (Johnson & Gueutal, 2011), like cloud-based HR software vendors that include Workday, SuccessFactors, and Oracle Taleo and Ultimate Software.

Web 2.0

Web 2.0 refers to a second generation of Web-related services focusing on creativity, collaboration, and sharing, in contrast to traditional isolated information silos. With Web 2.0, users not only access information but also generate, share, and distribute new content. According to Dario de Judicibus, "Web 2.0 is a knowledge-oriented environment where human interactions generate content that is published, managed and used through network applications in a service-oriented architecture" (as quoted in Deloitte Consulting LLP, 2008).

Examples of Web 2.0 technology include (McKinsey & Company, 2007):

- Social networking sites (e.g., Facebook, LinkedIn, Twitter)
- Wikis (collaborative, shared, Web dictionaries that enable users to contribute to online knowledge repositories, documents, or discussions)

- Blogs (short for Web logs, i.e., personal or corporate online journals or diaries hosted on a website)

- Mash-ups (Web applications that combine data from multiple sources into a single location, or application—e.g., pulling up a rental car booking site within an airline booking site)

- Podcasts (audio or video recordings)

- RSS (rich site summary/really simple syndication)—feeds which publish frequently updated sites such as blogs or news

- Personal websites

- Peer-to-peer networking (P2P)—file sharing (e.g., text, music, and videos)

- Collective intelligence (sharing knowledge to tap the expertise of a group)

- Web services (Web-enabled instant communication between users to update information or conduct transactions—e.g., a supplier and a retailer updating each other's inventory systems)

Web 2.0 has also encouraged businesses to promote user collaboration to share knowledge and to communicate with business partners, such as suppliers and outsourcing providers. With an emphasis on sharing, Web 2.0 can dramatically change the way in which employees communicate with each other and with customers. Using Web 2.0 will require the HR department to pay greater attention to the legal, ethical, and security implications of information exchange. Blogs are not only used to share information within the company and with external stakeholders but also to communicate organization culture and personality. Because organizational culture is based on the shared values of employees, informal communication such as this can help modify the company's culture, particularly during the development and implementation of a new HRIS.

Social Networking

As noted in the previous section, **social networking** (SNW) is one of the features of Web 2.0. Social networking tools such as Facebook, LinkedIn, and Twitter have become important tools for organizations, and human resources is not an exception. Although many of these networks were originally developed to enhance personal social connections, organizations are increasingly harnessing the power of SNW in the workplace. For example, tools such as wikis are being used by organizations to harness and centralize employee knowledge. Some companies are even requiring that employees contribute to the company wiki, making these contributions a formal component of various jobs. Many companies, such as IBM and Deloitte, are making social networking a central component of how they bring new employees into the organization, connecting them with current employees and easing their transition into the company. In addition, as discussed in Chapter 12, companies are increasingly turning to each of these tools to recruit and communicate with both passive and active candidates.

Another important purpose of SNW tools is to connect employees and facilitate information sharing. For example, EMC Corporation uses its social business network, EMC/One, to generate ideas from its employees for its annual innovation contest. After the employees post their innovation ideas on EMC/One, they can also vote for the best idea (Roberts, 2010). At AT&T, senior HR managers use its social business network, tSpace, to identify employees with special skills or knowledge, such as the ability to read or speak a foreign language. A recent SHRM study has found that 20% of organizations are using SNW tools for internal communications (SHRM, 2012). Through these tools, companies are seeking to make information more readily available and to increase employee engagement. Due to the growing use of social networking, HRIS vendors are developing applications within their product offerings to help support employee collaboration, onboarding, and learning. Figure 17.3 provides an illustration of how SAP Jam is designed to mimic such popular social tools as LinkedIn and Facebook to increase employee acceptance and reduce the employee learning curve.

The public nature of many social networking tools, particularly Facebook and Twitter, has created challenges for organizations as they determine appropriate use of the tools by employees at work and outside of work. Stories abound about individuals being fired or reprimanded for comments made on Facebook. More recent legal challenges, though, appear to be limiting the scope of an organization's ability to fire employees made by employees on personal time (Eidelson, 2013). Finally, adding to the complexity of using SNW tools, six states have recently passed legislation that limits an employer's ability to use and access applicant and employee accounts on tools such as Facebook (e.g., require employees to provide passwords to their accounts). Due to the fluid legal state of the use of SNW and because of the relative novelty and complexity of using social networking tools, it is important that your organization have a specific organizational use policy. Although many firms have a dedicated person who manages the company's SNW strategy, more organizations typically rely on HR to develop and enforce the corporate SNW strategy.

Enterprise Portals

Enterprise portal is the general term used to refer to the ways in which individuals can interact with each other. **Enterprise portals** can be information portals, collaboration portals, expertise and knowledge portals, operation portals, **social business networks**, or a combination of all of these. Within an HRIS, employee and manager self-service portals are powerful examples

Figure 17.3   SAP Jam

Source: © SuccessFactors, Inc. All Rights Reserved.

of the potential use of such portals (see Chapter 10). In the context of portals, two of the most commonly used standards are WSRP (Web Services for Remote Portlets) and JSR (Java Specification Request), although, as described in the previous section, companies are beginning to adopt software necessary to build social business networks. Although research has shown that over 60% of organizations have adopted HR portals, their use is continuing to grow, with over 20% of organizations planning to implement them (Towers Watson, 2012b).

Open-Source Software

As discussed throughout this text, traditionally, vendors developed software following a very structured approach. Software is often released in formal cycles, and, in each cycle, new functionality is added and errors from previous releases are fixed. Each cycle, then, culminates with a release date. In addition, vendors will often stop supporting older releases as they place more resources into newer releases. The software developed in this way is copyrighted, and the source code is neither open nor available for others to enhance. This approach to software development has been criticized by some developers as increasing the cost of software, stifling innovation, and encouraging developers to make previous versions obsolete, thus requiring companies to upgrade.

In response to these concerns, some software developers have agreed to a different approach to the development of software called open source. In an open-source approach to software development, the developers make the source code available for anyone to see and to change. This means that other companies or developers can then expand on the product or easily develop complementary products. **Open-source software** also costs much less than traditional (or proprietary) software and is sometimes provided for free. Open-source products are available for a wide variety of organizational needs. Examples of open-source products include Linux (an operating system), Apache (a Web server that plays a central role in the operation of the Web), OpenOffice (a free alternative to Microsoft Office), and MySQL (a database product). The major risk facing organizations considering open-source adoption is the long-term viability of the product, as the continued success of these products depends on the continuing interest of the developers. But, in many areas where needs are common across organizations, open-source products are finding strong support.

Open-source software should grow in importance for human resources in the near future. For example, many HR vendors such as Workday, Taleo, and Journeyx use open-source software in support of their product offerings. In addition, companies are starting to emerge that offer open-source HRIS. Some of these are integrated and some are more function specific. For example, TimeTrex is open-source software for time and attendance management, an important component of workforce and talent management (Chapter 11), and OrangeHRM also offers a more integrated HRIS. Both of these products are targeted at small to medium-sized businesses. Central to these companies' business model is not the sale of the software itself. Instead these companies focus on providing support services and customization support, which may include training for company employees. The business model thus changes from one of continual updates for profit to one of developing a long-term relationship with clients.

An Evolving Industry

Markets and industries are cyclical. Innovations drive change and create new opportunities. In response to these opportunities, new companies emerge that specialize in new innovations. For example, when ERP vendors first started introducing their products 15+ years ago, new opportunities arose for consultants, implementation partners, and other services surrounding their use. Over time the markets consolidated and vendors merged, leaving a few dominant HR ERP vendors such as SAP, Oracle/PeopleSoft, ADP, and Lawson.

This time, cloud-based HR software is driving industry change. Many of the original cloud-based HR vendors have offered a best of breed for a specific niche, such as Taleo's recruiting product. Today, though cloud vendors are beginning to merge not only with other cloud vendors to develop breadth across HR functions, but they are also being purchased by the major legacy vendors. For example in the last few years, SAP has purchased SuccessFactors, Workday has established a strategic alliance with Salesforce.com, Oracle has purchased Taleo, and IBM purchased Kenexa. In addition, mergers and acquisitions are continuing in the consulting area surrounding cloud-based HR. For example, OmniPoint Consulting, a specialized firm focused on Workday implementations, was recently purchased by Aon-Hewitt to bolster their Workday offerings. Because of these changes to the HRIS industry, it is important that you consider carefully a vendor's viability as you assess potential HR software options.

Evolving HRIS Technology Strategy

Along with the consolidation of the vendor and consultant landscape, organizations are reconsidering their HR delivery models. One of the challenges facing organizations is that many of them have historically chosen disparate best of breed approaches where different vendors are added to current offerings, leading to a situation where organizations have added technology support for automating more HR processes (as discussed in Chapters 10–15). But this has created two issues for organizations. First, organizations are faced with managing the complexity of working with multiple vendors. Second, although organizations may have added a large amount of technology to their processes, they have realized that they have not really reflected as to whether they are actually more effective in the delivery of HR services. Therefore in the next few years, we believe that organizations will spend more time and effort assessing the most effective portfolio of HR technology, and many will likely consider moving to some type of consolidated technology platform. Our assessment is supported by Towers Watson research that suggests that within the next few years nearly half of the organizations surveyed are planning to consolidate or reorganize their HR function (Towers Watson, 2012b).

HRIS Moves to Small Businesses

The last trend in HRIS that we focus on is the expanding options for small businesses. As short as five years ago, the idea that a small business would be able to adopt a full-scale HR ERP would have seemed unlikely. But these days, products are being made available at costs that make their attractiveness to small businesses high. One of the reasons for this change is the availability of cloud-based solutions. Companies no longer need the capital to invest in both hardware and software, and the IT expertise to manage the HRIS. Now, much of the risk and expertise for managing the hardware and software is with the vendor. Therefore, small businesses are not only able to afford access to the software, but they are also not burdened by the technological overhead required to implement legacy systems. Now, no company is too small to have their employees supported by HR software. Myco Portal even offers a time and attendance module for companies with fewer than 10 employees!

Future Trends in Workforce Technologies

The many future trends in the HRM, IT/IS, and HRIS fields can easily lead to confusion for organizations, management, vendors, and employees. A solution to this confusion has been proposed by Carden (2009), and we agree wholeheartedly: Technology should serve strategic goals. Carden notes that the increasing competition by organizations to improve their profitability has often led to the conclusion that *new technology will solve these issues,* but the reality is more complex than that. Organizations that are most successful are those who are able to leverage the technology that most closely links to a strong business and HRM strategy. With the recent global recession, the increasing pressure to remain competitive and survive has led to companies adopting technology to carefully diagnose what *strategic goals* the adoption of technology could support. "Even the most sophisticated software is rendered powerless without a solid business strategy behind it" (Carden, 2009, p. 20). Thus, as we consider the changes in workforce technologies, it is important to keep in mind that how effectively organizations are able to harness the power of these new technologies will depend on how well they link it to their HR strategy.

In the first edition of this book, we noted that Henson (2005) had made the following predictions about the future of workforce technologies:

- the technology of the future will be both collaborative and connected;

- there will be increased and more widespread use of intelligent self-service via employee portals;

- there will be increased use of HR scorecards coupled with workforce analytics and decision trees;

- there will be increases in process automation and the use of online analytical processing (OLAP) for processing raw data;

- faster and cheaper access to accurate real-time HR information will be possible due to advancements in communication tools; and

- the worker of the future will be able to work anywhere, any time, and on any device, which will not only help work-life balance but also turn the workplace into a 24/7 cycle.

As we examine the recent state of workforce technologies, we agree with Henson. Surprisingly, many of these predictions mentioned in 2005 have already been realized. Therefore, we decided to conclude this chapter by reporting the results of the latest *CedarCrestone 2010–2011 HR Systems Survey* (CedarCrestone, 2010) on "HR Technologies, Service Delivery Approaches, and Metrics."[2] The purpose of this survey was to provide "a worldwide benchmark of workforce technologies adoption and the value achieved from their use," so CedarCrestone broadened its "coverage scope for both HR technologies and emerging technologies . . . to explore over 40 applications concerning adoption, deployment options, vendor outlook, value achieved, and expenditures" (p. 1). The results of this systems survey are depicted in Figure 17.4.

Data for this report were collected in 2010 from 1,289 respondents representing more than 20 million employees. The sample represents companies from throughout the globe

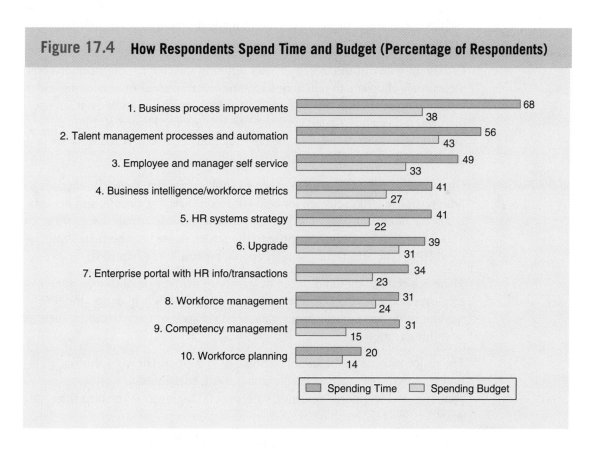

Figure 17.4   How Respondents Spend Time and Budget (Percentage of Respondents)

Source: CedarCrestone 2010–2011 HR Systems Survey: HR Technologies, Service Delivery Approaches, and Metrics, 13th Annual Edition (CedarCrestone, 2010).

including North America, Europe, Asia, and Australia. The major findings of this study are as follows:

1. As was reported in the first edition of this book, organizations that have more automation across all categories of technologies outperform those organizations with less automation on the important productivity measures of net income growth, sales growth, and sales per employee.

2. Due to recent economic conditions, the market was quite unstable for the organizations represented in the survey sample. However, the respondents in the survey reported that their organizations have had strong recoveries, and they forecasted a 100% growth in HRIS talent management, social media, and analytics and planning applications.

3. Organizations reported that business process improvement through techniques such as Six Sigma (Chapter 6) for recruiting new employees was their top initiative.

4. Consistent with our discussion of SaaS earlier in the chapter, organizations are increasingly choosing to rent access to applications instead of purchasing and installing these applications on site. This growth was noted to be even stronger than was indicated in CedarCrestone's previous survey. However, although sales are forecast to decrease in the next year, on-premise licensed software is still the leader across all HRIS applications.

5. Organizations are continuing to invest in applications across all HR functions. Administrative HRIS software for core HR record keeping, payroll, and benefits is still the dominant class of technology, with worldwide average use at 90%. This figure should not be a surprise to the reader, as we have been emphasizing these HRIS functions throughout this book, especially in Chapter 10.

6. There is a continuing trend to use new "service delivery" applications, such as employee and manager self-service systems, portals, HR help desks, and workforce life cycle management; this trend is expected to grow during the next three years.

7. The major increase in the use of technology to support HR will focus on programs and tools such as talent management, social media, workforce planning, and workforce analytics, with over 90% growth in the next three years.

8. Among organizations that have installed multiple talent management applications, that is, those for acquiring, developing, and retaining employees,

those companies with four or more applications installed outperformed those companies with three or fewer applications in terms of higher net income growth, sales growth, and sales per employee.

9. Organizations have begun preparing to use service-oriented architecture (SOA) to automate business processes such as applicant tracking. As discussed earlier in this chapter, SOA provides an overall service that is well defined, self-contained, and context and platform independent, and that adds value to the organization's business purpose.

10. Finally, the survey focused on choices and investments that are providing a strong return to companies. These choices include the following:

- *Focus on Career Development.* It is not simply technology that makes a difference for employees. By leveraging technology and HR practices, organizations that actively support employee professional development will find that employee loyalty will increase and turnover will be reduced.

- *Use **Workforce Optimization Technologies**.* There is continued growth of organizations adopting workforce planning and workforce analytics (see Chapter 11). Organizations that have adopted these applications outperform those that have not.

- *Choose an Integrated ERP-Based Talent Management Solution.* For the third year in a row, organizations pursuing a strategy that integrates multiple HR functions into a software solution have had the best financial performance out of all those firms participating in the study.

- *Adopt Social Networking.* Early evidence suggests that the adoption of social networking by organizations is leading to lower costs and improved organizational agility and responsiveness.

SUMMARY

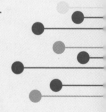

As noted early in this chapter, forecasting the future is very difficult. One reason for this difficulty is that the field of HRIS is not just about what might become technically possible. It is, essentially, about systems that serve humans and human enterprise. Students focusing on understanding the field

of HRIS must never forget the human issues involved in developing and implementing an HRIS. The field of HRIS continues to evolve, and it is important for those studying it not only to understand what is occurring today but also to look at the environmental and technological forces that will affect it in the coming years. If there is one central theme of our look toward the future, it is the importance of HR policies and programs matched with organizational change and technology; this alignment will have the greatest impact on the future success of HRIS and the organizations investing in these systems. For example, one of the findings from the CedarCrestone survey was the emphasis on change management—to which an entire chapter of this book was devoted (see Chapter 9). Technology is not a substitute for managerial competence and employee discretionary behavior (Armstrong, 2005). It can only be a messenger, not a message. It is also impractical to expect information systems to supplant the soft functions of the HR department, such as an online electronic tutor replacing a good executive coach (Stanton & Coovert, 2004). In sum, technology is extremely important in the field of HRIS, but people are simply more important.

KEY TERMS

cloud computing 565

enterprise portals 568

open-source software 570

service-oriented architecture (SOA) 563

social business networks 568

social networking 567

software as a service (SaaS) 565

virtual workspace 561

Web 2.0 566

workforce optimization technologies 575

STUDENT STUDY SITE

Visit the Student Study Site at **http://www.sagepub.com/kavanagh3e** for additional learning tools such as access to SAGE journal articles and related web resources.

NOTES

1. We would like to thank Damon Lovett, senior consultant at KnowledgeSource Consulting, for his thoughts as we developed this section.

2. We are reporting only part of the results of this survey due to its length; however, the entire survey may be obtained from CedarCrestone.

REFERENCES

Armstrong, G. (2005). Differentiation through people: How can HR move beyond business partner? *Human Resource Management, 44*(2), 195–199.

Asay, M. (2012, December 4). Revealed: The gift that keeps on giving to Oracle . . . is dying. *The Register*. Retrieved from http://www.theregister.co.uk/2012/12/04/open_and_shut_oracle/

Beaman, K. (2011). *2011–2012 going global report: HCM trends in globalization*. San Francisco: Jeitosa Group International.

Bureau of Labor Statistics, U.S. Department of Labor. (2008), *The Editor's Desk*, Projected growth in labor force participation of seniors, 2006–2016. Retrieved from http://www.bls.gov/opub/ted/2008/jul/wk4/art04.htm

Bureau of Labor Statistics. (2011). BLS spotlight on statistics: Women at work. Retrieved from http://www.bls.gov/spotlight/2011/women

Carden, M. (2009). Strategy first, technology second. IHRIM.*link, 14*(2), 20–22.

Cascio, W. F. (2013). *Managing human resources: Productivity, quality of work life, profits* (9th ed.). New York: McGraw-Hill.

CedarCrestone. (2010). *CedarCrestone 2010–2011 HR systems survey: HR technologies, service delivery approaches, and metrics* (13th annual ed.). Alpharetta, GA: Author.

CedarCrestone. (2011). *CedarCrestone 2011–2012 HR systems survey: HR technologies, service delivery approaches, and metrics* (14th annual ed.). Alpharetta, GA: Author.

Cisco. (2011). 2011 Cisco Connected World Technology Report. Retrieved from http://www.cisco.com/en/US/solutions/ns341/ns525/ns537/ns705/ns1120/2011-CCWTR-Chapter-3-All-Finding.pdf

Clark, M., & Schramm, J. (2012). *Future insights: The top trends according to SHRM's HR subject matter expert panels*. Alexandria, VA: Society for Human Resource Management, SHRM Research Department.

Collective HR Solutions. (2010, April). *HR technology implementation value survey*. San Francisco: Author.

Deloitte Consulting LLP. (2008, October 10). The maturing human network: Can you find me now? *ComputerWeekly.com,* sec. 4, para. 3.

Dery, K., & Wailes, N. (2005). Necessary but not sufficient: ERPs and strategic HRM. *Strategic Change, 14,* 265–272.

Eidelson, J. (2013). *Go ahead, complain about your job on Facebook*. Retrieved from http://www.slate.com/articles/news_and_politics/jurisprudence/2013/01/complaining_about_your_job_on_facebook_the_national_labor_relations_board.html

Forrester. (2012). The expanding role of mobility in the workplace. Retrieved from http://www.cisco.com/web/solutions/trends/unified_workspace/docs/Expanding_Role_of_Mobility_in_the_Workplace.pdf

Gartner. (2012). Gartner Identifies the Top 10 Strategic Technology Trends for 2013 Retrieved from http://www.gartner.com/newsroom/id/2209615

Grant, D., Newell, S., & Kavanagh, M. (2010, August). *Realizing the potential of an HRIS: Unintended consequences, human agency and the HR function*. Paper presented at the annual meeting of the Academy of Management Symposium, Montreal, Canada.

Haines, V. Y., & Lafleur, G. (2008). Information technology usage and human resource roles and effectiveness. *Human Resource Management, 47*(3), 525–540.

Henson, R. (2005). The next decade of HR: Trends, technologies and recommendations. In H. G. Gueutal & D. L. Stone (Eds.), *The brave new world of eHR* (pp. 255–292). San Francisco: Jossey Bass.

Hurley-Hanson, A. E., & Giannantonio, C. M. (2008). Human resource information systems in crises. *Proceedings of the Academy of Strategic Management, 7*(1), 23–27.

Johnson, R. D., & Gueutal, H. G. (2011). *Transforming HR through technology: The* use of eHR and human resource information systems in organizations (SHRM Effective Practice Guidelines Series). Alexandria, VA: The SHRM Foundation.

Kavanagh, M. J., & Thite, M. (Eds.). (2009). *Human resource information systems: Basics, applications, and future directions.* Thousand Oaks, CA: Sage.

Lengnick-Hall, C. A., & Lengnick-Hall, M. L. (2006). HR, ERP and knowledge for competitive advantage. *Human Resource Management, 45*(2), 179–194.

Lockwood, N. R. (2010). *Successfully transitioning to a virtual organization: Challenges, impact and technology.* Alexandria, VA: Society for Human Resource Management, HR Content Program, SHRM Research.

Macy, J. (2010, March). HR technology: IDE and modern application development. *HRinsights.* New York: Jeitosa Group International.

McKinsey & Company. (2007, March). How businesses are using Web 2.0: A McKinsey global survey [Electronic version]. *The McKinsey Quarterly.* Retrieved from http://www.mckinseyquarterly.com/How_businesses_are_using_Web_20_A_McKinsey_Global_Survey_1913

Morris, S. S., Wright, P. M., Trevor, J., Stiles, P., Stahl, G. K., Snell, S., . . . Farndale, E. (2009). Global challenges to replicating HR: The role of people, processes and systems. *Human Resource Management, 48*(6), 973–995.

Pew Hispanic Center. (2010). *A statistical portrait of Hispanics in the United States, 2008.* Retrieved from http://pewhispanic.org/factsheets/factsheet.php?FactsheetID=58

Pew Research Center. (2012). *The state of the news media 2012: An annual report on American journalism.* Retrieved from http://stateofthemedia.org/2012/newspapers-building-digital-revenues-proves-painfully-slow/newspapers-by-the-numbers/

Robert Half. (2012). CFO concerns: What are the top challenges facing today's financial executives. Retrieved from http://www.roberthalf.com/cfoconcerns

Roberts, B. (2006). New HR systems on the horizon. *HR Magazine, 51*(5), 103–107.

Roberts, B. (2010). Developing a social business network. *HR Magazine, 55*(10), 54–60.

Society for Human Resource Management (SHRM). (2012). *An Examination of How Social Media Is Embedded in Business Strategy and Operations.* Alexandria, VA: Society for Human Resource Management.

Stanton, J. M., & Coovert, M. D. (2004). Guest editors' note: Turbulent waters: The intersection of information technology and human resources. *Human Resource Management, 43*(2/3), 121–125.

Towers Watson. (2012a). 2011–1012 HR Service Delivery and Technology Research Report.

Towers Watson. (2012b). 2012 HR Service Delivery and Technology Survey Executive Summary Report

U.S. Census Bureau. (2010). Census Bureau homepage. Retrieved from http://www.census.gov

Zeidner, R. (2007). *SAAS identified as leading trend in HR tech* (SHRM White Paper). Alexandria, VA: Society of Human Resource Management.

APPENDIX

Additional Resources

Internet Resources

A collection of change theory sites: www.comminit.com/en/taxonomy/term/36%2C25

Academy of Management: www.aomonline.org/

Advantiv (DecisionDirector® software): www.advantiv.com

American Society for *Training* and Development: www.astd.org

Association of Change Management Professionals: www.acmp.info

Being First, Inc.—a change leadership development and transformational change consulting firm with lots of free resources for change leaders and consultants: www.beingfirst.com/

CedarCrestone: www.cedarcrestone.com

Change Management Learning Center: www.change-management.com

Economic Research Institute: www.erieri.com

Employee Benefit Research Institute (EBRI): www.ebri.org

Expert Choice: www.expertchoice.com

Gartner, Inc.—an information technology research and advisory company: www.gartner.com

The Hackett Group—a company offering business best practices, business benchmarking, and transformation consulting services: www.thehackettgroup.com

Hay Group—a global management consulting firm: www.haygroup.com

HR-Guide: www.hr-guide.com

Human Factors and Ergonomics Society: www.hfes.org

International Association for Human Resource Information Management: www.ihrim.org

International Foundation of Employee Benefit Plans: www.ifebp.org

iSix Sigma—a firm providing information on Six Sigma as a change process as well as educational opportunities in Six Sigma. The registration is free: www.isixsigma.com

Jeitosa Group International—a consultancy firm specializing in global human resource technology and management: www.jeitosa.com

Kaiser Associates—an international strategy consulting firm: www.kaiserassociates .com

Maritz—a sales and marketing services company specializing in employee motivation: www. maritz.com

Mercer—a company specializing in benefits administration: www.mercer.com

Organization for the Advancement of Structured Information Systems (OASIS): www.oasis-open.org

Privacy Rights Clearinghouse—an organization dedicated to educating and empowering individuals to protect their privacy: www.privacyrights.org

Salary.com—a tool to find salary data: www.salary.com

SalaryExpert.com—a tool providing reports on salaries and cost of living from compensation professionals: www.salaryexpert.com

PwC Saratoga—a division of PricewaterhouseCoopers specializing in the measurement and benchmarking of human capital: www.pwc.com/us/en/ hr-saratoga

Society for Human Resource Management: www.shrm.org

Society for Industrial & Organizational Psychology (SIOP): www.siop.org

Structured Analysis Wiki: http://yourdon.com/strucanalysis/wiki

Themanager.org provides an excellent collection of topics on change management: www .themanager.org/Knowledgebase/Management/Change.htm

Towers Watson—a firm offering solutions in the areas of employee benefits, talent management, rewards, and risk and capital management: www.towerswatson.com

U.S. Department of Labor: www.dol.gov

U.S. Department of Labor, Bureau of Labor Statistics: www.bls.gov

Wageweb.com: www.wageweb.com

WorldatWork (was ACA)—a nonprofit focusing on global human resources issues: www .worldatwork.org

Vendor Software:

http://www.adp.com/

www.ceridian.com/

www.cornerstoneondemand.com

www.infor.com/

www.mycoportal.com

www.orangehrm.com

www.oracle.com

www.kenexa.com

www.peoplefluent.com

www.sap.com

www.successfactors.com

www.sumtotalsystems.com

www.workday.com

Additional Readings

Abrahamson, E. (2004). *Change without pain.* Boston: Harvard Business School Press.

Adler, N. J. (2002). *International dimensions of organizational behavior.* Cincinnati, OH: South-Western.

Aguinis, H., Henle, C. A., & Beaty, J. C. (2001). Virtual reality technology: A new tool for personnel selection. *International Journal of Selection and Assessment, 9,* 70–83.

Alavi, M., & Leidner, D. E. (2001). Research commentary: Technology-mediated learning—A call for greater depth and breadth of research. *Information Systems Research, 12*(1), 1.

Allen, E. T., Melone, J. J., Rosenbloom, J. S., & Mahoney, D. F. (2007). *Retirement plans: 401(k)s, IRAs and other deferred compensation approaches.* New York: McGraw-Hill.

Anderson, N. (2003). Applicant and recruiter reactions to new technology in selection: A critical review and agenda for future research. *International Journal of Selection and Assessment, 11,* 121–136.

Anderson, D., & Anderson, L. (2010). *The change leader's roadmap: How to navigate your organization's transformation* (2nd ed.). San Francisco: Pfeiffer.

Armstrong, M. (2006). *Performance management: Key strategies and practical guidelines* (3rd ed.). London: Kogan Page.

Armstrong, M., & Stephens, T. (2005). *A handbook of employee reward management and practice.* London: Kogan Page.

Austin, R. D., & Darby, C. A. R. (2003). The myth of secure computing. *Harvard Business Review, 81*(6), 120–126.

Bartram, D. (2006). Testing on the Internet: Issues, challenges, and opportunities in the field of occupational assessment. In D. Bartram & R. K. Hambleton (Eds.), *Computer-based testing and the Internet: Issues and advances* (pp. 13–37). San Francisco: Wiley.

Battilana, J., Gilmartin, M., Sengul, M., Pache, A.-C., & Alexander, J. A. (2010). Leadership competencies for implementing planned organizational change. *The Leadership Quarterly, 21,* 422–438.

Bauer, T. N., Truxillo, D. M., & Paronto, M. E. (2004). Applicant reactions to different selection technology: Face-to-face, interactive voice response, and computer-assisted telephone screening interviews. *International Journal of Selection and Assessment, 12,* 135–148.

Bauer, T. N., Truxillo, D. M., Tucker, J. S., Weathers, V., Bertolino, M., Erdogan, B., & Campion, M. A. (2006). Selection in the information age: The impact of privacy concerns and computer experience on applicant reactions. *Journal of Management, 32,* 601–621.

Beatty, R. W., Huselid, M. A., & Schneier, C. E. (2003). New HR metrics: Scoring on the business scorecard. *Organizational Dynamics, 32*(2), 107–121.

Bebchuck, L., & Fried, J. (2004). *Pay without performance: The unfulfilled promise of executive compensation.* Cambridge, MA: Harvard University Press.

Becker, B. E., & Huselid, M. A. (2006). Strategic human resource management: Where do we go from here? *Journal of Management, 32*(6), 898–925.

Beer, M., & Nohria, N. (2000). *Breaking the code of change.* Boston: Harvard Business School Press.

Bieg, B. J. (2007). *Payroll accounting 2007.* Mason, OH: Thomson/South-Western.

Braddy, P. W., Meade, A. W., & Kroustalis, C. M. (2006). Organizational recruitment website effects on viewers' perceptions of organizational culture. *Journal of Business and Psychology, 20,* 525–543.

Bridges, W. (2003). *Managing transitions: Making the most of change.* Cambridge, MA: Da Capo Press.

Buckley, P., Minette, K., Joy, D., & Michaels, J. (2004). The use of an automated employment recruiting and screening system for temporary professional employees: A case study. *Human Resource Management, 43,* 233–241.

Burke, W. W. (2007). *Organization change: Theory and practice.* Thousand Oaks, CA: Sage.

Business & Legal Reports (BLR). (2007). *2007 survey of employee benefits.* Old Saybrook, CT: Author.

Cappelli, P. (2001). Making the most of online recruiting. *Harvard Business Review, 79,* 139–146.

Carr, D. K., Hard, K. J., & Trahant, W. J. (1996). *Managing the change process.* New York: McGraw-Hill.

Cascio, W. F. (2000). *Costing human resources: The financial impact of behavior in organizations* (4th ed.). Boston: Kent.

CedarCrestone (2011). *CedarCrestone 2011–2012 HR systems survey: HR technologies, service delivery approaches, and metrics* (14th annual ed.). Alpharetta, GA: Author.

Chan, D., & Schmitt, N. (2004). An agenda for future research on applicant reactions to selection procedures: A construct-oriented approach. *International Journal of Selection and Assessment, 12,* 9–23.

Cohen, D. S., & Kotter, J. P. (2005). *The heart of change field guide.* Boston: Harvard Business School Press.

Conner, M. L. (2002). How do I measure return on investment (ROI) for my learning program? *Learning and training FAQs.* Retrieved from http://www.learnativity.com

Davison, H. K., Maraist, C., & Bing, M. N. (2011). Friend or foe? The promise and pitfalls of using social networking sites for HR decisions. *Journal of Business and Psychology, 26,* 153–159.

Dennis, A. R., Wixom, B. H., & Roth, R. M. (2006). *Systems analysis and design* (3rd ed.). Hoboken, NJ: Wiley.

Dineen, B. R., & Noe, R. A. (2009). Effects of customization on application decisions and applicant pool characteristics in a web-based recruitment context. *Journal of Applied Psychology, 94,* 224–234.

Dowling, P. J., & Welch, D. E. (2005). *International human resource management: Managing people in a multinational context* (4th ed.). Mason, OH: Thomson South-Western.

Duck, J. D. (2001). *The change monster: The human forces that fuel or foil corporate transformation and change.* New York: Crown Business.

Eddy, E., Stone-Romero, E. F., & Stone, D. L. (1999). Effects of information management policies on reactions to human resource information systems: An integration of privacy and procedural justice perspectives. *Personnel Psychology, 52,* 335–358.

Ellig, B. R. (2002). *The complete guide to executive compensation.* New York: McGraw-Hill.

Ensher, E. A., Nielson, T. R., & Grant-Vallone, E. (2002). Tales from the hiring line: Effects of the internet and technology on HR processes. *Organizational Dynamics, 31,* 224–244.

Epstein, J., & Klinkenberg, W. D. (2001). From Eliza to Internet: A brief history of computerized assessment. *Computers in Human Behavior, 17,* 295–314.

Epstein, J., Klinkenberg, W. D., Wiley, D., & McKinley, L. (2001). Insuring sample equivalence across Internet and paper-and-pencil assessments. *Computers in Human Behavior, 17,* 339–346.

Feldman, D. C., & Klaas, B. S. (2002). Internet job hunting: A field study of applicant experiences with on-line recruiting. *Human Resource Management, 41,* 175–192.

Fitz-enz, J. (1995). *How to measure human resources management* (2nd ed.). New York: McGraw-Hill.

Fitz-enz, J., & Davidson, B. (2002). *How to measure human resource management* (3rd ed.). New York: McGraw-Hill.

Flannery, T. P., Hofrichter, D. A., & Platten, P. E. (1996). *People, performance, and pay.* New York: Free Press.

Galpin, T. J. (1996). *The human side of change.* San Francisco: Jossey-Bass.

Gane, C., & Sarson, T. (1979). *Structured systems analysis.* Englewood Cliffs, NJ: Prentice Hall.

Gerhart, B., & Rynes, S. L. (2003). *Compensation: Theory, evidence, and strategic implications.* Thousand Oaks, CA: Sage.

Gilley, J. W., Quatro, S. A., Hoekstra, E., Whittle, D. D., & Maycunich, A. (2001). *The manager as change agent.* Cambridge, MA: Perseus.

GLOBE Research Team. (2002). *Culture, leadership, and organizational practices: The GLOBE findings.* Thousand Oaks, CA: Sage.

Grant, D., Newell, S., & Kavanagh, M. J. (2010, August). *Realizing the potential of an HRIS: Unintended consequences, human agency and the HR function.* Symposium presented at the annual meeting of the Academy of Management, Montreal.

Gueutal, H. G., Marler, J. H., & Falbe, C. M. (2007). Skill sets for the e-HR world. *IHRIM Journal, 11*(2), 9–15.

Gueutal, H. G., Stone, D. L., & Salas, E. (2005). *The brave new world of eHR: Human resources in the digital age.* San Francisco: Jossey-Bass.

Harris, M. M. (2006). Internet testing: The examinee perspective. In D. Bartram & R. K. Hambleton (Eds.), *Computer-based testing and the Internet: Issues and advances* (pp. 115–133). San Francisco: Wiley.

Harris, M. A., & Weistroffer, H. R. (2009). A new look at the relationship between user involvement in systems development and system success. *Communications of the Association for Information Systems, 24*(42), 739–756.

Hiatt, J. M. (2006). *ADKAR: A model for change in business, government, and our community.* Loveland, CO: Prosci Learning Center Publications.

Hornik, S., Johnson, R. D., & Wu, Y. (2007). When technology does not support learning: Conflicts between epistemological beliefs and technology support in virtual learning environments. *Journal of Organizational and End User Computing, 19*(2), 23–46.

Hornke, L. F., & Kersting, M. (2006). Optimizing quality in the use of web-based and computer-based testing for personnel selection. In D. Bartram & R. K. Hambleton (Eds.), *Computer-based testing and the Internet: Issues and advances* (pp. 115–133). San Francisco: Wiley.

Huang, F., & Cappelli, P. (2010). Applicant screening and performance-related outcomes. *American Economic Review, 100,* 214–218.

Jellison, J. M. (2006). *Managing the dynamics of change.* New York: McGraw-Hill.

Johnson, R. D., & Gueutal, H. G. (2011). *Transforming HR through technology: The use of eHR and human resource information systems in organizations* (SHRM Effective Practice Guidelines Series). Alexandria, VA: The SHRM Foundation.

Johnson, R. D., Gueutal, H., & Falbe, C. (2009). Technology, trainees, metacognitive activity and e-learning effectiveness. *Journal of Managerial Psychology, 24*(6), 545–566.

Johnson, R. D., Hornik, S. R., & Salas, E. (2008). An empirical examination of factors contributing to the creation of successful e-learning environments. *International Journal of Human-Computer Studies, 66,* 356–369.

Jones, J. W., & Dages, K. D. (2003). Technology trends in staffing and assessment: A practice note. *International Journal of Selection and Assessment, 11,* 247–252.

Jones, S. D., & Schilling, D. J. (2000). *A step-by-step, customizable approach for managers, facilitators, and team leaders.* San Francisco: Jossey-Bass.

Kluemper, D. H., Rosen, P. A., & Mossholder, K. W. (2012). Social networking websites, personality ratings, and the organizational context: More than meets the eye? *Journal of Applied Social Psychology, 42,* 1143–1172.

Kotter, J. P. (1996). *Leading change.* Boston: Harvard Business School Press.

Kotter, J. P., & Cohen, D. S. (2002). *The heart of change.* Boston: Harvard Business School Press.

Lengnick-Hall, C. A., & Lengnick-Hall, M. L. (2006). HR, ERP and knowledge for competitive advantage. *Human Resource Management, 45*(2), 179–194.

Lievans, F., & Anseel, F. (2007). Creating alternate in-basket forms through cloning: Some preliminary results. *International Journal of Selection and Assessment, 15,* 428–433.

Lukaszewski, K. M., Stone, D. L., & Stone-Romero, E. F. (2008). The effects of the ability to choose the type of human resources system on perceptions of invasion of privacy and system satisfaction, *Journal of Business and Psychology, 23,* 73–86.

Marler, J. H., Liang, X., & Dulebohn, J. H. (2006). Training and effective employee information technology use. *Journal of Management, 32,* 721–743.

Marshak, R. J. (2006). *Covert processes at work.* San Francisco: Berrett-Koehler.

McCumber, J. (2005). *Assessing and managing security risk in IT systems: A structured methodology.* Boca Raton, FL: Auerbach Publications.

Meade, J. G. (2003). *The human resources software handbook: Evaluating technology solutions for your organization.* San Francisco: Jossey-Bass.

Milkovich, G., & Newman, J. (2007). *Compensation.* New York: McGraw-Hill.

Nadler, D. A. (1998). *Champions of change.* San Francisco: Jossey-Bass.

Piskurich, G. M. (2003). *The AMA handbook of e-learning.* New York: AMACOM.

Potosky, D., & Bobko, P. (2004). Selection testing via the internet: Practical considerations and exploratory empirical findings. *Personnel Psychology, 57,* 1003–1034.

Rynes, S. L., & Gerhart, B. (Eds.). (2000). *Compensation in organizations: Current research and practice.* Thousand Oaks, CA: Sage.

Salgado, J. F., & Moscoso, S. (2003). Internet-based personality testing: Equivalence of measures and assessees' perceptions and reactions. *International Journal of Selection and Assessment, 11,* 194–205.

Searle, R. H. (2006). New technology: The potential impact of surveillance techniques in recruitment practices. *Personnel Review, 35,* 336–351.

Selden, S., & Orenstein, J. (2011). Government e-recruiting web sites: The influence of e-recruitment content and usability on recruiting and hiring outcomes in US state governments. *International Journal of Selection and Assessment, 19,* 31–40.

Sitzmann, T., Kraiger, K., Stewart, D., & Wisher, R. (2006). The comparative effectiveness of web-based and classroom instruction: A meta-analysis. *Personnel Psychology, 59,* 623–664.

Smith, M., & Smith, P. (2005). E-selection: Computer-based assessment and interpretation. In M. Smith & P. Smith (Eds.), *Testing people at work* (pp. 220–237). Malden, MA: Blackwell.

Smither, J. W. (Ed.). (1998). *Performance appraisal: State of the art in practice.* San Francisco: Jossey-Bass.

Stone, D. L. (Ed.). (2003). *Advances in human performance and cognitive engineering research* (Vol. 3). New York: JAI Press.

Stone, D. L., Stone-Romero, E. F., & Lukaszewski, K. M. (2006). Factors affecting the acceptance and effectiveness of electronic human resource systems. *Human Resource Management Review, 16,* 229–244.

Stone, E. F., & Stone, D. L. (1990). Privacy in organizations: Theoretical issues, research findings, and protection strategies. In G. Ferris & K. Rowland (Eds.), *Research in personnel and human resources management* (Vol. 8, pp. 449–511). Greenwich, CT: JAI Press.

Strohmeier, S. (2007). Research in e-HRM: Review and implications. *Human Resource Management Review, 17*(1), 19–37.

Uggerslev, K. L, Fassina, N. E., & Kraichy, D. (2012). Recruiting through the stages: A meta-analytic test of predictors of applicant attraction at different stages of the recruiting process. *Personnel Psychology, 65,* 597–660.

Van Rooy, D. L., Alonso, A., & Fairchild, Z. (2003). In with the new, out with the old: Has the technological revolution eliminated the traditional job search process? *International Journal of Selection and Assessment, 11,* 170–174.

Wallace, J. C., Tye, M. G., & Vodanovich, S. J. (2000). Applying for jobs online: Examining the legality of Internet-based application forms. *Public Personnel Management, 29,* 497–503.

Weichmann, D., & Ryan, A. M. (2003). Reactions to computerized testing in selection contexts. *International Journal of Selection and Assessment, 11,* 215–229.

Whitman, M. E., & Mattord, H. J. (2011). *Principles of information security* (Vol. 4). Boston: Course Technology

Williamson, I. O., Lepak, D. P., & King, J. (2003). The effect of company recruitment website orientation on individuals' perceptions of organizational attractiveness. *Journal of Vocational Behavior, 63,* 242–263.

WorldatWork. (2007). *The WorldatWork handbook of compensation, benefits & total rewards.* New York: Wiley.

Zingheim, P. K., & Schuster, J. R. (2000). *Pay people right!* San Francisco: Jossey-Bass.

GLOSSARY

Ability test A standardized test of personal skills. Examples of ability tests include the Watson-Glaser Critical Thinking Appraisal that measures critical thinking skills, the Scholastic Aptitude Test (SAT), the Miller Analogies Test (MAT), and the Graduate Record Examination (GRE).

Action-research model A process model of the management of change in organizations. The basis of this model is the interaction of managerial or organizational action and research that both evaluates the action taken and provides data for future planning of the change effort.

Administrative process efficiency This kind of HR efficiency refers to the capacity to conduct existing HRM processes accurately and on time while minimizing costs. Centralizing certain HRM processes, for example, recruiting new employees, offers process efficiency benefits.

Aesthetic features of website The overall stylistic or innovative features of a website, such as contrasting colors, pictures, animation, and playfulness, that keep the user engaged while navigating through multiple Web pages.

Affirmative action plan (AAP) A written report detailing how an employer actively seeks to hire and promote individuals in protected classes. For employers with government contracts totaling $50,000 or more, the Office of Federal Contract Compliance Programs (OFCCP) requires that an AAP be completed.

Age Discrimination in Employment Act (ADEA) The 1967 federal legislation prohibiting illegal discrimination in employment against individuals 40 years of age and older.

Alliance Programs Partnerships between major HRIS vendors and small, independent vendors that allow organizations to implement fuller (or total) solutions for companies.

Americans with Disabilities Act (ADA) The 1990 federal legislation prohibiting illegal discrimination in employment against individuals with disabilities. A disability is defined as a physical or mental impairment that substantially limits one or more major life activities.

Analysis Phase The phase in the systems development life cycle (SDLC) where an organization's current capabilities are documented, new needs are identified, and the scope of an HRIS is determined.

Applicant-tracking system (ATS) A module in an HRIS that supports e-Recruiting and the processing of applicants electronically.

Application service provider (ASP) A third-party firm that hosts and provides access to a bundle of one or more software application services from a central location to multiple clients via the Internet. Clients pay a subscription fee, which generally entails data management and software upgrades. ASPs are often considered a cost-effective way for organizations to manage their information requirements. Many learning management systems are ASP based; that is, access to applications is available through ASPs.

Asynchronous communication Two-way communication in which transmission does not take place in real time. Examples include e-mail or Internet discussion forums. It is useful for collaboration across different time zones.

Attributes Characteristics of an entity, for example, attributes of an employee entity may be employee ID, last name, first name, phone number, and e-mail address.

Backsourcing The effort to bring functionality that had previously been outsourced back in-house.

Balanced scorecard A means of measuring strategic organizational performance that gives managers a chance to look at their company from the perspectives of stakeholders, including external customers, employees, and shareholders.

Balance sheet approach An approach for expatriate compensation that has as its goal the maintenance of a home-country living standard plus a financial inducement for accepting an international assignment.

Bandwidth This term refers to the rate and volume of data transfer, measured in bits per second.

Base pay The pay received by employees for doing their jobs, not taking into account overtime or bonuses. Base pay for some workers is stated in terms of pay per hour; for others, it is stated in terms of annual pay.

Benchmarking (also known as *best-practice benchmarking* or *process benchmarking*) A process used in management, and particularly in human resource management, to evaluate various aspects of the HR function, both activities and programs, usually within a firm's own market sector.

Best-fit This is an approach to strategic HRM where the organization adopts the practices that work most effectively for them rather than adopting industry-wide best practices.

Best-fit learning event model A model of the conditions necessary for the most successful learning outcomes.

Best of breed (BOB) An approach to acquiring HRIS capabilities where the company will pick the best application to support each functional area of HR. Thus, the technology architecture combines the best-fit products from multiple vendors.

Best-practice This is an approach to strategic HRM used by researchers where organizations adopt industry-recognized best practices and uses them in their organization.

Big Data A collection of very large and complex data, created by transaction processing systems, which are mined for hidden patterns of relationships regarding customers or employees.

Blended learning As the term implies, it "blends" various approaches to learning and could incorporate, for instance, face-to-face, formal, informal, and online learning methods.

Business application A set of one or more computer programs that serve as an intermediary between the user and the DBMS (database management system) while providing the "functions" or "tasks" that the user wants performed.

Business intelligence (BI) A broad category of business applications focused on helping organizations and HR collect, store, and analyze data. BI applications include tools such as decision support systems, query and reporting, statistical analysis, and data mining.

Business process reengineering The analysis and redesign of work flow to improve an organization's efficiency and effectiveness. Also, see **Six Sigma**.

Business process transformation The fundamental rethinking of how a business operates, in which the business redesigns its processes to improve its global competitiveness. Global companies must transform themselves to develop global workforce cultures, with better understanding of transnational teams, online collaboration, and globalization and standardization of their HR processes, such as recruiting.

"Caretaker" functions The early phase in the development of human resource management where HR was primarily involved in clerical record keeping of employees.

CBA guidelines A set of guidelines helping the cost-benefit analysis (CBA) team approach a CBA that provides them with an improved likelihood of making the best financial decision regarding an investment in an HRIS.

Change agent (also known as *change leader*) A person who is responsible for leading an organizational change or someone who is influential and can communicate and motivate others to accept a change by informal means.

Change management A structured approach to changing the mindset and perceptions of individuals, groups, and organizations to accept and implement new ideas and processes in an organization.

Cloud computing   The delivery of software functionality over the Internet where HRIS functionality is delivered to companies via the Web. For the company, there is no hardware and software to install. It is a specific type of software as a service.

Collaborative technologies   Software and hardware, such as groupware (electronic meeting software), instant messaging, e-mail, and so on, that help groups (and trainees) communicate, interact, make decisions, and learn more effectively.

Commercial off-the-shelf (COTS) software   Prewritten or developed software or hardware products that already exist for purchase.

Computer virus   A software program that inserts a copy of itself into another program and causes harm to a computer by altering data, erasing files, or other damage.

Content information   The degree to which the website hosts relevant information that the user deems valuable and informative in nature.

Context-level diagram   The highest-level data flow diagram that contains the least amount of detail. It is used to represent the system, its boundaries, and the external entities that interact with the system.

Core competency   A combination of some set of knowledge, skills, and abilities. Many industrial psychologists equate competencies with traits.

Corporate brand management   Long-term talent management strategies also need to be linked to corporate strategy. One very important strategy that must be maintained despite the state of the marketplace is corporate brand management. It has been confirmed repeatedly that the best labor talent is linked to highly regarded corporations that have excellent brand images.

Corporate culture   An organization's collective values, beliefs, experiences, and norms that shape the behavior of the group and the individuals within it.

Corporate social responsibility and sustainability (CRS)   A form of corporate self-regulation that demonstrates a commitment to ethics, sustainability, and social responsibility. There is an increasing need to incorporate the ethical values of an increasingly diverse and global workforce.

Corrective feedback   In performance management, information fed back to an employee pointing out the discrepancy between observed performance and a performance standard. The purpose is to solve any performance problem and increase performance level.

Cost-benefit analysis (CBA)   The financial analysis of the benefits and costs of implementing a new or upgraded system. Important calculations include the break-even point, net present value, return on investment, and the cost-benefit ratio.

Cost-benefit ratio (CBR)   A measurement that expresses the benefits of an HR project (e.g., implementation of an HRIS) as the numerator and the costs as the denominator; thus, values greater than one indicate a favorable ratio.

Countermeasures   Identification of mechanisms that can be used to protect data.

Critical path   The sequence or project network with the longest overall duration determining the shortest time possible to complete the project.

Critical Path Method (CPM)   A method for analyzing a project that calculates the starting and ending times for each activity and determines which activities are critical to the completion of a project (called the *critical path*) and which activities have "float time" (are less critical).

Cross-cultural suitability   This term refers to an attribute of an expatriate. It could include language ability, cultural empathy, adaptability, and a positive attitude toward the assignment in the specific country being considered.

Cross-tab query   A type of query available in MS Access that calculates a sum, average, or other type of aggregation and then groups the results by two sets of values.

Cultural norm A specific belief, attitude, or behavior that is defined as right or wrong, correct or incorrect, within a given culture in a country. Cultural norms are part of the cultural environment of a country.

Culture shock The feeling of uneasiness and discomfort experienced when going from one culture to another as well as the adjustment that occurs in a relatively short time when moving from one country to another.

Customization The modification of a software product to match specific organizational processes or needs.

Dashboards A type of interface for reporting HR data that use a visual, or graphical, representation of key HR data for view by managers.

Database management system A set of software applications that supports the processes of creating and managing the physical database, managing the data in the database (e.g., insert, read, update, and delete data from the database); maintaining data integrity and security; and preventing data from being lost by providing backup and recovery capabilities.

Data flow DFD (data flow diagram) component that represents the flow of data within the system. An arrow indicates the direction of flow, and the name of the flow indicates the type of data.

Data flow diagram (DFD) Graphical tool that represents the flow of data through a system and the various processes that manipulate or change the data.

Data migration The process of transferring employee data between storage types and computer systems or software applications.

Data mining The sophisticated statistical analysis of large data sets to identify recurring relationships and patterns. For example, data mining an employee database might reveal that most employees reside within a group of particular ZIP codes.

Data perspective A view of an HRIS that focuses on an analysis of what data the organization captures and uses, and on the definitions and relationships of the data, while ignoring how or where the data are used by the organization.

Data store A DFD (data flow diagram) component that represents the temporary or permanent storage of data within the system. A data store is represented by an open-ended rectangle in the data flow diagram.

Decision support systems (DSS) Software applications that are designed to support business professionals in their decision-making process. One such approach is the use of "what-if" analysis through which managers are able to review and compare various business scenarios and assess the benefits of one problem solution against other solutions.

Denial-of-service (DoS) A technique that attempts to make a computer, network, or service unavailable for legitimate users, often by flooding it with external communication requests.

Design Phase The phase in the SDLC where the detailed specifications for the final system are laid out and final vendor evaluation and selection occurs.

Desired information goals Ensuring that data is kept confidential, has not been manipulated, and is available to those who are authorized to access it.

Direct costs of expatriate failure These costs include the actual money spent on selecting and training, relocation costs for the expatriate (and family), and the salary of the expatriate.

Direct report The direct report is the employee whose job performance is being evaluated. At the broadest level, this definition of the performance would include any employee who fills the job position, that is, it describes the job performance expectations for any position in the organization.

Discrete HRO The outsourcing of only discrete, or selected, HR functions to third-party providers.

DMAIC See Six Sigma.

Economic feasibility System feasibility assessment tool that focuses on the financial and economic benefits and costs that a new system would bring to the organization.

e-learning   A type of training where trainees are often geographically distributed, communication and interaction occur via technology, and the training is provided in online repositories. Individuals can access the material via computers, kiosks, mobile devices, or other technology.

Electronic data processing (EDP)   The automation of business processes to perform routine, standardized sets of transactional activities.

Employee data warehouse   A centralized repository of a company's electronic data, specifically designed to facilitate reporting and analysis for decision making.

Employee master file   A record of all relevant employee information, central to all core HRIS functionality.

Employee self-service (ESS)   A structural approach to HR administration through HR portals that provides a means for employees to access their personal information and HR services and information.

Employment brand   An organization's well-known values or distinctive image and culture (think Southwest Airlines or Apple). A company often sets itself apart from competitors by means of its employment brand.

Enterprise portal   A framework or system that integrates information, communication, and processes, often through a single, web-based interface.

Enterprise resource planning (ERP) software   A set of integrated applications, or modules, that carry out the most common business functions, including human resources, general ledger, accounts payable, accounts receivable, order management, inventory control, and customer relationship management. ERP modules are integrated primarily through a common set of definitions and a common database.

Entity (database)   An object or thing of significance to an organization that have multiple characteristics of interest to the organization. For example, employees, dependents, managers, and health insurance plans are examples of entities in the human resources context.

Entity (Data Flow Diagram)   An external person, department, or agent that interacts with the system through receiving or sending data. An entity is represented as a square on the DFD (data flow diagram).

Equal Employment Opportunity (EEO)   The condition in which all individuals have an equal chance for employment, regardless of their race, color, religion, sex, age, disability, or national origin, as established in federal legislation and the U.S. Constitution and its amendments (13 and 14).

Equity Theory   A work motivation theory based on the perceived fairness of the employee-employer exchange.

Exempt Workers   Not subject to the provisions of the Fair Labor Standards Act. See **Nonexempt**.

Expatriate   A parent-country national (PCN) employee assigned to a subsidiary of a multinational enterprise (MNE) in another country.

Expatriate failure   The return of expatriates prior to the completion of their overseas assignments.

eXtensible Markup Language (XML)   A markup language or set of rules for encoding an electronic document.

Fair Labor Standards Act (FLSA)   The 1938 federal legislation that established a minimum wage for hourly workers, set the rate of pay for overtime work beyond the defined workweek of 40 hours, prohibited oppressive child labor by restricting hours of work for children below 16 years, and listed hazardous occupations too dangerous for children.

Family and Medical Leave Act (FMLA)   The federal legislation that requires organizations with 50 or more employees to provide up to 12 weeks of unpaid leave after childbirth or adoption, to care for a seriously ill family member, or for an employee's own serious illness.

Field   An attribute of an entity that is stored in a table. It appears as a column.

File-oriented data structures   Data-processing systems that performed record-keeping functions that mimicked the existing manual procedures. Thus, electronic data were stored in computers much the same way as they were stored in paper-based filing systems.

Firewall   A device or set of devices that will permit or deny all computer traffic between computers with different security requirements based on a set of rules.

Flex plan   (also known as cafeteria plans) A benefits plan in which an employee is provided with some core set of benefits and can then add on some dollar amount of additional benefits paid for by the providing organization.

Focus groups   A diverse group of organizational stakeholders that are brought together to provide data to analysts in support of the needs analysis of a new or upgraded HRIS.

Force-field analysis   A procedure to understand the forces during any organizational change that focuses on the forces that drive or support a change in an HRIS and the forces that will inhibit the change.

Foreign key   The primary key from one table that is stored as an attribute in another table. It represents a common key between two tables and is used to form a relationship between the two tables.

Form   A user-friendly window or screen in a database management system that contains multiple fields that can be used to view, change, update, delete, or print records in a more "structured" manner.

Functional experts   Employees with extensive knowledge of HR and IT processes. These employees can sometimes be referred to as the power users because of these skills.

Gantt chart   A popular type of bar chart that illustrates a project schedule. It provides a graphical representation of the duration of tasks against the progression of time in a project.

Gap analysis   An assessment of the differences between the current state of affairs in the organization and the desired future state.

Global Diversity Readiness Index (DRI)   An online spreadsheet tool that is available on the SHRM website (www.shrm.org/diversity). The DRI is used to rank 47 countries on 39 separate indicators, which combine to create diversity scores in five categories.

Goal-setting theory   A work motivation theory with the fundamental tenet that goals and intentions are responsible for human behavior on the job.

Going-rate approach   An approach to expatriate compensation that ties the base salary for international employees to the salary levels in the host country. For example, an expatriate would earn pay that is comparable with that earned by employees in the host country.

Hackers   Individuals who accesses a computer or computer network unlawfully.

Hierarchical access   A set of access rules that provides differential security for employees at different levels or roles in the organization.

Host-country nationals (HCNs)   Employees of the MNE who are citizens of a country in which a branch or subsidiary is located, but where the organization's headquarters is located in a different country.

HR balanced scorecard   An approach to measuring the value of the human resource function by identifying the key valued-added HR activities that contribute to business goals, measuring them, and evaluating the effectiveness of HR through them.

HRIS   Human resource information systems; systems used to acquire, store, manipulate, analyze, retrieve, and distribute information regarding an organization's human resources.

HRIS functionality   The number of programs or functions—such as recruiting, compensation, and job analysis—that are operational using the specific HRIS configuration, as well as the features of these programs that enhance their usability and capacity to affect outcomes.

HR metrics   Measures used to evaluate the functioning of HR programs and as benchmarks for the total HRM department.

HR workforce scorecard   See **HR balanced scorecard**.

Human capital   This encompasses "the knowledge, skills, competencies and attributes embodied in individuals that facilitate the creation of personal, social and economic well-being" (OECD, 2001, p. 18, cited in Chapter 13, this volume).

Human capital management (HCM)   Another term used for **talent management**.

Human resource management (HRM)   An integral part of the organizational system dealing with strategies, policies, and practices that aims to attract, develop, and retain high-quality intellectual capital.

Human resources outsourcing (HRO)   Moving a company's human resource function outside the organization to an external company.

Human resources planning (HRP)   A systematic approach to estimating the future needs of a company for human capital in terms of labor and supply.

HyperText Markup Language (HTML)   The predominant markup language for Web pages. It provides a means to describe the structure of text-based information in a document—by denoting certain text as links, headings, paragraphs, lists, and so on—and to supplement that text with *interactive forms,* embedded *images,* and other objects.

Implementation Phase   The phase in the SDLC where an HRIS is built, tested, and readied for actual rollout.

Implementation team   The team working with the project manager to complete the actual software implementation.

Incentive pay   Compensation provided for some performance achievement. Unlike merit pay, it is not added to base pay but is a one-off reward that must be re-earned to be received again.

Indirect benefits   The benefits associated with the implementation and use of a new HRIS that cannot be measured with certainty (also called intangible benefits). These can be factors such as improved HR reputation or employee morale.

Indirect costs   The costs associated with the implementation and use of a new HRIS that cannot be measured with certainty (also called intangible costs). These can be factors such as lost employee productivity or a short-term loss of HR goodwill as employees learn to use the new system.

Indirect costs of expatriate failure   Indirect costs are harder to quantify than direct costs, but they could include loss of market share in the country, negative reactions from the host-country government, and possible negative effects on local employee morale.

Infographs   A visual representation of data that may combine a number of data sources and data elements such as pictures, charts, and text.

Information   According to the *Oxford English Dictionary,* information is the act of informing or giving form or shape to the mind. Information provides "structure" and "meaning" to abstract data and is of potential value to organizations.

Information privacy   A human value consisting of four elements that refer to human rights, namely, solitude, anonymity, intimacy, and reserve. Information privacy concerns come to play wherever personally identifiable information is collected, stored, and used.

Information security   Ensuring the confidentiality, integrity, and availability of information.

Internal rate of return (IRR)   A capital budgeting metric that is the annualized effective compounded rate of return when the net present value of an investment is zero; it is an indicator of the efficiency of an investment.

International Association for Human Resource Information Management (IHRIM) The professional organization for specialists in both human resources and human resources technology.

International human resource management (IHRM) The profession and practice of HRM within an international or global corporation.

Internet-based training (IBT) Any Web-based training (WBT) or online learning or education.

IT architecture The basic hardware, software, and networking infrastructure of the organization.

Job analysis The process of systematically obtaining information about jobs by determining the duties, tasks, or activities of jobs, from which a set of KSA (knowledge, skills, and abilities) can be estimated.

Job description A written summary of the duties, tasks, responsibilities, and activities that define the working contract between the employee and the organization.

Job evaluation A rating or ranking system designed to create an internal hierarchy of job value. In many organizations, job evaluation results form the basis of the salary structure.

Knowledge Information in context, or the ability to understand the relations between the various pieces of information available.

Knowledge management (KM) A process for identifying, creating, collecting, processing, distributing, and using knowledge.

Knowledge, skills, and abilities (KSA) The requirements for each job in the organization. These provide the basis for HR planning and for the recruitment and selection of new employees.

Knowledge test A multiple-choice training posttest of knowledge of the tools, machines, and equipment used at a factory, designed to measure how well the new hire has learned essential job information taught in classroom training.

Kotter's eight-stage change model A model of organizational change developed by Dr. John Kotter that outlines eight steps that should be completed in order to manage change successfully and avoid the common pitfalls that have beset failed change programs.

Learning management system (LMS) A software application or Web-based technology that allows the creation, delivery, and management of learning resources and content. An LMS can perform a variety of functions, including training administration, performance management, competency management, skills-gap analysis, or resource allocation.

Learning organization A company that values, supports, and facilitates employee learning and development.

Legacy computing system A large, outdated computer system or application that is still being used, often because of the high cost of replacing such a system. The cost of maintaining such systems, which increases over time, is often a key driver for a new system investigation.

Legal and political feasibility A system feasibility assessment tool that focuses on the legal issues associated with the implementation of a new system and any political impacts that would emerge from its use.

Level 0 diagram The first-level DFD (data flow diagram) that outlines the major processes (functions) of the system, the basic sequence of these processes, the basic data stores, and the external entities that interact with the system.

Lewin's three-step change model One of the earliest and key contributions to organizational change, Lewin's framework serves as a general model for understanding planned change.

Load balancing A technique in computer networking that spreads work between computers, network links, or CPUs in order to get optimal resource utilization from the network.

Logical design A phase in the SDLC (systems development life cycle) in which a new system is designed without regard to the technology (e.g., hardware, software, networking) in which it will be implemented.

Logical model A model of the system that graphically illustrates what the system does, independent of any technological architecture (e.g., hardware, software, networking).

Maintenance Phase The phase in the SDLC where the implemented HRIS is refined and updated to prolong its useful life, to fix minor errors, and to improve functionality.

Management information systems (MIS) A type of information system designed to provide detailed data to aid managers in performing day-to-day activities.

Management reporting systems Software that (1) focuses on information aimed at middle managers; (2) integrates transaction-processing data by business function such as manufacturing, marketing, and human resources; and (3) provides reporting of summarized data.

Management sponsor The senior manager who is ultimately responsible for the successful completion of a project.

Market benchmarking A compensation practice designed to provide labor market rates for jobs in an organization. The labor markets may be local, regional, national, or global. The underlying rationale is that an organization should pay for a job roughly what other employers in the relevant market pay to attract and retain employees.

McCumber Cube A graphical model, or framework, of the architectural approach used when establishing or evaluating organizational security measures.

Middleware The general term for any computer programming that serves to "glue together" or mediate between two separate and often already existing programs.

Mobile learning The delivery of training/learning over mobile devices.

Multinational enterprise (MNE) A term applied to any organization that has a business presence in more than one country. A multinational enterprise is also called a multinational corporation.

Multiprocess HRO An approach to outsourcing HR administration, also known as *comprehensive* or *blended services outsourcing*. This approach involves outsourcing to niche, third-party providers all of one or more related HR functions, for example, recruitment and selection or defined and 401(k) retirement plan administration.

Nadler's congruence model An organizational performance model that is built on the view that organizations are systems and that only if there is congruence ("fit") between the various organizational subsystems can we expect optimal performance.

Navigability (of a website) The overall ease with which a user can browse through multiple Web pages to locate topics of interest.

Needs analysis In the analysis of an HR system, the process by which an organization determines and documents its current and future system needs. These needs become the targets or goals that the new system will attempt to satisfy. See also **requirements definition**.

Nonexempt Workers Subject to the requirements of the Fair Labor Standards Act. Employers of nonexempt employees must pay them at least minimum wage, pay overtime of 1.5 times the base pay rate for every hour worked in one week in excess of 40 hours with 2.5 allowed for meals, keep track of hours worked, and file reports with the U.S. Labor Department demonstrating compliance.

N-tier architectures The software and hardware configurations in which databases, applications, and other resources are distributed among many different computers around the world.

Occupational Assessor® software Software developed and supported by the Economic Research Institute (ERI), which was founded in 1987 to provide compensation research to organizations and consultants in the form of published reports and survey software.

Occupational Safety and Health Act (OSHA) The 1970 law that authorizes the federal government to establish and enforce occupational safety and health standards for all places of employment affecting interstate commerce.

Offshoring An organization's use of groups outside of its home country (e.g., India, Ireland, or China for U.S. corporations) to provide services (e.g., HR call centers) to achieve strategic organizational goals.

O*Net database (www.onetonline.org/) A database containing job descriptions for a large number of jobs in a variety of industries. It is a good starting point for a job analysis project.

Online recruiting (also known as *Web-based recruiting, Internet-based recruiting, cyber recruiting,* and *e-recruiting*) The use of the Internet in attracting job seekers to a company's job openings.

Open-source software An approach to software development in which the developers make the source code available for anyone to view, adapt, or change.

Operational experiments One of the most effective methods for developing the evidence on which to base managerial decisions.

Operational feasibility System feasibility assessment tool that focuses on how well the new system will fit within the organization and can be used to consider issues such as development schedule, extent of organizational change, and user responses to the system.

Optical character recognition (OCR) The translation of images of hand-written or printed text into computer-editable text, usually by a scanner.

Organizational culture A concept defined as a complex set of shared beliefs, guiding values, behavioral norms, and basic assumptions acquired over time that shape employees' thinking and behavior; they are part of the social fabric of the organization.

Outsourcing An organization's use of an outside group to provide services—from a few services (e.g., recruiting, compensation processing) up to a broad set of services (e.g., all HR functions)—to achieve strategic organizational goals.

Overall work plan A written time schedule of tasks and responsibilities with deadlines so that the HRIS project will be done in the total time allotted. Note, however, that the orientation of this plan is toward the management of the project itself, not the people who are responsible for the development and implementation of the HRIS.

Parent-country nationals (PCNs) Employees of the multinational organization (MNE) who are citizens of the country in which the parent, or headquarters, of the MNE is located.

Payback period A capital budgeting metric that calculates the number of years required for the flow of benefits returned by an investment to equal the cost of the investment.

Performance appraisal A retrospective system noting how an employee has performed during a previous period. Performance appraisal data usually form the basis for merit pay.

Performance criterion An outcome, behavior, or competency used in the performance management (or appraisal) process. Performance criteria are the factors on which an employee's performance is rated.

Performance evaluation and review technique (PERT) A method for analyzing the tasks involved in completing a given project, the time needed to complete each task, and the minimum time needed to complete the total project. Once the PERT analysis is completed, a Gantt chart can be constructed to guide the project.

Performance gaps Performance discrepancy between the current HR system, or HRIS, and the desired system.

Performance management A managerial process designed to improve employees' job performance. Performance management is broader than performance appraisal because it focuses on planning for performance, providing performance feedback to an employee, and rewarding changed job performance behavior.

Perquisite A reward based on job status. In the past, these were usually reserved for executives (corporate jet, executive dining room, special parking), but now they are frequently used as performance rewards for other workers.

Phishing Attempting to acquire usernames, passwords, account information, or other personal information by appearing to look like an authentic source with which the victim does business.

Physical design A phase in the SDLC (systems development life cycle) in which a new system is designed with particular focus on how the hardware, software, networking, activities, and so on will be implemented.

Planning Phase The phase in the SDLC where an organization reviews the existing technological and system capabilities and develops a general plan for adapting, upgrading, or changing these systems.

Position analysis questionnaire A research validated, structured/standardized job analysis tool consisting of 194 items that represent work behaviors, work conditions, and job characteristics.

Positive feedback Remarks made by a manager to a direct report concerning observed performance and designed to reinforce efforts leading to high performance.

Post-implementation evaluation report An important part of the final Project Management phase is project closeout, which involves the implementation, evaluation, documentation, and maintenance of the HRIS.

Power tests A type of test in which there is no designated time limit to create time pressure or in which the time limit is set such that most candidates will complete the test without working hastily.

Power user The most demanding user of HRIS who will use a large amount of the system functionality.

Predeparture training Training program for expatriates prior to taking an international position. See Table 15.1. Training program for expatriates prior to taking an international position.

Primary key An attribute of an entity that is used to uniquely identify a specific instance of that entity. For example, each employee has a unique employee ID and each dependent has a unique Social Security number.

Process A business function or activity through which data are created, manipulated, or transformed. A process is represented on a DFD (data flow diagram) by a square with rounded edges.

Process mapping The systematic documentation of organizational processes that directly relate to the ongoing project.

Process model A model that represents the key business processes or activities conducted by the organization.

Process perspective A perspective for analyzing an HRIS that focuses on the business processes and activities in which the organization engages and on how data flow through the HRIS.

Project charter A planning document that defines the scope of, and provides a basic "rule book" to facilitate completion of, a software implementation project.

Project concept This describes the key stakeholders and seeks to ensure that the right questions are asked so that the right problem is solved.

Project creep The addition of functionality beyond what was defined in the project scope. It is also called *scope creep*.

Project manager The person chosen by an organization to be responsible for the planning, execution, and evaluation of an HRIS implementation project.

Project proposal (also called a **project charter**) A description of the objectives and performance targets (e.g., cost, time, scope) for the HRIS project.

Project scope The portions of the information system that need to be completely operational to satisfy the needs of the various customers, employees, and senior management.

Project sponsor   Often, a member of the steering committee whose organizational unit has provided the fiscal resources for the development and implementation of the HRIS.

Psychological contract   Employees' beliefs about the reciprocal obligations and promises between them and their organizations.

Psychological safety   A feeling that refers to mitigating the anxiety that people feel whenever they are asked to do something different or new. People are concerned about losing their identities, looking dumb, and losing their effectiveness or self-esteem. This anxiety can be a significant restraining force to organizational change.

Pull systems   Procedures of making information available to managers so that they can access any of it at a point in time when it will be most useful for their decision making.

Push systems   Push communications channels, such as e-mail, actively push information and analyses to the attention of managers. These channels are used for information that is time critical or of which the manager is unaware. These are excellent for getting information to decision makers.

Query   A question you ask about the data stored in a database. For example, you may want to know which employees live within a specific ZIP code.

Rapid e-learning (REL)   The delivery of tailor-made e-learning content swiftly and inexpensively to a large number of learners, and the tracking of learning progress in order to stay abreast of rapidly changing knowledge and information needs.

Realistic job preview   A preview of what it is like to work for an organization that shows applicants both the positive and negative attributes of a job.

Recognition award   Any reward (whether cash or noncash) with the primary purpose of celebrating the specific performance achievements of individuals or groups by publicly rewarding them.

Record   In a relational database, it is a row in a table that represents an "instance" of the entity. For example, in an employee table, each row contains data about a particular employee.

Reengineering   See **business process reengineering**.

Relational database   A type of database that stores data in series of "related" tables, with each table representing one entity. Tables are related to each other through a common attribute or key.

Relationships   These are created by having the same attribute in two separate tables within the database. The relationships are created by matching the value of the attribute in each table. Most often, this is done by taking the **primary key** of one table and including it in the related table.

Repatriation   The process that occurs as the expatriate and family return to their homeland. It is critically important that repatriation programs be established since there is a readjustment (reverse culture shock) when individuals return to their home cultures.

Reports   Formatted presentations of data that help employees and managers make business decisions. Data are drawn from a table, multiple tables, or queries.

Request for proposal (RFP)   A document that solicits potential consultants or vendors to submit proposals and bids for proposed work.

Requirements definition   The process that occurs when an organization analyzes an HR system, whereby it determines and documents its current and future needs. These needs become the targets or goals that the new system will attempt to satisfy. Business requirements definition is similar to a **needs analysis**.

Resistance to change   A common response of employees to any major change initiative; individuals reject all or part of the change and strive to maintain the status quo.

Return on investment (ROI)   A capital budgeting metric in which the flow of benefits that result from an investment is compared with the cost of the investment, usually in the form of a ratio, using the cost of the investment as the denominator. ROI is generally expressed as a percentage of the *total benefits less total costs over the total costs, and it is usually determined by the following formula:

$$\frac{Total\ Benefits - Total\ Costs}{Total\ Costs} * 100$$

Return on workforce (ROW)   An HR metric that monitors and best reflects the value that the total talent returns to the organization. It is calculated as:

$$\frac{Operating\ Income}{Total\ Labor\ Costs}$$

Row-level security   A set of rules that define who can access (or is prohibited from accessing) data on specific employees; for example, a supervisor can access information on the employees in his group but not on employees under a different supervisor.

Security breaches   Illegal access to private data, services, networks, or devices by getting around security protections.

Selection ratio   The number of candidates who, based on the assessment, are chosen for the job divided by the number of candidates who are assessed.

Select query   This query allows you to retrieve data stored in one or more tables in a database.

Self-service portal   See **employee self-service**.

Service-oriented architecture (SOA)   A structure for organizing and utilizing distributed computing capabilities that may be under the control of different ownership domains.

Shared-service center (SSC)   A technology-enabled centralized group designed to provide excellent service to internal customers at reduced costs.

Single data truth   All enterprise data can be accessed by all users wherever and whenever needed.

Six Sigma   A structured approach for improving business (HR) processes through a step-by-step method labeled DMAIC, which stands for define,

measure, analyze, improve, and control. The DMAIC approach uses an assortment of statistical tools to reengineer business processes, and HRM processes such as recruiting, training, and compensating employees can be examined using this approach.

Social business networks   A type of enterprise portal built to provide tools for employees to connect, coordinate, and communicate within a specific company *only*.

Society for Human Resource Management (SHRM)   The largest worldwide professional organization for HR practitioners and academics.

Software as a service (SaaS)   An approach to the delivery and use of HR software where the software is hosted remotely and accessed via a private or public (e.g., the Internet) network, and is often accessed using a Web browser. Instead of owning the hardware and software, it is rented by the organization. See also **cloud computing**.

Sourcing partner   An external firm that partners with a company to provide some of its HR functionality, for example, recruitment or benefits management. Sourcing partners require certain information to complete these tasks, such as information about vacant positions including position description, job specifications, desired candidate competencies, potential salary range, and contact information. The information provided is limited to specific searches for open jobs and is updated as needed.

Spyware   Software installed on a computer that gathers information about a user's activities on the Web and transmits it to third parties

Stakeholders   Those who have a direct interest or involvement in the implementation of an HRIS, or those that are affected by its implementation.

State of information   The state in which data is currently residing. It can be in storage (data at rest, waiting to be accessed), in process (being actively examined or modified), or in transmission (data in motion).

Steering committee   A committee usually composed of the project manager, the senior management member who is the project sponsor, and the lead employee from each involved area (e.g., lead systems analyst, lead database administrator). Also on the steering committee are HR functional experts, whose role is to provide expertise about what HR data are needed, how the HR process maps should be interpreted, and what data are required for decision making.

Strategic HRM   The strategic alignment of the HR management function with organizational goals. It aims to harness the potential of people as a key competitive advantage through the use of their creativity and innovation.

Synchronous communication   "Real-time" or live communication using tools such as messenger services or videoconferencing.

Systems development life cycle (SDLC)   A formal process through which a system is analyzed, redesigned, and implemented. The SDLC will include phases such as analysis/evaluation, design/improvement, development, implementation, and maintenance of the system.

Tables   In a relational database, it is a collection of organized data about entities. One table is created for each entity.

Talent management (human capital management)   A strategic approach to the recruitment, selection, training, development, and management of employees, including the management of their performance and promotion, to meet the strategic objectives of a firm and, thus, improve the organization's competitiveness in the marketplace.

Technical feasibility   A system feasibility assessment tool that focuses on the technical capability of the organization and the availability of the technology necessary to implement a new system.

"Think global, act local"   The most common advice regarding the management of an MNE has been to "think global, act local." This advice applies to the total management process of an MNE—its strategy, operations, finance, marketing, and HR—and has been followed religiously for many years in international management. Beaman has argued that this approach is completely the inverse of how we should be developing and managing our global HRIS projects.

Third-country nationals (TCNs)   Employees of the MNE who are citizens of a country other than the parent or host country.

360° appraisal   Any system in which employee performance is rated by managers, peers, subordinates, and (possibly) outsiders and the employee as well.

3-tier architecture   A type of computer architecture in which a client computer interacts with two (or more) servers. One server usually maintains the database and data while the other server manages the processing logic.

Total HRO   An outsourcing approach that involves having all, or nearly all, HR functions handled by one or more external vendors. All traditional HR administrative and functional activities would be managed through third-party vendors.

Traditional HR activities   Traditional functions of an HR department, such as recruitment and training. They can add strategic value to the organization depending on how they are conducted.

Transactional HR activities   Routine, day-to-day activities of the HR department, such as record keeping, that are important but add little value to the competitive position of the organization.

Transaction cost theory   The idea that organizations can choose to purchase the goods and services they need in the competitive marketplace or make those goods and services internally.

Transaction processing systems   Software applications that process operational data and whose main functions are (1) data storage, processing, and flows at the daily operational level and (2) efficiency, accuracy, and speed.

Transformational HR activities   High-value-added programs or functions in the HR department, such as cultural change, which can significantly affect the strategic direction and long-term viability of the organization. A simple example would be a training program for marketing department employees designed to increase sales, and its effects.

Trojan   A type of malware that hides inside e-mail attachments or files and infects a user's computer when it is opened and/or executed. Trojans are named after the Trojan horse of Greek mythology in that they appear to be something positive, but are in reality doing something malicious.

2-tier (client server) architecture   A term to describe the software and hardware configuration that divides a business application into two tiers, typically with the user interface and some business logic on the user's computer, such as a PC (the client), and the database and mainstream parts of the application stored on a server.

Unauthorized access   To access employee (or other types) of data without permission or authority.

Unauthorized disclosure   The disclosure of employee information to third parties without the permission of the employee.

Unproctored testing   A form of selection testing where the job candidate is tested online at a location and time convenient to them and there is no proctoring of the exam by a test administrator.

Usability (of a website)   The extent to which users are able to use a website effectively. Web usability is often viewed as being comprised of a number of dimensions, including navigability, content and display of information, aesthetics, and ease of use.

User acceptance   The willingness of a user of a system to employ the new technology.

User interface   The communication boundary between the hardware device (e.g., computer, PDA, kiosk) and the user of that hardware. It is the point at which the user interacts with the system, providing inputs and receiving information or feedback from the system.

Validity coefficient   A statistical correlation that indicates the correspondence between test scores and job performance or some other important work outcomes.

Vanilla implementation   Implementing a software package without customizing it for a specific organization.

Virtual private network (VPN)   A "private" computer network across a public network that is enabled through the use of software controls. It can provide organizations with the privacy they seek without forcing them to build a separate network infrastructure for just their data or system.

Virtual workspace   A work environment where the employees of a company work away from company premises and communicate with their respective workplaces via telephone or computer devices.

Web 2.0   The second generation of Web-related services, focusing on creativity, collaboration, and sharing in contrast to traditional isolated information silos.

Work breakdown structure   A definition of the order in which activities, tasks, and jobs are to be performed that also establishes specific check or monitoring points.

Workforce analytics   Strategies for combining data elements into metrics and for examining relationships or changes in HR metrics.

Workforce modeling   A technique that attempts to understand how an organization's human capital needs would change as a function of some expected change in the organization's environment. This change may be a shift in the demand for the organization's product, entry into a new market, divestiture of one of the organization's businesses, or a pending acquisition of or merger with another organization.

Workforce optimization technologies   The use of workforce planning and workforce analytics (see Chapter 11) for which there is continued growth of organizations adopting these technologies. Organizations that have adopted these applications outperform those that have not.

Work packages   These define what must be done, by whom, using what resources, in what time, and at what cost to complete the HRIS project.

Work simulation   An in-basket exercise in which the examinee must examine a variety of types of information (correspondence, reports, and other information) and also interact with simulated coworkers, employees, or other business associates (whether computer simulated or role-played by actors over the telephone or in person). The examinee is evaluated on a variety of dimensions, from accuracy and the quality of decisions to work-related competencies, interpersonal skills, and other personal attributes.

Worms   A stand-alone software program that is meant to disrupt computer and network operations that can replicate itself to spread. Unlike viruses that require the spreading of an infected file, worms can spread by themselves without attaching to files.

Author Index

Giles, W. F., 381
Gilmartin, M., 257
Gleicher, D., 249
GLOBE Research Team, 506
GMAC Global Relocation Services, 507
Goh, M., 298
Goh, W.-K., 416
Goldstein, H. W., 380
Goldstein, I. L., 430
González, M. R., 443
Gould, D., 471
Graetz, F., 253
Graham, M. E., 381
Grant, D., 139, 149–150, 203, 557
Grant, R. M., 414, 416
Green, M., 248, 251
Greenberg, P., 270
Greer, C., 6
Gregersen, H. B., 513
Grossman, R. J., 147–148
Grossnickle, W. F., 374
Gueutal, H. G., 7, 19, 139, 199, 246, 284, 287, 294–295, 297, 519, 561, 566
Guion, R. M., 390, 392
Gunnigle, P., 415
Gur, Z., 52

Hackney, R., 138, 203
Hagan, C. M., 457
Haines, V. Y., 15, 557
Hall, M. E., 463
Hall, R., 139, 203
Halper, H., 542
Hamel, G., 414
Handy, C., 5
Hansen, G. W., 41–42, 55
Hansen, J. V., 41–42, 55
Harris, D., 519–520
Harris, M. A., 92, 269
Harris, R., 249–250
Harris, S. G., 259
Harrison, R., 414, 432
Hatch, P., 305
Hawk, R. H., 169
Hawver, T. H., 256
Hayashi, A., 430
Hendrickson, A. R., 61
Heneman, H. G., 376
Henle, C., 380

Henson, R., 154, 572–573
Heraty, N., 415
Herold, D. M., 242
Hersch, J., 308, 319
Hewitt, 301
Higgins, J. M., 266
Higgs, M., 256
Hill, W., 416
Hinde, S., 542
Hinojos, J. A., 122
Hite, J. M., 513
Hitt, L. M., 118
Hoffer, J., 41
Hofstede, G., 264, 505
Hogler, R. L., 380
Holland, S., 543
Hollenbeck, J., 313, 343, 492–493
Hollmann, R. W., 169–170
Holton, E. F., III, 416
Honey, P., 420
Hornik, S., 269
Howell, R., 256
Howes, P., 216
Hughes, A. A., 436
Humphrey, R. H., 256
Hunter, J. E., 223, 394–395, 400
Hurley-Hanson, A. E., 557
Huselid, M. A., 12–14, 20, 24–25, 175, 322, 349

IBM Global Business Services, 347, 350
Igneri, N., 425
International Association for Human Resources Information Management, 28, 496
Isenhour, L. C., 63, 282, 297, 379–380, 535, 605
Iyer, R., 490

Jackson, L. A., 379
Jackson, S. E., 24
Jacobs, R. W., 249
Jeitosa Group, 496, 524
Jessup, L., 74
Johns, K. M., 333, 605
Johnson, 566
Johnson, A. F., 537
Johnson, E. C., 382
Johnson, R. D., 2, 82, 106, 237, 379, 555, 561, 602
Jones, M., 263–264
Jones, S. D., 464
Josler, C., 140

Masia, B. B., 433
Mason, K., 496
Mattord, H. J., 539
May, D. R., 379
May, K. E., 457
Mayberry, E., 205
McCormack, J., 476
McCourt-Mooney, M., 377
McCreight, M. K., 244
McDonnell, S., 466, 471
McKinsey and Company, 337, 339, 376, 566
McMahan, G., 15–16, 284
McManus, M. A., 63, 379
McPherson, M. A., 428
Mead, A., 393
Meade, A. W., 375, 381
Meade, J., 39, 51
Meijerink, J., 139, 203
Mency, Y., 261
Mendenhall, M., 511
Menefee, J. A., 466
Mercer Delta Consulting, 250, 260
Mersino, A. C., 256
Meyer, G., 464
Michael, J. J., 375
Michaels, J., 372
Michel, J. W., 156, 430, 488, 607
Microsoft, 547
Millemann, M., 258
Miller, D., 242
Miller, J. S., 374
Miller, M., 122
Miller, M. S., 61
Mills, E., 533
Minette, K., 372
Mohamed, A. A., 377, 379
Mohrman, S. A., 14, 17
Mohun, V., 289
Moore, T., 543
Morgan, L., 271
Morley, M., 415
Morris, M. G., 270
Morris, S. S., 557
Morrison, E. W., 375
Mossholder, K. W., 384–385
Motowidlo, S. J., 513
Mourier, P., 258
Moynihan, J. J., 475
Mulvey, P. W., 381

Mumford, A., 420
Munsterberg, H., 169

Nadler, D., 250–251
Nardoni, R. E., 452, 607
Narisi, S., 538
Naughton, K., 350
Naylor, J. C., 399
Nelson, E., 139
Newell, S., 139, 203, 557
Ng, K. Y., 516
Nielsen, J, 381
Noe, R., 313, 343, 377, 382, 423, 431, 433,
    442–443, 492–493, 499, 503–504
Nohria, N, 240
Nonaka, I., 413
Norton, D. P., 14, 175, 319, 354, 434
Nossbaum, B., 356
Nunes, J. M., 428

O'Boyle, E. H., 256
O'Brien, J. A., 145
O'Connell, S., 315
O'Connor, B., 74
Oddou, G., 511
Office of the Auditor General, 238–239
OrangeHRM, 440
Orenstein, J., 383
Organisation for Economic Co-operation and
    Development (OECD), 414
Organizational Research Counselors (ORC),
    507–508
Organization for the Advancement of Structured
    Information Systems (OASIS), 288, 518
Orife, J. N., 377
Osle, H., 287
Otondo, R. F., 376
Overholt, M. H., 257, 271

Pache, A., 257
Page, S., 319
Panko, R., 541, 543, 547
Pascale, R., 258
Paskoff, S. M., 309
Patterson, D. C., 428
Patton, G. S., 108
Paul, L. G., 241, 259–260
Pazer, H. L., 149
Pedler, M., 414

Subject Index

Management information system (MIS), 11, 42, 594
Management reporting systems (MRSs), 38, 42–43, 594
Management support
  critical success factors for HRIS development and implementation, 156
  for needs analysis, 90
  management sponsor, 59, 78, 90
  reasons for system implementation failures, 255–257
  See also Senior management
Managers, HRIS users, 60, 61
Manager self-service (MSS), 286, 294–295, 574
  resistance to, 297–298
Market benchmarking, 466, 469, 594
Mash-ups, 567
Master file on employees, 39, 282, 284, 590
McCumber Cube, 538–541, 539f, 594
Meaning of work, 455
Measurement. *See* HR metrics
Media richness theory, 381
Medical benefits, 473
Medical information access, 534–535
Merit pay, 463, 466, 467
Microsoft Azure, 69
Middleware, 67, 594
Mobile computing, 563–564
Mobile learning, 421, 423, 594
Modeling information systems, 112–114
Model of organizational functioning, 24–25
Models of change process, 243–244
Monster.com, 64, 383
Motivation. *See* Employee motivation
MS Access, 48–51
MS SQL Server, 43
Multinational corporations, 493
Multinational enterprises (MNEs), 488, 594
  case study, 523–524
  compensation management, 514–517
  domestic HRM differences, 499–501
  expatriate failure issues, 489–490
  expatriate staffing, 493
  HRIS applications, 517–521
  managing different types of employees, 501–502
  offshoring, 305–307
  performance appraisals in, 512–514
  process of going global, 494–499
  types of employees, 499

types of international business operations, 492–494
  See also Globalization and global economy
Multiprocess human resource outsourcing (HRO), 303, 594
MySQL, 570

Nadler's congruence model, 250–252, 594
National culture envelope, 491
National Institute for Occupational Safety and Health (NIOSH), 313
National Security Telecommunications and Information Systems Security Committee (NSTISSC) security model, 538
Natural disasters, threats to security, 542
Navigability of websites, 381, 594
Needs analysis, 82, 84, 88–89, 594
  benefits program case study, 103–104
  consequences of not doing, 84–85, 88
  data collection, 95–99
  defining goals, 90
  defining needs, 93f
  evaluation, 99–100
  exploration, 95–99
  gap analysis, 94
  management support for, 90
  observation, 92–95
  planning, 89–92
  preliminary systems review document, 93f
  prioritization, 94, 99–100
  reporting, 100–101
  reviewing with management, 94–95
  stakeholders, 90, 91f
  tools and techniques, 91–92
  training needs analysis, 419, 431
Needs analysis team, 90
Nestlé, 154
Network database systems, 40
New employee orientation programs, 263–264
Nonexempt workers, 468, 594
North American Free Trade Agreement (NAFTA), 491
N-tier architectures, 43, 66, 67, 68–69, 68f, 520, 594

"Obamacare" (Patient Protection and Affordable Care Act), 558, 561
Observation, needs analysis process, 92–95
Occupational Assessor software, 286, 594

ABOUT THE EDITORS

Michael J. Kavanagh is currently Professor Emeritus of Management at the State University of New York at Albany. He also serves on the faculty of the Lorange School of Business Administration, Zurich, Switzerland. He is past editor of *Group & Organization Management* and a fellow of the American Psychological Association, the American Psychological Society, the Society for Industrial and Organizational Psychology, and the Eastern Academy of Management. He has been involved in the HRIS field since 1982. He established the HRIS MBA program at the University at Albany in 1984 and has taught numerous courses in the field of HRIS. In 2006, he received the Award for Career Excellence from the International Association for Human Resource Information Management (IHRIM). He received his PhD in industrial/organizational psychology from Iowa State University in 1969.

Mohan Thite is an associate professor at Griffith Business School, Griffith University, Brisbane, Australia. He has more than 25 years' experience as an HR professional, both in industry and in academia. He is a fellow of the Australian Human Resources Institute. He has been teaching HRIS for several years. His research interests include strategic HRM in the knowledge economy, HRIS, and HRM in multinational corporations from emerging economies. His publications include *Managing People in the New Economy* (Sage, India), a coedited book on HRM in the business process outsourcing industry in India, book chapters, and articles in international journals such as *Work, Employment, and Society,* the *International Journal of HRM,* and the *International Journal of Project Management.*

Richard D. Johnson is an associate professor and department chair of management at the University at Albany, State University of New York. Dr. Johnson's research interests focus on human resource information systems, psychological impacts of computing, training and e-learning, and issues surrounding the digital divide. He has published over 30 academic and practitioner articles in outlets such as *Information Systems Research, Human Resource Management Review,* the *Journal of Applied Social Psychology,* the *Journal of the Association for Information Systems,* the *International Journal of Human Computer Studies,* and the *Journal of Managerial Psychology.* He is also a certified Human Resource Information Professional and is co-director of the University at Albany's nationally recognized MBA concentration on HRIS. He received his PhD from the University of Maryland, College Park.

ABOUT THE CONTRIBUTORS

Michael D. Bedell is acting dean and professor of management at Northeastern Illinois University. He was previously a professor of management, MBA program director, AACSB Accreditation director, and past Bautzer University Advancement faculty member at California State University, Bakersfield. He has worked in the banking industry as a TQM expert focused on improving service quality. He has also worked for a *Fortune* 500 retailer in corporate organizational development, and his responsibilities included developing and validating selection methods, implementing a PeopleSoft HRIS, and training merchandising teams. His research and consulting interests are centered on HRIS, HR metrics, and HR strategy with a focus on small or family businesses. He is a member of numerous professional and academic organizations. He received his PhD in human resource management with a minor in operations management from Indiana University in 1996.

Ralf Burbach is the campus coordinator of the Wexford Campus of the Institute of Technology, Carlow, Ireland, where he previously lectured. He has also lectured at the National University of Ireland, Galway, and the Galway-Mayo Institute of Technology, Ireland. He has previously taught courses in organizational behavior, organizational change, industrial relations, strategic human resource management, international human resource management, and HRIS. He is a chartered member of the Chartered Institute of Personnel and Development, the United Kingdom's and Ireland's leading professional body for HR professionals. He has been carrying out research into HRIS since 2001, including a government-funded project on HRIS use in small enterprises. His current research interests include global HRIS, e-HRM, talent management systems, and international and comparative HRM.

Michael L. Canniff has worked in the IT field for more than 15 years, beginning with IBM as a software engineer and, most recently, as vice president, Development for Acuitrek. His time in the field also includes several years of developing leading-edge, Internet-based products and solutions as director of development for PeopleSoft. Currently, he is the acting chief technology officer with San Joaquin Regional Transit and provides strategic research for software companies such as SAP. He has specialized his career research in the areas of enterprise application integration and electronic commerce systems. He implemented cross-product XML integration standards while at PeopleSoft. He has published several papers on electronic commerce and business process management best practices.

Kevin D. Carlson is associate professor and director of graduate studies in the Department of Management at Virginia Tech. He has published research on a wide variety of topics related to the measurement and evaluation of individual, process, and organizational effectiveness. His work has been published in the *Journal of Applied Psychology, Personnel Psychology,* the *Journal of Management,* the *IHRIM Journal,* and *Personnel Review,* and he has presented papers to the Academy of Management, the Society for Industrial and Organizational Psychology, and the International Association for Human Resource Information Management (IHRIM). He is an associate editor for *Human Resource Management,* a member of the editorial board for the *Academy of Management Learning and Education,* and a member of the board of directors of IHRIM. His current research addresses how to use HR metrics and workforce analytics to enhance organizational performance.

David N. Dickter is senior manager, Talent Assessment at PSI. He is a consultant to *Fortune* 500 companies for the selection, assessment, and development of individuals at all levels. Previously, he was in the corporate organization effectiveness group at AT&T. His experience also includes personnel selection and research roles at Educational Testing Service and the United States Air Force. He has published and presented research and practical papers on selection and technology, turnover, decision making, and various other human resources topics. He received his PhD in industrial/organizational psychology from The Ohio State University.

James H. Dulebohn is an associate professor of human resource management and associate director at Michigan State University's School of Human Resources and Labor Relations. His research interests include decision making, HRIS, compensation and benefits, and HR systems. His articles have appeared in journals, including the *Academy of Management Journal, Personnel Psychology,* the *Journal of Management,* the *Journal of Risk and Insurance, Organizational Behavior and Human Decision Processes, Research in Higher Education,* and others. He has consulted for a variety of organizations, including Dow Chemical, Monsanto, Raytheon, TIAA-CREF, the State of Illinois, the State of Texas, and Marriott. He also served on PeopleSoft's Academic Advisory Committee and on the editorial board of the Society of Human Resource Planning. He earned his PhD and master's degrees from the University of Illinois at Urbana-Champaign.

Charles H. Fay is currently a professor of human resource management at the School of Management and Labor Relations, Rutgers University. He has taught undergraduate and graduate courses in rewards management, performance appraisal, HRIS, statistics, and labor economics. He has also taught rewards management, performance management, and HRIS in several executive and management education programs in the United States, Singapore, Malaysia, and Indonesia. His research focuses on rewards and performance management. He is the coauthor of several books, including *The Performance Imperative, New Strategies for Public Pay,* and *The Executive Handbook on Compensation.* He was a presidential appointee to the Federal Salary Commission and served as a consultant to the Bureau of Labor Statistics on the National Compensation Survey. He has earned certified compensation professional status from WorldatWork (formerly the American Compensation Association). He has served as an expert witness on compensation issues before the Presidential Emergency Board numerous times and testified before Congress on compensation and performance management issues. He has a PhD in management and organization behavior from the University of Washington.

Barry D. Floyd is currently Professor of Information Systems and Management at California Polytechnic State University–San Luis Obispo. He has designed and developed enterprise application software as well as consulted on ERP implementation projects. He has served as a member of academic advisory committees with PeopleSoft, Microsoft, and NetApp. Professor Floyd has presented at conferences and published articles on incorporating ERP systems into the business curriculum. His teaching efforts include courses on database design, systems analysis and design, e-commerce, enterprise resource planning, business negotiations, business planning and modeling, database auditing, and HRIS. He has been a visiting professor in Thailand, Vietnam, China, Finland, England, Italy, Spain, and more recently Germany, where he received a DAAD grant to teach and conduct research at the University of Potsdam. He received his PhD and MBA in computer and information systems from The University of Michigan.

Linda C. Isenhour is currently associate professor of management at Eastern Michigan University, where she develops and teaches courses in HR and technology. Her research interests include recruitment, cultural values, strategic human resource management, and human resource information systems. She has published articles and book chapters on HRM and technology, recruitment, HRM and cultural values, and HRM and privacy. In addition, she has presented scholarly papers to the Academy of Management, the Society of Industrial and Organizational Psychology, the Southern Management Association, and the Western Business and Management Association. A member of the Academy of Management, the Southern Management Association, and the Society for Human Resource Management, she has also earned certification as a Global Professional in Human Resources (GPHR) from the Society of Human Resource Management.

Kevin M. Johns is a business development and sales executive at IBM Corporation. His career with IBM began in 1982, and he has worked in sales, systems engineering, and consulting services, covering major clients of IBM in multiple industries such as telecommunications, life sciences, insurance, and government. Presently, he is responsible for global business partner alliances that sell industry solutions to joint clients. These solutions include ERP, CRM, HCM, and BI (business intelligence) systems. He has experience with ERP applications such as SAP and PeopleSoft. He has been a lecturer at the Rutgers School of Management and Labor Relations, and the Rutgers Business School. He received his undergraduate degree in economics and his MBA from Rutgers University.

Jerard F. Kehoe received his doctorate in quantitative psychology in 1975 from the University of Southern California. He joined AT&T in 1982 where he had responsibility for selection programs in manufacturing, customer service, sales, technical, management, and leadership jobs, assuming overall leadership and direction of that function in 1997. In September 2003, he founded Selection & Assessment Consulting and serves as president. Dr. Kehoe has been active professionally, with several publications, chapters, and conference presentations on selection and assessment topics, including computerized testing, fairness, scoring strategies, cut scores, and test validity. In 2000, he edited the Society for Industrial and Organizational Psychology's Professional Practice Series volume, *Managing Selection in Changing Organizations: Human Resource Strategies*. In 2001–2003, he served on the SIOP subcommittee that revised the *Principles for the Validation and Use of Employment Selection Procedures*.

Kimberly M. Lukaszewski is an associate professor of management at the State University of New York at New Paltz. Her research is focused on electronic human resources, privacy, and diversity issues. Her work has been published in journals such as the *Human Resource Management Review*, the *Journal of Business and Psychology*, the *Journal of Business Issues*, the *Journal of the Academy of Business Education*, the *Business Journal of Hispanic Research*, and the *International Association for Human Resources Information Management Journal*. She has written various book chapters published in the *Handbook of Workplace Diversity*, *The Brave New World of eHR: Human Resources Management in the Digital Age*, *The Influence of Culture on Human Resource Management Processes and Practices*, *The Handbook of Human Resource Management Education*, and *Advances in Human Performance and Cognitive Engineering Research*. She received her MBA in HRIS and her PhD in organizational studies from the University at Albany.

Brian D. Lyons is an associate professor of management in the Raj Soin College of Business at Wright State University. His research interests involve human resources certification, Web recruiting, the efficiency of selection instruments, counterproductive work and off-duty behavior, and leadership effectiveness. His research has been published in outlets such as *Human Resource Management*, *Human Performance*, *Journal of Occupational and Organizational Psychology*, *International Journal of Selection and Assessment*, and *Journal of Managerial Psychology*. His work has been featured in media outlets such as *ESPN*, *The Wall Street Journal*, *The Washington Post*, *Yahoo! Sports*, *CBS Sports*, *AOLnews.com*, the *Atlanta Journal-Constitution*, and the *New York Daily News*. Prior to entering academia, he conducted HR-related research for the Federal Bureau of Prisons and the American Institutes for Research. He earned his PhD in organizational studies from the University at Albany, State University of New York.

Janet H. Marler is currently associate professor at the University at Albany–State University of New York. She has served on both PeopleSoft and Oracle academic advisory boards and held visiting faculty appointments at the University of Pennsylvania's Wharton School and Rutgers School of Management and Labor. Her research, which centers on the strategic use of HR technology, compensation strategy, and alternative and flexible employment arrangements, has been published in leading scholarly journals and books including *Academy of Management Perspectives, Human Resource Management Review, International Journal of Human Resources, Journal of Management, Journal of Organizational Behavior, Journal of Vocational Behavior, Journal of Managerial Psychology, Personnel Psychology,* and *Strategic Management Journal.* She currently serves as an associate editor of the *International Journal of Human Resource Management* and is on the editorial boards of *Human Resource Management, Human Resource Management Review,* and *Academy of Management Perspectives.* A leader in the use of ERP systems technology in the classroom, she teaches MBA programs in HRIS, HRM, compensation strategy, and careers. She earned a PhD in human resource studies and industrial labor relations from Cornell University.

John W. Michel is an assistant professor of management in the Joseph A. Sellinger, S. J. School of Business and Management at Loyola University Maryland. His research interests include leadership and influence processes, supportive and fun workplace practices, employee selection and retention, and the utilization of HRIS in HRM. His research has appeared in the *Journal of Vocational Behavior, Human Performance, Journal of Service Management, Information & Management, Journal of Leadership & Organizational Studies,* and the *Cornell Hospitality Quarterly.* He received his PhD in organizational studies from the University at Albany, State University of New York.

Renato E. Nardoni is president of Nardoni Associates, Inc.—now known as Pilat HR Solutions, the internationally known succession planning and 360-degree assessment software company. He has consulted with clients such as Merrill Lynch, The World Bank, ConocoPhillips, Nike, Ericsson, RIM, Marriott, IBM, Exelon, Wellpoint Health, Philip Morris, Johnson & Johnson, Chase Manhattan, and AT&T. He has served on the board of directors of the New York IHRIM chapter and was the editor of its newsletter. He has been contributing editor to personnel magazines and computers in personnel. He spent more than 17 years with AT&T in a variety of IT, financial, and human resource positions. In 1982, as a founder of Human Resource Technologies, he designed and developed one of the first commercially available PC-based HRIS products.

Lisa M. Plantamura is associate professor, director of Instructional Design, and director of the MBA program at Centenary College in New Jersey, as well as the cofounder and vice president of Operations and Development for *Professors On Demand*. She spent over 20 years in human resource information systems management positions, working in a variety of industries and as an independent consultant. She was a cofounder and director of the Human Resources Information Management Society and a director for IHRIM, from which she received the prestigious Summit Award for significant, long-term contributions to the association's advancement, as well as the Professional of Human Resources Information designation. She currently serves on the HRIM Foundation Board. Dr. Plantamura has a DM in organizational leadership, a PhD in adult education, and an MBA.

Dianna L. Stone received her PhD from Purdue University and is currently professor of management at the University of Texas at San Antonio. Her research focuses on a variety of issues including electronic human resource management (eHRM), e-recruiting, e-selection, privacy, and diversity in organizations including issues of race, culture, disability, and immigrant status. Results of her research have been published in the *Journal of Applied Psychology, Personnel Psychology,* the *Academy of Management Review, Human Resource Management Review,* and the *Journal of Management.* She is the former editor of the *Journal of Managerial Psychology* and received the Lead Editor Award from Emerald Publishing in 2012. She also served as guest editor for multiple special issues of *Human Resource Management Review.* In 2012 she was awarded the Sage Scholarly Achievement Award for Research on Gender and Diversity. In addition, Dr. Stone is a fellow of the Society for Industrial and Organizational Psychology, the American Psychological Association, and the Association for Psychological Science.

Romuald A. Stone is a professor of civilian leader development at the Army Management Staff College, Fort Leavenworth, Kansas. He is also an online faculty member in the Keller Graduate School of Management, where he teaches leadership, organizational behavior, and change management. He has held previous professional appointments at James Madison University and George Mason University. His research and writings include numerous strategy case studies and practitioner-oriented articles. He is the coauthor of *Managing Organizational Change,* a change management textbook. His work has appeared in the *Academy of Management Executive, Psychological Reports,* the *Journal of Management Education, Computers in Human Behavior, Educational and Psychological Measurement, Business Horizons, Employment Relations Today,* the *SAM Advanced Management Journal,* and the *Journal of Applied Management and Entrepreneurship.* As a practitioner, he has more than 20 years of experience as a trainer and consultant in the areas of organizational management and leadership. He received his DBA from Nova Southeastern University in 1990.

Humayun Zafar is an assistant professor of information security and assurance, and director of the MAD Lab at Kennesaw State University. He received his doctorate from the University of Texas at San Antonio. His research interests include organizational security risk management, network security, and organizational performance. Some of his previous work has appeared in journals and conferences such as the *Communications of the Association for Information Systems, Information Resources Management Journal, Journal of Information Privacy and Security, Journal of Emerging Knowledge on Emerging Markets, Human Resource Management Review,* Hawaii International Conference on System Sciences, and Americas Conference on Information Systems.

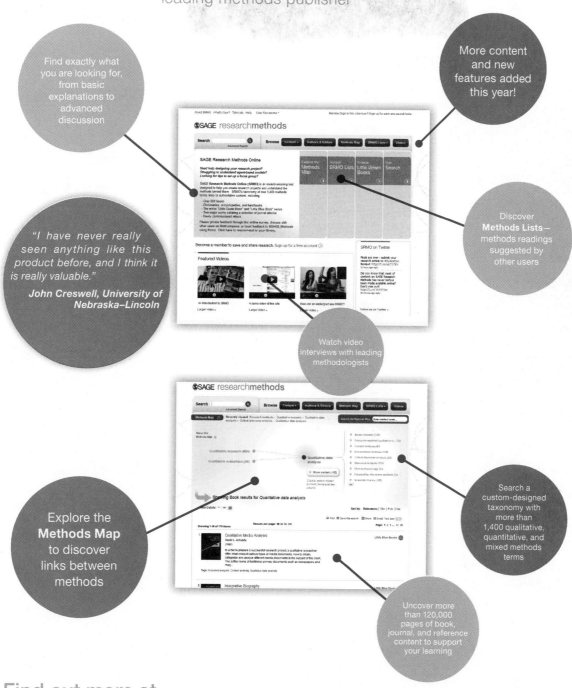

$SAGE researchmethods

The essential online tool for researchers from the world's leading methods publisher

Find exactly what you are looking for, from basic explanations to advanced discussion

More content and new features added this year!

"I have never really seen anything like this product before, and I think it is really valuable."

John Creswell, University of Nebraska–Lincoln

Discover **Methods Lists**— methods readings suggested by other users

Watch video interviews with leading methodologists

Explore the **Methods Map** to discover links between methods

Search a custom-designed taxonomy with more than 1,400 qualitative, quantitative, and mixed methods terms

Uncover more than 120,000 pages of book, journal, and reference content to support your learning

Find out more at
www.sageresearchmethods.com